Why Crime Rates Fall and Why They Don't

Why Crime Rates Fall and Why They Don't

Edited by Michael Tonry

Crime and Justice
A Review of Research
Edited by Michael Tonry

VOLUME 43

The University of Chicago Press, Chicago and London

The University of Chicago Press, Chicago 60637
The University of Chicago Press, Ltd., London

ISSN: 0192-3234

ISBN: 978-0-226-20863-3

LCN: 80-642217

Library of Congress Cataloging-in-Publication Data

Why crime rates fall and why they don't / edited by Michael Tonry.
    pages cm — (Crime and justice : a review of research; volume 43)
    ISBN 978-0-226-20863-3 (cl : alk. paper) — ISBN 978-0-226-20877-0 (pbk.) 1.
Crime—Western countries. 2. Criminal behavior—Western countries. 3. Criminal
statistics—Western countries. I. Tonry, Michael H., editor. II. Series: Crime and justice
(Chicago, Ill.) ; v. 43.
    HV6025.W459 2014
    364—dc23

                                                                    2014036003

The paper used in this publication meets the minimum requirements of American
National Standard for Information Sciences—Permanence of Paper for Printed
Library Materials, ANSI Z39.48-1984. ∞

Contents

Preface

Thematic volumes of *Crime and Justice* typically have long gestations. This one has had the longest. A small planning meeting is usually convened to decide whether a sufficiently ample literature has accumulated to justify pulling it together and synthesizing it and, if so, to decide what to commission and from whom. A conference attended by the writers and 10–15 other subject matter experts is convened to discuss and illuminate the drafts. After rewriting, they are distributed to paid referees for critical reactions. Those that are eventually published are substantially rewritten yet again.

This volume followed that pattern, with the important difference that three conferences were held—in 2010 in Amsterdam and in 2012 and 2013 in Bologna—to discuss successive drafts of the original papers and newly commissioned ones. That extended process resulted from the novelty and difficulty of the subject. Important historical work convincingly showing that homicide rates in Europe have been declining for many centuries, and that rates of all offenses fell from the early 1800s through the 1950s in some Western countries, was published only recently and was not widely known among nonhistorians. Rising crime rates in all developed Western countries in the 1970s and 1980s preoccupied criminologists. Few imagined that those decades were anomalous and were no more than a disruption in long-term trends.

In any case, even if scholars had understood, or wanted to know, what was happening, few attempts were made to analyze crime trends cross-nationally. Partly that is because few people have specialized in comparative and cross-national study of crime and criminal justice systems. Explanations include parochialism, language barriers, and the absence of international networks of scholars working on comparative subjects.

Equally importantly, reasonably reliable data were unavailable for use in cross-national analyses.

Those obstacles are declining. The emergence of English as the international language of science and sharply increased collaboration across national boundaries have made comparative and cross-national work easier and much more common. Formidable data problems persist, but more reliable sources have become available. These include the *European Sourcebooks on Crime and Criminal Justice Statistics*, Eurostat's improved data systems, and the International Crime Victimization Surveys. All of these have gradually been improving. The World Health Organization's homicide data, while still far from perfect, and often differing significantly from national police homicide data, have steadily improved.

Some of the writers of this volume, including the editor, believe that crime rates for all traditional violent and property offenses are falling in all developed Western countries. All of its writers agree that homicide and property crime rates are falling. Some, however, believe that there is no common pattern for nonlethal violent crimes, with official rates declining in the English-speaking and some European countries but apparently stable or rising elsewhere in Europe.

Assuming it is true that crime rates generally are falling, the implications are profound. One is that deep social forces affect people's offending proclivities in all developed Western countries in much the same way, and have for centuries. Another is that efforts in some countries to control and prevent crime through adoption of harsh policing and sanctioning policies have been largely epiphenomenal, importantly affecting the lives of individual human beings but having little effect on overall rates and patterns.

Inevitably many people played important roles in the development of this book. The Netherlands Institute for the Study of Crime and Law Enforcement supported the 2010 conference in Amsterdam. Henk Elffers and Catrien Bijleveld organized the event, and Gerben Bruinsma, then the institute's director, generously provided funding. Papers were presented by Marcelo Aebi, Ybo Buruma, Manuel Eisner, Henk Elffers and Ben Vollaard, Hanns von Hofer, Martin Killias, Tapio Lappi-Seppälä, and Sebastian Roché. Gerben Bruinsma, Anthony Doob, Jeffrey A. Fagan, Rosemary Gartner, Rossella Selmini, Michael E. Smith, and Terry Thornberry also attended.

The subsequent meetings in Bologna were remarkably useful and could not have happened so successfully had Rossella Selmini not pointed us to hotels, conference sites, and restaurants. They were organized by Adepeju Solarin, David Hanbury, and Robbi Strandemo. In addition to the writers whose works appear in this book, they were attended by Marcelo Aebi, Paulo Buonanno, Gerben Bruinsma, Asher Colombo, Philip J. Cook, Francesco Drago, Gary LaFree, David McDowall, Daniel Nagin, Peter Reuter, Rossella Selmini, and Nico Trajtenberg. Funding for the Bologna meetings was provided by the Robina Foundation through grants to the University of Minnesota Law School.

Final versions of papers were reviewed by at least three referees. Anonymity conventions preclude my naming and thanking them publicly. The reports by Europeans and North Americans from a wide range of disciplines including history, economics, sociology, psychology, public policy, and criminology were typically detailed and constructive. The papers went through many drafts and were substantially enriched by the process.

Many people worked hard to produce the volume. Writers exhibited remarkable patience and goodwill in hearing and reading critiques of their work through multiple drafts. Referees prepared reports substantially more detailed and reflective than is common. Participants in meetings did their reading ahead of time and appeared ready to offer advice and criticism. The administrative work required to carry out the venture was efficient and well done. I am enormously grateful to all of those people and to the organizations that provided funding, and to Su Smallen and Chad Pennington who oversaw preparation of the manuscripts. Su did her usual careful, painstaking work to make this volume better than it otherwise could have been.

Many of the essays in this volume will be landmarks that will influence and shape efforts to describe, understand, and explain crime rates and patterns for years to come. Most could not have been written even a few years ago. All were improved by the cross-fertilization that the series of meetings and referees' reports provided. The fundamental finding that all Western developed countries have experienced substantial drops in homicide and property crime is incontrovertible. Whether nonlethal violence has also dropped everywhere remains contested. That is one question that needs an authoritative answer. So does the larger question of why crime rates for most or all traditional crimes in all Western countries are declining.

Michael Tonry
Bologna, December 2014

Michael Tonry

Why Crime Rates Are Falling throughout the Western World

ABSTRACT

Crime rates have moved in parallel in Western societies since the late Middle Ages. Homicide rates declined from 20 to 100 per 100,000 population in western Europe to one per 100,000 in most Western countries by the beginning of the twentieth century. Crime rates in major cities and in countries fell from the early nineteenth century until the middle of the twentieth. From the 1960s to the 1990s, rates for violent and property crimes rose in all wealthy Western countries. Since then, rates in all have fallen precipitately for homicide, burglary, auto theft, and other property crimes. The patterns appear in both police and victimization data. Rates for nonlethal violence have fallen sharply in the English-speaking countries and parts of continental Europe. In other parts of Europe, nonlethal violence has been stable or increasing, but the data are probably wrong. Interacting changes in rates of reporting and recording and in cultural thresholds of tolerance of violence that occurred earlier in the English-speaking countries are the likeliest explanation for the appearance of crime rate increases. Diverse explanations have been offered for both the long- and short-term declines. Most agree that, whatever the explanations may be, they do not include direct effects of changes in policing or sanctioning policies.

Almost no one except a handful of academic specialists seems to have noticed that crime rates are falling throughout the Western world.

Electronically published October 29, 2014

Michael Tonry is professor of law and public policy, University of Minnesota. He is the grateful beneficiary of data, advice, and assistance from many people including Anthony N. Doob, Manuel Eisner, Mike Hough, Julian Roberts, Rossella Selmini, Tapio Lappi-Seppälä, and the late and sorely missed Hanns von Hofer.

1

That is curious. It should be seen everywhere as good news. Fewer people are victimized. Fewer are arrested, prosecuted, convicted, and punished. Hospital emergency rooms handle fewer intentional injuries. Insurance companies compensate fewer losses. Politicians have less incentive to propose and policy makers to adopt severe policies aimed at pleasing, placating, or pacifying an anxious public.

No one has a really good explanation for why crime rates are falling. Since few people have noticed that they are, this is not entirely surprising. Why crime rates are falling may in any case be the wrong question. The better question may be, Why did crime rates rise in all developed Western countries during the 1960s, 1970s, and 1980s before peaking and turning downward? There is nearly incontestable evidence that homicide rates fell dramatically and more or less continuously from the late Middle Ages through the middle of the twentieth century (Eisner 2003; Spierenburg 2008, 2012; Muchembled 2011). Few historians question that rates for other crimes fell from the early nineteenth century to the middle of the twentieth (e.g., Gurr, Grabosky, and Hula 1977). Those findings support a hypothesis that the rising rates of recent decades were an anomaly. The centuries-long downward trend has been interrupted before by profound social and economic dislocations. Crime rates usually fall during wars, for example, rise for a short period afterward, and then resume long-term patterns (Archer and Gartner 1976, 1984; Gurr 1981, pp. 344–46). Well-known social and economic dislocations of recent decades affected all developed countries and may simply have caused another short-term disruption to the long-term trend.

My aims in this essay are to demonstrate that crime rates have moved in parallel in the English-speaking countries and western Europe since the 1960s and to assess the main explanations for why they rose in the 1970s and 1980s and fell afterward.[1] The implications are important. One is that Western countries are much more closely linked in structural, social, and cultural ways than is commonly recognized. Many demographic patterns in recent decades have characterized most or all developed countries including rising life expectancies, female labor force participation, and income inequality and declining fertility, infant

---

[1] The "English-speaking countries and western Europe" are my primary focus. That lengthy phrase is mostly used in lead sentences. Proximate references to "countries" should be understood to refer to English-speaking countries and western Europe unless other countries or regions are explicitly mentioned.

mortality, and marriage rates. It would be odd if crime trends were not also common. All Western countries (and many others) appear to march to the same distant drummers without realizing that is what they are doing.

A second implication is that many of the things that governments have done to reduce crime rates in recent decades have been largely epiphenomenal—normatively and politically important, and having major effects on many people's lives, but pretty much beside the point in terms of crime rates and patterns. It is at least a little parochial, for example, that the US National Academy of Sciences twice in recent years has sought to explain recent American crime trends primarily in terms of distinctively American developments such as mass imprisonment, policing initiatives, legalization of abortion, and reduction in children's exposure to lead paint (e.g., Goldberger and Rosenfeld 2008; Rosenfeld 2014).

Comparison of American and Canadian developments makes the parochialism clear. Canadian crime rate patterns have closely paralleled America's since 1960, but Canada's imprisonment patterns and criminal justice policies have been starkly different (Webster and Doob 2007). Since 1960, the Canadian imprisonment rate has fluctuated around 100 per 100,000 population, while America's rose from 150 per 100,000 in 1970 to 756 in 2007. Canadian agencies have not emphasized zero-tolerance and other aggressive forms of policing, and the Canadian Parliament did not enact three-strikes, truth-in-sentencing, and life-without-possibility-of-parole laws. Only in the last couple of years have significant mandatory minimum sentence laws been enacted; they do not, however, require sentences measured in decades and lifetimes and are meeting strong resistance from the appellate courts (*R. v. Smickle*, 2013 Ontario Court of Appeals 677 [CanLII]; *R. v. Nur*, 2013 Ontario Court of Appeals 678 [CanLII]; Doob and Webster 2013).

Yet crime rates moved in tandem. Figure 1 shows US and Canadian homicide, robbery, and imprisonment rates since 1960. The US imprisonment rate nearly quintupled; the Canadian rate barely changed. Homicide rates, however, moved almost in lockstep. Robbery trends also were closely similar. Whatever caused homicide rates in the two countries to change in parallel, it was something other than changes in imprisonment rates and sentencing laws. Yet both US National

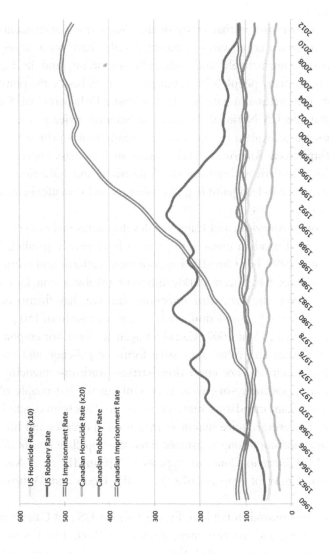

FIG. 1.—Imprisonment, homicide, and robbery rates per 100,000 population, Canada and United States, 1960–2012. Sources: Bureau of Justice Statistics; Statistics Canada; Walmsley (2013, table 1). US imprisonment rates do not include county jail inmates and understate total US imprisonment by approximately one-third. Reasonably reliable annual jail population data are unavailable before the 1980s.

Academy of Sciences initiatives have sought to explain American crime trends as if the reasons for them are uniquely American.

Reasonable arguments can be made that recent drops in property crime rates were influenced by improved security technologies in motor vehicles, residences, and retail stores (e.g., van Dijk, Tseloni, and Farrell 2012b; Farrell, Tilly, and Tseloni 2014). Those developments may explain minor differences in trends between countries that adopted them more and less extensively or at different times, but all developed countries experienced substantial declines. Few plausible arguments can be made, however, that technological or crime control policy changes have caused sharp parallel declines in homicide and other violent and sexual offending. Something more fundamental is happening.

The evidence that crime rates have moved in parallel in Western countries between the 1960s and 1990s, with occasional lags in particular countries, is overwhelming. No informed person disagrees that homicide rates rose from various starting points in the 1950s and 1960s, peaked in the 1990s, and have since fallen (e.g., Eisner 2008, 2014). No informed person disagrees that nonviolent property crime rates—burglary, theft, motor vehicle theft—in all Western countries have been falling at least since the 1990s (van Dijk and Tseloni 2012). In some countries including the United States, there are good reasons from victimization data to believe that property crime declines began earlier.[2] The declines in property crime rates are especially striking since they continued during the recessions that afflicted almost all Western countries beginning in 2008 and are continuing in many as these words are being written.

The disagreements concern trends in nonhomicidal violence and sexual offending since the early 1990s. In the English-speaking and some western European countries, both police and victimization data show that robbery, rape, and aggravated assault rates have fallen since the early to mid-1990s. In other western European countries, rates for nonhomicidal violence have not fallen since the early 1990s and in

[2] The Bureau of Justice Statistics (1994) published a report on victimization trends for 1973–92 (a major redesign of the National Crime Victimization Survey took effect the latter year). It showed that all forms of theft and household burglaries peaked in the early 1980s and then began the long-term trends that continue today. Rape and robbery peaked and began to fall in the mid-1980s but experienced small increases in the late 1980s, paralleling official data. Motor vehicle theft rates rose until the early 1990s. Only assault rates remained broadly stable.

some have increased (e.g., Aebi and Linde 2010, 2012). The challenge is to explain those divergent patterns.

The explanation is that there is no divergence. The appearance of one is misleading. The incidence not only of homicide but of all violent crime is almost certainly falling in all developed Western countries, but this is obscured in three interrelated ways. First, victims have become more likely to report incidents to the police, but the timing of the increases varies between countries. Victimization surveys regularly ask respondents to indicate whether they reported incidents to the police. In the American national surveys, reporting rates for rape and domestic violence increased in the 1970s; after the mid-1980s, reporting rates for violent and sexual offenses increased substantially. Among the effects are that apparent increases in violent crime in the 1970s and 1980s were exaggerated and recent declines have been substantially underestimated. The most comprehensive analysis concludes that, when changes in victim reporting are taken into account, nonlethal serious violence decreased by 51 percent between 1991 and 2005. Police data indicate only a 27 percent decline (Baumer and Lauritsen 2010, p. 173). Similar patterns of increased levels of reporting to the police have been documented in England and Wales and Scandinavia, other places where annual victimization surveys have long been conducted (Chaplin, Flatley, and Smith 2011; Kivivuori 2014). As in the United States, apparent rate increases in official crime data have been exaggerated and decreases underestimated.

Second, net of changes in victim reporting, police recording practices have changed in ways that artificially increase crime rates. Partly this is the result of professionalization of police management and the related shift over 40 years from paper to electronic record keeping (Reiss 1992; Mastrofsky and Willis 2010). Recording rates for most crimes have increased, but more for some than for others. Domestic violence and sexual offenses are the paradigm cases, but other violent offenses are affected. No one who has lived through recent decades can fail to recognize that people in Western societies (at least) have become much less tolerant of intimate violence, violence against women, and sexual offenses generally (Pierotti 2013). Both for public relations reasons—to forestall criticism of police insensitivity—and because police are part of society and inevitably are affected by changing cultural attitudes, some kinds of incidents have become more likely to be officially recorded as crimes.

In some countries, policy decisions have been made to increase recording rates. Two major recent changes were made in England and Wales. In 1998–99, counting rules were changed to record more minor, or "summary," offenses particularly for less serious violent crimes, frauds, and drug offenses. The Home Office estimated that the change increased crime statistics overall by 14 percent. However, there were wide variations by type of offense. Burglary and robbery were estimated to have been little affected but other violence against the person to have increased by 118 percent (Povey and Prime 1999). Hough, Mirrlees-Black, and Dale (2005, p. 28) later observed that the changes "would have taken several years to bed in . . . [and] will have artificially inflated the count of crimes each year."

In 2002, the National Crime Recording Standard was introduced. England and Wales shifted from operating an "output" system in which police apply established criteria before recording incidents as crimes to an "input" system in which citizens' reports are taken at face value. The aim was to make the process more victim-oriented. The Home Office estimated that the change increased total crime rates by 10 percent in 2002/3, but as with the 1998–99 change, the effects varied between types of crime and were predicted to be especially significant for violent crimes (Simmons and Dodd 2003).

Third, cultural thresholds of tolerance have been changing since at least the 1960s. Behaviors now regarded as appropriately reported to police were in earlier times often regarded as unpleasant, undesirable, or socially unacceptable but not as criminal. Well-known examples include violence within domestic relationships, fights between acquaintances or drinking partners, and unwanted sexual touching in public. If the cultural meanings of such behaviors change over time, people at different times will use the same words to describe wrongful acts but mean different things. Here, too, domestic violence and sexual assaults are the paradigm cases. Had there been national victimization surveys in the 1960s, for example, respondents would have been much less likely than now to have thought of a blow from a husband, wife, or partner as an assault. Many victims of domestic violence or of bar fights would not have considered themselves to be crime victims and said "no" if asked if they had been assaulted. Many more such people in the 1980s and even more in the 2000s would have answered "yes." Issues of reporting and recording by definition would not have been raised in the earlier period for behaviors not then thought of as crimes.

The social meaning of assault would have changed even though respondents themselves did not realize that they now considered behaviors to be criminal that earlier they would not have.

Similar changes are likely to have occurred concerning a wide range of sexual incidents especially including allegations of nonstranger rapes and attempted rapes in dating and acquaintance relationships. Feminists worked hard in the 1970s and 1980s to expand cultural conceptions and legal definitions of rape (Estrich 1987). No reasonable person can believe that their efforts were unsuccessful. Something similar occurred in relation to child abuse. Rates of reported child physical and sexual abuse increased enormously in the United States in the 1980s as the result of a succession of new laws requiring social workers, psychologists, nurses, doctors, and psychiatrists to report suspected incidents to the police (Garbarino 1989; Brosig and Kalichman 1992; Kalichman 1999). After the early 1990s, recorded rates of child physical and sexual abuse plummeted. Between 1992 and 2004, reported physical abuse fell by 43 percent and sexual abuse by 49 percent (Finkelhor and Jones 2006, fig. 1).

Taken together, changes in reporting, recording, and cultural thresholds of tolerance in recent decades have increased official crime rates substantially in all developed countries. Those increases are, however, likely to have occurred at different times in different places. Their effects on official crime rates were largely manifest in the United States and some other countries by the early and mid-1990s. In other places, including many western European countries, they occurred and are occurring later. It is difficult, for example, not to hypothesize that all three mechanisms are major causes of recent increases in rates of sexual offending and assaults in official data in the Scandinavian countries (Selmini and McElrath 2014). Sexual crimes are the targets of major social and political movements there and the subjects of important changes in criminal laws and practices (Skilbrei and Holmström 2011, 2013; Tham, Rönneling, and Rytterbro 2011). It would be astonishing if those initiatives had no effects on cultural attitudes, victim behavior, and police policies and practices.

In this essay, I provide evidence that supports the preceding assertions. Section I summarizes the literature concerning a many-centuries-long decline in homicide rates through the mid-1950s, after which rates increased in all developed Western countries. Section II documents declines in homicide rates beginning in the 1990s, declines in rates since then for all crimes in many countries, and discordant evidence of increases in violence rates in a few. Section III canvasses reasons why the apparent increases in violence rates in some countries are much more likely to be the effects of changes in recording, reporting, and cultural thresholds of tolerance than of real increases. Section IV briefly explores the underdeveloped literature that attempts to explain both long-term and recent falls in rates of property and violent crimes. The explanations are simultaneously simple and complex. The simple explanations center on secular subjects including situational crime prevention initiatives and target hardening, the bureaucratization of modern life, and cultural shifts that are denunciatory of crime and violence. The complex explanations concern interactions among cultural and secular changes that have influenced capacities for informal social control and individual self-control (Baumer and Wolff 2014; Eisner 2014).

I. The Long-Term Decline in Crime Rates

A massive body of evidence shows that crime rates have long been declining. For periods before the establishment of institutionalized systems of official data, mostly in the nineteenth and twentieth centuries, studies focus almost entirely on homicide. Work on periods after 1800 encompasses other violent and property crimes. In our time, official data series have been standardized and strengthened and in many countries have been augmented by data from representative national victimization surveys. Taken together, they show a steady decline of homicide rates over many centuries, declines in a wide range of offenses from the early nineteenth through the mid-twentieth century, rises in rates of all crimes during the 1970s and 1980s, and falls in property crimes and homicide since the early 1990s. The only disagreement concerns nonlethal violence and sexual offenses since the early 1990s.

There is nothing controversial about the assertion that homicide rates declined substantially and continuously after the late Middle Ages. Pioneering work by the Swiss historian Manuel Eisner (2003), recently popularized by Steven Pinker (2011), provides almost unchallengeable evidence through the nineteenth century. Work by American political scientist Ted Robert Gurr and others demonstrated remarkably parallel crime patterns in several Western countries from the early nineteenth century through the middle of the twentieth (Gurr et al. 1977).

In a classic *Crime and Justice* article, Gurr (1981) offered evidence of a long-term decline in homicide rates in England between the thirteenth and twentieth centuries. For the earliest periods, Gurr calculated homicide rates for a few years or decades on the basis of work by English historians reporting data from coroners' and court records. From the beginning of the nineteenth century, he drew on data from official records. Figure 2, reprinted from Gurr's article, shows the results. The dots represent estimates based on individual studies; the solid line beginning in the nineteenth century is based on official records. Homicide rates averaged more than 20 per 100,000 in the thirteenth century, fell below 10 in the seventeenth century, and reached approximately the modern level of one per 100,000 in most western European countries in the nineteenth century. Writings on Finland (Ylikangas 1976), England (Cockburn 1991), Norway (Naess 1982), Sweden (Osterburg and Lindstrom 1988; Osterburg 1996), and the Netherlands (Spierenburg 1996) documented similar long-term patterns.

In another classic *Crime and Justice* article, Eisner (2003) documented centuries-long homicide declines in Europe beginning in some places in the fourteenth century. In the 1990s Eisner created the History of Homicide Database, on which he and most subsequent historians of long-term homicide trends have since relied. He was motivated by Gurr's showing of an apparent long-term decline in English homicide, evidence of similar patterns elsewhere, and speculation that something similar had happened throughout Europe. By 2003, Eisner's database contained 390 estimates of premodern homicide rates based on more than 90 publications. Figure 3, reprinted from Eisner's essay, shows the English data. It resembles figure 2 from Gurr but is based on many more studies and estimates. Separate figures for Scandinavia, the Netherlands and Belgium, Germany and Switzerland, and Italy showed comparable declines throughout Europe. The broad pattern was everywhere the same, but the timing varied: homicide rates in Scandinavia reached the contemporary level of one per 100,000 earliest, by 1800, and in Italy reached that level last—only in the twentieth century. By 2014, the database included 823 estimates of homicide rates during the period before creation of official national data sets (Eisner 2014). Figure 4, using the updated database, shows long-term declining homicide rates for most regions in western Europe: the patterns are everywhere the same, but the timing varies.

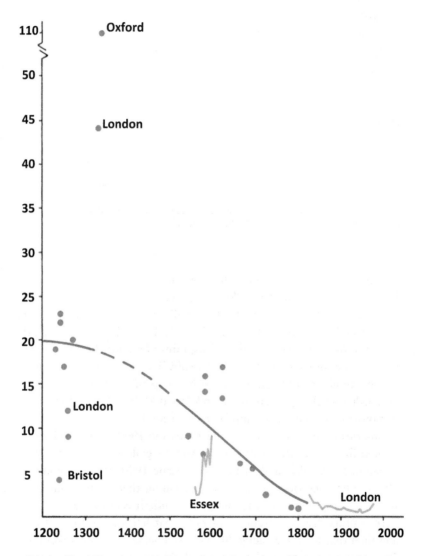

FIG. 2.—Homicide rates per 100,000 population, England, 1200–1980. Reprinted from Gurr (1981, p. 313, fig. 1). Each dot represents the estimated homicide rate for a city or county for periods ranging from several years to several decades. See Gurr (1981) for details on sources.

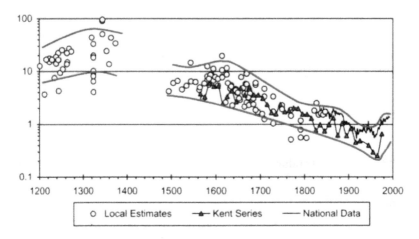

FIG. 3.—Homicide rates per 100,000 population, England, 1200–1990. Reprinted from Eisner (2003, p. 96, fig. 3). See Eisner (2003, 2014) for details on sources.

Gurr and colleagues had earlier looked at official data on crime in London, New South Wales (Sydney), and Stockholm and found that rates for all offenses declined substantially during the nineteenth and early twentieth centuries (Gurr et al. 1977). In England, which had the most extensive official record systems, rates of recorded crime, convictions, and imprisonment fell substantially. This was widely recognized in the late nineteenth century; French newspapers referred to it as the "English miracle" (Radzinowicz and Hood 1986). Zehr (1975, 1976) demonstrated a somewhat similar pattern for France.

American scholars writing in the 1980s and 1990s confirmed for the United States the pattern that Gurr and his colleagues had shown for London, Stockholm, and Sydney (e.g., Lane 1980, 1992; Monkkonen 1981). They described a "U-curve" of falling then rising crime rates from the early nineteenth to the mid-twentieth centuries and a twentieth-century "reverse J-curve" of rates that fell for the first 60 years and then rose for the ensuing 20. Now, of course, we know that official American rates continued to rise until 1991 and have fallen continuously since.

Criminal justice history is a small field and is not well known among social scientists who study crime. The field was even smaller in the 1980s. Even so, a handful of writers—Gurr, Lane, and James Q. Wilson—tried to make sense of the U- and reversed J-curves. All identified

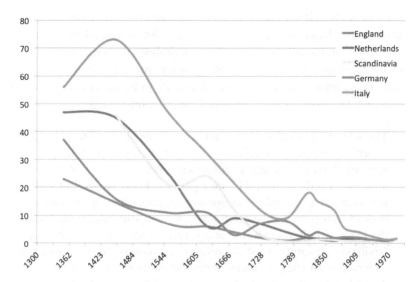

FIG. 4.—Homicide rates per 100,000 population, five European regions, 1300–2000. Source: History of Homicide Database. See Eisner (2003, 2014) for details on sources.

social or economic developments that, they argued, successively strengthened and then weakened individuals' capacities for self-control. In retrospect, they did pretty well, anticipating the most plausible theories offered in recent years (e.g., Fukuyama 1999; Pinker 2011; Eisner 2014).

For Gurr (1981, 1989) and Lane (1989, 1992) the fundamental explanation for the nineteenth-century decline was the development of institutions associated with modernization and the emergence of state and industrial bureaucracies. These included mandatory public education, the military, the factory, other economic institutions of the Industrial Revolution, and the expansion and bureaucratization of government. They also included the full range of modern criminal justice system institutions: professional police, juvenile training schools and later on the juvenile court, the reformatory and the prison, and parole and probation. Altogether, these institutions socialized individuals into conformity with important norms and helped create a disciplined environment characteristic of the industrializing cities of the nineteenth century. After the mid-twentieth century, buffeted by social and economic change, they lost their effectiveness.

Lane argued that the nineteenth-century changes altered people's capacities for self-control. They required more orderly, rational, and cooperative behavior than was necessary for independent farmers, craftsmen, and small merchants. In a preindustrial society, high levels of drunkenness, erratic or violent behavior, and unreliability affected only those immediately involved. Not so in an industrializing society, in which the work of each depended on what others did:

> The state was called in then, and cops in part created to help tame a formerly unruly population—with special emphasis on drunkenness, the kind of victimless crime that private citizens did not prosecute on their own. The new public schools taught not literacy so much as discipline, as youngsters preparing for regimented lives in factory or bureaucracy learned to sit still, take turns, mind the teacher, hold their water, and listen for the bell. The literally "civilizing" institutions of the nineteenth century, from temperance societies to a variety of incarcerating institutions, worked to make the industrial cities function smoothly as far as they did because they were going with the flow, reinforcing the felt needs of the new economic order, helping to create an appropriately new kind of mass social psychology. (Lane 1992, pp. 34–35)

Lane argued that rising crime rates after the 1950s reflected the shift from an industrial to a postindustrial society; its educational and technical demands left millions behind. Good blue-collar jobs were once available to most men who would accept industrial discipline. "It was never easy," Lane wrote, "to get young people—especially young males—to go along with that discipline, and now that there is little room for those who do not take to purely academic achievement, it is nearly impossible. The result is that the schools and cops, the injunctions to stay clear of the prevailing drugs, no longer work because they are no longer serving their former economic function, and much of the population, suffering from structural un- or underemployment, no longer accepts the kind of social psychology that built the industrial city" (1992, p. 35).

James Q. Wilson (1976; Wilson and Herrnstein 1985), by contrast, paid little attention to economic and structural changes. Instead, he focused almost entirely on Protestant and Catholic religious revivals that he argued strengthened socialization into moral norms of right behavior in the nineteenth century and later lost steam and influence. The revivals, which he believed improved capacities to delay gratification and resist violent and other wrongful impulses, rested on a Christian foundation that held during the nineteenth and early twentieth centuries. Once personal self-control was weakened by ideas of moral relativism and norms of hedonistic self-indulgence, things fell apart: "Parents could no longer socialize their children with the authority conferred by absolute moral standards, young folks lost the ability to control their impulses, the state, in effect, lost its nerve and will to punish effectively, and the result was and has been higher crime" (summarized in Lane [1992, p. 36]).

There the matter rested for a decade. It was only after the realization began to sink in early in the twenty-first century that crime rates had peaked in the United States in 1991 and around the same time or within a few years in other Western countries that scholars began once again to look for reasons for why crime rates fall.

II. The Recent Rise and Contemporary Fall in Crime Rates

The recent story is better known. Figure 5 shows homicide, rape, robbery, burglary, and motor vehicle theft rates per 100,000 population in the United States from 1960 through 2012. So that trends for the five offenses can be shown in one figure, homicide and rape rates have been multiplied by 10 and burglary rates divided by 10. With the exception of burglary, which peaked in 1981 and, despite a slight later increase, never again reached that level, the patterns for the five offenses are remarkably similar. They rise and fall, reach peaks and troughs, almost in lockstep. Rates rose from various dates in the 1960s until 1981, fell for 5 years, and except for burglary rose again until 1991.[3] Since then they have fallen more or less continuously, including in 2013.

The picture of recent declining crime rates is even more evident in

---

[3] Data from the National Crime Victimization Survey (NCVS) show broadly similar patterns (Bureau of Justice Statistics 1994). Robbery and assault victimization rates peaked in the early 1980s and again in 1991, falling afterward. Motor vehicle theft peaked in the early 1990s before beginning a long-term fall. Personal larceny, household larceny, and household burglary patterns are slightly different; all peaked in the early 1980s and fell continuously in subsequent years. Since the NCVS was redesigned in 1992, victimization rates have declined continuously for all offenses and especially steeply for violence (Truman and Planty 2012, fig. 3; Lauritsen and Rezey 2013). Victim reporting to the police increased gradually throughout the period 1973–92 (Bureau of Justice Statistics 1994, pp. 1–5) and more sharply from 1991 to 2005 (Baumer and Lauritsen 2010).

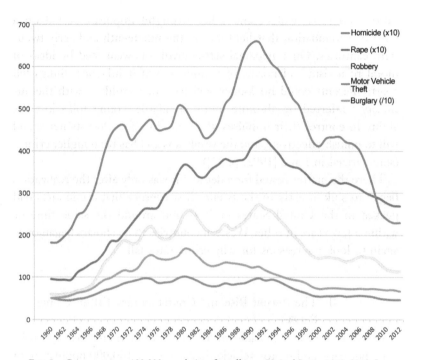

FIG. 5.—Crime rates per 100,000 population, five offenses, United States, 1960–2012. Source: Federal Bureau of Investigation, *Crime in the United States*, various years. To show trends for five offenses in one figure, homicide and rape rates per 100,000 population have been multiplied by 10. Rates for burglary have been divided by 10.

victimization data. Table 1, based on data from the 1993 and 2010 US NCVS, shows that reported victimization of individuals for most violent crimes fell by three-fourths during those years. Household victimizations for burglary, theft, and motor vehicle theft fell by two-thirds. The starting date is 1993 because that was the first year of data collection after a fundamental redesign of the survey. Victims' reports provide a broader indicator of the extent of victimization than do police data because they include both attempted and completed crimes, including many that victims did not consider serious enough to report to the police.

The rest of this section demonstrates three propositions. All aim to demonstrate that the national patterns shown by official data are accurate and that something fundamental was happening that affected all states and all developed Western countries. First, the American crime rate patterns shown in aggregate data are broadly representative of the

TABLE 1

Victimization and Prevalence Rates, per 1,000 Persons Aged 12 or Older (Violence) or per 1,000 Households (Property), by Type of Crime, 1993 and 2010

	Violence			Property	
	Victimization	Prevalence		Victimization	Prevalence
Total:			Total:		
1993	79.8	29.3	1993	351.8	171.6
2010	19.3	10.8	2010	125.4	89.2
Rape/sex assault:			Burglary:		
1993	7.7	2.6	1993	63.9	36.2
2010	1.9	1.0	2010	25.8	19.4
			Motor vehicle		
Robbery:			theft:		
1993	8.3	3.9	1993	19.3	12.1
2010	2.2	1.6	2010	4.9	4.3
Aggravated assault:			Theft:		
1993	16.5	7.6	1993	286.6	136.7
2010	3.4	2.2	2010	94.6	70.1
Simple assault:					
1993	50.7	18.4			
2010	12.7	6.9			

SOURCE.—Lauritsen and Rezey (2013).

experiences of individual American states and major cities. Second, American patterns of declining homicide and property crime rates characterize all western European and developed English-speaking countries. Third, patterns of nonlethal violent crime since the early 1990s appear—albeit misleadingly—to vary substantially between countries. In the English-speaking and some western European countries, rates for nonlethal violence have fallen substantially, paralleling homicide and property crime. In other western European countries, rates of nonlethal violent crime have either increased substantially or in any event not fallen (Aebi and Linde 2010, 2012; Selmini and McElrath 2014). In some countries, including those in Scandinavia, both police and victimization survey data show increases in rates of nonlethal violence. Kivivuori (2014) shows, however, that those figures should not be taken at face value.

A. American Crime Trends in States and Cities

The robustness of American crime rate declines can be seen by looking at patterns in states and cities. In this subsection, I present and briefly discuss homicide and robbery trends in the five largest states by population and homicide trends in the 10 largest cities. Because the

United States includes 50 states, the District of Columbia, Puerto Rico, and several smaller territories, "national averages" can be materially misleading. In the case of crime trends, they are not.

The problem can be illustrated by thinking about imprisonment rates. The overall state and federal imprisonment rate at year-end 2012, for example, was 480 per 100,000 population. The national rate, however, is afflicted by the sad tale of the statistician who drowned in a lake that was, on average, 3 inches deep. Means can mislead. There are huge differences in imprisonment rates between states. Maine's state imprisonment rate in 2012 was 145 per 100,000. When local jail inmates are taken into account, the total is about 200 per 100,000. That is well above the western European average but only slightly higher than the rates in England, New Zealand, and Spain and lower than those in much of eastern and central Europe. The highest rates, Louisiana's, were 893 per 100,000 when only state prisoners are counted and over 1,300 including jail inmates. Louisiana has by far the world's highest imprisonment rate, more than double those of Russia, Ukraine, and Belarus. Louisiana's rate in 2012 was also nearly double the total US rate, including jail inmates, of 717 per 100,000 (Carson and Golinelli 2013, table 8; Minton and Golinelli 2014, table 1). Imprisonment rates in all American states increased substantially after 1973, but the degree of increase and absolute rates varied enormously (Travis and Western 2014, chap. 2).

For comparison of crime trends, the relevant measure is not absolute rates but patterns of change. The patterns have been consistent throughout the United States. Figures 6 and 7 show changes in homicide and robbery rates for the five most populous states since 1980. More than a third of Americans live in them. Rates are standardized at one in 1980. Both figures follow the national patterns. Rates peaked in 1981–82, followed by a drop through the mid-1980s and a late 1980s climb to a higher peak in the early 1990s. After that the declines were continuous. In the most recent years, homicide rates were 40–60 percent lower than the starting point and a third to half their peaks. Robbery rates fell to levels 10–60 percent below the starting points and vastly below the intermediate peaks. The robbery data understate the declines. Homicide is the most reliably measured crime both because the indicator is unambiguous and because trends in police data can be validated with health statistics data on deaths from intentional injury. Robbery data are much more likely to be affected by changes in victim

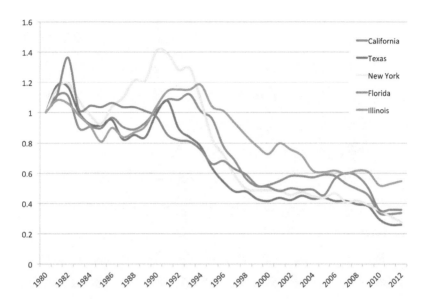

FIG. 6.—Standardized homicide rates per 100,000 population, five most populous American states, 1980–2012. Source: Federal Bureau of Investigation, *Crime in the United States,* various years. Rates have been standardized using state homicide rates in 1980 as bases valued as one. The figure shows trends in each state relative to its starting point.

reporting and police recording. They are also more likely to be affected by changes in criminal opportunities such as the increased prevalence of ownership of mobile telephones and other small electronic devices.

Figure 8 shows trends in homicide for the 10 most populous cities. Rates are standardized at one in 1990. Most cities experienced small increases in the early 1990s, followed by continuous falls through 2000. One clear implication is that "zero-tolerance" and "public order" policing in New York City played at most a small role in reducing homicide rates. During that decade of steep decline, rates in San Diego and Houston plummeted as precipitously. In the most recent years, every city's rate is at least 25 percent below the starting point, most are 60 percent below, and New York City's is 80 percent below. New York's anomalous 2001 rate results from the World Trade Center deaths.

B. Cross-National Measures of Victimization and Offending

Quantitative cross-national efforts to compare crime patterns pose formidable methodological challenges, some of which are discussed in

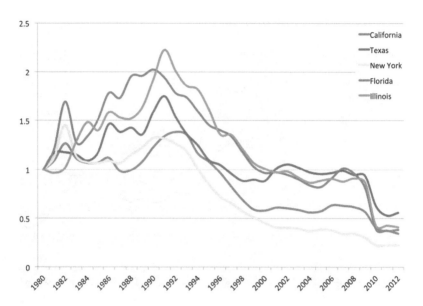

FIG. 7.—Standardized robbery rates per 100,000 population, five most populous American states, 1980–2012. Source: Federal Bureau of Investigation, *Crime in the United States*, various years. Rates have been standardized using state robbery rates in 1980 as bases valued as one. The figure shows trends in each state relative to its starting point.

following subsections. Efforts are being made to establish reasonably reliable cross-national data systems. These include the UN Surveys on Crime Trends and the Operations of Criminal Justice Systems (Harrendorf, Heiskanen, and Malby 2010), the *European Sourcebook of Crime and Criminal Justice Statistics* (Aebi et al. 2010), and the International Crime Victims Survey (ICVS; van Dijk, van Kesteren, and Smit 2007).[4] The first two remain relatively primitive because of basic cross-national differences in how crimes are defined and recorded (Alvazzi del Frate 2010 [UN data]; Harrendorf 2012 [*European Sourcebook*]).

The ICVS has been administered five times beginning in 1989 in a wide range of countries and cities. The core elements of the survey instrument are standardized though translated into appropriate languages. Questions ask about victimization experiences in everyday language and neither use nor assume knowledge of statutory offense def-

---

[4] The most successful such cross-national effort, though covering only the Scandinavian countries, is *Nordic Criminal Statistics, 1950–2010* (von Hofer, Lappi-Seppälä, and Westfelt 2012).

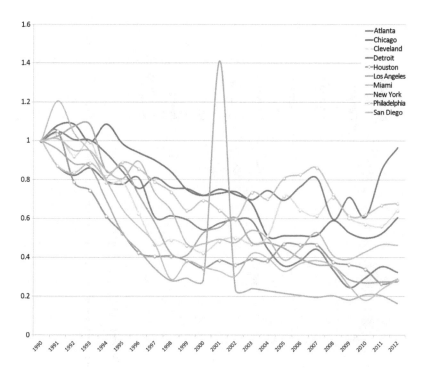

FIG. 8.—Standardized homicide rates per 100,000 population, 10 most populous American cities, 1990–2012. Source: Federal Bureau of Investigation, *Crime in the United States*, various years. Rates have been standardized using homicide rates in 1990 as bases valued as one. The figure shows trends in each state relative to its starting point.

initions. Surveys use representative national samples that average 2,000 subjects. Participation rates have varied over the years, typically ranging between 50 and 70 percent. Administering the surveys and analyzing the data of course pose significant methodological and statistical challenges. Nonetheless, the findings for developed Western countries are highly consistent and confirm the belief that crime rates have generally been falling since the early and mid-1990s.

Figures 9, 10, and 11 show the percentages of respondents reporting victimizations in seven English-speaking and European countries that participated in four or five ICVS waves. The green and white striped lines show averages for all countries (not only the seven shown). Figure 9 shows percentages reporting any crime victimization. Figures 10 and 11 show data for one violent offense (assault) and one property offense (burglary). Figures A1 and A2 in the appendix show results for the

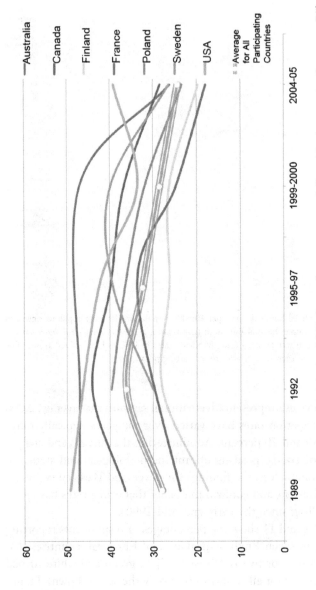

FIG. 9.—Percentages of respondents reporting any victimization, ICVS, four or five waves, seven and all participating countries. Source: van Dijk et al. (2007, table 5).

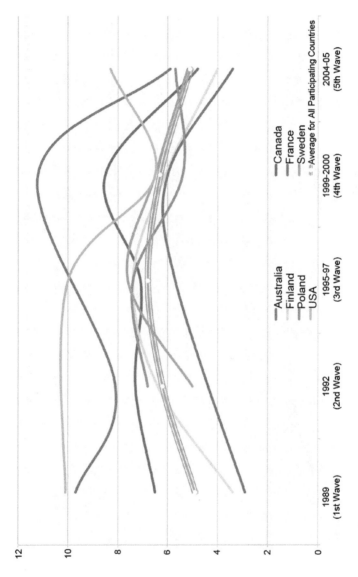

FIG. 10.—Percentages of respondents reporting assaults, ICVS, four or five waves, seven and all participating countries. Source: van Dijk et al. (2007, table 5)

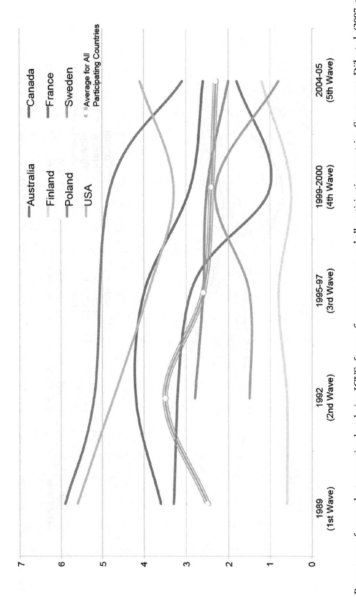

FIG. 11.—Percentages of respondents reporting burglaries, ICVS, four or five waves, seven and all participating countries. Source: van Dijk et al. (2007, table 5)

other two most commonly reported victimizations—auto theft and personal theft.

All the ICVS figures show the same thing, despite fluctuations attributable to the small sample sizes and—in some countries in some years—low participation rates: victimization rates rose in most countries after the 1989 wave of data collection, peaked in the early and mid-1990s, and have fallen since. This closely follows the patterns shown in American victimization (see table 1; Truman and Planty 2012, fig. 3) and police data (see fig. 5).

To round out this survey of broadly cross-national data, figure 12 shows data from the British Crime Survey from 1981 to 2010 for all property and violent offenses, for serious assaults (involving injuries), and for the three most common property crimes. England is the only country outside Scandinavia and the United States that has long conducted annual victimization surveys using large representative national samples. The patterns for all offenses are the same: rises in the 1980s, peaks in the early 1990s, and subsequent substantial continuing declines.

Take altogether, the American, English, and ICVS data lay a foundation for at least a tentative hypothesis that crime rates in recent decades have followed much the same patterns in Western countries for all crimes and separately for violent and property offenses.

C. Homicide and Property Crime Trends in Western Countries

There is now general agreement, at least for developed English-speaking countries and western Europe, that homicide patterns have moved in parallel since the 1950s (Eisner 2008). The precise timing of the declines has varied, but the common pattern is apparent. Homicide rates increased substantially from various dates in the 1960s, peaked in the early 1990s or slightly later, and have since fallen substantially. Property crime rates have declined everywhere since at least the early 1990s (Aebi and Linde 2010, 2012). I provide illustrative data for the English-speaking and Scandinavian countries because they, as groups of countries, provide polar cases.

1. *Homicide.* Figures 13 and 14 show Scandinavian and English-speaking country homicide rates, standardized at one on the 1960 rates.[5] There are no clear patterns in Scandinavia until the early 1970s,

---

[5] Except for Australia, for which reasonably reliable national data are available only from 1993 (Carcach 2005).

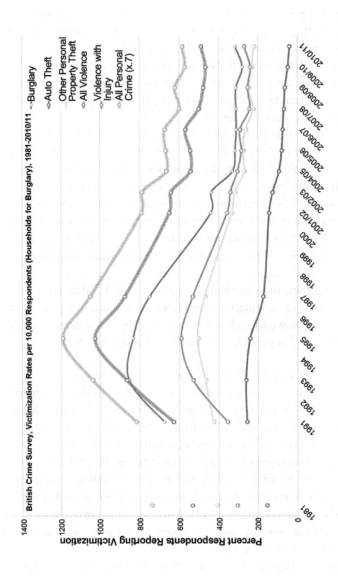

Fig. 12.—Victimization rates per 10,000 respondents aged 16 or over, or per 10,000 households, British Crime Survey, selected offenses, 1981–2010/11. Source: Chaplin et al. (2011, table 2.02).

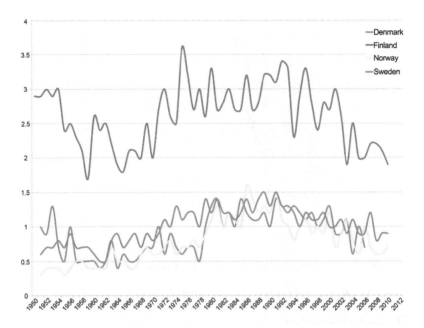

FIG. 13.—Homicide rates per 100,000 population, four Scandinavian countries, 1950–2012. Sources: 1950–2010: von Hofer et al. (2012, table 1); 2011–12: data provided by Tapio Lappi-Seppälä.

when rates began to rise in all four countries (least in Finland), peaking in the early 1990s, and dropping substantially since. Except in Finland, whose traditionally higher homicide rate ranged between 1.9 and 3.4 per 100,000 population, rates in the other Scandinavian countries fluctuate around one per 100,000. In recent decades they have usually been lower (von Hofer 2011; von Hofer and Lappi-Seppälä 2014). In countries of 4–8 million people, small differences in absolute numbers cause noticeable year-to-year rate fluctuations.

English-speaking patterns are similar, albeit with a lagged decline in England and Wales. Rates in Canada and the United States rose rapidly beginning in the mid-1960s, peaking around 1980, fluctuating at high levels during the 1980s, and peaking again in the early 1990s. After that, they fell sharply, as did Australia's after 1993. The pattern in England and Wales is similar except that the peak is a decade later. The English pattern is substantially affected by the case of Dr. Harold Shipman, who was convicted of killing 15 of his patients but was later established to have killed at least 215, with authoritative estimates that

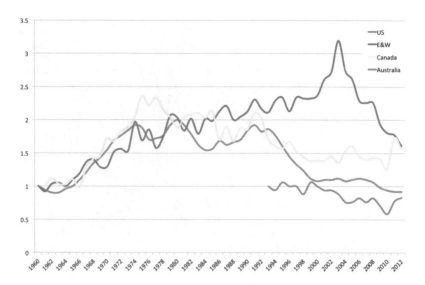

FIG. 14.—Standardized homicide rates per 100,000 population, four English-speaking countries, various years to 2012. Sources: Australia: Australian Bureau of Statistics; Canada: Statistics Canada; England and Wales: Office for National Statistics; United States: Federal Bureau of Investigation, *Crime in the United States*, various years. Rates have been standardized using homicide rates in 1960 in England and Wales and the United States, 1961 in Canada, and 1993 in Australia as bases valued as one. The figure shows trends in each country relative to its starting point.

altogether there may have been more than 260 (Smith 2003). England's homicide rate has fluctuated around one per 100,000 for the past 50 years. As in Scandinavia, comparatively small year-to-year differences in absolute numbers cause significant fluctuations in rates.[6] It is important to recall that figure 14 shows standardized data. American rates are typically four to eight times higher than those in England and Wales, three to four times those in Canada, and five to six times those in Australia.[7]

2. *Property Crime.* There is wide agreement that property crimes

---

[6] From 1990 to 1999, the annual number of homicides ranged between 669 and 750 (see table 2 below). After anomalous high absolute numbers in 2001 and 2002, the rate returned to the prior range and then declined, reaching 553 in 2011 and 552 in 2012 (Office of National Statistics 2013, table 6a).

[7] In 1993, e.g., the first year for which Australian data are shown, the American rate was 9.5 per 100,000, the English 1.31, the Canadian 2.19, and the Australian 1.7. In 2010, the American rate was 4.8, the English 1.12, the Canadian 1.62, and the Australian 1.0.

are declining in all developed countries, so I do not belabor the point (van Dijk, Tseloni, and Farrell 2012*a*). Figures 15 and 16 show trends for the United States, England and Wales, and the Scandinavian countries. First, however, a few words about cross-national comparison of official data are called for.

Countries vary substantially in police recording practices. Even homicide data can be suspect: validation against intentional homicide data in health statistics shows significant differences even in some developed countries and huge differences in many less developed countries (Smit, de Jong, and Bijleveld 2012; Lappi-Seppälä and Lehti 2014). Problems of data comparability are much greater, however, for other offenses (Aebi 2010; Harrendorf 2012). English-speaking common-law countries share roughly comparable legal definitions for offenses such as robbery, burglary, theft, and motor vehicle theft. So do the Scandinavians. The picture is vastly more complex in the rest of continental Europe. In some countries, burglary is a subset of theft and sometimes includes takings from houses, other buildings, and cars. "Motor vehicle theft" sometimes includes motorcycles, which in some countries are much more prevalent than in the English-speaking countries. "Robbery" is often not a separate category at all; offenses Americans would think of as robberies are distributed across a number of separate offense categories. And so on. Analyses of, for example, police data on motor vehicle thefts or burglaries in the United States and European countries are often apples-and-oranges comparisons and are bound to be misleading unless very careful adjustments are made (Tonry and Farrington 2005).[8] That is why I use English-speaking and Scandinavian countries to offer comparisons. Within each set of countries, offense definitions are broadly comparable.

Even within those sets of countries, figures showing comparative trend data cannot validly be used as a basis for drawing comparative

---

[8] This is the Achilles' heel of the admirable *European Sourcebook of Crime and Criminal Justice Statistics* (Aebi et al. 2010). The police data, compiled according to national offense definitions, are adjusted to make them comparable to standardized generic definitions and "checked" by national correspondents for each country: "Each correspondent would be an expert in crime and criminal justice statistics and would act as a helpline. They would also be entrusted with checking their country's data to ensure good quality. . . . They had full responsibility for the accuracy of the data provided by their respective countries" (p. 16). This means that the reliability of the "comparable" data eventually published depends critically on individuals in each country who must make adjustments to the official data and inevitably vary in their knowledge, sophistication, conscientiousness, and idiosyncrasies (Harrendorf 2012).

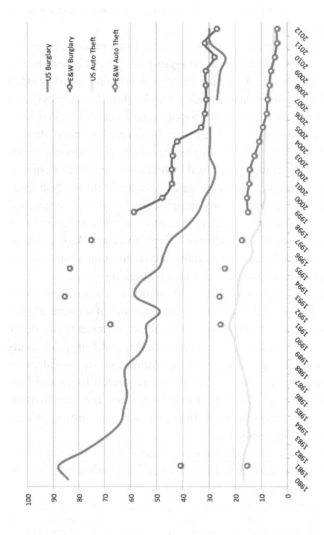

Fig. 15.—Victimization survey respondents reporting burglary or automobile theft, United States, since 1980. Sources: England and Wales: Chaplin et al. (2011, table 2.03); Office of National Statistics (2013, table 1.06); Bureau of Justice Statistics, NCVS. Rates in both countries are per 1,000 households.

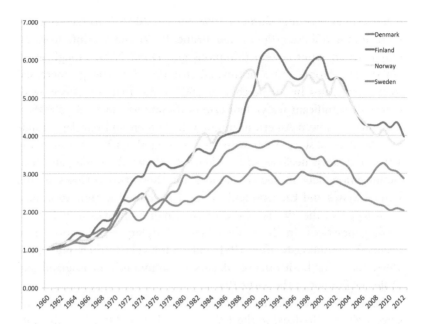

FIG. 16.—Thefts per 100,000 population, four Scandinavian countries, 1950–2012. Sources: 1950–2010: von Hofer et al. (2012, table 5); 2011–12: data provided by Tapio Lappi-Seppälä. Rates have been standardized using theft rates in 1960 as bases valued as one. The figure shows trends in each country relative to its starting point.

conclusions about crime levels. They can be used with greater confidence to compare trends. Crime-level comparisons cannot be made because recording practices vary. Minor thefts in some countries, for example, are commonly recorded in police data and in others they are not. The same differences exist for assaults.

Countries vary in how carefully they screen reported incidents before deciding whether to record them as crimes. Some operate "output" systems. This means that offenses are recorded only when police decide that the offense occurred and meets legal definitions. Others use "input" systems. This means that offenses are recorded as they are reported, without screening. Not surprisingly, input countries have higher crime levels than output countries (e.g., Aebi 2008, 2010; Harrendorf 2012).

Thus, even among sets of countries that use similar offense definitions, analyses of comparative trend data need to be sensitive to changes in recording policies. England and Wales, for example, made major crime-recording shifts in 1998–99 and 2002–3: to record many more minor offenses (Povey and Prime 1999) and to shift from an output to an input system (Simmons and Dodd 2003; Hough et al. 2005). The Home Office estimated that the 2002 change increased total crime rates by 10 percent in 2002/3 and that the effects were especially significant for violent crimes (Simmons and Dodd 2003).

Figure 5 showed American motor vehicle theft and burglary trends in official data since 1960 with rises during the 1960s through the 1980s and steep declines since. Figure 15 shows the same pattern in victimization data in recent decades for those two offenses in the United States and England and Wales. I have used victimization data so as to avoid the effects of the recent English changes in police recording practices. In the United States, burglary victimization rates declined continuously after 1981 and motor vehicle theft rates after 1991. Rates for both offenses declined continuously in England and Wales beginning in the early 1990s.

Figure 16 shows similar theft trends in official Scandinavian data since 1960 standardized to the 1960 rates. Theft and fraud are the only nonviolent property offenses for which time-series data are readily available (von Hofer et al. 2012). Rates rose continuously in all four countries to a peak in the early 1990s and have since fallen substantially.

3. *Nonlethal Violent Crime.* This is where things become more complicated. To this point, there is convincing evidence of steady, substantial declines in lethal violence in Western countries from the late Middle Ages to the nineteenth century, a continuing decline in rates for many offenses in selected countries through the mid-1950s, and rising rates for all major offenses in all developed Western countries through the early 1990s. Since then, there is convincing evidence of declines in homicide and the major property crimes in all developed Western countries (Baumer and Wolff 2014; Farrell et al. 2014; Lappi-Seppälä and Lehti 2014). Concerning nonlethal violence the evidence is mixed. In the English-speaking countries and some continental European countries, nonlethal violence as shown in official data is declining (Aebi and Linde 2010, 2012). Official data in other continental European countries, sometimes backed up by victimization data, show increases (see, e.g., Kivivuori 2014; Selmini and McElray 2014).

Figures 17–20 tell the tale. First the English-speaking countries. Figure 17 shows robbery rates per 100,000 population in official data from

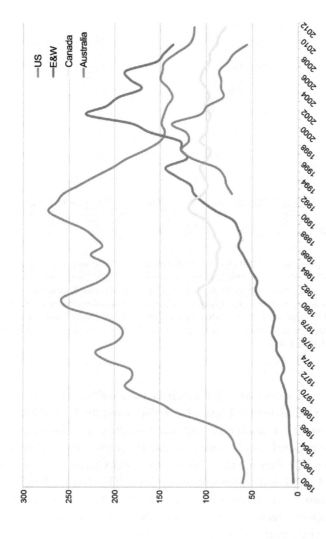

FIG. 17.—Robbery rates per 100,000 population, four English-speaking countries, various years to 2012. Sources: Australia: Australian Bureau of Statistics; Canada: Statistics Canada; England and Wales: Office for National Statistics; United States: Federal Bureau of Investigation, *Crime in the United States*, various years.

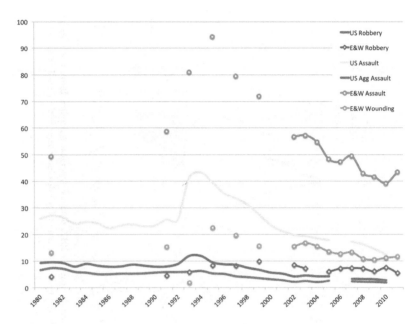

FIG. 18.—Respondents per 1,000 reporting victimization by robbery, assault, or aggravated assault, England and Wales since 1981 and United States since 1980. Sources: England and Wales: Chaplin et al. (2011, table 2.02); United States: Bureau of Justice Statistics, *Criminal Victimization*, various years; *Sourcebook of Criminal Justice Statistics Online* (http://www.albany.edu/sourcebook/pdf/t322010.pdf, table 3.2.2010). Victimization rates for England and Wales are per 1,000 population aged 16 and older. Victimization rates for the United States are per 1,000 population aged 12 and older.

1960 to the most recent dates for which data are available. Continuous time series are available for England and Wales and the United States. Data are shown for Canada and Australia from the years when reasonably reliable national data became available (Carcach 2005; Welsh and Irving 2005). The data for the United States and Canada show sharp rises through 1991 and significant drops since. The data for England and Wales show a continuous rise through 1996, followed by a drop and a subsequent steep rise that is no doubt attributable to the 1998 and 2002–3 changes in counting rules discussed above. After 2002, the English rates quickly fell by 50 percent. The Australian data show rises through the early 2000s, followed by a precipitate 60 percent drop.

Figure 18 shows victimization data for robbery, aggravated assault, and all assaults per 1,000 residents aged 16 and up for recent years in England and Wales and aged 12 and up in the United States. I use victimization data because they are not distorted by changes in English counting rules. Here the picture is much clearer than in the official data. In the United States, the trends for all three offenses parallel the trends shown in official data. The victimization data for England and Wales closely track the American pattern, with steady drops since the early 1990s.

As a whole, the data from the English-speaking countries tell a consistent story: violence rates rose substantially until the early and mid-1990s and dropped substantially afterward. Despite the complexities in the English data, all four countries show substantial declines in nonlethal violence in the 2000s.

The Scandinavian story is otherwise. Figure 19 shows robbery rates, standardized as one on the 1960 rate, from 1960 to 2010. Through the early 1990s, they parallel the English and American patterns, with steep rises through the early 1990s, followed by steep declines through the mid-1990s. After that, however, except arguably for Finland, the pattern is entirely different. Rates rise again in the late 1990s to peaks for three of the countries in 2000 and, except for Finland, where rates decline, fluctuate at the new higher level.

The Scandinavian difference is even more acute for assault, as the standardized data in figure 20 show.[9] Except for periods of decline in the 1990s in Finland and Denmark, the overall pattern is of continuous increases for 50 years, with the possibility of a change of direction in the early 2000s. That is too soon to tell.

So there it is. On the face of official data trends, the Scandinavians have experienced long-term and recent patterns in homicide and property crime that parallel those in the English-speaking countries. The same official data, however, show radically different trends in nonlethal violence since 1990. Either there are different stories to be told about crime trends in the English-speaking countries and Scandinavia (and other continental European countries) or there is one story but it is obscured by changes in reporting, recording, and changing cultural thresholds of tolerance. There is only one story: crime rates are falling throughout the developed Western world.

---

[9] The Scandinavian difference is especially marked concerning sexual offenses in official data (Selmini and McElray 2014).

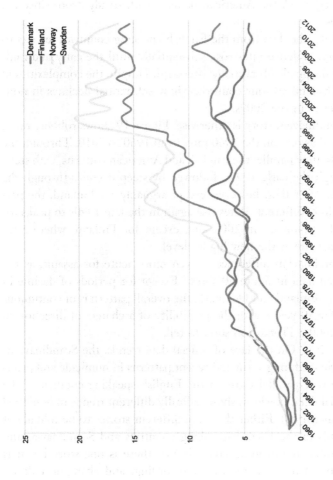

Fig. 19.—Standardized robbery rates per 100,000 population, four Scandinavian countries, 1950–2010. Sources: 1950–2010: von Hofer et al. (2012, table 4); 2011–12: data provided by Tapio Lappi-Seppälä. Rates have been standardized using robbery rates in 1960 as bases valued as one. The figure shows trends in each country relative to its starting point.

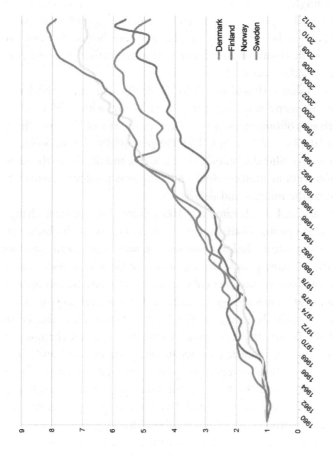

FIG. 20.—Standardized assault rates per 100,000 population, four Scandinavian countries, 1950–2010. Sources: 1950–2010: von Hofer et al. (2012, table 2); 2011–12: data provided by Tapio Lappi-Seppälä. Rates have been standardized using assault rates in 1960 as bases valued as one. The figure shows trends in each country relative to its starting point.

III. Why Apparent Rises in Violent Crime Are
Misleading

Changes in cultural thresholds of tolerance, victim reporting of incidents, and police recording of crimes are why violent crime rates appear, misleadingly, to be rising in some developed Western countries. In this section, I explain why the true incidence of violent crime is highly unlikely to be increasing in places where homicide rates are falling and briefly summarize evidence that suggests that apparent rises are artifacts of other social phenomena.

Nonlethal violence should be probabilistically associated with lethal violence in the same way that traffic deaths are with vehicle miles driven. Both sets of outcomes are products of the law of large numbers. In a particular place and period, 100,000 potentially violent incidents should produce predictable numbers of injuries and deaths in the same way that 100 million motor vehicle miles driven produce predictable numbers of traffic injuries and deaths.

Traffic injury and death rates per 100 million miles driven change slowly. They are probabilistic outcomes of driving skills, highway engineering, automotive design, medical trauma care, and random chance. With so many people driving so many kinds of vehicles on so many types of roads in any particular country, it would be astonishing if injury and death rates changed significantly from year to year. They have been gradually declining in the United States since the 1960s because all the factors that contribute to them have been changing in ways that reduce the incidence of accidents. Between 1981 and 2011, death rates fell by 0.03 percent per year (National Highway Traffic Safety Administration 2012, table 1). All developed countries including the United States have strengthened driver training requirements and targeted drunken driving; social norms about drinking and driving have changed; year by year, often under governmental mandates, automotive engineering changes have made cars safer; highway safety engineering has steadily improved; and the quality of treatment of traumatic injuries has improved. Without those changes, there is no reason to suppose that base rates of deaths and injuries would have changed at all.

And so it should be with homicide and nonlethal violence (e.g., Harris et al. 2002). Deaths should be probabilistically associated with the total number of potentially violent incidents. Franklin Zimring (1972) demonstrated this four decades ago in an article tellingly entitled "The Medium Is the Message: Firearm Caliber as a Determinant of Death from Assault." To investigate whether firearms affect the outcomes of violent crimes, he examined Chicago police reports for violent incidents in the late 1960s. He found that the likelihood of death occurring was probabilistically related to the tools available to an assailant. All else about an incident being equal, hands are less lethal than knives, which are less lethal than small-caliber firearms, which are less lethal than large-caliber firearms.

The data discussed in Section II demonstrate the probabilistic relationship between lethal and nonlethal violence in the English-speaking countries and demonstrate the existence of declining homicide rates in the Scandinavian countries. Baumer and Wolff (2014) and Lappi-Seppälä and Lehti (2014) demonstrate the existence of declining homicide rates in all developed Western countries. Nonlethal violence rates should be declining everywhere but appear in some places not to be. Either the law of large numbers does not apply in Scandinavia and in some other developed Western countries or the data are misleading.

The data are misleading. The fundamental reason is that there have been major shifts in cultural thresholds of tolerance of violence. One manifestation of this is that victims report larger percentages of incidents to the police. Victimization surveys almost always ask victims whether they have reported incidents to the police. In the United States and England and Wales, substantial increases in victim reporting have occurred for all offenses since the mid-1980s, but especially for sexual offenses and violence.

The most comprehensive and sophisticated analysis of NCVS data on victim reporting concluded that changes in victim reporting have led to substantial underestimates of the decline in the incidence of crime in the United States since 1991: "According to UCR data on nonlethal serious violence (i.e., rape, robbery, and aggravated assault), the number of violent crimes in the United States decreased by about 27 percent from 1991 to 2005. However, the NCVS suggested a much larger decrease for these same crimes—about 51 percent" (Baumer and Lauritsen 2010, p. 173). Because the point is so important, I quote their main findings:

> The overall empirical pattern that emerged from our research indicated that . . . an apparent widespread and important increase can be observed in the likelihood of police notification in the United States during the past 30 years. This increase seems to have been led by a rise in reporting for sex offenses and family vi-

olence, but we also observed significant increases in police notification since the early 1970s for burglary and motor vehicle theft as well as from the mid-to-late 1980s for nonsexual assaults, violence against both men and women, larceny, stranger and non-stranger assaults, [and] robberies committed by non-strangers. (P. 173)

No comparably sophisticated analysis of British Crime Survey data has been published. Responses to questions about reporting to the police since 1981, however, show substantial increases, especially for violence. Figure 21 shows relatively little change in victim reporting for burglary and motor vehicle theft but—especially relative to the 1981 base year—large ones for theft, minor assault (little or no injury), serious assaults (injury), and domestic violence (Chaplin et al. 2011, table 2.11). For domestic violence incidents, reporting to the police doubled, increasing from 20 percent in 1981 to 39 percent in 2010/11 and reaching 47 percent in 2009. Reporting of thefts, minor assaults, and serious assaults increased by half over the entire period and in some intervening years by more.

Comparably long-term, representative annual victimization surveys with large sample sizes are available in few other countries. Scandinavian countries are among them. There, as Kivivuori (2014) shows, victim reporting to the police has substantially increased since the early 1990s.

A second, multiplicative manifestation of the change in cultural thresholds is that the police record as crimes more of the incidents that come to their attention. This can happen as a matter of policy decisions or as a matter of unplanned—and unrecognized—changes in practice. Police in English-speaking countries traditionally operated output recording systems; a reported incident was recorded as a crime only if the police decided that the allegations were "founded," that is, if they satisfied legal criteria. An "unfounded" reported incident was not recorded as a crime. Input systems record reported incidents without independent confirmation by the police that a crime occurred. Not surprisingly, crime rates are higher in jurisdictions with input systems (Aebi 2008, 2010; Harrendorf 2012).

A number of countries have recently purposely switched from output to input recording systems. The 2002–3 English shift, which I discussed earlier, was predicted to increase crime rates generally but especially for violence (Simmons and Dodd 2003; Hough et al. 2005). As figure 17 shows for robbery, that is what happened. The principal

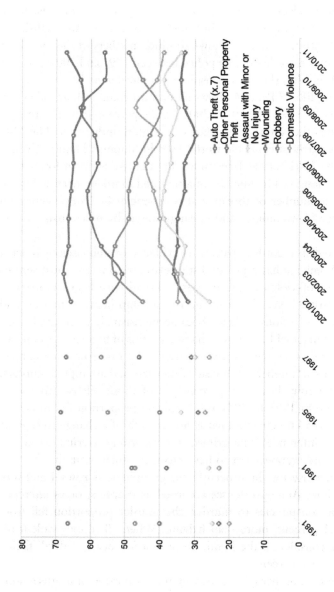

FIG. 21.—Percentages of respondents reporting victimization to the police, six offenses, England and Wales, 1981–2010/11. Source: Chaplin et al. (2011, table 2.01)

explanation for such shifts is that politicians want more incidents to be officially counted as crimes.

Police themselves, however, are no less likely than anyone else to be affected by changing cultural thresholds of tolerance. An English example is illustrative. Table 2 shows absolute numbers of the four most violent crimes recorded by the police between 1991 and 2001: murder, attempted murder, threat or conspiracy to murder, and "wounding or endangering life."[10] Panel A shows an upward trend in homicide from 669 deaths in 1991 to 850 in 2001—a 25 percent increase, though totals in the other intervening years were significantly lower. The 2001 increase is partly attributable to the Harold Shipman killings. Even if we take the 2001 rate at face value, the increase is much lower than for other offenses. The number of attempted murders increased by 50 percent, the number of threats and conspiracies by 250 percent, and the number of woundings and endangerments by more than 70 percent.

That English recording pattern is evidence of unconscious bracket creep. If homicide has a probabilistic relationship to the most serious other forms of violence, the increases should have been comparable for each. Instead, year by year, the relationship between murder and other forms of serious violence became increasingly attenuated. This can be seen in panel B. It shows changing ratios of homicides to various combinations of serious violent offenses. The first row, for example, shows the total numbers each year of murders and attempted murders. The second row shows the percentages of those offenses that were murders. From 1991 to 2001 the homicide proportion fell modestly, from 58.4 to 54.6 percent. That is not enough of a change to support any strong inference. The criteria for recording a crime as an attempted murder appear not to have changed much or at all.

It is otherwise for the other offense groupings, as rows 4 and 6 of panel B show. Among offenses recorded as murders, or as attempts, threats, or conspiracies to murder, the murder proportion fell from 12.6 to 5.4 percent, more than halving. When all serious violent offenses are considered, the homicide proportion nearly halved, falling from 4.7 to 2.7 percent.

There are a number of reasons why the proportion of deaths among

---

[10] The table stops in 2001 because the input recording system that took effect in 2002 was predicted to have substantial but unknown effects on recording patterns, especially for violence.

TABLE 2

England and Wales, Ratios of Murders to Other Violent Recorded Offences, 1990–2000/2001

	1990	1991	1992	1993	1994	1995	1996	1997	1997/98	1998/99	1998/99*	1999/ 2000*	2000/ 2001*
							A. Recorded Violent Crimes						
1. Murder	669	725	687	670	726	745	679	739	748	750	750	766	850
2. Attempted murder	476	555	568	661	651	634	674	652	661	676	676	750	708
3. Threat/conspiracy to murder	4,162	4,712	5,487	5,638	6,844	7,044	8,533	9,340	9,661	11,112	11,212	13,434	14,064
4. Wounding/ endangering life	8,920	9,408	10,741	10,701	11,033	10,445	12,169	12,531	12,833	13,960	14,006	15,135	15,662
						B. Ratios of Murders to Other Violent Crimes							
Total 1 + 2	1,145	1,280	1,255	1,331	1,377	1,379	1,353	1,391	1,409	1,426	1,426	1,516	1,558
1 ÷ (1 + 2)	.584	.566	.547	.503	.527	.540	.502	.531	.531	.526	.526	.505	.546
Total 1 + 2 + 3	5,307	5,992	6,742	6,969	8,221	8,423	9,886	10,731	11,070	12,538	12,638	14,950	15,622
1 ÷ (1 + 2 + 3)	.126	.121	.102	.096	.088	.088	.069	.069	.068	.060	.059	.081	.054
Total 1 + 2 + 3 + 4	14,227	15,400	17,483	17,670	19,254	18,868	22,055	23,262	23,903	26,498	26,644	30,085	31,284
1 ÷ (1 + 2 + 3 + 4)	.047	.047	.039	.038	.038	.039	.031	.032	.031	.028	.028	.025	.027

SOURCE.—Home Office (2001, table 2.15).

* Per revised classification scheme.

serious violent incidents might change. Just as changes in drivers' skills, drunk driving prevalence, automotive safety, highway engineering, and trauma care explain why highway injury and death rates have been declining, equivalent changes might be sought for serious violent incidents. Improvements in trauma care, for example, have made a huge difference in homicide rates over the past several hundred years and a significant one over the past 50 (Monkkonen 2001; Harris et al. 2002) but are unlikely to have caused major declines in deaths from intentional injuries in the past two decades. Changes in the technology of violence in England and Wales should have increased rather than decreased the proportion of fatal injuries; the prevalence of assaultive use of both guns and knives increased in England and Wales in the 1990s.[11] There are no close equivalents to changes in driving skills, automotive safety engineering, and the other contributors to the drop in automobile fatalities.

The proportion of homicides among serious violent incidents in England and Wales declined in the 1990s because the criteria police used to classify incidents gradually changed. Shifts in cultural attitudes toward violence, equivalent to shifts in cultural attitudes toward drunk driving, are the likeliest reason. British police increasingly classified incidents as very serious violence that in earlier years they would not have.

Something similar happened with less serious violent incidents. English civil servants have provided detailed statistical evidence that recording of minor assaults by the police increased substantially after 2000. They attribute the increases to the changes in counting rules discussed above and also to police responses to politicians' insistence that greater attention be given to minor violence (Britton et al. 2012).

Similar things have happened in many countries. In the conclusion to a recent book on the "international crime drop," Jan van Dijk and colleagues observe,

> In times of declining rates of crime, police forces are inclined to lower their thresholds for recording cases of less serious crime. Crime recording in our view tends to be counter-cyclical. This institutional mechanism seems to account for the remarkable divergences over the past ten or fifteen years between survey results on assault and police figures on less serious violent crime in the US,

---

[11] Their use has fallen significantly since 2000 (Chaplin et al. 2011).

Canada, several Western European countries, and Australia/New Zealand. Almost everywhere a degree of statistical net widening seems to have taken place, which has inflated the police count of violent crime. In our view, police figures of violent crime have, in recent years, been increasingly inflated. (Van Dijk et al. 2012*a*, p. 305)

Police are no less likely to be affected by shifts in prevailing cultural attitudes than anyone else. They watch the same films and television programs, read the same electronic and print media, and are affected by the same changes in prevailing political and cultural attitudes. Declining tolerance of wrongdoing caused crime victims in the United States, England and Wales, and Scandinavia to become increasingly likely in recent decades to report incidents to the police. In the United States, the principal reasons why prison populations rose in the 1970s and 1980s were that police arrested more people, prosecutors pursued cases they previously would have dropped and drove harder plea bargains, and judges sentenced more people to prison and for longer times (Blumstein and Beck 1999). Only later, in the 1990s, were harsher sentencing laws the primary driver of prison population changes (Raphael and Stoll 2013; Travis and Western 2014, chap. 3). Those laws also, however, reflected heightened intolerance of wrongdoing and more punitive attitudes to it.

If crime victims, police choosing whom to arrest, prosecutors making case processing decisions, and judges deciding sentences became more punitive, it would be astonishing if police-recorded crimes were unaffected by the attitudinal shifts that led to those changes. A rising sea lifts all things that float, including police boats.

There are thus good reasons to believe that rising official rates of crime in some countries are artifacts of cultural changes and not of real increases in violent incidents. The important question then becomes, Why have the offense amplification processes described in the preceding paragraphs occurred later in the Scandinavian (and some other European) countries than in the English-speaking countries? No one has been asking that question, so there is little research I can draw on to suggest answers.

One general hypothesis is that some countries are experiencing delayed responses to the rising crime rates of the 1970s and 1980s. Structural and cultural characteristics of the English-speaking countries caused them to respond earlier and more harshly. Repressive attitudes may both have risen and abated earlier than elsewhere. Tapio Lappi-Seppälä (2008) identified risk factors that especially characterize English-speaking countries in explaining why imprisonment rates rose substantially in some countries in recent decades but not in others. These include conflict versus consensus political systems, politically accountable prosecution and judicial systems versus apolitical civil service ones, expert versus political influence on policy making, and low versus high levels of trust by citizens in fellow citizens and government. Relative to most developed Western countries, England and Wales, New Zealand, the United States, and parts of Australia fall into the first of each paired set of alternative characteristics. In each, crime control was an important partisan political issue in the 1980s and especially the 1990s. This led to adoption and application of repressive crime control policies (and, with them, steeply rising prison populations).

A second, related general hypothesis is that the changes in cultural attitudes that caused long-term violence rates to fall also exacerbated public anger and resentments when short-term rates rose. The massive economic, social, and political changes of recent decades that affected all developed countries caused a several-decade disruption in long-term crime trends, as wars historically have. The gradual changes in social attitudes and values that caused violence rates to decline over centuries also raised thresholds of intolerance. In the English-speaking countries, especially the United States and England and Wales, politicians harnessed public anger to personal and partisan ends. The results in both countries included overheated political rhetoric, adoption of harsh crime control policies, and rising prison populations (Tonry 2004a, 2004b, 2010; Downes and Morgan 2012).

In much of Europe, by contrast, politicians and civil servants attempted rationally and humanely to address the challenges posed by rising crime, increased numbers of cases, enlarged budgets, and over-stretched facilities (Tonry 2004c, 2007; Lappi-Seppälä 2008). The English-speaking politicians acknowledged public anxiety and anger and, as David Garland (2001) argued, adopted severe expressive punishments in response. Politicians in some other countries attempted to manage and suppress public anger and anxiety. Scandinavian and some other European countries may now be experiencing the public upset that might have accompanied an immediate doubling or trebling of crime rates after the 1960s. Because crime rates rose gradually, and their practical consequences were managed effectively, in some countries public anxiety was delayed. It became manifest only during the recent decades of declining crime rates.

Delayed public anger and indignation about deviant behavior, leading to harsh attitudes and policies, have been documented in other settings. In each of three periods of alcohol and drug prohibition in the United States since 1850, the most punitive public attitudes, the harshest new laws, and the most aggressive enforcement practices occurred years after drug use peaked and began to decline. The leading drug policy historian, David J. Musto (1999), had an explanation. When drug use was not widely seen as a major problem, many people argued that it was not as dangerous as others believed and in any case was a private matter: in a free society, people should be able to do as they wish as long as they do not harm others. As drug use rose and its ill effects became more widely recognized, he argued, attitudes began to harden and prohibitionist sentiments became more prevalent. Social norms began to change and at a tipping point caused drug use to begin to decline. Fewer people used drugs partly because they feared legal consequences. Partly, however, they stopped because they came to believe drug use to be wrong. As the decline continued, attitudes became progressively harder. Few people any longer believed, or at least would publicly argue, that use of illicit drugs is acceptable or harmless.

This social consensus reinforced the decline in drug use, weakened opposition to harsh policies, and added a tone of fierce moralism to drug law enforcement. Musto also observed that attitudes began to soften during the first two prohibition eras, and policies and practices to moderate, 15–20 years after drug use began to fall. That model also fits the most recent "war on drugs." Drug use peaked in the late 1970s and early 1980s. The harshest policies were enacted between 1984 and 1996 (Tonry 2004b). A similar pattern characterizes American crime policy. Crime rates fell for 5 years after 1981, then rose until 1991, and have fallen almost continuously since. The harshest sentencing laws were enacted in the mid-1990s. As happened with drugs in the 1990s, much of the fervor has disappeared from the politics of crime and policies have begun to soften (Tonry 2013).

A third hypothesis is that distinctive cultural or political developments in some countries have caused crime to be treated as a substantively and symbolically more important issue in recent years, thereby exacerbating awareness of crime and deviance. One result is a process of amplification by which harms come to be seen as more serious than in earlier times. Since the late 1990s, sexual offenses in Scandinavian countries have received steadily increasing political and ideological attention (Skilbrei and Holmström 2011, 2013). In both political debates and the media, crime discourse in Scandinavia is increasingly victim-centered and moralistic (Tham et al. 2011). The recent emphases on victims and on sexual offenses may have made victims and police more sensitive than in earlier times to minor kinds of invasive behavior, citizens more likely to perceive incidents as assaultive when answering victimization surveys and to report incidents to the police, and police more likely to treat them as offenses. Selmini and McElrath (2014) show that sexual offense rates in Scandinavia continued rising long after they began to fall in many countries. Kangaspunta and Haen Marshall (2012) reviewed victimization survey data and police statistics on intimate violence in a number of countries. Surveys consistently showed declines in violence between intimates. Police statistics showed increases. They argued that increased recording of intimate violence has been influenced by worldwide campaigns to reduce violence against women. Van Dijk et al. (2012a, p. 305) suggest that this is a specific example of a more general mechanism of net widening by the police in a period when crime is falling.

The hypothesis that changes in cultural thresholds of tolerance of violence have amplified its salience is only recently becomingly recognized. The ideas that victim reporting and police recording change over time are well known and increasingly well documented. The more elusive idea that there are changes in cultural thresholds of tolerance, which are important contributors to higher victimization and crime rates, is less widely recognized. Kivivuori (2014) provides compelling evidence about it from the United States, England and Wales, France, and the Scandinavian countries.

IV. Making Sense of Declining Crime Rates

Substantial changes in crime rates ought to be an important social indicator. Sharp rises or falls or changes in long-term trends should tell us things about the health of social systems or about the nature and effects of major secular changes. This is the kind of subject about which men and women from Mars would expect there to be a sizable and sophisticated literature. They would be disappointed. Durkheim (e.g., [1893] 1933) had insightful things to say about crime as an organic outgrowth of social systems and about changes in levels and types of crime over time, but relatively few theorists have added much that is useful to his analysis. Garland (1990) stimulated renewed interest in Norbert Elias's ([1939] 1978) theory of a civilizing process that unfolded in Europe from the Middle Ages to modern times, bringing with it greater attention to hygiene, growing fastidiousness in serving and eating meat, and reduced use and acceptance of violence. Eisner showed (2003, 2008) that Elias's ideas provide at least part of a plausible explanation for the centuries-long decline in homicide rates.

Much of the theoretical work on explanation of crime trends until recently has been pretty primitive. That was probably inevitable since even somewhat reliable cross-national data, pertaining mostly to wealthy developed countries, have only recently become available. Most theorizing as a result has had to be a priori. Two competing cross-national sets of theories contended: a "Durkheimian" anomie theory that modernization weakened primary social bonds and with them inhibitions against egoistic behavior[12] and a Marxissant conflict theory that exploitative international patterns of economic development weakened social bonds and systems, and with that social control, especially in underdeveloped countries (Neuman and Berger 1988; LaFree 1999). Gary LaFree (2005), analyzing 45 years of homicide data from 34 countries, tested "modernization" and conflict theories. He concluded that homicide trends were becoming more similar in wealthy developed countries but not in less developed countries and concluded that an "elite convergence" was occurring.

The articles mentioned in the preceding paragraph are not, of course, the only ones on the subject, but they are among the most cited and they give a flavor of the nature of recent theorizing.[13] They

[12] This is slightly odd. The assumption that modernization and urbanization bring heightened crime rates with them contradicts the well-known historic pattern that crime rates were typically lower in the emerging cities of the modern era than in the countryside (Eisner 2003, pp. 105–6). In another of his intellectual hats, Durkheim (1982) famously argued that crime is a necessary social construct that every society needs in order to reinforce core values. As societies change, the content of "crime" necessarily changes, but the concept would exist even in a society of saints. Thus as societies evolve, conceptions of crime should change, but the amount of "crime" should be more or less constant.

[13] Another recent theoretical approach has been to test crime trend hypotheses derived from etiological theories of crime. The study by Kivivuori, Savolainen, and Danielsson (2012) is an especially comprehensive example.

and others like them have largely been passed by. The historical work on long-term trends was much less well known when they were written. As a result they sought short-term explanations to what we now know to have been only modulations in long-term trends. Likewise, the now sizable literature documenting parallelism in homicide trends in wealthy Western countries did not exist (e.g., Eisner 2008), so their authors could not have known about it.

The near-absence of a theoretical literature on crime trends is astonishing. Hundreds of thousands of people have spent their lives studying crime and criminal justice systems, but only comparatively few have seriously attempted to explain the most striking and consequential crime developments of the past 50 years: the steep increase in crime rates in all developed Western countries beginning in the 1960s and the steep decreases since the early 1990s.

The most persuasive theories are the simplest and hark back to the writing of Ted Robert Gurr, Roger Lane, and James Q. Wilson in the 1980s. All of them looked for explanations for the U- and reverse J-curves in social and economic changes likely to have affected social control processes and shaped capacities for self-control. Eisner showed that homicide rates fell throughout western Europe more or less continuously from the late Middle Ages. The timing and trajectories of decline varied, but most regions converged on a rate of one per 100,000 inhabitants by the beginning of the nineteenth century and almost all reached it by the beginning of the twentieth. Eisner's (2003) early explanations drew elements from Elias's ideas about a "civilizing process." Later he focused on Max Weber's ideas about the influence of the Protestant Ethic in shaping norms and values (Eisner 2008). The relevant mechanisms included state formation with a state near-monopoly on legal violence, creation of institutions and processes that obviated needs for self-help, urbanization, and increasing social interdependence (Johnson and Monkkonen 1996; Eisner 2003).

Ted Gurr and others (Gurr et al. 1977; Gurr 1981) showed that crime rates declined generally in major Western cities in the nineteenth century and the beginning of the twentieth. Gurr's major early works were written before Eisner's findings became known, and he therefore sought not to locate nineteenth-century developments into longer patterns but to explain developments in the period he studied. In retrospect his explanations fit well with Eisner's synthesis. The major contributing causes were increases in social control and self-control associated with industrialization, urbanization, modernization, and bureaucratization. The archetypal institutions socializing individuals into conformity included the public school, the newly invented criminal justice institutions, the factory, the army, and the bureaucratic institutions of the modernizing state. Lane's (1980, 1992) explanations focused on interdependence and the need for individuals to learn to function cooperatively. Wilson (e.g., Wilson and Herrnstein 1985) focused more on the normative underpinnings of cooperative behavior and found them in religious revivals in the nineteenth century that strengthened social and self-control by means of socialization into strengthened moral norms of right behavior.[14]

Put together, those accounts cumulate into an intuitively plausible story of how human beings at least in developed countries gradually became less larcenous and less violent. They do not explain what went wrong in the 1960s. Francis Fukuyama (1999) provides a plausible account. Postwar economic expansions produced prosperous and peaceable years in the 1950s. However, in short order came decolonization of most of Africa, much of the Caribbean, and parts of South America and the Middle East; the Vietnam War and youthful rebellions of the 1960s; the civil, women's, and gay rights movements; economic transformations including the OPEC oil embargos of the 1970s, massive economic restructuring, and globalization; and vastly increased movements of people between countries. In retrospect it was all too much to be absorbed in a short time. As Chinua Achebe (1958) described colonial Nigeria, *Things Fall Apart*. Crime rates rose as did support in many countries for neoliberal and xenophobic political movements. That harsh crime policies emerged in some countries is not surprising.

By the 1990s, however, in most wealthy developed countries the effects of the preceding decades' disruptions had largely been absorbed. Crime rates peaked and began what proved to be precipitate falls. The historic long-term trend resumed after a several-decade disruption.

Most of the theorizing by social scientists has largely missed the big

[14] This is not very different from how Eisner (2008, p. 270) summarized Weber's ideas: "Weber used the term *Lebensführung* . . . or conduct of life [to refer] to a much wider cultural script encompassing work, politics, beliefs, education, and individual character. These models of conduct of life become reinforced and stabilized through institutions such as schools, families, the church, and bureaucracies. In *The Protestant Ethic and the Spirit of Capitalism* Weber [(1930) 1982] argued that models of conduct of life can be enormously powerful forces that mold the details of daily action and shape the trajectories of economic life."

picture by focusing only on the aberrational decades of the 1970s and 1980s and the subsequent steep declines.[15] By doing so, they miss the significance of the long-term patterns. Graham Farrell and his colleagues (2014), for example, adopt primarily opportunity and routine activities explanations for the post-1960s crime rise. The argument is that rates rose because larger quantities of valuable portable goods were available to be stolen, fewer people were at home during the day to guard them, and more people moved in public places and thereby became more vulnerable to personal victimization. The post-1990 declines are posited to be the effect of situational crime prevention initiatives including, notably, automobile theft prevention hardware, greatly increased use of home security hardware, and a wide variety of target-hardening and guardianship-enhancing initiatives. There are two insuperable difficulties. One is that the routine activities arguments and the situational initiatives, though plausibly related to changes in burglary and theft rates, are impossibly hard to relate to changes in rates of lethal and sexual violence. Arguments can be made that reducing property crime rates through instrumental means might delay, alter, or prevent onset of criminal careers and thereby affect the incidence of other kinds of crimes. However, the notion that there is a sizable causal relation between involvement in stealing cars or committing burglaries and the incidence of rape or murder is not credible. The second problem is that homicide rates in developed countries have moved in parallel for 50 years. Take-up and timing of situational crime prevention initiatives have varied widely over time and space. They cannot be the independent variable that explains changes in homicide rates.

A separate set of theories focusing on the influence of economic variables suffers from similar problems.[16] Efforts have been made to

---

[15] Farrell et al. (2014) identify 17 theories that have been offered to explain recently rising crime rates and evaluate them using four tests. These include that the theory has cross-national validity and must be reconcilable with the crime rate increases of the 1970s and 1980s. Only one theory passes all four tests.

[16] Dills, Miron, and Summers (2008, p. 3) tested all the prevailing American explanations for the fall in crime rates and found that none was generalizable cross-nationally: "Based on this evaluation, we argue that economists know little about the empirically relevant determinants of crime. This conclusion applies both to policy variables like arrest rates or capital punishment and to indirect factors such as abortion or gun laws. The reason is that even hypotheses that find some support in U.S. data for recent decades are inconsistent with data over longer horizons or across countries. Thus, these hypotheses are less persuasive than a focus on recent U.S. evidence might suggest."

explain property crime rates specifically and crime rates generally, and changes in them, on the basis of national differences in economic variables such as unemployment, inflation, and economic growth (e.g., Rosenfeld and Messner 2009; Buonanno, Drago, and Galbiati 2014; Rosenfeld 2014). Such variables may or may not explain marginal differences in property crime rates over time, or even cross-nationally, but by definition, differences in them cannot explain common cross-national trends in homicide and other violent crimes. The problem is the same as that confronting the opportunity theories: the causal chain from greater or lesser incentives to commit burglaries or thefts to commission of killings and rapes is impossible to draw. Deeper forces of causal cross-national salience are at work.

Finally, it is no longer reasonable even to hypothesize that crime patterns can be explained in terms of punishment policies or imprisonment rates, although many academics, especially economists, try to do so (e.g., Buonanno et al. 2011). Figure 1, showing nearly identical homicide and robbery patterns in the United States and Canada but stable Canadian imprisonment rates and an American quintupling, is but one of many demonstrations (e.g., Tonry 2007; Lappi-Seppälä 2008). The most exhaustive recent analyses reach the same conclusion (Baumer and Wolff 2014; Lappi-Seppälä and Lehti 2014).

Lane (1992, p. 33) rightly and presciently observed, at a time when American crime rates appeared to be rising inexorably, and when little information was available about crime patterns elsewhere, as follows:

> That this is an international phenomenon suggests that most of the usual parochial explanations for rising crime, whether of the left or right, do not apply. It is important to stress that neither the decisions of the Supreme Court of the United States, the increasingly black complexion of American cities, nor our national gun culture have much to do with rising rates in Scandinavia or Australia. That the curve was down during the previous century suggests also that neither massive economic change, the disruption of traditional society, nor waves of immigration, all modern phenomena first experienced during the nineteenth century, can explain the upsurge either.

What are left to explain long-term and recent trends are broad-based theories of social control and self-control (e.g., Baumer and Wolff 2014; Eisner 2014).

As was true in Europe beginning in the late Middle Ages, crime rates move to deep and broad social forces, and move in parallel, even if sometimes with lags. That is what happened with major Western cities in the nineteenth and twentieth centuries and in all developed Western countries from the 1960s to the 1990s. Since then, rates for all the traditional crimes of property and violence have fallen substantially in many countries. The appearance of recently rising rates of nonlethal violence in some European countries will in time be revealed as an illusion. If I am right, apparent increases in violent crime rates in Europe should soon peak and then fall, making it clear that trends are moving in parallel not only in the English-speaking countries but in all the Western world.

APPENDIX

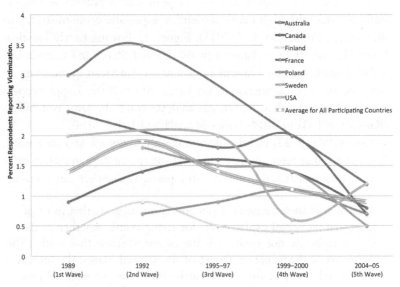

FIG. A1.—Percentages of respondents reporting automobile theft, ICVS, four or five waves, seven and all participating countries. Source: van Dijk et al. (2007, table 5).

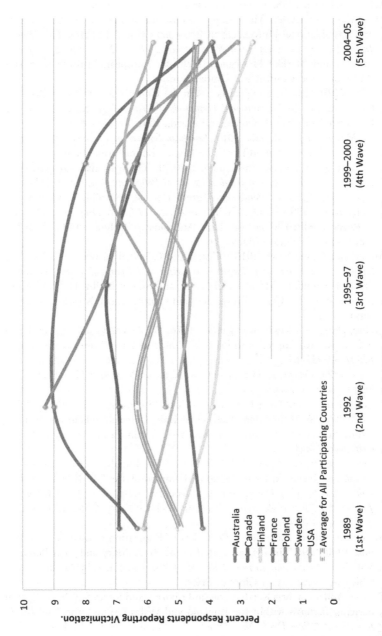

FIG. A2.—Percentages of respondents reporting personal theft, ICVS, four or five waves, seven and all participating countries. Source: van Dijk et al. (2007, table 5).

REFERENCES

Achebe, Chinua. 1958. *Things Fall Apart*. London: Heinemann.

Aebi, Marcelo F. 2008. "Measuring the Influence of Statistical Counting Rules on Cross-National Differences in Recorded Crime." In *Crime and Criminal Justice Systems in Europe and North America, 1995–2004*, edited by Kauko Aromaa and Markku Heiskanen. Helsinki: European Institute for Crime Prevention and Control and United Nations.

———. 2010. "Methodological Issues in the Comparison of Police-Recorded Crime Rates." In *International Handbook of Criminology*, edited by Shlomo Giora Shoham, Paul Knepper, and Martin Kett. London: CRC Press.

Aebi, Marcelo F., et al., eds. 2010. *European Sourcebook of Crime and Criminal Justice Statistics—2010*. 4th ed. The Hague: Boom Juridische uitgevers.

Aebi, Marcelo F., and Antonia Linde. 2010. "Is There a Crime Drop in Western Europe?" *European Journal of Criminal Policy and Research* 16:251–77.

———. 2012. "Crime Trends in Western Europe According to Official Statistics from 1990 to 2007." In *The International Crime Drop: New Directions in Research*, edited by Jan van Dijk, Andromachi Tseloni, and Graham Farrell. London: Palgrave Macmillan.

Alvazzi del Frate, Anna. 2010. "Crime and Criminal Justice Statistics Challenges." In *International Statistics on Crime and Criminal Justice*, edited by Stefan Harrendorf, Markku Heiskanen, and Steven Malby. Helsinki: European Institute for Crime Prevention and Control and UN Office on Drugs and Crime.

Archer, Dane, and Rosemary Gartner. 1976. "Violent Acts and Violent Times: A Comparative Approach to Postwar Homicide Rates." *American Sociological Review* 41:937–63.

———. 1984. *Violence and Crime in Cross-National Perspective*. New Haven, CT: Yale University Press.

Baumer, Eric P., and Janet L. Lauritsen. 2010. "Reporting Crime to the Police, 1973–2005: A Multivariate Analysis of Long-Term Trends in the National Crime Survey (NCS) and National Crime Victimization Survey (NCVS)." *Criminology* 48:131–85.

Baumer, Eric P., and Kevin T. Wolff. 2014. "The Breadth and Causes of Contemporary Trends in Cross-National Homicide Rates." In *Why Crime Rates Fall and Why They Don't*, edited by Michael Tonry. Vol. 43 of *Crime and Justice: A Review of Research*, edited by Michael Tonry. Chicago: University of Chicago Press.

Blumstein, Alfred, and Allen J. Beck. 1999. "Population Growth in U.S. Prisons, 1980–1996." In *Prisons*, edited by Michael Tonry and Joan Petersilia. Vol. 26 of *Crime and Justice: A Review of Research*, edited by Michael Tonry. Chicago: University of Chicago Press.

Britton, Andrew, Chris Kershaw, Sarah Osborne, and Kevin Smith. 2012. "Underlying Patterns within the England and Wales Crime Drop." In *The International Crime Drop: New Directions in Research*, edited by Jan van Dijk, Andromachi Tseloni, and Graham Farrell. London: Palgrave Macmillan.

Brosig, Cheryl L., and Seth C. Kalichman. 1992. "Clinicians' Reporting of

Suspected Child Abuse: A Review of the Empirical Literature." *Clinical Psychology Review* 12(2):155–68.

Buonanno, Paolo, Francesco Drago, and Roberto Galbiati. 2014. "Response of Crime to Unemployment: An International Comparison." *Journal of Contemporary Criminal Justice* 30(1):29–40.

Buonanno, Paolo, Francesco Drago, Roberto Galbiati, and Giulio Zanella. 2011. "Crime in Europe and the United States: Dissecting the 'Reversal of Misfortunes.'" *Economic Policy Journal* 26:347–85.

Bureau of Justice Statistics. 1994. *Criminal Victimization in the United States: 1973–1992 Trends*. Washington, DC: US Department of Justice, Bureau of Justice Statistics.

Carcach, Carlos. 2005. "Crime and Punishment in Australia, 1980–2000." In *Crime and Punishment in Western Countries, 1980–1999*, edited by Michael Tonry and David P. Farrington. Vol. 33 of *Crime and Justice: A Review of Research*, edited by Michael Tonry. Chicago: University of Chicago Press.

Carson, E. Ann, and Daniela Golinelli. 2013. *Prisoners in 2012—Advance Counts*. Washington, DC: US Department of Justice, Bureau of Justice Statistics.

Chaplin, Rupert, John Flatley, and Kevin Smith, eds. 2011. *Crime in England and Wales, 2010/11: Findings from the British Crime Survey and Police Recorded Crime*. 2nd ed. London: Home Office Statistics.

Cockburn, J. S. 1991. "Patterns of Violence in English Society: Homicide in Kent, 1560–1985." *Past and Present* 130:70–106.

Dills, Angela K., Jeffrey A. Miron, and Garrett Summers. 2008. "What Do Economists Know about Crime?" NBER Working Paper no. 13759. Cambridge, MA: National Bureau of Economic Research.

Doob, Anthony M., and Cheryl Marie Webster. 2013. "'Truth in Sentencing' Act: The Triumph of Form over Substance." *Canadian Criminal Law Review* 17:365–92.

Downes, David, and Rod Morgan. 2012. "Overtaking on the Left: The Politics of Law and Order in the 'Big' Society." In *The Oxford Handbook of Criminology*, 5th ed., edited by Mike Maguire, Rod Morgan, and Robert Reiner. Oxford: Oxford University Press.

Durkheim, Emile. 1933. *The Division of Labor in Society*. Translated by George Simpson. New York: Macmillan. (Originally published 1893.)

———. 1982. "Rules for the Distinction of the Normal from the Pathological." In *The Rules of Sociological Method*, translated by W. D. Halls. New York: Free Press.

Eisner, Manuel. 2003. "Long-Term Historical Trends in Violent Crime." In *Crime and Justice: A Review of Research*, vol. 30, edited by Michael Tonry. Chicago: University of Chicago Press.

———. 2008. "Modernity Strikes Back? A Historical Perspective on the Latest Increase of Interpersonal Violence (1960–1990)." *International Journal of Conflict and Violence* 2:288–316.

———. 2014. "From Swords to Words: Does Macro-Level Change in Self-Control Predict Long-Term Variation in Levels of Homicide?" In *Why*

Crime Rates Fall and Why They Don't, edited by Michael Tonry. Vol. 43 of *Crime and Justice: A Review of Research*, edited by Michael Tonry. Chicago: University of Chicago Press.

Elias, Norbert. 1978. *The Civilising Process*. 2 vols. Translated by Edmund Jephcott. New York: Urizen. (Originally published 1939.)

Estrich, Susan. 1987. *Real Rape*. Cambridge, MA: Harvard University Press.

Farrell, Graham, Nick Tilly, and Andromachi Tseloni. 2014. "Why Did Crime Drop?" In *Why Crime Rates Fall and Why They Don't*, edited by Michael Tonry. Vol. 43 of *Crime and Justice: A Review of Research*, edited by Michael Tonry. Chicago: University of Chicago Press.

Finkelhor, David, and Lisa Jones. 2006. "Why Have Child Maltreatment and Child Victimization Declined?" *Journal of Social Issues* 62(4):685–716.

Fukuyama, Francis. 1999. *The Great Disruption: Human Nature and the Reconstruction of Social Order*. New York: Free Press.

Garbarino, James. 1989. "The Incidence and Prevalence of Child Maltreatment." In *Family Violence*, edited by Lloyd Ohlin and Michael Tonry. Vol. 11 of *Crime and Justice: A Review of Research*, edited by Michael Tonry and Norval Morris. Chicago: University of Chicago Press.

Garland, David. 1990. *Punishment in Modern Society—a Study in Social Theory*. Chicago: University of Chicago Press.

———. 2001. *The Culture of Control*. Chicago: University of Chicago Press.

Goldberger, Arthur S., and Richard Rosenfeld, eds. 2008. *Understanding Crime Trends: Workshop Report*. National Research Council, Division of Behavioral and Social Sciences and Education, Committee on Understanding Crime Trends, Committee on Law and Justice. Washington, DC: National Academies Press.

Gurr, Ted Robert. 1981. "Historical Trends in Violent Crime: A Critical Review of the Evidence." In *Crime and Justice: An Annual Review of Research*, vol. 3, edited by Michael Tonry and Norval Morris. Chicago: University of Chicago Press.

———. 1989. "Historical Trends of Violent Crime." In *Violence in America*, vol. 1, *The History of Crime*, edited by Ted Robert Gurr. Newbury Park, CA: Sage.

Gurr, Ted Robert, Peter N. Grabosky, and Richard C. Hula. 1977. *The Politics of Crime and Conflict: A Comparative History of Four Cities*. Beverly Hills, CA: Sage.

Harrendorf, Stefan. 2012. "Offence Definitions in the *European Sourcebook of Crime and Criminal Justice Statistics* and Their Influence on Data Quality and Comparability." *European Journal of Criminal Policy and Research* 18:23–53.

Harrendorf, Stefan, Markku Heiskanen, and Steven Malby, eds. 2010. *International Statistics on Crime and Criminal Justice*. Helsinki: European Institute for Crime Prevention and Control and UN Office on Drugs and Crime.

Harris, Anthony R., Stephen H. Thomas, Gene A. Fisher, and David J. Hirsch. 2002. "Murder and Medicine: The Lethality of Criminal Assault 1960–1999." *Homicide Studies* 6:128–66.

Home Office. 2001. *Criminal Statistics, England and Wales, 2000*. London: Home Office, Research, Development, and Statistics Directorate.

Hough, Michael, Catriona Mirrlees-Black, and Michael Dale. 2005. *Trends in Violent Crime since 1999/2000*. London: King's College, Institute for Criminal Policy Research.

Johnson, Eric A., and Erik H. Monkkonen. 1996. "Introduction." In *The Civilization of Crime: Violence in Town and Country since the Middle Ages*, edited by Eric A. Johnson and Erik H. Monkkonen. Urbana: University of Illinois Press.

Kalichman, Seth C. 1999. *Mandated Reporting of Suspected Child Abuse: Ethics, Law, and Policy*. 2nd ed. Washington, DC: American Psychological Association.

Kangaspunta, Kristiina, and Ineke Haen Marshall. 2012. "Trends in Violence against Women: Some Good News and Some Bad News." In *The International Crime Drop: New Directions in Research*, edited by Jan van Dijk, Andromachi Tseloni, and Graham Farrell. London: Palgrave Macmillan.

Kivivuori, Janne. 2014. "Understanding Trends in Personal Violence: Does Cultural Sensitivity Matter?" In *Why Crime Rates Fall and Why They Don't*, edited by Michael Tonry. Vol. 43 of *Crime and Justice: A Review of Research*, edited by Michael Tonry. Chicago: University of Chicago Press.

Kivivuori, Janne, Jukka Savolainen, and Petri Danielsson. 2012. "Theory and Explanation in Contemporary European Homicide Research." In *The Handbook of European Homicide Research*, edited by Marieke C. A. Liem and William Alex Pridemore. New York: Springer.

LaFree, Gary. 1999. "A Summary and Review of Cross-National Comparative Studies of Homicide." In *Homicide: A Sourcebook of Social Research*, edited by M. Dwayne Smith and Margaret A. Zahn. Thousand Oaks, CA: Sage.

———. 2005. "Evidence for Elite Convergence in Cross-National Homicide Victimization Trends, 1956 to 2000." *Sociological Quarterly* 46:191–211.

Lane, Roger. 1980. "Urban Police and Crime in Nineteenth-Century America." In *Crime and Justice: An Annual Review of Research*, vol. 2, edited by Norval Morris and Michael Tonry. Chicago: University of Chicago Press.

———. 1989. "On the Social Meaning of Homicide Trends in America." In *Violence in America*, vol. 1, *The History of Crime*, edited by Ted Robert Gurr. Newbury Park, CA: Sage.

———. 1992. "Urban Police and Crime in Nineteenth-Century America." In *Modern Policing*, edited by Michael Tonry and Norval Morris. Vol. 15 of *Crime and Justice: A Review of Research*, edited by Michael Tonry. Chicago: University of Chicago Press.

Lappi-Seppälä, Tapio. 2008. "Trust, Welfare, and Political Culture: Explaining Differences in National Penal Policies." In *Crime and Justice: A Review of Research*, vol. 37, edited by Michael Tonry. Chicago: University of Chicago Press.

Lappi-Seppälä, Tapio, and Martti Lehti. 2014. "Cross-Comparative Perspectives on Global Homicide Trends." In *Why Crime Rates Fall and Why They*

Don't, edited by Michael Tonry. Vol. 43 of *Crime and Justice: A Review of Research*, edited by Michael Tonry. Chicago: University of Chicago Press.

Lauritsen, Janet L., and Maribeth L. Rezey. 2013. *Measuring the Prevalence of Crime with the National Victimization Survey*. Washington, DC: US Department of Justice, Bureau of Justice Statistics.

Mastrofsky, Stephen D., and James J. Willis. 2010. "Police Organization Continuity and Change: Into the Twenty-First Century." In *Crime and Justice: A Review of Research*, vol. 39, edited by Michael Tonry. Chicago: University of Chicago Press.

Minton, Todd D., and Daniela Golinelli. 2014. *Jail Inmates at Midyear 2013—Statistical Tables*. Washington, DC: US Department of Justice, Bureau of Justice Statistics.

Monkkonen, Eric H. 1981. *Police in Urban America, 1860–1920*. Cambridge: Cambridge University Press.

———. 2001. "New Standards for Historical Homicide Research." *Crime, History and Society* 5(2):7–26.

Muchembled, Robert. 2011. *A History of Violence: From the End of the Middle Ages to the Present*. Cambridge: Polity.

Musto, David J. 1999. *The American Disease: The Origins of Narcotic Control*. 3rd ed. New York: Oxford University Press.

Naess, Hans Eyvind. 1982. *Trolldomsprosessene i Norge pa 1500–1600-tallet: En retts- og sosialhistorisk undersiikelse*. Oslo: Universiteits Forlaget.

National Highway Traffic Safety Administration. 2012. *2011 Motor Vehicle Crashes: An Overview*. Washington, DC: US Department of Transportation, National Highway Traffic Safety Administration.

Neuman, W. Lawrence, and Ronald J. Berger. 1988. "Competing Perspectives on Cross-National Crime: An Evaluation of Theory and Evidence." *Sociological Quarterly* 29:281–313.

Office of National Statistics. 2013. *Crime in England and Wales, Year Ending March 2013*. London: Office of National Statistics.

Osterberg, Eva. 1996. "Criminality, Social Control, and the Early Modern State: Evidence and Interpretations in Scandinavian Historiography." In *The Civilization of Crime: Violence in Town and Country since the Middle Ages*, edited by Eric A. Johnson and Eric H. Monkkonen. Urbana: University of Illinois Press.

Osterberg, Eva, and Dag Lindstrom. 1988. *Crime and Social Control in Medieval and Early Modern Swedish Towns*. Uppsala: Academia Upsaliensis.

Pierotti, Rachael S. 2013. "Increasing Rejection of Intimate Partner Violence: Evidence of Global Cultural Diffusion." *American Sociological Review* 78:240–65.

Pinker, Steven. 2011. *The Better Angels of Our Nature: Why Violence Has Declined*. New York: Viking.

Povey, David, and Julian Prime. 1999. *Recorded Crime Statistics England and Wales: April 1998–March 1999*. Home Office Statistical Bulletin 18/99. London: H.M. Stationery Office.

Radzinowicz, Leon, and Roger Hood. 1986. *The Emergence of Penal Policy in Victorian and Edwardian England.* London: Stevens.

Raphael, Steven, and Michael A. Stoll. 2013. *Why Are So Many Americans in Prison?* New York: Russell Sage Foundation.

Reiss, Albert J., Jr. 1992. "Police Organization in the Twentieth Century." In *Modern Policing,* edited by Michael Tonry and Norval Morris. Vol. 15 of *Crime and Justice: A Review of Research,* edited by Michael Tonry. Chicago: University of Chicago Press.

Rosenfeld, Richard. 2014. "Crime and Inflation in Cross-National Perspective." In *Why Crime Rates Fall and Why They Don't,* edited by Michael Tonry. Vol. 43 of *Crime and Justice: A Review of Research,* edited by Michael Tonry. Chicago: University of Chicago Press.

———. 2014. "The Crime Trends Roundtable." *Criminologist* 39(1).

Rosenfeld, Richard, and Steven F. Messner. 2009. "The Crime Drop in Comparative Perspective: The Impact of the Economy and Imprisonment on American and European Burglary Rates." *British Journal of Sociology* 60(3): 445–71.

Selmini, Rossella, and Suzy McElrath. 2014. "Violent Female Victimization Trends in Europe, Canada, and the United States." In *Why Crime Rates Fall and Why They Don't,* edited by Michael Tonry. Vol. 43 of *Crime and Justice: A Review of Research,* edited by Michael Tonry. Chicago: University of Chicago Press.

Simmons, Jon, and Tricia Dodd. 2003. *Crime in England and Wales, 2002–2003.* Home Office Statistical Bulletin 07/03. London: H.M. Stationery Office.

Skilbrei, May-Len, and Charlotta Holmström. 2011. "Is There a Nordic Prostitution Regime?" In *Crime and Justice in Scandinavia,* edited by Michael Tonry and Tapio Lappi-Seppälä. Vol. 40 of *Crime and Justice: A Review of Research,* edited by Michael Tonry. Chicago: University of Chicago Press.

———. 2013. *Prostitution Policy in the Nordic Region: Ambiguous Sympathies.* Farnham, Surrey, UK: Ashgate.

Smit, Paul R., Rinke R. de Jong, and Catrien C. J. H. Bijleveld. 2012. "Homicide Data in Europe: Definitions, Sources, and Statistics." In *The Handbook of European Homicide Research,* edited by Marieke C. A. Liem and William Alex Pridemore. New York: Springer.

Smith, Dame Janet. 2003. *The Shipman Enquiry, Third Report: Death Certification and the Investigation of Deaths by Coroners.* Presented to Parliament by the Secretary of State for the Home Department and the Secretary of State for Health by Command of Her Majesty. CM 5854. London: Home Office and Department of Health.

Spierenburg, Peter. 1996. "Long-Term Trends in Homicide: Theoretical Reflections and Dutch Evidence, Fifteenth to Twentieth Centuries." In *The Civilization of Crime: Violence in Town and Country since the Middle Ages,* edited by Eric A. Johnson and Eric H. Monkkonen. Urbana: University of Illinois Press.

———. 2008. *A History of Murder: Personal Violence in Europe from the Middle Ages to the Present.* Cambridge: Polity.

———. 2012. "Long-Term Historical Trends of Homicide in Europe." In *The Handbook of European Homicide Research*, edited by Marieke C. A. Liem and William Alex Pridemore. New York: Springer.

Tham, Henrik, Anita Rönneling, and Lise-Lotte Rytterbro. 2011. "The Emergence of the Crime Victim: Sweden in a Scandinavian Context." In *Crime and Justice in Scandinavia*, edited by Michael Tonry and Tapio Lappi-Seppälä. Vol. 40 of *Crime and Justice: A Review of Research*, edited by Michael Tonry. Chicago: University of Chicago Press.

Tonry, Michael. 2004a. *Punishment and Politics: Evidence and Emulation in the Making of English Crime Control Policy*. Cullompton, Devon, UK: Willan.

———. 2004b. *Thinking about Crime: Sense and Sensibility in American Penal Culture*. Oxford: Oxford University Press.

———. 2004c. "Why Aren't German Penal Policies Harsher and Imprisonment Rates Higher?" *German Law Review* 5:1187–1206.

———. 2007. "Determinants of Penal Policies." In *Crime, Punishment, and Politics in Comparative Perspective*, edited by Michael Tonry. Vol. 36 of *Crime and Justice: A Review of Research*, edited by Michael Tonry. Chicago: University of Chicago Press.

———. 2010. "The Costly Consequences of Populist Posturing: ASBOs, Victims, 'Rebalancing,' and Diminution of Support for Civil Liberties." *Punishment and Society* 12(4):387–413.

———. 2013. "Sentencing in America, 1975–2025." In *Crime and Justice in America, 1975–2025*, edited by Michael Tonry. Vol. 42 of *Crime and Justice: A Review of Research*, edited by Michael Tonry. Chicago: University of Chicago Press.

Tonry, Michael, and David P. Farrington. 2005. "Punishment and Crime across Space and Time." In *Crime and Punishment in Western Countries, 1980–1999*, edited by Michael Tonry and David P. Farrington. Vol. 33 of *Crime and Justice: A Review of Research*, edited by Michael Tonry. Chicago: University of Chicago Press.

Travis, Jeremy, and Bruce Western. 2014. *The Growth of Incarceration in the United States: Exploring Causes and Consequences*. National Research Council Committee on Law and Justice. Washington DC: National Academies Press.

Truman, Jennifer L., and Michael Planty. 2012. *Criminal Victimization, 2011*. Washington, DC: US: Department of Justice, Bureau of Justice Statistics.

van Dijk, Jan, and Andromachi Tseloni. 2012. "Global Overview: International Trends in Victimization and Recorded Crime." In *The International Crime Drop: New Directions in Research*, edited by Jan van Dijk, Andromachi Tseloni, and Graham Farrell. London: Palgrave Macmillan.

van Dijk, Jan, Andromachi Tseloni, and Graham Farrell. 2012a. "Conclusions—Understanding International Crime Trends: A Summing Up." In *The International Crime Drop: New Directions in Research*, edited by Jan van Dijk, Andromachi Tseloni, and Graham Farrell. London: Palgrave Macmillan.

———, eds. 2012b. *The International Crime Drop: New Directions in Research*. London: Palgrave Macmillan.

van Dijk, Jan, John van Kesteren, and Paul Smit. 2007. *Criminal Victimisation in International Perspective: Key Findings from the 2004–2005 ICVS and EU ICS*. The Hague: Netherlands Ministry of Justice.

von Hofer, Hanns. 2011. "Punishment and Crime in Scandinavia, 1750–2008." In *Crime and Justice in Scandinavia*, edited by Michael Tonry and Tapio Lappi-Seppälä. Vol. 40 of *Crime and Justice: A Review of Research*, edited by Michael Tonry. Chicago: University of Chicago Press.

von Hofer, Hanns, and Tapio Lappi-Seppälä. 2014. "The Development of Crime in Light of Finnish and Swedish Criminal Justice Statistics, Circa 1750–2010." *European Journal of Criminology* 11(2):169–94.

von Hofer, Hanns, Tapio Lappi-Seppälä, and Lars Westfelt. 2012. *Nordic Criminal Statistics, 1950–2010: Summary of a Report*. 8th ed. Stockholm: Stockholm University, Kriminologiska institutionen.

Walmsley, Roy. 2013. *World Prison Population List*. 10th ed. Essex: International Centre for Prison Studies.

Weber, Max 1982. *The Protestant Ethic and the Spirit of Capitalism*. London: Routledge. (Originally published 1930, translated by Talcott Parsons, by Charles Scribner's Sons.)

Webster, Cheryl, and Anthony Doob. 2007. "Punitive Trends and Stable Imprisonment Rates in Canada." In *Crime, Punishment, and Politics in a Comparative Perspective*, edited by Michael Tonry. Vol. 36 of *Crime and Justice: A Review of Research*, edited by Michael Tonry. Chicago: University of Chicago Press.

Welsh, Brandon, and Mark H. Irving. 2005. "Crime and Punishment in Canada, 1981–1999." In *Crime and Punishment in Western Countries, 1980–1999*, edited by Michael Tonry and David P. Farrington. Vol. 33 of *Crime and Justice: A Review of Research*, edited by Michael Tonry. Chicago: University of Chicago Press.

Wilson, James Q. 1976. *Thinking about Crime*. New York: Basic Books.

Wilson, James Q., and Richard J. Herrnstein. 1985. *Crime and Human Nature*. New York: Simon & Schuster.

Ylikangas, Heikki. 1976. "Major Fluctuations in Crimes of Violence in Finland: A Historical Analysis." *Scandinavian Journal of History* 1:81–103.

Zehr, Howard. 1975. "The Modernization of Crime in Germany and France, 1830–1913." *Journal of Social History* 8:117–41.

———. 1976. *Crime and the Development of Modern Society: Patterns of Criminality in Nineteenth Century Germany and France*. Totowa, NJ: Rowman & Littlefield.

Zimring Franklin E. 1972. "The Medium Is the Message: Firearm Caliber as a Determinant of Death from Assault." *Journal of Legal Studies* 1:97–123.

Manuel Eisner

From Swords to Words: Does Macro-Level Change in Self-Control Predict Long-Term Variation in Levels of Homicide?

ABSTRACT

Over the past decade the idea that Europe experienced a centuries-long decline in homicide, interrupted by recurrent surges and at different speeds in different parts of the continent, became widely acknowledged. So far explanations have relied mostly on anecdotal evidence, usually broadly relying on Norbert Elias's theory of the "civilizing process." One major general theory of large-scale fluctuations in homicide rates, self-control theory, offers a wide range of hypotheses that can be tested with rigorous quantitative analyses. A number of macro-level indicators for societal efforts to promote civility, self-discipline, and long-sightedness have been examined and appear to be strongly associated with fluctuations in homicide rates over the past six centuries.

Electronically published October 1, 2014

Manuel Eisner is professor of comparative and developmental criminology, University of Cambridge; deputy director of the Cambridge Institute of Criminology; and director of the university's Social Science Research Methods Programme and of its Violence Research Centre. Earlier versions of this paper were presented at the "Cross-National Crime Rate Trends" seminar in Bologna, May 24–25, 2013; the first US National Academy of Sciences "Roundtable on Crime Trends" meeting in Washington, June 25–26, 2013; and the Arizona State University "The Origin of Violence: From the Brain to World Wars" seminar on April 3–6, 2014, in Scottsdale. Helpful comments on earlier drafts were obtained by Maarten van Dick, Daniel Nagin, Randolph Roth, Pieter Spierenburg, Michael Tonry, Nico Trajtenberg, and anonymous reviewers.

Homicide rates in the United States have dropped by at least 40 percent since 1991, mirroring a much broader downturn of violent crime that includes assault, robbery, rape, bullying, and child abuse (Blumstein and Wallman 2000). But while the US decline has long been known, experts only recently began to realize that something similar is happening across the Western world. Homicide rates in most European countries have declined considerably since the early 1990s (Eisner 2008), and overall crime levels have been moving along a downward trend for the past 20 years (van Dijk, Tseloni, and Farrell 2012).

The phenomenon of a largely synchronized decline in violent crime across the Western world has puzzled researchers. Initial explanations had mainly focused on the United States, but as the evidence for the similarities mounts, scholars find that attention must be paid to mechanisms that account for the astonishing commonalities. One such approach interprets the past two decades as one of several extended historical periods during which interpersonal violence was in retreat. They are believed to be part of a broader civilizing process—a long dynamic toward the growing concentration of the legitimate use of force in the hands of the state; expansion of methodical and rationalized self-control; and rising abhorrence of judicial torture, maltreatment of children, cruelty against animals, and bullying in schools (Eisner 2003; Muchembled 2008; Spierenburg 2008; Pinker 2011). In this view trends in violence are similar across Western societies, because the macro-level forces that shape patterns of daily discipline and self-control easily transgress national boundaries.

A prominent example of this perspective is found in Steven Pinker's monumental *The Better Angels of Our Nature* (2011), which develops a comprehensive theoretical framework for understanding the decline of violence since the early beginnings of state-organized societies in the Neolithic age. Within this framework Pinker sees the rise in violent crime between the 1960s and the 1980s mainly as a side effect of the assault on self-control in the pleasure-seeking, self-indulging, and substance-abusing youth countercultures of the generation that came of age in the 1960s (p. 106). But by the early 1990s the civilizing process stopped its temporary reverse gear and was restored to its forward direction in what Pinker calls a "recivilizing process." Communities began recivilizing their young men, the criminal justice system became more predictable, self-control became increasingly central to crime prevention programs, and society returned to glorifying the value of responsibility. Others have told a similar story. Fifteen years ago the political scientist Francis Fukuyama (1999) argued that in the early 1990s the United States entered a phase of re-anchoring beliefs in a civil society that values self-control and responsibility. Ouimet (2002) saw a new "ethos of moderation" contributing to the crime decline in Canada and the United States (also see Mishra and Lalumiere 2009). Kivivuori and Bernburg (2011) suggested that young people in Finland increasingly perceive substance users and delinquents as "losers" or "jerks"—a trend that they interpret as a growing condemnation of uncontrolled behavior.

That the Western world lost self-control in a decivilizing crisis of the 1960s and returned to a trajectory of increasing civility in the 1990s is a plausible story. The problem is that there is a lack of empirical support for the hypothesis, especially in the shape of robust quantitative indicators. And a similar problem also holds for the substantial European homicide decline in interpersonal violence over centuries, which took levels of lethal encounters from rates of 20–50 per 100,000 in late medieval cities to rates below one per 100,000 in many of the great European metropolises by the mid-twentieth century (Eisner 2001). While the descriptive pattern is now broadly accepted, little empirical evidence has yet been produced about whether indicators of presumed causal mechanisms corroborate current theories (but see, e.g., Pinker 2011; Roth 2012).

It is therefore time to move beyond the description of historical trends and to assess more formally the mechanisms that may have been involved in the big homicide decline. This essay presents a first attempt in this direction. In the first two sections, I review the evidence by presenting new findings based on the History of Homicide Database, the most comprehensive collection of quantitative estimates of homicide levels from 1200 to the present. In Section III, I introduce an interpretive framework that links the decline in violence to a sequence of civilizing offensives, historically specific bundles of techniques that target both the inner self (i.e., self-control) and the mechanisms of social control. In Section IV, the core of this essay, I examine the empirical evidence related to five theoretically important questions for which meaningful quantifiable indicators can be collected: Was the decline in interpersonal violence preceded by an even longer dynamic toward the pacification of the elites? Was the long trend in homicide associated with change in punitive practices as measured by the frequency of executions? Were trajectories in the early modern decline of violence associated with the diffusion of the written word and literacy? Were nineteenth- and twentieth-century fluctuations in homicide rates associated with coordinated attempts to promote temperance and self-control as measured by levels of alcohol consumption? And is there any evidence to support the notion that the long wave of homicide since the early 1960s was a result of cultural shifts that reflect the loss and return of self-control? Section V wraps up the discussion.

I. Measuring Homicide Trends since the Middle Ages

In 1981 political scientist Ted Robert Gurr plotted findings from several primary studies of historical crime in a graph to describe what happened to homicide over the centuries since the Middle Ages (1981, p. 313). The graph was based on just a handful of studies mainly relating to the south of England, but the conclusion of a long-term decline between the thirteenth and the twentieth centuries still stands today. In two studies published in the early 2000s, I followed his lead with a more systematic review of the historical evidence across Europe from around 1200 onward (Eisner 2001, 2003). The main idea was to compile all available historical scholarship that had produced homicide counts for some period and place in Europe and then to examine emerging patterns across the estimates. By 2001 the History of Homicide Database comprised 390 estimates of homicide rates for the pre-1800 period, retrieved from 90 publications. For the age of statistics, I had collected national time series for 10 countries, primarily based on mortality statistics. These data allowed me to identify trends in five major regions, namely, England, the Netherlands, Scandinavia, Germany and Switzerland, and Italy. I proposed several generalizations. First, the data suggested a long-term declining trend in homicide across Europe from about 1500 until the mid-twentieth century, which took homicide rates from about 30 per 100,000 to about one per 100,000 (Eisner 2003, p. 99). Second, I argued that the evidence supports the notion of substantial geographic variation in the timing of the decline, with England and the Netherlands leading the way, Sweden remaining high until the early seventeenth century and experiencing a steep decline from then onward, and Italy following a trajectory with high levels of homicide until the early nineteenth century, followed by a steep decline from then onward. For Germany and Switzerland, I suggested a middling path between the north and the south, while noting a lack of sufficiently clear data. I therefore interpreted the pattern of homicide rates visible in the second half of the nineteenth century: low rates across the wealthier and more advanced northern and central Europe (i.e., mainly including Germany, France, Scandinavia, and the British Isles) and high rates in the south and the east as the result of a center-periphery difference that had gradually developed since the seventeenth century. Finally, I suggested that the development between the 1860s and the mid-1990s was best understood as a U-shaped pattern with a decline until the 1950s and a substantial increase since. I also interpreted the data as being suggestive of a center-periphery pattern with the decline in homicide occurring earlier among the pioneers of European modernization, the Netherlands and England, and a much tardier decline at the rims of European modernity.

Since then the History of Homicide Database could be expanded considerably. It now comprises twice as many observation points for the pre-1800 period, national time series for more countries and longer time periods, and a wealth of information on contextual aspects (e.g., age, sex, location, time, weapon, and social class) of homicide over the past 800 years. Not all of this material can be presented here. Rather, I limit myself to a selective update with a focus on describing the current structure of the database and an overview of the core findings relating to the major long-term trends.

A. The History of Homicide Database

Addressing questions about the causes for the long-term homicide decline requires quantitative indicators that track the historical change in levels of interpersonal violence and data that index long-term trajectories of theoretically relevant processes. This is the primary goal of the History of Homicide Database, an ongoing project aimed at the systematic collection of numerical data related to levels and characteristics of homicide in Europe since the Middle Ages. It currently comprises four main groups of data. The "premodern homicide data set" includes estimates of homicide rates extracted from local historical studies from 1200 until the onset of national statistics. The "modern homicide data set" comprises time series of national homicide data for 18 European countries over the longest time periods for which data could be found. The "contextual homicide characteristics data set" is a comprehensive collection of quantitative data on a variety of contextual characteristics of homicide over the past 800 years. Core variables include information about the sex of perpetrators; the sex of victims; offender-victim relationships; the age of perpetrators and victims; the distribution of homicides by location, day, and time; as well as data on weapons used and the time elapsed between the incident and the death. The "homicide correlates" database, finally, retrieves macro-level time series of information on potentially relevant predictors including, for example, long-term serial data on levels of elite violence, the frequency of executions, urbanization, book production, literacy, wage levels, alcohol consumption, and life expectancy.

I briefly describe the premodern and modern homicide databases.

1. *Premodern Homicide Data Set.* The logic of collecting information for the premodern homicide data set has remained the same as the approach described in more detail in Eisner (2003). In a first stage, primary historical research on homicide, violence, and crime is retrieved. Systematic searches are conducted in English, French, German, Italian, and Spanish, but more limited searches also include publications in Dutch and Swedish. The search strategy is flexible and uses electronic catalogues of national libraries, the backtracking of references in recent publications, and various other search strategies. Conventional databases (e.g., *Criminal Justice Abstracts*) are of limited value as they rarely index more specialist literature in non-English languages. Publications that include statistical tables of the number of cases recorded in the underlying source are then carefully read to understand better the nature of the primary source, the geographic area the data refer to, and the classification of crimes. The data are finally entered into the Homicide Database if the study includes homicide counts and the source is assessed as reflecting a substantial proportion of actual homicides.

When primary studies present series of annual data over longer time spans, the data are aggregated to 10-year time units—the preferred length of observations in the premodern homicide data set. For each observation the entered data include the region, the exact location, the time period, the count of homicides, the population estimate, a description of the data source, information about whether infanticide is included, and references to the source of the homicide count and the population estimate. Rates are expressed as homicides per 100,000 inhabitants. Generally, a preference is given to estimates that include infanticide (as few studies make the distinction between infanticide and other homicides), but infanticides are almost entirely absent from judicial records before the seventeenth century.

In 2003 the premodern homicide data set comprised 390 observation points. Since then the size has more than doubled and currently encompasses 823 local estimates between 1200 and the beginning of national data series. Estimates are derived from a total of 115 historical studies. A considerable part of the growth in estimates is due to the inclusion of data for regions that were not covered in Eisner (2003), namely, Spain, the southern Low Countries, France, and a set of estimates relating to Sardinia and Corsica. All together the data represent 10,570 place-years of data, and each observation covers, on average, 13.2 years (standard deviation 16.9). The number of observation points per century increases over time, moving from $N = 28$ and $N = 70$ in the thirteenth and fourteenth centuries to $N = 192$ and $N = 213$ in the seventeenth and eighteenth centuries.

2. *Modern Homicide Time-Series Data Set.* In addition to the evidence derived from local studies, the History of Homicide Database includes a data set of national series of recorded homicide, usually based on mortality statistics or statistics on police-recorded homicides. The data and the sources are described in more detail in Eisner (2008). The longest data series come from Sweden and Finland, which introduced the first national death registration system in 1754 (Kivivuori and Lehti 2011); the series for France, England and Wales, Scotland, Ireland, and Prussia (subsumed under the series for Germany) start in the first half of the nineteenth century; and all other series start in the second half of the nineteenth century or around 1900. In some cases only conviction statistics were available (e.g., for the Netherlands before 1900). In these cases the conviction rates were multiplied with a constant of 1.65. The conversion coefficient is based on a sample of nineteenth-century periods in different countries where overlapping police or mortality statistics and conviction statistics exist. They suggest that conviction rates are typically about 60 percent of the rates based on either mortality or police statistics.

In total, the modern homicide time-series data set currently comprises 2,705 data points covering 19 geographic units. In addition to series described in Eisner (2001, 2003), the data set includes series starting in the nineteenth century for Spain, Portugal, Austria, Hungary, Serbia, Romania, and Norway.

B. *Sources of Bias*

Historians of crime rightly warn that figures emerging from analyses of historical records are fraught with uncertainty and that they may in various ways systematically over- or underestimate the true occurrence of assaults leading to death (e.g., Schwerhoff 2002). Such bias may vary over time, leading to erroneous conclusions about true time trends. However, we are beginning to understand some of these biases better, meaning that we can assess their likely effects on estimates over time. I briefly examine five relevant issues, namely, geographic bias, incomplete records, changing age structure, wound treatment, and the lethality of weapons.

1. *Disproportionate Representation of Cities.* Especially during the first few centuries, most data for areas other than England (where data are available for whole counties) come from cities—bustling places with markets, taverns, and brothels that attracted problem groups such as students and vagrants in large numbers (Dean 2001). However, only a small fraction of the medieval population lived in urban settlements, and we know much less about crime and violence in the more typical rural areas. In the few instances in which such information is available, historians have sometimes found lower homicide rates (Hanawalt 1979; van Dijck 2007). This is corroborated by findings from the premodern historical homicide data set, where average homicide estimates for the urban centers in the period between 1200 and 1500 are 32 per 100,000, falling to 27 per 100,000 for other towns and cities, and to 15 per 100,000 for territorial units such as counties or bailiwicks. However, it is currently impossible to say with confidence whether the tendency toward lower rates in rural areas reflects incomplete records because of the absence of criminal justice institutions or whether violence was effectively concentrated in urban centers.

2. *Incomplete Records.* For several reasons the surviving records likely give an incomplete picture of the incidence of homicide across historical times. For example, during the first centuries covered here, only part of all homicides ended up in criminal courts because cases of manslaughter could still be dealt with via private compensation and because prosecution in court sometimes required accusation by a family member of the victim (Rousseaux 1999). Also, late medieval and early modern criminal justice was a web of competing systems in which, for example, large fractions of homicide cases could be diverted away from the urban justices if perpetrators submitted a request for pardon to

their king (Muchembled 1992). This means that surviving records of any one judicial institution may reflect only part of even those cases that were known and that this proportion may have undergone significant shifts over time.

Also, a substantial proportion of data come from trials in criminal courts, which would happen only if a suspect was identified. But arrest was probably rare during much of the earlier period. Spierenburg (1994) and van Dijck (2007) have compared early modern autopsy reports and criminal justice records. They suggest that only about 10–20 percent of medieval and early modern killers ended up in a court, the others fleeing somewhere else or finding an extrajudicial settlement. To account for this problem at least to some extent, the database does not include data from sources that are clearly incomplete such as the medieval gaol delivery rolls in England, which comprise only trials of offenders arrested and kept in jail (Bellamy 1998).

Finally, some common subcategories of homicide are almost entirely absent from medieval records. This is particularly blatant for infanticide, which starts to find its way into the criminal courts only from the seventeenth century onward, and even then was likely practiced much more widely than judicial records suggest (Hanlon 2003). Some historians of crime hence believe that in medieval societies, infanticide was regarded as a sin rather than as a punishable crime (e.g., Trexler 1973). True levels of infanticide over time are probably impossible to determine empirically. But by the nineteenth century, when authorities made systematic attempts to bring infanticide under control, mortality statistics from France, England, and Switzerland suggest that about one-third of recorded homicides concerned victims at ages below 12 months.

3. *Changing Age Structure.* In all known societies, males aged 16–30 are most likely to commit homicides. Changes in demographic composition will therefore affect findings on long-term trends, with homicide rates appearing to be higher in periods when the proportion of young males is elevated.

To estimate the effects of a changing demographic structure on homicide rates, two crude ideal-type age pyramids were constructed, one reflecting the demographic regime of the Middle Ages and the early modern period and one typical for a late modern society. For the first demographic structure, an age pyramid was assumed where 25 percent of children died within the first 4 years of age and subsequently 1.2

TABLE 1

Modeled Demographic Regimes in Two Time Periods and Estimated
Effect on Overall Homicide Rate

| | Hypothetical Demographic Regime | |
	Medieval and Early Modern	Late 20th Century
Underlying assumed characteristics:		
Life expectancy at birth (years)	25.3	75.2
Infant mortality (< 4 years; %)	25	.4
% aged 50+ (%)	9.5	35.2
Crime-relevant characteristics:		
% aged 16–30 of total population (%)	25.5	18.2
% aged 16–30 of population aged 16+ (%)	43.2	23.0
Age-standardized homicide rate*	112	100

NOTE.—Model populations were created using 22 4-year age brackets (0–3, 4–7, 8–11, etc.). The medieval age-standardized rate was modeled using the age distribution across age brackets as weights and assuming a stable age-homicide curve in both periods.

* Assumes a constant homicide-age curve (index = 100 for the late twentieth-century demographic structure).

percent of the population died in each year of life. The average life expectancy at birth in this demographic model is 25.3 years, which is close to the empirical estimates suggested by demographic research on premodern societies. The late modern demographic structure assumes an infant mortality rate of 0.4 percent, an average risk of death of 0.1 percent for each year of life until age 60, and a steep increase in mortality between ages 72 and 90. The average life expectancy in this model would be about 75 years, and about 35 percent of the population would be at age 50 and above. These characteristics are close to those found empirically in highly developed societies in the late twentieth century.

I consider two indicators for assessing the possible effect of different demographic regimes on homicide rates. First, we can estimate the proportion of those aged 16–30 (the age group found to be at the highest risk of criminal violence across all known societies) in both model populations. As table 1 shows, their share of the population was considerably higher in a premodern society. This is especially true of the share of 16–30-year-olds among those aged 16 and above, which was around 40–45 percent in medieval and early modern societies and typically ranges around 20–25 percent in a contemporary society. This is an important difference. Young men accounted for a much larger proportion of the medieval and early modern public than is the case in a contemporary society.

Second, we can assess the direct effect of the demographic structure by estimating age-standardized homicide rates. To do so, I assumed a constant crime-age curve for homicide perpetrators, with a steep increase between ages 12 and 20, a peak age of offending at age 24, and a decline in the offending rate to half its peak value by age 37. This standard curve was developed on the basis of 36 empirical homicide age curves collected from samples covering nine countries (Germany, Norway, Sweden, England, Portugal, France, Austria, Italy, and Switzerland) between 1830 and 2010 (Eisner 2014). Accepting this as a general age pattern of homicide offenders, we can then estimate an age-standardized homicide rate for the premodern demographic structure by summing up the products of the homicide rate for each age group times the demographic weight of the group. The result shown in table 1 suggests that premodern homicide rates are probably only 12 percent higher than they would have been with a late modern age distribution of the population.

In interpreting this finding, it is important to bear in mind that this exercise takes into account only the direct linear bias introduced by differences in the population weight of various age groups. It does not account for possible nonlinear effects such as a greater likelihood of conflictive interactions in a society where the population share of young men was twice as high as it is in a typical modern society. It is plausible that such effects exist, but we do not currently have any way of estimating their size. They would primarily change the picture during the course of the twentieth century, when the bulk of the demographic change occurred. Finally, one should note that the effective age distribution of homicide perpetrators in the Middle Ages is unknown and that there could have been both short- and long-term variation in the peak age of violent offending.

4. *Wound Treatment.* An important source of bias over long periods of time is progress in healing technology, including rapid transportation to a hospital, easily available emergency services, and better wound treatment including antibiotics and trauma medicine (Monkkonen 2001). Data collected as part of the History of Homicide Database allow us to estimate the timing and the size of this factor by examining information on the time between the event and the occurrence of death

TABLE 2

Distribution between Assault and Time of Death, Seven Samples
between 1300 and 2010 (%)

Location	Period	Time to Death				N
		Immediate	< 24 Hours	1–7 Days	8+ Days	
London	1300–1340	33	25	35	7	117
Gascony	1360–1526		62		38	101
Spain	1623–99	37	36	14	13	188
Middlesex	1667–84	41	16	22	22	74
East Sussex	1750–1838	38	29	16	16	84
Philadelphia	1839–1901		67		33	1,359
Finland	2003–8	79	19	2		549

SOURCE.—London, Middlesex, and East Sussex: own analyses based on coroner's records and assize records. Spain: Chaulet (1997); Gascony: Prétou (2010); Philadelphia: Lane (1979, p. 79). Finland: Granath et al. (2011).

over eight centuries. Table 2 shows a sample of estimates derived from prior historical scholarship as well as from the coding of some additional English sources.

The data show a consistent picture. Until the early twentieth century, some 35–40 percent of the victims died "immediately," 15–35 percent died within the first 24 hours after the incident, and 30–45 percent died more than 24 hours later, often suffering for days or weeks until they died. This approximate shape of the survival curve remained essentially unchanged between the fourteenth and the late nineteenth centuries, suggesting that improved wound treatment is not a plausible source of bias before 1900. But over the past 100 years, advances in healing technology have had a major impact. Its size order can be estimated if we assume that none of those who died immediately could be rescued with modern technology, that half of those who died within the first 24 hours could be rescued, and that probably almost all of those who survived for a day could be treated with modern technology. Applying such crude weights suggests that the percentage of serious injuries before 1900 that would not result in death with modern technology is about 50 percent. When considering long-term trends, we therefore need to take into account that any change during the twentieth century is biased toward lower rates.

5. *Lethality of Weapons.* Homicide rates may change over time because people's access to suitable killing instruments in situations of altercation varies. Although this source of variability does not consti-

TABLE 3

Method of Killing, England, Fourteenth to Twenty-First
Centuries (%)

Location	Period	Instrument					
		Sharp	Blunt	Shooting	Any Manual	Any Other	N
London	1300–1348	67	19	1	7	5	153
Northamptonshire	1300–1348	63	29	6	1	1	472
Kent	1560–99	32	31	2	14	21	231
Kent	1600–1649	28	32	2	23	15	209
Kent	1650–99	19	20	8	37	16	254
Kent	1700–1749	14	19	14	38	14	140
Kent	1750–99	13	13	21	37	16	154
Kent	1800–1849	12	11	15	37	26	197
England	1956–66	31	12	9	34	13	1,400
England	2000–2009	37	9	8	29	17	5,292

SOURCE.—London, 1300–1349: coroner's record, own coding. Northamptonshire: Hanawalt (1976). Kent: Cockburn (1991, p. 80). England, 1956–66: Morris and Blom-Cooper (1979). England, 2000–2009: Smith et al. (2012, p. 34).

NOTE.—Sharp instrument: axe, hatchet, knife, sword; blunt instrument: staff, stick, stone; shooting instrument: arrow, firearm; any manual: hit, kick, push, strangulate; other: drown, burn, poison.

tute bias in the same sense as incomplete records, it is desirable to have estimates of access to killing technology such as swords, knives, or guns over time. While access to weapons is difficult to establish empirically, data on weapon use in homicides provide a good proxy.

The History of Homicide Database includes a scattering of estimates of weapon use for several regions. The only region for which we can currently establish trends with some degree of confidence over time is southern England, where a series of data points provide a picture of the long-term trend over the past 800 years. Table 3 shows selected data across eight centuries.

Almost all homicides in medieval London were committed with some fighting instrument. The weapons of choice were swords, fighting knives such as the *anelace* or the *misericorde*, and staffs—long, thick wooden poles whose end was often reinforced with a metal tip. The medieval coroner's records make it clear that we are looking at a society of well-armed men who were well trained in the fighting technologies of the day (e.g., Sharpe 1913).

From the fourteenth to the eighteenth century, the data suggest one big trend in weapon use. As overall levels of homicides declined, the proportion of those committed with weapons also went down, and a larger share of the dwindling number of homicides was committed without weapons. By the second half of the eighteenth century and during the nineteenth century, 30–50 percent of homicides in southern England were committed by bare hands or feet, suggesting that in conflictive encounters people either did not have a weapon at hand or were unwilling to use it. From this we can conclude that a dispropor- tionately large part of the overall decline in homicide was due to sit- uations that involved weapons, which probably suggests that weapons generally disappeared from routine activities in public space (on the sword going out of fashion in the 1720s, see, e.g., Shoemaker [2002]).

The situation has changed quite considerably since the 1950s. In particular, an increase in the proportion of homicides committed with knives and a decrease of those committed with bare hands and legs suggest a return to a situation in which violence-prone groups carry fighting instruments in expectation of violent clashes.

II. European Homicide from 1200 to 2011

Quantifying the course of interpersonal violence over centuries will always remain an exercise fraught with doubts about the comparability of data over time and space and limitations regarding homicide as a leading indicator for violence more generally. But combining data over large spaces and long periods has important benefits. It makes big dy- namics visible that are hard to see with a case study approach anchored in specialist knowledge of any one place in one period. In this section, I provide a condensed overview of the main trends in homicide as they emerge from the updated and extended data collection.

I present the main results in two ways. Table 4 shows an overview of estimates from 1200 through 2012 for 11 large geographic areas of Europe in which estimates based on local studies and national series provide enough information to make a substantive interpretation de- fensible. All data for the periods before 1800 (with the exception of Sweden, where national series start in 1754) are based on averages of local estimates, aggregated over 50-year periods. For the periods 1750– 99, 1800–1849, and 1850–74, I present local estimates only if no na- tional data series are available. From 1850 onward, the data in table 4 are based on national data series and aggregated by 25-year periods. I present combined data for Corsica and Sardinia in a separate row to illustrate a long-term trajectory that is very different from that in continental Europe. Estimates based on local data are usually displayed only if at least two local estimates were available. Some exceptions were made either where local estimates are based on a reasonably good series of data (e.g., the series of recorded homicide in Geneva as a proxy for Switzerland in the seventeenth century) or where the data refer to a big part of a regional unit (e.g., the data for Sardinia in the late eighteenth century that cover a large proportion of the island).

Figures 1–3 present trend data based on national statistics since 1750. The data have been aggregated in 10-year periods to give a better idea of medium-term fluctuations over the past 250 years. Similar to the long series in table 4, the data have been arranged in three geographic clusters, namely, northern Europe (Finland, Sweden, Norway, Denmark, England and Wales, Scotland, Ireland), central western Europe (France, Belgium, Netherlands, Germany), and southern and eastern Europe (Austria, Hungary, Italy, Spain, Portugal, Switzerland). Periods when a war was fought on the respective territory (e.g., Finnish War 1808–9, Italy 1942–45) were excluded in the calculation of the estimates. War years usually show massive spikes in homicide rates recorded in the mortality statistics, but it is currently unclear to what extent these spikes reflect war-related deaths, for example, deaths inflicted on resistance fighters.

A. The Big Picture

I first want to draw attention to the big picture over the past 800 years as it emerges from the findings presented in table 4. It shows essentially two main trend periods. The first period covers the first 250 years or so, from 1200 to about 1450. During this period the average estimates of homicide rates for each region typically range between 15 and 60 per 100,000 inhabitants, with little evidence of systematic trends in either direction. Across the continent, estimates converge at a rate of about 27 per 100,000. There was, of course, much variation at the level of cities and smaller areas, and most probably such variation reflects true variability. Medieval cities and rural areas likely oscillated between being rather orderly places with well-functioning institutions and including periods when they were riddled with feuds, unrest, banditry, and antagonistic groups engaged in serious conflicts.

The second trend period starts in the first half of the fifteenth cen-

TABLE 4

Mean Homicide Rates in 11 European Regions, 1250–2012, by 50-Year Intervals until 1849, 25-Year Intervals for 1850–2012

	1200–1299	1300–1349	1350–99	1400–1449	1450–99	1500–1549	1550–99	1600–1649	1650–99	1700–1749	1750–99	1800–1849	1850–74	1875–99	1900–1925	1925–49	1950–75	1975–99	2000–2012
North:																			
England and Wales	14.7 (23)	21.4 (14)	13.0 (4)	…	…	…	5.2 (16)	5.8 (17)	3.5 (25)	2.0 (20)	1.4 (19)	1.6	1.6	1.3	.8	.8	.8	1.3	1.5
Ireland	…	…	…	…	…	…	…	…	…	5.9 (3)	4.2 (4)	2.3	1.7	1.9	1.2	.4	.4	1.0	1.5
Sweden and Finland	…	…	…	…	38.3 (7)	18.4 (5)	23.3 (20)	22.3 (28)	9.0 (17)	4.2 (6)	1.1* (4)	1.6*	1.7*	1.6*	1.3*	.8*	.8*	1.2*	.9*
Center:																			
France	…	…	…	…	…	20.2 (5)	7.2 (10)	13.6 (8)	6.0 (11)	2.9 (8)	2.3 (4)	1.5	1.4	1.4	1.5	1.1	1.1	1.1	.7
Belgium	…	…	16.4 (12)	20.5 (14)	22.5 (19)	13.2 (22)	8.8 (19)	14.6 (12)	5.7 (19)	4.3 (14)	2.4 (18)	.8	1.7	1.8	2.2	1.6	.8	1.6	1.4
Netherlands	…	…	20.7 (3)	59.1 (3)	…	35.9 (2)	8.9 (7)	7.6 (5)	3.1 (8)	3.4 (8)	1.9 (9)	…	.8	.9	.6	.8	.5	1.0	1.0
Germany	39.4 (4)	26.8 (9)	30.1 (20)	6.6 (2)	18.6 (4)	…	9.0 (7)	10.1 (9)	3.1 (6)	5.0 (10)	4.6 (9)	2.4	1.5	1.6	2.1	1.8	1.1	1.1	.6

80

South:

Switzerland	…	…	56.8 (3)	13.6 (4)	4.0 (1)	…	6.8 (1)	10.4 (1)	5.3 (1)	4.3 (2)	5.1 (4)	4.7†	1.7†	3.0	2.1	1.4	.8	1.1	.8
Italy	22.4 (2)	…	71.7 (6)	62.0 (1)	…	…	38.7 (10)	39.1 (3)	10.2 (3)	16.9 (3)	7.1 (10)	8.0 (5)	7.0 (3)	5.7	3.9	2.0	1.3	1.7	1.0
Spain	…	…	32.3 (3)	…	12.6 (3)	7.9 (8)	4.7 (5)	8.6 (9)	5.9 (9)	4.2 (20)	8.8 (16)	8.3	5.5	4.5	1.4	.3	.9	.9	
Corsica and Sardinia	…	…	…	…	…	…	…	28.1 (9)	42.2 (3)	49.1 (1)	22.8‡	29.2‡	14.1‡	10.0‡	…	…		2.5‡	2.0‡
Average§	25.8	23.4	32.7	32.4	20.9	20.1	12.8	12.0	6.1	5.5	3.8	3.5	2.7	2.5	2.0	1.2	.8	1.2	1.0

NOTE.—Averages of local estimates. Numbers of estimates are in parentheses. Figures for 1800–2012 are based on national statistics except for Italy in 1800–1849 and Spain in 1800–1849. Estimates for France and Italy exclude Corsica and Sardinia, which are shown as a separate unit.

 * National series for Sweden only.
 † Canton of Zurich only.
 ‡ Estimates for Sardinia only.
 § Without Corsica and Sardinia.

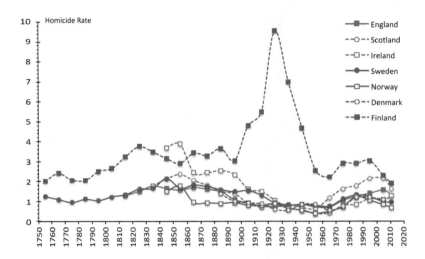

Fig. 1.—Modern homicide trends in northern Europe. Source: History of Homicide Database.

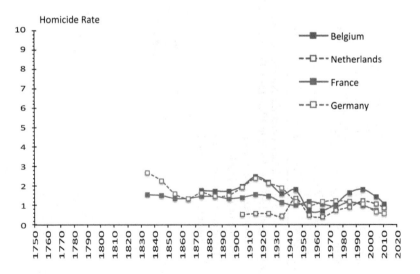

Fig. 2.—Modern homicide trends in central Europe. Source: History of Homicide Database

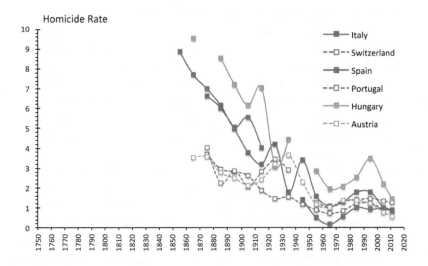

F<small>IG</small>. 3.—Modern homicide trends in southern and eastern Europe. Source: History of Homicide Database.

tury and continues essentially unbroken until the early twenty-first century. During this period the data suggest a long declining trend. Consider the grand average homicide rate across the local estimates at the beginning of each century as an approximation for the overall European trend: 20.1 (1500–1549), 12.0 (1600–1649), 5.5 (1700–1749), 3.5 (1800–1825), 2.0 (1900–1924), and 1.0 (2000–2012). This is a remarkable sequence of numbers. What it suggests is that over a period of 500 years the peacetime criminal homicide rate in Europe fell by half every century, corresponding to a rather stable average rate of decline of about 0.5 percent per year.

B. Emerging Regional Differences

While the overall decline is the dominant trend across Europe, the data shown in table 4 and figures 1–3 also suggest some important regional differences emerging during the early modern period. Considering the period until 1800 first, the data suggest that estimates for England were already lower than those for the rest of Europe during the Middle Ages and that estimates for the late sixteenth and seventeenth centuries continued to be lower than those on the continent. This may suggest an early entry into a trajectory of declining violence in England, but it is also possible that the lower estimates result from the more comprehensive geographic coverage of whole countries rather than cities, as is usually the case on the continent. In Scandinavia the clusters of estimates for Stockholm and a range of smaller cities suggest persistent homicide rates of around 20–50 per 100,000 until the mid-seventeenth century. Then homicide begins to decline with an average rate of 3 percent per year over a period of 100 years, taking rates in Stockholm from 26 per 100,000 to 1.4 over the period (for an overview, see Karonen [2001]). From the start of national statistics onward, the data suggest a high similarity in the trends across the whole north of Europe with periods of increasing homicide from the 1770s to the 1830s or 1840 and again from the early 1960s to the early 1990s. The major exception is the massive peak in Finland between about 1910 and 1940, which has been associated with the sustained period of civil strife and the political legitimacy crisis before and after the Finnish Civil War of 1918 (Kivivuori and Lehti 2011).

Across central Europe, few systematic differences emerge, and the main impression is of a largely parallel movement in France, Belgium, the Netherlands, and Germany. From about 1600 until 1800 and beyond, the rates in the Netherlands appear to have been somewhat lower than those in other regions in this cluster. This may be indicative of a somewhat stronger decline in the Calvinist-dominated north of the Dutch provinces, where a combination of economic prosperity during the Dutch Golden Age and the Protestant emphasis on a methodic conduct of life may have helped to accelerate the decline in homicide (Spierenburg 2007*b*). However, the differences from the Catholic south (which also remained politically subjected to Habsburg rule) were relatively small. Van Dijck (2007) has argued that hardly any meaningful differences existed.

In southern Europe the new estimates confirm that Italy had consistently higher rates than those in northern Europe. Mean homicide rates around 1800 are considerably lower than those found before 1650, suggesting a declining trend that may have begun around the mid-seventeenth century and continued throughout the nineteenth and early twentieth centuries (see fig. 3). In contrast, the new data emerging from research in Spain are at best partly in line with what I expected. Thus, I would have assumed that the early modern trajectory in Spain would follow a "southern" pattern, with homicide rates remaining high until the late nineteenth century and then gradually falling to levels found in the rest of Europe. During the nineteenth century, homicide statistics for Spain do suggest a high level of lethal interpersonal violence, similar to those in other countries at the periphery of Europe such as Italy, Greece, or Hungary during this period. However, early modern data based on court records in Madrid (Alloza 2000) and Navarra (Berraondo 2012) suggest homicide levels in the seventeenth and eighteenth centuries that were closer to those in London or Paris than to those in Rome. Limitations of the data may be important here. In both cases, the records of cases recorded by the judicial authorities may be far off the true mark because of a lack of reporting, inefficient policing, and inadequate forensic expertise. Especially striking are the persistently high rates on the Mediterranean islands of Corsica and Sardinia, where homicide rates were around 30–50 per 100,000 in the eighteenth century and started to decline only during the nineteenth century.

C. Differential Trends for Types of Homicide

Homicides can occur in a mix of different situational contexts and for a variety of different reasons. For explanations it is therefore important to understand which subtypes of interpersonal violence contributed most to the long-term declining trend. Findings presented in Eisner (2003) on this issue suggested that over the centuries the proportion of male victims declined and similarly that the proportion of nondomestic homicides (i.e., between acquaintances and strangers) tended to fall over time, suggesting that the strongest decline was related to fights between men. However, no direct evidence of this hypothesis was presented then.

Additional data now allow for a more direct test of the hypothesis that big falls in homicide are primarily due to a reduction in male-to-male fighting. For example, data relating to noninfant homicide in London can be broken down by the sex of perpetrators and victims over 700 years (with a gap in the fifteenth and sixteenth centuries).

Findings suggest, first, that homicide in London declined by about 98 percent between the early fourteenth century and the turn of the twentieth century. It also suggests that over this long period the rates of both male and female perpetrators declined. See table 5. However, the decline was considerably stronger for male perpetrators, which fell from an estimated rate of about 46 per 100,000 in the fourteenth century to about 0.9 around 1900. The over-proportionate fall in male

TABLE 5

Homicide Rates per 100,000 by Sex of Perpetrators and Victims,
London, 1300–1909

	1300–1340 (1)	1680–99 (2)	1740–59 (3)	1780–99 (4)	1830–49 (5)	1890–1909 (6)	Change (%) (Col. 6 − Col. 1)
Perpetrators:							
Male	46.37	10.72	3.01	1.47	2.14	.90	−98
Female	3.63	.88	.47	.13	.46	.30	−92
Male/female							
ratio	12.78	12.23	6.33	11.47	4.60	3.06	
Victims:							
Male	45.42	9.82	2.51	1.21	1.67	.67	−99
Female	4.58	1.78	.97	.39	.93	.53	−88
Male/female							
ratio	9.93	5.51	2.58	3.05	1.78	1.26	
Homicide rate	25.0	5.80	1.74	.8	1.3	.60	−98

SOURCE.—1300–1340: coroner's rolls, own data collection; 1680–1909: data for calculations derived from Old Bailey Online, http://www.oldbaileyonline.org.

offenders is reflected in the male/female perpetrator ratio, which fell over the centuries from about 13 : 1 to about 3 : 1.

The differential change is even more pronounced for victims, for whom the risk of a lethal assault had fallen by about 99 percent in 1900 as compared with the situation in the early fourteenth century. The risk for women to be killed also fell over the centuries, but "only" by 88 percent. Over the centuries these differential changes are indexed well by the ratio of male to female victims, which fell along a clear trend from about 10 : 1 in the fourteenth century to an almost equal risk around 1900.

The data presented in Eisner (2003) suggest that trends in the proportion of female victims were similar in other areas in which a homicide decline occurred, implying that any covariates that may explain the long-term decline in homicide must probably focus on the pacification of unrelated male-to-male interactions in public spaces.

D. The Western World, 1950–2011

Figures 1–3 show that by the mid-twentieth century, homicide rates across most of western Europe had converged to a narrow range of 0.5 to two cases per 100,000 inhabitants, with only a few areas at the outer fringes of the continent—most notably the southern parts of Italy

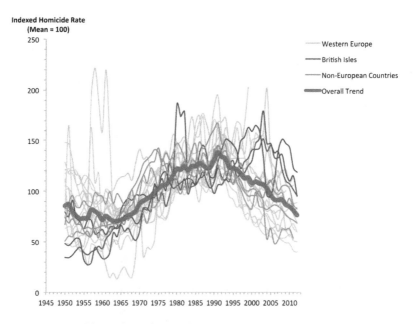

FIG. 4.—Shared homicide trend across the Western world, 1950–2012. Homicide rates for Australia, Austria, Belgium, Canada, Denmark, England and Wales, France, Germany, Finland, Hungary, Ireland, Italy, Netherlands, New Zealand, Norway, Portugal, Spain, Switzerland, and the United States. Each series is standardized by its own mean, $M = 100$. Series for countries with a population less than 10 million in 2000 were smoothed with 3-year moving averages. Source: History of Homicide Database.

and Corsica—still experiencing a substantially higher incidence of lethal interpersonal violence. Since then, homicide trends in various European countries have by and large been variations of one long cyclical movement that embraced all of the Western world. To illustrate this movement, figure 4 shows the trend in homicide rates across 18 Western societies, including data series for almost all European countries as well as Australia, Canada, New Zealand, and the United States. Northern Ireland was excluded because official records include an unknown proportion of deaths related to the violent ethnonationalist conflict that began in the late 1960s. All series have been standardized to their own mean = 100, and series for countries with a population of less than 10 million in 2000 were smoothed with 3-year moving averages to reduce random variation due to small numbers. The thick orange line represents the averages across all 18 series.

The figure shows a common long-term movement of increasing ho-

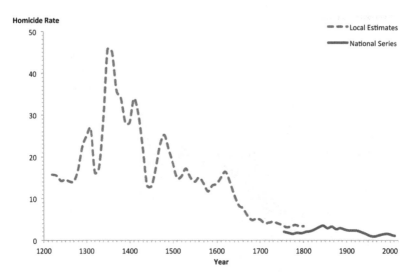

FIG. 5.—European homicide trend, 1200–2010. Source: History of Homicide Database

micide between about 1965 and 1992 and a shared declining trend from 1992 onward. The average correlation of the 18 series with the shared trend is $r = .69$, with 16 correlations ranging between .50 and .94. The lowest correlation with the shared trend was found for France ($r = .07$), where the Algerian War of Independence between 1954 and 1962 spilled over to mainland France and led to a spike in homicides during a period when levels in most other countries were at a low.

E. The European Trend and Its Variations, 1200–2012

A critical requirement for assessing the facial plausibility of potential quantitative covariates that may guide the explanation of the long homicide drop is the availability of acceptable estimates of the "outcome" variable over time. In Section IV, I explore a number of indicators for social processes associated with changes in self-control that may contribute to the explanation of the decline in homicide. To this purpose the information that is now available in the History of Homicide Database was condensed into one overall time series of homicide levels in Europe between 1200 and 2012 (see fig. 5). The series consists of two parts. The first is based on averages of the local estimates and the second on averages of the national time series. For the first part, I used all local estimates other than those for Corsica and Sardinia, because

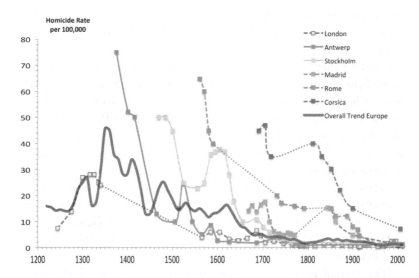

FIG. 6.—European homicide trend and selected local variations, 1300–2010. Source: History of Homicide Database.

estimates for these areas start relatively late and because they are distinct outliers in comparison with the rest of Europe. All other estimates were first ordered chronologically by the mean year of the underlying time span. I then computed means for overlapping 20-year time periods, for example, 1400–1419, 1410–29, 1420–39, and so forth. No corrections were made for differences in the underlying population size, variation in the geographic coverage over time, or the quality of the underlying data. In principle, such "corrections" would be desirable, but I do not think that our present understanding of various potential biases is advanced enough to make a weighting of observations a defensible approach.

For the modern period, I compute means of the 10-year average homicide rates for 14 European countries: England and Wales, Scotland, Ireland, Sweden, Norway, Denmark, Belgium, the Netherlands, France, Germany, Italy, Switzerland, Spain, and Portugal. For most countries, national series became available only during the 1850s and 1860s. I therefore linked the early decades of the overall series based on fewer countries using a correction coefficient based on the earliest decade for which data from all countries were available.

Figure 6 shows the overall European trend over 800 years that results from the two data series—the series that I use as a reference series in Section IV of this essay. In addition to the long-term declining trend, it suggests a number of fluctuations. For many of them it is unclear whether they represent genuine variations in homicide levels or whether they are due to freak movements in the available data. This is particularly true of the early increase in homicide rates during the second half of the fourteenth century and the various ups and downs in the data until about 1600. Considering that for this period great uncertainties surround the data points, geographic coverage is patchy, and mean estimates are based on relatively few observation points, it is doubtful whether these fluctuations have any substantial meaning. In contrast, the evidence for an increase during the last decade of the sixteenth and the early seventeenth centuries, and the rather rapid decline from about 1620 to 1700, is probably quite robust. Also, two subsequent periods of increasing homicide occurred around 1780–1840 and between 1960 and 1990.

The second main message emerging from the updated History of Homicide Database is that the overall European trend should be seen as a latent dynamic that affected all corners of the continent but that different places had their own trajectories. This is illustrated in figure 6, which shows trajectories for six geographic places with extended time series against the common European trend. If we follow these data, London probably was the first city in Europe where homicide declined to levels below 10 per 100,000, possibly as early as the late sixteenth century. Antwerp appears to have followed somewhat later with major declines in the sixteenth century. The next city in the figure to join the decline was Stockholm, where a good series of data suggests a major drop between 1620 and the late eighteenth century. In contrast, homicide rates in Rome remained much higher throughout the eighteenth and nineteenth centuries. Corsica, finally, began a gradual decline only during the nineteenth century but has remained far above the European average to the present day. The pattern for Madrid is unusual. Various estimates for the nineteenth century suggest that Madrid closely followed the southern European pattern of high levels of homicide. However, the earlier series of data based on court records suggest that levels in the late seventeenth and eighteenth centuries were only marginally higher than those in the north.

III. Civilizing Offensives and the Decline in Violence

The big decline in homicide was real. It occurred everywhere in western Europe, crossing national boundaries and gradually embodying a joint movement toward equally low rates by the mid-twentieth century. It began at different periods in different locations, roughly following a gradient from the centers of European modernity to the more peripheral areas. It probably started in the late Middle Ages, but certainly gained momentum from the early seventeenth century, preceding other macrochanges such as the Industrial Revolution and the demographic transformation by centuries. It was not smooth. There were booms and busts, some possibly synchronized across geographically distant places since the sixteenth century, some being more local and depending on specific circumstances. Its main component was the decline in intermale violence in public space, although other types of serious violence may have followed a similar path. Its length, ubiquity, and size rank it among the most significant features of European modernity, on a par with other big dynamics such as urbanization, individualization, and state building.

Why did it happen? The most influential theoretical anchor remains Norbert Elias's (1978) theory of the "civilizing process," which links the rise of civilized behavior to the macro-level dynamics of state building and the changing structure of social relations (Linklater and Mennell 2010). The core hypothesis is that European societies over many centuries went through a dynamic whereby average levels of self-control, standards of decency, and disgust for open displays of cruelty tended to increase. Prima facie, this is an attractive starting point for criminologists as lacking self-control and the moral neutralization of violence have been shown to be strong individual-level risk factors for violent behavior (Gottfredson and Hirschi 1990; Piquero, Jennings, and Farrington 2010; Ribeaud and Eisner 2010). Bridging sociological theory, macrotheory, and psychological insight, Elias held that two macrodynamics promoted this change (1978, p. 322): the expansion of the state with its monopoly of violence and the extension of the market economy with its effects on interdependency. In respect of the first factor, Elias argued that the European experience from the early Middle Ages onward entailed a long-term movement toward an increasing concentration of the legitimate use of force in the state and its institutions. This process started with the transformation of the elites of the knightly warrior societies of the Middle Ages into relatively pacified courtiers, where elaborate manners and intrigue rather than fighting strength came to determine political success (Elias 1983). As the centralization and monopolization of state functions extended over time, more and larger social spaces became relatively free of violent disruptions, leading to a dampening of emotions and a distaste for public displays of cruelty.

Elias's second argument was that self-control flourishes in networks of functional interdependency. It borrows heavily from Enlightenment philosophers such as Adam Smith, Adam Ferguson, and David Hume, who believed that commerce and manufacture promote civility by introducing "order and good government, and with them, the liberty and security of individuals" (Smith 1776, sec. III.iii, p. 8). Interdependence does not necessarily foster affection for a trading partner, but it promotes "diplomacy" and sober "indifference" by making people focus on what matters for a profitable interaction to be continued. Also, it gives actors more opportunities to inflict costs on others by nonviolent means, for example, by withdrawing from an exchange of goods and choosing a different trading partner. This creates incentives for actors to be disciplined and good-mannered, as manifestations of low self-control and being unreliable are poisonous to the maintenance of complex networks.

While Elias assumed that the growth of self-control was due to the unintentional workings of structural forces, other scholars have followed Max Weber's (1982) analysis of the Protestant disciplinary ethos and emphasized the relevance of intentional man-made cultural change in disciplinary techniques. Different terms have been proposed to describe this idea. Many historians working on the change in daily life during the early modern age have found the notion of social disciplining useful. Developed in the late 1960s by the German historian Gerhard Oestreich (1982), social disciplining refers to a set of strategies through which the early modern state sought to discipline, rationalize, and organize its subjects' behavior in order to facilitate well-ordered government and to improve the strength of the army (van Krieken 1990; Ogilvie 2006).

The sociologist Philip Gorski (2003, pp. 32–33) proposed the related notion of disciplining revolutions. By disciplining revolution, Gorski means the introduction and diffusion of a set of disciplinary techniques and strategies that reorder the relationship between the individual, the community, and the state. His framework distinguishes four types of discipline, namely, self-discipline (individual and normative), correctional discipline, communal discipline, and judicial or institutional discipline. Disciplinary revolutions are then packages of techniques that combine strategies for organizing social control with offensives that aim to modify the behaviors and beliefs of subjects in the direction of higher self-control. While examining the sixteenth- and seventeenth-century disciplinary revolution in the Netherlands and Prussia, Gorski emphasized that the notion of disciplinary revolutions can be generalized to different periods and societies.

Finally, Dutch sociologists working under the influence of Elias have developed the notion of civilizing offensives (Powell 2013). Civilizing offensives are conscious and deliberate attempts by powerful groups to attack behaviors of common people that are considered immoral, licentious, or uncivilized and to promote a life of self-control, temperance, orderliness, and respectability. They aim to change the political economy of prudence and self-control by means of a combination of punishment, monitoring, individual reform, restructuring of daily activities, and moral betterment. Among others, they change standards of manners and courtesy, those rules of daily interaction that "vex or soothe, corrupt or purify, exalt or debase, barbarise or refine us" through their constant, steady, uniform, insensible operation (Burke 1796, p. 38). Such change is particularly relevant here as many homicides originate in what Wolfgang (1958) called "altercations of relatively trivial origin"—conflicts that arise from signs of disrespect, insults, or improper public behavior, which lead to humiliation or embarrassment.

Civilizing offensives are associated with change in standards of emotional expression. For example, European elites in the seventeenth and eighteenth centuries increasingly regarded manifestations of emotional spontaneity (e.g., in dancing, at carnivals, during sports, in theaters) including expressions of anger as vulgar and disorderly, leading to the launch of a variety of disciplinary and legal measures designed to curb spontaneity (Stearns 2008, p. 20). At the same time, there was an increasing emphasis on the cultivation of an inner-directed and self-reflexive self, within which managing emotions rather than expressing them became a virtuous ability (Stearns and Stearns 1986; Stearns 2008, p. 25).

In awareness of the risk of oversimplifying a complex historical process, table 6 offers a schematic overview of six main "civilizing offensives" that social historians have described. The first process refers to the courtization of the nobility during the eleventh to thirteenth centuries. Jaeger (1985), for example, describes the rise of courtly ideals during the eleventh and twelfth centuries and interprets them as an expression of the beginning subordination of the nobility by the emerging royal courts. The twelfth and thirteenth centuries also are the period of the transition from a justice system based on private reconciliation and revenge to the development of a "criminal justice" idea that increasingly imposed the compulsory involvement of judicial authorities (Dean 2007).

A second period of intensified strategies to control daily behaviors has been associated with the "new monarchies" of the late fifteenth and sixteenth centuries, whose rise led to the absolutist states. Especially Tilly (1985, 1992) argues that the late fifteenth century experienced an invigorated thrust to monopolize the extortion of protection rent through regular taxes and to bring subjects under tighter control. In respect to the penal climate, this period saw what Lenman and Parker (1980) have termed the judicial revolution, the beginning of a more systematic attempt to expand the reach of a bureaucratic and formalized criminal justice system, manifest, for example, in the abolition of sanctuary protection of perpetrators (Shoemaker 2011).

The period of the late sixteenth and early seventeenth centuries has long been regarded as a turning point in the disciplinary techniques of the European elites. There are two main versions of the argument. In the tradition of Weber (1982), Gorski (2003, p. xvi) argues that the Protestant revolution, especially in its Calvinist version, was pivotal in creating a new model of self-discipline. By refining and diffusing a toolbox of disciplining techniques, Calvin and his followers created a structure of intensive religious governance and control that fundamentally altered the relationship between the individual and the state. Its core technology was observation: self-observation, mutual observation, and hierarchical observation.

Researchers in the tradition of Oestreich (1982), by contrast, hold that the movement toward social disciplining was part of a much broader cultural and ideological change that originated in the Neo-stoicist movement and deeply changed the behavior of authorities in the direction of an intensified, deeper, more thorough regulation of daily life. By the end of the sixteenth century, the elites of western European towns saw the explosion of social behavior regulations, including Sunday observance; blasphemy; expenditure on weddings, christenings, and funerals, as well as the time spent on them; the upbringing of children; breaches of the peace; begging; almsgiving; and so forth (van Krieken 1990).

The Victorian Age is the next period for which historical research suggests the emergence of a bundle of disciplining technologies that target civility and self-control. For England, for example, Wood (2004) has described the nineteenth-century civilizing process as a self-conscious moral crusade by the English middle classes, supported by bourgeois mentalities, the expansion of state bureaucracies, and the rise of a professionalized police force. It included, among others, the increasing emphasis on respectability as an ideal of masculine identity, the belief in progressive betterment and moral reform of society and individuals, moral entrepreneurs who aimed to eliminate disorderly behaviors and alcohol consumption, and the emergence of a planned professional social control of public space by police officers. As Joseph Kidd, a Victorian journalist and activist of the temperance movement said in 1879, "To be able to rule self and transmit to children an organization [i.e., Victorian England] accustomed to self-restraint and moderation in all things is one of the chief delights and aspirations to the moral nature of a true man" (cited in Smith 1993).

A logical extension of this argument is that the latest in a series of civilizing offensives that bundle technologies of social and self-control occurred in the 1980s and 1990s. Traces of such an idea can be found, for example, in Garland's (2001) analysis of change in patterns of social control since the 1970s. His analyses suggest a confluence of shifts in ideas that can be called a new disciplinary regime. Emphasizing the criminal justice system, he highlights the emergence of a more punitive justice system, increased demands for protection and retribution, extended use of surveillance technologies, more intensive control of antisocial behaviors and enforcement of discipline, and an expanding infrastructure of crime prevention and community safety (also see Tonry 2004). But change in the direction of tighter control was not limited to the criminal justice system. Similar moves toward tighter controls over daily behavior since the 1980s have also been documented for drunk driving and other controls of traffic behaviors (Voas, Tippetts, and Fell 2000), moves to build more incentives for finding work into welfare benefits systems, an expansion of disciplinary models in schools including zero-tolerance regimes (Hirschfield 2008), and policies em-

TABLE 6

Schematic Overview of Major "Civilizing Offensives," Eleventh to Twenty-First Centuries

Period	Core Characteristics	Selected Proponents
Courtization of warriors (11th–13th centuries)	Disappearance of "free warriors" Increasing dependence of nobility Courtliness (modesty, patience, restraint, and elegance) as new ethic God's peace and king's peace limit private retaliation rights Beginning monopolization over legitimate use of force Criminalization of killing, institutionalized death penalty Beginning of state-run criminal justice based on written procedure	Elias (1983), Jaeger (1985)
Early absolutist state (late 15th–17th centuries)	Limitation of power of feudal aristocracy, fight against feuding Centralized taxation Monopolization of protection business Standing army Centralization of judicial powers State punitiveness focused on suffering and pain	Lenman and Parker (1980), Tilly (1992), Ertman (1997)

Period	Characteristics	References
Social disciplining revolution (mid-16th–18th centuries)	Police ordinances expand state control over daily behaviors Emphasis on frugality, duty, deference, orderliness Confessionalization and church discipline intensify social control and promote conscience and ethic of inner control Fight against disorderly pastimes and behaviors Reformation of the poor, workhouses, orphanages	Oestreich (1982), Hsia (1992), Gorski (1993)
Bourgeois civilizing offensive (1830–1900)	Disciplining of working classes in factories (time and work discipline) Universal schooling and mass conscription armies Professional national police forces "Temperance movement" emphasizes self-control "Rational recreation" promotes civilized leisure activities Ideal of domesticity and respectability promote inner-directed family harmony	Thompson and Longstreth (1988), Wiener (2004), Powell (2013)
Securitization and new culture of control (1980s to present)	Extended use of surveillance technologies More intensive control of antisocial behaviors Enforcement of discipline and propriety Expanding infrastructure of crime prevention and community Initiatives against welfare dependency	Garland (2001), Tonry (2004), Farrell et al. (2011)

anating from public health strategies in respect of alcohol and tobacco consumption, physical exercise, and sexual behavior.

IV. Correlates of the Long Homicide Decline

The notion of subsequent civilizing offensives implies that the ways in which powerful actors try to shape the daily practice of self-discipline vary over time and that different aspects of social life are targeted in different periods. In the following sections, I examine relationships between trends in lethal violence and selected quantitative indicators of long-term change in social control and self-control. Such an endeavor is becoming possible because social historians generate a growing array of quantitative data that track processes associated with the rise of European modernity (de Vries 1984; De Long and Shleifer 1993; Allen 2001; Buringh and van Zanden 2009; Eisner 2011). The role of such indicators is not to replace in-depth historical analyses. Their function is to provide a frame of data that can inform further analysis and interpretation.

With this purpose in mind, I explore five covariates of homicide rates. Each relates to a facet of social disciplining and self-control that was outlined in the previous section. I start with examining whether the decline in homicide rates among the general population was preceded by an even longer process of declining elite violence between AD 600 and 1800. This is important because the theory of the civilizing process predicts that the taming of warrior elites is necessary (but not sufficient) for the pacification of social interactions more generally (Elias 1978). I then explore the association between homicide trends and a key indicator of change in Europe's punitive regime, namely, the frequency of capital punishments between 1200 and 1800. This matters because the transition from a punitive regime based on public rituals of suffering to one founded on confinement and correction played an essential part in the disciplinary transition of the early modern age (Foucault 1975; Spierenburg 2007a). Next, I examine the spread of the book and the growth of literacy from the invention of the printing press in 1453–1900. Arguably, literacy played a vital role in the cultivation of self-discipline and reflexive conscience during this period, and I explore the extent to which the retreat of homicide was associated with the advance of books. Fourth, I consider links between macro-level change in alcohol consumption and homicide, focusing on countries in northern Europe between 1800 and 2000. I interpret alcohol consumption as an indicator that tracks the extent to which the bourgeois civilizing offensive of the nineteenth century was successful in promoting temperance and self-control. Finally, I return to the issue raised by Pinker (2011), namely, whether the up and down of homicide since the 1950s was associated with the loss and reconquest of self-control. Exploring the contents of 5 million English-language books indexed in the Google NGRAM database, I investigate whether one can find traces of a cluster of ideas around self-control and discipline that could have been involved in the decline in violence since the early 1990s.

The analyses are at the descriptive level of plotting trends, supported by bivariate correlations as indications of the strength of relationships. No formal tests of causal relationships are performed. Such tests do not seem adequate in an exploratory analysis of data in which all measures are affected by considerable systematic and unsystematic error, indicators at best indirectly capture processes for which no direct measurement is possible, and we lack good theory that could guide the selection of predictors for which more rigorous tests could be promising.

A. The Pacification of the Elites: 600–1800

In *The Civilizing Process*, Norbert Elias (1978) argued that the development of "courtoisie," the medieval code of refined manners, generosity, and respect among peers, and the wider pacification of society first and foremost require the subordination of local warlords under rulers who successfully assert a monopoly of legitimate violence. The idea is that individuals are more likely to invest in long-sighted behavior, cultivate self-discipline, and engage in cooperation with nonrelatives if they live in a polity where life, limb, and livelihood are protected. In contrast, infighting among political elites, robbery attacks against adversaries, and feuds among bitterly opposed factions propagate the revenge and retaliation mechanisms that are rooted in our evolutionary past (Boehm 1984; Roth 2011), while hindering the cultivation of skills related to long-term planning, cooperation, dispassionate interaction guided by politeness, and empathetic perspective taking. Conceptually, the argument is similar to observations by Rotberg (2003) about the link between criminal violence and state failure. State failure manifest in armed political factions, violent ethnic cleavages, and widespread private protection entrepreneurs leads to explosions of conventional criminal violence while the restoration of legitimate authority that ties elites to compliance with shared rules is a prime precondition for the restoration of order.

But is there any quantitative evidence for a movement toward more stable power structures at the top of the power hierarchy even before the decline in homicide began? There is one indicator that may serve as a defensible proxy, namely, data on the proportion of monarchs whose rule ended prematurely as a result of removal by murder. I recently developed and presented pertinent data (Eisner 2011). They are derived from an analysis of all 1,628 monarchs who ruled one of 34 territorial units across Europe between 600 and 1800. In a first step, continuous lists of rulers were created. In a second step, all cases of alleged violent death were coded and further subdivided into battle death, accident, legal execution, and murder. Multiple sources were used to optimize validity.

The subcategory of regicide—the murder of monarchs—is of particular relevance. It is an indicator of the pacification of the elites because most regicides were not committed by outsiders but by members of the elite who saw a chance to remove an ineffective ruler, perceived their life to be at threat through the machinations of some other faction in the court, or were angered by monarchs who raped, robbed, or killed. Regicides have more in common with modern coups d'état—a good proxy of lacking political stability and failed control over power elites (McGowan 2003)—than with spur-of-the-moment manslaughter. They are best interpreted as cost-effective means for enforced power transition. The assassins had a good chance of providing the next monarch, although they subsequently exposed themselves to an increased risk of being murdered (Eisner 2011).

Despite the small population of just above 1,600 individuals (among whom fewer than one homicide would be expected in contemporary society), the data set has enough statistical power to examine overall trends over time. The reason is that over the entire period, 218 of all rulers were murdered, corresponding to 14 percent of the sample. Calculated as a homicide rate per ruler-year, the risk of being killed amounts to 1,003 per 100,000, making "monarch" the most dangerous occupation known in criminological research (for some comparative modern data on occupational homicide risks, see, e.g., Castillo and Jenkins [1994]).

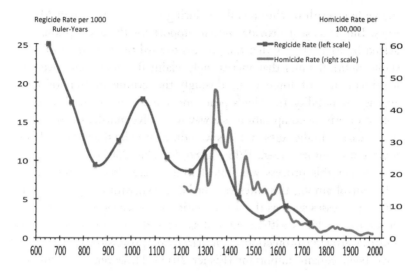

FIG. 7.—Elite violence (600–1800) versus European trend in homicide rates (1250–2012). Source: All series are from the History of Homicide Database.

However, the probability of regicide varied significantly over time. Figure 7 shows the long-term trend in European regicide rates by century between the seventh and the eighteenth centuries. The data document a linear long-term trend that takes the average annual occupational risk for a European ruler to be murdered from about 2,000 per 100,000 (i.e., a risk of about 1 : 50 per year in office) in the seventh and eighth centuries to about 200 per 100,000 in the eighteenth century. A linear trend regression line is highly significant and accounts for 56 percent of the variance.

For comparison, figure 7 also shows the European trend in homicide rates since 1200. For the period in which the two series overlap, there is considerable similarity in the declining trend. Apparently, as the probability that rulers would be removed by competitors dropped, the mean risk that conventional people would be killed on the streets also declined.

Importantly, however, the regicide series suggests a trend toward declining elite violence long before the first written records document the operations of the criminal justice system from around 1200. At this stage, it is unclear whether the quantitative trend in regicides can be generalized to wider trends in levels of violence among the elites, although future research may lead to better data that describe trends in the violent death of elite members during the early and High Middle Ages. But at least it provides initial support for the assumption, suggested by Elias (1978), that the process toward the formation of more stable political units that increasingly claimed a monopoly over the legitimate use of force (e.g., through the criminalization of feuds among the nobility, the king's peace movement, or the gradual elimination of private composition as a way to resolve murder cases) started in the early Middle Ages and was well on its way by the thirteenth and fourteenth centuries (e.g., White 1986; Fletcher 2002).

Whether this process was linked to an increasing commitment to self-control among the elites cannot be shown with the present data. Other processes such as the formalization of succession rules, the tendency to vest kings with an aura of sacral authority and divine rights, and the growing protection of monarchs by professional guards may have been equally important (Eisner 2011). However, the finding is certainly in line with results from contemporary cross-national research that societies with high levels of criminal interpersonal violence tend to be societies in which the right to rule is contested, elites use violent means to secure access to power and resources, and power transfer takes the form of violent removal (Chu and Tusalem 2013).

B. The Vanishing Theatre of Horror: 1200–1800

Foucault (1975) and Elias (1978) saw a transition in the early modern period from a model of punishment based on the primacy of public infliction of pain and suffering to one that uses confinement to promote discipline and fight idleness and villainy. The opposition of these ideal types has been criticized for oversimplifying the historical dynamics, but the scheme remains a useful framework for interpreting the change in penal practice between about 1500 and 1900 (Spierenburg 1987, 1991). An important turning point in this process is the emergence of houses of correction for beggars and vagrants in England and the Netherlands around 1600, which symbolize a new disciplining technology and a changing attitude toward the maintenance of public order and control over the poor. In seventeenth-century Amsterdam, the new houses of correction were a major attraction for international visitors, who spread knowledge about the innovative model of disciplinary policy to other parts of Europe (Spierenburg 1987).

Rituals of public executions were probably the most prominent sign of the older disciplinary model (van Dülmen 1990). The public confession, pastoral support provided by confraternities (Terpstra 2008), publication of "Last Dying Speeches" (Sharpe 1985), humiliating processions through large crowds of people, and symbolic mirroring of the wrongdoing and the mode of execution make executions a focal point of a punitive regime that was built on the publicly visible infliction of pain and suffering as a symbol of the repressive potential of the state (Spierenburg 1984).

Serial data on public executions go back to the thirteenth century and are available for a large number of cities across Europe (less is known about capital punishment in rural areas). They were sometimes kept by financial authorities to record payments to the hangman; in other places including Italy, confraternities of volunteers who provided consolation to the sinners kept detailed lists. Owing to their wide availability over long periods of time, execution data are prime quantitative indicators for the rise and fall of a punitive model anchored in the public infliction of suffering and its gradual substitution with a model premised on reform and discipline.

The Homicide Database currently comprises 18 time series, retrieved from primary historical research, on the frequency of executions in various cities and regions. They cover a range of geographic areas including, for example, Rome, Bologna, Venice, and Pamplona in southern Europe; Frankfort, Zurich, Antwerp, and Wrocław/Breslau in central Europe; and the counties of Cheshire and Essex and London in the British Isles. Wherever a meaningful denominator existed, the figures have been standardized to rates per 100,000. However, sometimes the areas from which malefactors were brought to the public executions in the big cities are not entirely clear. Where this was the case, I used the absolute numbers per year and multiplied the series with a constant to bring it roughly in line with the other series. While this standardization makes common trends more easily visible, it means that variation in levels between the series cannot be interpreted.

To illustrate the main European trend, figure 8 shows all series combined without distinguishing between individual locations. Overall, the data suggest very high levels of capital punishments in the High Middle Ages and the early modern period. For example, between 1280 and 1360, the small kingdom of Navarra on the Spanish side of the Pyrenees had about 20 executions per year, peaking at around 50 executions in the mid-fourteenth century (Urra 2007). Scholars estimate that the kingdom had some 40,000 hearths, which may correspond to a maxi-

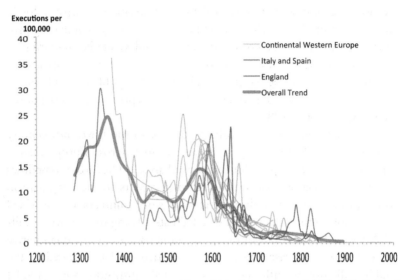

FIG. 8.—Executions in 18 European cities and joint long-term trend, 1200–1900. Series of executions include Mechelen (1370–1800), Antwerp (1400–1690), Augsburg (1545–1806), Breslau (1445–1800), Danzig (1558–1731), Frankfurt (1360–1696), Nuremberg (1503–1743), Zurich (1400–1900), Essex (1620–79), Chester (1580–1709), London (1701–1840), Sweden (1750–1940), Amsterdam (1524–1800), Bologna (1540–1799), Venice (1600–1798), Navarra (1280–1360), Lucerne (1550–1798), and Rome (1500–1870).

mum of 200,000 adults (Lazcano 2005; Urra 2007). This equals an execution rate of at least 10–25 per 100,000. Similarly, van Dijck (2007) estimates that execution rates in late medieval and early modern cities in Brabant (Antwerp, Mechelen, s'Hertogenbosch) fluctuated around 10–20 per 100,000 inhabitants between 1370 and 1570. Average rates of over 10 executions per 100,000 inhabitants seem to have been common—rates that would translate into 32,000 executions annually in the present-day United States or 700,000 executions worldwide.

Data on the common trend in executions suggest a wave-like pattern between the thirteenth and the sixteenth centuries, with a decline between 1350 and 1500 followed by a peak in the late sixteenth century. However, the very small number of time series before 1450 renders generalizations for the earlier period highly speculative. In contrast, the larger number of series from the mid-fifteenth century onward offers firmer ground for generalizing descriptions. The most outstanding feature is a strong tendency toward a joint decline after about 1590 in most European areas. In Bologna, the peak level of executions oc-

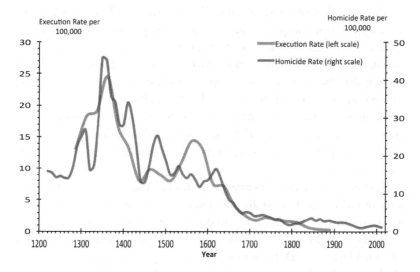

FIG. 9.—European trend in executions versus trend in homicide rates, 1200–1900

curred in 1580–89; in Rome it was 1590–99; Zurich, Nuremberg, and Augsburg in the south of German-speaking Europe had the peak number of executions in 1575–99; and in Antwerp and Mechelen the peak occurred in the 1560s and 1570s. In contrast, the situation may have been somewhat different in England. The series for the palatinate of Chester and Essex County start only around 1600, but both show an increase in the first decades of the seventeenth century and a pronounced spike around 1630, about 40–70 years later than seems to have been the case in continental Europe.

In figure 9, I project the European trend in capital punishment against the trend in homicide rates. It indicates an astonishingly strong correlation over the period between 1300 and 1800. Both curves show a peak in the late fourteenth century, a possible minor spike in the second half of the fifteenth century, and a long decline in the seventeenth and eighteenth centuries, which seems to have started earlier for the practice of state-sanctioned hanging and beheading than for criminal homicide. In interpreting this association, one should bear three issues in mind. First, the two groups of data come from different types of sources. It is therefore unlikely that the association reflects shared methodological bias. Second, the spatial coverage of the execution series and the homicide series differs considerably. While most of the execution series relate to Italian, German, and Dutch cities, the homicide series comprise a geographically larger and more varied set of data. Considering this lack of spatial congruity, it may even be more astonishing that the overall patterns are so similar. Finally, it is worth noting that the overlap is not a direct result of murder trials resulting in executions. Across Europe, the death penalty was a common punishment for a wide range of felonies including larceny, robbery, burglary, arson, and witchcraft (Spierenburg 1984; Bellamy 1998). Offenders convicted of homicide typically accounted for only a small proportion of all executions.

The correlated trend between executions and homicide raises several questions that need further inquiry. For one, the shared trend could mean that the declining frequency of executions signals the increasing capacity of early modern governments to gain control over their subjects. Van Dülmen (1995), for example, has suggested that the decline in capital punishments in Germany since the late sixteenth century is largely a result of the drop in actual crime levels, with the authorities gradually gaining control over the social disorder of the seventeenth century. This is not an argument in support of a direct deterrent effect of executions. Rather, it would suggest that the bundle of disciplinary techniques that spread through Europe in the wake of the late sixteenth-century social disciplining offensive gradually brought violent and criminal behavior under control, making executions a less likely event even if the tariff (i.e., the likelihood of capital punishment given a certain crime) had remained constant.

But the similarity in trends could also be seen as evidence that homicide and capital punishment were two sides of the same coin and that their simultaneous decline up to 1800 reflects a more fundamental shift that affected elite attitudes away from approving the spectacle of human beings being debased, tortured, killed, and publicly displayed to large audiences as much as the sense of respectability, frugality, and moderation that influenced increasing segments of the evolving civil society (Spierenburg 1984).

C. Books and the Reading Revolution, 1450–1900

A theoretical framework that links the long homicide decline to increased self-control warrants indicators of investment in discipline, long-sightedness, and perspective taking. For the early modern period, two such indicators are the spread of books and literacy. They index self-control for several reasons. The rise of the book is intimately linked to the European historical epicenter of self-discipline, the monasteries, in which the mastery over greed (poverty), over physical desires (chastity), and over self-interest (obedience) were core pillars of ascetic life (Lawrence 2001). This was especially so until Johannes Gutenberg's idea of printing hit the market in 1453, which freed the encounter with ideas stored on parchment or paper from the century-old confines of monastic libraries. Also, reading and writing skills were mainly acquired in the schools, the foremost producer of discipline and compliance. This is true even if in some rural areas such as Sweden and Switzerland the spread of literacy largely relied on learning at home (Houston 1988). But schools were not only about providing knowledge. Authorities were convinced that lack of education bred immorality and crime and that schools could keep vice in check by promoting obedience, restraint, and discipline (Graff 1977, p. 245).

Furthermore, literacy was linked to self-control via the contents that readers read. In seventeenth-century Spanish bookshops, for example, popular books would include religious titles such as the *Exercitatorio de la vida spiritual* (An exercise book in spiritual life), liturgical literature, sermons, and editions of the holy scriptures and commentaries, although more practical advice literature and cheap broadsheets were also in high demand (Nalle 1989). Similarly, the Swedish and Scottish literacy campaigns of the late seventeenth and eighteenth centuries were entirely designed to support the reading of the scriptures and the catechism (Houston 1987). Finally, reading and writing are in themselves training sessions in self-control. They require mastery over abilities such as sitting still, fine-motor control of hand movements, self-directed information processing, and training of mnemonic and thinking skills—all of which are core components of self-control. Moreover, for many centuries the acquisition of literacy was a costly investment in human capital (Schofield 1973; Baten and van Zanden 2008). It promised returns in prestige or wealth in the long run only, thus possibly creating a rational incentive for long-sightedness and careful planning.

Buringh and van Zanden (2009) have recently presented an extraordinary series of estimates, based on extensive searches of catalogues and corrections for missing information, on the volume of manuscripts and printed books produced from 600 to 1800. They argue that book

TABLE 7

Book Production per 1,000 Inhabitants, 1453–1799

Country				Period			
	1453–99	1500–1549	1550–99	1600–1649	1650–99	1700–1749	1750–99
Great Britain	2.0	14.6	27.3	80.0	191.8	168.3	192.0
Ireland	0	0	.1	3.8	14.2	61.7	77.7
Sweden	.2	.8	1.1	39.7	58.5	83.8	208.9
France	3.2	29.9	33.7	52.2	70.1	58.7	117.9
Belgium	4.7	17.7	48.2	33.2	73.6	30.7	44.5
Netherlands	7.9	14.2	33.5	139.0	259.4	391.3	488.3
Germany	4.1	21.2	43.4	54.0	78.7	99.7	122.4
Switzerland	9.3	48.1	78.5	9.3	14.6	14.2	32.3
Italy	6.8	21.3	51.0	42.1	56.3	48.4	86.5
Spain	.9	4.2	4.3	8.8	14.3	18.5	28.3
Poland	0	.2	.5	5.7	6.2	9.9	22.5
Western Europe	3.1	17.5	29.1	40.6	66.7	66.7	122.4

SOURCE.—Data from Buringh and van Zanden (2009).

production is a core indicator of human capital formation and that it is closely correlated with the spread of literacy across the continent.

Between 1453 and 1800, their estimates on the production of printed books in 50-year intervals distinguish 13 European regions within contemporary boundaries. The data show that the volume of printed books increased about 40-fold across Europe from 3.1 per 1,000 inhabitants in 1453–99 to 122.4 per 1,000 inhabitants in 1750–99 (see table 7). Moreover, they found substantial differences in the trajectories between regions. According to their estimates, France, Belgium, Germany, Switzerland, and Italy were early pioneers of the printing press in the sixteenth century but lost relative importance in the seventeenth and eighteenth centuries. In contrast, the two dominating military and economic powers of the seventeenth and eighteenth centuries, the Netherlands and Britain, experienced a fast growth in book production during the seventeenth century. By the second half of the century, they produced more than twice as many books per capita as any other European country, signaling a massive lead in academic and literary book production. Sweden followed suit during the eighteenth century, establishing itself as one of the major producers of books by the late eighteenth century. In contrast, the economically backward regions of Poland and Spain lagged far behind the European average throughout the early modern period.

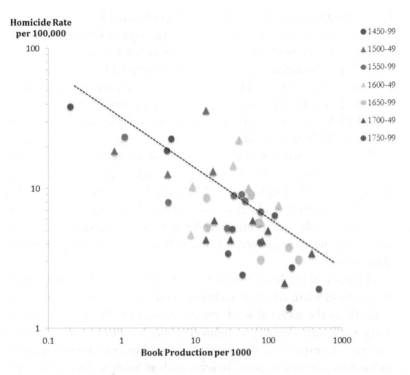

FIG. 10.—Log-log relationship between book production and homicide rates in western Europe, 1450–1800, 50-year periods. Data on book production are based on Buringh and van Zanden (2009). Homicide data are as shown above in table 1. Regression model: HomRate = $22.3 \times \text{BookProd}^{-0.345}$; $R^2 = 53.7$ percent; $N = 42$.

The data by Buringh and van Zanden (2009) permit an empirical assessment of the dynamic link between the spread of books and levels of homicide. To examine this association, I matched their 50-year estimates of per capita book production with corresponding estimates from the History of Homicide Database. Forty-two observation points representing eight regions between 1450–99 and 1750–99 have information on both variables, forming the basis for the visualization of the relationship in figure 10. The results are shown in a log-log plot, in which logarithmic scales are used on both the horizontal and the vertical axes. Because the data relate to different time periods and places, I present the findings so that observations for each 50-year time period are coded with a different label.

The data show a strong negative association across all 42 observations. I fitted an equation of the form $y = ax^k$, which represents the linear relationship between the two logged variables, with k representing the elasticity estimate. The findings suggest that every 10 percent increase in book production was associated with a 3.4 percent reduction in homicide rates and that the two variables share almost 54 percent of the variance. The main historical movement suggested by the data is a shift of European societies from the upper-left-hand corner of high homicide and low literacy toward the lower-right-hand corner of high literacy and low homicide, with an evolving cross-sectional association between the two variables. For example, the countries that had moved to the highest per capita book production by 1750–99, namely, England, the Netherlands, and Sweden, had also reached the lowest levels of homicide rates. By comparison, in countries such as Italy and Spain, where literacy and book production lagged behind by the late eighteenth century, homicide rates were considerably higher.

The story of the literacy-homicide link does not end in 1800. From the 1850s onward, relatively continuous estimates of illiteracy rates are available at the national level, usually as part of the national census. They show that illiteracy continued to decline during this period in line with the expansion of compulsory schooling, but with considerable differences between regions. In areas such as Sweden, Denmark, Norway, the Netherlands, Prussia, Switzerland, and Scotland, literacy rates were already above 80 percent in the middle of the nineteenth century and converged to below 5 percent before World War I. In the south and east of Europe, however, very considerable proportions of the population were illiterate in the middle of the century. And although illiteracy fell rapidly in the following decades, countries such as Italy, Spain, Portugal, and Hungary continued to have illiteracy rates above 25 percent around 1910 (Flora and Alber 1983).

To further examine the link between the fall in illiteracy and the decline in homicide rates, figure 11 shows the trajectory of homicide rates against illiteracy rates over subsequent 5-year periods in five selected countries. Arrows indicate the time order of observations to allow the reader to follow the time path within each country.

It suggests a consistent pattern of falling homicide rates as literacy rates increased. Furthermore, one may note that the inverse association between literacy and homicide is stronger in the middle range of literacy rates, between 70 and 30 percent, while the association is flatter as literacy rates approach 100 percent. This might be suggestive of the

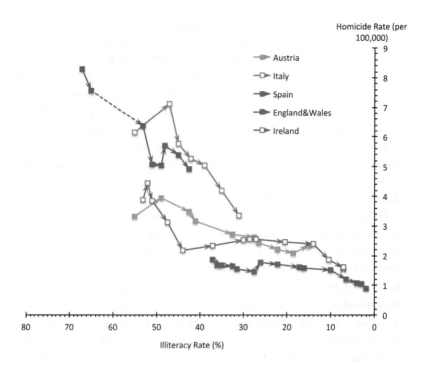

FIG. 11.—Trajectories of literacy rates versus homicide rates over time in five selected countries, 1845–1910, 5-year intervals. Arrows indicate the direction of time, starting between 1845 (England and Wales) and 1875 (Italy) and ending in 1910–14. Source: Homicide rates are from the History of Homicide Database. Illiteracy rates are from 1845 based on Flora and Alber (1983) and UNESCO (1953).

notion that the self-control-enhancing effect of literacy became weaker as the skill became more widely disseminated and literacy ceased to be a valuable capital.

Again, it is important to note that these associations do not demonstrate causation. As literacy rates were monotonically falling in every country during the period from 1850 to 1914, very little can be said statistically about the relationship other than that there was an association in the expected direction over time and that at each specific time there was considerable cross-sectional correlation between literacy rates and homicide rates. Literacy and book production share the problem of all macro-level indicators in social science research, namely, that they index several theoretically meaningful constructs, and their societal meaning and significance can change over time. If the correlational link with homicide is more than a coincidence, it could reflect the growth of self-control, the rise of modern individualism, the accumulation of human capital, or something else that may be associated with books. Which of these mechanisms was involved cannot be determined on the basis of macro-level indicators alone. In the present world, macro-level differences in literacy rates have not generally been found to be systematically associated with differences in homicide rates, although they were a substantial regional and national covariate in the nineteenth century (e.g., Nivette 2011). This probably underlines the point that macro-level quantitative indicators need to be interpreted in their historical and social contexts.

Despite these limitations, I believe that the findings presented here are the best available quantitative support for the hypothesis that investment in self-control was one of the driving forces behind the decline of homicide rates in Europe during the four centuries from about 1500 until about 1900. The overall decline in homicide rates as well as regional differences in the trajectories track the rise in literacy rates. Areas such as England and the Netherlands, where reading and writing spread earlier, were areas where homicide declined earlier. In areas such as Sweden, where there was a national literacy campaign during the second half of the seventeenth and the first half of the eighteenth centuries, the homicide decline coincided with the expansion of the ability to read the Bible and the Lutheran catechisms. Throughout the nineteenth century there existed a notable correlation, at both national and regional levels, between the diffusion of reading skills and levels of homicide rates. And, finally, the convergence of homicide rates across Europe toward the end of the nineteenth century coincides with the generalization of schooling across almost all areas of at least western Europe. In sum, populations that could read were less likely to have lethal fights and societies where the spread of literacy occurred earlier tended to experience an earlier drop in homicide.

D. Promoting Temperance and Controlling Alcohol Consumption: 1850–2000

Civilizing revolutions are not restricted to techniques that mold people's inner selves. Rather, mindful of the fragility of human self-discipline, their carriers likewise try to curtail the subjects' exposure to temptations and frictions that imperil a virtuous life. To put it in economic terms, disciplining revolutions are also aimed at lowering the demand for self-control by reducing exposure to brothels, taverns, or uncontrolled gatherings of festive crowds. One prime target of such efforts has been alcohol—the big seducer of men that writers from the Middle Ages onward have accused of ruining self-control and breeding lewdness, aggressiveness, madness, and disrespect for authorities (Warner 1997). Or, as the Elizabethan pamphleteer Thomas Nashe (1567–1601) put it, the drunkard "flings the pots about the house, calls his Hostesse whore, breakes the glasse windowes with his dagger, and is apt to quarrell with any man that speaks to him" (cited in Warner 1997, p. 1792).

Attempts to reduce excessive alcohol consumption go back to the Middle Ages. In medieval Augsburg, for example, the city council imposed tavern bans as a kind of antisocial behavior order against men who were known for domestic violence (Tlusty 1994). But the first coordinated attempt at large-scale reduction in excessive alcohol use was associated with the disciplining initiatives of Protestant and Catholic reformers from the late sixteenth century onward (Martin 2009). English Puritans such as Phillip Stubbes in his "Anatomy of Abuses" were vociferous in condemning drinking. Reformers denounced, for example, the traditional "church ales," festivals at which ale was sold to raise money for church expenses and the relief of the poor, as "mere excuses for bullbeatings, bowlings, drunkenness, dancings and such like" (Nicholls 2008, p. 194).

Some evidence suggests that alcohol consumption did decrease in the seventeenth and eighteenth centuries (Martin 2009), but it is impossible to assess its extent and timing with any greater degree of precision. The situation is much better from the mid-nineteenth century onward, when national data become available for a number of countries. I focus here on northern Europe, where temperance movements, fueled by evangelical and utilitarian motives, became a supporting pillar of the drive toward moral betterment between about 1850 and 1930 (Levine 1993; Yeomans 2011). Their target was self-control. Alcohol, the argument went, weakened the moral and higher proportions of the brain, produced a "disease of the will," and caused irrational harm both to oneself and to others. Sobriety, thrift, and self-discipline, by contrast, characterized the respectable "true man" who is in full possession of his willpower. Across the Protestant north of Europe these movements were highly influential, helping to shape early public health pol-

FIG. 12.—Homicide rate and alcohol consumption in England and Wales, 1840–2010. Source: Alcohol data until 1922 are from Wilson (1940). Homicide rates were smoothed with 3-year moving averages.

icies, social welfare policies, and the shifts in public opinion toward an increasing moral denunciation of alcoholic beverages.

Figures 12–15 chart the level of alcohol consumption according to official statistics in Sweden, Norway, Denmark, and England and Wales from the 1840s onward. They show that alcohol consumption fell by at least 50 percent in all four countries between the 1880s and the 1920s. Remarkably, this decline occurred despite increasing spending power and a growth in leisure time due to declining working hours. In Denmark, for example, per capita intake dwindled to less than 4 liters of pure alcohol in the 1930s, about 3 pints of beer per week. There is little doubt that the combination of state control (e.g., the purchasing rationing regime in Sweden from 1917 to 1955) and private moral entrepreneurship was pivotal in achieving this sobering of whole societies. It was closely watched by contemporaries and seen as a success in the promotion of civilized behavior (e.g., Carter 1932). But by the 1930s the temperance movement had lost its momentum, and across northern Europe, levels of alcohol consumption rose steadily until around 1980, when a new plateau of consumption levels was reached, with fluctuations in each country probably reflecting national differences in alcohol policy (e.g., Bentzen, Eriksson, and Smith 1999).

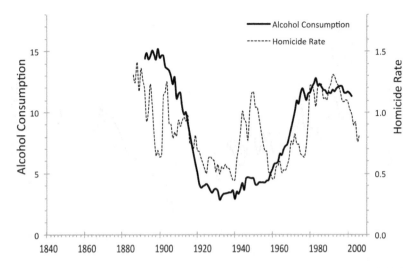

FIG. 13.—Homicide rate and alcohol consumption in Denmark, 1880–2010. Source: Alcohol data: personal communication Jan Bentzen, Aarhus University. Homicide rates were smoothed with 3-year moving averages.

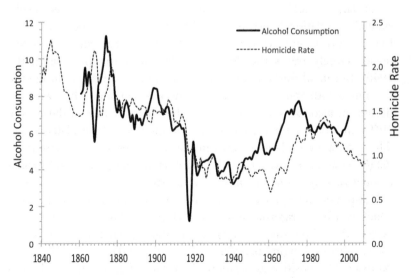

FIG. 14.—Homicide rate and alcohol consumption in Sweden, 1870–2010. Source: Alcohol data: personal communication Jan Bentzen, Aarhus University. Homicide rates were smoothed with 3-year moving averages.

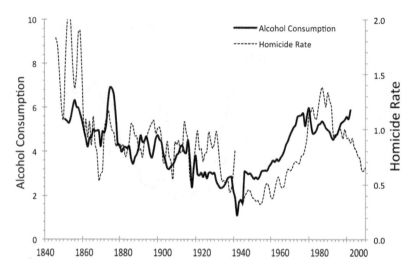

FIG. 15.—Homicide rate and alcohol consumption in Norway, 1850–2010. Source: Alcohol consumption: personal communication Jan Bentzen, Aarhus University. Homicide rates were smoothed with 3-year moving averages.

Figures 12–15 also show trends in homicide rates over the periods when data on alcohol consumption are available. They suggest a substantial correlation between alcohol trends and homicide rates in all four countries—most convincingly in Norway and Sweden, where homicide closely tracks the decline in alcohol consumption until the 1940s. But in all four countries, homicide rates went down during the late nineteenth and early twentieth centuries roughly in line with the decline in alcohol consumption, and they increased again during the 1960s and 1970s, when alcohol became more widely available again. The bivariate correlations between the raw series are .59 (Denmark), .62 (Norway), .73 (Sweden), and .69 (England), suggesting a substantial amount of shared variance in the overall trend.

I also examined associations between the first-differenced series, which is a more rigorous test of causal effects. Over the entire time period, they show small correlations in the expected direction for all four countries, ranging between $r = .10$ for England and $r = .16$ for Norway. The positive association disappears when the homicide data are lagged by 1 or 2 years, suggesting that any causal effect is short-term and likely operates within the same year (also see Lenke 1990). However, the issue of whether alcohol consumption has a direct causal effect on homicide is not central to my argument. Rather, my primary interest is in sobriety as an indirect indicator for the success of the civilizing offensives by elites that aimed to change the moral economy of their populations.

Certainly, the Victorian drive to improve self-control was not limited to alcohol. Rather, constraining alcohol use was part of a wider effort to promote self-discipline, perseverance, responsibility, and honesty. In Victorian England, different threads came together under the umbrella term of "rational recreation," a prevention strategy that aimed at clearing the hot spots of unmoral pastimes, especially rowdy and undisciplined street games, and substituting for them pastimes that were respectable and morally improving (Bailey 1978). By around 1850, the brutal tradition of prizefighting in open space came to be replaced by the more regulated sport of boxing, which was subject to strict rules and came to be seen as having an educational value in fostering efficient and muscular Christians (Wiener 2004). Approximately in the same period, the medieval game of football, essentially an open-end organized fight of two large groups of villagers around an inflated pig bladder, became sanitized as a rule-bound sport that came to be seen as promoting fair play, self-reliance, endurance, and sobriety (Vorspan 2000).

The decline of alcohol consumption during the period thus should be seen as indexing a wider civilizing offensive that targeted behaviors both in public and at home. It contributed to northern Europe experiencing some of the lowest homicide rates ever recorded in human history between the 1920s and the 1950s. Despite much less effective wound treatment and a considerably larger proportion of young men than today, homicide levels typically ranged between 0.3 and 0.6 per 100,000—roughly a 1 : 100 reduction over medieval levels and substantially less than contemporary rates in Europe would be if medical technology and demographic structure could be held constant.

E. Self-Control Lost and Regained? 1950–2010

I return to the "culture shift" argument set out at the beginning of this essay. Is there evidence for the notion that violent crime exploded in the 1960s because cultural shifts undermined the motivational fabric of self-control and that a reconfigured emphasis on self-control stabilized and then reduced crime since the early 1990s?

Finding quantitative data on this issue is difficult. While time series for economic and social variables proliferated in recent decades, quantitative indicators for cultural change remain scarce. I therefore turn to a new source of data on cultural trends, namely, the Google Books NGRAM corpus (Michel et al. 2011). Launched in 2010, NGRAM is a database of 8 million digitized books published between 1500 and 2008, corresponding to about 4 percent of all books ever printed. The interface allows users to track the frequency of any group of words as a percentage of all words in the corpus over a specified period of time. Its popularity as a source for cultural information has soared recently. For example, Greenfield (2013) used it to track changes in psychological characteristics during the transition from rural to urban society between 1800 and 2000, and Roth (2012) used NGRAM to trace shifts in group identities associated with major fluctuations in US homicide rates during the eighteenth and nineteenth centuries. But can this huge collection of English-language texts help to back up the postulated rise and decline in self-control?

NGRAM has important limitations as a source for cultural indicators. Book genres can be only partly separated, making it impossible to determine how change in the proportion of, for example, science and engineering texts affects the results. Also, it is hard to say what changing word frequencies mean. If the word "disrespectful" became more often used since the late 1980s, does this indicate that people became more disrespectful, that showing respect became more highly valued, or that talking about respect became more fashionable? Finally, Google Books mostly indexes academic work. The focus of our interest, namely, change in popular youth culture, is hence filtered through the vagaries of academic writing, publishers' decisions, and publication delays.

Despite these limitations, the NGRAM viewer is probably our best bet for exploring macro-level cultural change over the past 60 years. I focus on three domains. The first is three groups of words that tap into hedonistic preferences claimed to have been responsible for the growth in crime, namely, the occupation with "sex," "drugs," and "narcissism." The second domain is four groups of words that relate to self-control, namely, "shame," "politeness and good manners," "conscientiousness," and "honesty." Finally, I examine the career of three words that represent elements of the new culture of control proposed by Garland (2001), namely, "CCTV (closed-circuit television)," "zero tolerance," and "anger management." All analyses were conducted on

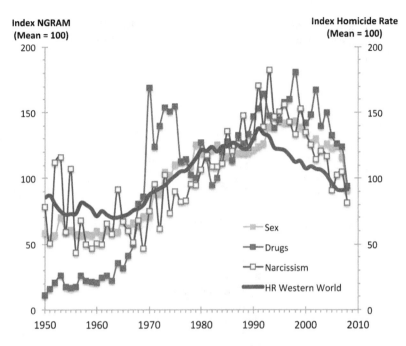

FIG. 16.—NGRAM frequency of "sex," "drugs," and "narcissism" versus indexed homicide rates, Western world, 1950–2008. Lexical entries used in NGRAM search: "drugs": cannabis, marijuana, heroin, cocaine; "narcissim": narcissism, narcissistic; "sex": sex, sexual, sexually.

the 2013 "English" corpus of NGRAM, the most comprehensive corpus of books published in English.

Figures 16–18 show the trends in the three groups of indicators in comparison with the shared homicide trend across Western societies described in figure 4. The shared trend (rather than the series for the United States, England, or Australia) was chosen because English-language publications continued to have a major influence on cultural trends across most Western societies.

Figure 16 suggests that the three indicators of more hedonistic interests show similar trends. Broadly in line with the culture shift hypothesis, sex, drugs, and narcissist self-interest became increasingly popular subjects in English-language books from the 1960s onward. In the early 1980s, typical book titles that fed the increase included *All about Sex Therapy*, *Sex Tips for Girls*, *Psychoactive Drugs and Sex*, or *Love and Narcissism in Psychoanalytic Practice*. The trend continued until the mid-1990s. But from about 1996 onward, all three topics began to lose

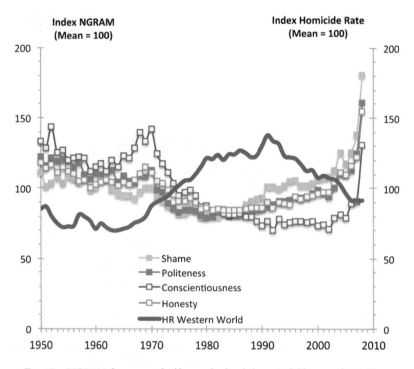

FIG. 17.—NGRAM frequency of self-control-related thematic fields versus homicide rate, Western world, 1950–2008. Lexical entries used in NGRAM search: "shame": shame, ashamed, shaming; "honesty": honesty, honest, trustworthiness, trustworthy, truthfulness, truthful; "politeness": politeness, polite, respectfulness, respectful, thoughtful, manners, etiquette, civility; "conscientiousness": conscientiousness, conscientious, diligent, industrious, self control.

importance in the English-language book market. A comparison of these indicators with the homicide trend in the Western world suggests a broadly parallel movement with a good coincidence of the upward turn in the late 1960s and the shift toward declining trends in the early 1990s. The bivariate correlations with the Western world homicide trend are $r = .74$, $r = .80$, and $r = .85$ for the topics of sex, drugs, and narcissist self-interest as measured in NGRAM, respectively.

Figure 17 shows the frequency of word fields that may be indicative of self-control, namely, shame, politeness, conscientiousness, and honesty. As the arguments brought forth by commentators such as Himmelfarb (1995) and Fukuyama (1999) would lead us to expect, the late 1960s and the early 1970s saw some decline in the frequency of word strings that express preoccupation with the kinds of moral issues and

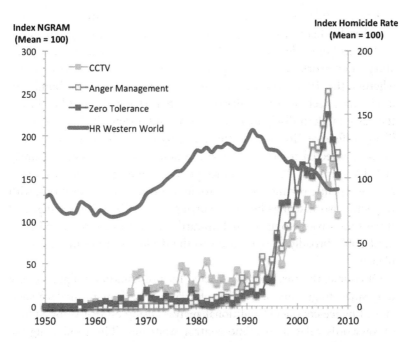

FIG. 18.—NGRAM frequency of "CCTV," "zero tolerance," and "anger management" versus homicide rates, Western world, 1950–2008. Lexical entries used in NGRAM search were CCTV, anger management, and zero tolerance.

norms of conduct that had been of such concern in the Victorian period. Subsequently, all four indicators essentially follow a long U-shaped curve with a trough roughly in the mid-1980s. Since then, issues related to honesty, shame, and politeness slowly recovered some of the ground they had lost in the early 1970s, with a notable acceleration of interest in self-control-related topics since about 2003. Titles that relate to these thematic fields around 2005–8 include a fair proportion of popular advice literature such as, for example, *Be Honest and Tell the Truth*, *Becoming a Trustworthy Leader*, *Shameful Behaviors*, *It's Time for Good Manners*, or *Good Manners: A Passport to Success*. Taken together they reflect an increasing preoccupation with exercising what psychologist Roy Baumeister called the "moral muscle of self-control" (Baumeister and Exline 1999). The associations with the trend in homicide rates are in the predicted direction, with bivariate correlations of −.29, −.73, −.84, and −.71 between homicide and shame, politeness, conscientiousness, and honesty, respectively.

The general return of values that emphasize self-control, civility, and moral individualism is one possible explanation for the synchronized decline in homicide across the Western world. But within the explanatory framework of this essay, it is equally important to consider whether the 1990s saw the introduction of an innovative bundle of disciplinary techniques, similar to those that changed social life during the early modern disciplinary revolution and during the Victorian civilizing offensive. To examine this issue, figure 18 shows the frequency of three selected topics related to the new culture of control, namely "CCTV cameras," "zero-tolerance policies," and "anger management" as a therapeutic regime. All three topics were genuine innovations, with respective word strings hardly occurring before 1990. Interestingly, all three topics rose along parallel upward trajectories from around 1992 until 2007, broadly in opposition to the declining trend in serious violence.

Of course, the three topics selected for presentation in figure 18 are only small fragments of the disciplinary mechanisms in modern societies. I hence conducted additional analyses using NGRAM for a range of keywords related to crime-control strategies. The results suggest that a much broader range of techniques that shape the current criminological discussion took off at some stage in the 1990s. This includes, among others, the keywords "DNA profiling," "offender management," "electronic tagging," "curfew orders," "boot camps," "three strikes," "community" and "problem-oriented" policing, "early childhood intervention," "evidence-based prevention," and "violence prevention." These thematic fields are at best tenuously related to each other. But in conjunction they seem to signal a broad underlying swing toward a new disciplinary paradigm.

So what do these data tell us about the link between cultural shifts away from and then back toward self-control, and trends in violent crime rates? Assuming that the shown indicators are crude, but roughly correct, measures of change in moral climate, the findings lend themselves to three conclusions. First, they suggest a drift toward more hedonistic expectations during the 1960s, 1970s, and 1980s and a return of more traditional preoccupations during the 1990s and 2000s. This is in line with the "culture shift" argument proposed by observers such as Fukuyama (1999) and Pinker (2011). The amplitude of the swings was moderate, and changes were gradual rather than abrupt. Maybe this is an artifact of the source used, however. The themes covered in NGRAM capture change as seen through the eyes of adult academics and publishers, whose decision-making processes may delay and smooth out more significant change in popular culture.

Second, the indicators suggest a broad link between culture shifts and change in homicide rates since World War II, although the indicators of culture change do not track specific turning points in violent crime. This does not mean that the inverse correlation between the rise and fall of crime and cultural interest in self-control was purely coincidental. Rather, it probably suggests that the shifts in values, expectations, and themes that characterized the cultural history of the Western world since the 1950s should be seen as a kind of long-term background radiation that affected the longer trends in crime levels rather than the specifics of short-term variation and differences between countries.

Third, I note a good correspondence between the beginning of the crime decline in the 1990s and the diffusion of the three indicators of a new culture of control, namely, CCTV surveillance, zero-tolerance policies in policing and schools, and a focus on anger management as a self-control-based therapeutic strategy (fig. 18). Their increasing popularity is part of a broader bundle of disciplinary topics that were booming in the 1990s, which include aspects of technical surveillance, more effective formal social control, and early and evidence-based prevention and risk-focused intervention. This probably supports the plausibility of claims that securitization (Farrell et al. 2011) and a new culture of control (Garland 2001) played a role in bringing about the change in crime trends during the early 1990s.

From the long-term perspective that I have taken in this essay, this should not come as a surprise. If the conclusion from the analyses presented here is that a combination of wider cultural shifts with more specific innovative technologies of outer social control (e.g., CCTV cameras) and inner control (e.g., anger management as just one manifestation of self-control-focused intervention strategies) contributed to the turning point in the early 1990s, then the constellation would be somewhat similar to that of the early seventeenth-century disciplinary revolution and the Victorian assault on crime and vice around the mid-nineteenth century.

One limitation of NGRAM is that it remains unclear whether change observed at the level of words used in books bears any relationship to beliefs and preferences in the general population. This would require survey data over long enough periods. Currently, I have found only one set of data with repeated measurements that reflect wider change in values and beliefs related to parenting. The largest opinion poll organization in Germany, the Allensbach Institute for Public Opinion Research, has produced a series of survey data on parenting values from 1967 to 2010 (Petersen 2011). Over more than 40 years representative samples of the population were asked which values they consider particularly important for helping their children in their later life. Three items are particularly important here as they directly bear on self-control, namely, "politeness and good manners," "doing work diligently and properly," and "being thrifty in money matters." These questions were asked to representative samples of the general population, and they were not specifically about parenting practices, but about general goals thought to be important in life. I therefore believe that they are best interpreted as broader measures of value change than as more proximal measures of actual parenting.

Figure 19 shows the average proportion of respondents who did not agree to any one of these items. It suggests that in Germany the tendency to reject self-control values as being important in life increased substantially between the mid-1960s and the early 1990s. In contrast, since 1990 the data suggest a tendency for larger proportions of respondents to endorse values that are arguably associated with self-control. The change in trends is broadly similar to findings reported by Collishaw et al. (2012) on parenting values in the United Kingdom, based on large nationally representative surveys that study tracked changes in parental practices that are likely to be related to self-control. The study found that between 1986 and 2006, parental expectations about "being polite to parents" and "doing homework" had increased significantly.

Figure 19 also shows the average annual homicide rates in Germany and the neighboring (mostly) German-speaking countries Austria and Switzerland. The data suggest a close association between change in "self-control" as a public value and variation in homicide rates. The bivariate correlation is $r = .80$.

As always, such associations do not demonstrate causal impact. Also, the lack of similar indicators for other countries makes it impossible to say whether trends in homicide rates are more generally associated with change in the extent to which politeness, diligence, and thriftiness are emphasized as broad values in the general population.

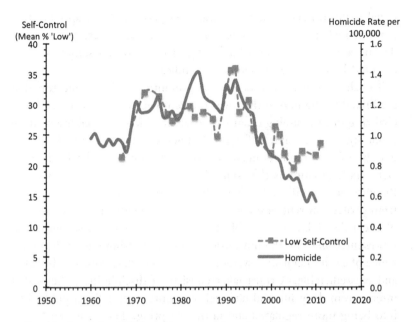

FIG. 19.—Promoting "self control" as a parenting value in Germany and mean homicide trends in German-speaking countries. The "low self-control" score is based on three items, namely, importance of promoting "politeness and good manners," "doing work diligently," and "being thrifty and saving money," mean percentage not agreeing to these items. Source: Parenting values: Petersen (2011). Homicide rates are the unweighted average for Germany, Austria, and Switzerland.

V. Conclusions and Outlook

It is not merely a scientific embarrassment for criminology that we still barely understand why homicide rates have declined consistently across the Western world over the past 20 years. Understanding why the decline occurred could also be a critical achievement. It might provide clues about how to make declining trends happen in the future. This is especially so if one assumes that all major violence declines, in all places, at all times, are triggered by similar universal mechanisms and that at least some of these mechanisms are due to man-made policies (irrespective of whether they are intended to reduce violence) rather than to anonymous social forces.

In this essay, I focused on the longest, biggest, and best-documented drop in interpersonal violence, namely, the long European homicide decline between the late Middle Ages and the mid-twentieth century, which according to the evidence presented here comprised a drop in lethal male-to-male fighting by about 99 percent. More specifically, I examined whether it is possible to go beyond a mere description of the decline and to move toward a testing of theoretical assumptions represented by macro-level quantitative indicators.

To achieve this goal, I focused on presenting various indicators that are linked to the notion that over the centuries Europe saw a series of civilizing or disciplining offensives, each of which changed the political economy of social and self-control. They can be interpreted as a hierarchy of requirements needed to promote pacified behavior in a society. Its foundation is the establishment of a state where members of the elite do not kill each other, where entrepreneurs who seek profits from protection rents are kept in check, and where at least some level of the rule of law is available to common citizens. A second layer, represented here by the indicator of capital punishments, is the emergence of a criminal justice system that is not cruel, is governed by rules, and is predictable. A third layer consists of disciplining policies that intervene in daily life and channel behaviors, especially in public life, into being more regulated and norm-accepting. The Victorian "rational recreation" movement with its links to temperance and alcohol control was an example. A fourth layer consists of the resources that support the formation of conscience and self-control as an inner moral muscle, exemplified here by the diffusion of reading and writing abilities.

I have reiterated throughout this essay that the display of correlated curves is not sufficient to make any claims for causal mechanisms. And it may be necessary to state it again here. But I believe that the data presented here open up a range of possibilities for further empirical inquiry. In particular, the continuing development of an ever denser set of indicators on the economic, social, cultural, and political dynamics of Europe over the past centuries will bring us to the stage where we can subject theoretically based hypotheses on the long-term development of interpersonal violence to meaningful, more rigorous empirical tests. It is quite possible that measures of interpersonal violence will turn out to index important behavioral change that is intimately linked to (and predictive of) the rise of modern society.

Much more could be done, of course, beyond further improving the scope and quality of historical homicide data. For example, national biographies in various languages would lend themselves to the construction of comparative quantitative indicators about political violence among elites over long periods of time. Similarly, the early modern wave of social disciplining has left a mass of traces in the shape of ordinances and other behavioral regulations, whose trend over time could be examined.

Finally, the long-term perspective adopted here brought forth some evidence in support of the hypothesis that the decline of homicide in the Western world over the past 20 years shares some important characteristics with earlier declines. In particular, the early 1990s, on top of the broader pendulum swing back toward a higher emphasis on self-control, was characterized by emergence of a bundle of disciplining techniques similar to the social disciplining technologies of the late sixteenth and early seventeenth centuries or the Victorian civilizing offensive.

REFERENCES

Allen, Robert C. 2001. "The Great Divergence in European Wages and Prices from the Middle Ages to the First World War." *Explorations in Economic History* 38(4):411–47.

Alloza, Ángel. 2000. *La vara quebrada de la justicia: Un estudio histórico sobre la delincuencia madrileña entre los siglos XVI y XVIII.* Madrid: Catarata.

Bailey, Peter. 1978. *Leisure and Class in Victorian England: Rational Recreation and the Contest for Control, 1830–1885.* London: Routledge.

Baten, Joerg, and Jan van Zanden. 2008. "Book Production and the Onset of Modern Economic Growth." *Journal of Economic Growth* 13(3):217–35.

Baumeister, Roy F., and Julia J. Exline. 1999. "Virtue, Personality, and Social Relations: Self-Control as the Moral Muscle." *Journal of Personality* 67(6): 1165–94.

Bellamy, John G. 1998. *The Criminal Trial in Later Medieval England: Felony before the Courts from Edward I to the Sixteenth Century.* Toronto: University of Toronto Press.

Bentzen, Jan, Tor Eriksson, and Valdemar Smith. 1999. "Rational Addiction and Alcohol Consumption: Evidence from the Nordic Countries." *Journal of Consumer Policy* 22(3):257–79.

Berraondo, Mikel. 2012. "La violencia interpersonal en la Navarra moderna (siglos XVI–XVII)." PhD diss., Universidad de Navarra.

Blumstein, Alfred, and Joel Wallman, eds. 2000. *The Crime Drop in America.* Cambridge: Cambridge University Press.

Boehm, Christopher. 1984. *Blood Revenge: The Enactment and Management of Conflict in Montenegro and Other Tribal Societies.* Lawrence: University Press of Kansas.

Buringh, Eltjo, and Jan Luiten van Zanden. 2009. "Charting the 'Rise of the West': Manuscripts and Printed Books in Europe, a Long-Term Perspective from the Sixth through Eighteenth Centuries." *Journal of Economic History* 69(2):409–45.

Burke, Edmund. 1796. *First Letter on a Regicide Peace.* London: F. and C. Rivington.

Carter, Henry. 1932. "The Drink Problem in Great Britain." *Annals of the American Academy of Political and Social Science* 163:197–205.

Castillo, Dawn N., and E. Lynn Jenkins. 1994. "Industries and Occupations at High Risk for Work-Related Homicide." *Journal of Occupational and Environmental Medicine* 36(2):125–32.

Chaulet, Rudy. 1997. "La violence en Castille au XVIIe siècle à travers les indultos de viernes santo (1623–1699)." *Crime, Histoire et Société* 1(2):5–27.

Chu, Doris C., and Rollin F. Tusalem. 2013. "The Role of the State on Cross-National Homicide Rates." *International Criminal Justice Review* 23(3):252–79.

Cockburn, James S. 1991. "Patterns of Violence in English Society: Homicide in Kent, 1560–1985." *Past and Present* 130:70–106.

Collishaw, Stephan, Frances Gardner, Barbara Maughan, Jacqueline Scott, and Andrew Pickles. 2012. "Do Historical Changes in Parent-Child Relationships Explain Increases in Youth Conduct Problems?" *Journal of Abnormal Child Psychology* 40(1):119–32.

Dean, Trevor. 2001. *Crime in Medieval Europe, 1200–1550.* London: Pearson.

———. 2007. *Crime and Justice in Late Medieval Italy.* Cambridge: Cambridge University Press.

De Long, J. Bradford, and Andrei Shleifer. 1993. *Princes and Merchants: European City Growth before the Industrial Revolution.* Cambridge, MA: National Bureau of Economic Research.

de Vries, Jan. 1984. *European Urbanization, 1500–1800.* London: Methuen.

Eisner, Manuel. 2001. "Modernization, Self-Control and Lethal Violence: The Long-Term Dynamics of European Homicide Rates in Theoretical Perspective." *British Journal of Criminology* 41(4):618–48.

———. 2003. "Long-Term Historical Trends in Violent Crime." In *Crime and Justice: A Review of Research,* vol. 30, edited by Michael Tonry. Chicago: University of Chicago Press.

———. 2008. "Modernity Strikes Back? A Historical Perspective on the Latest Increase in Interpersonal Violence (1960–1990)." *International Journal of Conflict and Violence* 2(2):289–316.

———. 2011. "Killing Kings: Patterns of Regicide in Europe, AD 600–1800." *British Journal of Criminology* 51(3):556–77.

———. 2014. "Evolutionary Boundaries to the Historical Variability of Violence: Sex and Age Characteristics of Homicide Perpetrators." Unpublished manuscript. Cambridge University.

Elias, Norbert. 1978. *The Civilizing Process.* 2 vols. Oxford: Oxford University Press.

———. 1983. *Die Höfische Gesellschaft: Untersuchungen zu einer Soziologie des Königtums und der höfischen Aristokratie*. Frankfurt am Main: Suhrkamp.

Ertman, Thomas. 1997. *Birth of the Leviathan: Building States and Regimes in Medieval and Early Modern Europe*. Cambridge: Cambridge University Press.

Farrell, Graham, Andromachi Tseloni, Jen Mailley, and Nick Tilley. 2011. "The Crime Drop and the Security Hypothesis." *Journal of Research in Crime and Delinquency* 48(2):147–75.

Fletcher, Richard. 2002. *Bloodfeud: Murder and Revenge in Anglo-Saxon England*. London: Penguin.

Flora, Peter, and Jens Alber. 1983. *State, Economy, and Society in Western Europe, 1815–1975: A Data Handbook in Two Volumes*. Frankfurt am Main: Campus.

Foucault, Michel. 1975. *Surveiller et punir: La naissance de la prison*. Paris: Galimard.

Fukuyama, Francis. 1999. *The Great Disruption: Human Nature and the Reconstitution of Social Order*. New York: Free Press.

Garland, David. 2001. *The Culture of Control: Crime and Social Order in Contemporary Society*. Oxford: Oxford University Press.

Gorski, Philip S. 1993. "The Protestant Ethic Revisited: Disciplinary Revolution and State Formation in Holland and Prussia." *American Journal of Sociology* 99(2):265–316.

———. 2003. *The Disciplinary Revolution: Calvinism and the Rise of the State in Early Modern Europe*. Chicago: University of Chicago Press.

Gottfredson, Michael T., and Travis Hirschi. 1990. *A General Theory of Crime*. Stanford, CA: Stanford University Press.

Graff, Harvey J. 1977. "'Pauperism, Misery, and Vice': Illiteracy and Criminality in the Nineteenth Century." *Journal of Social History* 11(2):245–68.

Granath, Sven, Johanna Hagstedt, Janne Kivivuori, Martti Lehti, Soenita Ganpat, Marieke Liem, and Paul Nieuwperta. 2011. *Homicide in Finland, the Netherlands and Sweden: A First Study on the European Homicide Monitor Data*. Stockholm: Swedish National Council for Crime Prevention.

Greenfield, Patricia M. 2013. "The Changing Psychology of Culture from 1800 through 2000." *Psychological Science* 24(9):1722–31.

Gurr, Ted R. 1981. "Historical Trends in Violent Crime: A Critical Review of the Evidence." In *Crime and Justice: An Annual Review of Research*, vol. 3, edited by Michael Tonry and Norval Morris. Chicago: University of Chicago Press.

Hanawalt, Barbara A. 1976. "Violent Death in Fourteenth and Early Fifteenth Century England." *Comparative Studies in Society and History* 18:297–320.

———. 1979. *Crime and Conflict in English Communities, 1300–1348*. Cambridge: Cambridge University Press.

Hanlon, Gregory. 2003. "L'infanticidio di coppie sposate in Toscana nella prima età moderna." *Quaderni Storici* 38(2):453–98.

Himmelfarb, Gertrude. 1995. *The Demoralization of Society: From Victorian Virtues to Modern Values*. New York: Random House.

Hirschfield, Paul J. 2008. "Preparing for Prison? The Criminalization of School Discipline in the USA." *Theoretical Criminology* 12(1):79–101.

Houston, Rab. 1987. "The Literacy Campaign in Scotland, 1560–1803." In *National Literacy Campaigns: Historical and Comparative Perspectives*, edited by Robert F. Arnove and Harvey J. Graff. New York: Springer.

Houston, Robert A. 1988. *Literacy in Early Modern Europe: Culture and Education, 1500–1800*. London: Longman.

Hsia, Po-Chia. 1992. *Social Disciplining in the Reformation: Central Europe, 1550–1750*. London: Routledge.

Jaeger, C. Stephen. 1985. *The Origins of Courtliness: Civilizing Trends and the Formation of Courtly Ideals, 939–1210*. Philadelphia: University of Pennsylvania Press.

Karonen, Petri. 2001. "A Life for a Life versus Christian Reconciliation: Violence and the Process of Civilization in the Kingdom of Sweden, 1540–1700." In *Five Centuries of Violence in Finland and the Baltic Area*, edited by Heikki Ylikangas, Petri Karonen, and Martti Lehti. Columbus: Ohio State University Press.

Kivivuori, Janne, and Jón G. Bernburg. 2011. "Delinquency Research in the Nordic Countries." In *Crime and Justice in Scandinavia*, edited by Michael Tonry and Tapio Lappi-Seppälä. Vol. 40 of *Crime and Justice: A Review of Research*, edited by Michael Tonry. Chicago: University of Chicago Press.

Kivivuori, Janne, and Martti Lehti. 2011. "Homicide in Finland and Sweden." In *Crime and Justice in Scandinavia*, edited by Michael Tonry and Tapio Lappi-Seppälä. Vol. 40 of *Crime and Justice: A Review of Research*, edited by Michael Tonry. Chicago: University of Chicago Press.

Lane, Roger. 1979. *Violent Death in the City: Suicide, Accident and Murder in Nineteenth Century Philadelphia*. Cambridge: Cambridge University Press.

Lawrence, Clifford H. 2001. *Medieval Monasticism: Forms of Religious Life in Western Europe in the Middle Ages*. Harlow, UK: Pearson Education.

Lazcano, Marcelino B. 2005. *Crimen y castigo en Navarra bajo el reinado de los primeros evreux (1328–1349)*. Pamplona: Universidad Pública de Navarra.

Lenke, Leif. 1990. *Alcohol and Criminal Violence: Time Series Analyses in a Comparative Perspective*. Stockholm: Almqvist & Wiksell.

Lenman, Bruce, and Geoffrey Parker. 1980. "The State, the Community and the Criminal Law in Early Modern Europe." In *Crime and the Law: The Social History of Crime in Western Europe since 1500*, edited by V. A. C. Gatrell, Bruce Lenman, and Geoffrey Parker. London: Europa.

Levine, Harry G. 1993. "Temperance Cultures: Alcohol as a Problem in Nordic and English-Speaking Cultures." In *The Nature of Alcohol and Drug-Related Problems*, edited by Malcom Lader, Griffith Edwards, and D. Colin Drummon. New York: Oxford University Press.

Linklater, Andrew, and Stephen Mennell. 2010. "Norbert Elias, the Civilizing Process: Sociogenetic and Psychogenetic Investigations; an Overview and Assessment." *History and Theory* 49(3):384–411.

Martin, Austin L. 2009. *Alcohol, Violence, and Disorder in Traditional Europe*. Kirksville, MO: Truman State University Press.

McGowan, Patrick J. 2003. "African Military Coups d'Etat, 1956–2001: Frequency, Trends, and Distribution." *Journal of Modern African Studies* 41(3): 339–70.

Michel, Jean-Baptiste, et al. 2011. "Quantitative Analysis of Culture Using Millions of Digitized Books." *Science* 331(6014):176–82.

Mishra, Sandeep, and Martin Lalumiere. 2009. "Is the Crime Drop of the 1990s in Canada and the USA Associated with a General Decline in Risky and Health-Related Behavior?" *Social Science and Medicine* 68(1):39–48.

Monkkonen, Eric. 2001. *Murder in New York City*. Berkeley: University of California Press.

Morris, Terence, and Louis Jacques Blom-Cooper. 1979. *Murder in England and Wales since 1957*. London: Observer.

Muchembled, Robert. 1992. *Le temps des supplices; de l'obéissance sous les rois absolus: Xve–Xviiie siècle*. Paris: Armand Colin.

———. 2008. *Une histoire de la violence*. Paris: Editions du Seuil.

Nalle, Sara T. 1989. "Literacy and Culture in Early Modern Castile." *Past and Present* 125:65–96.

Nicholls, James. 2008. "Vinum Britannicum: The 'Drink Question' in Early Modern England." *Social History of Alcohol and Drugs* 22(2):190–208.

Nivette, Amy E. 2011. "Cross-National Predictors of Homicide: A Meta-Analysis." *Homicide Studies* 15(2):103–31.

Oestreich, Gerhard. 1982. *Neostoicism and the Early Modern State*. Cambridge: Cambridge University Press.

Ogilvie, Sheilagh. 2006. "'So That Every Subject Knows How to Behave': Social Disciplining in Early Modern Bohemia." *Comparative Studies in Society and History* 48(1):38–78.

Ouimet, Marc. 2002. "Explaining the American and Canadian Crime 'Drop' in the 1990's." *Canadian Journal of Criminology—Revue Canadienne de Criminologie* 44(1):33–50.

Petersen, Thomas. 2011. *Die Bewältigung der Diktatur in den Familien*. Eine Dokumentation des Beitrags von Dr. Thomas Petersen in der Frankfurter Allgemeinen Zeitung Nr. 63 vom 16, März 2011. http://www.ifd-allensbach .de/uploads/tx_reportsndocs/Maerz11_Wertewandel.pdf.

Pinker, Steven. 2011. *The Better Angels of Our Nature: Why Violence Has Declined*. London: Viking.

Piquero, Alex R., Wesley G. Jennings, and David P. Farrington. 2010. "On the Malleability of Self-Control: Theoretical and Policy Implications Regarding a General Theory of Crime." *Justice Quarterly* 27(6):803–34.

Powell, Ryan. 2013. "The Theoretical Concept of the 'Civilising Offensive' (Beschavingsoffensief): Notes on Its Origins and Uses." *Human Figurations* 2(2):1–15.

Prétou, Pierre. 2010. *Crime et justice en Gascogne à la fin du moyen age (1360–1526)*. Rennes: Presses Universitaires de Rennes.

Ribeaud, Denis, and Manuel Eisner. 2010. "Are Moral Disengagement, Neutralization Techniques, and Self-Serving Cognitive Distortions the Same? Developing a Unified Scale of Moral Neutralization of Aggression." *International Journal of Conflict and Violence* 4(2):298–315.

Rotberg, Robert I. 2003. "Failed States, Collapsed States, Weak States: Causes and Indicators." In *State Failure and State Weakness in a Time of Terror*, edited by Robert I. Rotberg. Washington, DC: Brookings Institution Press.

Roth, Randolph. 2011. "Biology and the Deep History of Homicide." *British Journal of Criminology* 51(3):535–55.

———. 2012. "Measuring Feelings and Beliefs That May Facilitate (or Deter) Homicide: A Research Note on the Causes of Historic Fluctuations in Homicide Rates in the United States." *Homicide Studies* 16(2):197–216.

Rousseaux, Xavier. 1999. "From Case to Crime: Homicide Regulation in Medieval and Modern Europe." In *Die Enstehung Des Öffentlichen Strafrechts; Bestandsaufnahme Eines Europäischen Forschungsproblems*, edited by Dietmar Willoweit. Köln: Böhlau Verlag.

Schofield, Roger S. 1973. "Dimensions of Illiteracy, 1750–1850." *Explorations in Economic History* 10(4):437–54.

Schwerhoff, Gerd. 2002. "Criminalized Violence and the Civilizing Process: A Reappraisal." *Crime, Histoire et Société* 6(2):103–26.

Sharpe, James A. 1985. "'Last Dying Speeches': Religion and Public Execution in Seventeenth-Century England." *Past and Present* 107:144–67.

Sharpe, Reginald R. 1913. *Calendar of Coroners Rolls of the City of London, A.D. 1300–1378*. London: Clay & Sons.

Shoemaker, Karl. 2011. *Sanctuary and Crime in the Middle Ages, 400–1500*. New York: Fordham University Press.

Shoemaker, Robert B. 2002. "The Taming of the Duel: Masculinity, Honour and Ritual Violence in London, 1660–1800." *Historical Journal* 45(3):525–45.

Smith, Adam. 1776. *An Inquiry into the Nature and Causes of the Wealth of Nations*. London: Strahan & Cadell.

Smith, Kevin, Sarah Osborne, Ivy Lau, and Andrew Britton. 2012. *Crime in England and Wales, 2010/11*. Supp. vol. 2, *Homicides, Firearm Offences and Intimate Violence, 2010/11*. Statistical Bulletin 02/12. London: Home Office.

Smith, Rebecca. 1993. "The Temperance Movement and Class Struggle in Victorian England." *Student Historical Journal Loyola University*. http://www.loyno.edu/~history/journal/1992-3/smith-r.htm.

Spierenburg, Pieter. 1984. *The Spectacle of Suffering: Executions and the Evolution or Repression; from a Preindustrial Metropolis to the European Experience*. Cambridge: Cambridge University Press.

———. 1987. "From Amsterdam to Auburn an Explanation for the Rise of the Prison in Seventeenth-Century Holland and Nineteenth-Century America." *Journal of Social History* 20(3):439–61.

———. 1991. *The Prison Experience: Disciplinary Institutions and Their Inmates in Early Modern Europe*. New Brunswick, NJ: Rutgers University Press.

———. 1994. "Faces of Violence: Homicide Trends and Cultural Meanings: Amsterdam, 1431–1816." *Journal of Social History* 27:701–16.

———. 2007a. *The Prison Experience: Disciplinary Institutions and Their Inmates in Early Modern Europe*. Amsterdam: Amsterdam University Press.

———. 2007*b*. "Protestant Attitudes to Violence: The Early Dutch Republic." *Crime, Histoire et Société* 10:5–31.

———. 2008. *A History of Murder: Personal Violence in Europe from the Middle Ages to the Present.* Cambridge: Polity.

Stearns, Carol Z., and Peter N. Stearns. 1986. *Anger: The Struggle for Emotional Control in America's History.* Chicago: University of Chicago Press.

Stearns, Peter N. 2008. "History of Emotions." In *Handbook of Emotions*, edited by Michael Lewis, Jeannette M. Haviland-Jones, and Lisa Feldman Barrett. New York: Guilford.

Terpstra, Nicholas, ed. 2008. *The Art of Executing Well: Rituals of Execution in Renaissance Italy.* Vol. 1. Kirksville, MO: Truman State University Press.

Thompson, Francis, and Michael Longstreth. 1988. *The Rise of Respectable Society: A Social History of Victorian Britain, 1830–1900.* Cambridge, MA: Harvard University Press.

Tilly, Charles. 1985. "War Making and State Making as Organized Crime." In *Bringing the State Back In*, edited by Peter Evans, Dietrich Rueschemeyer, and Theda Skocpol. Cambridge: Cambridge University Press.

———. 1992. *Coercion, Capital, and European States, AD 990–1992.* Cambridge, MA: Blackwell.

Tlusty, Beverly A. 1994. "Gender and Alcohol Use in Early Modern Augsburg." *Social History* 27(54):241–59.

Tonry, Michael H. 2004. *Punishment and Politics: Evidence and Emulation in the Making of English Crime Control Policy.* Cullompton, Devon, UK: Willan.

Trexler, Richard C. 1973. "Infanticide in Florence: New Sources and First Results." *Journal of Psychohistory* 1(1):98–116.

UNESCO. 1953. *Progress in Literacy in Various Countries: A Preliminary Statistical Study of Available Census Data since 1900.* Paris: UNESCO.

Urra, Félix S. 2007. "La pena de muerte en la Navarra medieval." *Clío y Crímen: Revista del Centro de Historia del Crimen de Durango* 4:277–305.

van Dijck, Maarten. 2007. "De Pacificering van de Europese Samenleving; Repressie, Gedragspatronen en Verstedelijking in Brabant Tijdens de Lange Zestiende Eeuw." PhD thesis, University of Antwerp.

van Dijk, Jan, Andromachi Tseloni, and Graham Farrell, eds. 2012. *The International Crime Drop: New Directions in Research.* Basingstoke, UK: Palgrave Macmillan.

van Dülmen, Richard. 1990. *Theatre of Horror: Crime and Punishment in Early Modern Germany.* Cambridge: Cambridge University Press.

———. 1995. *Theater des Schreckens: Gerichtspraxis und Strafrituale in der Frühen Neuzeit.* München: Beck'sche Verlagsbuchhandlung.

van Krieken, Robert. 1990. "Social Discipline and State Formation: Weber and Oestreich on the Historical Sociology of Subjectivity." *Amsterdams Sociologisch Tijdschrift* 17(1):3–28.

Voas, Robert B., A. Scott Tippetts, and James Fell. 2000. "The Relationship of Alcohol Safety Laws to Drinking Drivers in Fatal Crashes." *Accident Analysis and Prevention* 32(4):483–92.

Vorspan, Rachel. 2000. "Rational Recreation and the Law: The Transformation of Popular Urban Leisure in Victorian England." *McGill Law Journal* 45: 891–973.

Warner, Jessica. 1997. "Shifting Categories of the Social Harms Associated with Alcohol: Examples from Late Medieval and Early Modern England." *American Journal of Public Health* 87(11):1788–97.

Weber, Max. 1982. *The Protestant Ethic and the Spirit of Capitalism*. London: Routledge.

White, Stephen D. 1986. "Feuding and Peace-Making in the Touraine around the Year 1100." *Traditio* 42:195–263.

Wiener, Martin J. 2004. *Men of Blood: Violence, Manliness and Criminal Justice in Victorian England*. Cambridge: Cambridge University Press.

Wilson, George B. 1940. *Alcohol and the Nation*. London: Nicholson & Watson.

Wolfgang, Marvin E. 1958. *Patterns in Criminal Homicide*. Philadelphia: Wiley.

Wood, J. Carter. 2004. *Violence and Crime in Nineteenth Century England: The Shadow of Our Refinement*. London: Routledge.

Yeomans, Henry. 2011. "What Did the British Temperance Movement Accomplish? Attitudes to Alcohol, the Law and Moral Regulation." *Sociology* 45(1): 38–53.

Tapio Lappi-Seppälä and Martti Lehti

Cross-Comparative Perspectives on Global Homicide Trends

ABSTRACT

Data are available on homicide trends and patterns for 235 countries from six continents from 1950 to 2010. Recent rates range from fewer than 0.5 victim per 100,000 population to 80 and regionally from around one in Scandinavia to around 30 in Central America. Countries that share cultural, political, and social traditions usually have similar crime trends. In Western countries, lethal violence increased in the 1960s through the early 1990s, followed by declines. Elsewhere, trends may have been different as a result of local political configurations and social developments. In eastern Europe, the development of crime was affected by political turmoil after the fall of the Soviet Union and in several Latin American and Caribbean countries by unstable political conditions and the drug industry. Homicide is not decreasing in parts of the Americas and the Caribbean. Cross-sectional analyses confirm the interdependency of lethal violence with socioeconomic and political factors. The level of lethal violence is heavily dependent on the rule of law, the quality and integrity of governance, the level of democracy, and social and economic equality. No signs were detected of the effects of sanctions practices. Use of capital punishment, high rates of imprisonment, and long sentences coincide with high and increasing homicide rates—and not the other way around.

Homicides have been a primary target for comparative and historical criminological studies since the beginnings of modern criminal statistics. Adolphe Quetelet observed in the nineteenth century that almost

Electronically published November 11, 2014
Tapio Lappi-Seppälä is director and Martti Lehti is senior research analyst at the National Research Institute of Legal Policy, Helsinki.

135

all homicides were recorded by the authorities, making them a suitable object of studies of crime, and especially of trends. It was not by chance that the founders of modern criminology, including Enrico Ferri, Franz von Liszt, Cesare Lombroso, Veli Verkko, and others, had great interest in homicides. Aided by the collection and steady expansion of data sets collected by international organizations, there has been a steady growth of comparative statistical analyses since then, especially in the recent few decades.[1] Much recent research has been centered around the United States (e.g., Hsieh and Pugh 1993; LaFree 1999; Pratt and Cullen 2005; Nivette 2011; Trent and Pridemore 2012).

The major aims of cross-national homicide research have been to search for explanations for differences and for trends. Research has usually sought to explain variations in homicide patterns in terms of factors related to strain, disorganization, and social deprivation theories. These perspectives have also guided the selection of predictors used in the analyses. Thus, social disorganization theory calls attention to racial heterogeneity, family disruption, and urbanism; (institutional) anomie theory to the strength of noneconomic institutions, divorce rates, and decommodification; social support theories to welfare expenditures, investments in health care, and education; and economic and resource deprivation theories to poverty (absolute deprivation) and income inequality (relative deprivation). Modernization and development theories add predictors such as circulation and reading of newspapers, energy consumption, cell phones, access to education, literacy, school enrollment, gross domestic product (GDP), and human development. In this essay we offer examples from all these perspectives.

Historical works based on long-term historical time series, by contrast, have followed different lines. These works have stressed both structural and cultural explanations and a more qualitative approach.[2] In the Nordic context, alcohol has been a major focus since the early works of Veli Verkko in Finland (Verkko 1931, 1951).

This essay combines elements from both approaches. We provide a statistical description and analyses of differences in lethal violence us-

---

[1] The most encompassing publication based on this material to date is the UN Office on Drugs and Crime (UNODC) *Global Study on Homicide*, with 207 countries and data starting from 1995 (see UNODC 2011).

[2] See, e.g., the studies of Monkkonen (1975), Gurr (1981, 1989), Österberg and Lindstrom (1988), Österberg (1991, 1996), Sharpe (1996), Spierenburg (1996, 1998, 1999, 2008, 2012), Eisner (2003, 2008), and Lindström (2008). For a structural approach, see especially the works of Ylikangas (1976, 2001).

ing the most encompassing comparative data yet published. The sample covers 235 nations and self-governing regions. In trend analyses we use data from the 1950s onward in 187 countries. We first draw a global cross-sectional picture of the levels of lethal violence disaggregated by continents and subregions. Results reveal huge variation in national homicide rates ranging from fewer than 0.5 victim per 100,000 population to 80. An almost equivalent scale of variance exists regionally, with the level of homicides varying from around one in Scandinavia to around 30 in Central America. Trend analyses from 1950 to 2010 show that countries that share the same cultural, political, and social traditions usually share more or less similar crime trends. Western countries largely follow patterns detected in earlier studies: first a fall of lethal violence lasting until the 1950s or 1960s, then an increase starting in the 1960s, followed by a decline from the early 1990s onward (e.g., Eisner 2008). For other parts of the world, this model fits less well. The further we move from Europe, the United States, and the English-speaking developed countries, the harder it is to fit nations into this general pattern.

Having documented these differences and trends, we explore explanations for them. The factors discussed fall into four main groups. The first includes macro-level social and structural indicators that are usually associated with strain, disorganization, and deprivation theories. The second consists of state-level political indicators, including political structures and the style and quality of governance. The third consists of cultural variables, including social values and attitudes. Finally, we look for the effects of sanctioning practices. High-crime societies are characterized by gross income differences, meager welfare state, high corruption, low social trust, and less effective government. High lethal violence associates also with stronger authoritarian and conservative moral views, more collectivist cultures, and lower long-term cultural orientations. Age structure and ethnic diversity play much lesser roles compared to these social-structural, political, and cultural variables. Severe sanction practices (the use of capital punishment, high rates of imprisonment, and extensive use of life sentences) coincide with high and increasing homicide rates—and not the other way around.

This essay has six sections. Section I presents the data and sources. Section II gives an overall view of present homicide rates and trends from 1950 to 2010 for nations, subregions, and continents. Section III explores the relations between lethal violence and social, economic, political, and cultural factors. The relation between sanction practices and crime will be discussed in Section IV. Section V continues the analyses with multivariate statistical models. Conclusions and discussion of findings follow in Section VI.

I. Data and Sources

We use homicide data from a data collection project in the National Research Institute of Legal Policy in Helsinki.[3] The data set is based on public health and criminal justice system sources. Health authorities produce data certifying causes of death; by law, enforcement authorities collect data in the process of recording and investigating a crime. At present, the data set covers 235 nations and self-governing regions with the most recent updating from 2013. For trend analyses, data are available from the 1950s in 187 countries.

When national time series were being compiled, priority was given to cause-of-death data (COD), as they should in principle have been compiled according to similar classifications and standards during the period examined. COD data are generally superior to criminal justice data but have their own problems (Aebi and Linde 2012).[4] Related reliability problems have received comparatively little attention in the literature (see Smit, de Jong, and Bijleveld 2012; Trent and Pride-

---

[3] The Comparative Homicide Time Series (CHTS) data set has been compiled by Martti Lehti of the National Research Institute of Legal Policy in Finland. The data have been obtained mainly from published official national or international statistics. Five main sources have been used: (1) National statistics homepages: most European states, Australia, Canada, South Korea, Taiwan, and the United States. (2) World Health Organization (WHO) Mortality Database: South and Central American states, Brunei, Philippines, Hong Kong, Israel, Russia and countries in the former Soviet region, Japan, Mauritius, Rodrigues, Seychelles, Thailand, and New-Zealand. (3) UNODC international homicide database, mortality rates: all other countries, except the following groups 4 and 5 (for which there were no data or clear reliability problems within the WHO). (4) South Africa and Jamaica local police statistics, Fiji general crime statistics, Guam coroner's statistics, and Samoa judicial statistics. (5) The last group is countries that provided data only through online-media crime reports and news: Cook Islands, Falkland Islands, Niue, Pitcairn, Saint Helena, and Tuvalu. The UNODC figures are based on cause-of-death statistics or WHO estimates, concerning in all cases the years 2004, 2008, or both. For details, see Lehti (2013). We are grateful to Manuel Eisner for sharing data and source information, which has greatly enriched the data set.

[4] Information on infant homicides is especially unreliable in both COD and criminal justice statistics (Yarwood 2004; Tursz and Cook 2011; Höynck, Zähringer, and Behnsen 2012).

more 2012). National studies indicate that there can be substantial differences in the reliability of COD statistics even in Europe (where both COD and criminal justice statistics are generally of high quality). Differences in detection rates affect both COD and criminal justice statistics in a similar way. In Europe, for example, forensic medical examination practices differ considerably between countries. In Scandinavia, almost all violent deaths lead to a forensic medical examination, while in continental and eastern Europe, examination rates are much lower. Because of this, it has been suggested that there may be considerable numbers of undetected noninfant homicides in continental Europe (Smit et al. 2012, p. 19). In Germany and the Netherlands, for example, it has been suggested that the estimated annual numbers of undetected homicides are more or less the same as the numbers of detected homicides. The detection rate can vary also because of structural differences in types of homicide. It is probable, for example, that a country in which most homicides are related to drinking brawls and are not usually premeditated will have a much higher detection rate than a country in which a large percentage of homicides are related to organized-crime activities.

In appendix A we provide information about the percentage-level differences between COD and crime statistics for countries in which this information could be obtained for the years 1960–70 and 2000–2010. In general, the smaller the difference between the figures from these two independent sources, the more reliable the information should be in both. The COD rates are typically lower. The difference in most cases is less than 20 percent. However, there are notable exceptions, even in Europe. In France and England and Wales, criminal justice statistics report twice as many homicides as the health authorities. In some regions, COD rates are higher, as in the Baltic countries and Africa. Again the difference is usually less than 20 percent, but there are notable exceptions. A difference of 10–20 percent is tolerable, but larger deviations cause problems (such as in Jamaica, where health authorities report fewer than one victim per 100,000 population but police report more than 50). We have treated COD statistics as the primary source. However, when these figures are implausible because of inconsistencies in trends (huge jumps up and down) or stark differences between comparable countries in the region, or for some other reason (such as ruined or demolished health care systems), we use criminal justice data, predominantly police data and in some cases conviction data. Sources used are listed in appendix B.

Trend comparisons (as opposed to level comparisons) are somewhat less of a problem. For this purpose, COD statistics and criminal justice statistics, if recording and reporting practices and definitions of crimes in individual countries have not changed substantially during the study period, both provide reasonably reliable bases to study trends (Aebi and Linde 2012; von Hofer and Lappi-Seppälä 2014). There is no indication of critical changes in the classifications in the COD statistics.[5] Operational changes in public health care or criminal justice systems in individual countries may also influence the comparability of COD data over time.[6]

We have made general checks of data source changes within the time period examined to ensure their comparability and reliability by comparing the average crime levels shown by the different time series for overlapping periods or periods otherwise near in time (separated by no more than a decade). If the COD data and police or court data overlap with less than a 10 percent level difference, the series have been combined without further adjustments. If the level difference was much larger than 10 percent, the secondary series has been correspondingly adjusted to the level of the primary series.[7]

---

[5] During the period we examined, all the included countries used International Statistical Classification of Diseases and Related Health Problems (ICD; published by the WHO) or its national adaptations in their COD statistics. The ICD classification changed three times during the review period: from ICD-7 to ICD-8 in 1968–70, from ICD-8 to ICD-9 in 1979–95, and from ICD-9 to ICD-10 in the years following 1994. The changes took place in different years in different countries. Changes in the definition of a death caused by an intentional assault in all four classifications were, however, negligible. Earlier analyses suggest that the first classification change from ICD-7 to ICD-8 influenced infanticide levels but not other child or adult homicide levels in some industrialized countries (Jason, Carpenter, and Tyler 1983). The later classification changes seem not to have had any effect even on infanticide levels (Kääriäinen et al. 2014).

[6] These kinds of changes when known have been reported in the detailed data source descriptions (see Lehti 2013).

[7] Sources for each individual country are explained in Lehti (2013). Smit et al. (2012) provide a good general overview of current homicide data sources and their differences in Europe, as does Spierenburg (2012) on historical sources; Smit and Zahn (1999) provide a comprehensive overview of international data sources and methodological questions.

TABLE 1

Homicide Levels, 2008–12, by Continent and Region, Weighted and Unweighted Means

	Mean	
Region	Unweighted	Weighted
Europe	1.9	4.1
Scandinavia	.9	1.1
Western Europe	.8	.8
Southern Europe	1.3	2.0
Eastern Europe	2.9	1.7
Europe/Asia (including former Soviet region)	6.0	10.2
Americas	19.1	17.3
North America	5.6	5.3
Central America	34.6	27.3
South America	17.2	24.0
Caribbean	17.8	17.1
Africa	15.4	13.6
North Africa	6.5	6.7
Western Africa	15.0	10.6
Central Africa	19.2	19.7
Eastern Africa	13.5	14.8
Southern Africa	15.5	33.2
Asia	3.8	2.9
Western Asia	1.8	2.4
Southern Asia	3.1	4.3
Southeast Asia	6.7	3.6
East Asia	2.1	1.2
Oceania	2.7	6.6
Total	9.3	6.6

II. Trends and Differences

This section gives an overview of levels and trends in homicide disaggregated by continents, regions, and individual countries. The first subsection gives a condensed overview of present levels. The next two subsections deal with trends and changes.

A. Homicide Rates in 2008–12

The global unweighted mean of homicides per 100,000 population in 235 countries and self-governing regions in 2010 (2008–12) was 9.3. The median was 4.3. The weighted mean (adjusting for population size) was 6.6. High homicide rates in numerous small countries lifted the overall mean. Weighted and unweighted means by regions and continents are displayed in table 1. Homicide rates are highest in the Americas (unweighted mean 19.1), followed by Africa (15.4). The lowest rates are in Europe (mean 1.9). Subregional differences vary from 0.9 (Scandinavia) to 34.6 (Central America).

Homicide rates by continents, regions, and countries in 2008–12 are shown in detail in appendix A. The table contains only countries with at least 50,000 inhabitants. Means are counted for all observations available from 2008 to 2012. Countries are listed from the lowest to the highest rates by subregions.

Countries in Europe have been divided in appendix A into three blocks (western, southern, and eastern Europe), with further subregions based on geographic, historical, linguistic, and cultural traditions. Western Europe has been divided into the Nordic countries (Scandinavia), the British Isles (Ireland, England and Wales, and Scotland), German-speaking continental Europe, France and the Benelux countries, southwestern Europe, and southeastern Europe. Rates for western Europe range from 0.3 in Iceland to 1.9 in Finland. Southwestern countries rate equally low from 0.6 (Slovenia) to 1.2 (Andorra), but southeastern countries range from 1.2 (Cyprus) to 2.9 (Turkey).

Eastern Europe is divided into three regions: the Baltic countries, the former socialist countries, and the former Soviet Union region (also including associated central Asian states). The Baltic countries rate highest in the European context. Rates in the former socialist countries are on the same level as those in southeastern Europe (0.8–2.3). The highest rates are in the former Soviet region, with Russia highest (14.9). However, there is considerable variation within this region, from lows of 0.5 in Georgia and 1.5 in Armenia.

The American continent is divided into North, Central, and South America plus the Caribbean islands. In North America, Canadian rates are the lowest (1.7). The US rate is fairly low for the region (5.4). Rates in Central America range from 10 to almost 80 and in South America from six to 50. Most Caribbean islands report rates of over 10, with Jamaica highest (50).

Asia covers a large area from the southeastern corner of Europe to Japan in the east and Indonesia in the south. Rates are fairly low in most parts of Asia, with the exception of some parts of southeast Asia and North Korea (the reliability of the latter is questionable). Developed Asian countries, including Japan, Hong Kong, Taiwan, Korea, Singapore, and Malaysia, have rates below 1.0.

Data for the African countries are limited. For most countries, figures are available for only one year (2008). All African countries report huge differences and generally very high rates, with a partial exception of northern (Islamic) Africa. The highest rates are in the 40–50 range

TABLE 2

Changes in Homicide Levels in 1960–2010 in Three Sets of Countries

	Mean		
	50 Nations 1960–	85 Nations 1990–	122 Nations 2000–
1960–62	4.2		
1970–72	4.4		
1990–92	7.0	6.8	
2000–2002	6.3	7.5	9.0
2008–11	7.2	7.1	8.7

(Zambia, Ivory Coast, and Swaziland). A majority of African countries have rates between 15 and 30.[8]

Oceania consists of Australia and New Zealand, along with a large number of small islands (many of which are not included in the table because of the 50,000-population limit). Homicide rates in Australia and New Zealand and in many islands are modest (1.3–1.6), with the exception of Papua New Guinea.

B. Overview of Changes, 1960–2010

Changes can be expressed either as percentage changes (e.g., 10 percent increase/decrease) or as changes in rates relative to population (e.g., increase from 2.5 per 100,000 population to 3.5). The first comparison in table 2 shows rate changes from 1960 to around 2010. Since the composition of countries affects the results, rates have been counted for the same countries and for three periods: 1960–90, 1970/72–1990/92, and 1990/92–2008/11. All means in this section are unweighted (each country is given the same weight in the calculations).

Global homicide rates increased, on average, by 60–70 percent from 1970 to 1990 and declined from 1990 to 2010 by 4 percent, using unweighted means. Data are available from 50 nations. In these countries, mean homicide rates remained fairly stable from 1960 to 1970 (a 5 percent increase from 4.2 to 4.4 per 100,000). From 1970 to 1990, rates increased by 59 percent, from 4.4 to 7.0. There was a slight decrease from 1990 to 2000 and a return to the 1990 level in 2010. In

[8] Most African COD rates are based on WHO estimates, not on national statistics. These estimates are usually much higher than the rates shown in national police statistics (the only form of national homicide data available in most African countries).

TABLE 3

Percentage Changes in Homicide Rates, 1960–2010,* by Continents

Continent	Change 1960/62–1990/92 Decrease N (%) Increase N			Change 1970/72–1990/92 Decrease N (%) Increase N			Change 1990/92–2008/11 Decrease N (%) Increase N		
Europe	2	+136%	23	2	+71%	24	37	−37%	4
Americas	6	+68%	12	7	+54%	15	10	+79%	19
Asia	3	+72%	4	4	+18%	4	10	−26%	2
Oceania	0	+87%	2	0	+67%	2	3	−37%	0

* Ending dates vary slightly between countries.

85 countries for which data are available since 1990–92, the average homicide rate rose 10.3 percent from 1990 to 2000 from 6.8 to 7.5 per 100,000 and fell thereafter by 4 percent. In the 122 nations for which data are available from 2000–2002, the mean average homicide rate fell from 9.0 to 8.7 (−3.6 percent) by around 2010.

Rate and trend differences between the samples result from differences in the composition of the three groups of countries. Longer data series are available mainly from developed countries. Thus, the shorter the time span and the larger the sample, the higher the proportion of low-income and developing countries (and, as will be seen, development and homicide are strongly associated).

Regional Patterns.   Table 3 displays percentage changes in homicide rates by continents and numbers of countries in each with rising or falling rates. In Europe, homicide rates increased 136 percent from 1960 to 1990 and by 71 percent from 1970 to 1990. In both periods, homicide rates increased in all but two countries. Between 1990 and 2010 there was an average drop of 37 percent (37 countries in decline, four increasing). The pattern is similar for Oceania. In Asia, increases were smoother, and the numbers of countries with increasing and decreasing rates remained about the same from 1960 to 1990, while from 1990 to 2010 rates were decreasing in 10 out of 12 countries. In the Americas, homicide rates increased also from 1990 to 2010 in two out of three countries.

Regional analyses would show that in 1970–90, homicide rates increased in 12 out of 14 subregions, on average, by 30–100 percent. Since the 1990s, they have declined in 11 subregions but increased in parts of the Americas, Asia, and Africa.

Figure 1 illustrates differences between European and American

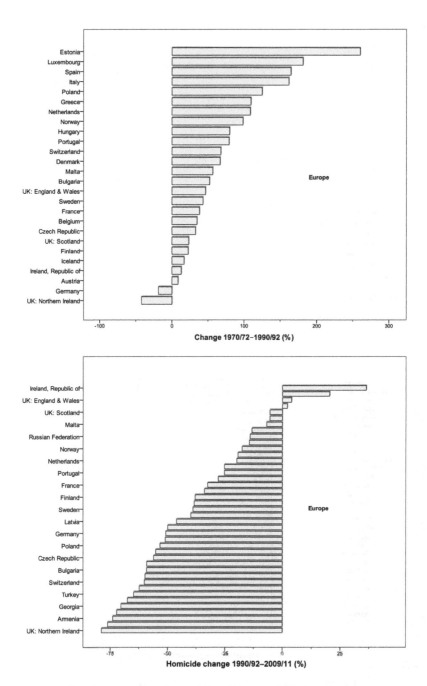

FIG. 1*A*.—Percentage changes in homicide rates, 1960–2010, Europe

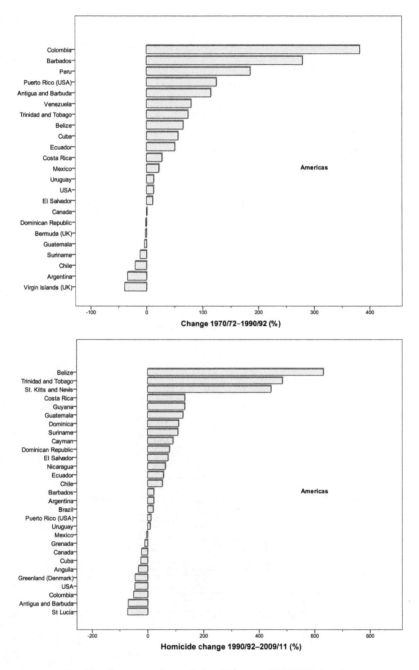

FIG. 1*B*.—Percentage changes in homicide rates, 1960–2010, Americas

regions. In Europe, almost all countries experienced increasing rates from 1970 to 1990; the only exceptions were Northern Ireland and West Germany (before reunification). From the mid-1990s to 2010, rates decreased in 37 European countries and increased only in four.

In the Americas, a clear majority of countries experienced rising rates from 1970 to 1990. In contrast to Europe, the same overall trend continued from 1990 to 2010. However, trends in the United States and Canada parallel those in Europe. The much more numerous Latin American countries determine the general trend for the Americas.

C. Trends by Regions and Countries, 1950–2010

In this subsection, we examine homicide trends from selected countries in six continents in 1950–2010. With few exceptions, in order to minimize disruptions from single-year deviations, data are presented as 3-year moving averages. The patterns vary substantially.

1. *Europe.*   Variations in trends exist within Europe. In western Europe, most countries experienced rises during the 1970s and 1980s and subsequent falls. The timing of the falls varies between the early 1990s and the early 2000s. Eastern European patterns vary between countries but share a common characteristic of sharp rises in the early 1990s after the fall of the communist regimes.

a. Western Europe.   Six western European blocks display three patterns, with some variations. Figure 2 shows the data. Scandinavia, the German-speaking countries, France, and the Benelux countries have similar profiles. All experienced declining rates from 1950 through the mid-1960s followed by an almost doubling through 1990. Since then, rates have fallen to the levels of the early 1960s. The most conspicuous deviation from this pattern is the sharp peak in France in 1957–62 associated with the Algerian war.[9] There are slight differences concerning timing. In Austria, France, Germany, Norway, and Sweden, the peak was in the mid- or late 1980s; in Denmark and Finland, in the early 1990s; and in Belgium, Switzerland, and the Netherlands, in the late 1990s.

In southwestern Europe, Italy fits the general western European

---

[9] Since the data are based on COD statistics, the figures should include only civilian victims. Northern Algeria was an integral part of France until 1962 and its French inhabitants (unlike the Arab population) were French citizens. The statistics accordingly include fatalities among the Algerian French. The French peak in the late 1950s and early 1960s was probably composed mainly of people killed in Algeria.

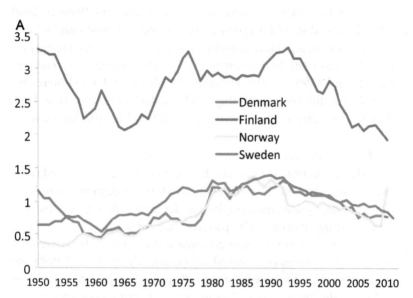

A

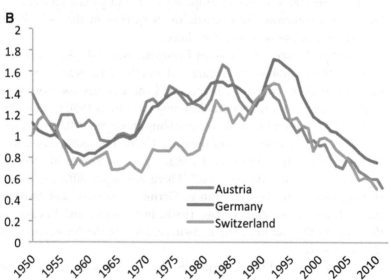

B

FIG. 2A.—Western Europe: six blocks. Source: CHTS database, Lehti (2013)

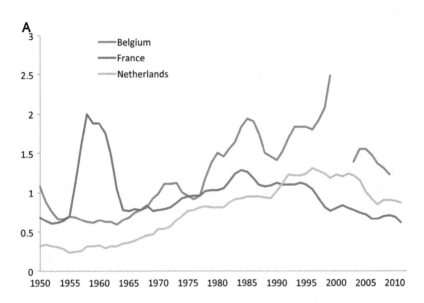

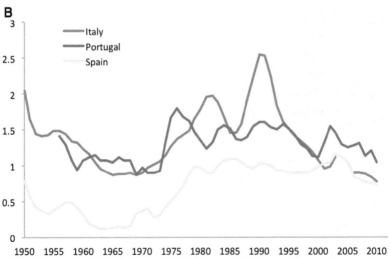

FIG. 2B.—Western Europe: six blocks. Source: CHTS database, Lehti (2013)

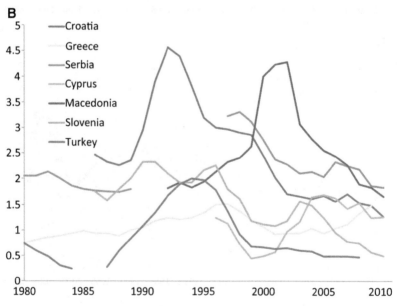

Fig. 2C.—Western Europe: six blocks. Source: CHTS database, Lehti (2013)

profile, but with much sharper changes. The postwar peak lasted from 1976 until 1992 and included victims of left- and right-wing political violence. In Spain and Portugal, the lowest levels were reached in the 1960s and early 1970s. Both experienced a substantial increase in homicide rates from the mid-1970s to the mid-1980s, after the fall of authoritarian regimes. Since the 1980s, rates have been stable or slightly declining.

In southeastern Europe, most countries experienced ongoing political crises in the 1980s and 1990s, which are reflected in their homicide rates. During the past decade, all had declining homicide levels, but the timing differed (for Croatia since 1990, Slovenia since 1995, and Macedonia since 2000).

The pattern in the British Isles, especially its timing, is distinctive, compared with the rest of western and northern Europe. In England and Wales and Scotland, rates increased steadily from the 1960s until the early 2000s but have since dropped markedly. In Ireland, the increase was stable from the 1980s onward.[10]

b. Eastern Europe. We divided eastern Europe into three regions: the former socialist countries in central Europe, the Baltic countries, and countries that were socialist republics in the Soviet Union. The first two groups are shown in figure 3. In the formerly socialist countries of central Europe, homicide rates have followed a similar pattern since the early 1950s. At their lowest in the 1960s, rates began to rise in the 1970s, peaking in the late 1980s and early 1990s when regime changes (and the collapse of the Soviet Union) were associated with steep but short increases. Since then, rates dropped rapidly and are today lower than in the 1960s or at the same level.

The Baltic countries have had much higher homicide levels than in central Europe and more abrupt rate changes. Both features, presumably, reflect the repressive influence of the Soviet period. The very high homicide rates in Estonia in the early 1950s reflect the last phases of armed resistance against Soviet occupation (the situation was probably

---

[10] The extraordinarily high 2003 figure for England and Wales is related to killings by Harold Shipman, a doctor to whom 172 homicides were attributed. In Ireland, the high figure in 1981 is related to the Stardust nightclub fire in Dublin with 48 fatalities. Even more drastic changes took place in Northern Ireland, where the homicide trend was relatively stable until the 1970s, but there were annually 100–300 extra homicide deaths related to the conflict during the civil unrest of 1971–81. During 1972–76, the annual average homicide rate rose to 17 per 100,000 population (in the 1960s, the average rate was 0.43).

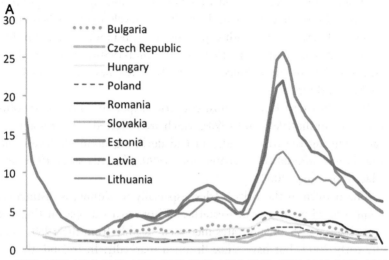

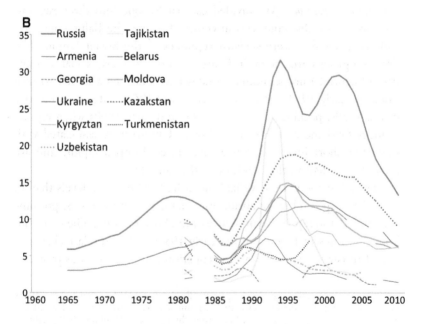

FIG. 3.—Eastern Europe. Special sources: Russia 1965–94: Meslé et al. (1996); Ukraine 1965–84: Meslé and Vallin (2012); Latvia 1966–79: Central Statistical Bureau of Latvia by personal correspondence with Sandra Vitola, March 13, 2014.

similar in the other Baltic countries). Unstable conditions of the period immediately after World War II also led to an increase in nonpolitical criminal homicides. Armed resistance in the Baltics ended around 1950 after many people had been deported to Siberia. Peaks in the early 1990s in all three countries were related to the collapse of the Soviet Union and consequent regime changes.[11] Since the mid-1990s, rates have dropped but remain well above the levels of the first half of the 1960s.

The former Soviet region includes Russia and former socialist republics of the Soviet Union (Belarus, Ukraine, Armenia, Azerbaijan, Kazakhstan, Kyrgyzstan, Tajikistan, Turkmenistan, and Uzbekistan). Regime changes in all these countries in the early 1990s led to drastic increases in homicide rates. In Russia (and probably in the other countries also), this was related partly to an increase in organized-crime activity but more broadly to increases in all types of homicide. The bulk of homicides continued to be alcohol-related as they had been during the Soviet era (Lysova, Shchitov, and Pridemore 2012). Rates have been decreasing since the late 1990s and early 2000s but, especially in Russia, Ukraine, and Belarus, are still higher than before the homicide wave of the 1990s began.[12]

2. *The Americas and the Caribbean.*   Figure 4 provides data about countries in North, Central, and South America since 1950. In contrast to Europe, there is no single general pattern. Figure 4 divides the countries into four areas.

North American figures for the United States and Canada are shown on different scales in order to underline the strong similarities in these two countries: crime trends have been practically identical, even though the base levels are different. In the United States, the postwar increase started in the mid-1960s, between 1975 and 1995 rates fluctuated, and they decreased steadily afterward. The pattern in Canada was similar except that rates peaked in the late 1970s.[13]

---

[11] Many homicides during this period were related to organized crime, but the bulk involved alcohol-related violence, the main type of lethal violence in the region during the Soviet period and in the decades before World War II (see Lehti 1997, 2002; Salla, Ceccato, and Ahven 2012).

[12] Two extraordinary peaks (even for this group) in Azerbaijan (not included in the figure) and Tajikistan are explainable by wars after the fall of the Soviet Union (the Armenian-Azerbaijan war over Nagorno-Karabakh and civil war in Tajikistan).

[13] There are substantial variations in timing among US states, although the basic profile is the same in almost all.

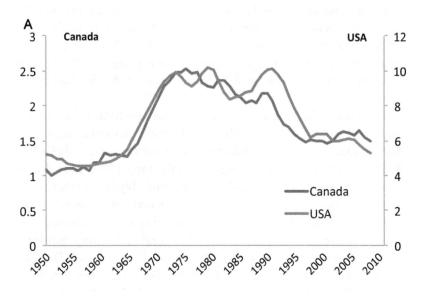

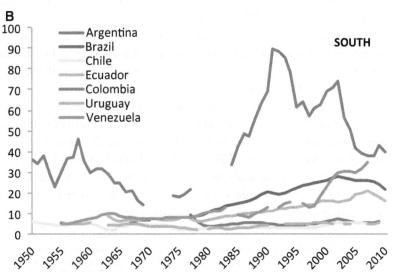

Fig. 4.4.—Americas and the Caribbean, 1950–2010. Source: CHTS database, Lehti (2013)

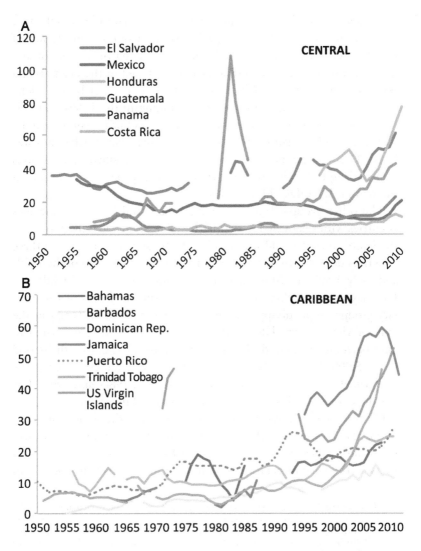

FIG. 4B.—Americas and the Caribbean, 1950–2010. Source: CHTS database, Lehti (2013)

South American countries can be divided roughly into two groups. Countries with high and rising homicide rates include Colombia, Venezuela, Brazil, and Ecuador (although in Colombia, Brazil, and Ecuador, rates have decreased substantially in the last decade). Colombian homicide rates were the highest in South America during the whole postwar period, with two peaks: from the late 1940s until the early

1960s and a second very violent period from the late 1980s to the first years of the 2000s. The latter peak resulted from a combination of violence related to cocaine trafficking and related operations of and conflicts among organized-crime groups occupied in the business and political violence that had its roots in the long conflict between left-wing guerrillas and the government beginning in the 1960s.[14] Homicide rates decreased sharply in the last 15 years but remain two and a half times higher than in the early 1970s, when they reached postwar lows. The decline has been attributed to intensified state actions against drug trafficking (Colombia is the main producer of cocaine in the region; UNODC 2011, p. 54).

The other group—Argentina, Chile, Peru, and Uruguay—includes countries with relatively low and fairly stable homicide rates. However, the figures must be read with caution. COD statistics in some of these countries do not include most victims of political violence of the 1970s and early 1980s. In Argentina (but to some extent also in Chile and Uruguay), most of those killed by the government forces or paramilitary groups simply disappeared and were never found. In Uruguay, the bulk of victims were killed abroad. The total numbers estimated to have been killed in political violence (on both sides) during the period were 15,000–45,000 in Argentina, 3,000 in Chile, and 200 in Uruguay. In Peru, about 70,000 persons were killed in the 1980s and 1990s during the conflict against the communist group Shining Path.[15]

Central American rates were high throughout the period, and it is impossible to find any clear general trend. For example, in Mexico, homicide rates decreased in two stages from the 1950s until the first years of the current century, reaching the lowest levels in 2001–7. In

---

[14] It is hard to distinguish between the two types of violence because many politically motivated guerrilla groups degenerated into criminal gangs active in cocaine trafficking. A brief armistice between the main paramilitary groups and the government in the early 1990s led to a short but marked decrease in homicide. The estimated number of victims of political violence in the 1940s and 1950s is 200,000–300,000 and over 50,000 during the 1990s (LeGrand 2003; Lopez 2011).

[15] For Argentina, see http://www.desaparecidos.org/nuncamas/web/english/library/nevagain/nevagain_001.htm; "Argentina's Dirty War: The Museum of Horrors," *Daily Telegraph*, May 17, 2008 (http://www.telegraph.co.uk/culture/3673470/Argentinas-dirty-war-the-museum-of-horrors.html); "Argentina's Forgotten Terror Victims," *Wall Street Journal*, January 3, 2011 (http://online.wsj.com/news/articles/SB10001424052970203513204576047680350412562). For Chile: "Chile Recognises 9,800 More Victims of Pinochet's Rule," *BBC News*, August 8, 2011 (http://www.bbc.co.uk/news/world-latin-america-14584095). For Uruguay: "New Find in Uruguay 'Missing' Dig," *BBC News*, December 3, 2005 (http://news.bbc.co.uk/2/hi/4494286.stm). For Peru: Comisión de la Verdad y Reconciliación (2003, p. 17).

recent years, rates increased rapidly. In Costa Rica and Panama, the base levels throughout the postwar period were the lowest in the region. In Costa Rica, homicide rates increased continuously from the 1950s until 2009 but have dropped in the last few years. In Panama, the trend has fluctuated, but rates generally increased during the whole period. Among the countries with the highest base levels are El Salvador, Guatemala, and Honduras. In El Salvador, homicide rates decreased moderately from the mid-1950s to the mid-1970s; in Guatemala they increased. In both countries, internal conflicts during the 1980s caused marked increases and extremely high rates of 50–100 victims per 100,000 population.

The Caribbean states generally had rising rates throughout the entire period, and especially since the 1990s. In Puerto Rico, rates began to increase in the beginning of the 1970s and peaked in the 1990s. After a steep but short decrease in the late 1990s, rates resumed their ascent. In Trinidad and Tobago, the number of annual homicides leaped from 5–10 per 100,000 to 40–50 in the last decade, and similar increases occurred in many of the smaller Caribbean states. These changes exemplify the role of the illicit drug industry in lethal violence. Much of lethal violence in this region is affected by drug trafficking and changing drug markets. The Caribbean region has been losing its position as the central drug route to Central America, which has intensified competition between the drug-trafficking organizations fighting for their share of the diminished market (UNODC 2011, pp. 52–53). However, the relation between violence and drug industry is not linear. High-volume drug trafficking and undisturbed markets may well coincide with lower levels of violence, but the situation may change when the balance of powers changes or competition in the business increases. The sharp increase in homicide numbers in the last few years in Mexico also seems to be related to the intensified state actions against organized drug smugglers, which have led to territorial disputes regarding the control of the most lucrative drug routes (UNODC 2011, pp. 51–52).

3. *Asia.* On the basis of their political development during the last half century, Asian countries can be divided roughly into two groups: stable and the crisis-ridden (see fig. 5). Our examples of stable countries come from east (Japan and Hong Kong) and southeast Asia (Singapore). Examples from crisis-ridden countries come from southeast (Thailand), south central (Sri Lanka), and west Asia (Israel).

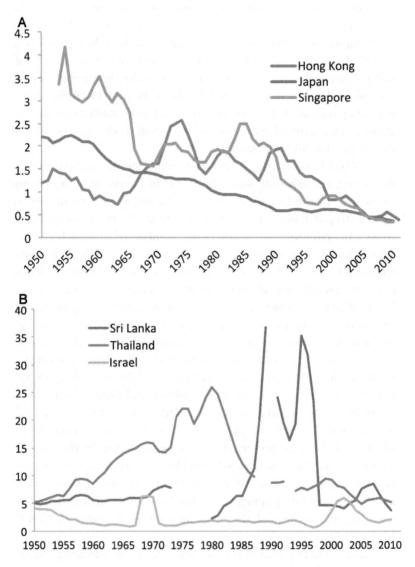

FIG. 5.—Asia: stable societies (*top*) and countries with crises (*bottom*). Source: CHTS database, Lehti (2013).

Japanese homicide rates have been declining since the early 1960s; likewise in Singapore, where rates have decreased continuously since the late 1950s. Hong Kong experienced a sharp increase in homicides beginning in the second half of the 1960s; they peaked, however, in the early 1970s. After that, rates fluctuated in a narrow range until the beginning of the 1990s, when they began to decrease.

In Thailand, rates increased from the 1950s until the 1970s. Peaks in the 1970s and 1980s coincided with the unstable period following the end of the Vietnam War. There was an internal war against communist groups, and at the same time, Khmer guerrilla groups based in Thailand fought Vietnamese troops in Cambodia. The 1970s were also a period of student unrest in Thailand that included "student massacres" by the military in 1973 and 1976. After the late 1990s, rates decreased considerably to the levels of the early 1950s. High peaks in Sri Lanka in 1987–96 and 2006–8 are associated with the civil war between Tamil rebels and the Singhalese government. The war lasted from summer 1983 to spring 2009 but had many phases including a 4-year cease-fire in 2002–5.[16] In Israel, contemporary homicide rates are twice as high as in the mid-1960s. There were two periods of extraordinarily high rates during the last 50 years: a steep peak in 1969 and a longer increase in 2001–5, peaking in 2002. The first peak was related to the War of Attrition in 1969–70 launched by the Egyptian army and the second to the Palestinian Second Intifada beginning in 2000. Both periods included intensive attacks against civilians in Israel.

4. *Oceania and Africa.* Figure 6 illustrates patterns for Oceania and Africa. Postwar patterns in Australia and New Zealand were largely similar. In both countries, rates increased from the 1950s until the late 1980s and early 1990s. After that, rates decreased. Especially during the last decade, the drop has been much steeper in Australia than in New Zealand.

It is not possible on the basis of scattered African data to characterize a general African trend even for the last few decades. Homicide rates and trends seem to have varied widely between countries and subregions. The most visible change is a dramatic fall in homicide rates in

---

[16] Data for 1977–2004 are COD data, and it is not known whether their reliability varied over that period. The year 1987 marked a change in Liberation Tigers of Tamil Eelam (LTTE) tactics when it started a campaign of suicide attacks on civilian targets; however, there is no obvious reason for the huge drop in rates in 1997. Although the nature of the war changed toward a battle between regular forces with clear frontlines in the late 1990s, the LTTE continued its campaign against civilian targets.

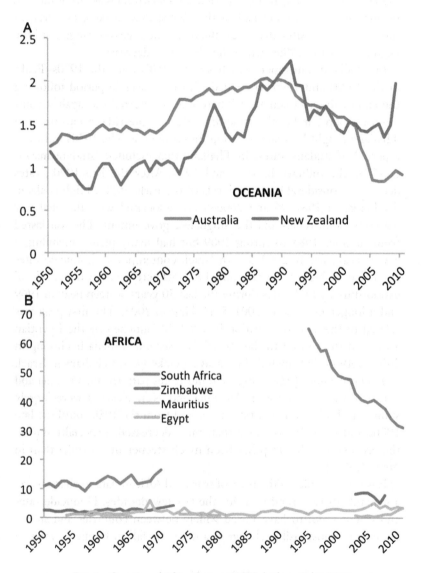

FIG. 6.—Oceania and Africa. Source: CHTS database, Lehti (2013)

South Africa since the mid-1990s from 65 per 100,000 population to 31.[17]

Fairly reliable data are available from three other countries for longer periods. In Mauritius, homicide rates were broadly stable between the late 1950s and the mid-1960s. They then increased considerably until the early 1970s, then decreased, and started to increase again in the mid-1980s. In Zimbabwe, rates increased from the late 1950s until the 1970s. Data from the mid-1970s to the early 2000s are not available. Current rates are nearly twice as high as in the 1970s, but it is not known how well preindependence data covered all population groups. In Egypt, homicide rates were fairly stable from the 1950s until the 1970s. Only scattered data have been available since the 1980s, but even they show rather stable crime levels. During the political uprising in 2010–11, annual homicide rates in Egypt increased from about one per 100,000 to over three. Hence, the effects of the "Arab spring" in Egypt have been similar to the higher violent crime rates associated with regime changes in eastern Europe in the 1990s.

D. Summary

Manuel Eisner (2008, p. 298) distinguishes three main phases in the evolution of serious violence in recent centuries in industrialized Western countries: decline and convergence from the mid-1800s to the 1950s, a common upward trend from the 1960s to the 1990s, and a decline since the early 1990s. The period discussed in this essay covers the last two stages of Eisner's model.

Western and northern Europe follow those two stages. In the south, Spain and Portugal largely missed the third, declining stage. In the southeast, data have been available only since the 1980s, but they indicate a different profile with sharp and quickly returning peaks in the 1990s and 2000s. The British Isles have distinct patterns with either increasing (England and Scotland) or stable (Ireland) homicide rates until the early 2000s, followed by a decline.

Eastern Europe and the former Soviet region largely share a common pattern. Rates in the former socialist central European countries were relatively stable until the 1990s. The Baltic countries' rates in-

---

[17] However, the level in 2011 was still twice that in 1970. The pre-1970 data are conviction data and thus should be lower crime rates than in post-1990 police data. However, it is not known how fully the conviction data of the apartheid period cover all population groups.

creased from the 1960s to the 1980s, followed by a short period of decline during the Gorbachev years. All countries in that region experienced sharp increases in the early 1990s after the fall of the Soviet Union. This was especially the case in the countries that were part of the former Soviet Union (including the Baltic countries). In the course of the 2000s this peak has largely passed, and countries have returned (or are returning) to their pre-1990s levels. The shapes of the eastern European homicide curves resemble the western European ones, but the timing and backgrounds differ.

The United States and Canada in North America are paradigmatic representatives of phases 2 and 3. However, all other American regions seem to follow different patterns, at least in timing. Most countries in Central and South America and the Caribbean experienced constantly increasing homicide rates beginning in the 1960s or 1970s, escalating in the 2000s. High peaks and individual profile differences in the region are related to civil unrest, political instability, or transformations in the drug market (or all of these factors).

In Asia, none of the countries for which longer time series are available followed Eisner's three stages. In some Asian countries, homicide rates have been declining, but this trend started in the 1950s (Japan and Singapore) or 1970s (Hong Kong). Other countries in the region experienced steep peaks in the 1960s, 1970s, or 1990s caused by political conflicts.

In Oceania, both Australia and New Zealand neatly followed stages 2 and 3. In Africa, the only country with long-term comparable statistical data (Mauritius) experienced a constant increase from the 1980s onward. The marked decline in South African homicide fits stage 3 (but questions exist about the reliability of the data, especially during the earlier decades).

Whether the trends observed by Eisner in western Europe and the non-European English-speaking industrialized countries are global ones is partly a matter of judgment, partly a matter of definition. Homicide rates went up and are now going down in most parts of the world, but this has taken place at different times, with different backgrounds, and probably for different reasons.

Those few Asian and African countries with published long-term data have distinctive patterns. In the industrialized east Asian countries, the second stage is largely missing: homicide rates have declined steadily since World War II. In other parts of Asia and in Africa, rates have been stable or increased, with trends interrupted often by short-term shocks associated with political factors. Similar crisis-related peaks are evident in postwar patterns of eastern Europe and the former Soviet region. The breakdown of the communist regimes was followed by clear increases in homicide rates, probably due to the loosening of formal controls and subsequent social turbulence and structural change.[18]

Political and civil unrest seems to have had a strong influence on homicide rate trends in almost all countries in Latin America. Organized crime has comparably affected trends in many places outside the western European and English-speaking countries, especially in Latin America. In recent decades, changes in the drug markets also appear to have radically influenced homicide rates in the Americas and the Caribbean.

Civil unrest, severe political or socioeconomic crises, and transformations in organized crime often overwhelm the effects of theoretically grounded, explanatory variables typically included in cross-national statistical analyses of crime. The effects of these crises can be relatively long-lasting, influencing base-level homicide rates for decades, even after the crisis is long past and largely forgotten.

III. Exploring the Correlates

In this section we explore possible explanations for national homicide trends and differences over time and between countries. Most of the analyses are cross-sectional and exploratory; we examine a wide range of promising explanatory variables rather than test specific criminological hypotheses or theories. The factors investigated fall into four main groups. The first are macro-level social and structural indicators discussed traditionally in the contexts of strain-disorganization and deprivation theories. The second consists of state-level political indicators, including political structures and the style and quality of governance. The third consists of cultural variables, including social values and at-

---

[18] In South America, the very low homicide rates during the military regimes in the 1970s seem to have been caused by manipulation of statistics, a factor that cannot be ruled out completely in eastern or southern Europe. In the communist bloc, criminal justice data were manipulated heavily during the communist period, but COD data only moderately; we have found no information for this essay concerning the situation in the authoritarian states of southern Europe (Lehti 1997, 2002).

titudes.[19] The fourth—formal controls and sanctioning practices—is discussed separately in Section V.

The sample used in the following analyses includes the 222 nations from the CHTS data set that also provide data on imprisonment rates. The sample was divided into three subsamples according to classifications in the 2012 UN Human Development Index (HDI) in order to examine patterns across different levels of development (for a similar solution, see Ouimet [2012]). Some of the analyses use data from the 50 US states.

A. Social and Economic Indicators

In this subsection we examine correlations between homicide rates and a wide range of factors. These include demographic composition, various measures of inequality, social policy characteristics, and cultural factors including marital stability, firearms, and alcohol consumption. Analyses of some of these indicators use US state data.

Table 4 displays bivariate correlations for all social and economic indicators (seven groups altogether) discussed in this section. The figures are presented separately for all 222 countries and for the three HDI groups. Each group of indicators will be commented on separately.

1. *Demographics, Poverty, and Development.* Age structure and the ratio of males to females matter, as most homicides in most countries involve young males. Demographic composition, ethnic diversity, and urbanization are important from the perspectives of both social disorganization and control theories: the more urban or diverse the population, the higher the risks of social disruption and of ineffective social controls.

GDP per population (or gross national product) has been used both as a measure of poverty (for which there are better indicators; see Pridemore 2011) and as a measure of average well-being or development. The UN HDI provides a more encompassing measure for development that includes conditions in health, education, and economic achievement.[20] A new multiple poverty index (MPI) from the UN

---

[19] About the "theoretical affiliation" of these predictors, see the introduction.

[20] The three basic dimensions are life expectancy at birth, as an index of population health and longevity; knowledge and education, as measured by the adult literacy rate (with two-thirds weighting) and the combined primary, secondary, and tertiary school gross enrollment ratio (with one-third weighting); and standard of living, as measured by the natural logarithm of GDP per capita at purchasing power parity in US dollars.

covers the same dimension but is better suited to developing countries. Absolute deprivation and poverty are measured by earnings-based indicators (the percentage of the population earning less than US$1.25 per day in the late 2000s). Previous research has used the infant mortality rate as a proxy for poverty.

As displayed in table 4, the percentage of young males and ethnic diversity ("fractionalization") are positively correlated with lethal violence in the basic sample, as anticipated. Urbanization points in the opposite direction (contrary to the social disorganization hypothesis). When countries are disaggregated into the three HDI blocks, the correlations are weaker. In the low-HDI group the share of young males correlates negatively with homicide. However, none of the correlations in the subsamples pass the .01 or .05 significance tests. Nor does unemployment, which was unrelated to homicide in all samples.

Development and poverty measures (group 3) correlate strongly with homicide levels in most samples. The HDI correlates strongly with homicide rates in both the high- and low-HDI groups. However, earnings-related poverty measures and the infant mortality rate were even more highly correlated in the low-HDI group. The results for the HDI index are shown in figure 7 for countries and regions (with logged homicide scales). Many (but not all) Asian subregions have lower than predicted homicide rates, while the African and South and Central American regions have higher than predicted rates.

2. *Social Equality and Social Policy.*   Indicators under the label "social equality" try to map the distribution of wealth and measures of social justice. Together with "health and education" indicators, they measure states' activities and efforts to alleviate consequences of poverty and economic distress.

Income inequality (fig. 8) may be used as an indicator of relative deprivation, but it may also be interpreted as an indicator of concerns for social equality or social support. The Gini index is the most commonly used measure of income distribution. Distributive social policy and investments in social support are measured by the GDP share of social expenditures.

The Gini index and homicide rates correlate strongly across all samples. This is the most consistent finding in our analyses. Individual upward exceptions include nations in the Caribbean and Africa. Downward exceptions are found in Asia, South America, and

TABLE 4

Social Indicators and Lethal Violence, Bivariate Correlations: Homicide 2004–12 (Mean)

Socioeconomic and Structural Indicators	All (222) Correlation	N	High HDI (62) Correlation	N	Middle HDI (62) Correlation	N	Low HDI (61) Correlation	N
1. Demographics:								
Males, 15–29, % (2005)	.210**	207	.155	62	.022	61	−.183	59
Urban population (% of total, World Bank 2007)	−.244**	177	−.072	60	.125	60	−.033	55
Ethnic fractionalization (Alesina et al. 2002)	.268**	177	.185	60	.075	59	.173	53
2. Unemployment:								
Total	.043	131	.079	54	.018	40	−.037	22
Male	.013	130	.084	54	−.052	39	−.039	22
3. Development and poverty:								
GDP per capita PPP 2006 (World Bank 2007)	−.347**	180	−.369**	60	.05	60	−.101	55
HDI 2012 (UN)	−.448**	185	−.502**	62	−.131	62	−.398**	61
Multiple poverty index (MPI late 2000s, UN)	.316**	102			.308	38	.400**	52
MPI—poor (% of population, UN)	.319**	102			.288	38	.417**	52
Earning less than US$1.25/day (%, UN)	.371**	97			.273	36	.531**	50

4. Social equality:								
Public social expenditure 2002–7, % of GDP (IMF)	−.459**	82	−.437**	46	−.253	21	.13	15
Gini coefficient (UNDP 2004)	.571**	121	.651**	43	.510**	39	.513**	39
5. Health and education:								
Combined gross school enrollment ratio (% 2002, UNDP 2004)	−.339**	171	−.208	56	−.027	58	−.181	55
Education (LPI)	.491**	104	.443**	46	.462**	34	.257	23
Infant mortality rate 2010 (World Bank)	.482**	138	.531**	32	.266	54	.579**	52
Health (LPI)	.463**	104	.667**	46	.141	34	.17	23
6. Family relations:								
Divorces/population	−.208	82	.071	51	−.106	27		
Divorces/marriages	.252	40	.247	32	.961**	8		
7. Alcohol:								
Total (absolute liters) 2003	−.456**	44	−.248	38	.223	6		
Spirits (absolute liters) 2003	−.042	44	.393*	38	−.815*	6		
Ownership of firearms (%)	.17	42	.133	29	.15	11		

SOURCE.—See app. B.

* Significant at the .05 level (two-tailed).

** Significant at the .01 level (two-tailed).

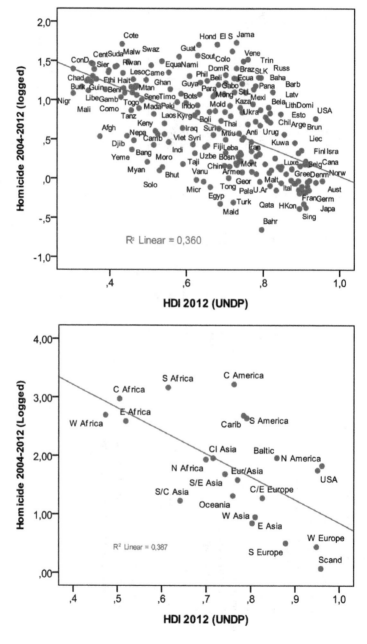

FIG. 7.—Homicide and human development

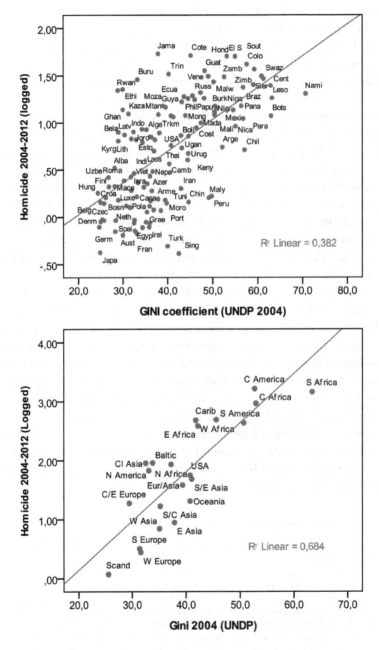

FIG. 8.—Income inequality

Africa.[21] Investments in social welfare also correlate strongly in the total sample and in the high-HDI group.

Public investments in education, educational achievement, and equal opportunities were measured by school enrollment and by the Legatum Prosperity Index (LPI) of Educational Performance (fig. 9). The latter includes school enrollment rates (measuring access to education), educational expenditures, average years of schooling, and female educational participation. Issues related to health and well-being are measured by the infant mortality rate and the Legatum Prosperity Index on Health and Well-Being (including, in addition to infant mortality, health satisfaction, number of health professionals, health-adjusted life expectancy, number of hospital beds, experienced physical pain, and experienced health problems). All indicators correlated strongly in most samples. No systematic differences could be found between different HDI groups. There is much less lethal violence in countries that invest more than average in social welfare, education, and health services than in countries that invest less than average.

3. *Comparing Social Indicators with US States.* Table 5 and figure 10 display correlations with the US murder rate in 2011 of selected indicators including demographic composition measured as percentage African Americans, the unemployment rate, the poverty level (percentage of population below the nationally defined poverty line), and GDP. The generosity of welfare support is measure by the maximum monthly Temporary Assistance for Needy Families (TANF) benefit for a family with three children and a composite index of social spending.[22] Educational attainment and investment (measuring both social inclusion and equality in opportunity) are measured by the percentage of the population with a high school (or higher) diploma.[23] General development is measured by the American HDI. The index measures the

[21] Because the Gini index is sensitive to changes at the top of the income scale, alternative measures were also tested. Comparisons for 78 nations between the poorest and the richest percentiles of the population (10 and 20 percent) gave practically identical results.

[22] The index is published by an information service, WallSt 24/7. Items in the index include unemployment benefits, state spending on education per student, income inequality (Gini coefficient), Medicaid spending per recipient, the average state employee pension benefits, welfare cash assistance to families with dependent children (TANF), and costs of living. For details, see Stockdale, Sauter, and Allen (2011).

[23] See Secretary of Health and Human Services (2008 Indicators of Welfare Dependence, Annual Report to Congress 2008, http://aspe.hhs.gov/hsp/indicators08/apa.shtml#ftanf2.

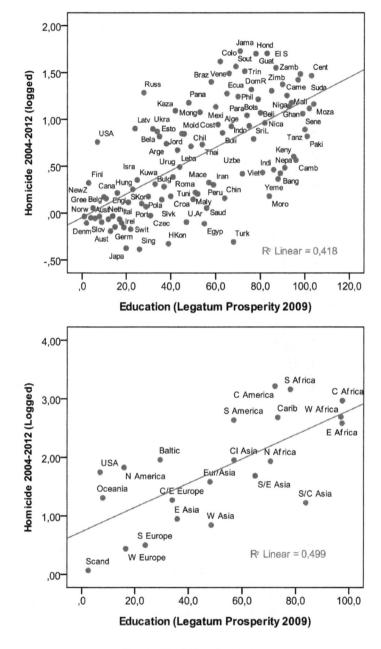

Fig. 9.—Homicide and education

TABLE 5
Social Indicators Nation-States and US States in Comparison, Bivariate Correlations

US Indicators	US Murder Rate 2011 (DPIC)	Global Homicide Rate 2004–12 (Global)	Global Indicators
Demographic indicators:			
African American population (% 2010)	.739**	. . .	
Unemployment	.348*	.043	Unemployment total
Poverty and development:			
GDP 2010/population ($)	−.248	−.347**	GDP/population 2006
American HDI 2010	−.480**	−.448**	UN HDI 2012
Poverty 2010	.645**	.371**	Earning less than $1.25 per day
Infant mortality rate 2005	.682**	.459**	Infant mortality rate 2010
Social equality and social policy:			
Gini	.495**	.571**	Gini UNDP 2004
Max monthly TANF benefit for family with 3 children 2009 (NCCP)	−.539**	. . .	
Social spending rank ca. 2010 (WallSt 24/7)	.514**	.459**	Social expenditures 2002–7
High school or higher 2004 % (US census)	−.576**	−.339**	Combined school enrollment

SOURCE.—See app. B.

* Significant at the .05 level (two-tailed).

** Significant at the .01 level (two-tailed).

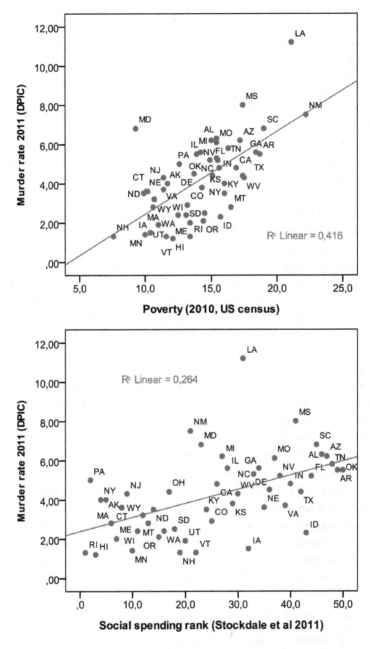

FIG. 10.—Poverty, social spending, and homicide rates in the United States. Source: Stockdale et al. (2011).

three basic dimensions but uses different indicators to reflect the US context and to maximize use of available data.[24] For the sake of comparison, the right-hand column presents results from the (roughly) comparable indicators for the basic sample.

The findings for countries and for US states are broadly consistent. Except for unemployment, the similarities are astonishing. The strongest correlation demonstrates one distinctive US-specific feature, the black/white homicide gap. The right-hand figure adds a social dimension. Homicide rates correlate with the black population percentage and correlate almost equally strongly with all poverty-related measures, income inequality, and all measures of welfare investments.

4. *Cultural Sensitivity: Family Disruption, Guns, and Alcohol.* The last two sections in table 4 include information for indicators that need to be discussed separately and that may have different meanings in different cultural contexts.

Guns are a culturally sensitive factor. The only available comparable data for firearm ownership come from the International Crime Victimization Survey (see van Dijk, van Kesteren, and Smit 2007). Homicide rates were only weakly (and nonsignificantly) related to national ownership rates of firearms (.170). The relevance of gun ownership for homicide levels appears to be dependent in part on differences in national homicide profiles and the types of guns people possess. In a setting in which victims are often killed with knives and in which guns in private homes are mainly hunting weapons, high firearm ownership may be irrelevant to the incidence of homicide. However, where homicides are generally committed with easily accessible handguns, gun control may play a more important role.

Alcohol is the second culturally sensitive predictor. Since the studies of Verkko (1931, 1951) in Finland, the relation of alcohol and violence has been a key issue in Nordic criminology. Several studies indicate a strong association between overall alcohol consumption and violent crime. An annual per capita change of 1 liter of pure alcohol consumed led to an annual change of 16 percent in violent crime in Norway during the years 1932–77 (Skog and Björk 1988). For the years 1950–

---

[24] The American HDI uses life expectancy calculated from official US government mortality data to measure longevity, a combination of educational attainment and school enrollment to measure knowledge, and median personal earnings to measure standard of living. The scores and rankings of the American HDI are not comparable to those of the global UN Development Program (UNDP) HDI (http://www .measureofamerica.org/the-measure-of-america-2010-2011-book/).

80 and 1921–84 in Sweden, a similar change in alcohol consumption led to a 6 percent change in assault rates and an 11 percent change in homicide rates (Lenke 1990). According to a study in Finland for the years 1950–2000, a 1-liter change in alcohol consumption led to a 3–6 percent change in the assault rate (Sirén 2000). Nothing in the correlates in table 4 would suggest this type of interdependency.

In the basic sample, total consumption of alcohol correlates negatively with violence. One explanation might be that the relation between alcohol consumption and violent crime is strongly culturally related, at least in Europe (see Rossow 2001; for Russia, see Pridemore and Chamlin [2006]). In most European wine-making countries, alcohol consumption levels or level changes seem to have only a very weak or nonexistent connection to violent crime. However, there are high-violence cultures, especially outside Europe, in which alcohol- or drug-related violence plays a subordinate role in homicidal crime. Thus the figures in table 4 may point to misleading general conclusions.

Even if there is a general inverse relationship between total alcohol consumption and violence, alcohol and problem drinking may be important risk factors in specific cultural environments, for example, where drinking takes place in risky situations, with hard liquor and in bad company with the intent to get as drunk as possible. In other words, the role of alcohol may be dependent not only on quantity but on culturally specific drinking and dining habits.

Is there evidence that would support a hypothesized connection between alcohol and homicide? Figure 11 compares trends in homicide rates and alcohol consumption (for wine countries, only hard spirits) in seven countries from 1960 to 2010 and in Sweden from 1860 to 2010. The shapes of these curves suggest that alcohol and alcohol consumption level changes should not be excluded from the list of possible explanations of long-term homicide rate changes.[25]

---

[25] A third, contextually sensitive factor relates to family disruption (as measured by divorce rates). It has a central position in US homicide research as a variable related to social disorganization theory (see Pratt and Cullen 2005; Nivette 2011, p. 116). This association has occurred over time: The US divorce rate more than doubled as the homicide rate increased from 1966 to 1980 but has fallen since the early 1990s in parallel with the homicide rate decline (La Free 1998, p. 144). However, attempts to test associations between lethal violence and family disruption with cross-comparative divorce rate data proved difficult. Data for divorce rates were accessible for 82 nations relative to population and for 40 relative to marriages. As table 4 shows, these two measures gave opposite results, most probably as a result of sample selection. As divorce rates are also affected by legislative and cultural side constraints, one may ask whether they measure the same phenomena in different countries.

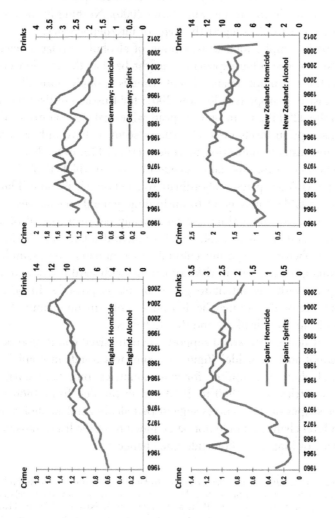

FIG. 11.*A.*—Alcohol and lethal violence in eight countries. Sources: CHTS database, Lehti (2013), with updates for Russia 1965–94 (Meslé et al. 1996); World Advertising Research Center (2005); von Hofer (2012).

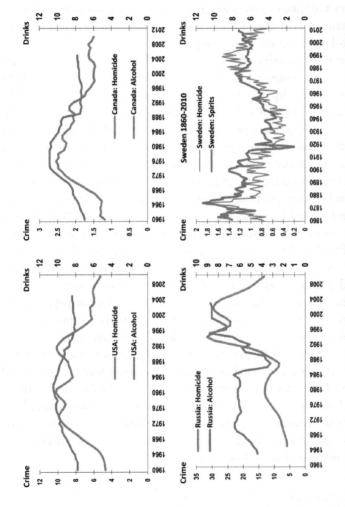

FIG. 113.—Alcohol and lethal violence in eight countries. Sources: CHTS database, Lehti (2013), with updates for Russia 1965-94 (Meslé et al. 1996); World Advertising Research Center (2005); von Hofer (2012).

B. Political Indicators: Democracy and Good Governance

Political factors receive surprisingly little attention in cross-national analyses of violent crime.[26] The importance of the stability of state for the incidence of violence is self-evident in times of civil unrest. Political structures and state organization may also be important in less dramatic circumstances. Historical evidence underlines the interdependency of lethal violence and the legitimacy of state power. Compliance with legal norms, as theories of normative compliance propose, may be dependent on the perceived fairness of criminal justice processes and the legitimacy of the legal order in citizens' eyes (see, e.g., Tyler 2003). Democracy is defended and praised precisely because of its capacity to achieve social security, equality, and well-being, all closely connected with lethal violence. Corrupt governments, autocratic civil servants, and badly run justice systems not only foster anger, resentment, and lack of cooperation but also are ineffective at maintaining social order.

This subsection examines relations between four democracy indicators and homicide levels. The most widely used Polity IV indicators measure constitutional dimensions of democracy. The equally well-known Freedom House indicators measure democracy "from the bottom up" by focusing on the extent to which individuals are entitled to civil and political rights ("liberal democracy"). Both measures have been criticized for "thinness" and formality and for not paying sufficient attention to the extent to which these rights are honored and exercised in practice. An alternative index of "effective democracy" developed by World Bank researchers aims to measure to what extent these liberties are respected by political elites and how much control over their lives people have in practice. Finally, the Economist Intelligence Unit democracy index places emphasis on "substantive" dimensions of democracy expressed along five dimensions: electoral process and pluralism, civil liberties, the functioning of government, political participation, and political culture.[27]

---

[26] A notable exception to this generalization is LaFree's (1998) study on relations between homicide rates and the legitimacy of social institutions. The importance of state-level political factors was pointed out by Gartner (1990) and LaFree (1999) in the 1990s. In general, though, state-level factors have begun to receive significant attention only recently (e.g., Pampel and Gartner 1995; Chamlin and Cochran 2006; Chu and Tusalem 2013; Eisner and Nivette 2013; Nivette and Eisner 2013).

[27] Polity IV database: http://www.systemicpeace.org/polity/polity4.htm; Freedom House database: http://www.freedomhouse.org; the Economist Intelligence Unit democracy index: Ståhlberg 2008; Economist Intelligence Unit Database, http://www.eiu.com.

The quality and integrity of governance have been measured by the Governance Matters project of the World Bank (Kaufmann, Kraay, and Mastruzzi 2006). All indicators are based on subjective or perceptions-based data reflecting the views of informed stakeholders, household and firm survey respondents, experts working in the private sector, nongovernmental organizations, and public-sector agencies (see table 6). These indexes in different ways measure the quality of public and civil services and policy formulation and the extent to which respondents have confidence in and abide by the rules of society. Indicators capture six key dimensions of governance (voice and accountability, political stability and lack of violence, government effectiveness, regulatory quality, rule of law, and control of corruption). Here we discuss three indicators: rule of law, control of corruption, and a summary index of good governance. Rule of law refers to perceptions of the extent to which respondents have confidence in and abide by the rules of society, including the quality of contract enforcement, property rights, the police, and the courts; it also encompasses the likelihood of crime and violence. Control of corruption measures perceptions of corruption. The summary index of good governance combines measures of corruption, government effectiveness, political participation, liberty rights, and political stability. It measures both how governments are selected and monitored and the capacity of governments to formulate and implement sound policies.

As figure 12 illustrates, Freedom House and Polity IV indicators are either unrelated or only weakly correlated with homicide rates. However, substantive democracy indicators show much stronger correlations. The explanation for these differences is to be found from the shape of the correlation. The correlation with the Polity indicator is highly skewed (a reverse "U"), indicating that homicide levels are low both in well-developed democracies and in autocracies. The reasons, however, may be very different.[28] Another indication of this phenomenon is that the democracy index correlates negatively with homicide in the high-HDI group but positively in the middle group (note that the Freedom House indicator uses reversed indicators). This parallels LaFree and Tseloni's (2006) findings that crime rates increased in transitional democracies but declined as democratization continued.

---

[28] The reliability of official homicide data may differ between autocracies and democracies.

TABLE 6
Political Indicators, Bivariate Correlations: Homicide 2004–12 (Mean)

Political Indicators	All (222)		High HDI (62)		Middle HDI (62)		Low HDI (61)	
	Correlation	N	Correlation	N	Correlation	N	Correlation	N
1. Democracy:								
Freedom House rating of democracy 2008	.126	180	.109	60	−.269*	60	.04	55
Constitutional democracy 2006 (Polity IV)	.037	144	.027	48	.391**	45	−.003	50
Democracy, Economist 2008	−.168*	156	−.210	54	.392**	48	−.061	53
Effective democracy 2000–2006 (Welzel)	−.303**	177	−.271*	59	.166	56	−.063	58
2. Good governance:								
Kaufmann rule of law 2006	−.419**	179	−.420**	60	−.242	59	−.106	55
Kaufmann corruption 2006	−.352**	176	−.392**	59	−.0355	59	−.033	55
Summary good governance 1996 (Kaufmann et al.)	−.320**	143	−.373**	55	.177	46	−.120	41

SOURCE.—See app. B.

* Significant at the .05 level (two-tailed).

** Significant at the .01 level (two-tailed).

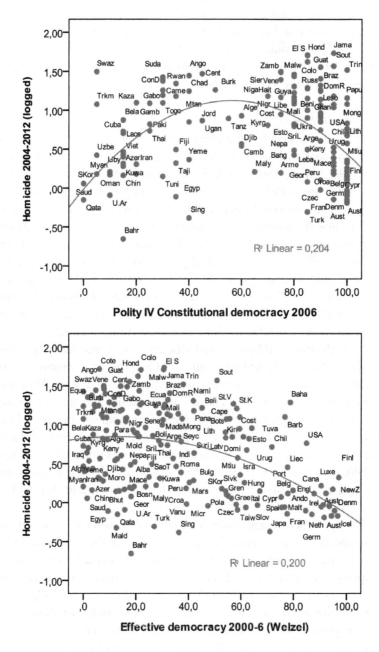

Fig. 12.—Homicide and democracy

Of the good governance indicators, rule of law behaves consistently, with a strong negative correlation in all groups. The shape of the correlation is clear and consistent at both national and regional levels (see fig. 13). Lethal violence levels are lower in well-functioning uncorrupted democracies. Upward outliers include South Africa, the Baltic countries, and the United States.

C. Cultural Factors

The need to include cultural variables and other "soft" predictors in cross-national analyses of crime has long been recognized (e.g., Gartner 1990; LaFree 1999, pp. 135–36). This tendency has increased as Norbert Elias's (1994) theory of civilization processes has gained attention. For example, Eisner (2008) argues that the long-term historical decline in violence was primarily the result of a change in the "cultural model" of daily life. This included three elements: "an emphasis on *self-control* as an ideal of personality; domesticity and *familialism* as guidelines for private life; and *respectability* as the yardstick for public appearance" (p. 303; emphasis in original). He asserts that this model and these values were reinforced and reproduced through social institutions such as schools, church, and the family. The values of self-control, thriftiness, diligence, and sobriety were reiterated by parents, teachers, the church, and labor unions. They were also precipitants of successful efforts to reduce the consumption of alcohol. Men and women should root their identities in the family and the upbringing of children. Respectability and fear of embarrassment constrained behavior in the expanding area of leisure time. All these elements reduced the risk of violence between young males. Gurr (1981, 1989), Sharpe (1996), and Spierenburg (1996, 1998, 1999) offer similar explanations for long-term declines in homicide rates since the Middle Ages in England, the Netherlands, and Scandinavia.

The special challenge concerning cultural theories is to operationalize and test them empirically. Elias's civilization theory directs attention to hard-to-measure moral sensibilities and cultural traits such as empathy, self-discipline, and acceptance of violence; individualism; the existence of a "culture of honor"; modernization; and "cosmopolitanism." In the absence of direct measures, existing studies have employed various proxies. Below we suggest a couple of new ones.

1. *Acceptance of Violence.* "Cultural acceptance of violence" is a popular explanation for high violence rates but, without indicators other

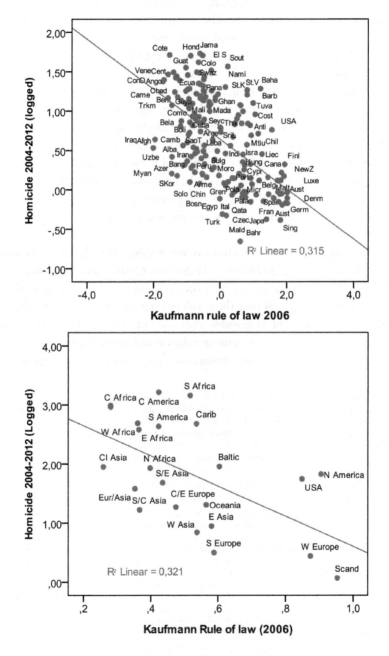

Fig. 13.—Homicide, rule of law, and good governance

than crime itself, is tautological.[29] We tested two indicators of cultural acceptance of violence. The first relates to cultural effects of violent experiences caused by internal armed conflicts and civil unrest. The second measures the extent to which corporal punishment is allowed in school, families, and child welfare institutions.[30]

2. *Values and Moral Views.* Values surveys measure cross-national differences between attitudes and values. However, none of them includes a direct measurement of what might be characterized as the "culture of honor" (Altheimer 2012). We sought proxies. Inglehart and Welzel's (2005) dimension of traditional versus secular values, including elements of inflexibility, moral conservatism, national pride, and respect for formal authority, is one possible proxy for the culture of honor (and the willingness to protect one's reputation and property with force).[31]

3. *National Cultures.* Culture is about values but also about behavior, dispositions, and abilities.[32] Hofstede's (2001) cultural dimensions theory describes the effects of a society's culture on the values of its members and explains how those values relate to behavior. His cultural indexes can be used as possible measures of cultural differences that have been viewed as important in relation to Elias's civilization theory.

Three of Hofstede's six dimensions appear especially salient to vi-

[29] Small-scale comparisons from 14 nations indicate that acceptance of killing correlates positively with homicide rates (McAlister 2006), but we were unable to detect surveys using larger samples of nations. Cultural acceptability of violence can also be reflected in the ways the legal system treats killings as justifiable actions. Daly and Wilson (1988, pp. 289–90) report that one-quarter of intentional killings in some states of the United States have been characterized as justifiable. In Scandinavian legal practice, by contrast, justified homicides are exceedingly rare.

[30] The index is based on Ståhlberg's (2008) reworking of the UNICEF *World Report on Violence against Children* (Pinheiro 2006).

[31] The work of Inglehart and Welzel is based on the assumption that values and beliefs play a central role in social, economic, and political development (while being at the same time dependent on material conditions and these same socioeconomic developments and traditions). The authors distinguish two major dimensions of cultural variation: traditional vs. secular and survival vs. self-expression values (2005, pp. 48–49). While the text does not imply that there should be any apparent link between violent behavior and these dimensions, items in traditional values cover elements familiar to both the hypotheses of culture of honor (national pride, respect for authority) and the Durkheimian hypothesis about the connection between homicide and sentiments related to collective things (God, religion, family; for discussion, see Dicristina [2004]).

[32] According to Altheimer (2012, p. 847), "a toolkit of symbols, stories, rituals, and worldviews that configures strategies of action that people draw from to solve certain problems."

olent behavior: Individualism, as the opposite of collectivism, stands for a society in which ties between individuals are loose: a person is expected to look after only himself or herself and his or her immediate family. Collectivism stands for a society in which people are integrated into strong, cohesive in-groups, which continue to protect them throughout their lifetime in exchange for unquestioning loyalty (0–10: collectivist to individualist). The presumed effect of individualism is partly disputed. While Durkheim (1951, 1957) interpreted the historical decline of homicide rates primarily as the product of liberation from collective bonds, subsequent writers have attributed the increase of late twentieth-century homicide rates in many countries to "excessive" or "expressive" individualism (Eisner 2003, pp. 123–32; 2008, pp. 309–10). Whether the rise of youth cultures and gang criminality—often linked with visions of increased crime—reflects the rise of individualism in the Durkheimian sense is more than a little doubtful (Eisner 2008, p. 310).

Masculinity for Hofstede refers to the distribution of emotional roles between men and women. Masculinity stands for a society in which social gender roles are clearly distinct: men are supposed to be assertive, tough, and focused on material success and women to be modest, tender, and concerned with the quality of life. Femininity stands for a society in which social gender roles overlap: both men and women are supposed to be modest, tender, and concerned with the quality of life (0–100: feminine to masculine).

Long-term orientation for Hofstede stands for a society that fosters virtues oriented toward future rewards, in particular, adaptation, perseverance, and thrift. Short-term orientation stands for a society that fosters virtues related to the past and present, in particular, respect for tradition, preservation of "face," and fulfillment of social obligations (0–100: short-term oriented to long-term oriented).

4. *Social Trust.* The fourth candidate for a cultural predictor is social trust. Social trust has been linked with crime through theories of social capital (Lederman, Loayza, and Menéndez 2002) and collective efficacy (Sampson 2006), including the existence of social networks and shared values that inhibit lawbreaking and support norm compliance (Halpern 2005, pp. 135–36). Measurements of social trust are based on the World Values Survey (WVS; http://www.worldvaluessurvey.org).

5. *Regional Dummies.* Regional dummies have been used to take

cultural processes or differences into account (e.g., Neapolitan's [1998] "machismo-effect" in South America).

Results for all indicators are shown in table 7 and figure 14. Countries with (internal) armed conflicts experience higher levels of "civilian" lethal violence. This might be interpreted as tentative evidence of a civil war effect (although, if so, the mechanisms might be many and heterogeneous—not only cultural but also related to the dissolution of legal institutions, availability of firearms, etc.). Countries that have rejected or banned the use of corporal punishment in schools, education, and in different institutions have lower homicide levels. Lethal violence rates are also lower in countries with less punitive populations and higher in countries that share traditional, religion-based, and authoritarian moral views. The question remains, however, whether these values have independent causal importance or whether lower levels of violence and the growth of postmaterialist secular and rational values result from the same underlying socioeconomic developments (see also Inglehart and Welzel 2005, p. 22).

Results from the Hofstede index indicate that cultural individualism correlates inversely with homicide levels. Contrary to expectations, masculinity seems to be unrelated to lethal violence. However, there are differences between HDI groups. In the high-HDI group, the correlation is negative, but in the middle group it is positive. The same pattern repeats for long-term orientation. With the exception of individualism, cultural differences have the greatest relevance for the middle group. The direction of this association fits well with civilization theory: short-term orientation, the importance of "preservation of face," and masculinity are associated with higher violent crime rates. The question remains why these correlations prevail in lower but not in higher HDI-level groups.

Social trust correlates inversely with homicide rates in all samples. The results, however, are statistically significant only for the basic sample because of the small number of countries. Correlation diagrams are consistent on both country and regional levels (see fig. 14).

All regional dummies correlate strongly with lethal violence. Whether this demonstrates the existence of a specific trait of "machismo" (see Neapolitan 1998) is discussed below.

TABLE 7
Cultural Indicators, Bivariate Correlations: Homicide 2004–12 (Mean)

Cultural Indicators	All (222) Correlation	N	High HDI (62) Correlation	N	Middle HDI (62) Correlation	N	Low HDI (61) Correlation	N
1. Acceptance of violence:								
Number of conflicts (2000)	.186*	180	.310*	60	.002	60	.157	55
Major conflict (1,000+ deaths per year [2000])	.257**	180	.469**	60	.137	60	.298*	55
Corporal punishment index	−.259**	98	−.380**	52	−.042	39	−.409	7
2. Culture and moral views:								
Punitivity (ICVS)	.465**	75	.463**	43	.128	19	.264	12
Traditional/secular-rational values (Inglehart and Welzel 2005)	−.580**	93	−.142	48	−.617**	27	−.316	18
3. National cultures and behavior (Hofstede):								
Individualism index	−.391**	71	−.416**	45	.029	18	−.633	7
Masculinity index	.139	71	−.123	45	.512*	18	−.72	7
Long-term orientation index	−.426**	93	.030	47	−.463*	27	−.396	17
4. Social trust:								
Trust in people (WVS)	−.381**	79	−.255	44	−.372	23	−.477	11
5. Culture—regions:								
Africa dummy	.365**	222	.08	62	.063	62	.531**	61
South America dummy	.341**	222	.549**	62	.564**	62	.154	61
Western Europe dummy	−.250**	196	−.311*	61	...	61	...	60

SOURCE.—See app. B.

* Significant at the .05 level (two-tailed).

** Significant at the .01 level (two-tailed).

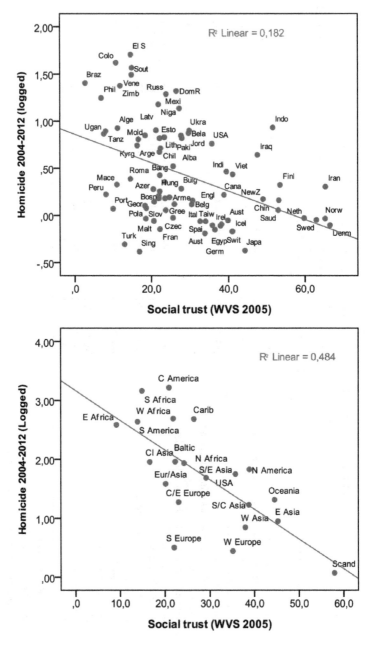

FIG. 14.—Homicide and trust

TABLE 8

Demographics and Lethal Violence: US States, Bivariate Correlations

Cultural Factors: US States	Murder Rate 2011 (DPIC)
Attitudes social values:	
In favor of death penalty (DDB, 1 disagree, 6 agree)	.059
Police should use whatever force is necessary to maintain law and order (DDB, 1 disagree, 6 agree)	.562**
There should be a gun in every home (DBB, 1 disagree, 6 agree)	.388**
More important: fight against crime (1) or humane society (2) (DDB)	−.375**
Most people are honest (DDB, 1 disagree, 6 agree)	−.615**
Regions:	
Northeast dummy	−.316*
South dummy	.503**
Slave state, non–slave state	−.317*

SOURCE.—See app. B.

* Significant at the .05 level (two-tailed).

** Significant at the .01 level (two-tailed).

D. Homicide and Cultural and Social Values in the United States

A North-South homicide gap has deep roots in American history. Data collected by Nisbett and Cohen (1996), Roth (2009), and Pinker (2011) attribute this difference to the periods of colonization and state formation from the seventeenth century onward, traditions of a weak state and reliance on self-help, and the culture of honor in the South. The origins of the culture of honor have been linked to the herding background of southern settlers as "herdsmen the world over tend to be capable of great aggressiveness and violence because of their vulnerability to losing their primary resource, the animals, while the settlers in the North came from farming communities where cooperation with neighbors was essential and the need to have reputation for strength less important" (Nisbett and Cohen 1996, p. xv). Whether an association between herding or farming and violence holds today cross-nationally is disputable (Altheimer 2012), but there is a clear North-South difference in attitudes toward violence (Nisbett and Cohen 1996, pp. 25–26). And there is a strong and significant correlation between regional dummies, as is shown in table 8.

State-level attitudinal data come from the DDB Needham Lifestyles

Survey.[33] The survey provides comparable results for social trust. Other measurements deal with attitudes toward the death penalty, police powers, the importance of crime prevention crime, and the presence of guns in homes (see fig. 15).

With the exception of support for the death penalty, all correlations are strong and significant. Conservative procontrol values (including importance of crime prevention and support for extensive police powers) correlate positively with lethal violence. Social trust, in turn, correlates inversely and strongly with homicide. Regional patterns are clear and familiar from several former studies. Southern states have, on average, more than double the homicide rate (5.8 per 100,000 population a year) of that in the Northeast (2.8).

IV. Deterrence and Formal Control

Differences in sentencing practices and police effectiveness, from a criminal justice policy perspective, are sources of hypotheses about differences in homicide rates. Testing this is difficult because of a lack of comparative data. The sanctioning of homicide varies across countries, but there are few, if any, quantifiable measures of this variation with the exception of capital punishment. Other possible indicators are the relative use of imprisonment and police numbers per capita.

A. General Remarks

Table 9 includes data for three indicators related to deterrence and formal control: use of the death penalty, imprisonment rates relative to population, and the number of police officers relative to population. The use of capital punishment has been measured with a four-point scale adopted from Amnesty International (http://www.amnesty.org): abolitionist for all crimes (99 states out of 199), allowing use of capital punishment in exceptional circumstances (but not practicing it; eight states); abolitionist in practice (34 states); and retentionist (retaining capital punishment for ordinary crimes and not included in the

---

[33] See http://www.icpsr.umich.edu/icpsrweb/instructors/icsc/datasets.jsp. Since 1975 the survey has measured Americans' values, attitudes, and ways of living. Most measurements are based on a six-point scale. Surveys were conducted in each state with a national total sample of 3,500–4,000. Since state-level samples in small states are too low for meaningful analysis, results are based on cumulative (pooled) data from surveys conducted between 1988 and 1996. Data are available also from http://bowlingalone .com/?page_id=7.

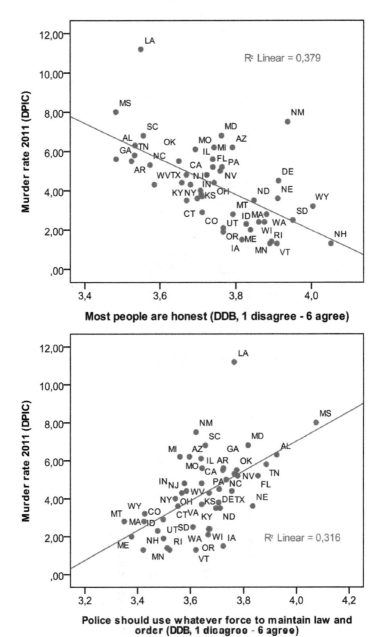

FIG. 15.—Homicide and social values (United States)

TABLE 9
Deterrence and Formal Control, Bivariate Correlations: Homicide 2004–12 (Mean)

Deterrence and Formal Control	All (222)		High HDI (62)		Middle HDI (62)		Low HDI (61)	
	Correlation	N	Correlation	N	Correlation	N	Correlation	N
Death penalty (1 = no, 4 = yes)	.189**	199	.233	61	-.079	62	.117	61
Prisoners 2010–13 (mean)	.062	221	.650**	62	.211	62	.086	61
Police officers (Harrendorf and Smit 2010)	-.179	96	.053	51	-.299	30	.324	13

SOURCE.—See app. B.

* Significant at the .05 level (two-tailed).

** Significant at the .01 level (two-tailed).

previous category; 58 nations).[34] Numbers of police officers per capita come from Harrendorf and Smit (2010). Correlations are shown in table 9.

Homicide rates and use of capital punishment correlate positively in the global sample (199 nations), but the correlation is nonsignificant in subsamples. Homicide rates are lowest among abolitionist states. There are fewer differences among the other groups. The mean homicide rate among abolitionist nations was 6.8 per 100,000 population. The median was 2.2. For retentionist states the corresponding figures were 11.1 and 6.8. Those results justify skepticism about the deterrent effectiveness of capital punishment (e.g., Fagan 2006). The positive correlation may have a cultural explanation. Capital punishment may be a form of violence by which the state undermines respect for the value of human life and thereby indirectly encourages violent behavior.

Imprisonment and homicide rates covary positively among more developed nations but show a zero correlation in the global sample. The strong positive correlation in the high-HDI group is influenced strongly by strong observations from the United States and the former Soviet region. Figure 16 illustrates correlations for countries and regions between the number of prisoners per 100,000 population in 2010–13 and homicide rates in 2004–13 (most data from 2010–12) in the global sample (log scales, 222 nations).

In the global sample the correlation between imprisonment and homicide is slightly positive. A regional analysis shows a zero correlation (with the United States as a clear, high-rate outlier in use of imprisonment).

None of these results supports the deterrence hypothesis. The only results giving partial support were negative. Correlations between homicide rates and the number of police officers in the middle-HDI group were nonsignificant.

Long Prison Sentences. European sources provide some data on penal responses other than capital punishment, especially for homicide. Aebi and Delgrande (2012) report the percentages and numbers of prisoners serving sentences for homicide or serving a life sentence or otherwise long prison term. The former figures are of little use for our

---

[34] States considered abolitionist in practice are those that have not executed anyone in the past 10 years and are believed to have a policy or established practice of not carrying out executions; see http://www.amnesty.org/en/death-penalty/abolitionist-and-retentionist-countries#retentionist.

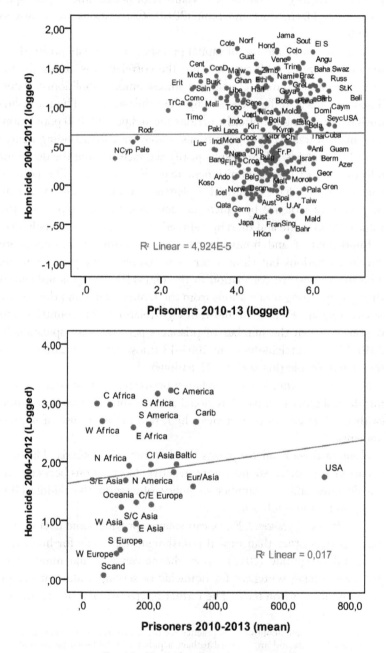

FIG. 16.—Homicide and imprisonment rates

TABLE 10

Long-Term Prisoners and Homicide, Bivariate Correlations:
Homicide 2008–12 (Mean)

Long-Term Prison Sentences	Europe 2010 (45)	
	Correlation	N
Prisoners serving a life sentence (/100,000 population)	.077	44
Prisoners serving more than 20 years or a life sentence (/100,000 population)	.198	44
Prisoners serving more than 10 years or a life sentence (/100,000 population)	.770**	45
All prisoners	.585**	45

* Significant at the .05 level (two-tailed).
** Significant at the .01 level (two-tailed).

purpose (Campbell 2012), but the number of long-term prisoners relative to population may be informative as life imprisonment is imposed in most countries mainly for homicide or murder. Correlations in table 10 compare the rates of long-term prisoners against the level of lethal violence.

The number of prisoners serving life sentences does not correlate with homicide rates. Countries with many life prisoners, such as England and Wales, have few homicides, but so do countries with few life prisoners such as Denmark and Germany (fig. 17). However, correlations become stronger when other long-term prisoners are included in the analyses: the more long-term prisoners relative to population, the higher the homicide rates. The reason may be that high levels of violence lead to harsher sentencing practices. But it is equally possible that the social, political, and cultural factors that contribute to high levels of violence also influence the severity of crime control policies and the overall use of imprisonment.[35] In that case, homicide and imprisonment rates should move in parallel rather than inversely (as is assumed by adherents of the deterrence hypothesis).

[35] This assumption is supported by comparison of factors discussed in this essay and by factors that explain cross-national differences in the use of imprisonment and penal attitudes (Lappi-Seppälä 2008, 2013).

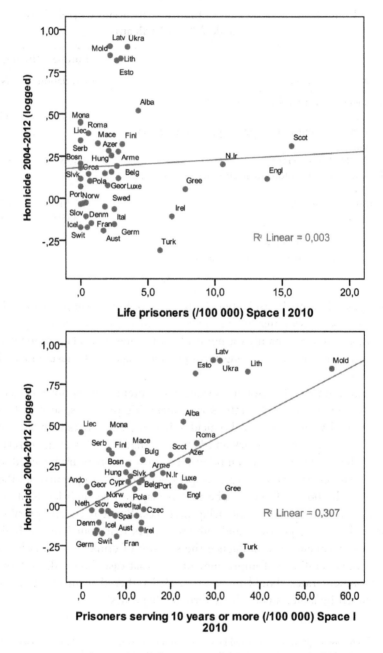

FIG. 17.—Homicide and long-term prisoners

B. Imprisonment and Homicide in Europe, 1960–2012

Figure 18 illustrates trends in homicide and imprisonment in eight European countries, the United States, and Canada from 1960 to 2010. Homicide rates in the Nordic countries moved in parallel during the period: an increase from 1960 to the early 1990s, followed by a drop. Imprisonment rates evolved similarly in Denmark, Sweden, and Norway, but completely differently in Finland until the early 1990s. Finland thus shared a homicide curve with the other three countries but had a very different prison curve.

Homicide in England and Wales increased from 1960 until the early 2000s. Imprisonment rates also increased until at least 2010. In Germany, the homicide trend was stable or declining. Imprisonment rates also were stable or declining. Following the deterrence hypothesis, Germany and England should have switched their crime curves: declining rates for England because of the deterrent effects of stiffer prison sentences and rising rates for Germany because of its less harsh prison sentences. But that did not happen.

Homicide followed the same curve in France, Belgium, and the Netherlands, with some differences in timing: first, a period of increasing homicide rates in France till the mid-1980s, in Belgium until the mid-1980s or early 2000s, and in the Netherlands till 1995–2000, followed in each case by a clear drop. Imprisonment rate trends were similar except in the Netherlands (a steeper increase from a lower level, followed by a clear drop in the 2000s).

For southern Europe, prison data are available only from the 1980s onward. In Spain, homicide rates rose after the regime change in the mid-1970s. Since then, rates have been stable. Homicide rates in Italy increased through the early 1990s followed by a clear drop. Imprisonment rates in Spain increased systematically throughout the period. In Italy, imprisonment rates fluctuated (partly as a result of amnesties), but the overall profile has resembled Spain's. The two countries have similar prison profiles but very different crime profiles.

C. Imprisonment and Homicide in Seven Countries 1910–2012

Six nations (Sweden, Norway, Finland, Japan, New Zealand, England and Wales, and the United States) provide uninterrupted data on homicide and imprisonment rates since 1910. A century-long comparison in figure 19 shows that, if anything, homicide and imprisonment move together. This was especially visible during the first half of

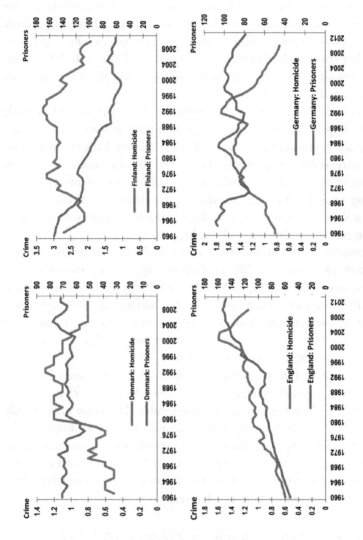

FIG. 18.4.—Homicide rates and imprisonment, 1960–2010: western Europe

198

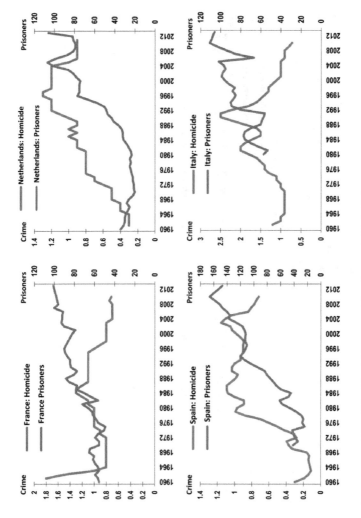

Fig. 18*B*.—Homicide rates and imprisonment, 1960–2010: western Europe

199

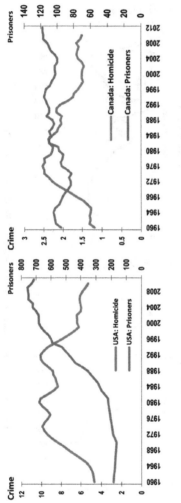

FIG. 18C.—Homicide rates and imprisonment, 1960–2010: United States and Canada

the twentieth century in Sweden, Finland, Norway, Japan, and the United States, before the great decline in crime in the 1940s.

During the second half of the century the profiles differ. In Finland, New Zealand, and Japan, the curves followed each other until around 1990. From 1990 to 2005, homicide and imprisonment rates moved in opposite directions in Japan. In Norway, homicide rates increased from 1960 to 1990, but imprisonment rates were stable; in Sweden, the homicide trend paralleled Norway's, but imprisonment rates fluctuated. In the United States, homicide rates doubled from 1960 to 1980 while imprisonment rates were broadly stable; in the 1980s, homicide rates fell through 1985 but rose again until 1991; in the 1990s, homicide rates fell steeply and imprisonment rates continued to climb.

The early 1990s mark the turning point when homicide trends and imprisonment rate trends took a different turn in all but one country in the group (Finland). While from 1910 to 1990 both trends had more or less followed each other, paths departed during the most recent 20 years. This serves as a warning for cross-national analyses that employ data only from 1990 onward. This has been the only period when homicide and imprisonment rates have generally followed different routes (and in a manner that some would support the deterrence hypothesis) in the Western industrialized countries.

Changes in lethal violence in Western countries cannot credibly be linked to changes in the use of imprisonment. In the first half of the twentieth century, imprisonment and homicide trends moved roughly in parallel in western Europe and the United States. Since then, the picture has become more complex. Homicide trends have converged in western Europe and the English-speaking countries, but imprisonment trends have not. Explaining differences and changes in homicide and imprisonment rates is a distinct challenge. Some background factors, such as the strength of the welfare state and the legitimacy of the political system, on theoretical grounds ought to have relevance for both, but evidently not everywhere. None of the evidence surveyed in this essay supports the view that national differences in lethal violence are inversely related to imprisonment rates. If there is a correlation, it is a positive one.[36]

---

[36] See also Aebi and Kuhn (2000). With regard to the Nordic countries, there is strong historical evidence that changes in the use of imprisonment (and the use of the death penalty in the case of murder) did not influence the development of crime convictions to a tangible degree. This conclusion is derived from four different offense

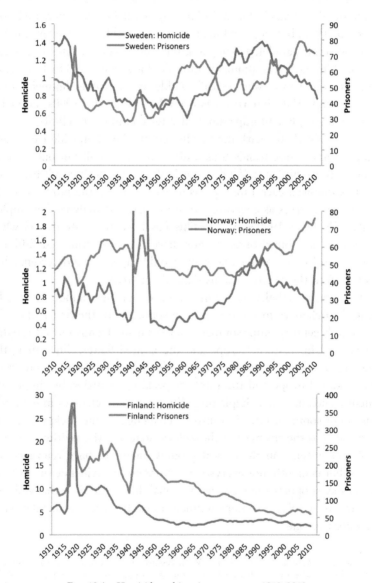

Fig. 19A.—Homicide and imprisonment rates 1910–2012

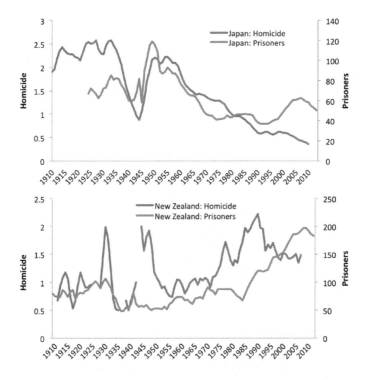

FIG. 19B.—Homicide and imprisonment rates 1910–2012

V. Explaining Trends and Differences?

So far the examination has been restricted to correlational analyses and graphical trend descriptions. The next logical step is use of multivariate statistical models. There are predictable difficulties in doing this: a data set with around 200 nations and over 50 variables covering a varying number of nations for different periods of time allows practically an indefinite number of different models. They all would be statistically defensible but give different results depending on sample, period, and variable selections. Thus, one may have some doubts about reaching the "final explanation" with a statistical model. Still, they may be helpful in testing the relative weight and relevance of the three groups of factors included in the previous analyses.

types in two countries over long periods of time from the early 1800s onward using simple but robust graphical methods. See von Hofer and Lappi-Seppälä (2014).

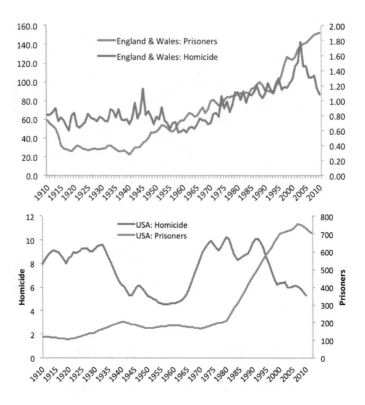

FIG. 19C.—Homicide and imprisonment rates 1910–2012

A. Explaining Differences

We look first at how much social and structural factors, political factors, and cultural factors as a group explain total variance. After that, we look at what the result would be when the strongest predictors from each group are combined in the same model.

This is done in table 11. Models 1–3 deal with social, political, and cultural variables, respectively. Model 4 combines the most powerful predictors from models 1–3. In addition, each model is complemented with two regional/cultural dummies (Africa and South America). Two demographic variables are included as controls (the share of young males and ethnic diversity [fractionalization]).

Model 1 covers central social indicators with 117 countries. Without regional dummies, HDI, Gini, and ethnic fractionalization explain 56 percent of variance. The South American dummy increases the power of the model to 65 percent, with the result that income inequality drops out.

Political indicators in model 2 cover the largest set of countries ($N = 147$). Rule of law and democracy explain 51 percent of the variance. When regional dummies are included, the R^2 increases to 69 percent.

Cultural model 3 covers the smallest set of countries ($N = 56$). The model explains only 36 percent of the variance without dummies. In addition, only one of the cultural variables (social trust) passed the significance test (meaning that the explanatory power of the model came mainly from the demographic controls). Adding the regional dummies raises the power of the model to 47 percent, but the cultural variables remain insignificant.

The last model, 4 ($N = 116$), includes both social (HDI, Gini) and political indicators (rule of law and democracy). The model explains 66 percent of the variance without the regional dummies. All predictors were statistically significant (with rule of law and democracy in the lead). Adding the dummies brings only a slight improvement in the model (from .647 to .664). This indicates that the variables in the model have succeeded in capturing much of the South American machismo effect. Two control variables, ethnic fractionalization and share of young males, did not pass the significance level in any of the eight models. All models passed the collinearity test (but in model 4B, the largest variable inflation factor [VIF] was 4.4).

Thus model 4, the strongest (explaining 69 percent), included the two political predictors supplemented by regional dummies (2B). However, the information value of this model is diminished because about half of the predictive power resulted from regional dummies, and we can only guess what might lie behind these dummies. The assumption that a culturally specific element of machismo would play a significant role is uncertain since the introduction of the South American dummy in model 4 had only a marginal effect. Model 4A may be the most informative. Its message is that the level of lethal violence is dependent first and foremost on the rule of law, the quality and integrity of governance, and the level of democracy.[37]

These results alter the picture from earlier studies by placing polit-

---

[37] Several of the good governance indicators produced practically the same result. Rule of law was the strongest (adjusted R^2 .664, β −.381, significance .001), but a summary index of good governance (.650, −.364, .007) and a corruption index (.650, −.271, .014) came quite close.

TABLE 11
Regression Analyses

	A			B		
	β	t	Significance	β	t	Significance
Model 1: Social (N = 117):						
Adjusted R²	.561			.650		
Constant		−.223	.824		.478	.634
Males 15–29 (%)	.148	1.779	.078	.151	1.968	.052
Ethnic fractionalization (Alesina et al. 2002)	.158*	2.188	.031	.116	1.766	.080
HDI 2012	−.302**	−3.493	.001	−.283**	−2.814	.006
Gini (UNDP 2004)				.137	1.773	.079
Africa dummy				.222*	2.398	.018
South America dummy	.365**	5.059	.000	.385***	5.551	.000
Model 2: Political (N = 147):						
Adjusted R²	.509			.691		
Constant		−2.477	.014		−1.808	.073
Males 15–29 (% 2005)	.164*	2.127	.035	.113	1.802	.074
Ethnic fractionalization (Alesina et al. 2002)	.253**	3.907	.000	.075	1.350	.179
Kaufmann rule of law 2006	−.786**	−9.495	.000	−.566**	−7.693	.000
Democracy, Economist 2008				.323**	3.857	.000
Africa dummy				.479**	8.646	.000
South America dummy	.475**	4.996	.000	.324**	5.907	.000

Model 3: Cultural (N = 56):

Adjusted R²	.363			.471		
Constant		−.037	.971		−1.02	.313
Males 15–29 (% 2005)	.252	1.555	.126	.299	1.914	.062
Ethnic fractionalization (Alesina et al. 2002)	.273*	2.207	.032	.214	1.866	.068
Individualism index	−.029	−.202	.84	.079	.544	.589
Masculinity index	−.086	−.764	.448	−.097	−.938	.353
Long-term orientation index	−.171	−1.444	.155	.017	.138	.891
Social trust (WVS)	−.255*	−2.117	.039	−.127	−1.095	.279
Africa dummy				.184	1.687	.098
South America dummy				.412**	3.158	.003

Model 4: Combined (N = 116):

Adjusted R²	.647			.664		
Constant		−1.489	.139		−.191	.849
Males 15–29 (% 2005)	.137	1.508	.134	.118	1.332	.186
Ethnic fractionalization (Alesina et al. 2002)	.126	1.920	.057	.125	1.958	.053
Kaufmann rule of law 2006	−.525**	−5.186	.000	−.381**	−3.347	.001
HDI 2012	−.264**	−2.944	.004	−.348**	−3.723	.000
Gini (UNDP 2004)	.286**	4.138	.000	.212**	2.890	.005
Democracy, Economist 2008	.416**	4.131	.000	.305**	2.833	.005
South America dummy				.187*	2.551	.012

SOURCE.—See app. B.

NOTE.—Dependent variable: all models, homicide 2004–12, logged mean.

* Significant at the .05 level (two-tailed).

** Significant at the .01 level (two-tailed).

ical predictors over social factors. Among the latter group of factors, income inequality remains among the most powerful indicators. This, however, has been contested recently by Pridemore (2011). His reanalyses of older data sets, together with his own original analyses, indicate that including poverty, measured as child mortality, in the model would increase the power of the model and eventually either diminish or altogether remove the effect of income inequality. To test the effect of poverty-related variables in the model, table 12 presents alternative models for model 4A. In model 5, Gini has been replaced by earnings-based poverty (earning less than US$1.25 per day). Model 6 replaces Gini with child mortality and model 7 with GDP.

These modifications do not improve the results. Model 5 explains only 35 percent of the variation. Model 6 with child mortality explains 58 percent, which is less than in model 4A. Model 6 with GDP explains 55 percent, but the chosen poverty measure remains insignificant.[38] This does not mean that poverty does not matter; it does, as has been illustrated above. But including poverty measures in the analyses does not render the aspects and arguments behind income and social inequality meaningless. They seem to maintain their central position, not as the most important factor but still crucial.

B. Explaining Trends?

What has been done so far is merely cross-sectional. There are strong reasons to assume that many of the factors detected in cross-sectional analyses are relevant also for the changes. But to test that, we would need a different methodology. An initial step in testing the relevance of examined variables for changes is to examine how these factors correlate with percentage changes in homicide. Even if this does not give a causal explanation, it does tell what is typical of societies in which violence has increased and what is common for countries in which violence has decreased. The strongest bivariate correlations with key indicators and changes in lethal violence in 1990/92–2008/11 are displayed in table 13.

Strong correlations exist between country characteristics and trends in lethal violence. Educational achievement, modernization (measured

---

[38] Keeping Gini in the model would not have altered the end result. In this case, Gini would have remained in the model as a significant predictor, but none of the alternatives would have passed the significance test. The overall power of the models would have slightly increased, but all would have remained below model 4A.

TABLE 12
Regression Analyses: Testing Gini and Poverty Measures

	Model 4A: Gini			Model 5: Earning < $1.25/Day (%)			Model 6: Infant Mortality			Model 7: GDP		
	N	Adjusted R²	VIF	N	Adjusted R²	VIF	N	Adjusted R²	VIF	N	Adjusted R²	VIF
	117	.631	3.4	87	.354	2.7	147	.582	3.9	147	.547	4.5
	β	t	Signif.	β	t	Signif.	β	t	Signif.	β	t	Signif.
Constant		−3.480	.001		−2.171	.033		−3.884	.000		−2.642	.009
Males 15–29 (% 2005)	.109	1.138	.257	.215	2.08	.041	.219	2.900	.004	.125	1.636	.104
Ethnic fractionalization (Alesina et al. 2002)	.173	2.587	.011	.278	3.009	.003	.142	2.203	.029	.201	3.102	.002
Kaufmann rule of law 2006	−.579	−5.659	.000	−.335	−3.122	.002	−.633	−7.295	.000	−.581	−4.891	.000
HDI 2012	.123	1.329	.186	−.131	−.926	.357	.027	.261	.795	.259	3.091	.002
Democracy, Economist 2008	.364	3.535	.001	.38	3.515	.001	.57	6.277	.000	.479	5.120	.000
Gini coefficient (UNDP 2004)	.321	4.662	.000									
Earning less than $1.25/day (%)				.415	3.651	.000						
Infant mortality rate (2010)							.356	3.516	.001			
GDP per capita PPP 2006 (World Bank)										−.087	−.852	.395

Source.—See app. B.

Note.—Dependent variable: homicide 2004–12 (mean, log).

TABLE 13

Key Correlates and Changes in Homicide, 1990–2008: Bivariate
Correlations

	Correlation
South America dummy	.524**
Education (LPI)	.461**
Globalization index 2005 (KOF)	−.439**
Males 15–29 (% 2005)	.408**
Gini coefficient (UNDP 2004)	.384**
Long-term orientation index	−.375**
Individualism index	−.351**
Infant mortality rate	.343*
Public social expenditures, 2002–7 % of GDP (IMF)	−.343*
Urban population (% of total) 2006, World Bank 2007	−.327**
HDI 2012	−.310**

SOURCE.—See app. B.

* Significant at the .05 level (two-tailed).

** Significant at the .01 level (two-tailed).

by the globalization index), income distribution, and cultural characteristics of long-term orientation and individualism are among the
most powerful correlates with changes in lethal violence.

C. *Comparing Homicide Levels and Percentage Changes by Key Predictors*

The last comparison combines results from rate analyses and trend
analyses. Figure 20 illustrates associations between key indicators with
both the levels and changes in homicide rates. Countries are grouped
according to each indicator into three groups (high, middle, and low).
Mean homicide rates and mean percentage changes are reported for
each group and according to each indicator.

Thus, for example, in the high-HDI group (upper-left corner), the
mean homicide rate was three and crime decreased by 26 percent, while
in the low-HDI group, the mean rate was 13 and homicide increased
by 27 percent. In this case the association was not completely systematic, since homicide increased even more in the middle group.

With regard to the four other indicators—education, social expenditure, income inequality, and trust in police—all associations are systematic. Crime was higher and changes less favorable in countries that
invested less in education and social welfare, had larger income differences, and had lower levels of trust in the police.

The last indicator, democracy, shows a different pattern. Well-

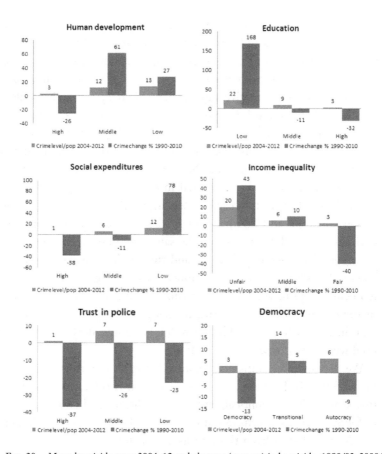

FIG. 20.—Mean homicide rates 2004–12 and changes (percent) in homicide, 1990/92–2008/11 according to key indicators.

developed democracies had the lowest homicide rates (about three) and the largest decline (−13 percent). However, the level of crime was lower in autocracies when compared to the middle groups consisting of developing democracies (six compared to 14). And in autocracies, crime was declining (−9 percent) but rising in the middle group (+5 percent). This confirms the pattern discussed earlier of increasing crime rates in developing democracies.

VI. What Next?

We seek in this essay to do three things. The first is to provide a global picture of rates and trends in lethal violence using the most reliable and comprehensive statistical data available. Results showed huge variation in homicide rates from below 0.5 victim per 100,000 population to 80. Similar variance exists regionally, with homicide rates varying from around one in Scandinavia to around 30 in Central America.

Our second aim is to give a global view of changes in lethal violence from the 1950s onward. Our results reaffirm earlier observations of a general crime decline, taking place since the beginning of the 1990s (Eisner 2008). This drop seems to have been restricted mainly to western Europe, Canada, Australia, New Zealand, and the United States. Homicide rates have also decreased in east Asia, eastern Europe, and South Africa, but starting earlier (Asia in the 1950s and 1960s) or later (eastern Europe and South Africa in the mid- or late 1990s). These declines may well not be part of the same phenomenon with the same background factors as in Europe and the English-speaking countries. There also seems to have been much variation in the timing of the homicide drops in Western industrialized countries. The decline began in some countries in the 1980s, in many in the 1990s, and in some only in the early 2000s. The term "global crime decline" should be used with strong reservations, if at all.

We do not offer statistically controlled explanations for the causes of these trends. However, analyses in Section II offer clues. Countries that share cultural, political, and social traditions and conditions seem to follow similar patterns in crime. Searches for the reasons behind the trends should start from those traits and patterns.

Our third aim is accordingly to explore reasons and factors that today explain huge national and regional differences in lethal violence. Cross-sectional analyses with a large set of countries and a variety of social, political, and cultural factors provide strong and consistent indications that lethal violence is far more common in countries with large income differences and less well-developed social welfare states. Lethal violence is lower in developed democracies, but also in autocracies (and obviously for different reasons). Homicide is lower under more effective governments and in less corrupt environments. High-crime societies are characterized by stronger authoritarian and conservative moral views, more collectivist cultures, and lower long-term cultural orientations. Demographic considerations—the age structure and ethnic diversity—play much lesser roles than social-structural, political, and cultural variables. The same patterns apply regardless of whether homicide victims are male or female.[39] Use of capital punishment, high rates of imprisonment, and extensive use of life sentences are usually associated with high and increasing homicide rates—and not the other way around.

These associations recur across continents and across countries at different levels of human development. Similar patterns also appear among US states. Our analyses do not provide systematic controlled explanations for trends, but they do indicate that the factors associated with differences in homicide rates are also relevant to changes in them. Crime has declined more in countries with better social services, smaller income differences, higher levels of trust, and well-functioning democratic political systems. Most structural indicators show the opposite values in countries with increasing violence.

[39] Factors influencing homicide levels globally seem to be gender-neutral. High male and female homicide mortality rates are explainable by the same factors. No systematic differences were detected between gender-specific and general predictors.

Average Homicide Levels

TABLE A1

Average Homicide Levels in 2008–12 by Country and Region: Europe

Region/Country	Mean	Region/Country	Mean	Region/Country	Mean
Western Europe:		Southern Europe:		Eastern Europe:	
Nordic:		Southwest:		Baltic countries:	
Iceland 3	.3	Slovenia 3	.6	Estonia 3.1	5.5
Denmark 3	.8	Spain 3	.8	Lithuania 3	5.7
Sweden 3.1	.8	Italy 3	.8	Latvia 3.1	6.7
				Former socialist	
Norway 3.1	1.0	Malta 3	.8	countries:	
Finland 3.1	1.9	Portugal 3	1.1	Czech 3	.8
France/Benelux:		Andorra 3	1.2	Poland 3	1.1
France 3	.7	Southeast:		Slovakia 3	1.2
Netherlands 3	.9	Cyprus 3	1.2	Hungary 3.1	1.6
Belgium 3	1.2	Kosovo 3	1.3	Bulgaria 3	1.6
Luxembourg 3	1.4	Bosnia 3	1.3	Romania 3	2.3
				Former Soviet	
German speaking:		Croatia 3	1.4	region:	
Germany 3.1	.6	Greece 3	1.4	Georgia 3	.5
Austria 3.1	.6	Northern Cyprus 4	1.4	Armenia 3	1.5
Switzerland 3	.6	Macedonia 3	1.7	Tajikistan 3	2.3
British Isles:		Serbia 3.2	1.9	Azerbaijan 3	2.4
UK England 3.1	.6	Montenegro 3	2.3	Uzbekistan 3	2.4
Ireland 3.1	.9	Albania 3	2.5	Kyrgyztan 3	6.0
Jersey 2	1.4	Turkey 3.3	2.9	Belarus 3	6.4
UK Scotland 3	1.5			Moldova 3	6.6
UK Northern Ireland 3	1.8			Ukraine 3	6.7
				Kazakstan 3	10.0
				Turkmenistan 3	11.8
				Russia 3.1	14.9

SOURCE.—Lehti (2013). Keys for sources: 1 = court and prosecutor, 2 = police, 3 = health statistics (COD), 4 = specific source.

TABLE A2

Average Homicide Levels in 2008–12 by Country and Region: Americas and Caribbean

Region/Country	Mean	Region/Country	Mean	Region/Country	Mean
North America:		South America:		Caribbean:	
Canada 2	1.7	Argentina 2	5.7	Martinique 3	3.0
USA 3.1	5.4	Suriname 2	6.5	Guadeloupe 3	4.4
Bermuda 2	8.2	Uruguay 2	6.7	Cuba 3	4.7
Greenland 2.1	12.9	Chile 2.1	7.0	Aruba 3	6.4
Central America:		Peru 2	10.0	Haiti 2	7.4
Costa Rica 2	10.3	French Guyana 3	10.1	Barbados 2	9.3
Nicaragua 2	12.9	Paraguay 2	11.9	Grenada 2	11.9
Mexico 2	17.6	Ecuador 2	17.2	Antigua 2.1	13.6
Panama 2	19.1	Guyana 2	17.9	Dominica 2	15.6
Belize 2	38.2	Brazil 2	21.7	Saint Vincent 2	20.2
Guatemala 2	41.4	Bolivia 2.1	37.0	Saint Lucia 2	23.7
El Salvador 2	59.6	Colombia 3.1	40.2	Dominican Rep. 2.2	23.8
Honduras 2.2	77.8	Venezuela 2	49.6	Puerto Rico 2	25.9
				Bahamas 2	28.0
				Trinidad Tobago 2	33.7
				US Virgin Islands 3	47.8
				Jamaica 2	50.5

SOURCE.—Lehti (2013). Keys for sources: 1 = court and prosecutor, 2 = police, 3 = health statistics (COD), 4 = specific source.

TABLE A3

Average Homicide Levels in 2008–12 by Country and Region: Asia

Region/Country	Mean	Region/Country	Mean	Region/Country	Mean
West:		South:		Southeast:	
Bahrain 3.1	.0	Maldives 3	.5	Brunei 3	.0
UAE 3	.3	Bhutan 2	1.1	Singapore 3	.4
Qatar 3	.6	Iran 3.2	1.4	Indonesia 3	.5
Kuwait 3	.7	Bangladesh 2	2.7	Malaysia 3.1	.9
Iraq 3	2.0	Nepal 2	3.0	Laos 3	4.6
Israel 3	2.0	Afganistan 3	3.4	Thailand 2	5.5
Yemen 3	2.1	India 2.2	3.8	Timor Leste 3	6.9
Jordan 3.1	2.1	Sri Lanka 2	4.7	Myanmar 3	10.2
Oman 3.2	2.2	Pakistan 2	7.3	Philippines 3	13.9
Syria 2	2.6	East:		Cambodia 3	21.5
Saudi Arabia 3	2.7	Japan 3.1	.4		
Palestine 3	3.0	Hong Kong 2	.5		
Lebanon 2	3.4	Taiwan 3	.7		
		Korea 3	1.3		

Region/Country	Mean	Region/Country	Mean	Region/Country	Mean
		Vietnam 3	1.6		
		China 3	1.6		
		Macao 3.2	1.7		
		Mongolia 3.1	8.6		
		North Korea 3	15.2		

SOURCES.—Lehti (2013). Keys for sources: 1 = court and prosecutor, 2 = police, 3 = health statistics (COD), 4 = specific source.

TABLE A4

Average Homicide Levels in 2008–12 by Country and Region: Africa

Region/Country	Mean	Region/Country	Mean	Region/Country	Mean
North Africa:		East Africa:		West Africa:	
Tunisia 3	1.1	Reunion 3	1.8	Niger 3	3.8
Morocco 2	1.4	Rodrigues 3	3.3	Mali 3	8.0
Egypt 2	2.0	Djibouti 3	3.4	Senegal 3	8.7
Libya 3	2.9	Mauritius 3	3.6	Liberia 3	10.1
Algeria 3	7.2	Kenya 2.2	4.0	Gambia 3	10.8
Sudan 3	24.2	Uganda 2	7.4	Togo 3	10.9
Central Africa:		Tanzania 2	8.0	Nigeria 3	12.2
Sao Tome 3	1.9	Madagascar 3	8.1	Cape Verde 3	13.1
Gabon 3	13.8	Mozambique 3	8.8	Mauritania 3	14.7
Chad 3	15.8	Comoros 3	12.2	Sierra Leone 3	14.9
Angola 3	19.0	Seychelles 2	12.8	Benin 3	15.1
Cameroon 3	19.7	Zimbabwe 3	14.3	Ghana 3	15.7
Equatorial Guinea 3	20.7	Rwanda 3	17.1	Burkina Faso 3	18.0
Congo Kinshasa 3	21.7	Eritrea 3	17.8	Guinea Bissau 3	20.2
CAR 3	29.3	Burundi 3	21.7	Guinea 3	22.5
Congo Brazzaville 3	30.8	Ethiopia 3	25.5	Ivory Coast 3	56.9
		Malawi 3	36.0	South Africa:	
		Zambia 3	38.0	Botswana 2.2	10.5
				Lesotho 3	22.9
				Namibia 3	27.4
				Rep. of South Africa 2	33.6
				Swaziland 3	41.0

SOURCE.—Lehti (2013). Keys for sources: 1 = court and prosecutor, 2 = police, 3 = health statistics (COD), 4 = specific source.

TABLE A5

Average Homicide Levels in 2008–12 by Country and Region: Oceania

Region/Country	Mean	Region/Country	Mean	Region/Country	Mean
Australia 4	1.3	Niue 4	.0	Northern Mariana Isl. 3	1.8
New Zealand 3.1	1.6	Pitcairn 4	.0	Samoa 1.1	2.1
		Micronesia 3	.9	New Caledonia 1.2	2.5
		Vanuatu 3	.9	American Samoa 3.2	2.5
		Solomon Islands 3	1.0	Fiji 2	2.7
		Tonga 3	1.0	Guam 3.2	2.9
		Marshall Islands 3	1.8	French Polynesia 2	3.4
				Kiribati 3	7.3
				Papua New Guinea 3	13.0

SOURCE.—Lehti (2013). Keys for sources: 1 = court and prosecutor, 2 = police, 3 = health statistics (COD), 4 = specific source.

TABLE A6

Average Annual Homicide Levels in COD and Crime Statistics in 2000–2010 by Country and Region

Region/Country	COD	Crime	Difference Percent COD/Crime	Region/Country	COD	Crime	Difference Percent COD/Crime
Europe:				Asia:			
Scandinavia			94%	W, S, and S.E. Asia			72%
Denmark	.88	.92	96%	Bahrain	.04	.67	6%
Finland	2.27	2.91	78%	India	4.95	4.04	123%
Norway	.81	.76	107%	Israel	3.35	2.55	131%
Sweden	.96	1.02	94%	Pakistan	3.6	6.7	54%
W. Europe:			70%	Sri Lanka	3.33	8.06	41%
France	.75	1.57	48%	Thailand	5.98	7.5	80%
Germany	.62	.94	66%	E. Asia			100%
Italy	.93	1.12	83%	Hong Kong	.63	.6	105%
Netherlands	1.12	1.32	85%	Japan	.57	.6	95%
British Isles			76%	Africa			192%
E and W	.65	1.39	47%	Kenya	4.22	3.91	108%
N. Ireland	1.86	2.01	93%	Mauritius	3.34	3.19	105%
Scotland	1.87	2.14	87%	South Africa	10.55	38.4	364%
E. Europe			126%	Oceania			107%
Estonia	9.17	8.17	112%	Australia	1.44	1.47	98%

218

Latvia	9.65	6.92	139%
Americas:			
N. America			98%
Canada	1.57	1.85	85%
USA	5.98	5.4	111%
C. America			93%
Belize	18.96	28.68	66%
Costa Rica	7.82	8.17	96%
El Salvador	52.62	60.03	88%
Guatemala	30.3	38.87	78%
Mexico	11.34	13.02	87%
Nicaragua	15.3	11.52	133%
Panama	13.32	13.18	101%
S. America			78%
Argentina	6.06	6.55	93%
Brazil	25.96	23.67	110%
Chile	5.19	7.94	65%
Colombia	50.94	47.81	107%
Ecuador	17.67	16.68	106%
Guyana	17.14	18.72	92%
Paraguay	11.56	18.14	64%
Peru	1.59	7.13	22%
Suriname	4.21	11.76	36%
Uruguay	5.6	6.29	89%
Venezuela	29.96	39.81	75%
New Zealand	1.48	1.28	116%
Caribbean			63%
Antigua	3.62	10.55	34%
Bahamas	18.32	18.19	101%
Barbados	12.2	10.59	115%
Dominica	5.68	10.34	55%
Dominican Republic	5.28	18.24	29%
Grenada	.62	10.81	6%
Jamaica	.71	50.32	1%
Puerto Rico	20.51	21.11	97%
Saint Kitts and Nevis	12.03	22.98	54%
Saint Lucia	16.3	22.08	74%
Saint Vincent and Gr.	15.79	19.49	81%
Trinidad and Tobago	24.9	22.11	113%

APPENDIX B
Sources for Tables
Table 4:

- Males, 15–29 % (2005): UN Department of Economic and Social Affairs, World Population database (http://esa.un.org/unpd/wpp/unpp/p2k0data .asp)
- Urban population (% of total, World Bank 2007): World Bank database (http://data.worldbank.org/indicator)
- Ethnic fractionalization: Alesina et al. (2002)
- Unemployment, total: World Bank database (http://data.worldbank.org/ indicator)
- Unemployment, male: World Bank database (http://data.worldbank.org/ indicator)
- GDP per capita, purchasing power parity (PPP) 2006, World Bank (2007): World Bank database (http://data.worldbank.org/indicator)
- HDI 2012 (UN): UNDP Human Development Reports database (http://hdr.undp.org/en/data)
- Multiple poverty index (MPI, late 2000s): UNDP Human Development Reports database (http://hdr.undp.org/en/data)
- MPI—poor (% of population): UNDP Human Development Reports database (http://hdr.undp.org/en/data)
- Earning less than US$1.25day (%): UNDP Human Development Reports database (http://hdr.undp.org/en/data)
- Public social expenditures 2002–7, % of GDP (International Monetary Fund): http://www.ilo.org/dyn/sesame/ifpses.socialdbexp
- Gini coefficient (UNDP 2004): UNDP Human Development Reports database (http://hdr.undp.org/en/data)
- Combined gross school enrollment ratio (% 2002, UNDP 2004): UNDP Human Development Reports database (http://hdr.undp.org/en/data)
- Education (LPI): Legatum Institute Prosperity Index (http://www .prosperity.com)
- Infant mortality rates (per 1,000 female adults 2005, World Bank 2007): World Bank database (http://data.worldbank.org/indicator)
- Health (LPI): Legatum Institute Prosperity Index (http://www .prosperity.com)
- Divorces/population 2008–12: UN Statistical Division, Demographic and Social Statistics database (http://unstats.un.org/unsd/Demographic/ sconcerns/mar/default.htm)
- Births to mothers <20 years (%), 1991–97: Pippa Norris database
- Alcohol: total (absolute liters, 2003): WHO Global Information System on Alcohol and Health database (http://www.who.int/gho/alcohol/en/)
- Alcohol: spirits (absolute liters, 2003: WHO Global Information System on Alcohol and Health database (http://www.who.int/gho/alcohol/en/)
- Ownership of firearms (%): van Dijk et al. 2007

Table 5:
US indicators:

- African American population (% 2010): US Census Bureau (http://www.census.gov)
- Unemployment 2013: Bureau of Labor Statistics (http://www.bls.gov)
- GDP 2010/population ($): US Bureau of Economic Analysis (http://www.bea.gov)
- American Human Development Index (HDI) 2010: http://www.measureofamerica.org/human-development/
- Poverty 2010: http://www.census.gov
- Infant mortality rate 2005: National Center for Health Statistics (http://www.census.gov/statab/ranks/rank17.html; http://www.cdc.gov)
- Gini: US Census Bureau (http://www.census.gov)
- Max monthly TANF benefit for family with three children (NCCP): National Center for Children in Poverty database (http://www.nccp.org)
- Social spending rank: Stockdale et al. (2011)
- Educational attainment (high school or higher): Secretary of Health and Human Services (2008 Indicators of Welfare Dependence, Annual Report to Congress 2008, http://aspe.hhs.gov/hsp/indicators08/apa.shtml#ftanf2)

Global indicators:

- Unemployment total: World Bank database (http://data.worldbank.org/indicator)
- GDP/population 2006: World Bank database (http://data.worldbank.org/indicator)
- UN HDI 2012: UNDP Human Development Reports database (http://hdr.undp.org/en/data)
- Earnings less than $1.25: UNDP Human Development Reports database (http://hdr.undp.org/en/data)
- Infant mortality 2010: World Bank database (http://data.worldbank.org/indicator/SP.DYN.IMRT.IN/countries?display=default)
- Gini, UNDP 2004: UNDP Human Development Reports database (http://hdr.undp.org/en/data)
- Social expenditure 2002–7: http://www.ilo.org/dyn/sesame/ifpses.socialdbexp
- Combined school enrollment: UNDP Human Development Reports database (http://hdr.undp.org/en/data)

Table 6:

- Freedom House Rating of Democracy (2008): Freedom House Database (http://www.freedomhouse.org)
- Constitutional democracy: Polity IV Project database (http://www.systemicpeace.org/polity/polity4.htm)
- Democracy, Economist 2008: Economist Intelligence Unit Database (http://www.eiu.com)
- Effective democracy 2002–6. Alexander, Inglehart, and Welzel (2011)

- Kaufmann rule of law: Kaufmann et al. (2006)
- Kaufmann corruption: Kaufmann et al. (2006)
- Summary of good governance 1996: Kaufmann et al. (2006)

Table 7:

- Number of conflicts (2000): Peace Research Institute, Oslo (http://www .prio.org/)
- Major conflict (2000): Peace Research Institute, Oslo (http://www .prio.org/)
- Corporal punishment index: Pinheiro (2006), Ståhlberg (2008)
- Punitivity (ICVS database, http://www.unicri)
- Traditional/secular-rational values: Inglehart and Welzel (2005)
- Individualism index: Hofstede Centre database (http://geert-hofstede .com/)
- Masculinity index: Hofstede Centre database (http://geert-hofstede.com/)
- Long-term orientation index: Hofstede Centre Database (http://geert-hofstede.com/)
- Trust in people: World Values Survey database (http://www.world valuessurvey.org)

Table 8:

- Murder rate 2011: DPIC: Death Penalty Information Center Database (http://www.deathpenaltyinfo.org/)
- In favor of death penalty
- Police should use whatever force is necessary to maintain law and order
- There should be a gun in every home
- More important: fight against crime (1) or humane society (2)
- Most people are honest
- Source for all: DDB Needham Lifestyles Survey (http://www.icpsr .umich.edu/icpsrweb/instructors/icsc/datasets.jsp)

Table 11:

- Males 15–29 % (2005): UN DESA World Population database (http:// esa.un.org/unpd/wpp/unpp/p2k0data.asp)
- Ethnic fractionalization: Alesina et al. (2002)
- 2012 HDI value: UNDP Human Development Reports database (http://hdr.undp.org/en/data)
- Gini coefficient (UNDP 2004): UNDP Human Development Reports database (http://hdr.undp.org/en/data)
- Kaufmann rule of law: Kaufmann et al. (2006)
- Democracy, Economist 2008: Economist Intelligence Unit Database (http://www.eiu.com)
- Individualism index: Hofstede Centre database (http://geert-hofstede .com/)
- Masculinity index: Hofstede Centre database (http://geert-hofstede.com/)

- Long-term orientation index: Hofstede Centre Database (http://geert-hofstede.com/)
- Indulgence vs. restrain index: Hofstede Centre Database (http://geert-hofstede.com/)

Table 12:

- Males 15–29 % (2005): UN DESA World Population Database (http://esa.un.org/unpd/wpp/unpp/p2k0data.asp)
- Ethnic fractionalization: Alesina et al. (2002)
- Rule of law: Kaufmann et al. (2006)
- HDI: UNDP Human Development Reports database (http://hdr.undp.org/en/data)
- Democracy: Economist Intelligence Unit database (http://www.eiu.com)
- Gini: UNDP Human Development Reports database (http://hdr.undp.org/en/data)
- Earning below $1.25: UNDP Human Development Reports database (http://hdr.undp.org/en/data)
- Child mortality: World Bank database (http://data.worldbank.org/indicator)
- GDP: World Bank database (http://data.worldbank.org/indicator)

Table 13:

- Education (LPI): Legatum Institute Prosperity Index (http://www.prosperity.com)
- Globalization Index 2005 (KOF): KOF Index of Globalization (http://globalization.kof.ethz.ch/)
- Males 15–29, % (2005): UN DESA World Population database (http://esa.un.org/unpd/wpp/unpp/p2k0data.asp)
- Gini coefficient (UNDP 2004): UNDP Human Development Reports database (http://hdr.undp.org/en/data)
- Long-term orientation index: Hofstede Centre database (http://geert-hofstede.com/)
- Individualism index: Hofstede Centre database (http://geert-hofstede.com/)
- Infant mortality rate: World Bank Database (http://data.worldbank.org/indicator)
- Public social expenditures 2002–7 percent of GDP (International Monetary Fund): http://www.ilo.org/dyn/sesame/ifpses.socialdbexp
- Urban population (percent of total) 2006 (World Bank 2007): World Bank database (http://data.worldbank.org/indicator)
- 2012 HDI value: UNDP Human Development Reports database (http://hdr.undp.org/en/data)

REFERENCES

Aebi, Marcelo F., and Natalia Delgrande. 2012. *Council of Europe SPACE 1: 2010 Survey on Prison Populations.* Document PC-CP (2012). Strasbourg: Council of Europe.

Aebi, Marcelo F., and André Kuhn. 2000. "Influences on the Prisoner Rate: Number of Entries into Prison, Length of Sentences and Crime Rate." *European Journal on Criminal Policy and Research* 8:65–75.

Aebi, Marcelo F., and A. Linde. 2012. "Crime Trends in Western Europe According to Official Statistics from 1990 to 2007." In *The International Crime Drop: New Trends in Research*, edited by Jan van Dijk, Andromachi Tseloni, and Graham Farrell. New York: Palgrave Macmillan.

Alesina, A., A. Devleeschauwer, W. Easterly, S. Kurlat, and R. Wacziarg. 2002. "Fractionalization." NBER Working Paper no. 9411. Cambridge, MA: National Bureau of Economic Research. http://www.nber.org/papers/w9411.

Alexander, A. C., R. Inglehart, and C. Welzel. 2011. "Measuring Effective Democracy: A Defense." *World Values Research* 4(1):1–40. http://www.world valuessurvey.org.

Altheimer, lrshad. 2012. "Cultural Processes and Homicide across Nations." *International Journal of Offender Therapy and Comparative Criminology* 57(7): 842–63.

Campbell, Michael C. 2012. "Homicide and Punishment in Europe: Examining National Variation." In *Handbook of European Homicide Research: Patterns, Explanations, and Country Studies*, edited by C. Marieke, A. Liem, and William Alex Pridemore. New York: Springer.

Chamlin, Mitchell B., and John K. Cochran. 2006. "Economic Inequality, Legitimacy, and Cross-National Homicide Rates." *Homicide Studies* 10(4):231–52.

Chu, Doris C., and Rollin F. Tusalem. 2013. "The Role of the State on Cross-National Homicide Rates." *International Criminal Justice Review* 23(3):252–79.

Comisíon de la Verdad y Reconciliación. 2003. "Cuantos peruanos murieron? Estimación del total de víctimas causadas por el conflicto armado interno entre 1980 y el 2000." Anexo 2. http://cverdad.org.pe/ifinal/pdf/Tomo percent20-percent20ANEXOS/ANEXOpercent202.pdf.

Daly, Martin, and Margo Wilson. 1988. *Homicide.* New Brunswick, NJ: Transaction.

Dicristina, Bruce. 2004. "Durkheim's Theory of Homicide and the Confusion of the Empirical Literature." *Theoretical Criminology* 8:57–91.

Durkheim, Emile. 1951. *Suicide: A Study in Sociology.* New York: Free Press.

———. 1957. *Professional Ethics and Civic Morals.* New York: Routledge.

Eisner, Manuel. 2003. "Long-Term Historical Trend in Violent Crime." In *Crime and Justice: A Review of Research*, vol. 30, edited by Michael Tonry. Chicago: University of Chicago Press.

———. 2008. "Modernity Strikes Back? A Historical Perspective on the Latest Increase in Interpersonal Violence (1960–1990)." *International Journal of Conflict and Violence* 2(2):288–316.

Eisner, Manuel, and Amy Nivette. 2013. "Does Low Legitimacy Cause Crime? A Review of the Evidence." In *Legitimacy and Criminal Justice: An International Exploration*, edited by Anthony Bottoms, Alison Liebling, and Justice Tankebe. Oxford: Oxford University Press.

Elias, Norbert. 1994. *State Formation and Civilization: The Civilizing Process*. Guildford, UK: Biddles.

Fagan, Jeffrey. 2006. "Death and Deterrence Redux: Science, Law and Causal Reasoning on Capital Punishment." *Ohio State Journal of Criminal Law* 4: 255–322.

Gartner, Rosemary. 1990. "The Victims of Homicide: A Temporal and Cross-National Comparison." *American Sociological Review* 55:92–106.

Gurr, Ted Robert. 1981. "Historical Trends in Violent Crime: A Critical Review of the Evidence." In *Crime and Justice: An Annual Review of Research*, vol. 3, edited by Michael Tonry and Norval Morris. Chicago: University of Chicago Press.

———. 1989. "Historical Trends in Violent Crime: Europe and the United States." In *Violence in America*, vol. 1, *The History of Crime*, edited by Ted Robert Gurr. Newbury Park, CA: Sage.

Halpern, David. 2005. *Social Capital*. Malden, MA: Polity.

Harrendorf, Stefan, and Paul Smit. 2010. "Attributes of Criminal Justice Systems: Resources, Performance and Punitivity." In *International Statistics on Crime and Justice*, edited by Stefan Harrendorf, Markku Heiskanen, and Steven Malby. Helsinki: European Institute for Crime Prevention and Control and UN Office on Drugs and Control.

Hofstede, Geert. 2001. *Culture's Consequences: Comparing Values, Behaviors, Institutions and Organizations across Nations*. 2nd ed. Thousand Oaks, CA: Sage.

Höynck, T., U. Zähringer, and M. Behnsen. 2012. *Neonatizid: Expertise im Rahmen des Projekts "Anonyme Geburt und Babyklappen in Deutschland—Fallzahlen, Angebote, Kontexte."* München: Deutsches Jugendinstitut.

Hsieh, Ching-Chi, and M. D. Pugh. 1993. "Poverty, Income Inequality, and Violent Crime: A Meta-Analysis of Recent Aggregate Data Studies." *Criminal Justice Review* 19(2):182–202.

Inglehart, Ronald, and Christian Welzel. 2005. *Modernization, Cultural Change, and Democracy: The Human Development Sequence*. Cambridge: Cambridge University Press.

Jason, J., M. M. Carpenter, and C. W. Tyler Jr. 1983. "Underrecording of Infant Homicide in the United States." *American Journal of Public Health* 73(2):195–97.

Kääriäinen, Juha, Martti Lehti, Mikko Aaltonen, and Noora Ellonen. 2014. "Trends of Infanticides 1960–2009: Comparisons between 28 Countries." Unpublished manuscript. Helsinki: National Research Institute of Legal Policy.

Kaufmann, Daniel, Aart Kraay, and Massimo Mastruzzi. 2006. "Governance Matters V: Aggregate and Individual Governance Indicators for 1996–2005." World Bank Policy Research Working Paper no. 4012. Washington, DC: World Bank.

LaFree, Gary. 1998. *Losing Legitimacy: Street Crime and the Decline of Social Institutions in America.* Boulder, CO: Westview.

———. 1999. "A Summary and Review of Cross-National Comparative Studies on Homicide." In *Homicide Studies: A Sourcebook of Social Research,* edited by D. Smith and M. A. Zahn. Thousand Oaks, CA: Sage.

LaFree, Gary, and Andromachi Tseloni. 2006. "Democracy and Crime: A Multilevel Analysis of Homicide Trends in Forty-Four Countries, 1950–2000." *Annals of the American Academy of Political and Social Science* 605:26–49.

Lappi-Seppälä, Tapio. 2008. "Trust, Welfare, and Political Culture: Explaining Difference in National Penal Policies." In *Crime and Justice: A Review of Research,* vol. 37, edited by Michael Tonry. Chicago: University of Chicago Press.

———. 2013. "Imprisonment and Penal Demands: Exploring the Dimensions and Drivers of Systemic and Attitudinal Punitivity." In *The Routledge Handbook of European Criminology,* edited by Sophie Body-Gendrot, Mike Hough, Klara Kerezsi, René Lévy, and Sonja Snacken. New York: Routledge.

Lederman, Daniel, Norman Loayza, and Maria Menéndez. 2002. "Violent Crime: Does Social Capital Matter?" *Economic Development and Cultural Change* 50(3):509–39.

LeGrand, Catherine. 2003. "The Colombian Crisis in Historical Perspective: Part 1, Record in Progress." *Canadian Journal of Latin American and Caribbean Studies* 28(55/5):165–209. http://bailey83221.livejournal.com/58817 .html.

Lehti, Martti. 1997. *Viron henkirikollisuus 1990-luvulla.* Oikeuspoliittisen tutkimuslaitoksen julkaisuja 148. Helsinki: Oikeuspoliittinen tutkimuslaitos.

———. 2002. "Trends in Homicidal Crime in Estonia 1919–1999." In *Manslaughter, Fornication and Sectarianism: Norm-Breaking in Finland and the Baltic Area from Mediaeval to Modern Times.* Suomen tiedeakatemian toimituksia, Humaniora 319. Saarijärvi: Suomen tiedeakatemia.

———. 2013. *NRILP Comparative Homicide Time Series (NRILP-CHTS).* National Research Institute of Legal Policy Research Brief 32/2013. Helsinki: National Research Institute of Legal Policy. http://www.optula.om.fi/1368802881488.

Lenke, Leif. 1990. *Alcohol and Criminal Violence: Time Series Analyses in a Comparative Perspective.* Stockholm: Almqvist & Wicksell.

Lindström, Dag. 2008. "Homicide in Scandinavia: Long-Term Trends and Their Interpretations." In *Violence in Europe: Historical and Contemporary Perspectives,* edited by Sophie Body-Gendrot and Pieter Spierenburg. New York: Springer.

Lopez, Giselle. 2011. "The Colombian Civil War: Potential for Justice in a Culture of Violence." http://depts.washington.edu/jsjweb/wp-content/uploads/2011/05/JSJPRINTv1n2.-Lopez-G.pdf.

Lysova, Alexandra V., Nikolay G. Shchitov, and William Alex Pridemore. 2012. "Homicide in Russia, Ukraine, and Belarus." In *Handbook of European Homicide Research: Patterns, Explanations, and Country Studies,* edited by C. Marieke, A. Liem, and William Alex Pridemore. New York: Springer.

McAlister, Alfred L. 2006. "Acceptance of Killing and Homicide Rates in Nineteen Nations." *European Journal of Public Heath* 16(3):259–65.

Meslé, France, Valdimir M. Shkolnikov, Véronique Hertrich, and Jacques Vallin. 1996. *Tendances récentes de la mortalité par cause en Russie, 1965–1994.* Paris: INED.

Meslé, France, and Jacques Vallin. 2012. *Mortality and Causes of Death in 20th Century Ukraine.* Paris: INED.

Monkkonen, Eric H. 1975. *The Dangerous Class: Crime and Poverty in Columbus, Ohio, 1860–1885.* Cambridge, MA: Harvard University Press

Neapolitan, Jerome L. 1998. "Cross-National Variation in Homicides: Is Race a Factor?" *Criminology* 36(1):139–56.

Nisbett, Richard E., and Dov Cohen. 1996. *Culture of Honor: The Psychology of Violence in the South.* New York: Westview.

Nivette, Amy E. 2011. "Cross-National Predictors of Crime: A Meta-Analysis." *Homicide Studies: An Interdisciplinary and International Journal* 15(2):103–31.

Nivette, Amy E., and Manuel Eisner. 2013. "Do Legitimate Polities Have Fewer Homicides? A Cross-National Analysis." *Homicide Studies: An Interdisciplinary and International Journal* 17(1):3–26.

Österberg, Eva. 1991. "Kontroll och kriminalitet I Sverige från medeltid till nutid: Tendenser och tolkningar." *Scandia* 57:66–87.

———. 1996. "Criminality, Social Control, and the Early Modern State: Evidence and Interpretations in Scandinavian Historiography." In *The Civilization of Crime: Violence in Town and Country since the Middle Ages*, edited by Eric A. Johnson and Eric H. Monkkonen. Urbana: University of Illinois Press.

Österberg, Eva, and Dag Lindström. 1988. *Crime and Social Control in Medieval and Early Modern Swedish Towns.* Acta Universitatis Upsaliensis 152. Uppsala: Almqvist & Wiksell.

Ouimet, Mark. 2012. "A World of Homicides: The Effect of Economic Development, Income Inequality, and Excess Infant Mortality on the Homicide Rate for 165 Countries in 2010." *Homicide Studies: An Interdisciplinary and International Journal* 16(3):238–58.

Pampel, Fred C., and Rosemary Gartner. 1995. "Age Structure, Socio-political Institutions, and National Homicide Rates." *European Sociological Review* 11(3):243–60.

Pinheiro, Paulo Sérgio 2006. *World Report on Violence against Children.* http://www.unesco.org/new/en/social-and-human-sciences/themes/fight-against-discrimination/education-of-children-in-need/sv9/news/world_report_on_violence_against_children/.

Pinker, Steven. 2011. *The Better Angels of Our Nature: Why Violence Has Declined.* New York: Viking.

Pratt, Travis C., and Francis T. Cullen. 2005. "Assessing Macro-Level Predictors and Theories of Crime: A Meta-Analysis." In *Crime and Justice: A Review of Research*, vol. 32, edited by Michael Tonry. Chicago: University of Chicago Press.

Pridemore, William Alex. 2011. "Poverty Matters: A Reassessment of the Inequality-Homicide Relationship in Cross-National Studies." *British Journal of Criminology* 51:739–72.

Pridemore, William Alex, and Mitchell B. Chamlin. 2006. "A Time-Series Analysis of the Impact of Heavy Drinking on Homicide and Suicide Mortality in Russia, 1956–2002." *Addiction* 101:1719–29.

Rossow, I. 2001. "Alcohol and Homicide: A Cross-Cultural Comparison of the Relationship in 14 European Countries." *Addiction* 96(suppl. 1):S77–S92.

Roth, Randolph. 2009. *American Homicide*. Cambridge, MA: Harvard University Press.

Salla, Jako, Vania Ceccato, and Andri Ahven. 2012. "Homicide in Estonia." In *Handbook of European Homicide Research: Patterns, Explanations, and Country Studies*, edited by C. Marieke, A. Liem, and William Alex Pridemore. New York: Springer.

Sampson, Robert. 2006. "Collective Efficacy Theory: Lessons Learned and Directions for Future Inquiry." In *Taking Stock: The Status of Criminological Theory*, edited by Francis T. Cullen, John Paul Wright, and Kristie R. Blevins. London: Transaction.

Sharpe, James A. 1996. "Crime in England: Long-Term Trends and the Problem of Modernization." In *The Civilization of Crime: Violence in Town and Country since the Middle Ages*, edited by Eric A. Johnson and Eric H. Monkkonen. Urbana: University of Illinois Press.

Sirén, R. 2000. *Pahoinpitelyrikollisuus 1950–1997: Kehityspiirteitä ja kehitystä selittäviä tekijöitä*. Oikeuspoliittisen tutkimuslaitoksen julkaisuja 169. Helsinki: Oikeuspoliittinen tutkimuslaitos.

Skog, O.-J., and E. Björk. 1988. "Alkohol og voldskriminalitet: En analyse av utviklingen i Norge 1931–82." *Nordisk Tidsskrift for Kriminalvidenskab* 1988: 123.

Smit, M. D., and M. A. Zahn, eds. 1999. *Homicide: A Sourcebook of Social Research*. Thousand Oaks, CA: Sage.

Smit, Paul R., Rinke R. de Jong, and Catrien C. J. H. Bijleveld. 2012. "Homicide Data in Europe: Definitions, Sources, and Statistics." In *Handbook of European Homicide Research: Patterns, Explanations, and Country Studies*, edited by C. Marieke, A. Liem and William Alex Pridemore. New York: Springer.

Spierenburg, Pieter. 1996. "Long-Term Trends in Homicide: Theoretical Reflections and Dutch Evidence, Fifteenth to Twentieth Centuries." In *The Civilization of Crime: Violence in Town and Country since the Middle Ages*, edited by Eric A. Johnson and Eric H. Monkkonen. Urbana: University of Illinois Press.

———. 1998. "Knife Fighting and Popular Codes of Honor in Early Modern Amsterdam." In *Men and Violence: Gender, Honor, and Rituals in Modern Europe and America*, edited by Pieter Spierenburg. Columbus: Ohio State University Press.

———. 1999. "Sailors and Violence in Amsterdam, 17th–18th Centuries." In *Crime and Control in Europe from the Past to the Present*, edited by Mirkka

Lappalainen and Pekka Hirvonen. Publications of the History of Criminality Research Project. Helsinki: Helsinki University Press.

———. 2008. *A History of Murder: Personal Violence in Europe from the Middle Ages to the Present.* Cambridge: Polity.

———. 2012. "Long-Term Historical Trends of Homicide in Europe." In *Handbook of European Homicide Research: Patterns, Explanations, and Country Studies*, edited by C. Marieke, A. Liem, and William Alex Pridemore. New York: Springer.

Ståhlberg, Pia. 2008. "Lasten pahoinpitely. Kansainvälinen laki, kansalliset säädökset ja yhteiskuntatodellisuus. Pro gradu -työ. Oikeustieteellinen tiedekunta." Master's thesis, University of Helsinki, Faculty of Law.

Stockdale, Charles B., Michael B. Sauter, and Ashley C. Allen. 2011. "The States Doing the Most (and Least) to Spread the Wealth." http://247wallst.com/investing/2011/11/11/the-states-doing-the-most-and-least-to-spread-the-wealth/#ixzz329VXPnXR.

Trent, Carol L. S., and Alex Pridemore. 2012. "A Review of the Cross-National Empirical Literature on Social Structure and Homicide." In *Handbook of European Homicide Research: Patterns, Explanations, and Country Studies*, edited by C. Marieke, A. Liem, and William Alex Pridemore. New York: Springer.

Tursz, A., and J. M. Cook. 2011. "A Population-Based Survey of Neonaticides Using Judicial Data." *Archives of Disease in Childhood—Fetal and Neonatal Edition* 96(4):F259–F263.

Tyler, Tom. 2003. "Procedural Justice, Legitimacy, and the Effective Rule of Law." In *Crime and Justice: A Review of Research*, vol. 30, edited by Michael Tonry. Chicago: University of Chicago Press.

UNODC (UN Office on Drugs and Crime). 2011. *Global Study on Homicide: Trends, Contexts, Data.* Vienna: UNODC.

van Dijk, Jan, John van Kesteren, and Paul Smit. 2007. *Criminal Victimisation in International Perspective: Key Findings from the 2004–2005 ICVS and EU ICS.* The Hague: WODC.

Verkko, Veli. 1931. *Henki- ja pahoinpitelyrikollisuuden kehityssuunnan ja tason määräytymisestä. I ja II. Tilastollis metodologinen tutkimus.* Helsinki: Valtioneuvoston Kirjapain.

———. 1951. *Homicides and Suicides in Finland and Their Dependence on National Character.* Scandinavian Studies in Sociology, vol. 3. Copenhagen: G. E. C. Gads Forlag.

von Hofer, Hanns. 2012. *Brott och Straff i Sverige: Historisk kriminalstatistik 1750–2010. Diagram, tabeller och kommentarer.* Stockholm: Kriminologiska institutionen Stockholms universitet.

von Hofer, Hanns, and Tapio Lappi-Seppälä. 2014. "The Development of Crime in Light of Finnish and Swedish Criminal Justice Statistics, ca. 1750–2010." *European Journal of Criminology* 11(2):169–94.

World Advertising Research Center. 2005. *World Drink Trends, 2005.* Henley-on-Thames, UK: World Advertising Research Center.

Yarwood, D. J. 2004. *Child Homicide: Review of Statistics and Studies.* Ascot, UK: Dewar Research. http://www.dewar4research.org.

Ylikangas, Heikki. 1976. *Puukkojunkkareiden esiinmarssi: Väkivaltarikollisuus Etelä-Pohjanmaalla 1790–1825.* Keuruu, Finland: Otava.

———. 2001. "What Happened to Violence? An Analysis of the Development of Violence from Medieval Times to the Early Modern Era Based on Finnish Source Material." In *Five Centuries of Violence in Finland and the Baltic Area.* Columbus: Ohio State University Press.

Eric P. Baumer and Kevin T. Wolff

The Breadth and Causes of Contemporary Cross-National Homicide Trends

ABSTRACT

Analysis of international homicide trends from the late 1980s through the late 2000s for a relatively large sample of nations showed that trends did not vary substantially by victim sex or age. There was, however, significant regional variation in overall trends during the 1990s, suggesting that there was not a global drop in lethal violence during this period, or at least not something that occurred everywhere simultaneously. During the 2000s there appears to be growing convergence across nations, with notable declines in most by the middle of the decade. Multivariate analyses indicate that the observed declines are most strongly linked to reductions in poverty and urbanization and an increase in "youth oversight," the ratio of older to younger persons. No significant associations were observed between homicide trends and recent shifts in immigration, growth in imprisonment rates, and use of cellular phones and personal computers.

There is now an emerging consensus that rates of several forms of crime, including homicide, have fallen significantly since the early to mid-1990s in many parts of the world (LaFree and Drass 2001, 2002; LaFree 2005; LaFree and Tseloni 2006; Zimring 2007; Eisner 2008; Tseloni et al. 2010; Baumer 2011; van Dijk, Tseloni, and Farrell 2012). Yet, perhaps because the infrastructure for cross-national data analyses remains underdeveloped, the bulk of research on the possibility of a

Electronically published September 19, 2014
Eric P. Baumer is the Allen E. Liska Professor of Criminology and Criminal Justice, Florida State University. Kevin T. Wolff is assistant professor, John Jay College of Criminal Justice.

"global" crime drop during the 1990s and 2000s has focused on relatively narrow descriptions of the scope and magnitude of observed crime trends in a limited number of nations. Only a small body of studies has been directed at systematically identifying the key sources of those trends in a multinational, multivariate context (e.g., Neumayer 2003; Jacobs and Richardson 2008; Rosenfeld and Messner 2009; Buonanno et al. 2011; Messner et al. 2011; van Dijk, Tseloni, and Farrell 2012). In this analysis, we capitalize on recent expansions in the available data to attempt to contribute to existing knowledge of descriptive and explanatory dimensions of recent cross-national crime trends. We restrict our attention to lethal violence. Doing so minimizes concerns that patterns we uncover are due to differences in reporting and recording, which have been shown to be problematic in police-based data on nonlethal crimes (Aebi 2010). Focusing on homicide also enables us to assess contemporary trends across a relatively large sample of nations, an objective that is fundamental and is not currently possible with data on nonlethal victimization (Baumer 2011).

We pursue two avenues of inquiry. First, we consider in greater detail the breadth of the assumed contemporary cross-national drop in lethal violence, focusing on the nature of shifts in homicide during the past two decades across most of the major world regions and also across theoretically informative demographic groups. Our goal for this analysis is purely descriptive. We begin by posing the straightforward question of whether the observed temporal variation in homicide rates across nations during the past two decades yields a widely shared "global" pattern or whether instead there is evidence of divergent trends across world regions. This is an expansion of the geographic scope of much research on cross-national crime trends, which tends to be limited to relatively small samples of nations dominated by North America and Europe (for an exception based on police data, see Alvazzi del Frate and Mugellini [2012]). We also consider whether recent international trends in lethal violence are unique across demographic groups, focusing on possible sex and age differences. Some of the explanations proffered for recent homicide trends imply shifts that may have been unique to homicides against males and to lethal violence involving young persons. We explore that possibility by considering whether comparable homicide victimization trends are evident across nations since the late 1980s for males and females and for youths and young, middle-aged, and older adults. To our knowledge, previous research has not reported on these disaggregated homicide trends, at least for a relatively large number of nations.

Second, we expand existing assessments of factors that may be responsible for the recent cross-national decline in homicide. We do so by exploring whether some relatively neglected shifts in demography (e.g., age structure balance, immigration), lifestyle (trends in home computing and cell phone subscriptions), and collective sentiment (i.e., social trust, faith in government) that have occurred since the late 1980s in many parts of the world offer meaningful insights into the observed cross-national trends in homicide rates over this period, while also considering the more "usual suspects" (e.g., changes in poverty and wealth, income inequality, population size, sex ratios, urbanicity, and imprisonment rates).

We pursue these dual objectives by integrating data on levels of homicide from the World Health Organization and the National Research Institute of Legal Policy Comparative Homicide Time Series with data on potential explanatory factors from a wide variety of sources, including the World Bank, the United Nations, the European Values Survey, and the World Values Survey. The essay has five sections. Section I briefly summarizes existing knowledge about the nature of cross-national crime trends and illuminates some important gaps in prior descriptive research. The overarching focus of Section II is on identifying neglected subjects in the cross-national crime research portfolio. Section III describes the data assembled for our analysis. Results germane to the two general issues addressed are summarized in Section IV. In Section V, we outline our primary conclusions and describe what we see as the most pertinent needs for future research.

Three significant results emerge. First, we find uniform patterns in homicide victimization trends among males and females and among youths, young adults, and older adults from the late 1980s through the late 2000s. That pattern characterizes the vast majority of the nations included in our sample. This suggests that the major forces that underlie recent shifts in lethal violence are not highly specific to particular gender or age groups. This finding is especially informative as it adds to the body of evidence that calls into question the utility of cohort-based explanations of the crime drop, including those that emphasize the effects on particular cohorts of shifts in abortion laws and lead abatement (Anderson and Wells 2008; Kahane, Paton, and Simmons

2008; Dills, Miron, and Summers 2010; Buonnano et al. 2011; Farrell 2013).

Second, our analysis uncovers significant regional variation in overall homicide trends, especially during the 1990s, leading us to conclude that the widely chronicled drop in homicide during this period was not a global phenomenon. Since 2000, though, there appears to be growing convergence across nations, with most nations (even many in the Caribbean and South America) experiencing notable declines by the middle of the decade.

Third, we find little support for the idea that homicide trends are associated with recent shifts in immigration, growth in imprisonment, or the use of cellular phones and personal computers. We find that changes in cross-national homicide rates are most strongly linked to shifts in poverty, urbanization, and the ratio of older persons to younger persons, which we refer to as "youth oversight." Social scientific research has documented notable improvements in economic conditions across many nations during the period we looked at, including reductions in poverty (United Nations 2010; Chandy and Gertz 2011) and increases in gross domestic product (Bureau of Labor Statistics 2012). It is widely known that many societies have undergone significant demographic transitions, with older age cohorts growing in size and younger ones shrinking (UN Secretariat 2005). Also, while there is considerable cross-national variability with respect to patterns of urbanization, the proportions of populations residing in urban areas have declined in many nations during the past few decades (OECD 2010). These trends have been accompanied by significant reductions in overall homicide rates. Collectively, these factors help to account for a significant fraction of observed regional differences in homicide trends and explain a notable portion of the estimated linear change in homicide observed since the late 1980s.

These results lead us to conclude that shifting age structure balances, declines in urbanization, and reductions in poverty have played important roles in recent reductions in lethal violence that have been observed internationally. However, we acknowledge that additional research is needed before drawing strong conclusions. We included a fairly comprehensive empirical specification compared to previous studies, including nation and year fixed effects, but lacked complete time-varying indicators of some measures (e.g., faith in government) and could not include indicators of other factors that might be important (e.g., data on routine activities, parenting practices, morality, security measures). Additionally, even with more complete data, several complex methodological issues are inherent in analyzing multiple conditions over time and across places that can serve as obstacles to arriving at valid and reliable inferences (Greenberg 2014). Some of the potential culprits (e.g., issues of nonstationarity and cointegration) are probably not highly problematic in assessments of change over a relatively small number of time periods, which describes our effort, but others (e.g., endogeneity) are ubiquitous to the endeavor and fully satisfactory resolutions are very difficult to identify with nonexperimental designs.

We do not think that our findings regarding the roles of shifting age structure balance, urbanization, and poverty can be easily written off because of concerns about endogeneity, but we urge others to assess further the robustness of our results to alternative measures and analytical strategies. Finally, it is possible that some factors are associated with crime reductions in some nations but not in others. Most cross-national crime studies, including ours, assume invariant slopes across nations, which may be naïve and could have significant influence for the conclusions drawn. For instance, increases in imprisonment may reduce crime in places where the justice system is considered legitimate but may increase it in areas where there is deep suspicion regarding government authority. Similar propositions about cross-national variability in estimated slopes can be derived for other factors, too, and yet most cross-national studies of crime trends, including ours, assume that the measured factors have uniform effects across nations.

I. Contemporary Cross-National Homicide Trends

The collective image that emerges from the quickly growing cross-national literature on crime trends, though important nuances and exceptions have been documented, is that many nations have experienced a significant reduction in both violent and property crimes since the early to mid-1990s. This is least controversial in the United States, where many scholars have documented substantial declines in all forms of street crime since at least the early 1990s (Levitt 2004; Blumstein and Wallman 2006; Baumer 2008). Zimring (2007) chronicles the large crime drop that has occurred in New York City and many other US cities, dubbing the phenomenon "the Great American Crime Decline."

He also acknowledges, however, that Canada has experienced declines in most forms of crime since the early 1990s that closely resemble those observed in the United States.

Several sources indicate significant crime declines in many European nations since approximately the mid-1990s based on both victimization data and state-recorded data from police and medical examiners (van Dijk, van Kesteren, and Smit 2007; Walker et al. 2009). The observed declines, however, do not appear to have been uniform across all types of crime in Europe, especially with regard to nonlethal violence (e.g., van Dijk, Tseloni, and Farrell 2012). Moreover, there are noteworthy differences in timing and magnitude of the observed declines across nations that warrant close scrutiny (e.g., Messner et al. 2011). Yet, the general portrait that emerges is that levels of many forms of property crime and rates of lethal violence have declined significantly during the 1990s and 2000s, at least in North America, Europe, Oceania, and selected other nations elsewhere that have been included in samples that thus far have been scrutinized. The evidence of a fairly widespread crime decline is most clearly evident for lethal violence, for which Eisner (2008, pp. 310–11) concludes that since the early 1990s, "homicide rates in most European countries have been falling, in some cases quite dramatically." More recently, Messner et al. (2011) and Alvazzi del Frate and Mugellini (2012) document distinct downward trends in lethal violence during the 1990s among European nations and selected countries from other world regions, while also highlighting notable differences in the onset of the observed declines.

Taken as a whole, there is an abundant set of relatively rich descriptions of contemporary cross-national crime trends. These include a handful of multinational assessments of victimization and government-recorded data and several nation-specific analyses, many of which have produced insightful information (Baumer 2011). Nonetheless, important questions remain regarding the breadth of recent crime drops across nations and forms of crime. Two fundamental dimensions have been neglected: first, the degree to which contemporary trends in lethal violence have been comparable across different regions of the world and, second, whether observed declines in lethal violence have been shared across different demographic groups within various societies. In addition, other interesting descriptive questions remain largely unaddressed within a cross-national context because of data limitations, including whether there is a systematic pattern of timing and magnitude of recent crime trends across world regions and whether observed declines vary by situational features of crime, such as location in physical space, relationship between perpetrator and victim.

Regarding the comparability of homicide trends across nations, in our analysis, we expand the geographic breadth of previous descriptive analyses of cross-national trends by using data on lethal violence from a number of sources. Most of the recent research on international crime trends has focused on relatively small samples of nations dominated by North American and European societies, which is understandable but not very valuable for addressing whether the trends observed in these areas reflect more general global patterns. Indeed, recent studies of individual nations (Greenberg and Agozino 2012) and multinational studies (Alvazzi del Frate and Mugellini 2012) reveal reasons to suspect significant variability across nations. We go beyond recent assessments of the geographic breadth of the recent drop in lethal violence (Messner et al. 2011) by studying a relatively large sample of nations ($n = 86$) that span most regions of the world. Building on Alvazzi del Frate and Mugellini's (2012) recent analysis of data on police-recorded intentional homicides across 100 societies based on data obtained from the UN Survey of Crime Trends and Operations of Criminal Justice Systems, we adopt a more systematic assessment of homicide trends for a comparatively similar number of nations, and we focus on homicide rates measured through public health data systems, which yield fewer measurement concerns than police-based sources.

For a subsample of our cross-national sample, we also consider demographic differences in contemporary crime trends; these have not been extensively studied in the international literature. Although many forms of disaggregation are potentially of interest, sex- and age-specific patterns represent two fundamental considerations that have yet to be examined closely. Most explanations for contemporary crime trends are not uniquely applicable to violence against men, but much of the research at least implicitly assumes that recent temporal trends primarily reflect male-on-male violence. We thus consider whether there are notable differences in homicide victimization trends among males and females over the past two decades.

The potential theoretical value of considering age-specific trends is even greater. Such analyses can help to illuminate whether observed trends are a function mainly of things germane to particular age cohorts or whether, instead, they reflect shifting period conditions that operate on persons across cohorts. Research on US crime patterns indicates that the crime drop observed since the early 1990s has been prominent among both youths and adults (Cook and Laub 1998, 2002), suggesting that something about this era has shaped outcomes across multiple cohorts, and not just those who entered high-crime ages at that time. It is unclear, however, whether similar patterns are evident cross-nationally, which is a notable gap in knowledge given that some of the proposed explanations both in the United States and cross-nationally emphasize shifts (e.g., lead exposure and the abortion dividend) that are germane to particular age cohorts (Donohue and Levitt 2001; Nevin 2007; Kahane, Paton, and Simmons 2008), while most others are more general in scope (see Baumer and Wolff 2014). One objective of our analysis is to contribute to ongoing debates about such matters by broadening the descriptive assessment of contemporary cross-national homicide trends by examining whether comparable patterns are observed for youths and young adults, middle-aged adults, and older adults.

II. Explaining Contemporary Cross-National Homicide Trends

A second objective of this study is more general and also comparatively much more challenging: to evaluate whether selected, theoretically relevant factors have contributed to the observed cross-national crime trend patterns. There is a fairly substantial theoretical and empirical literature on cross-national crime trends, but much of it focuses on post–World War II crime trends and predates the contemporary period in which crime rates appear to have dropped significantly in many societies (e.g., Cohen and Felson 1979; Cantor and Land 1985; Cook and Zarkin 1985; Marvell and Moody 1991; LaFree 1998; Levitt 1999; Roberts and LaFree 2004). The recent crime drop has attracted quite a lot of insightful commentary about possible causal influences (Fukuyama 1999; LaFree 1999; Thome and Birkel 2007; Zimring 2007; Eisner 2008). However, this has translated into only a modest body of systematic empirical research, a good deal of which has focused on a small number of nations, and most frequently on the United States. Indeed, we could locate just a handful of multivariate studies that have focused on explaining the 1990s and 2000s crime drop across a relatively large sample of nations (e.g., Neumayer 2003; Jacobs and Richardson 2008; Rosenfeld and Messner 2009; Buonanno et al. 2011; Messner et al. 2011; van Dijk, Tseloni, and Farrell 2012). The dearth of systematic explanatory research makes the ongoing conversation interesting but also unsatisfying.

The literature is replete with theoretical discussions of possible explanations for the drop in crime rates that appears to have unfolded in many societies over the past two decades. Baumer and Wolff (2014) have organized the various explanations in terms, first, of conditions that constrain or channel the conduct of a population away from illegitimate activities; second, of shifts in physical or social settings or both that decrease the degree to which criminal propensities are activated or that permit existing constraints to operate more effectively; and, third, of conditions that serve to reduce the criminal motivation or propensities of the population at given times. The first two domains invoke factors such as demographic and economic conditions, cultural shifts, routine activities and lifestyle attributes, and criminal justice interventions that may exert widespread effects across many age groups within a particular period. The latter refers to early life experiences of a particular cohort that are realized in the form of lower rates of crime in subsequent periods as the cohort enters high-rate offending ages. For instance, some have argued that children born in the mid-1970s and beyond may have lower criminal propensities than their predecessors because of improved birthing conditions (Donohue and Levitt 2001), reduced lead exposure (Nevin 2007), or cultural shifts in child rearing that brought an increased focus on instilling self-control and discipline (Eisner 2008), each of which may have generated higher levels of self-control—a common marker of criminal propensity—among youths and young adults in the 1990s.

While many of the proposed explanations may have merit for advancing understanding of contemporary crime trends, some are likely to be particularly relevant for distinctive trends within particular nations (e.g., shifting policing and punishment strategies), while others are probably better situated for explaining changes in crime that are more "global" in nature (demographic changes, technological shifts, cultural change). In other words, some perspectives are better suited than others to explaining conditions that characterize many nations even if they unfold at different times and magnitudes (Baumer and Wolff 2014). The last observation parallels conclusions reached both from historical scholarship on broadly shared violence trends (Lane

1992) and from a recent assessment of the conceptual and empirical logic of theoretical explanations of the 1990s crime drop (Farrell 2013).

Drawing on these insights, we include in our analysis both factors that exhibit shifts that are highly variable across nations (e.g., imprisonment) and factors for which there is some evidence of meaningful shared changes across nations (e.g., economic output and demographic shifts). Both types of factors are important to consider because, as we report below, recent cross-national homicide trends reflect both a shared component and potentially important country differences. We consider a variety of commonly contemplated factors, including changes in poverty and wealth, divorce rates, income inequality, imprisonment rates, population growth, and urbanicity. However, drawing from contemporary discussions of multinational sociodemographic trends and key contributions to the crime trends literature, we also examine the effects of three additional sets of potentially germane factors that have exhibited notable changes in recent decades, can be measured from the currently available data, and have been largely neglected in prior cross-national crime trends research.

First, we highlight two major demographic shifts that may have enhanced social control, lessened the motivation for crime, or both since the late 1980s or early 1990s. These include a shifting "age structure balance" that may have promoted greater adult oversight of young persons, who tend to exhibit the highest crime rates in most societies, and changes in immigration levels, which have been linked to enhanced levels of social control through a variety of mechanisms. Second, we highlight selected technological innovations that could have reduced the attractiveness of potential crime targets and enhanced guardianship, such as increasing possession of mobile phones and use of personal home computers. Finally, we emphasize shifts in collective sentiments that could have reduced motivations for crime and strengthened social controls, focusing on changes in collective sentiment about fellow citizens and governments. We elaborate briefly on these issues below.[1]

---

[1] Other changes in contemporary society may also have had substantial effects on cross-national crime trends, including development of a largely "cashless society," systematic changes in how and where people spend their leisure time, widespread increases in levels of self-control, and shifts in use of security measures. We do not discuss these in depth here. As far as we know, these are untestable hypotheses in the context of a large-scale cross-national study, at least retrospectively.

A. Demographic Transitions

Demographic shifts are often included among possible explanatory candidates when crime rates exhibit notable changes, in part because demographic trends are routinely monitored but also because some elements of the demographic profile in a population, most notably its age structure, have been strongly linked to offending and victimization rates. For a variety of reasons including both motivational and constraint mechanisms (Greenberg 1977), crime tends to be disproportionately committed by and against teenagers and young adults, while rates of offending and victimization among older persons tend to be relatively low. It stands to reason, then, that when the average age in a population increases, aggregate crime rates should decline, at least in the absence of major shifts in cohort criminal propensities.

The "graying" of many nations in recent decades (UN Secretariat 2005) makes it understandable that shifts in age structure have been highlighted in discussions about the crime drop (O'Brien, Stockard, and Isaacson 1999; Phillips 2006). This is, however, a relatively simplistic demographic argument, especially in light of the nuanced ways in which age structure could affect other features of social life. In particular, economists and demographers routinely highlight not only gross numbers of persons within selected age groups but also the importance of age structure balance. This arises most often in the context of discussions about dependency or support ratios. For example, one concern stemming from the economics literature is the implication that large older cohorts in combination with relatively small younger cohorts raise questions about the availability of sufficient economic resources for support for the retirement generations (e.g., Cohen and Land 1987).

A similar logic might be usefully applied to analysis of cross-national trends in crime. The apparent reductions in crime rates may have occurred simply because there are fewer persons in age groups that are especially criminally active, but it also seems plausible that crime may be suppressed most significantly when there are relatively few persons in high-crime age groups and relatively many in age groups that are well equipped to provide social control of youths and young adults. We explore this possibility by integrating into our analysis of cross-national homicide trends the ratio of persons aged 45–64 to persons aged 15–24. Recent research (Baumer 2013) has shown that this measure, which we label *youth oversight*, exhibits trends that parallel in a converse manner homicide rates from 1960 through 2010 in selected nations, including those in which homicide rose and fell over this period (e.g., the United States) and places (e.g., Japan) that diverged notably from that pattern (Roberts and LaFree 2004). In preliminary analyses, we observed that the indicator of youth oversight that we use increased considerably in many nations over the period encompassed in our study. Below, we evaluate whether it yields the anticipated inverse relationship with recent homicide trends, net of other factors.

Another demographic feature that has been linked to recent crime trends in the United States (Stowell et al. 2009) and elsewhere (Bircan and Hooghe 2011; Buonanno et al. 2011; Bianchi, Buonanno, and Pinotti 2012) is the level of immigration. As with age structure, arguments link immigration to crime trends through both motivational and constraint mechanisms (Sampson 2008; Ousey and Kubrin 2009). Although some early theoretical framing and historical assessments of US trends drew attention to links between the co-occurrence of major immigration waves and crime increases in America (e.g., Shaw and McKay 1942; Gurr 1989), the empirical evidence has long indicated that in most settings immigrants tend to exhibit crime rates comparable to and, in many instances, lower than those of natives (Tonry 1997). More recent studies have bolstered the empirical basis for the latter conclusion during the contemporary era (Sampson, Morenoff, and Raudenbush 2005). This has led to speculation that increases in immigrant populations during the 1990s may have yielded crime reductions through positive selection processes (e.g., Ousey and Kubrin 2009). Others have suggested that the rise in immigration rates in the 1990s may have reduced crime in America by bringing a heavy dose of prosocial norms about conflict resolution, increasing family stability and collective efficacy, and bolstering economies in areas in which immigrants settled, thereby increasing informal social control and reducing pressures to engage in illicit conduct (see Sampson 2008). Though the specific causal mechanisms remain uncertain, several empirical studies of recent US crime trends find evidence consistent with the prediction of a significant inverse association between immigration and crime (Ousey and Kubrin 2009; Stowell et al. 2009; Martinez, Stowell, and Lee 2010; Wadsworth 2010; Harris and Feldmeyer 2013).

Relatively few studies of cross-national crime trends have incorporated data on immigration levels (for an exception, see Bianchi, Buonanno, and Pinotti [2012]), though there is a fairly robust literature on the causes and consequences of international migration on other out-comes, including the structure and functioning of labor markets, set-tlement patterns, social integration, and economic development (e.g., Sanderson 2013). A clear image emerges from that literature that par-allels the nuanced findings that tend to emerge in studies of immigra-tion and crime: the influence of increased levels of international mi-gration on a wide spectrum of outcomes is likely to be highly contingent on a variety of internal national dynamics. A general pre-diction that follows is that immigration tends to yield positive conse-quences when prevailing conditions are more conducive to the social and economic integration of recent migrants. For example, Sanderson (2013) documents how the influence of international migration on eco-nomic development is likely to depend on the pace of recent popula-tion growth from other sources, namely, fertility levels. As he puts it, countries with "slower population growth rates might have more ca-pacity to absorb cumulative immigration inflows, allowing the positive effects of immigration to become apparent over time . . . [while in] . . . countries with higher population growth rates, immigration might place additional burdens on host social structures, further straining health and education infrastructures, exacerbating unemployment, heightening competition in labour markets and lowering aggregate wages" (p. 8). If one were to apply a similar logic to crime trends, the implication would be that the effect of increases in international mi-gration on crime trends may be contingent on recent population growth rates.

Immigration scholars have adopted a similar "conditioning" logic in relation to the role of economic structures in channeling the conse-quences of heightened immigration (Martinez and Lee 2000). The for-mal economy understandably has received the greatest attention in this regard, with the basic idea being that immigrants are more apt to thrive and yield greater benefits for communities when they have a steady stream of good opportunities in the conventional economy. Thus, im-migration may be less likely to yield negative outcomes (e.g., social and economic disruption and heightened levels of crime) and more likely to have positive impacts (e.g., enhanced social cohesion, elevated in-formal social control, and reduced crime) when it occurs in a context of thriving economic conditions. This reasoning need not be restricted to the formal economy, however. For example, some economists have suggested that a more robust informal or hidden economy can provide an important safety net for vulnerable populations who may not have easy access to the formal economy, a situation that often characterizes recent migrants in many national settings (see Kus 2010). Taken together, the insights summarized herein suggest that any effects of international migration trends on cross-national crime may be contingent on the nature of recent population growth and the health of both formal and informal economic structures. We explore these possibilities by examining both the main effect of international migration on homicide trends and whether the observed effect differs notably across time and space, specifically, whether it is moderated by broader population changes and common metrics of the performance of the formal and informal economic sectors.

B. Changes in Lifestyle

Though a large portion of the scholarly discussion of the crime drop has focused on changes in offender motivation and the amount of social control applied to offenders or those contemplating crime, substantial drops in crime could occur without major changes in these things (Cohen and Felson 1979). This could be the case if there were notable shifts in the physical surroundings and social settings in which crime may flourish. It has been well documented that there were significant changes in such factors during the 1970s and 1980s as crime increased in many parts of the world. Among others, Cohen and Felson (1979) document and make a compelling case that among the key elements of the shifting social context during this period was a substantial movement in daily activities away from the home and various technological advances (e.g., smaller electronic goods) that combined to yield more plentiful and more attractive opportunities for crime. These broad social trends were observed across many parts of the developed world, as were crime increases (Eisner 2008).

Since the mid- to late 1980s, a variety of broad shifts in lifestyle, technology, and social organization have proliferated that can be described as countertrends to the movement of people away from homes and surveillance sources during the 1960s and 1970s. Putnam (2000) suggests that social interactions have shifted increasingly from the public to the private (and virtual) sphere during the past several decades, a process that has been driven to some degree by the increased use of computers in the home and the "Internet revolution." In theory, such patterns could reduce the exposure of individuals to motivated offenders and increase the guardianship of homes, both of which have been tied to elevated levels of crime, including lethal violence (Cohen and Felson 1979). Another modern technological innovation that has been relatively widespread across nations is the increased use of mobile phones. The prevalence of mobile telephone subscriptions increased considerably during the 1990s and 2000s, and this may have yielded lower crime rates by creating a public environment with greater "guardianship" for individuals than was the case in previous eras and also by enhancing the deterrent capacity of criminal justice approaches (Klick, MacDonald, and Stratmann 2012). Orrick and Piquero's (forthcoming) national-level analysis provides some evidence of a significant negative association between cell phone subscription rates and property crime rates (but not violence) from 1984 through 2009, but the findings appear to be highly sensitive to empirical specification. Klick, MacDonald, and Stratmann provide a more rigorous assessment in a panel analysis of American states from 1997 through 2007, observing a fairly robust negative relationship between cell phone subscription rates and violent crime rates, but not property crime. We extend recent research efforts by evaluating whether contemporary cross-national crime trends have been responsive to trends in cell phone subscriptions, while also considering the possible role of growth in home computing, which to our knowledge has not been considered in prior studies.

C. Changes in Collective Sentiments

Prominent accounts of historical and contemporary shifts in crime, including homicide, posit that changes in collective sentiments and attachments may be an important component of the cross-national crime trends puzzle (e.g., Elias 1978; LaFree 1998; Garland 2001; Roth 2009; Messner et al. 2011). LaFree (1999) made a compelling case that the crime boom of the 1960s and 1970s was in part a function of declining faith in government, an argument he later suggested as potentially relevant to the 1990s US crime "bust" as well. Roth (2009) echoes such sentiments in a rich historical account of major shifts in homicide in America and elsewhere, highlighting also the potential importance of trust among individuals (see also Rosenfeld, Messner, and Baumer 2001). More recently, Karstedt (2013) has blended these ideas with insights from research and theory about the mutually reinforcing tendencies of collective sentiments about trust and the efficacy of political institutions (e.g., Robbins 2012). Karstedt suggests that societal arrangements that promote social trust and enhance the fidelity of government-citizen interactions yield a "thick" institutional context in which cross-national differences in more peaceful relationships emerge and interpersonal violence is reduced.

Collectively, this body of literature suggests that increasing levels of social trust and faith in government may be part of the explanation for recently observed reductions in lethal violence across nations. The theoretical arguments point to possible independent effects of social trust among citizens and faith in government but also that these dimensions of collective sentiment may interact in producing lower levels of violence. These possibilities are intriguing, but their empirical validity is not well established. Aside from some persuasive historical accounts (Roth 2009) and suggestive anecdotal evidence (LaFree 1998; Karstedt 2013), there has been relatively little systematic research on the link between homicide rates and indicators that gauge faith or confidence in government. Prior research has devoted greater attention to assessing the link between social trust and homicide in cross-national samples. The evidence from the handful of existing studies is somewhat mixed (see Lederman, Loayza, and Menendez 2002; Robbins and Pettinicchio 2012), but the most rigorous research suggests that homicide rates and indicators of generalized social trust are not significantly associated once other factors are considered (Robbins 2013). We extend inquiry in this area by evaluating the violence reduction potential of social trust and faith in government, considering both additive and possible multiplicative effects. We specifically consider whether recent cross-national homicide trends differ according to observed changes in levels of social trust and faith in government by integrating aggregate-level survey responses from a database that integrates the European Values Survey and the World Values Survey.

III. Data and Methods

We address the issues outlined above by integrating data from a variety of sources and analyzing both descriptive trends and explanatory models. In this section, we describe how we approach these objectives, including the time frame and samples used, the measures included, and the analytical strategies applied.

A. General Approach

Our analysis focuses on modeling overall and demographic-specific homicide victimization trends from the late 1980s through the late 2000s. We examine average homicide trends for this period, the nature of any observed variation across nations, and the capacity of several explanatory variables to account for the observed temporal patterns. These objectives are pursued by merging data on total intentional homicides from the National Research Institute of Legal Policy Comparative Homicide Time Series (NRILP-CHTS; Lehti 2013), data on age-specific homicide from the World Health Organization (WHO), and national-level indicators of changes in demography, technological innovation, and collective sentiment from a variety of sources.[2]

B. Time Frame and Samples

The descriptive portion of our analysis is based on analyses of annual homicide data from 1989–2008. Our assessment of trends in total homicide rates from the NRILP-CHTS encompasses 86 nations, which represent the maximum sample for which we can discern temporal variability in homicide trends across nations from the sources we consider to be most appropriate for the task at hand (i.e., public health data collections) with a minimal number of missing observations within nations.[3] We obtained homicide data disaggregated by victim sex from the NRILP-CHTS for 67 of these nations and age-specific homicide victimization data from the WHO for 46 of the nations. These are the largest samples for which we could locate the requisite annual homicide data for purposes of describing contemporary trends.

We focus our analysis of explanatory factors on total homicide rates. This component of our analysis is structured differently than the descriptive portion. Because many of the explanatory variables of interest are not available on an annual basis, and in some cases are available only sporadically over the study period, we define a set of grouped periods (i.e., waves) that serve as time points for our explanatory analysis of cross-national homicide trends. We use the annual homicide

---

[2] A description of the homicide data and details about how they can be accessed are available at http://www.optula.om.fi/material/attachments/optula/julkaisut/verkko katsauksia-sarja/w2p2O9sqF/kansainv_linen_henkirikollisuus_32_eng.pdf. WHO data are available at http://www.who.int/violence_injury_prevention/surveillance/databases/mortality/en/.

[3] We include nations in our descriptive analysis only if data are available for at least 15 of the 20 years observed.

data to construct 3-year average homicide rates, which we then analyze over five multiyear periods: 1989–91, 1993–95, 1997–99, 2001–3, and 2005–7. These are the periods for which we observe levels of homicide; as we elaborate below, we integrate explanatory variables that are lagged by 1 year in relation to these defined time points to satisfy the logic of the implied theoretical mechanisms.

We were able to locate data for most of the explanatory variables of interest for 65 of the 86 nations that represent the maximum sample assessed in our descriptive analyses. We lose some additional cases, however, when we consider more comprehensive models that include measures for which valid data are less widely available. In general, our multivariate models of homicide trends are based on samples ranging from about 40 nations to 65 nations. We provide details below.

C. Measures

Table 1 provides definitions and sources for the dependent, control, and explanatory variables considered in our analysis. We elaborate briefly in the text to clarify a few points and explain the logic of some of the measures.

Our measures of total and sex-specific homicide rates are drawn from the NRILP-CHTS (Lehti 2013), while age-specific homicide rates were obtained from the WHO. The total homicide rate in our analysis reflects the number of intentional homicides per 100,000 residents recorded by national or international public health organizations. We separately consider homicide victimization rates against males and females and against youths/young adults (ages 15–29), middle-aged adults (ages 30–44), and older adults (ages 45–59), all represented as victimizations per 100,000 residents in these demographic groups. We log each of the homicide measures in our analysis because they exhibit significant skewness.

We include several national-level indicators of recent shifts in demography, socioeconomics, lifestyle, and collective sentiment. The original sources of the measures are listed in table 1, but in many instances we were able to gain access to the data though a reputable online data portal (Gapminder World) that is highly useful for cross-national research.[4] In general, we incorporate variables that reflect con-

---

[4] Gapminder World centralizes cross-national data from a wide variety of sources, including the WHO, the UN, the World Bank, and various other sources (see http://www.gapminder.org).

ditions approximately 2 years prior to the periods in which we observe the homicide measures. In most instances, as we elaborate below, we incorporate in our analysis a measure of each variable that reflects the mean value across the five time periods and a measure that reflects a centered value (around this mean) for each time period. The former represent between-country differences in the explanatory variables within each wave, while the latter reflect within-nation variation in those variables over time. Our emphasis is on the latter time-varying measures and their relationships with changes in homicide rates.

Some of the variables listed in table 1 are treated as "control variables," but this should not be construed as a judgment that they are theoretically unimportant. Instead, they are simply not a major focus of our study for various reasons. In some cases, the reason is that the measures are often included in studies of cross-national crime rates and thus need not be discussed extensively. These include income inequality, divorce rates, the sex ratio, logged population size, and the percentage of the population that resides in urban areas. The same comment applies to two indicators—gross domestic product (GDP) and infant mortality rates—that exhibited a strong inverse correlation in our data and thus were combined into a factor variable that we label "poverty" (GDP was reverse coded). This decision builds on recent studies that have included GDP but also have used infant mortality rates as a proxy for poverty levels (Pridemore 2008; Messner et al. 2011). Some of the other control variables (e.g., female labor force participation, imprisonment rates) have infrequently been assessed in cross-national studies of crime trends, especially research that encompasses several nations (e.g., Jacobs and Kleban 2003), but are included because they have been linked to homicide and are commonly encompassed in cross-sectional research (Nivette 2011).

A few of the explanatory variables considered are variations on fairly standard themes (e.g., the ratio of older to younger persons) and need not be elaborated beyond the description provided in table 1. But others have not been dealt with as extensively in prior cross-national crime research, and so we comment briefly on them.

We measure recent immigration with data on trends in international migration stock obtained from the UN Population Division (Bell and Edwards 2013), which is at the present time the most global and comparable source of international migration available (Sanderson 2013). The UN defines an international migrant as one who is living in a

TABLE 1

Description of Variables Included in Analysis of Cross-National Crime Trends

Variable	Definition and Source
Dependent variables:	
Logged homicide rate	Number of homicides per 100,000 residents (source: NIRLP Public Health Data)
Logged male and female homicide rates	Number of homicide victimizations per 100,000 males and per 100,000 females (source: NIRLP Public Health Data)
Logged youth, young adult, and adult homicide rates	Number of homicide victimizations among 15–29-year-olds, 30–44-year-olds, and 45–59-year-olds per 100,000 within each age group (source: WHO)
Control variables:	
Poverty	Two-item factor that combines infant mortality rates per 1,000 live births and the national GDP per capita (reverse coded) (source: World Bank)
Gini index of income inequality	Gini index of inequality of household disposable income (source: Standardized World Income Inequality Database, vers. 3.1; Solt 2009)
Female labor force participation	Percentage of females aged 15–64 in labor force (source: International Labor Organization, accessed through Gapminder World)
Sex ratio	Number of males per 100 females (source: United Nations)
% urban	Percentage of total population in urban areas (source: World Bank)
Logged population	Logged population (source: United Nations)
Logged imprisonment rate	Logged number of persons in prison per 100,000 (sources: Eurostat, OECD, various others)
Divorce rate	Number of divorces per 1,000 persons (sources: United Nations, various others)
Explanatory variables:	
Youth oversight	Ratio of the older population to the younger population (45–64/15–24) (source: United Nations)
Recent immigration	Change in percentage foreign-born during prior 5 years (source: United Nations)
Informal economy	Difference in annual changes of electric consumption and annual changes in GDP (sources: US Energy Information Administration, World Bank)
Cell phone subscription rate	Mobile cellular subscriptions per 100 people (source: World Bank)
Personal computers per capita	Personal computers being used per 100 people (source: United Nations)
Social trust	Change in the percentage of respondents who indicate they trust others (source: EVS/WVS)

TABLE 1 (*Continued*)

Variable	Definition and Source
Faith in government	Three-item factor that combines changes in the percentage of respondents who indicate they have quite a lot or a great deal of confidence in parliament, the justice system, and the police (source: EVS/WVS)

SOURCE.—US Energy Information Administration: http://www.eia.gov/countries/ data.cfm; NRILP-CHTS: Lehti (2013); OECD: http://statlinks.oecdcode.org/30201 0061P1T111.XLS%29; United Nations: http://unstats.un.org/unsd/databases.htm; World Bank: http://data.worldbank.org/indicator; EVS/WVS: http://www.wvsevsdb .com/wvs/WVSIntegratedEVSWVS.jsp?Idioma = I; WHO: http://www.who.int/ violence_injury_prevention/surveillance/databases/mortality/en/index.html; Gapminder World: http://www.gapminder.org/data/; Eurostat: http://epp.eurostat.ec.europa.eu/ statistics_explained/index.php/Crime_statistics.

country that is not her or his country of birth, which in the majority of instances is determined by questions on foreign-born status in national censuses but in some cases is based instead on reports of national citizenship. In geopolitical contexts in which there are substantial numbers of refugees who are unlikely to be counted in official census tabulations, the UN adjusts total counts of international migrants with data on the presence of refugees from several sources (e.g., the UN High Commissioner for Refugees, UN Relief and Works Agency for Palestinian Refugees in the Near East). The UN has published estimates of the international migration stock for 10-year intervals for a large number of nations spanning the period 1950–2010. Though stock measures of immigration are potentially meaningful for studies of crime, measures of recent immigration flows strike us as more germane. Thus, we used available data from 1980–2010 to interpolate annual estimates of the foreign-born population and then computed the percentage change over the 5 years preceding each wave of our analysis to define recent immigration.

The volume of informal economic activity in nations has not been used extensively in extant studies of crime trends, but we explore whether a proxy measure of this phenomenon conditions the effects of recent international migration on crime. There is a sizable literature on the problems and prospects of various direct and indirect approaches to identifying the volume of unrecorded, hidden economic activity in a nation (e.g., Williams 2004; Feige and Urban 2008; Kus 2010). For the purposes of our analysis, we measure changes in the size of hidden economic activity across time and nations using the "electricity method." Several studies have documented that electric consumption is a highly valid indicator of overall economic activity in many societies, and thus one indication of growth in unofficial or un-recorded economic activity can be derived by subtracting growth in official GDP from growth in electric consumption; if the latter expands or contracts at a greater rate than the former, it is assumed to reflect "hidden" economic activities. We apply this logic, measuring temporal shifts in the size of the informal economy by computing the difference between annual changes in electric consumption and annual changes in GDP per capita. Higher values are assumed to reflect greater growth in the volume of informal economic activity.

Finally, as described in table 1, we obtained indicators of changes in interpersonal trust and faith/confidence in government institutions from a database that integrates the European Values Survey (EVS) and the World Values Survey (WVS). The measure of trust is based on a single item in which respondents from different nations are asked whether they trust others. We aggregate responses within nations to construct the percentage of respondents within each nation who in-dicated that most people can be trusted, a measure we label "changes in social trust." The integrated EVS/WVS database yields measures of social trust for differing samples of nations on five separate occasions from the early 1980s through the end of our observation period, but only a very small number of nations in our sample participated in every wave. Thus, it is not feasible to construct wave-specific time-varying indicators of social trust for our analysis. In lieu of doing that, we created a cross-sectional (i.e., static) measure that reflects the percent-age change between the earliest and latest waves in which each nation participated. In the majority of instances, this enables us to gauge changes in social trust from the early to mid-1980s through the mid-2000s, and our analysis evaluates whether trends in homicide differ across nations that exhibit varying degrees of changes in levels of social trust.

The EVS/WVS integrated database also serves as the source for our measure of "faith in government," which we construct using proce-dures similar to those described for the indicator of social trust. One difference, however, is that we use three survey items to measure faith in government. Specifically, we obtained from the EVS/WVS data on the degree of confidence respondents have in parliament, the justice system, and the police, respectively. We aggregated responses to the items within nations to compute the percentage of respondents who indicated that they have quite a lot or a great deal of confidence in these government entities and then in each case computed cross-sectional measures of change between the earliest and last waves available. We then conducted a factor analysis of the static measures of change in levels of confidence in parliament, the justice system, and the police, finding that each loaded strongly on a single dimension, which we label "changes in government confidence."

D. Analytic Strategy

We use a mixed-model regression approach to pursue our descriptive and explanatory objectives. To assess cross-national trends in total and demographically disaggregated homicide, we estimate a series of two-level hierarchical linear models in which temporal observations are nested within nations. This approach is fairly common in crime trends research (e.g., Rosenfeld, Fornango, and Baumer 2005; Phillips and Greenberg 2008; LaFree, Baumer, and O'Brien 2010). It is particularly attractive for our purposes because it provides an accessible and efficient means by which to summarize average homicide trends for the sample of nations in our study and to illuminate the degree of variability in those trends across nations. The mixed-modeling strategy is quite flexible: it is robust to unbalanced panels that arise from missing data on covariates, and it allows us to estimate coefficients for both time-varying and time-stable explanatory variables. The latter is important because it enables us efficiently to consider regional differences in trends and also key explanatory variables of interest, such as the cross-sectional indicators of changes in social trust and government confidence.

The descriptive section of our analysis is summarized well by a series of simple two-level mixed models in which time-varying logged homicide rates are nested within nations. This component of our analysis is structured annually. Homicide rates are observed for each nation for a minimum of 15 and a maximum of 20 years of data for the period 1989–2008 (complete data are available for the vast majority of nations). Using this criterion, we report below estimated trends in total homicide rates for 86 nations; gender- and age-specific trends are estimated for 67 and 46 nations, respectively.

We also estimate two-level hierarchical linear models for the explanatory component of our analysis. To facilitate this, we focus on modeling logged homicide rates across the five waves (i.e., 1989–91, 1993–95, 1997–99, 2001–3, and 2005–7) as a function of explanatory and control variables that are lagged by 1 year in relation to these defined time points. As noted earlier, the bulk of the analysis is based on 65 nations, but we also present results from models based on smaller samples because data on a specified measure were unavailable for some countries.

The general specification we adopt in the explanatory models includes time period dummies, mean-centered time-varying covariates, and corresponding mean levels for all of the covariates. By mean-centering the time-varying indicators and including nation-specific (i.e., time-invariant) means in these indicators, the model parallels a fixed-effects specification and eliminates the potential that the estimates are confounded with country differences in the explanatory variables (see also Phillips and Greenberg 2008; LaFree, Baumer, and O'Brien 2010). Preliminary analysis revealed significant serial correlation, so we also include in our models an AR(1) error term. Additionally, for all estimations presented below, we report standard errors clustered by nation, which accounts for the nonindependence of observations within countries and minimizes potential bias associated with serial correlation and nonstationarity (Greenberg 2014). With this specification, temporal variation in logged homicide rates across the five waves included in our study is modeled as a function of nation-specific time-varying circumstances, controlling for unobserved temporal changes that are shared across nations.

IV. Results

We focus on two general empirical issues: whether contemporary cross-national homicide trends exhibit similar patterns across world regions and different demographic groups and whether selected indicators of changing demography, lifestyle, and collective sentiment have been importantly associated with the observed trends in homicide cross-nationally.

A. Overall Trends and Geographic Variation in Homicide Rates

Table 2 reports the mixed-model estimated trend (i.e., linear and quadratic) parameters for total logged homicide rates observed an-

TABLE 2

Logged Homicide Rates Regressed on Linear and
Quadratic Time Variables for 86 Nations
(1989–2008)

	Model 1	Model 2
Fixed effects:		
Year	−.008	.039*
	(.006)	(.015)
Year^2	. . .	−.002*
		(.0007)
Intercept	1.28*	1.14*
	(.132)	(.133)
Random effects variances:		
Nation	1.15*	1.15*
Year	.044*	.040*
Year^2	. . .	.001*
Residual	.815*	.810*
Nation sample	86	86
Nation-period sample	1,628	1,628

* $p \leq .05$.

nually from 1989 through 2008. The best-fitting equation (model 2) indicates a significant curvilinear average trend in logged homicide rates, which is denoted by the fixed effects for year and year squared. The random-effects variance parameters also reveal, however, statistically significant and substantively important variability across nations both in logged homicide rates at the beginning of the time period (designated by the significant "nation" random effect) and in the predicted homicide trend parameters (designated by the significant random effects for year and year squared). The average trend across nations implied by the estimated parameters shown in table 2 is plotted in figure 1, which illuminates a pattern that should not be surprising: homicide rates generally increased through the mid-1990s but have since fallen considerably.

Perhaps the most important findings reported in table 2 are the significant cross-country variance trend parameters, which suggest meaningful departures across nations in the pattern displayed in figure 1. We explored cross-national variability in homicide trends by estimating parallel mixed models for 11 distinct world regions reflected in our sample, as defined by the UN. To minimize potential distortions that can arise from estimated homicide trends in smaller nations, we

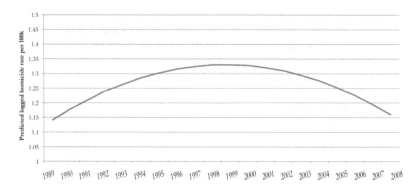

FIG. 1.—Estimated trend in logged homicide rates across 86-nation sample, 1989–2008

weight the data within regions by country population size. The results are displayed in table 3.

We highlight two overall conclusions from table 3. The first is that, in contrast to the idea that there has been a uniform "global" drop in lethal violence during the past two decades, we observe significant heterogeneity in the nature of changes in logged homicide rates from 1989 to 2008 (see also Alvazzi del Frate and Mugellini 2012). For instance, many European nations exhibit a steady linear decline in homicide throughout this period (see panels 1–3), but this is not evident for eastern Europe (panel 4), which instead experienced rising homicide through the 1990s and early 2000s, with decreases observed only during the 2000s. More generally, while there is clear evidence that several regions exhibit marked declines in lethal violence over this period, there is substantial variation in the estimated trends across nations. We illuminate the essence of that variability by grouping together regions that yield comparable trend parameters in table 3, reestimating the models based on the nations contained within those groupings and computing the trends implied by the estimates. We converted the group-specific predicted trends into z-scores to facilitate meaningful comparisons, which are presented in figure 2.

Figure 2 illuminates the noted significant steady decreases in logged homicide rates observed in the sampled nations from Oceania and western, southern, and northern Europe, a group that parallels observed trends in the 14 Asian nations included in our analysis so closely that the line designating the latter is hidden by the former. North America also experienced large decreases over this period, but they

TABLE 3

Logged Homicide Rates Regressed on Linear and Quadratic Time Variables for Selected World Regions (1989–2008)

	Model 1	Model 2		Model 1	Model 2
1. Western Europe ($n = 6$):			7. Central America ($n = 6$):		
Year	−.035*	−.011	Year	−.021	−.014
	(.005)	(.011)		(.016)	(.018)
Year^2	. . .	−.001	Year^2	. . .	−.0004
		(.0007)			(.0004)
Intercept	.254*	.185*	Intercept	2.91*	2.89*
	(.027)	(.025)		(.117)	(.126)
2. Southern Europe ($n = 8$):			8. South America ($n = 11$):		
Year	−.032*	−.040	Year	.020*	.055*
	(.016)	(.041)		(.009)	(.012)
Year^2	. . .	.0004	Year^2	. . .	−.002*
		(.001)			(.0006)
Intercept	.577*	.597*	Intercept	2.72*	2.61*
	(.237)	(.297)		(.326)	(.296)
3. Northern Europe ($n = 10$):			9. Western and central Asia ($n = 8$):		
Year	−.013*	−.002	Year	−.053*	.029
	(.004)	(.010)		(.013)	(.026)
Year^2	. . .	−.0006	Year^2	. . .	−.005*
		(.0006)			(.001)
Intercept	.315	.282	Intercept	1.35	1.12*
	(.271)	(.239)		(.456)	(.449)
4. Eastern Europe ($n = 10$):			10. Eastern and southern Asia ($n = 6$):		
Year	−.007	.113*	Year	−.026*	.010
	(.010)	(.026)		(.012)	(.018)
Year^2	. . .	−.006*	Year^2	. . .	−.002*
		(.0009)			(.0005)
Intercept	2.35*	2.00*	Intercept	.696	.588
	(.400)	(.353)		(.718)	(.708)
5. North America ($n = 3$):			11. Oceania ($n = 2$):		
Year	−.031*	−.061*	Year	−.043*	−.002
	(.003)	(.002)		(.006)	(.017)
Year^2	. . .	.002*	Year^2	. . .	−.002
		(.0002)			(.001)
Intercept	2.15*	2.24*	Intercept	.819*	.696
	(.248)	(.236)		(.024)	(.045)
6. Caribbean ($n = 16$):					
Year	.003	.066			
	(.015)	(.039)			
Year^2	. . .	−.003*			
		(.002)			
Intercept	2.14*	1.91*			
	(.167)	(.206)			

NOTE.—All models include random effects for the time variables.

* $p \leq .05$.

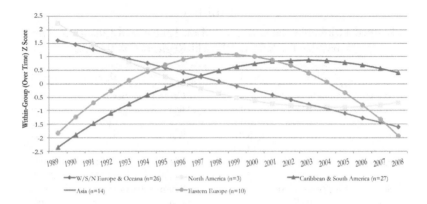

FIG. 2.—Estimated trends in logged homicide rates from 1989 to 2008 across 86-nation sample, by region.

have slowed during the 2000s (this is evidenced by the significant positive quadratic parameter reported in table 3). As noted, however, trends in lethal violence for eastern Europe diverge from these patterns. Additionally, the estimated trends for the Caribbean and South American nations in our sample are quite different from those observed in the other groupings. There was an upward trend in logged homicide during the 1990s in both of these divergent instances, with declines beginning in eastern Europe later than in most other nations (in the late 1990s and early 2000s) and only slight evidence of the beginnings of a downward trend in the Caribbean and Southern American nations during the 2000s.

On balance, these results indicate that cross-national trends in homicide rates do not follow a uniform pattern and, more to the point, that the contemporary drop in homicide rates observed in some parts of the world is not a global phenomenon, at least not in the sense of a widespread shared decline that occurred more or less simultaneously over the period assessed in our study.[5] It is worth highlighting, how-

[5] We reached a similar conclusion from a supplementary analysis in which we applied methods advanced by McDowall and Loftin (2009) for parsing shared and unique temporal variation in crime trends. This method entails the estimation of two econometric panel models of crime rates (in our case, logged homicide rates) for a sample of cross-sectional units (one with only cross-sectional fixed effects and one with these plus period fixed effects) and evaluation of the percentage of the variation explained by the period fixed effects (which reflect shared trends across the cross-sectional units) that remains after accounting for cross-sectional heterogeneity, which can be summarized in the form of a squared partial correlation. We applied this method to the

ever, that during the 2000s there appears to be greater convergence across nations, with most exhibiting notable decreases by this time. It should prove interesting to see if this trend continues over the next decade or so, and if it does, we would modify our conclusion about the global nature of contemporary homicide reductions. Such an outcome would suggest that homicide reductions have merely come more slowly to the Caribbean and South America than to other world regions and that the contemporary drop in homicide may reflect a globally shared phenomenon with varying starting and ending points across nations. As this longer-horizon view plays out, it would be instructive to consider whether there is a predictive pattern to what could represent a geographic diffusion of declining violence.

A second conclusion we draw is that, while in the majority of cases the estimates reported for given regions are fairly uniform across nations, there also is significant variability in contemporary homicide trends within some regions. This is particularly true among the Central American countries in our data. For instance, we observe overall no significant trend in contemporary homicide rates for the six Central American nations considered, but this result masks significant increases over the period in Belize and a comparable decline for Mexico (which, of course, experienced significant increases in homicide in the years after our study period closed). This underscores the need for a more general and expanded approach to explaining cross-national variation in homicide trends. This serves as motivation not only to develop explanatory models of cross-national homicide in the present study that isolate germane causal factors but also to evaluate the extent to which the models we develop can account for the observed cross-national variation in homicide trends. Results pertinent to both issues are discussed in subsection C below.

B. Sex- and Age-Specific Homicide Rate Trends

Are contemporary trends in homicide victimization comparable across demographic groups, or are distinct patterns revealed when the data are disaggregated by victim sex and age? Results relevant to this

---

cross-national trends in logged homicide rates for the 86 nations in our maximum sample using the annual data and also 3-year moving averages across the period. The results suggest only a relatively modest degree of commonality in international homicide trends, with squared partial correlations ranging from .05 to .20. This reinforces the conclusion that recent trends in cross-national homicide rates do not appear to yield a globally shared, simultaneous, phenomenon.

TABLE 4

Sex- and Age-Disaggregated Logged Homicide Victimization Rates Regressed on Linear and Quadratic Time Variables, 1989–2008

	A. Sex-Specific Homicide Victimization Sample ($n = 67$)			B. Age-Specific Homicide Victimization Sample ($n = 46$)	
	Model 1	Model 2		Model 1	Model 2
1. Total homicide:			1. Total homicide:		
Year	−.018*	.025*	Year	−.016*	.019*
	(.005)	(.010)		(.004)	(.009)
Year^2	. . .	−.002*	Year^2	. . .	−.002*
		(.0005)			(.0005)
Intercept	1.40*	1.27*	Intercept	1.31*	1.20*
	(.139)	(.134)		(.164)	(.155)
2. Male victims:			2. Victims aged 15–29:		
Year	−.020*	.021$^+$	Year	−.023*	.007
	(.005)	(.011)		(.006)	(.010)
Year^2	. . .	−.002*	Year^2	. . .	−.002*
		(.0006)			(.0006)
Intercept	1.79*	1.67*	Intercept	1.50*	1.41*
	(.151)	(.149)		(.186)	(.177)
3. Female victims:			3. Victims aged 30–44:		
Year	−.015*	.016$^+$	Year	−.022*	.015
	(.004)	(.010)		(.005)	(.011)
Year^2	. . .	−.002*	Year^2	. . .	−.002*
		(.0004)			(.0006)
Intercept	.565*	.470*	Intercept	1.71*	1.60*
	(.108)	(.106)		(.181)	(.174)
			4. Victims aged 45–59:		
			Year	−.018*	.017
				(.004)	(.014)
			Year^2	. . .	−.002*
					(.0007)
			Intercept	1.47*	1.37*
				(.170)	(.164)

NOTE.—All models include random effects for the time variables.

* $p \leq .05$.

$^+$ $p \leq .10$.

question are reported in table 4. Panel A reports the mixed-model estimated trend parameters overall and separately for male and female victims for 67 nations. Panel B displays a parallel set of results for 46 nations in which we were able to locate data on homicide victimization rates among people aged 15–29, 30–44, and 45–59. The story that emerges from both panels is very clear and easy to summarize un-

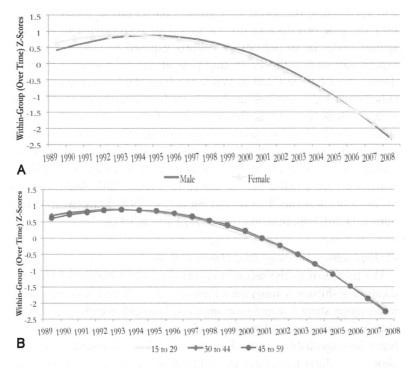

FIG. 3.—Estimated trend in logged homicide victimization rates across 67 nations, 1989–2008: *A*, sex specific; *B*, age specific.

equivocally: the estimated trends in logged homicide from the late 1980s through the late 2000s are uniform across the specified demographic groups considered.

To illustrate the patterns summarized in table 4, we computed the predicted average trends in logged homicide rates for males and females and for each of the age groupings represented, using in each case the parameters obtained from the quadratic specifications (i.e., model 2 in panels A and B). We then converted the predicted trends into within-group z-scores to diminish distortions that might arise from comparing trends across groups with substantially different levels of homicide. The within-group z-scores are plotted in figures 3A and 3B. As these figures show, the predicted trends in logged homicide victimization rates are very similar for males and females and also for young and older persons. For the vast majority of nations included in our analysis, trends in lethal violence are highly parallel across victim sex and age.[6] Thus, the forces that yielded reductions in lethal violence over the past two decades do not appear to be restricted to violence against males or to persons or cohorts exposed to unique early life experiences during the 1970s that yielded unusually large reductions during the 1990s and 2000s. While the latter finding cannot rule out cohort-based explanations of the recent homicide drops observed in many nations, it suggests that the major forces that underlie recent shifts are not unique to particular age groups. The findings thus add to the body of evidence that calls into question propositions that factors unique to certain age cohorts, such as shifts in abortion laws and lead abatement, are a major part of the story (Nevin 2007; Anderson and Wells 2008; Kahane, Paton, and Simmons 2008; Dills, Miron, and Summers 2010; Buonnano et al. 2011; Farrell 2013).

C. Explanatory Models of Total Homicide Rates

We now turn to the second general question: whether selected indicators of shifting demography, lifestyle, and collective sentiment have importantly shaped recent cross-national homicide trends. The factors that influence youth homicide trends and those relevant to domestic homicides (probably many of the female victim homicides analyzed above) may differ from those that affect adult homicide trends and male victim homicides (Goldberger and Rosenfeld 2008), and it may be worthwhile to consider explanatory models for demographic-disaggregated homicide rates. But given the highly uniform temporal patterns observed across sex and age groups in the analysis presented above, coupled with sample size considerations, we restrict our multivariate analysis of explanatory factors to total logged homicide rates. This strikes us as a good focal point for evaluating temporal trends in recent homicide rates cross-nationally, and it also enables us to retain a significantly larger sample of nations ($n = 65$) than would otherwise be the case.

The nations for which we were able to obtain data on homicide rates, the control variables, and selected explanatory variables are listed in appendix table A1. This sample encompasses a wide variety of nations that span the regions of North America, Europe, Central and South

---

[6] For example, the average within-nation (over-time) Pearson's correlation between male and female homicide victimization rates and between homicide victimization rates across the three age categories considered is greater than $r = .85$, and in most nations trends across these demographic designations are above $r = .90$.

America, Asia, and Oceania. Data for a few of the explanatory variables are not available for all of these nations, so the sample size and composition vary depending on model specification.

Table 5 displays descriptive statistics for all of the measures considered in our analysis of cross-national homicide trends, both for each of the five waves separately and across all waves (the final column). Some of the variables considered do not exhibit notable (aggregate) shifts over the five waves, including sex ratios and logged population. Other variables exhibit modest shifts over time overall but also exhibit considerable variability within waves across nations. One such variable is the indicator of recent immigration, which shows relatively little average change over the period across all nations, but this masks considerable heterogeneity. Some nations experienced growth in rates of recent immigration across the period, some exhibited steady reductions, and many saw initial increases followed by sharp reductions in immigration in the post-2000 period (e.g., the United States). Table 5 also reveals several factors that yield substantial and more consistent trends over the two decades covered in our study, including notable reductions in poverty (as measured by infant mortality rates and GDP, with the latter reverse coded) and increases in youth oversight, imprisonment, cell phone subscriptions, and personal computers per capita.

Are any of these shifts summarized in table 5 associated with cross-national trends in lethal violence? We explore this general question in a series of mixed regression models, the results of which we present in tables 6 and 7. Five models are presented in table 6. Model 1 is a "baseline" two-level regression model, which includes just the control variables. The subsequent four models add to this baseline model the explanatory variables highlighted in our study that gauge shifts in lifestyle innovations (models 2 and 3) and those that integrate measures of potentially important demographic changes (models 4 and 5). In each case, we present results only for the centered time-varying indicators. Note that all of the models also include static (mean-level) indicators of the time-varying measures and dummy variables for periods (with one omitted), but since our focus is the influence of observables on within-nation changes in homicide, we limit the tabular presentation to the time-varying indicators.

As revealed in model 1, we find no evidence for this sample of nations ($n = 65$) that homicide rate trends are associated with changes

TABLE 5
Descriptive Statistics for Variables Used in the Analysis

	Wave					Across Waves
	Wave 1	Wave 2	Wave 3	Wave 4	Wave 5	
Dependent variable:						
Logged homicide rate	1.28	1.38	1.31	1.31	1.16	1.29
	(1.05)	(1.27)	(1.22)	(1.26)	(1.33)	(1.22)
Control variables:						
Poverty	.169	.142	.041	−.095	−.230	.000
	(.867)	(.884)	(.928)	(.938)	(.916)	(.915)
Gini index of income inequality	39.63	41.83	44.39	44.45	44.47	43.00
	(8.15)	(7.40)	(6.36)	(6.25)	(7.05)	(7.73)
Female labor force participation	48.50	48.22	48.21	49.56	50.94	49.09
	(12.38)	(10.28)	(9.36)	(8.81)	(8.34)	(9.93)
Divorce rate	1.60	1.66	1.70	1.75	1.85	1.71
	(1.20)	(1.22)	(1.22)	(1.12)	(1.08)	(1.16)
Sex ratio	96.64	96.55	96.36	96.16	96.10	96.36
	(4.28)	(4.03)	(4.00)	(4.07)	(4.25)	(4.11)
% urban	64.98	66.16	67.09	67.90	68.79	66.98
	(17.57)	(17.52)	(17.56)	(17.65)	(17.82)	(17.57)

	(1)	(2)	(3)	(4)	(5)	(6)
Logged population	16.16	16.20	16.230	16.257	16.284	16.23
	(1.43)	(1.42)	(1.42)	(1.42)	(1.43)	(1.42)
Logged imprisonment rate	4.54	4.67	4.80	4.89	4.99	4.78
	(.607)	(.627)	(.671)	(.653)	(.609)	(.650)
Explanatory variables:						
Youth oversight	1.13	1.18	1.25	1.35	1.57	1.30
	(.438)	(.444)	(.484)	(.527)	(.559)	(.514)
Recent immigration	.728	.534	.402	.650	-.365	.388
	(2.03)	(1.24)	(1.46)	(1.28)	(.999)	(1.49)
Informal economy	-296.98	-81.79	-236.67	-383.38	-308.00	-267.96
	(388.78)	(368.97)	(306.63)	(526.73)	(328.37)	(402.29)
Cell phone subscription rate	.265	.959	4.981	27.529	56.98	18.25
	(.679)	(1.72)	(6.69)	(23.23)	(32.10)	(28.30)
Personal computers per capita	2.07	6.24	11.16	18.51	26.36	14.33
	(3.12)	(5.92)	(10.88)	(16.80)	(23.45)	(17.37)
Social trust	-1.28	-1.28	-1.28	-1.28	-1.28	-1.28
	(8.09)	(8.09)	(8.09)	(8.09)	(8.089)	(8.09)
Faith in government	.000	.000	.000	.000	.000	.000
	(.784)	(.784)	(.784)	(.784)	(.784)	(.784)

NOTE.—Standard deviations are in parentheses. For the dependent variable, wave 1 = 1989–91, wave 2 = 1993–95, wave 3 = 1997–99, wave 4 = 2001–3, and wave 5 = 2005–7. For the explanatory and control variables, wave 1 = 1987–88, wave 2 = 1991–92, wave 3 = 1995–96, wave 4 = 1999–2000, and wave 5 = 2003–4.

TABLE 6

Logged Homicide Rates Regressed on Time-Varying Control and Explanatory Variables

Fixed Effects	Model 1	Model 2	Model 3	Model 4	Model 5
Time-varying indicators:					
Intercept	1.53	3.98	2.95	11.00*	10.79
	(3.22)	(3.26)	(3.03)	(3.94)	(5.21)
Poverty	.547*	.551*	.362$^+$	.416$^+$	.584$^+$
	(.241)	(.267)	(.221)	(.238)	(.338)
Gini index of income in-					
equality	.0002	.0004	.001	−.0009	−.004
	(.005)	(.005)	(.004)	(.005)	(.005)
Female labor force par-					
ticipation	.009	.009	.029*	.009	.011
	(.008)	(.008)	(.007)	(.008)	(.010)
Sex ratio	−.018	−.017	.006	.003	.011
	(.029)	(.031)	(.031)	(.029)	(.036)
% urban	.036*	.036*	.028$^+$	.036*	.034*
	(.016)	(.017)	(.015)	(.015)	(.016)
Logged population	.842	.848	.357	.823	.929
	(.650)	(.678)	(.579)	(.592)	(.630)
Logged imprisonment					
rate	−.040	−.040	−.215	−.050	−.218
	(.100)	(.098)	(.138)	(.099)	(.151)
Divorce rate	.133$^+$	.132$^+$	.050	.152$^+$	.130
	(.008)	(.081)	(.071)	(.081)	(.104)
Cell phone subscription					
rate	...	−.00004	...	...	...
		(.002)			
Personal computers per					
capita	...	...	−.004	...	...
			(.003)		
Youth oversight	...	...	...	−.386*	−.404*
				(.130)	(.150)
Recent immigration	...	...	...	...	.025
					(.017)
Nation sample	65	65	59	65	51
Nation-period sample	288	286	246	288	235

NOTE.—Models also include static (mean) indicators of each time-varying measure, plus dummy variables for waves.

* $p \leq .05$.

$^+$ $p \leq .10$.

in income inequality or imprisonment rates, nor do we find significant effects on homicide of the sex ratio or female labor force participation. Two time-varying indicators are significantly associated with logged homicide rates in this model at conventional levels of statistical significance: changes in poverty and percent urban exhibit positive, significant associations with changes in logged homicide rates. This suggests that recent decreases in homicide have been greater in societies where there have been greater reductions in poverty and where urban population shares have declined. The results in model 1 also reveal a marginally significant positive association between divorce rates and logged homicide rates ($p = .10$, two-tailed test), a finding that parallels results generated from Messner et al.'s (2011) cross-national study. However, we do not find consistent evidence across models for a significant effect of the divorce rates, suggesting that conclusions about its role are contingent on sample composition and model specification.

In models 2 and 3, we expand the baseline analysis by considering shifts in technology. Specifically, we add the indicator of cell phone subscriptions in model 2 and the indicator of personal computer ownership in model 3. In preliminary estimations (not shown) that excluded the control variables, both indicators exhibited significant negative effects on logged homicide, which is consistent with theoretical expectations and some US-based research (Klick, MacDonald, and Stratmann 2012; Orrick and Piquero, forthcoming). However, as the results in models 2 and 3 reveal, though we observe the anticipated negative association between homicide trends and growth in cell phone subscriptions and personal computer ownership, the estimated relationships are not statistically significant once the other factors are considered. This suggests that the dramatic increases observed in many nations in computing and mobile telephony have not translated into differential trends in homicide.

Models 4 and 5 focus on different dimensions of recent demographic change. In model 4, we expand on the baseline model by integrating the time-varying indicator of youth oversight described earlier (i.e., the ratio of persons aged 45–64 to persons aged 15–24). The results indicate that trends in youth oversight exhibit a statistically significant inverse association with logged homicide trends, a pattern that is robust across the many different specifications we explored in the study. This result emerges net of the other time-varying indicators and year dummies, which reduces the chances that it is a spurious finding. The results are thus highly suggestive that a major demographic shift that has occurred in many nations over the past several decades—shrinking populations of young persons and major growth in older populations—is an important part of the cross-national story of contemporary trends in lethal violence.

As model 5 of table 6 shows, we find no support that the other major demographic factor considered—recent immigration—is associated with trends in lethal violence after controlling for other factors, at least across the pooled international sample for which we could obtain the requisite data (51 nations). These findings parallel those that have emerged thus far from the small body of cross-national research on the link between trends in immigration and crime (e.g., Buonanno et al. 2011), which suggests a null relationship. We acknowledge the possibility that the estimated effect of recent immigration could suffer from endogeneity bias, but we suspect that this is not a major confounder for our cross-national analysis. As Bianchi, Buonanno, and Pinotti (2012) aptly note, immigrants may be more likely to select into higher-crime areas, or places with attributes that are positively associated with crime (e.g., poverty), and failing to account for such processes may confound efforts to evaluate the hypothesized negative causal impact of immigration on crime trends. However, while such selection processes may be quite influential for shaping immigrant settlement within nations, it seems unlikely to us that they would be a major determinant of cross-national migration patterns.

Under the continued (untested) assumption of exogeneity, we explored the possibility that the effect of recent international migration on logged homicide may be contingent on other conditions, including population growth, changes in GDP, and changes in the volume of informal economic activity. The results of these conditional models (not shown in tabular form) do not support the prediction derived from Sanderson's (2013) research that the consequences of international migration are contingent on other dimensions of population growth, nor do we see evidence that a higher volume of formal economic activity (e.g., shifts in GDP) significantly moderates the effects of recent immigration on logged homicide trends. We do observe a statistically significant interaction between trends in immigration and an indicator of changes in the size of the informal economy (measured by residual electricity output not accounted for by the formal economy) that is consistent with theoretical expectations outlined earlier. We replicated these results, finding a similar pattern, using an alternative measure of shifts in the magnitude of the informal economy that has been high-lighted in the economics literature, the discrepancy between national income and expenditures (see Schneider 2005). In both cases, the mag-nitude of the interaction effect (not shown) is relatively small, but it would be worthwhile to explore in future research whether more direct measures of the informal economy yield a more substantial condition-ing impact on immigration.

We now turn to the matter of whether recent trends in homicide are associated with changes in levels of social trust among people or levels of confidence/faith they have in their governments. Because we lack time-varying indicators of social trust and faith in government, we adopt a somewhat different modeling strategy for this assessment. Spe-cifically, we capitalize on our mixed-modeling approach and include time-invariant indicators of changes in the percentage of national re-spondents who report that they trust others and changes in the per-centage who say that they have confidence in parliament, the justice system, and the police. As described earlier, the latter is a three-item composite measure. To assess whether recent cross-national reductions are more pronounced in nations that have experienced more substantial increases in social trust and confidence in government, we estimate three two-level regression models, the results of which are reported in table 7.

Model 1 parallels our earlier specifications except for replacing the time dummies with nation-specific linear and quadratic time trends (i.e., wave and wave squared). We include all of the controls, plus the indicator of youth oversight, which exerted consistently significant ef-fects on logged homicide in our earlier analysis. This model shows that the alternative specification and smaller sample used for the assessment of whether trends in homicide are associated with trends in collective sentiment yield results quite similar to those reported above (compare to table 6, model 4). The model also reaffirms the significant quadratic trend in logged homicide rates reported in our more detailed annual trend analysis (fig. 2).

Models 2 and 3 explore whether there is any evidence that the estimated trend parameters vary significantly as a function of country differences in the degree of changes observed in social trust and gov-ernment confidence. We do so by estimating the effects of the indi-cators of change in social trust and change in government confidence,

TABLE 7

Logged Homicide Rates Regressed on Indicators of Social Trust and Confidence in Government ($n = 40$)

Fixed Effects	Model 1	Model 2	Model 3
Time-varying indicators:			
Intercept	9.311+	1.043*	10.310+
	(5.324)	(.182)	(5.763)
Poverty	.458*	. . .	.526*
	(.208)		(.208)
Gini index of income inequality	.001	. . .	.00003
	(.004)		(.004)
Female labor force participation	.018*	. . .	.020*
	(.008)		(.007)
Sex ratio	.004	. . .	.010
	(.015)		(.017)
% urban	.028*	. . .	.029*
	(.012)		(.013)
Logged population	.016	. . .	−.221
	(.706)		(.679)
Logged imprisonment rate	−.047	. . .	−.025
	(.190)		(.181)
Divorce rate	.001	. . .	−.014
	(.057)		(.064)
Youth oversight	−.238*	. . .	−.186
	(.107)		(.138)
Wave	. . .	.063	.078
		(.041)	(.050)
Wave^2	. . .	−.035*	−.025*
		(.008)	(.009)
Static indicators:			
Change in social trust	. . .	.024	.033*
		(.023)	(.010)
Change in government confidence	. . .	−.371	−.156+
		(.196)	(.093)
Cross-level interactions:			
Change in social trust × wave	. . .	−.004	−.006
		(.005)	(.005)
Change in social trust × wave^2	. . .	.0004	.0005
		(.001)	(.001)
Change in government confidence × wave	. . .	−.023	−.016
		(.052)	(.046)
Change in government confidence × wave^2	. . .	.009	.007
		(.010)	(.009)
Nation sample	40	40	40
Nation-period sample	186	186	186

NOTE.—Models also include static (mean) indicators of each time-varying measure.

* $p \le .05$.

+ $p \le .10$.

along with product terms between these measures and the time trend variables. The latter serve as our focal point, as they provide the pertinent information about whether estimated trends in homicide differ across nations that vary on the measures of collective sentiment considered. We present results both without (model 2) and with (model 3) the time-varying control variables. The results are similar across the two specifications: none of the product terms attains statistical significance, indicating that the estimated trends in logged homicide rates from the late 1980s through the late 2000s are not significantly influenced by changes in social trust or government confidence. We obtained similar results from alternative specifications in which each of the product terms was considered separately and in models that included the three individual measures of government confidence separately. Finally, drawing insights from Karstedt (2013), we estimated additional models that tested for possible three-way interactions between the time parameters and the indicators of social trust and government confidence. We found no evidence for the idea that logged homicide trends over the past two decades were conditioned by the joint influence of changes in social trust and government confidence. Overall, these results are consistent with several other recent analyses of social trust and homicide based on different samples and alternative empirical strategies (Robbins and Pettinicchio 2012; Robbins 2013).

We close by considering two additional, overarching issues that tie together the various themes addressed in our research: first, how well do the studied factors perform in explaining cross-national variability in homicide trends overall; and, second, can the explanatory factors considered account for some of the specific forms of regional variability in homicide trends described earlier, most notably the divergent patterns observed in eastern Europe and the South American and Caribbean nations included in our sample? To address these questions, we estimated supplementary models that parallel the econometric specification applied in table 6 (model 4) for our maximum sample ($n = 65$), except that we substituted random linear and quadratic time effects in lieu of the time dummies (see Rosenfeld, Fornango, and Baumer [2005] for a similar strategy). This specification includes all of the control variables plus the indicator of youth oversight, which yielded consistently significant effects in our analysis (we omit the indicators of immigration, technological shifts, and collective sentiment because they did not yield significant effects on logged homicide rates and because including them would have reduced the sample considerably). By omitting the time dummies, this modeling approach reduces our capacity to account for shared unobserved temporal effects, but the findings are quite similar to those obtained above; importantly, this alternative strategy permits a direct assessment of the variance explained in estimated homicide trends across nations under different modeling scenarios.

The four random coefficient models reported in table 8 address whether the factors included in our study account for overall cross-national variability in homicide trends. The first two models in the table assume linear trends in logged homicide, showing both the estimated coefficients and variance components for this parameter without controlling for other factors (model 1) and then with the covariates included (model 2). Models 3 and 4 parallel these specifications, except that we include both linear and quadratic time variables in them. Both specifications yield the same conclusion, though the quadratic specifications (models 3 and 4) yield a better fit to the underlying trends in our sample. The coefficients for the time variables in model 3 reveal the now-familiar curvilinear trend in logged homicide observed for the period under investigation and the nations we consider. Though this model collapses the data to five waves over the study period, the pattern we observe is comparable to the one that emerges from our analysis of annual overall homicide trends (see fig. 1). Additionally, the random-effects variance components for model 3, reported at the bottom of the table, indicate that the estimated linear change in homicide over the period varies significantly across nations (variance of .012), while the quadratic variance component is quite small and does not reach statistical significance (variance of .001). The former indicates that, as shown earlier, some nations exhibited significant declines during the 1990s and early 2000s while others did not.

Do the covariates considered in our most comprehensive specification for the maximum sample account for the observed cross-national variation in linear homicide trends? The answer to this query can be found by comparing the variance components from model 3 (which does not include the covariates) with those from model 4 (which includes the covariates). Doing so reveals a substantial (approximately 92 percent) reduction in variation across nations in the estimated linear change in logged homicide rates over the study period. Further, the remaining cross-national variance in the estimated linear parameter,

TABLE 8

Logged Homicide Rates Regressed on Time Trends and Other
Factors ($n = 65$)

Fixed Effects	Model 1	Model 2	Model 3	Model 4
Time-varying indicators:				
Intercept	1.330*	10.565*	1.330*	10.555*
	(.145)	(3.92)	(.145)	(3.939)
Wave	−.047*	−.021	.047	.002
	(.020)	(.033)	(.043)	(.047)
Wave^2	. . .	. . .	−.022*	−.005
			(.009)	(.009)
Poverty	. . .	.370$^+$	. . .	.380$^+$
		(.229)		(.228)
Gini index of income inequality	. . .	−.001	. . .	−.001
		(.005)		(.005)
Female labor force participation	. . .	.009	. . .	.010
		(.008)		(.008)
Sex ratio	. . .	.007	. . .	.005
		(.027)		(.028)
% urban	. . .	.033*	. . .	.033*
		(.015)		(.015)
Logged population	. . .	.898	. . .	.824
		(.574)		(.589)
Logged imprisonment rate	. . .	−.053	. . .	−.052
		(.098)		(.098)
Divorce rate	. . .	.164*	. . .	.164*
		(.083)		(.081)
Youth oversight	. . .	−.463*	. . .	−.438*
		(.128)		(.143)
Random-effects variances:				
Nation	1.297*	.344*	1.280*	.347*
Wave	.011*	.002	.012*	.00009
Wave^2	. . .	. . .	.0001	.0001
Nation sample	65	65	65	65
Nation-period sample	288	288	288	288

NOTE.—Models also include static (mean) indicators of each time-varying measure.

* $p \leq .05$.

$^+$ $p \leq .10$.

after controlling for the covariates, is not statistically significant. Thus, the factors considered in our analysis explain most of the variation we observe across nations in estimated linear changes in logged homicide over the past two decades.

The results in table 8 speak to cross-national variability in logged homicide trends generally, but what about the more specific regional

TABLE 9

Regional Variation in Logged Homicide Trends with and without
Controlling for Selected Covariates ($n = 65$)

Fixed Effects	Without Covariates		With Covariates	
	Model 1	Model 2	Model 3	Model 4
Time-varying indicators:				
Intercept	1.067*	1.041*	10.366*	10.188*
	(.172)	(.175)	(4.490)	(4.460)
Wave	−.063*	−.015	−.018	−.047
	(.023)	(.052)	(.040)	(.059)
Wave^2	. . .	−.011	. . .	−.0003
		(.010)		(.010)
Wave × South America/Caribbean	.148*	.163*	.033	.080
	(.044)	(.076)	(.058)	(.071)
Wave^2 × South America/Caribbean	. . .	−.003	. . .	−.008
		(.021)		(.022)
Wave × eastern Europe	−.066*	.245*	−.023	.237
	(.032)	(.098)	(.045)	(.124)
Wave^2 × eastern Europe	. . .	−.069*	. . .	−.055*
		(.019)		(.021)
Nation sample	65	65	65	65
Nation-period sample	288	288	288	288

NOTE.—Models also include static (mean) indicators of each time-varying measure
and dummy variables distinguishing South American/Caribbean and eastern European
nations from others.

* $p \leq .05$.

patterns we reported earlier? Recall from figure 2 that, in our analysis
of annual logged homicide trends, the nations of eastern Europe, the
Caribbean, and South America exhibited divergent trends in homicide
from nations in other parts of the world. Other nations in our sample
exhibited estimated declines in lethal violence from the late 1980s onward, but these regions continued to experience increases in homicide
during the 1990s, and that trend reversed in the South American and
Caribbean nations only in the mid-2000s. Do the factors included in
our analysis help to account for these regional differences? We evaluate
this question by estimating a series of mixed-model regressions, the
results of which we report in table 9. These models parallel the analysis
presented in table 8, except that we include region-time interactions.
We again report models assuming different functional forms for the
estimated trends (i.e., linear and quadratic), and in each case we consider models both with and without covariates so that we can assess

whether any observed regional differences in trends are explained by the factors included in our analysis.

Models 1 and 2 in table 9, which do not contain any covariates aside from region, time, and region-time interactions, confirm the story conveyed in figure 2 above regarding the divergence in trends observed for eastern Europe, South America, and the Caribbean from those in other regions. Both models show that the estimated linear changes in logged homicide over the period were significantly different in the South American and Caribbean nations in our analysis. Models 3 and 4 reveal, however, that after we include the control variables plus the indicator of youth oversight, the product terms that represent the difference in the estimated linear trend in homicide between South American and Caribbean nations and other (non–eastern European) areas is reduced considerably and is no longer statistically significant.

These findings demonstrate that the factors considered in our research account for the majority of the divergence in contemporary homicide trends observed in South American and Caribbean nations. Further analyses (not shown) revealed that the bulk of this can be attributed to differential regional trends in our indicators of poverty (a composite of infant mortality and GDP, with the latter reverse coded) and youth oversight. As measured, poverty declined and youth oversight increased significantly overall, but these homicide-reducing shifts were significantly smaller in South American and Caribbean nations.

Our model is less well equipped to account for the divergence in homicide trends observed between eastern European countries and other (non-Caribbean and South American) nations. This can be seen most clearly by comparing models 2 and 4 in table 9. Consistent with our assessment of annual homicide trends (see fig. 2), model 2 shows that logged homicide trends in eastern European nations deviate from the average trend in both the magnitude of the estimated linear increase and the estimated deceleration parameter (i.e., the quadratic time component). Controlling for the covariates (model 4) explains only a small fraction of that divergence, as evidenced by the fact that the linear and quadratic time coefficients in this model are only slightly reduced from model 2. We found similar results when we reestimated the model after removing the other regional variables (i.e., the South American and Caribbean indicators). Thus, even after we hold constant shifts in poverty, youth oversight, and the other factors considered, the estimated homicide trends in eastern Europe diverge significantly from those observed in other nations. The implications of this finding are discussed below.

V. Summary and Conclusions

In this essay, we report findings from new analyses of whether the observed temporal variation in homicide rates from the late 1980s through the mid-2000s is consistent with a widely shared "global" pattern or whether instead there is evidence of divergent trends across regions. We also considered whether comparable trends are evident across nations over this period among male and female victims and among youths and young adult, middle-aged adult, and older adult victims. Finally, we explored whether selected elements of demographic change, technology-related lifestyle shifts, and trends in collective sentiment since the 1980s yielded fresh insights into the observed cross-national trends in homicide rates. Integrating data from several sources for a relatively large sample of nations, our analysis revealed three noteworthy findings.

First, we found uniform trends in homicide by victim gender and age, patterns that do not vary substantially across nations. This finding adds to the body of evidence that calls into question the utility of cohort-based explanations of the crime drop, including those that emphasize shifts in abortion laws and lead abatement.

Second, our analysis revealed significant regional variation in overall homicide trends, especially during the 1990s, leading us to conclude that the widely chronicled drop in homicide during this period was not a global phenomenon or at least not something that occurred everywhere simultaneously. An important caveat, though, is that during the 2000s there appears to be growing convergence across nations, with most nations revealing notable declines by the middle of the decade. Thus, an alternative interpretation of our data is that there has been a widespread reduction in lethal violence over the past several decades, with homicide declines merely coming more slowly to eastern Europe, the Caribbean, and South America than to other world regions. In other words, the contemporary drop in homicide may reflect a globally shared phenomenon with varying starting and ending points.

Third, though our multivariate analysis suggests a limited role for recent shifts in immigration, growth in imprisonment and the use of cellular phones and personal computers, and changes in social trust and government confidence in explaining cross-national homicide trends, the results revealed consistent evidence that trends in poverty, urbanization, and youth oversight were consequential. These results make sense in light of findings from research on global patterns of urbanization, poverty, and age structure.

Many nations have experienced steady, albeit small, increases in urbanization over the past two decades, but consistent with patterns reported elsewhere, several nations in our sample exhibit notable declines in urbanization or initial increases followed by decreases over this period (OECD 2010, pp. 22–24). Though de-urbanization would, from many theoretical angles, yield predictions for reductions in crime, this has not been a major component of ongoing dialogues about the factors that may be pertinent to crime reductions seen in many parts of the world.

Our indicator of "poverty" combines two proxies for changes in the economic status of nations that were highly correlated in our data: infant mortality and GDP. Existing research reveals fairly widespread declines in poverty and increases in GDP across many nations in recent decades (e.g., United Nations 2010; Chandy and Gertz 2011; Bureau of Labor Statistics 2012), and our analysis suggests that such trends are significantly associated with recent homicide trends. These findings reinforce conclusions drawn by Rosenfeld and Messner (2009) regarding the importance of improving economic conditions for explaining recent crime trends in Europe and America.

Our results also reveal a prominent role for shifts in age structure and, in particular, the ratio of older persons to younger persons, which has increased considerably in many nations in recent decades (UN Secretariat 2005). Though many prior studies of crime trends have considered more basic shifts in the proportion of the population that falls in high-crime age groups (e.g., ages 15–24), we suggest that the potentially important role of age structure imbalance has been underappreciated. In many societies, population dynamics have shifted in ways that simultaneously yield significant increases in the number of older persons (i.e., 45 and up) and significant decreases in the number of younger persons (i.e., 15–24). One consequence of such shifts is a progressive reduction in the sizes of cohorts that tend to exhibit the highest crime rates, but another consequence that we think may be even more important is that the ratio of older people who provide significant social control to younger people has increased considerably. Thus, the age structure in many societies has shifted so that there are relatively few persons in high-crime age groups and relatively many in age groups that are well equipped to provide social control of youths and young adults. Our analysis suggests that this balance has important implications for recent cross-national trends in homicide.

Collectively, the factors considered whose effects we examined, and in particular trends in urbanization, poverty, and age structure imbalance, account for a significant fraction of the observed cross-national and much of the observed regional variations in recent homicide trends. Eastern Europe is the exception. Our explanatory models were unable to explain why homicide trends there diverge significantly from those observed in other regions. We showed that these nations diverge from others primarily in their having a notably later decline in homicide. Other regions experienced declines during the early 1990s whereas declines in eastern European nations did not begin until the late 1990s and early 2000s. There could be several reasons why our model is unable to account for the divergence in homicide trends observed in eastern Europe. One that seems particularly plausible is that the political instability and transitions that affected much of eastern Europe beginning in the late 1980s may have delayed the processes that generated crime declines observed elsewhere.

Additional research is needed before firm conclusions can be drawn about the causes of recent cross-national homicide trends. Though we included a fairly comprehensive empirical specification compared to previous studies, including nation and year fixed effects, we lacked complete time-varying indicators of some measures (e.g., data on routine activities, parenting practices, morality, security measures) that might be important (Farrell 2013). Even with more complete data, complex methodological issues inherent in analyzing multiple conditions over time and space can serve as obstacles to arriving at valid and reliable inferences (Greenberg 2014). Some of the potential culprits (e.g., issues of nonstationarity and cointegration) are probably not highly problematic in assessments of change over a relatively small number of time periods, which describes our effort, but others (e.g., endogeneity) are ubiquitous, and fully satisfactory resolutions are very difficult to identify with nonexperimental designs. We do not believe that our findings regarding the roles of shifting age structure balance, urbanization, and poverty can be easily written off over concerns about endogeneity, but we urge future research to build on our analysis to assess further the robustness of our results to alternative measures and analytical strategies.

Finally, though we make some important strides in the analysis discussed in this essay, many questions remain unaddressed. For example, do patterns we observed for homicide characterize trends in other crimes, including nonlethal violence and property crime? Replicating our analysis with data from the International Crime Victimization Survey would permit an assessment of this issue. Are there distinctive groupings of crime "trajectories" across nations that go beyond a priori regional designations? Contemporary homicide trends in Mexico (a Central American nation), for instance, are much more similar to those in the United States than they are to other Central American nations. Similarly, eastern Europe looks more like some of its neighbors to the east than it does like other European nations. It would be informative if future research explored whether theoretically meaningful crime trend "groupings" emerged that were independent of regional or other classifications, an approach that has proven productive in the analysis of crime trajectories within nations (Stults 2010).

Cross-national crime research also could usefully be extended in two other ways. One would be to evaluate whether cross-national differences in recent crime trends are associated with shifts in values and beliefs beyond social trust and confidence in government, such as trends in morality and manners, which Eisner (2008) has suggested are a potentially important part of the story. Such issues could be explored by extending our analysis to include other survey-based measures from the WVS, EVS, and similar sources from other regions of the world (e.g., Robbins 2013).

Second, our analysis could be enriched by considering cross-national variability in the role of specified explanatory factors. Our analysis by design assumed that the explanatory factors we considered exerted uniform effects across nations. This assumption conformed to our objective of exploring general patterns in cross-national homicide trends and is common in other cross-national studies, but it may be both naïve and influential for the conclusions drawn (Baumer and Wolff 2014). For instance, we concluded that growth in imprisonment was unrelated to homicide trends, but this finding describes the overall pooled pattern that emerges across our sample of nations. Drawing insights from theories of legitimacy and procedural justice, we acknowledge the possibility that this null effect could mask offsetting effects across nations:

increases in imprisonment could yield homicide reductions in nations where the justice system is considered legitimate, while they could yield increases where there is deep suspicion regarding government authority.

Similar propositions about cross-national variability in estimated slopes can be derived for several other factors. Thus, it would be useful to reconsider the assumption of uniform covariate effects. The practical steps for doing so are fairly straightforward, as it merely requires the estimation of random-slope models for specified time-varying indicators. The more significant challenge, though, is developing a strong theoretical rationale for random effects and identifying the data and measures that can account for any observed slope variability. These and other issues must be addressed if we are meaningfully to enhance understanding of contemporary cross-national crime trends.

APPENDIX

TABLE A1

Nations Included in Baseline Regression Models of Cross-National Homicide Trends ($n = 65$)

	Nation		Nation
1	Argentina	34	Sri Lanka
2	Austria	35	Lithuania
3	Australia	36	Luxembourg
4	Azerbaijan	37	Latvia
5	Belgium	38	Moldova
6	Bulgaria	39	Macedonia
7	Brazil	40	Mauritius
8	Belarus	41	Mexico
9	Canada	42	Nicaragua
10	Switzerland	43	Nepal
11	Chile	44	Norway
12	Colombia	45	New Zealand
13	Costa Rica	46	Panama
14	Czech Republic	47	Peru
15	Germany	48	Poland
16	Denmark	49	Portugal
17	Dominican Republic	50	Paraguay
18	Ecuador	51	Romania
19	Estonia	52	Russian Federation
20	Spain	53	Sweden
21	Finland	54	Singapore
22	France	55	Slovenia
23	United Kingdom	56	Slovakia
24	Greece	57	El Salvador
25	Guatemala	58	Thailand
26	Hungary	59	Turkey
27	Ireland	60	Trinidad and Tobago
28	Israel	61	Ukraine
29	Iceland	62	United States of America
30	Italy	63	Uruguay
31	Japan	64	Uzbekistan
32	Korea, Republic of	65	Venezuela
33	Kazakhstan		

REFERENCES

Aebi, Marcelo F. 2010. "Methodological Issues in the Comparison of Police-Recorded Crime Rates." In *International Handbook of Criminology*, edited by

Shlomo Shoham, Paul Knepper, and Martin Kett. New York: Taylor & Francis.

Alvazzi del Frate, Anna, and Giulia Mugellini. 2012. "The Crime Drop in 'Non-Western' Countries." In *The International Crime Drop: New Directions in Research*, edited by Jan van Dijk, Andromachi Tseloni, and Graham Farrell. New York: Palgrave Macmillan.

Anderson, William, and Martin T. Wells. 2008. "Numerical Analysis in Least Squares Regression with an Application to the Abortion-Crime Debate." *Journal of Empirical Legal Studies* 5:647–81.

Baumer, Eric P. 2008. "An Empirical Assessment of the Contemporary Crime Trends Puzzle: A Modest Step toward a More Comprehensive Research Agenda." In *Understanding Crime Trends*, edited by Arthur Goldberger and Richard Rosenfeld. Washington, DC: National Academies Press.

———. 2011. "Describing and Explaining Crime Trends: An Assessment of Key Issues, Current Knowledge, and Future Directions of Scientific Inquiry." In *Oxford Handbook on Crime and Criminal Justice*, edited by Michael Tonry. New York: Oxford University Press.

———. 2013. "Lead and Crime: A Critical Assessment of the Evidence and Alternative Arguments." Presentation to the National Academies of Science Roundtable on Crime Trends, Washington, DC.

Baumer, Eric P., and Kevin T. Wolff. 2014. "Evaluating Contemporary Crime Drops in America, New York City, and Many Other Places." *Justice Quarterly* 31(1):5–38.

Bell, Martin, and Elin Edwards. 2013. *Cross-National Comparisons of Internal Migration: An Update on Global Patters and Trends.*" Report. New York: United Nations, Department of Economic and Social Affairs.

Bianchi, Milo, Paolo Buonanno, and Paolo Pinotti. 2012. "Do Immigrants Cause Crime?" *Journal of the European Economic Association* 10:1318–47.

Bircan, Tuba, and Marc Hooghe. 2011. "Immigration, Diversity and Crime: An Analysis of Belgian National Crime Statistics, 2001–2006." *European Journal of Criminology* 8(3):198–212.

Blumstein, Alfred, and Joel Wallman, eds. 2006. *The Crime Drop in America.* Rev. ed. New York: Cambridge University Press.

Buonnano, Paolo, Francesco Drago, Roberto Galbiati, and Giulio Zanella. 2011. "Crime in Europe and in the US: Dissecting the 'Reversal of Misfortunes.'" *Economic Policy* 26:347–85.

Bureau of Labor Statistics. 2012. *International Comparison of GDP per Capita and per Hour, 1960–2011.* Washington, DC: Bureau of Labor Statistics, Division of International Labor Comparisons. http://www.bls.gov/fls/intl_gdp _capita_gdp_hour.pdf.

Cantor, David, and Kenneth Land. 1985. "Unemployment and Crime Rates in the Post–World War II United States: A Theoretical and Empirical Analysis." *American Sociological Review* 50:317–32.

Chandy, Laurence, and Geoffrey Gertz. 2011. *Two Trends in Global Poverty.* Report. Washington, DC: Brookings Institution.

Cohen, Lawrence, and Marcus Felson. 1979. "Social Change and Crime Rate

Trends: A Routine Activity Approach." *American Sociological Review* 44:588–608.

Cohen, Lawrence, and Kenneth Land. 1987. "Age Structure and Crime: Symmetry vs. Asymmetry, and Projections of Crime Rates through the 1990's." *American Sociological Review* 52(2):170–83.

Cook, Phillip, and John Laub. 1998. "The Unprecedented Epidemic in Youth Violence." In *Youth Violence*, edited by Michael Tonry and Mark Moore. Vol. 24 of *Crime and Justice: A Review of Research*, edited by Michael Tonry. Chicago: University of Chicago Press.

———. 2002. "After the Epidemic: Recent Trends in Youth Violence in the United States." In *Crime and Justice: A Review of Research*, vol. 29, edited by Michael Tonry. Chicago: University of Chicago Press.

Cook, Philip, and Gary Zarkin. 1985. "Crime and the Business Cycle." *Journal of Legal Studies* 14(1):115–28.

Dills, Angela, Jeffrey Miron, and Garrett Summers. 2010. "What Do Economists Know about Crime?" In *The Economics of Crime: Lessons for and from Latin America*, edited by Rafael Di Tella, Sebastian Edwards, and Ernesto Schargrodsky. National Bureau of Economic Research Conference Report. Chicago: University of Chicago Press.

Donohue, John, and Steven Levitt. 2001. "The Impact of Legalized Abortion on Crime." *Quarterly Journal of Economics* 116:379–420.

Eisner, Manuel. 2008. "Modernity Strikes Back? A Historical Perspective on the Latest Increase in Interpersonal Violence (1960–1990)." *International Journal of Conflict and Violence* 2:268–316.

Elias, Norbert. 1978. *The Civilizing Process*. Vols. 1 and 2. Oxford: Oxford University Press.

Farrell, Graham. 2013. "Five Tests for a Theory of the Crime Drop." *Crime Science* 2:5. DOI:10.1186/2193-7680-2-5.

Feige, Edgar, and Ivica Urban. 2008. "Measuring Underground (Unobserved, Non-observed, Unrecorded) Economies in Transition Countries: Can We Trust the GDP?" *Journal of Comparative Economics* 36:287–306.

Fukuyama, Francis. 1999. *The Great Disruption: Human Nature and the Reconstitution of Social Order*. New York: Free Press.

Garland, David. 2001. *The Culture of Control: Crime and Social Order in Contemporary Society*. Chicago: University of Chicago Press.

Goldberger, Arthur, and Richard Rosenfeld, eds. 2008. *Understanding Crime Trends*. Washington, DC: National Academies Press.

Greenberg, David F. 1977. "Delinquency and the Age Structure of Society." *Contemporary Crises* 1:189–224.

———. 2014. "Studying New York City's Crime Decline: Methodological Issues." *Justice Quarterly* 31:153–88.

Greenberg, David F., and Onwobiko Agozino. 2012. "Executions, Imprisonment and Crime in Trinidad and Tobago." *British Journal of Criminology* 52:113–40.

Gurr, Ted R. 1989. "The History of Violent Crime in America." In *Violence in America*, vol. 1, edited by Ted R. Gurr. Newbury Park, CA: Sage.

Harris, Casey, and Ben Feldmeyer. 2013. "Recent Hispanic Immigration and Violent Crime in Traditional and Non-traditional Destinations." *Social Science Research* 42:202–16.

Jacobs, David, and Richard Kleban. 2003. "Political Institutions, Minorities, and Punishment: A Pooled Cross-National Analysis of Imprisonment Rates." *Social Forces* 82:725–55.

Jacobs, David, and Amber M. Richardson. 2008. "Economic Inequality and Homicide in the Developed Nations from 1975–1995." *Homicide Studies* 12: 28–45.

Kahane, Leo H., David Paton, and Rob Simmons. 2008. "The Abortion-Crime Link: Evidence from England and Wales." *Economica* 75:1–21.

Karstedt, Suzanne. 2013. "Does Democracy Matter for Criminologists? Situating Crime in the Institutional Context of the Polity." Paper presented in Presidential Panel, annual meeting of the American Society of Criminology, Atlanta.

Klick, Jonathan, John MacDonald, and Thomas Stratmann. 2012. "Mobile Phones and Crime Deterrence: An Underappreciated Link." In *Research Handbook on the Economics of Criminal Law*, edited by Alon Harel and Keith N. Hylton. Northampton, MA.: Elgar.

Kus, Basak. 2010. "Regulatory Governance and the Informal Economy: Cross-National Comparisons." *Socio-economic Review* 8:487–510.

LaFree, Gary. 1998. *Losing Legitimacy: Street Crime and the Decline of Institutions in America*. Boulder, CO: Westview.

———. 1999. "Declining Violent Crime Rates in the 1990's: Predicting Crime Booms and Busts." *Annual Review of Sociology* 25:145–68.

———. 2005. "Evidence for Elite Convergence in Cross-National Homicide Victimization Trends, 1956 to 2000." *Sociological Quarterly* 46:191–211.

LaFree, Gary, Eric P. Baumer, and Bob O'Brien. 2010. "Social Context and the Racial Gap in Violence: A City-Level Analysis of Changes in Black-White Homicide Arrest Ratios, 1960–2000." *American Sociological Review* 75: 75–100.

LaFree, Gary, and Kriss A. Drass. 2001. "Homicide Trends in Finland and 33 Other Nations since 1955: Is Finland Still Exceptional?" *In Homicide Trends in Finland*, edited by Tapio Lappi-Seppälä. Helsinki: National Research Institute of Legal Policy.

———. 2002. "Counting Crime Booms among Nations: Evidence for Homicide Victimization Rates, 1956 to 1998." *Criminology* 40:769–99.

LaFree, Gary, and Andromachi Tseloni. 2006. "Democracy and Crime: A Multilevel Analysis of Homicide Trends in Forty-Four Countries, 1950–2000." *Annals of the American Academy of Political and Social Science* 605:25–49.

Lane, Roger. 1992. "Urban Police and Crime in Nineteenth-Century America." In *Crime and Justice: A Review of Research*, vol. 15, edited by Michael Tonry. Chicago: University of Chicago Press.

Lederman, Daniel, Norman Loayza, and Ana Maria Menendez. 2002. "Violent Crime: Does Social Capital Matter?" *Economic Development and Cultural Change* 50:509–39.

Lehti, Martii. 2013. *National Research Institute of Legal Policy Comparative Homicide Time Series.* Research Brief. Helsinki: National Research Institute of Legal Policy.

Levitt, Steven. 1999. "The Limited Role of Changing Age Structure in Explaining Aggregate Crime Rates." *Criminology* 37:581–97.

———. 2004. "Understanding Why Crime Fell in the 1990s: Four Factors That Explain the Decline and Six That Do Not." *Journal of Economic Perspectives* 18:163–90.

Martinez, Ramiro, Jr., and Matthew Lee. 2000. "On Immigration and Crime." *Criminal Justice* 1:485–524.

Martinez, Ramiro, Jr., Jacob I. Stowell, and Matthew T. Lee. 2010. "Immigration and Crime in an Era of Transformation: A Longitudinal Analysis of Homicides in San Diego Neighborhoods, 1980–2010." *Criminology* 48:801–34.

Marvell, Thomas, and Carlisle Moody. 1991. "Age Structure and Crime Rates: The Conflicting Evidence." *Journal of Quantitative Criminology* 7:237–73.

McDowall, David, and Colin Loftin. 2009. "Do US City Crime Rates Follow a National Trend? The Influence of Nationwide Conditions on Local Crime Patterns." *Journal of Quantitative Criminology* 25:307–24.

Messner, Steven, Benjamin Pearson-Nelson, Lawrence Raffalovich, and Zachary Miner. 2011. "Cross-National Homicide Trends in the Latter Decades of the Twentieth Century: Losses and Gains in Institutional Control?" In *Control of Violence: Historical and International Perspectives on Violence in Modern Societies,* edited by Wilhelm Heitmeyer, Heinz-Gerhard Haupt, Stefan Malthaner, and Andrea Kirschner. New York: Springer Science+Business Media.

Neumayer, Eric. 2003. "Good Policy Can Lower Violent Crime: Evidence from a Cross-National Panel of Homicide Rates, 1980–97." *Journal of Peace Research* 40:619–40.

Nevin, Rick. 2007. "Understanding International Crime Trends: The Legacy of Preschool Lead Exposure." *Environmental Research* 104:315–36.

Nivette, Amy. 2011. "Cross-National Predictors of Crime: A Meta-Analysis." *Homicide Studies* 15:103–31.

O'Brien, Robert, Jen Stockard, and Lynne Isaacson. 1999. "The Enduring Effects of Cohort Characteristics on Age-Specific Homicide Rates, 1960–1995." *American Journal of Sociology* 104:1061–95.

OECD. 2010. *OECD Factbook 2010: Economic, Environmental and Social Statistics.* Paris: OECD Publishing.

Orrick, Erin A., and Alex R. Piquero. Forthcoming. "Were Cell Phones Associated with Lower Crime in the 1990s and 2000s?" *Journal of Crime and Justice.*

Ousey, Graham, and Charis Kubrin. 2009. "Exploring the Connection between Immigration and Violent Crime Rates in US Cities, 1980–2000." *Social Problems* 56:447–73.

Phillips, Julie. 2006. "The Relationship between Age Structure and Homicide Rates in the United States, 1970–1999." *Journal of Research in Crime and Delinquency* 43:230–60.

Phillips, Julie, and David Greenberg. 2008. "A Comparison of Methods for Analyzing Criminological Panel Data." *Journal of Quantitative Criminology* 24:51–72.

Pridemore, William A. 2008. "A Methodological Addition to the Cross-National Empirical Literature on Social Structure and Homicide: A First Test of the Poverty-Homicide Thesis." *Criminology* 46:133–54.

Putnam, Robert. 2000. *Bowling Alone: The Collapse and Revival of American Community*. New York: Simon & Schuster.

Robbins, Blaine. 2012. "Institutional Quality and Generalized Trust: A Nonrecursive Causal Model." *Social Indicators Research* 107:235–58.

———. 2013. "Cooperation without Culture? The Null Effect of Generalized Trust on Intentional Homicide: A Cross-National Panel Analysis, 1995–2009." *PLoS ONE* 8:e59511.

Robbins, Blaine, and David Pettinicchio. 2012. "Social Capital, Economic Development, and Homicide: A Cross-National Investigation." *Social Indicators Research* 105:519–40.

Roberts, Aki, and Gary LaFree. 2004. "Explaining Japan's Postwar Violent Crime Trends." *Criminology* 42:179–209.

Rosenfeld, Richard, Robert Fornango, and Eric Baumer. 2005. "Did Ceasefire, Compstat and Exile Reduce Homicide?" *Criminology* 4:419–50.

Rosenfeld, Richard, and Steven Messner. 2009. "The Crime Drop in Comparative Perspective: The Impact of the Economy and Imprisonment on American and European Burglary Rates." *British Journal of Sociology* 60:445–71.

Rosenfeld, Richard, Steven Messner, and Eric Baumer. 2001. "Social Capital and Homicide." *Social Forces* 80:283–310.

Roth, Randolph. 2009. *American Homicide*. Cambridge, MA: Harvard University Press.

Sampson, Robert. 2008. "Rethinking Immigration and Crime." *Contexts* 7:28–33.

Sampson, Robert, Jeffery Morenoff, and Stephen Raudenbush. 2005. "Social Anatomy of Racial and Ethnic Disparities in Violence." *American Journal of Public Health* 95:224–32.

Sanderson, Matthew. 2013. "Does Immigration Promote Long-Term Economic Development? A Global and Regional Cross-National Analysis, 1965–2005." *Journal of Ethnic and Migration Studies* 39:1–30.

Schneider, Frederick. 2005. "Shadow Economies around the World: What Do We Really Know?" *European Journal of Political Economy* 21:598–642.

Shaw, Clifford R., and Henry D. McKay. 1942. *Juvenile Delinquency and Urban Areas*. Chicago: University of Chicago Press.

Solt, Frederick. 2009. "Standardizing the World Income Inequality Database." *Social Science Quarterly* 90:231–42.

Stowell, Jacob, Steven Messner, Kelly McGeever, and Lawrence Raffalovich. 2009. "Immigration and the Recent Violent Crime Drop in the United States: A Pooled, Cross-Sectional Time-Series Analysis of Metropolitan Areas." *Criminology* 47:889–928.

Stults, Brian. 2010. "Determinants of Chicago Neighborhood Homicide Trajectories: 1965–1995." *Homicide Studies* 14:244–67.

Thome, Helmut, and Christoph Birkel. 2007. *Social Change and Violent Crime.* Weisbaden: VS Verlag fur Sozialwissenschaften.

Tonry, Michael. 1997. "Ethnicity, Crime, and Immigration." In *Ethnicity, Crime, and Immigration*, edited by Michael Tonry. Vol. 21 of *Crime and Justice: A Review of Research*, edited by Michael Tonry. Chicago: University of Chicago Press.

Tseloni, Andromachi, Jen Mailley, Graham Farrell, and Nick Tilley. 2010. "Exploring the International Decline in Crime Rates." *European Journal of Criminology* 7:375–94.

United Nations. 2010. *Rethinking Poverty: Report on the World Social Situation, 2010.* New York: United Nations, Department of Economic and Social Affairs.

UN Secretariat. 2005. *The Diversity of Changing Population Age Structures in the World.* Buenos Aires: United Nations, Population Division.

van Dijk, Jan, Andromachi Tseloni, and Graham Farrell, eds. 2012. *The International Crime Drop: New Directions in Research.* New York: Palgrave Macmillan.

van Dijk, Jan, John van Kesteren, and Paul Smit. 2007. *Criminal Victimisation in International Perspective: Key Findings from the 2004–2005 ICVS and EU ICS.* The Hague: Boom Legal Publishers.

Wadsworth, Tim. 2010. "Is Immigration Responsible for the Crime Drop? An Assessment of the Influence of Immigration on Changes in Violent Crime between 1990 and 2000." *Social Science Quarterly* 91:531–53.

Walker, Allison, John Flatley, Chris Kershaw, and Debbie Moon. 2009. *Crime in England and Wales, 2008/09.* Statistical Bulletin. London: Home Office.

Williams, Colin. 2004. "Beyond Proxy Indicators: From Indirect to Direct Measures of the Underground Sector in East-Central Europe." *International Journal of Economic Development* 6:158–98.

Zimring, Franklin. 2007. *The Great American Crime Decline.* Oxford: Oxford University Press.

Janne Kivivuori

Understanding Trends in Personal Violence: Does Cultural Sensitivity Matter?

ABSTRACT

Sociological theorists have suggested, at least in Western affluent societies, a societal change toward increasing sensitivity to violence. Possible causes include increasing affluence, security, medical victories over infectious diseases, increasing life expectancy, and feminization of society. A trend toward increasing sensitivity could have implications for understanding crime trends. If some conflicts are newly perceived as violence, this can create a false impression of rising crime, or a crime drop can be rendered invisible. Prior research and new analyses suggest that people in the West have become more sensitive toward violence. There are social differences in sensitivity, and these differences are consistent with theories of increasing sensitivity. Increasing sensitivity is expressed in heightened likelihood of reporting offenses to the police and to the crime victim surveyors.

The sociologist Emile Durkheim famously suggested that the amount of crime in society is a homeostatic constant: if there were too few crimes, people would have to adjust their views to make room for more. He suggested a thought experiment: Would a society of saints have crimes? According to Durkheim, it would. In a "perfect cloister of exemplary individuals," conventional crimes would be unknown, but

Electronically published September 12, 2014

Janne Kivivuori is research director, National Research Institute of Legal Policy. I am grateful for critical comments and suggestions from Michael Tonry, participants in the "Crime Drop" seminars in Bologna, and anonymous reviewers. I thank Mikko Aaltonen, Petri Danielsson, Hannu Niemi, and Reino Sirén for comments and assistance. The work was funded jointly by the Finnish Ministry of Justice and the National Research Institute of Legal Policy.

289

"faults which appear venial to the layman will create there the same scandal that the ordinary offense does in ordinary consciousness. If, then, this society has the power to judge and punish, it will define these acts as criminal and will treat them as such" (Durkheim [1895] 1982, p. 68). Durkheim suggested that the concept of crime could contract and expand; its power to subsume phenomena was a historical and social variable.

In an application of Durkheimian theory, US Senator Daniel Patrick Moynihan (1993) noted the increase in crime from the 1960s to the early 1990s and claimed that the crime rise led to attempts to "define deviance down": since it was not possible to quell crime, the homeostatic functioning of the social system meant that some behaviors fell out of the sphere of deviance. Moynihan would likely have predicted that a future crime drop would symmetrically lead to an expansion of conceptions of violence and an increasing cultural propensity to define interpersonal conflicts as violence.

In Durkheim's saint example, changes in crime caused changes in cultural interpretations. Society "needed" a certain amount of crime, not more and not less, and cultural definitions would expand or contract accordingly. Social theory in recent decades has again explored the links between cultural definitions and crime. Theorists have suggested that modern societies manifest increasing sensitivity and proneness to define conflicts and ambivalent situations as criminal. In these theories, the tendency to define phenomena as crimes is seen, following Durkheim, as an outcome of social processes. While Durkheim focused on crime as the sole cause of this trend, more recent theorists have also linked crime perception sensitivity to multiple structural and cultural factors.

In this essay, I examine the role and implications of changes in sensitivity to and conceptions of violence to interpretation of data on crime trends, emphasizing the *cultural-interpretive aspects* of how violence is construed by ordinary people. It is clear that the propensity of people to report offenses to the police is an important filter that affects trends in recorded crime (Baumer and Lauritsen 2010). In this essay, however, in addition to examining reporting propensity, I go one step back to the moment when a conflict or altercation is perceived as "violence." This moment of recognition is influenced by the general cultural context in which people live. In Section I, I discuss three criminologically relevant grand theories that link cultural changes to sensitivity of violence perception. Ulrich Beck coined the expression "risk society" to characterize societies obsessed with awareness of a wide variety of risks. Frank Furedi developed the notion of "culture of fear" to help understand societies obsessed with various kinds of threats, including crime. David Garland, the criminologist, wrote about the "high-crime society" in which people almost paradoxically are accustomed to high levels of crime but also are emotionally aroused by it. Key concepts in these theories differ, but all suggest that people in developed nations have become more sensitive to seeing phenomena as violent or criminal. These theories thus predict that the conceptual contents of notions such as "violence" and "crime" are expanding.

Little research has studied changes in sensitivity to and conceptions of violence over time. In Section I, I further examine candidate variables that could be used as proxies for changing sensitivities. The propensity to report offenses to the police is problematic because reporting propensity reflects a range of factors in addition to sensitivity. These include technological changes in police notification, technologies that provide new forms of evidence (e.g., threats made by text messages or by e-mail), reforms of penal law, and changes in the nature and culture of the police.

Other ways to explore changes in sensitivity are then examined, including survey data on justifications of crime and critical analyses of crime statistics. Surveys with repeated sweeps provide results consistent with hypotheses that sensitivity has been increasing. Europeans appear to have become more intolerant of petty infractions, and surveys document drastic reductions in the proportions of youths who see juvenile offending as "normal" and therefore excusable. Critical analyses based on trends in recorded offenses also indirectly point toward increasing sensitivity to lesser forms of violence. The logic of such analyses is discussed using selected examples based on Finnish, US, and UK crime data. These analyses contrast a baseline of "true" violence (usually homicide) with more volatile types of crime that are more susceptible to changing cultural sensitivity thresholds. The discrepancy between the baseline and the sensitivity measure is then interpreted as reflecting cultural sensitivity. The results of these analyses are consistent with the existence of conceptual expansions of what is seen as violence or crime.

Section II shifts attention to studies focusing on cross-sectional social differences in cultural sensitivity to violence. Some studies incorporate direct measures of sensitivity. Two subfields of criminology

stand out: domestic violence and public disorder. Studies in both indicate that sensitivity to seeing phenomena as violence (or crime) is
socially embedded. For instance, the perception of domestic conflicts
as violence appears to be linked to education. The perception of disorder in a neighborhood is linked to the demographic composition of
the local population. These two fields also approximate and highlight
two mechanisms that drive changes in cultural sensitivity: conscious
efforts by advocacy groups and social structural processes that unfold
without a steering hand.

The domestic violence and public disorder studies, however, largely
fail to address the question of changes in general as opposed to
domain-specific sensitivities. To remedy this, I turn in Section III to
the Finnish Crime Victim Survey (FCVS), which incorporates a general violence interpretation scale. FCVS data corroborate social differ-
entiation in cultural violence perception. Not surprisingly, females are
more sensitive than males to seeing conflicts as violence. Similarly,
higher education is a robust correlate of general violence-seeing sensitivity. Neighborhood social composition appears to be relevant also
in a comparatively homogeneous Nordic environment, while age and
immigration status appear to be differentially related to types of violence. Personal prior victimization appears to make people less prone
to define conflicts as violence.

Violence perception sensitivity is clearly socially patterned. The
question remains, are social differentials relevant for the understanding
of trends in personal violence? I examine this in Section IV, again by
conducting exploratory analyses with new survey data. Cultural sensitivity to seeing conflicts as violence could affect crime statistics in two
ways: by influencing the likelihood that offenses are reported to the
police and by influencing the likelihood that respondents in victim
surveys report phenomena as violence. Both are tentatively explored in
Section IV, using data from the Finnish Experimental Victim Survey.
Findings indicate that sensitivity and education are associated with
both police and survey reporting propensity. This casts a shadow on
the use of victim surveys to control for the effects of cultural sensitivity
effects on official data. The victim-offender gender constellation affects
reporting propensity, net of general cultural sensitivity and education.

I conclude by discussing these findings in relation to theories of
cultural change and to techniques of crime measurement. The evidence
from prior research, volatility baseline indicators of recorded crimes,

and explorative analyses of survey data is consistent with the hypothesis that cultural sensitivities are changing in ways that affect what "counts" as violence. These findings present considerable but not insurmountable challenges to efforts to understand crime trends. Thus, crime drops can be self-camouflaging if highly educated and nonvictimized people manifest heightened sensitivity to defining phenomena as violent and criminal. As "old" crimes decrease, new ones take their place in a process of cultural change that parallels Durkheim's classic thought experiment.

I. Are People Increasingly Likely to Perceive Conflicts as Violence?

Substantial evidence indicates that contemporary Western cultures are characterized by decreasing tolerance of interpersonal conflict and a correspondingly increasing tendency to see conflicts as violence or crime. In this section, prior research dealing with possible changes in cultural sensitivity is described. Sociological theories are briefly discussed before attention moves to variables that could be used as proxies for changes in cultural sensitivity in the study of trends.

A. Theories of Cultural Change

Several influential sociological theories suggest that there has been a shift toward increasing violence sensitivity among citizens of developed nations. Theories concerning *risk society*, *culture of fear*, and *high-crime society* incorporate a dimension of interpretive sensitivity as something analytically distinct from physical crime and violence.

Beck (2006, p. 332) suggests that modern society has become a risk society because it is increasingly debating, preventing, and managing risks that it itself has created. The risk society is characterized by an "obsession with risk" in regard to crime-related phenomena (Krahmann 2011). There is a paradox involved since developed societies appear to have achieved unprecedented levels of safety. But this paradox is resolved because the "risk" of risk society refers to anticipated risks rather than to risks that already exist. Beck also suggests that risk exposure and differential power to define risks are replacing class as the principal sources of inequality in contemporary society (2006, p. 333). He also sees the mass media as a central force creating and sustaining the omnipresence of risks.

Furedi's (2006) culture of fear theory also sees fears as culturally constructed rather than as determined by objective external risk (Walklate and Mythen 2010, p. 49). He argues that fear has become a general cultural perspective we draw on to make sense of our lives. A core feature is the belief that humans are constantly confronted by threats and risks. These can emerge from a variety of sources ranging from nature and food to people, including ourselves. Western societies are therefore constantly afflicted by crime-related panics that make the world seem more insecure (Furedi 2006, pp. 31–32). The theory comes close to encompassing sensitivity phenomena by emphasizing the centrality of vulnerability in current worldviews. According to Furedi (2008), vulnerability haunts public imagination. Thinking about risks shifts from a probabilistic to a possibilistic mode in which the worst-case scenario dominates. People who feel vulnerable are potentially also likely to see conflicts as violence.

Garland's theory of high-crime society refers to changes in cultural sensibility as an explanation for the post–welfare state criminal policies characterized by crime prevention and expressive punitivity. Owing to postwar increases in crime and because of multiple sources of insecurity in the labor market and family domains, people's wish to control risks and uncertainties, and to stave off insecurity, became "ever-more urgent aspects of middle-class psychology and culture" (Garland 2000, p. 361). Citizens have thus become increasingly "crime conscious" and "attuned to the crime problem." Phenomena such as these could be associated with an expansion of the breadth of concepts of crime and violence. Garland describes the rise of the new sensibility as a counter-reaction to the postwar historical phase that "defined deviance down" (p. 362; see also Moynihan 1993). The high-crime society is a society that defines deviance up because of a complex constellation of social, structural, cultural, and political factors.[1]

The Beckian and Furedian theories devote much attention to emerging awareness of environmental crisis, war, and terrorism and other "universal threats of catastrophic future" (Walklate and Mythen 2010, p. 52). It is sociologically interesting if people fear nuclear war, massive

---

[1] Another perspective sees similar phenomena as more abrupt moral panics, often explained by short-term interests such as electoral campaigns (see Mooney and Young 2006). The theories here described focus on more slowly emerging cultural shifts, but the approaches are neither mutually exclusive nor contradictory. Indeed, moral panics theory can be seen as analyzing extreme cases of sensitivity shifts (see Sec. I.C below).

terror attacks, or pandemics more than before, but such aspects of risk society are beyond the scope of this essay. In what follows, the question whether the increasing sensitivity hypothesis can be empirically anchored in criminological research and data is addressed. Much of the following discussion refers to Nordic countries, which are not usually regarded as the most "panicked" about crime. These countries can therefore be seen as test cases for the study of the more deeply embedded structural foundations of sensitivity to violence, as distinct from media scandals and punitive political campaigning.

B. Reporting Propensity as an Indicator of Cultural Sensitivity

The propensity of people to report offenses and incidents to the police has been a long-standing challenge for criminology. Because people's propensity to report particular kinds of incidents varies over space and over time, using official crime statistics may be seriously misleading. The early nineteenth-century criminologists sometimes used the concept of criminal irritability, *kriminelle Reizbarkeit*, to describe this phenomenon (Aschaffenburg 1903; Kivivuori 2011). The term is vivid: individuals, social groups, geographic areas, and historical periods differ in how much "irritation" crime causes and how much people are "aroused" by perceived or experienced crimes. The term is clearly related to the notion of sensitivity. Crime is constituted as a statistical reality by cultural and subjective sensitivity thresholds.

Sensitivity to seeing conflicts as violence is not the same thing as reporting propensity. Rather, perception precedes the possibility of reporting. However, since direct measures of sensitivity are rare, it is worthwhile to inspect reporting propensity as a proxy measure for cultural sensitivity to defining behaviors as violence or crime. Reporting propensity has been studied by means of surveys. Thus, Baumer and Lauritsen (2010) observed a widespread and important increase of police notification in the United States during the past 30 years, a process that started with sexual and family violence before spreading to other forms of crime and violence. In Finland, there has been a steady increase in reporting propensity since 1980 (see fig. 1).

Institutions also can manifest changing sensitivity toward violence. The Finnish Self-Report Delinquency Survey (FSRD), a national youth survey with nationally representative sweeps since 1995, has indicated a consistent increase in the likelihood of shoplifters becoming known to the police, a trend that reflects businesses' policies to "report

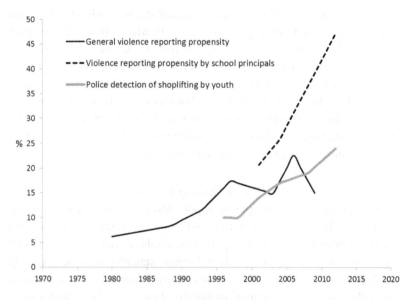

FIG. 1.—Police reporting propensity in Finland: general population (percentage of incidents involving at least hitting reported to the police), school incidents (percentage of FSRD school principals reporting a hypothetical incident to the police), and business theft reporting (percentage of shoplifters becoming known to the police for that offense). Sources: Sirén et al. 2010; Kivivuori, Salmi, and Jouhki 2013; Salmi 2012. Lines are interpolated from available survey sweeps.

all cases" to the police. Similar developments have taken place in educational institutions. In Sweden and Finland, the propensity of schools to report student conflicts to the police has increased (Estrada 2001; Kivivuori, Salmi, and Jouhki 2013). Finnish trends are summarized in figure 1. The figure is based on three separate survey data sets: the Finnish Security Survey (FSS; the percentage of people who reported an incident involving at least hitting to the police), the FSRD (the percentage of shoplifters who became known to the police for shoplifting), and the FSRD principal's module asking principals to assess whether the propensity to report incidents to the police has increased in their school over the last year.[2] As can be seen, violence reporting propensity increased gradually toward the turn of the century

[2] The FSS 1980–2009 was a national crime victim survey targeting 15–74-year-olds (Sirén, Aaltonen, and Kääriäinen 2010). The FSRD targets 15–16-year-olds in schools whose principals also respond to a short reporting propensity query (Kivivuori, Salmi, and Jouhki 2013).

but has not increased since then. In contrast, school and business decisions to involve the police show consistent increases continuing to the most recent observations.

Increases in police reporting propensity can reflect increasing sensitivity to seeing conflicts as violence and as something that should be reported to authorities. Even the policies of schools and businesses are shaped by individuals. Thus, Finnish research has indicated that the increasing propensity of schools to report student conflicts reflects parental pressure toward headmasters. Parents want to judicialize social conflicts such as bullying, and headmasters do so in part to defend themselves against charges of indifference and risks of litigation (Kivivuori Salmi, and Jouhki 2013). Similarly, the reporting behavior of business owners may reflect at least in part the expectations and rising security needs of customers. The increasing likelihood of educational institutions and businesses of reporting incidents to the police may reflect a general cultural shift toward decreasing acceptance of conflicts and disruptions.

While changing sensitivity is likely one factor driving police reporting trends, there are problems in using such trends as measures for cultural sensitivity. Reporting to the police is influenced by a plethora of factors including the technical means of reporting (Internet, cell phones), people's trust toward the police, the proneness of the police to accept reports, and the prominence of victim services and movements (see also Baumer and Lauritsen 2010, pp. 136–41).

C. Changes in Justifying or Excusing Crime

According to neutralization theory, offenders are subjectively able to break norms by deploying culturally available excuses and justifications (Sykes and Matza 1957; Maruna and Copes 2005). All neutralizations seek to influence the way others perceive an offense; a successful neutralization would redefine the behavior as not belonging to the category of "crime" or "violence" at all. Modern neutralization resources include political justifications and psychologically and statistically oriented "normality" rhetoric (Kivivuori 2011). Importantly, since offenders and onlookers share membership in a common culture, both use the same cultural resources to "understand" behaviors. Neutralization items tapping cultural notions of crime can therefore be used as measures of crime or violence perception. If culture is changing so as to make people more prone to define events as crimes or violence, this should be reflected in a decreasing propensity to see offenses as excusable or justifiable.

In Nordic youth studies, crime-related attitudes have been measured by means of neutralization scales. The rationale for using such scales has been to measure patterns and changes in the general culture of social control. Thus, the FSRD survey has included neutralization items such as "during puberty it is normal to break the law" and "youths breaking the law are merely acting out their inner problems." These attitude measurement items capture descriptive yet evaluative cultural notions that are instrumental in constructing or deconstructing the criminality of behaviors. The basic finding on cultural trends is that the propensity of youths to accept such neutralizing beliefs decreased consistently in the 1990s and early 2000s (Kivivuori 2007, pp. 96–97; Kivivuori and Bernburg 2011, pp. 419–20). For instance, the percentage of Finnish youths agreeing that "during puberty it is normal to break the law" decreased from 65 percent to 44 percent between 1995 and 2012, a finding that reflects both changing cultural attitudes and decreasing crime (Salmi 2012, p. 28). Overall, youths became less tolerant of justifications and excuses: the sphere of perceived criminality expanded rather than contracted.

Findings on adult European populations appear to be consistent with findings of Nordic youth crime studies. A recent Dutch "perception of small crime" survey used questions probing whether people consider relatively petty (nonviolent) transgressions to be justifiable (Douhou, Magnus, and von Soest 2011). Results from 1999 and 2008 suggested that Europeans became less willing to characterize minor transgressions as justifiable. In principle, a change like that could happen in the absence of changes in violence meanings and perceptions. However, the finding is consistent with the hypothesis that the boundary between transgression and nontransgression might also be shifting to include more less serious interactions. A small-scale US study indicated that the percentage of people regarding domestic violence as "always wrong" (never justified) increased from 1987 to 1997 (Johnson and Sigler 2000, p. 173). Increasing percentages of people regarded multiple behaviors ranging from never staying at home to beating the wife with a stick as always wrong. These findings are consistent with increasing sensitivity toward violence in the Western world. A recent large-scale study suggests that similar developments concerning domestic violence are occurring in developing countries as well, reflecting a global cultural shift (Pierotti 2013).

D. Recorded Crime Trends as Reflections of Cultural Sensitivity Shift

The question of sensitivity can be indirectly studied by contrasting different data sources on crime trends. The standard approach is to present crime trends based on police statistics and then add information that suggests that the change reflects social control–related factors rather than increases in criminal events (Kivivuori and Bernburg 2011, pp. 426–27, 459). While these studies typically do not directly deal with the problem of violence sensitivity, they often refer to increasing intolerance of disorderly behaviors and to increasingly sensitive perceptions of deviance. In other words, this research tradition invokes cultural sensitivity shifts as an interpretation of crime trend changes. Sensitivity is thus examined as a cause of an increasing number of recorded crimes. Studies from Sweden and France illustrate how the comparative method seeks to assess the subjective component in the constitution of crime trends.

1. *Sweden.* Von Hofer (2000) documented an "enforcement wave" against juveniles in Sweden and explained it as a consequence of a large-scale social transformation. First, increasing safety against problems such as hunger and disease-based death has lowered the sensitivity threshold of Swedes against all disruptions of everyday routines. Von Hofer theorized that the rise of the welfare state had improved security and raised expectations that led to increasing demands for additional control of disruptive phenomena. He also proposed that the feminization of society contributed to increasing antiviolence sentiment, so that making violence illegal was a "concrete expression of the status attained by female anti-violence values within the societal norm system" (2000, p. 67). Von Hofer mainly discussed the perception and control of serious juvenile violence, but his theory seems also germane to violence definition thresholds at the lower end of the seriousness continuum. His analysis would be consistent with a culturally expanding conception of violence. Hypotheses regarding social variation in conceptions of violence can be drawn from his theory. People with higher economic security and longer life expectancy should be more prone to define conflicts and borderline incidents as violence. Similarly, women should be more sensitive than men.

The overall shifts in violence sensitivity can also be seen in specific types of crime such as work-related violence. In Sweden, Estrada et al. (2010, 2014) studied the rise of work-related violence and specified two causal processes explaining the rise. First, changes in working conditions and the rise of new kinds of offenders resulted in real increases in violence. Second, increasing sensitivity to defining conflicts, threats, and altercations as violence and therefore as something that should be reported to the police also shaped the recorded trend. These two processes were likely to be mutually reinforcing.

2. *France.* Mucchielli (2010) conducted a similar analysis for France. Like von Hofer, he discerned increasing perceptions of unruliness, increasing sensitivity, and decreasing tolerance of interpersonal conflict and violence. He hypothesized a trend in which the scope of the violence concept expanded, so that previously subviolent interactions were increasingly subsumed under the conceptual umbrella of violence. What was previously defined as normal became abnormal, and what was private became public (pp. 813–14). As explanatory factors, Mucchielli referred to increasing standards of living and improvements in life expectancy and also to the feminization of society. He saw feminist movements as moral entrepreneurs who demanded the expansion of the violence concept (p. 813). Mucchielli was unaware of von Hofer's analysis, so his work can be seen as an independent replication and verification of the "increasing sensitivity" hypothesis.

3. *Finland.* There are at least three ways in which the "sensitivity-laden" nature of crime trends can be examined in critical examinations of recorded crime trends. All aim to compare crime types that are presumed to be differentially susceptible to interpretation effects. First, police statistics can be compared with external survey indicators that are presumed to be less influenced by cultural and control-related factors (but see the analysis in Sec. IV below). Second, survey sources can be analyzed internally by contrasting items that are believed to be differentially susceptible to the interpretive component. Third, police statistics can be similarly used to contrast offenses that are immune to interpretive factors with offenses that have a higher interpretive component. The studies from Sweden and France (von Hofer 2000; Estrada et al. 2010, 2014; Mucchielli 2010) used a mix of such strategies.

An *internal analysis of surveys* can be used to contrast injury-causing violence and less serious forms of conflicts. The Finnish Security Survey can be used to compare trends in physical injury–causing violence

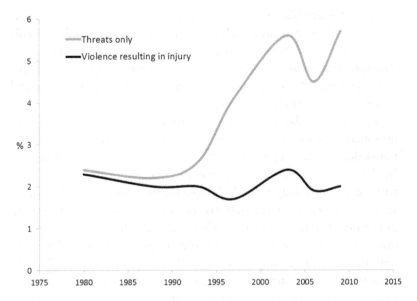

FIG. 2.—Prevalence of injury-causing violence and threats, 1980–2009, percentage of 15–74-year-olds, Finland. Source: Sirén et al. (2010). Lines are interpolated from available survey sweeps.

and threats.[3] The main observation is that physical violence has remained almost constant over the period 1980–2009, while threats increased drastically during the 1990s (fig. 2).[4] Such a divergence could be caused by changes in sensitivity that caused more phenomena to be defined as threatening. If a broader violence concept emerged during the 1990s, it could have been reflected in additional reports of threats only, while having no impact on the reported prevalence of injury-causing violence. However, this is a hypothesis: behavioral changes (increasing threats) cannot be excluded as an explanation of why reported threats increased from 1993 to 2003.

The internal analysis of official statistics is an alternative because, like surveys, official crime statistics incorporate offenses whose sensitivity-ladenness varies. I discuss two examples. In both, the rate of

[3] In this essay, the Finnish Security Survey (FSS) refers to the old victim survey (1980–2009), while the Finnish Crime Victim Survey (FCVS, 2012–) refers to the new one.

[4] The Finnish case is consistent with Aebi and Linde's (2010) observation that violence is an exception to the Western crime drop phenomenon.

completed homicide is taken to reflect the real violence level. This baseline is then compared with two offenses more susceptible to cultural definitions: defamation (fig. 3) and nonlethal violence (figs. 4–6). The following examination is intended as an initial exploration of analytic strategies that could provide openings for the analysis of cultural sensitivity differentials and trends.

Defamation in the penal law code criminalizes the "spread of false information or a false insinuation" or "disparaging another." The literal translation of the Finnish term (*kunnianloukkaus*) is breach of honor.[5] In the current context, the offense of defamation can be used as a particularly sensitivity-laden behavior. Furthermore, it has been previously used as a theoretical test case by Nordic criminologists. Writing in the mid-1970s, Nils Christie observed that crimes against people's honor were decreasing in the Nordic countries. He saw this as an indicator of an increasingly atomized and anomic society (1977, p. 6). In other words, he suggested that the decrease of defamation offenses signified a turn toward decreasing sensitivity to slanders and affronts that people no longer minded. In figure 3, Finland's completed homicide trend is contrasted with the number of defamations reported to the police. As can be seen, defamation skyrocketed at a time when completed homicides decreased. This could reflect cultural changes that made people increasingly sensitive to slurs, insults, and rude speaking. The historical trend depicted by Christie has reversed as people appear to be increasingly sensitive to insults in a period of decreasing "hard" violence.

If cultural sensitivity to seeing violence changes, this might be reflected in how many less serious crimes of violence are recorded for each case of lethal violence. Figure 4 compares trends in three types of violent crime to completed homicide in Finland. Since the offenses differ in absolute frequency, the figure focuses on trends (1980 = 100). There has been quite a consistent net-widening development: in relation to completed homicide, all types of violent crime have increased. Since the auxiliary assumption was that homicide stands for real violence, this can be taken to capture the forward march of cultural sensitivity in a Nordic welfare state. That all three offense types have increased in relation to homicide might suggest that technical statutory

[5] An unofficial transation of the 1889 Criminal Code of Finland is available at http://www.finlex.fi/fi/laki/kaannokset/1889/en18890039.pdf, 24:9.

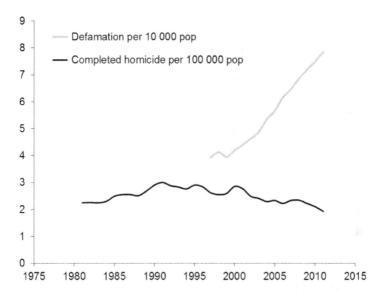

FIG. 3.—Defamation and completed homicide, Finland, 1980–2012 (3-year moving average). Source: Statistics Finland (http://193.166.171.75/database/statfin/oik/polrik/polrik_fi.asp) and National Research Institute of Legal Policy; data on defamation are available from 1996.

explanations are implausible. That the least serious type of violence (petty assault) has increased the most in relation to homicide is consistent with the cultural sensitivity hypothesis. Finland appears to have experienced a massive sensitivity shift since the beginning of the 1990s.

Completed homicide is the "gold standard" in terms of not only crime trend comparisons but also international comparisons. Comparisons analogous to those for Finland could be attempted in cross-national comparisons. The major difficulty is that while completed homicide is defined fairly similarly in different nations, crimes susceptible to cultural sensitivity are often defined differently. To illustrate the argument, I offer some examples. Thus, figure 5 compares the number of aggravated assaults per completed homicide in Finland and the United States. In Finland, the crime category of aggravated assault is the most stable of all assault offenses, which explains the rather moderate rise during the recent decade. In the United States, the criminal justice system caught more aggravated assaults for each completed homicide until the late 1990s, after which the assault-homicide ratio started to decrease. Needless to say, this comparison is highly abstract

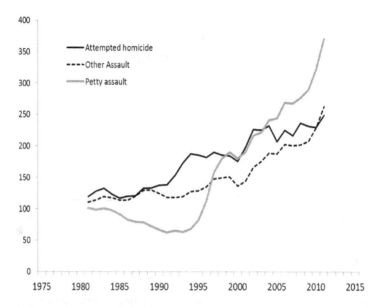

FIG. 4.—Ratio of attempted homicide, other assault, and petty assault to completed homicide, Finland, 1980–2012, 1980 = 100 (3-year moving average). Source: Statistics Finland (http://193.166.171.75/database/statfin/oik/polrik/polrik_fi.asp) and National Research Institute of Legal Policy.

and tentative as very many factors influence the number of aggravated assaults.

Aggravated assaults are hardly an ideal instrument to use to try to capture the cultural sensitivity of people to seeing conflicts as violence. What would be needed are types of offenses that are just above the official line between noncrime and crime. Such offenses are probably particularly divergent in definitions and practices. To illustrate the point, figure 6 compares "other wounding" in the United Kingdom with the Finnish crime category of petty assault (the lines stand for the number of such recorded offenses per one completed homicide).[6] It is immediately seen that the nearer we are to the crime/noncrime divide, the volatility of the crime indicator increases. These crime categories are clearly subject to changes in law and crime recording standards.

[6] Categories included are "other wounding," "less serious wounding," and "less serious wounding (including minor injury)"; from 2009, "inflicting actual bodily harm without intent," "actual bodily harm with injury," with and without racial motivation (Home Office 2013a, 2013b).

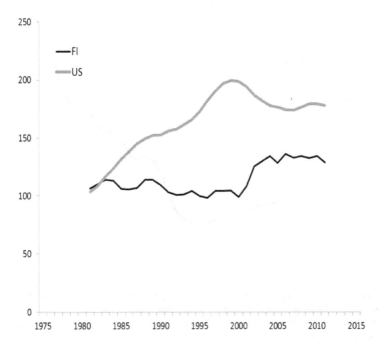

FIG. 5.—Ratio of aggravated assaults to completed homicide in Finland and the United States, 1980–2012, 1980 = 100 (3-year moving average). Source: Statistics Finland (http://193.166 .171.75/database/statfin/oik/polrik/polrik_fi.asp) and Uniform Crime Reports (http://www .ucrdatatool.gov/).

Both the UK and the Finnish series are also consistent with considerable net-widening in official control. It appears likely that such abrupt shifts are a complex result of "law and order" politics (Mooney and Young 2006) and moral campaigning taking place in the context of shifts toward increasing cultural sensitivity. Figures 5 and 6 also suggest that the timing of the sensitivity turn could be different in various nations. If the abrupt rise of the UK curve 10 years ago reflects technical changes in counting rules, the UK "sensitivity curve" could be interpreted as reaching its climax in the mid-1990s, as was also suggested by the US trend. In contrast, Finland would be a latecomer to the cultural sensitivity wave. This interpretation is consistent with policy fashions spreading from centers of innovation to countries that follow. Such diffusions can also be related to cultural trends.

Comparisons are instructive, but they should be interpreted with extreme caution. Analyses contrasting completed homicide trends and

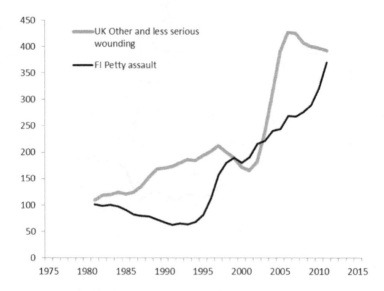

FIG. 6.—Ratio of other and less serious wounding and petty assault to completed homicide in the United Kingdom and Finland, 1980–2012, 1980 = 100 (3-year moving average). Source: Home Office 2013*a*, 2013*b*; Statistics Finland (http://193.166.171.75/database/statfin/oik/polrik/polrik_fi.asp).

other (more subjective) crime types suffer from the problem that the trends of the "subjective" crimes are influenced by multiple factors and not only changes in cultural sensitivity of people to defining conflicts as crimes or violence. Other relevant factors include at least the propensity of the police to register offenses, the bureaucratic and organizational efficiency of the police, people's trust in the police, and changes in law and victim services (Baumer and Lauritsen 2010).

Technical changes can make it difficult to disentangle possible cultural sensitivity effects. For instance, Finland has made it possible to report minor crimes by the Internet. Cell phones also may have affected the reporting of violence by victims and bystanders. Offenses such as defamation and unlawful threat using text messages or e-mail are probably increasingly reported because such offenses increasingly leave evidence when threats and insults are made. If it is technically easier to report minor incidents and if minor incidents leave incriminating evidence as never before, can we say that people's sensitivity is increasing? The interpretation is difficult also because technical changes can complexly and intricately interact with cultural sensitivity-related factors. Thus, "virtual interaction" may increase people's sensitivity, for instance, because moderating facial cues are not available. The increasing trends of the more "interpretive" crimes may reflect multiple sources, not only the cultural propensity of people to see conflicts as violence. This may also explain why the "sensitivity crimes" of figures 2–6 appear to increase at different times rather than being synchronized. It may be impossible to quantify the sensitivity component as distinct from the influence of the plethora of such factors so that it can be analyzed apart from the unique historical-institutional context.

II. Social Differences in Violence Perception Sensitivity

Above, research traditions addressing the existence and nature of the trend toward increasing sensitivity were described. In this section, research addressing social differentials in violence perception is discussed in this section. Both questions are relevant for the craft of crime measurement because both temporal and social differences in violent crime can be influenced by perceptual factors. Furthermore, social differences in violence perception can be interpreted from the point of view of probable cultural changes. For instance, if we know that higher education is linked to sensitivity, it is likely that the rising prevalence of higher education is a factor driving the cultural trend toward sensitivity.

There are relatively few studies examining social differences in people's sensitivity to seeing conflicts as violence. I discuss selected studies that have yielded information on the general social structural correlates of violence/crime perception. First, studies on domestic violence perception are discussed. Second, the related field of public disorder perception is addressed.

A. Perceptions of Domestic Violence

The relatively few studies on violence perception often stem from domestic violence studies. Thus, using a local sample from a London working-class suburb, Mooney (2000) asked her respondents to indicate whether selected incident descriptions would count as violence. For instance, she asked female respondents to agree or disagree with the statement "domestic violence includes being threatened with physical force or violence, even though no actual physical violence occurs" (p. 155). Of the respondents, 68 percent regarded this behavior as domestic violence, while one-third did not. There were sociodemographic differences. The oldest age group was least prone to define behaviors as violence. Women from professional classes were most prone to define behaviors as violence while working-class women were least prone to do so (p. 158). These cross-sectional differentials are consistent with increasing sensitivity if younger cohorts remain more sensitive as they age and if more women enter professional and non-manual working conditions.

A later US study on domestic violence perception (Carlson and Worden 2005) corroborated some but not all of the findings detected by Mooney. Women were more prone than men to define domestic conflicts as violence, and older persons were less likely than younger persons to define slapping as violence. In contrast, income was unre-lated to sensitivity to seeing conflicts as domestic violence. There were some indications that education might increase the propensity to see conflicts as violence (Carlson and Worden 2005, p. 1214).

Chamberland, Fortin, and Laporte (2007) pioneered an audiovisual approach to measuring violence interpretation. They had men watch films in which professional actors play the role of heterosexual couples in conflict situations, a method that is more realistic and subtle than the standard survey and vignette-based approaches. The men in the study represented three groups: violent men about to begin a treatment program for violent spouses, men who had completed such a program and stopped being violent, and nonviolent men from the general pop-ulation. The second group showed the broadest definition of violence, consistent with the fact that they had graduated from programs that sought to increase their awareness of it. Education was associated with a greater likelihood of seeing conflicts as violence.

The question of domestic violence perception has been directly stud-ied in regard to strategically important professions such as law enforce-ment and social work. McMullan, Carlan, and Nored (2010) examined students aspiring to these professions and detected that women, whites, and graduate students were more likely than others to describe do-mestic violence incidents as violence. Participation in a domestic vio-lence course was not linked to violence perception sensitivity, a finding that may reflect the self-selected nature of the sample (people who had decided to study law enforcement or social work).

B. Perception of Disorder

Research on what is perceived as "incivility" and "public disorder" (Innes 2004) is also relevant. Like interpersonal conflicts, threat experiences, and defamation, incivilities occupy the gray area between crime and noncrime and may be susceptible to differential and changing interpretive frames. Studies that have measured both perceptions of disorder and objective measures of disorder suggest that the extent of disorder is socially constructed. Visual cues of disorder and incivilities are ambiguous to a degree that allows room for variation and change in what counts as "disorder." This research tradition also warrants attention because it has acknowledged the local social structural embeddedness of seeing disorder.

US studies have shown that the percentage of young black males in an area is associated with the tendency to perceive crime among the residents of the same areas, independently of actual crime levels (Quillian and Pager 2001). Similarly, concentration of minority groups in specific areas increases the sensitivity of residents to seeing disorder such as litter/trash, graffiti, dilapidated housing, drinking in public places, and loitering teenagers (Sampson and Raudenbush 2004). Subsequent research has corroborated analogous findings, showing that neighborhood poverty and low social cohesion of neighborhoods are related to increased sensitivity to disorder in a manner that cannot be fully explained by objective levels of disorder (Franzini et al. 2008; Wickes et al. 2013). These studies thus indicate that social context affects the perception of crime, net of objective and independently observed disorder.

These findings are to some extent ambivalent concerning theories on general cultural change toward increased sensitivity. The minority concentration effect is consistent with the sensitivity hypothesis. Especially in Europe, ethnic diversity has increased greatly during recent decades. It is thus possible that the emergence of ethnic diversity and minority concentration increases sensitivity to seeing crime, net of its real occurrences.

The disorder perception studies appear to suggest that sensitivity is linked to poverty. That would go against the typical sensitivity theory that associates sensitivity with increasing affluence and security. However, it is possible that the poverty effect largely reflects the special conditions in which disorder studies have been conducted. Much of the literature is based on localities in which poverty is associated with ethnic and immigration-related segregation. It is therefore possible that the detected sensitivity effects are mainly due to ethnic composition factors rather than to economic factors. In any case, the disorder perception studies show the importance of conceptualizing perceived crime as distinct from actual crime (Quillian and Pager 2001, p. 720; Sampson and Raudenbush 2004, p. 322).

C. *Changing Violence Definition as Process and Project*

When differential or changing sensitivity to defining conflicts as violence is explained, several possible factors emerge from the literature. These can be roughly divided into two categories. One type of causal factor relates to cultural processes that are independent of the explicit aims and conscious intentions of individuals and groups. Durkheim's classic version ([1895] 1982) saw sensitivity as a function of crime: more crime meant less sensitivity, and less crime meant more sensitivity. Later variants point to rising affluence and security as causes of increasing sensitivity (von Hofer 2000). Even the findings of disorder perception studies can be seen as process explanations: people see more disorder net of real disorder when the neighborhood becomes ethnically diverse, a process that mostly works "behind the backs" of the human agents. In all process explanations, changes in sensitivity, and differences in sensitivity between social groups, emerge from social and cultural processes as opposed to conscious decisions to expand the conceptions of violence.

The second main type of explanation refers to political and pressure groups whose explicit aim is to expand the conceptions of violence. The feminist movement is an example of a pressure group that has consistently aimed at expanding violence definitions. It is probably true for most, if not all, Western developed nations that "policy makers and victim advocates have expended substantial energy in educating the public about the nature and causes of partner violence, focusing on reducing society's tolerance for violence" (Carlson and Worden 2005, p. 1198). An important part of this effort has been the aim to expand definitions of violence, especially in regard to domestic and sexual conflicts. It is also believed that raising community awareness about violence helps to reduce violence (Signal and Taylor 2008). For similar reasons, the concept of violence has been expanded to subsume a variety of behaviors such as emotional abuse, making a person feel bad, slanders, and control of economic resources (Muehlenhard and Kimes

1999, pp. 238–40; see also Mucchielli 2010).[7] The project to change conceptions regarding domestic violence has global reach and very likely has succeeded in changing cultural values in a manner that is not reducible to structural and demographic processes (Pierotti 2013).

There is thus a distinction between feminization as a cultural and structural process (von Hofer 2000; Mucchielli 2010) and the effects of feminist movements as projects to expand the violence definition. The cultural process refers to general value changes of all members of society, while the project factor relates to explicit aims of social movements. These process and project aspects are also likely to be interacting and may be mutually reinforcing. There is some evidence that successful completion of a domestic violence treatment program can result in broader violence definitions (Chamberland et al. 2007). Furthermore, experimental studies suggest that a feminist or violence-against-women framework can elicit more victimization reports in experimental surveys (Galesic and Tourangeau 2007; Kivivuori, Sirén, and Danielsson 2012), testifying to the possibility that such frames trigger expanded violence definitions in the general population.

The project explanation has been applied by critical criminologists studying various "law and order" movements. An example is the emergence of "antisocial behavior" as an officially regulated type of behavior in the United Kingdom (Tonry 2004; Mooney and Young 2006; see also fig. 6 in this essay). However, the critical approaches have focused more on legal definitions, police control, and enforcement waves rather than on how people's cultural sensitivity to perceiving violence changes over time. Nevertheless, there is reason to acknowledge that the generally increasing sensitivity toward violence could be partly explained by the educational and campaigning efforts of social movements, that is, by "project" factors, in conjunction with more structural and unintended factors.

III. Social Correlates of Violence Sensitivity in Finland

Social differentials in the propensity to see conflicts as violence can be studied empirically by collecting appropriate qualitative or quantitative data. Much of the existing literature concerns domestic violence and

---

[7] As an extreme example, Muehlenhard and Kimes (1999, pp. 239–40) discuss at length a movement that attempted to include consensual sex under the definitional umbrella of violence.

abuse. While domestic conflicts differ from other types of crime and violence in that there has been a strong and global cultural project to expand its definitions, there is no a priori reason to believe that definitional and cultural factors are exclusively limited to that sphere. Indeed, the grand theories of increasing sensitivity predict that there should be a more general expansion of conceptions of violence so that they encompass more interpersonal conflicts. Therefore, there is a need to study violence-seeing propensity more generally.

This section examines the question whether different social groups entertain differential thresholds of seeing conflicts as violence. The analysis draws on a nationally representative Finnish crime victim survey that incorporates measures of violence perception. I first describe the data set and its core dependent variable. Next, the bivariate association of sensitivity with gender and age is examined. After that, an exploratory multivariate analysis is conducted to ascertain the associations in a mutually adjusted model. In this stage, a selection of social structural variables such as white-collar status, education, family composition, and immigration status are included in the analysis. The analyses shown build on prior research but add to them by using a national sample, a relatively wide selection of independent variables, and general violence perception as a dependent variable. Since a considerable part of prior research stems from the Anglophone world, observations made in a Nordic welfare state setting provide an additional test case for sensitivity theorizing.

The main finding is that general violence perception is patterned according to sociodemographic differences in the population. The extent to which these differences reflect, let alone drive, secular trends postulated by grand sociological theories is open to debate. While cross-sectional data cannot be used to ascertain temporal changes, findings on social differentials can be analyzed to see how they relate to long-term structural changes and the suggested increase of sensitivity.

A. Data and Variables

The new Finnish Crime Victim Survey is a nationally representative survey of 15–74-year-old individuals ($N = 7{,}746$; response rate: 54 percent in the 2012 sweep). The survey instrument incorporates a direct question on what activities are perceived as violence. The purpose of this instrument is to measure cultural shifts over time.

1. *Dependent Variable.* In the FCVS, a list of 12 conflict descrip-

TABLE 1

Percentage of Respondents Regarding the Incident "Absolutely as Violence," Finland 2012

		Gender		Age		
	All	Males	Females	15–34	35–54	55–74
Noncontact conflicts:						
A knowingly blocks a doorway so that B cannot pass	11.5	8.4	14.5	6.8	13.3	14.6
Over the phone, A threatens to harm B physically	23.9	20.4	27.3	17.5	27.7	26.6
A threatens B with physical violence in a face-to-face situation	34.8	27.8	41.7	27.1	38.2	39.4
Contact conflicts:						
A knowingly pushes B	39.1	32.3	45.9	42.6	43.1	30.7
A grabs and shoves B	50.6	43	58.3	51.7	55.6	43.8
A slaps B in the face	63.8	57.7	69.9	66.3	69.5	54.6
A hits B so that the hit does not cause a visible sign or injury	65.1	59.7	70.5	68.1	70.9	55.6
A hits B so that a bruise results	77.8	75.6	80.1	80.1	84.2	68.1
A attacks B hitting with a hard object	94.6	94	95.3*	96.5	95.9	91.1
Sexual conflicts:						
A grabs or touches B in a way that is felt by B as sexually offensive	61.6	53.5	69.7	66.6	64.9	52.3
A tries to force B into sexual intercourse without succeeding	77.9	73.6	82.1	78.5	80.7	73.9
A forces his/her spouse into sexual intercourse	83.2	79.5	86.9	86.2	86.4	76.2
Observations	7,221	3,604	3,617	2,472	2,523	2,226

SOURCE.—FCVS 2012.

NOTE.—For data descriptives, see app. table A1. All gender and age differences are significant at $p < .001$, except for the one noted.

* $p < .05$.

tions is shown and respondents are asked to indicate to what extent they feel that the word "violence" can be applied to the listed incidents (incident descriptions are shown in table 1).[8] It is explicitly said that the parties to the incidents (A and B) are both adults, but otherwise they have no social characteristics. In the instruction, the respondent is directly asked to say whether "you think that the word 'violence' can

---

[8] The concept "conflict" is used to denote the FCVS incident scenarios even though many of them are legally clearly violent offenses. Since the study was to measure the perception of violence, it seems appropriate to describe the incidents as conflicts. The scale resembles, but is not identical with, the instrument used by McMullan et al. (2010).

be used to describe the incident." The most immediate question is, "Is A's action toward B violence in your view?" There are four response options: "no," "to some extent," "to a large extent," and "absolutely is."

Responses are intended to capture variation in people's propensity to define conflict interactions as violence, and the instruction orients respondents to think about the semantics of the word "violence."[9] Over time, responses to this question will create a time series of cultural interpretations of, and sensitivity toward, violence. Currently, the 2012 measurement is available, and therefore, only cross-sectional analysis is possible. In this analysis, the 12 items of the interpretation scale are divided into three subscales corresponding to noncontact conflicts, contact conflicts, and sexual conflicts (see table 1 and app. table A1).[10]

2. *Independent Variables.* The FCVS has been designed to serve as a "light" (and relatively inexpensive) annually repeated instrument. It contains a limited number of mainly basic structural variables capturing the social and economic position of the respondent. However, some of these variables are useful as they tap into phenomena that are relevant for the increasing sensitivity hypothesis. On the basis of that hypothesis, it can be predicted that female gender, young age, high education, white-collar position, affluence, and being a native (not an immigrant) are positively associated with sensitivity to seeing conflicts as violence. These variables are meaningful from the point of view of temporal change. Thus, age structure is changing so that there are more old persons,[11] while the number of educated, white-collar, and affluent people has also increased. Immigration has also increased, and there are more divorces. The available variables can thus be discussed as current manifestations of structural change. Most of the correlates were entered as dichotomous variables (Farrington and Loeber 2000). Basic descriptive information on all variables is shown in table A1.

---

[9] These questions do not directly pertain to standard survey responses because victim surveys never or rarely ask whether people have been "victims of violence"; the typical questions are more explicitly behavioral without recourse to general or legal concepts (see the concluding discussion below).

[10] Respondents replying "no" to all 12 incidents (reflecting response fatigue or joking intent) were excluded from all analyses. Some of the limitations of the sensitivity indicator are discussed in the conclusion.

[11] The current cross-sectional analysis is most inadequate in regard to age as changes of views over the life course and stable cohort sensitivity cannot be separated.

B. Seeing Violence by Gender and Age

Table 1 shows the percentage of respondents who regarded the incidents "absolutely as violence." In the questionnaire, the incidents were in random order; here the items are grouped into three subdimensions: noncontact conflicts, contact conflicts, and sexual conflicts. Within these dimensions, the items are listed in the order of overall prevalence of "absolute" violence attribution. As can be seen, there is a nearly total consensus (95 percent) that hitting a person with a hard object qualifies "absolutely" as violence, while only one in 10 respondents (12 percent) regarded the obstruction of movement as violence.

Females are more prone than males to define all 12 conflict incidents absolutely as violence. It should be noted that the FCVS items were gender neutral, with merely A and B designating the offender and the victim. It is conceivable that females intuitively think of the victim as a woman while males similarly think of men. A recent US study based on a quite similar methodology used separate items such as (would you consider it domestic violence for) "a husband to punch his wife with his fist" and "a wife to punch her husband with fist?" Of the respondents in that study, 99 percent responded "yes" to the first question and 90 percent to the second (Carlson and Worden 2005)

The link between age and violence appears to be somewhat more complex. In noncontact conflicts, the youngest age group is least prone to define the incidents absolutely as violence. In regard to contact conflicts and sexual conflicts, the oldest age group stands out as, on average, less prone to see the incidents as violence.

C. Exploratory Multivariate Analysis

To examine the correlates of people's propensity to define conflicts as violence, an exploratory ordinary least squares regression analysis was conducted. Sum scales corresponding to the three dimensions shown in table 1 were used as dependent variables.

1. *Gender.* Both von Hofer (2000) and Mucchielli (2010) explained the increasing sensitivity trend with reference to the feminization of society, a process that was simultaneously a cultural-structural process and a project of specific social movements. The current findings are consistent with this as female gender is robustly related to increased propensity to define conflicts as violence (tables 1 and 2). The gender effect is independent, not an expression of women being more edu-

TABLE 2

Propensity to Apply the Concept of Violence to Conflicts, Regressed on Key Variables: Standardized Regression Coefficients, Finland

	Noncontact Conflict		Contact Conflict		Sexual Conflict	
	β	p	β	p	β	p
Age	.12	.000	−.19	.000	−.13	.000
Gender (female)	.16	.000	.14	.000	.15	.000
University education	.07	.000	.09	.000	.04	.002
White-collar position	.03	.008	.05	.000	.05	.000
Income affluence	−.02	.100	.02	.063	.01	.480
Immigrant background	.04	.001	−.02	.094	−.05	.000
Divorced or separated	.02	.082	−.01	.302	−.02	.107
Unmarried	−.03	.038	−.09	.000	−.07	.000
Urbanization	−.02	.400	−.02	.180	.02	.404
Corresponding victimization	−.02	.148	−.07	.000	−.08	.000
Area educational level	−.03	.027	−.04	.002	.00	.929
Area income level	.00	.983	−.03	.038	−.02	.143
Area % of immigrants	.01	.660	.04	.006	.01	.699
Constant	6.42	.000	22.26	.000	10.86	.000
R^2	.06		.08		.05	

SOURCE.—FCVS 2012 data.

NOTE.—$N = 7,361$. For data descriptives, see app. table A1.

cated, more often in white-collar positions, or more often victimized than men.

2. *Age.* Age relates to violence interpretation differently depending on the type of conflict. Old age is associated with increased proneness to define noncontact conflict as violence but with reduced proneness to define contact and sexual conflicts as violence. One may speculate that the noncontact finding could reflect the traditional standards of "politeness" by which older people judge verbal expression; they would thus be more prone to see verbal insults, rude speaking, and threats as violent.

The cross-sectional links of age to violence sensitivity are difficult to interpret from the point of view of presumed temporal change. If age groups are seen as cohorts carrying stable violence interpretation styles, the demise of old cohorts would make the current violence semantics of younger generations more prevalent (increasing the perception of contact and sexual conflicts as violence). In contrast, noncontact conflicts would be less often defined as violence. If the differences reflect pure age or "maturing" effects, the hypothesis is not the same.

3. *Social Structural Position.*   Overall, the findings indicate that high or secure social position is associated with sensitivity to seeing conflicts as violence, net of other factors in the model, including victimization. Theories on sensitization often link the expansion of the violence concept to increasing social protection and affluence. The current cross-sectional findings appear to be consistent with this. University education and white-collar position in the labor market are associated with sensitivity. The finding that high education is linked to increased sensitivity to seeing all kinds of conflicts as violence is consistent with prior findings in domestic violence studies. Thus, Mooney (2000) found that professional women were most prone to see scenarios as domestic violence, while Nabors, Dietz, and Jasinski (2006) observed that the duration of stay at the university was linked to an expanded violence perception. The current analysis shows that the same is true in a Nordic country like Finland and for general violence perception, which is not limited to domestic violence.

4. *Immigrant Background.*   Immigrants had above-average proneness to define noncontact conflicts as violence. However, they are less prone than natives to construe sexual conflicts as violence, net of other structural features and prior corresponding victimizations.[12] Conceivably, the noncontact finding might be explained by the reality and expectation of racist slurs and threats, even though corresponding noncontact victimizations are adjusted for in the model (it is possible that tacit racism is not captured by the threat victimization items). The relative insensitivity to defining sexual conflicts as violence cannot be explained by sexual victimization that is controlled. Maybe many of the immigrants come from cultures that are less sensitive toward sexual affronts than is common among people socialized within the Finnish/Nordic culture. It will be interesting to explore whether immigrants become more sensitive toward violence as they live longer in a Nordic culture (something that cannot be done with the current data set).

5. *Family Situation.*   The family situation of the respondents was measured by two variables showing whether the respondent was separated/divorced or unmarried (single). Being divorced or separated was

[12] The direction of the effect in sexual conflicts is the same as in contact violence ($p < .10$).

not related to violence sensitivity. In contrast, being unmarried was linked to reduced sensitivity to seeing conflicts as violence.

6. *Urban Residence.* Living in an urban area was not related in the current analysis to sensitivity to seeing conflicts as violence. The reason may be that a number of social structural variables were controlled for in the analyses. In the absence of educational and other relevant controls, urban residence could be related to sensitivity due to population compositional effects.

7. *Prior Victimization.* Regarding contact violence and sexual conflicts, those respondents who have themselves experienced analogous forms of victimization appear to be less prone than others to define related scenarios as violence.[13] In noncontact violence (mainly threats), there is no corresponding association. The relative "insensitivity" of violence victims requires further scrutiny. Possibly people who have been victimized judge the hypothetical conflict scenarios against the backdrop of what happened to them. Their prior victimization experience could thus benchmark for them what counts as violence, making their violence interpretation style comparatively restrictive (see the discussion section).

8. *Area Variables.* Area factors were measured by linking register-based postal code–specific population data to each respondent.[14] In relation to defining contact conflicts as violence, these area variables emerged as relevant. Living in areas characterized by low income or low education was associated with reduced sensitivity to seeing conflicts as violence. The interpretation could be the same as for prior victimization if people living in disadvantaged areas apply different criteria to incident interpretation. In contrast, concentration of immigrants in the area was associated with increased tendency to define contact conflicts as violence. This suggests that people (irrespective of whether they are immigrants or natives themselves) are more sensitive in high-immigration neighborhoods, net of personal victimization. As such, this finding resembles findings from US studies showing that immigration increases disorder perception net of real disorder and crime

---

[13] In table 2, the prior victimization variables tap into noncontact, contact, and sexual victimization in the three models. When a total victimization scale was used, prior victimization was also linked to decreased propensity to see noncontact conflicts as violence.

[14] Because of the small number of respondents in postal code areas, these data were technically treated as individual-level variables.

victimization (Quillian and Pager 2001; Sampson and Raudenbush 2004). If interpreted in relation to social trends, immigration appears to be complexly related to cultural sensitivity. Immigrants themselves may be less sensitive to seeing violence, but their presence in the area appears to be linked to increased sensitivity to seeing violence.

Taken together, these explorative analyses indicate that men and women, people of different ages, and people from different ladders of social stratification differ in their average propensity to see interpersonal conflicts as violence. Immigration was complexly related to sensitivity. For instance, there were indications that immigrants may be less prone to see sexual conflicts as violence, but people living in areas of high immigration were more sensitive to seeing physical contact conflicts as violence, net of personal victimization and personal immigration status. Personal victimization was associated with reduced sensitivity to seeing conflicts as violence. The limitations of these analyses are discussed in Section V.B.

IV. Social Consequences of Sensitivity in Relation to Police Records and Victim Surveys

Many of the social categories associated with increased sensitivity to defining conflicts as violence are becoming numerically more prevalent in modernizing societies, such as people with higher educational credentials. This and prior research suggests that sensitivity is increasing. But is the rise of cultural sensitivity relevant for the social construction of official and survey-based statistics on crime?

The main question is whether cultural sensitivity translates into recorded crime trends through the propensity of people to report incidents. In subsection A, the data and the measurement of key constructs are described. Next, the findings are shown separately for police reporting propensity and survey reporting propensity. The main finding is that there is a robust association between violence perception sensitivity and reporting propensity and that this link is roughly the same for police reporting and survey reporting. Importantly, the current analyses are based on people's self-reported intention to report hypothetical violent incidents when asked to imagine that they themselves were so victimized.

A. Data and Variables

In this subsection, the link of violence perception to crime reporting is tentatively examined separately for police reporting and survey reporting. The data are drawn from the FEVS. Reporting propensity was explored by using incident vignettes designed for that purpose (Kivivuori, Sirén, and Danielsson 2012).

1. *Dependent Variables.* To measure self-assessed police reporting propensity, four vignettes were used, depicting workplace violence, street violence, home violence, and sexual harassment.[15] In each scenario, the violent incident caused a bruise to the victim (but did not cause more serious injury), as exemplified by the street violence scenario:

> A was returning from the movies and was queuing to a kiosk which was open at night-time hours. B was in the same queue. A and B did not know each other previously. They started to quarrel about which one had been first in the line. B pushed A so that A hit the vendor and got a bruise on his/her arm.

The victim-offender gender combinations were varied in the vignettes. Thus, all respondents reacted to vignettes depicting workplace, home, and street violence, but the gender of the victim and the offender was (randomly) varied.

After each incident scenario, the respondent was asked how likely he or she would be to report the incident to the police or, in a victim survey, if he or she had been the scenario victim. The response alternatives were "would not," "maybe," "likely," and "certainly." While it appears natural to see violence perception sensitivity as a continuum, the decision to report or not to report an incident is, ultimately in real life, a forced "dichotomous" choice. For the purpose of this analysis, people responding "likely" and "certainly" were therefore defined as manifesting high reporting propensity (coded 1) and compared with the others (coded 0) in logistic regression models. Since there were four violence type scenarios and for each of these both police reporting and survey reporting propensities were asked, there were altogether

---

[15] The sexual violence scenario came in only one victim-offender gender combination (female victim and male offender), explaining the reduced respondent number (see tables 4, 5, and A2). The FEVS was a stage in the project to develop the FCVS.

TABLE 3

Percentage of Respondents Who Would Likely or Certainly Report the Offense, if Victimized in Street Violence, by General Sensitivity to Regarding Conflicts as Violence, Finland

	General Violence Perception Sensitivity			
	Low	Intermediate	High	p
If victimized, would report street violence in a victim survey	35	60	77	.000
If victimized, would report street violence to the police	16	27	36	.002
Observations	123	249	146	

SOURCE.—FEVS survey.

NOTE.—Based on the scenario depicting male-to-female violence. For data descriptives, see app. table A2.

eight dependent variables. The corresponding logistic regression models are shown in tables 4 and 5 below.

2. *Independent Variables.*   The aim of this explorative analysis was to probe the link between violence perception sensitivity and reporting propensity. Since the FEVS contained the first version of the FCVS violence interpretation scale, it was available as an operationalization of cultural perceptions. Here the sensitivity scale was dichotomized to flag a high sensitivity perception style. Since prior research on violence sensitivity has suggested that educational level is related to sensitivity to seeing conflicts as violence (Mooney 2000; Carlson and Worden 2005; Chamberland et al. 2007), this tentative analysis sought to disentangle the effects of sensitivity and education. For this purpose, an education-sensitivity combination variable was created (1 = neither high education nor high sensitivity, 2 = high education without high sensitivity, 3 = high sensitivity without high education, and 4 = high education and high sensitivity). Since the victim-offender gender combinations were varied in the study design, these framing stimuli were controlled in the models. The associations between victim-offender gender combinations and reporting propensity are shown in the models as they are of interest in their own right. Additionally, key sociodemographic variables were adjusted for in the analyses (for the basic descriptives of the FEVS variables used in the following analyses, see app. table A2).

To give a bivariate illustration, table 3 shows the percentage of respondents saying that they would likely or certainly report a case of street violence (as described in the vignette shown above), disaggregated by general violence reporting propensity. The bivariate association between self-assessed reporting behavior and interpretive sensitivity is strong. The more sensitive a respondent is, the more likely he or she would report a street violence incident. Recall that this is about self-assessed reporting behavior in a hypothetical incident in which the respondent is cued to see himself or herself as the victim.

As can be seen, self-assessed survey reporting was more prevalent than self-assessed police reporting. This is consistent with the well-known finding that surveys elicit responses concerning incidents that for many persons are below the police reporting threshold. However, this type of indirect analysis suggests that even in victim surveys, some respondents may see pushing in the street (with minor injury) as below the threshold of what counts as violence.

B. Sensitivity and Reporting Offenses to the Police

To explore how combinations of sensitivity and high education relate to self-assessed police reporting behavior, four logistic regression analyses were conducted, one for each type of violence included in the FEVS study. Table 4 shows the basic findings of the logistic regression analyses in which the outcome was the likely or certain reporting of the offense to the police.

The education-sensitivity combinations variable was associated with police reporting propensity. High education alone did not increase reporting propensity, but interpretive sensitivity appears to be capable of doing that without high education. Furthermore, the combination of high sensitivity and high education was linked to police reporting propensity. These associations were robust in the presence of multiple control variables capturing basic sociodemographic factors, economic adjustment, and past victimizations. The finding tentatively suggests that if increasing education is the driving force behind the rising police reporting propensity, its effect "needs" sensitivity to manifest itself. The existing data do not make it possible to specify the details of this mechanism. It is possible that higher education makes only sensitive people prone to report violence or that higher education affects reporting only to the extent that it succeeds in "social marketing" of sensitivity.

The analyses yield other findings that merit attention. Females were

TABLE 4
Propensity to Report an Incident Causing Bruising to the Police, Regressed on Sensitivity-Education Combinations: Binary Logistic Regression Models for Four Outcomes, Finland

	Workplace Violence		Home Violence		Street Violence		Sexual Violence	
	Odds Ratio	p	Odds Ratio	p	Odds Ratio	p	Odds Ratio	p
Interaction of sensitivity and education:								
High education only	1.09	.718	.43	.195	1.00	1.000	.59	.225
High sensitivity only	2.48	.000	4.63	.000	3.23	.000	3.12	.000
High education and high sensitivity	1.99	.032	3.38	.018	2.30	.010	2.95	.047
Gender:								
Female	1.47	.006	1.20	.479	1.12	.419	1.36	.217
Age:								
35–54-year-olds	1.91	.000	.77	.411	.74	.079	.23	.000
55–74-year-olds	1.49	.040	.93	.829	.69	.040	.31	.000
Violence type:								
Male-to-female violence	1.36	.042	2.60	.001	1.68	.001		
Female-to-male violence	.50	.000	.75	.440	.61	.006		
Constant	−1.397		−3.078		−1.127		−1.823	
Nagelkerke R^2	.10		.134		.102		.145	
Observations	1,519		1,519		1,519		522	

SOURCE.—FEVS data, 2011.

NOTE.—Additionally adjusted: white-collar position, affluence, divorced/separated, urbanization of residence, and past victimizations. Reference categories: neither high education nor high sensitivity; males, 18–34-year-olds; and male-to-male violence, no past victimization. For data descriptives, see app. table A2.

more prone to report workplace violence to the police, but not so for other violence types. When compared with young adults, middle-aged persons and the elderly were more likely to report workplace violence but less likely to report street and sexual violence. The gender combination of the victim and the offender (in the assessed vignette scenario) had a consistent link to police reporting propensity. Compared with all-male incidents, male-to-female violence was more likely to be reported, while female-to-male violence was less likely to be reported. This finding is consistent with prior research (Felson and Feld 2009), but here the main point is that the sensitivity-education effect exists net of the perceived victim-offender gender combination effects.

This analysis indicates that high sensitivity to seeing conflicts as violence is associated with proneness to report conflict incidents to the police, net of gender, age, core socioeconomic status variables, prior victimization, and victim-offender gender constellation in the judged incident. The link emerges in all four types of violence.[16] Clearly, if cultural sensitivity is increasing and if increasing numbers of people are receiving higher education, this should translate into more conflicts being reported to the police. This in turn would influence trends in recorded crime.

C. Sensitivity and Survey Responding

The analyses shown above indicate that official statistics about violence are partially influenced by cultural and social factors that affect the propensity of individuals to report conflicts to the police. Oftentimes, the conclusion is that crime should instead be measured by recourse to survey method. Indeed, the very idea that crime should be measured by surveys was born from the critique of official statistics. The early criminologists of the nineteenth century understood that official statistics excluded the vast realm of hidden crime. Most of them also knew that the propensity of people to report offenses to the police was not a constant, even though they paid lip service to the so-called constant ratio doctrine. Their dream was to break the official control barrier of crime measurement, a goal that was finally achieved in the 1930s with the advent of crime surveys (Kivivuori 2011). But the question remains, are surveys free from culturally variant sensitivity effects?

[16] In the FEVS, violence type vignettes were all shown in the same questionnaire, so consistency in police reporting or survey reporting across violence types partially emerges from this design feature.

Table 5 shows the findings from regression models in which the dependent variable is the likelihood of reporting the incident in a survey context. The independent variables are the same as in the previous model on police reporting. As can be seen, the education-sensitivity combinations variable was highly correlated with people's self-assessed likelihood of reporting conflicts as violence in a victim survey. Both high education and high sensitivity are linked to increased survey reporting propensity, and this is so for all four types of violence. Thus, survey reporting differs from police reporting in that higher education alone appears to be sufficient to increase survey reporting likelihood. As in police reporting, high definitional sensitivity alone similarly connects with increased survey reporting propensity. Furthermore, people who have both higher education and an expanded violence notion are particularly prone to report conflict phenomena as violence, when compared with people who lack both of these attributes.

As in police reporting, respondent gender does not influence the likelihood of survey reporting. Age behaves differently in survey reporting: the elderly were less likely than the youngest age group to report work violence, home violence, and street violence in a survey, a finding raising the possibility that victim surveys underestimate the victimization of older age groups. In regard to the gender combinations of the judged vignette scenarios, the findings are the same as in the police reporting analysis: male-to-female conflicts are more likely to trigger survey reporting than all-male incidents.

These explorative analyses suggest that high general sensitivity to seeing conflicts as violence is linked to the likelihood of reporting conflicts as violence in victim surveys. Definitional sensitivity appears to have a link to reporting behavior in combination with higher education (or vice versa). There is no reason to believe that surveys as such would be less influenced by social structural and cultural processes affecting the sensitivity to seeing conflicts as violence (see also Tonry and Farrington 2005, p. 14).

V. Concluding Discussion

Several social theorists have suggested that, on average, people have become more sensitive toward various hazards and threats, including crime and violence (Garland 2000; von Hofer 2000; Furedi 2006; Mucchielli 2010). If such a turn has taken place, it is potentially of great

TABLE 5

Propensity to Report an Incident Causing Bruising in a Crime Victim Survey, Regressed on Sensitivity-Education Combinations: Binary Logistic Regression Models for Four Outcomes, Finland

	Workplace Violence		Home Violence		Street Violence		Sexual Violence	
	Odds Ratio	p	Odds Ratio	p	Odds Ratio	p	Odds Ratio	p
Interaction of sensitivity and education:								
High education only	1.55	.011	1.40	.094	1.55	.010	1.78	.047
High sensitivity only	2.59	.000	4.15	.000	2.99	.000	4.82	.000
High education and high sensitivity	6.76	.000	6.06	.000	6.26	.000	7.36	.000
Gender:								
Female	1.17	.170	1.03	.847	.90	.351	1.17	.430
Age:								
35–54-year-olds	1.29	.067	.91	.530	.79	.086	.70	.153
55–74-year-olds	.72	.025	.49	.000	.52	.000	.90	.694
Violence type:								
Male-to-female violence	1.27	.071	3.33	.000	1.91	.000		
Female-to-male violence	.79	.079	1.62	.004	.98	.849		
Constant	.258		−.671		.712		.082	
Nagelkerke R^2	.12		.172		.129		.146	
Observations	1,519		1,519		1,519		522	

SOURCE.—FEVS data, 2011.

NOTE.—Additionally adjusted: white-collar position, affluence, divorced/separated, urbanization of residence, and past victimizations. Reference categories: neither high education nor high sensitivity; males, 18–34-year-olds; and male-to-male violence, no past victimization. For data descriptives, see app. table A2.

importance for scholars who seek to understand trends in interpersonal violence. This is so because sensitivity to seeing violence can influence the number of offenses reported to the police or to survey researchers. In this essay, the question of increasing sensitivity to counting conflict phenomena as violence has been examined by reviewing the relevant literature and by using survey data to explore the social correlates of violence definition sensitivity.

There is a shortage of research examining the question, what counts as violence, directly and empirically. An area in which this dimension has been probed is domestic violence research. Researchers in that field clearly deserve praise for paying attention to definitional issues as social variables. Studies on the perception of disorder are another specialty in which key contributions have been made. These studies suggest that various social groups have differential violence definitions and that the community context affects how disorder is seen. There are very few, if any, studies using direct questions on violence perception with repeated sweeps to ascertain cultural shifts in sensitivity toward crime, but Finland's new national crime victim survey will remedy that situation in that country. The greatest shortage of research pertains to ascertaining the trends of cultural sensitivity, and certainly more research is needed in that regard. In this essay, that aspect was explored with reference to prior historical-institutional analyses of enforcement waves, and discussing social differentials in sensitivity from the perspective of social structural change.

A. Findings

The current findings can be summarized by tentative answers to three questions: Is there a trend toward increasing sensitivity? What social factors drive that trend? And is there reason to believe that cultural sensitivity translates into official statistics of recorded crime, thus influencing observed crime trends?

1. *Is There a Trend of Increasing Sensitivity?*   Grand sociological theory suggests that such a trend exists. This body of literature clearly provides a hypothesis that has not been very robustly tested, but the theorists have not developed their views in a vacuum. Scholars such as Beck, Furedi, and Garland have marshaled much evidence to support the idea of increasing sensitivity. Similarly, historical-institutional analyses by criminologists clearly support the claim that cultural sensitivity matters in interpreting crime trends over recent decades. Such histor-

ical-institutional analyses of crime trends often rely on assessing the concurrent validity of differential indicators of crime. In so doing they treat one indicator as a criterion, a "gold standard" against which other crime trend indicators are judged. Several specific types of contrast have been used. Thus, analysts have compared official statistics with survey indicators, showing, for instance, that sublethal forms of recorded violence increase while surveys indicate stability. Another approach makes internal comparisons within surveys, contrasting injury-causing violence with more subjective forms of violence. Yet another method has been the internal analysis of official statistics, which contrasts more solid crime categories with more subjective categories.

At least in Sweden, Finland, and France, such historical-institutional analyses support the role of increasing discrepancies between the criteria (lethal violence or injury-causing violence) and the assessed crime data source (von Hofer 2000; Estrada et al. 2010, 2014; Mucchielli 2010). But can this discrepancy be attributed to a change of cultural sensitivity? This is a difficult question to answer solely by means of historical-institutional and comparative analyses of various indicators. This is so because the discrepancy between the more volatile indicators (assumed to be proxies for sensitivity) and the criterion indicators (lethal violence and injury-causing violence) can result from multiple and overlapping social processes. Cultural sensitivity is clearly one such process. But the list of alternative or additional factors is long. For instance, if the sensitivity turn exists, it is probably embedded in a technological framework. The Internet has allowed new means of expressing rudeness in a manner that produces evidence. The same applies to text messages: a threat is easy to make, the phone can be used in a police report, and the text provides evidence. The rise of hate talk and rudeness is probably a combination of real rudeness and sensitivity.

It is also possible that some of the discrepancies between objective criteria crime types and more volatile crime types reflect local conditions instead of general cultural developments. For instance, the increase of work-related violence and threatening behavior in Finland and Sweden partially reflected real changes in the working conditions of specific professions such as social work, the health sector, and education. Increasing attention to the problem was relevant, but real changes mattered as well (Estrada et al. 2010, 2014; see also fig. 2 above). This dual interpretation appears to be a fairly common result in historical-institutional analyses of crime trends.

2. *Which Social Factors Are Related to Sensitivity to Seeing Conflicts as Violence?*   The data discussed in this essay illustrated some of the analytic potential of direct sensitivity studies by recourse to survey data. The findings indicate that multiple social structural variables are associated with proneness to interpret conflicts as violence, net of past victimization. Female gender, young age, university education, and a white-collar job were related to proneness to see conflicts as violence. Some of the findings corroborated prior results from domestic violence studies, at least in regard to education and professional status, which have been shown to be linked with sensitivity to seeing domestic conflicts as violence (Mooney 2000; Chamberland et al. 2007). A recent study on attitudes in developing countries indicated that education, and higher education in particular, was related to rejection of domestic violence (Pierotti 2013, p. 255). My analysis shows that higher education is analogously associated with violence perception sensitivity in an advanced welfare state context. In judging this result, it should be noted that Finnish campuses and universities are not so permeated by a security culture and crime prevention campaigning as are comparable institutions in some other countries (Furedi 2006, pp. 127–31). The education effect may capture more fundamental social processes than what is actually taught in the universities.

The correlation of age with sensitivity is difficult to interpret, given the limitations of the data. Middle-aged and old people were more prone to see noncontact conflicts as violence, while old people were less prone to interpret contact and sexual conflicts as violence. Immigrant background was also differentially related to sensitivity depending on the type of conflict. Immigrants were more prone to see noncontact conflicts (mainly threats) as violence but less prone to see sexual conflicts as violence. Do elderly people and immigrants share something? It might be speculated that their primary socialization to cultural values has taken place in another age or in another place. Maybe that "cultural lag" explains, for instance, lower sensitivity to sexual conflicts.

People who have been victimized had narrower violence definitions than others. In other words, violence victims were less sensitive to judging conflicts as violence than nonvictims. Possibly they judged the hypothetical scenarios against the backdrop of their own past experiences. Additionally, the relative "insensitivity" of crime victims could reflect the correlation between victimization and offending. Since the FCVS does not have questions about the offenses of the respondents, victimization items may partially capture variation related to offending propensity. Studies in the field of intimate partner violence have indicated that offenders are less prone to see conflicts as violence (Miller and Bukva 2001; Chamberland et al. 2007, p. 421).

Many of the detected associations were such that the relevant "risk factor" is something that has been increasing in the overall societal development. Thus, while the current analysis of FCVS data cannot directly say anything about temporal change, the findings appear to be consistent with the increasing sensitivity hypothesis (von Hofer 2000; Mucchielli 2010).

3. *Does Sensitivity Influence Police Statistics and Survey Responding?*
This question is crucial for the specification and understanding trends in interpersonal violence. Changes in sensitivity affect crime measurement only insofar as they translate into official and survey-based statistics.

I observed above that general sensitivity to seeing conflicts as violence is associated with propensity to report hypothetical violence cases to the police. Since it is known that the propensity to report offenses to the police has increased over the recent decades, it appears plausible that rising educational levels and rising culture of sensitivity together have contributed to that trend. Furthermore, reporting propensity is particularly strong for incidents involving a female victim and a male offender. This introduces some vexing questions related to interpreting trends of recorded crime. Maybe sensitivity effects on apparent crime trends are specific in terms of victim-offender relationships rather than general.

These findings appeared to be roughly the same for the propensity to report incidents as violence in a victim survey; in this regard, the combination of cultural sensitivity and high education appeared to be particularly strongly associated with victim survey responding.

B. Limitations and Future Research Needs

In the analysis of factors related to sensitivity, the findings were interpreted and discussed from the angle of temporal change, even though the survey-based analyses were cross-sectional. If education is linked to sensitivity, it can be inferred that rising sensitivity could be driven by the higher-education expansion as reflected in population composition. Needless to say, one should be cautious in drawing such inferences. For instance, it is possible that higher education flags individual receptivity to global cultural projects whose aim has been to expand the scope of the violence concept. Studies suggest that attitude change can be swift in a way that cannot be completely explained by changes in population composition or cohort turnover (Pierotti 2013). Needless to say, longitudinal analyses should be conducted in the study of general violence perception propensity. In that way, the social causes and crime reporting consequences of violence perception could be more robustly assessed in a single study frame.

Apart from its cross-sectional nature, the Finnish data on which I draw have some flaws that limit their uses in theoretically oriented analysis. Thus, the FCVS lacks variables on people's routine activities and personality traits. In the absence of personality variables, some other variables such as education may partially capture self-selection processes based on individual traits. It would be interesting to know more about the links between self-control and violence perception sensitivity. While self-control is a relatively stable trait, it is also a reflection of historically variant socialization practices (Eisner 2008; see also Eisner 2014). Such practices could be predictors of both violent behavior and sensitivity toward violence. The hypothesis would therefore be that self-control is correlated with heightened sensitivity to construing interpersonal conflicts as violence. Furthermore, it would be useful to have a measure of punitive attitudes to examine their link to sensitivity. This could help to tease out the possible difference between cultural-cognitive sensitivity and intolerance toward deviation.[17]

There are also shortcomings in the outcome variable (the instrument used to capture variation in sensitivity). Especially in the contact violence scale and in the sexual violence scale, the response distributions were skewed to the right, reflecting the fact that many respondents regard the incidents largely or absolutely as violence. Items on less serious types of conflict manifest higher dispersion of respondent scores.[18] Overall, it appears that the basic sensitivity indicator would benefit from the inclusion of more nonserious incident scenarios to introduce more variation. Furthermore, it is noteworthy that the mul-

---

[17] Thus, Lane (1992, p. 32) uses rising levels of recorded crimes as indicators of "intolerance" rather than sensitivity. Von Hofer's (2000) concept of "enforcement wave" also rhymes with that. Consider also the "moral panic" tradition, which predicts abrupt changes in sensitivity (Mooney and Young 2006).

[18] This is consistent with findings from offense seriousness ranking studies (Stylianou 2003).

tivariate models explained little variance, a finding shared by other studies in this field (e.g., Carlson and Worden 2005, p. 1209). Probably there are unmeasured factors that are causally relevant, the personality of the respondents among these.

When the relevance of current findings for crime victim surveys is discussed, there is reason to note that survey research questions rarely (if ever) use the notion of violence in the actual wording of questions. Rather, the questions are much more behavioral (hitting, slapping, making threats, etc.). Changes in the semantics of the violence concept should therefore not be exaggerated as validity threats for victim surveys. Moreover, the findings on the sensitivity-reporting link were based on hypothetical questions triggered by scenarios; this is a rather indirect way of exploring how sensitivity relates to reporting behavior in real-life victimization situations. However, it does seem to be the case that seeing behavioral items as violence is associated with an elevated probability of reporting incidents to survey researchers. Furthermore, there is some evidence that cultural frames also affect "real" survey responding as opposed to self-assessed survey responding (Galesic and Tourangeau 2007; Kivivuori, Sirén, and Danielsson 2012).

The field of violence perception studies has been dominated by domestic and intimate partner violence research. It has been an important criminological contribution of domestic violence researchers to address the question of violence perceptions. The other side of the coin is that analogous questions have been neglected among other criminologists.

Some research has examined whether intimate partner violence perceptions are correlated with perceptions regarding violence against children (Chamberland, Fortin, and Laporte 2007). Sensitivity to different types of violence was found to correlate, meaning that sensitive cognitive style transcends specific victim-offender relationships. Yet even these important findings remain within the family domain. There is thus need to examine violence perceptions more generally, something I have attempted in this essay. Overall, the current findings on sensitivity are about general sensitivity, not about domain-specific sensitivity. Furthermore, this suggests that interpersonal violence and domestic violence–related findings may reflect more general processes rather than domain-specific phenomena. Additionally, it is possible that the causal arrow runs from domain-specific campaigning to more general sensitivity, as has been suggested in relation to police reporting propensity (Baumer and Lauritsen 2010). Further research is also needed on whether general violence perception sensitivity affects how people relate to violence among socially disadvantaged persons.

C. Contrary Hypotheses and Observations

There are traditions and observations that appear to contradict the "increase of sensitivity" hypothesis. In future research, these competing or alternative approaches and observations should be addressed. Conceivably, societal development harbors several and countervailing forces that may partially suppress how the move toward sensitivity is expressed generally and in local conditions.

Media researchers have suggested that the rise of violent entertainment leads to desensitization. This means that people's emotional responsiveness to violence is reduced as a response to a repeated exposure to images of violence (Krahé et al. 2011, p. 631). Studies in laboratory settings indicate that this is really the case, even though such studies have not used violence definitions as outcomes. Yet it appears plausible that media exposure could involve changes in what is counted as violence in the first place. Of course, societal processes are complex, and observed phenomena can reflect multiple and countervailing factors.

Fear of crime researchers have observed that citizens of socially protective welfare state regimes manifest, on average, lower levels of fear of crime (Hummelsheim et al. 2011). This to some extent contradicts von Hofer's theory according to which increasing social protection leads to sensitivity and "enforcement waves." Fear of crime, however, is not identical with the more fundamental question of what counts as crime or violence. In principle, it could be possible that increasing social protection reduces fear of traditional crimes representing the "old core" of the crime/violence concept but simultaneously expands the application area of the violence concept so that increasingly non-serious incidents qualify as violence for an increasing number of people.

D. Implications for Crime Measurement

My analysis suggests that there has been a cultural change toward increasing sensitivity in the Western world and that cultural sensitivity influences the likelihood of incidents being reported to the police and in surveys. It appears to be beyond doubt that such cultural processes are relevant for the understanding of trends in interpersonal violence. However, criminology is not powerless in the face of this challenge.

Several options are open to increase the validity of crime measurement. First, crime trend analyses can rely on objective measures that are relatively immune to interpretive shifts. The most important of these is statistics on lethal violence. Second, survey measures can be used to complement official statistics. The major caveat is that, as shown here, survey responding is also subject to cultural influences. Therefore, surveys themselves should make every effort to emphasize objective measures. The most important means of doing that is to use the physical injury criterion in surveys. Like death, physical injury is not as susceptible to cultural interpretation as are less serious types of violence.

The analyses tentatively suggested that prior victimization may be related, on average, to a reduced propensity to see hypothetical conflict incidents as violence. If this finding reflects social realities, it suggests an interesting "Durkheimian" logic. People with personal experience as victims were less prone to see conflicts as meriting the label of violence, net of other sensitizing factors. This finding may have some implications for understanding violence trends. If injury-causing and physical forms of violence decrease in a society, there are more people who lack such violent experiences and who manifest heightened sensitivity to violence interpretation. Decrease of violence would feed the expansion of the violence concept. Successes in the reduction of violence could trigger cultural processes expanding violence perceptions to previously subviolent phenomena. Crime drops could thus have a distinct self-camouflaging quality: if violence drops, people compensate by expanding the violence concept.[19] This logic could also explain some of the energies that drive enforcement waves and criminalization of behaviors. Increasing control, surveillance, crime prevention, and punitiveness can be among the causes of the crime drop; but they can also be among the consequences of the crime drop through the Durkheimian sensitivity mechanism. Maybe we really are witnessing the homeostatic autoregulation of deviance at play. Maybe we are moving toward a "society of saints" whose threat detection radars are increasingly sensitive in the face of decreasing crime.

[19] This would be the reverse of the process described by Moynihan (1993).

TABLE A1

Descriptives of FCVS Variables Used in the Analyses

	Min	Max	Mean	SD	Skewness	Items	α
Dependent variables:							
Noncontact conflict interpretation scale	3	12	8.03	2.30	−.11	3	.84
Contact conflict interpretion scale	6	24	20.97	3.31	-1.35	6	.92
Sexual conflict interpretation scale	3	12	10.92	1.64	−2.11	3	.87
Independent variables:							
Age	15	75	44.25	16.44	.04	...	...
Gender	1	2	1.50	.50	−.01	...	...
University education	0	1	.18	.39	1.62	...	...
White-collar position	0	1	.34	.47	.68	...	...
Affluence (satisfaction with income)	0	1	.23	.42	1.29	...	...
Immigrant	0	1	.04	.19	4.97	...	...
Divorced or separated	0	1	.12	.32	2.41	...	...
Unmarried	0	1	.29	.45	.94	...	...
Urbanization of residence	1	4	2.77	.94	−.59	...	...
Noncontact victimization scale (items 1–3)	0	3	.20	.58	3.21	3	.70
Contact victimization scale (items 4–9 and 13)	0	7	.17	.73	6.01	7	.86
Sexual offense victimization scale (items 10–12)	0	3	.03	.26	10.11	3	.90
Area: % of low-income population	9.14	62.26	24.85	6.63	.76	...	...
Area: % of only basic education	11.53	61.62	29.11	7.57	.15	...	...
Area: % of residents speak foreign langauge	0	56.9	4.66	4.72	2.05	...	...

SOURCE.—Sirén et al. (2013).
NOTE.—N = 7,463.

TABLE A2

Descriptives of FEVS Variables Used in the Analyses

	Min	Max	Mean	SD
Dependent variables:				
Police reporting propensity:				
Work violence scenario	0	1	.19	.40
Home violence scenario	0	1	.05	.22
Street violence scenario	0	1	.2	.40
Sexual harassment scenario	0	1	.19	.40
Survey reporting propensity:				
Work violence scenario	0	1	.45	.50
Home violence scenario	0	1	.25	.44
Street violence scenario	0	1	.49	.50
Sexual harassment scenario	0	1	.43	.50
Independent variables:				
High propensity to see conflicts as violence*	0	1	.19	.39
Higher education	0	1	.17	.38
Combinations of high propensity and high education	1	4	1.56	.89
Gender	0	1	.5	.50
Age (3 groups)	1	3	2.04	.79
Victim-offender combination in the scenario	4	6	4.99	.81
White-collar occupation	0	1	.33	.47
Affluence (easy or very easy to cover expenses)	0	1	.29	.46
Divorced or separated	0	1	.08	.27
Urbanization of living area	1	4	2.62	.98
Past victimization (4 categories)	0	3	.44	.86

SOURCE.—Kivivuori, Sirén, and Danielsson (2012).
NOTE.—$N = 1,545$ except in sexual harrassment analyses, where $N = 528$.
* Highest quintile of a sum variable with 12 items and $\alpha = .898$.

REFERENCES

Aebi, Marcelo, and Antonia Linde. 2010. "Is There a Crime Drop in Western Europe?" *European Journal of Criminal Policy and Research* 16:251–77.

Aschaffenburg, G. 1903. *Das Verbrechen und seine Bekämpfung: Kriminalpsychologie für Mediziner, Juristen und Soziologen, ein Beitrag zur Reform der Strafgesetzgebung.* Heidelberg: Carl Winters Universitätsbuchhandlung.

Baumer, Eric P., and Janet L. Lauritsen. 2010. "Reporting Crime to the Police,

1973–2005: A Multivariate Analysis of Long-Term Trends in the National Crime Survey (NCS) and National Crime Victimization Survey (NCVS)." *Criminology* 48:131–85.

Beck, Ulrich. 2006. "Living in the World Risk Society." *Economy and Society* 35:329–45.

Carlson, Bonnie E., and Alissa Pollitz Worden. 2005. "Attitudes and Beliefs about Domestic Violence: Results of a Public Opinion Survey: I. Definitions of Domestic Violence, Criminal Domestic Violence, and Prevalence." *Journal of Interpersonal Violence* 20:1197–1218.

Chamberland, Claire, Andrée Fortin, and Lise Laporte. 2007. "Establishing a Relationship between Behavior and Cognition: Violence against Women and Children within the Family." *Journal of Family Violence* 22:383–95.

Chamberland, Claire, Andrée Fortin, Joane Turgeon, and Lise Laporte. 2007. "Men's Recognition of Violence against Women and Spousal Abuse: Comparison of Three Groups of Men." *Violence and Victims* 22:419–36.

Christie, Nils. 1977. "Conflicts as Property." *British Journal of Criminology* 17: 1–15.

Douhou, Salima, Jan R. Magnus, and Arthur von Soest. 2011. "The Perception of Small Crime." *European Journal of Political Economy* 27:749–63.

Durkheim, Emile. 1982. *The Rules of Sociological Method*. Edited with introduction by Steven Lukes. New York: Free Press, Macmillan. (Originally published 1895.)

Eisner, Manuel. 2008. "Modernity Strikes Back? A Historical Perspective on the Latest Increase of Interpersonal Violence (1960–1990)." *International Journal of Conflict and Violence* 2:288–316.

———. 2014. "From Swords to Words: Does Macro-Level Change in Self-Control Predict Long-Term Variation in Levels of Homicide?" In *Explaining Declining Crime Rates in Western Countries*, edited by Michael Tonry. Vol. 43 of *Crime and Justice: A Review of Research*, edited by Michael Tonry. Chicago: University of Chicago Press.

Estrada, Felipe. 2001. "Juvenile Violence as a Social Problem: Trends, Media Attention, and Societal Response." *British Journal of Criminology* 41:639–55.

Estrada, Felipe, Janne Flyghed, Anders Nilsson, and Karin Bäckman. 2014. "Why Are Occupational Safety Crimes Increasing?" *Journal of Scandinavian Studies in Criminology and Crime Prevention* 15:3–18.

Estrada, Felipe, Anders Nilsson, Kristina Jerre, and Sofia Wikman. 2010. "Violence at Work: The Emergence of a Social Problem." *Journal of Scandinavian Studies in Criminology and Crime Prevention* 11:46–65.

Farrington, David P., and Rolf Loeber. 2000. "Some Benefits of Dichotomization in Psychiatric and Criminological Research." *Criminal Behavior and Mental Health* 10:100–122.

Felson, Richard B., and Scott L. Feld. 2009. "When a Man Hits a Woman: Moral Evaluations and Reporting Violence to the Police." *Aggressive Behavior* 35:477–88.

Franzini, Luisa, Margaret O'Brien Caughy, Saundra Murray Nettles, and Patricia O'Campo. 2008. "Perceptions of Disorder: Contributions of Neighborhood Characteristics to Subjective Perceptions of Disorder." *Journal of Environmental Psychology* 28:83–93.

Furedi, Frank. 2006. *Culture of Fear Revisited: Risk-Taking and the Morality of Low Expectation*. New York: Continuum.

———. 2008. "Fear and Security: A Vulnerability-Led Policy Response." *Social Policy and Administration* 42:645–61.

Galesic, Mirta, and Roger Tourangeau. 2007. "What Is Sexual Harassment? It Depends on Who Asks! Framing Effects on Survey Responses." *Applied Cognitive Psychology* 21:189–202.

Garland, David. 2000. "The Culture of High Crime Societies." *British Journal of Criminology* 40:347–75.

Home Office. 2013a. *A Summary of Recorded Crime Data from 1898 to 2001/02*. London: Home Office. https://www.gov.uk/government/publications/historical-crime-data.

———. 2013b. *A Summary of Recorded Crime Data from 2002/03 to 2012/2013*. London: Home Office. https://www.gov.uk/government/publications/historical-crime-data.

Hummelsheim, Dina, Helmut J. Hirtenlehner, Jonathan Jackson, and Dietrich Oberwittler. 2011. "Social Insecurities and Fear of Crime: A Cross-National Study on the Impact of Welfare State Policies on Crime-Related Anxieties." *European Sociological Review* 27:327–45.

Innes, Martin. 2004. "Signal Crimes and Signal Disorders: Notes on Deviance as Communicative Action." *British Journal of Sociology* 55:335–55.

Johnson, Ida M., and Robert T. Sigler. 2000. "The Stability of the Public's Endorsements of the Definition and Criminalization of the Abuse of Women." *Journal of Criminal Justice* 28:165–79.

Kivivuori, Janne. 2007. *Delinquent Behavior in Nordic Capital Cities*. Scandinavian Research Council for Criminology and National Research Institute of Legal Policy, Publication 227. Helsinki: National Research Institute of Legal Policy.

———. 2011. *Discovery of Hidden Crime: Self-Report Delinquency Surveys in Criminal Policy Context*. Oxford: Oxford University Press.

Kivivuori, Janne, and Jon Gunnar Bernburg. 2011. "Delinquency Research in the Nordic Countries." In *Crime and Justice in Scandinavia*, edited by Michael Tonry and Tapio Lappi-Seppälä. Vol. 40 of *Crime and Justice: A Review of Research*, edited by Michael Tonry. Chicago: University of Chicago Press.

Kivivuori, Janne, Venla Salmi, and Virpi Jouhki. 2013. "Oikeudellistuva sosiaalinen kontrolli: Esimerkkinä koulujen alttius ilmoittaa oppilaiden tekoja poliisille." In *Suomalainen kriminaalipolitiikka: Näkökulmia teoriaan ja käytäntöön*, edited by Ville Hinkkanen and Leena Mäkipää. Forum Iuris. Helsinki: University of Helsinki Law Faculty.

Kivivuori, Janne, Reino Sirén, and Petri Danielsson. 2012. "Gender Framing Effects in Victim Surveys." *European Journal of Criminology* 9:142–58.

Krahé, Barbara, Ingrid Möller, L. Rowell Huessmann, Lucyna Kirwil, Juliane Ferber, and Anja Berger. 2011. "Desensitization to Media Violence: Links with Habitual Media Violence Exposure, Aggressive Cognitions, and Aggressive Behavior." *Journal of Personality and Social Psychology* 100:530–646.

Krahmann, Elke. 2011. "Beck and Beyond: Selling Security in the World Risk Society." *Review of International Studies* 37:349–72.

Lane, Roger. 1992. "Urban Police and Crime in Nineteenth-Century America." In *Crime and Justice: A Review of Research*, vol. 15, edited by Michael Tonry. Chicago: University of Chicago Press.

Maruna, Shadd, and Heith Copes. 2005. "What Have We Learned from Five Decades of Neutralization Research?" In *Crime and Justice: A Review of Research*, vol. 32, edited by Michael Tonry. Chicago: University of Chicago Press.

McMullan, Elizabeth C., Philip E. Carlan, and Lisa S. Nored. 2010. "Future Law Enforcement Officers and Social Workers: Perceptions of Domestic Violence." *Journal of Interpersonal Violence* 25:1367–87.

Miller, Joann, and Kathy Bukva. 2001. "Intimate Violence Perceptions: Young Adults' Judgements of Abuse Escalating from Verbal Arguments." *Journal of Interpersonal Violence* 16:133–50.

Mooney, Jayne. 2000. *Gender, Violence, and the Social Order*. London: Macmillan.

Mooney, Jayne, and Jock Young. 2006. "The Decline in Crime and the Rise of Anti-social Behavior." *Probation Journal* 53:397–407.

Moynihan, Daniel Patrick. 1993. "Defining Deviancy Down." *American Scholar* 62:1.

Mucchielli, Laurent. 2010. "Are We Living in a More Violent Society? A Socio-historical Analysis of Interpersonal Violence in France, 1970s–Present." *British Journal of Criminology* 50:808–29.

Muehlenhard, Charlene L., and Leigh Ann Kimes. 1999. "The Social Construction of Violence: The Case of Sexual and Domestic Violence." *Personality and Social Psychology Review* 3:234–45.

Nabors, Erin L., Tracy L. Dietz, and Jana L. Jasinski. 2006. "Domestic Violence Beliefs and Perceptions among College Students." *Violence and Victims* 21:779–95.

Pierotti, Rachael S. 2013. "Increasing Rejection of Intimate Partner Violence: Evidence of Global Cultural Diffusion." *American Sociological Review* 78:240–65.

Quillian, Lincoln, and Devah Pager. 2001. "Black Neighbors, Higher Crime? The Role of Racial Stereotypes in Evaluations of Neighborhood Crime." *American Journal of Sociology* 107:717–67.

Salmi, Venla. 2012. *Nuorten rikoskäyttäytyminen ja uhrikokemukset 2012*. Oikeuspoliittisen tutkimuslaitoksen tutkimustiedonantoja 113. Helsinki: Oikeuspoliittinen tutkimuslaitos.

Sampson, Robert J., and Stephen W. Raudenbush. 2004. "Seeing Disorder: Neighborhood Stigma and the Social Construction of 'Broken Windows.'" *Social Psychology Quarterly* 67:319–42.

Signal, Tania, and Nicola Taylor. 2008. "Propensity to Report Intimate Partner

Violence in Australia: Community Demographics." *Behavior and Social Issues* 17:8–19.

Sirén, Reino, Mikko Aaltonen, and Juha Kääriäinen. 2010. *Suomalaisten väkivaltakokemukset, 1980–2009: Kansallisen uhritutkimuksen tuloksia.* Helsinki: Oikeuspoliittinen tutkimuslaitos.

Sirén, Reino, Petri Danielsson, and Janne Kivivuori. 2013. *Suomalaiset väkivallan ja omaisuusrikosten kohteena 2012.* Oikeuspoliittisen tutkimuslaitoksen verkkokatsauksia 28/2013. Helsinki: Oikeuspoliittinen tutkimuslaitos.

Stylianou, Stelios. 2003. "Measuring Crime Seriousness Perceptions: What Have We Learned and What Else Do We Want to Know?" *Journal of Criminal Justice* 31:37–56.

Sykes, Gresham, and David Matza. 1957. "Techniques of Neutralization: A Theory of Delinquency." *American Sociological Review* 22:664–73.

Tonry, Michael. 2004. *Punishment and Politics: Evidence and Emulation in the Making of English Crime Control Policy.* Cullompton, Devon, UK: Willan.

Tonry, Michael, and David P. Farrington. 2005. "Punishment and Crime across Space and Time." In *Crime and Punishment in the Western Countries, 1980–1999*, edited by Michael Tonry and David P. Farrington. Vol. 33 of *Crime and Justice: A Review of Research*, edited by Michael Tonry. Chicago: University of Chicago Press.

von Hofer, Hanns. 2000. "Criminal Violence and Youth in Sweden: A Long-Term Perspective." *Journal of Scandinavian Studies in Criminology and Crime Prevention* 1:56–72.

Walklate, Sandra, and Gabriel Mythen. 2010. "Agency, Reflexivity and Risk: Cosmopolitan, Neurotic or Prudential Citizen?" *British Journal of Sociology* 61:45–62.

Wickes, Rebecca, John H. Hipp, Renee Zahnow, and Lorraine Mazerolle. 2013. "'Seeing' Minorities and Perceptions of Disorder: Explicating the Mediating and Moderating Mechanisms of Social Cohesion." *Criminology* 51:519–60.

Richard Rosenfeld

Crime and Inflation in Cross-National Perspective

ABSTRACT

Inflation belongs in the repertoire of economic indicators used in research on crime patterns. A resurgence of research on the relationship between economic conditions and crime has occurred in recent years, most of it showing crime increases during economic downturns and declines during recoveries. The so-called Great Recession of 2008–9 broke this pattern; crime rates fell or were flat. Historical scholarship on long-term crime increases during "price revolutions" and scattered empirical research on the relationship between short-run changes in crime and inflation suggest that low inflation rates help explain the absence of crime increases during the recent recession. Inflation, net of other economic conditions, had significant effects on homicide, robbery, and burglary rates in several European nations and the United States from the early 1980s to 2010. Inflation may be connected to crime through the dynamics of markets for stolen goods. As prices rise, the demand for cheap stolen goods grows, which strengthens incentives to increase the supply of stolen merchandises. Property crime rates increase. Violent crimes also increase as transactions multiply in "stateless" locations beyond the purview of formal authorities. The process operates in reverse as price increases diminish.

The role of inflation has not figured centrally in recent research on the effects of economic conditions on changes in crime rates over time. That research is dominated by studies of the effect of unemployment on crime rates, with some attention also devoted to the effects of total economic output, wages, and consumer sentiment (Chiricos 1987;

Electronically published September 12, 2014

Richard Rosenfeld is Founders' Professor of Criminology and Criminal Justice, University of Missouri–St. Louis.

341

Gould, Weinberg, and Mustard 2002; Arvanites and Defina 2006; Rosenfeld and Fornango 2007). There is a body of research that examines the contribution of inflation to crime rates, but it is small, scattered, theoretically underdeveloped, and limited to the United States. Building on that literature, in this essay I examine the connection between inflation and crime rates in cross-national context during the late twentieth and early twenty-first century, compare the effects of inflation with those of other macroeconomic conditions, and offer a theoretical foundation to guide future research on the role of price changes in the production of crime.

Historical research discloses a close connection between price increases and long-term increases in crime (Fischer 1996). That research, however, has made no noticeable impression on criminologists and other social scientists who study the relationship between economic conditions and crime trends. They have focused, first and foremost, on the effects of unemployment, with more recent attention devoted to wages, economic growth, and consumer sentiment. A small and somewhat dated body of research on inflation and crime shows a significant and positive relationship, but inflation has not been part of the recent research revival on the economy and crime, probably because prices have been impressively stable for the past two decades in the United States and most of Europe. Receding inflationary pressures may be an important reason why crime rates have fallen in Europe and the United States since the mid-1990s up to and through the Great Recession.

An analysis of homicide, robbery, and burglary trends in the United States and several European nations between the early 1980s and 2010 supports this expectation. Changes in consumer prices are associated with changes in these offenses, controlling for the effects of unemployment, economic growth, the age composition of the population, urbanization, and a measure of poverty. This analysis extends to other developed nations the results of prior research on inflation and crime in the United States.

The analysis also contributes to research on the economy and crime by offering an explanation for the effects of inflation, over and above those of other economic conditions, on both property and violent crime. Inflation spurs consumers to search for low-cost goods and services. When aggregate prices increase, retail outlets offering cut-rate prices do comparatively well—including those where consumers can find cheap stolen goods. As demand grows and transactions multiply in these underground locales, both property and violent crime rates increase. When prices stabilize, the demand for stolen goods shrinks, and crime rates fall. Inflation belongs in the suite of empirical indicators used to study changes in crime rates over time because it produces stress and discontent, as historians and sociologists have proposed, but also because it has a direct and immediate effect on the demand for stolen goods. This argument, firmly grounded in classical economic theory, merits attention in future research on the economy and crime.

The narrative unfolds as follows. Section I summarizes the historian David Hackett Fischer's argument and evidence linking upturns in social disorder and crime to four major "price revolutions" in Western history. Section II reviews prior research connecting crime increases to economic downturns and discusses the seeming paradox of the 2008–9 Great Recession, during which crime rates in the United States and most of Europe were flat or fell. The key to the puzzle is that inflation rates were running at historic lows during the Great Recession. The modest research literature on the relationship between inflation and crime supports this interpretation, but it is limited in theoretical depth and empirical scope. Section III augments existing explanations by highlighting the connection between aggregate price changes and the dynamics of demand in underground markets. As prices rise, demand for cheap stolen goods increases, and crime rates follow suit. Crime rates reverse course as underground markets shrink.

The following sections augment the empirical range of prior research on crime and inflation. The data and methods used in the current research are described in Section IV, and the results of a multivariate analysis of the relationship between inflation and homicide, robbery, and burglary rates are presented in Section V. The results reveal a significant and sizable impact of price changes on the crime trends over a 30-year period. The limitations of the analysis reported here are discussed in Section VI, guidelines for future research are suggested, and provisional policy guidance is offered.

I. Price Revolutions and Long Swings in Crime
The economic historian David Hackett Fischer has documented surges in crime that accompanied four "great waves" of price increases in the history of the Western world: the price revolutions of the fourteenth,

sixteenth, eighteenth, and twentieth centuries (Fischer 1996). During each period, rates of violent and property crime rose, especially in the latter stages of price inflation, and then fell during an extended period of "equilibrium" following each price revolution. Differing in particulars, the four price revolutions share several basic features: all began during periods of prosperity and were driven by expansions in demand for goods, usually resulting from population growth; they produced and were augmented by rising economic inequality; and they hit most European nations and, later, North America at the same time.

The latter point is especially pertinent. Bouts of sustained inflation are generally cross-national in timing and effect. For example, "the price-revolution of the twentieth century was not peculiar to any national economy or monetary system. It was a global event" (Fischer 1996, p. 188). Its social consequences were similarly global in scope. "Crime increased rapidly around the world during the period from 1965 to 1993. These movements correlated very closely with rates of inflation" (p. 225). As inflation rates began to fall in the early 1990s, so did crime rates in both Europe and the United States. Writing before the end of the twentieth century, Fischer was uncertain whether the most recent price revolution had come to an end. Nearly two decades later, we are in a better position to judge whether the Western world has entered a new period of price equilibrium and social peace.

II. Research on Crime and the Economy

Fischer's (1996) book on price revolutions was widely and positively reviewed, yet it has not had any discernible influence on contemporary criminological research, including comparative studies of crime trends. The role of inflation is conspicuous by its absence from recent research on crime and economic conditions.

A. New Consensus[1]

The long-standing research literature on the relationship between economic conditions and crime trends was puzzling at best and grim at worst. Puzzling because studies consistently returned mixed results. Grim because the results could be used to support almost any conclusion about how, or whether, the economy affects crime rates (Bushway

[1] This discussion is adapted from Rosenfeld and Messner (2013).

2011; Rosenfeld 2011). Around the turn of the current century, however, the "consensus of doubt" (Chiricos 1987) began to give way to a new research consensus regarding the relationship between the economy and crime.

Several studies confirmed the ages-old belief that worsening economic conditions produce disorder and crime. The new consensus was fueled, in part, by replacement or supplementation of the unemployment rate, the long-standing economic indicator of choice in research on crime trends, with other economic indicators. A good bit of the groundwork for the recent research on the economy and crime was established in an early paper by Cook and Zarkin (1985; see also Bushway, Cook, and Phillips 2013), who found that rates of robbery and property crime tend to increase during recessions and decline during recoveries. More recently, Arvanites and Defina (2006) found that state-level gross domestic product per capita is significantly related to property crime trends in US states in the expected direction: As output falls, crime rates increase. The researchers found no significant effect of unemployment on property crime. Rosenfeld and Fornango (2007) replicated these results and also found that collective perceptions of economic change, or "consumer sentiment," are significantly associated with regional property crime trends (see also Lauritsen and Heimer 2010). During periods of rising consumer confidence and optimism, crime rates fall, and when confidence wanes, crime rates rise. Similar results for the effects of consumer sentiment were reported in a comparative study of burglary rates in the United States and European nations (Rosenfeld and Messner 2009).

Grogger (1998) and Gould, Weinberg, and Mustard (2002) found an inverse relationship between wages and youth crime in the United States, and some studies even showed the expected positive effect of unemployment on crime trends (e.g., Raphael and Winter-Ebmer 2001; Gould, Weinberg, and Mustard 2002). The new consensus in findings concerning the relationship between economic conditions and property crime is matched by equal convergence in results showing little or no direct relationship with violent crime (for an exception, see Lauritsen and Heimer 2010). Finally, in an analysis of US cities, Baumer (2008) found evidence of asymmetry in the temporal relationship between crime and economic conditions, with economic factors contributing more to the 1990s crime drop than to the preceding rise during the 1980s.

B. Great Recession

And then came the "Great Recession" of 2008 and 2009. Economic output plunged, unemployment soared, and consumer confidence hit historical lows across the developed world. But crime rates did not rise in response as they had in the past. At the very least, these seemingly anomalous patterns pose a challenge to the new research consensus on crime and the economy. If deteriorating economic conditions drive up crime, how are we to explain falling crime rates during a severe recession?

A key difference between the 2008–9 recession and those of the past several decades, especially the "stagflation" period of the 1970s and early 1980s, is the absence of inflationary pressures during the recent downturn. Some economists warned that falling prices in the United States could deepen the recession (e.g., *Economist* 2010; Krugman 2010). Fischer (1996) has presented a suggestive historical case that changing crime rates coincide with price changes. As prices fell during the 1930s, in the United States and elsewhere, crime rates did as well. We might then add price deflation to the list of proposed solutions to the riddle of why crime dropped during the Great Depression (see, e.g., Johnson, Kantor, and Fishback 2007). Both crime and consumer prices were at historic lows during the 1950s. And what of the paradox of "crime amidst plenty" in the 1960s (Wilson 1985)? In fact, prices in the United States began a steep rise in the mid-1960s, and crime rates followed suit (Fischer 1996; LaFree 1998). While intriguing, these historical parallels offer only impressionistic evidence of the connection between short-run inflation and crime. The connection is confirmed, however, by more systematic empirical studies, although the relevant research is modest in both size and theoretical depth.

C. Crime and Inflation

Several studies report a significant and positive association between inflation and crime rates in the United States. Tang and Lean (2007) found a positive relationship between inflation and crime rates for the period 1960 to 2005 and concluded that the causal direction of the association is from inflation to crime. Allen (1996) examined the effects of inflation and several other socioeconomic indicators in time-series models of robbery, burglary, and motor vehicle theft rates between 1959 and 1992. The study reports a significant and positive inflation effect on all three types of offense and concludes that "inflation motivates criminal behavior independently of other socioeconomic conditions" (p. 303). Ralston (1999) reported a similar result for inflation in an analysis of burglary, larceny, and motor vehicle theft rates between 1958 and 1995. LaFree and Drass (1996) found positive effects of inflation on black and white arrest rates for robbery, burglary, and homicide between 1957 and 1990.[2]

Each of these studies treats the relationship between crime and inflation as if it were strictly linear, with changes in inflation giving rise to changes in crime rates of the same direction and magnitude regardless of whether inflation levels are high or low. There are reasons to suppose, however, that the association between inflation and crime may be curvilinear. Fischer (1996) observes that the first stage of each price revolution in Western history was one of "silent beginnings" characterized by small price increases well within the range of previous fluctuations and a general mood of confidence and optimism. This implies that crime rates should not increase appreciably, and may even decline, until inflation reaches a minimum threshold and breaks "through the boundaries of the previous equilibrium" (Fischer 1996, p. 237). The same logic of escalating effects on crime may also apply to other economic conditions, such as unemployment and economic growth.

The lack of attention to the possible nonlinear effects of inflation on crime rates reflects the atheoretical character of prior research. An exception is an early study by Devine, Sheley, and Smith (1988), which considers inflation and unemployment to be the two main macroeconomic indicators that influence US crime trends. The researchers argued that "inflation unleashes distributional conflict and undermines confidence in existing institutional arrangements" (Devine, Sheley, and Smith 1988, p. 408). This point is echoed in LaFree's (1998) account of the role of inflation in increasing crime by eroding institutional legitimacy. Finally, Fischer (1996) attributes upswings in crime to the deprivation, discontent, and stress brought about by inflation.

These arguments are quite plausible, but they rarely distinguish on theoretical grounds the effects of inflation from other measures of economic adversity, such as unemployment or weak economic growth, nor do they exhaust the theoretical significance of inflation as a cause of

---

[2] See Lafree, Drass, and O'Day (1992) for similar results; see also Cohen and Felson (1979).

crime. Inflation also may lead to crime increases by strengthening demand for cheap stolen goods.

III. The Dynamics of Demand and Supply in Illegal Markets

> . . . if there were no bargain hunting citizens the market
> for stolen goods would shrink enormously. (Sutton, Hodgkinson, and Levi 2008, p. 5)

Persons engaged in income-producing crime must have a way of disposing of the goods they steal that they do not consume. They can give them away, sell them for cash, or exchange them for something else of value. Gifts aside, property offenders perforce must become involved in underground or "off-the-books" transactions because it is illegal to buy and sell stolen goods. Applying standard economic theory, the greater the demand for stolen goods, the higher the returns to acquisitive crime (Becker 1968; Ehrlich 1973). The key issue in understanding the influence of underground markets on acquisitive crime, then, concerns the conditions that shape the demand for stolen goods.

Generally speaking, when aggregate incomes fall or prices rise, consumers search for cheaper goods and services; economists refer to this as "trading down." For example, as prices increase, midlevel retail outlets typically lose customers to those selling the same or similar goods at discount prices, such as Walmart and other "big-box" discount outlets, "dollar" stores, and the retail shops operated by Goodwill Industries and the Salvation Army. As a result, such businesses do comparatively well during economic downturns (Burke 2008; Rosenbloom 2008; Jackson and Feld 2011).

But where do those who had been shopping at Dollar General or Goodwill trade down when the economy sours? Although the evidence trail leaves off at the bottom rungs of the formal retail market, a reasonable inference is that more consumers enter the underground economy, including the market for stolen goods, in search of lower prices. The cardinal quality of stolen merchandise is that it is cheap. If it were not, it would attract few consumers away from legal markets that sell the same products with purity and quality guarantees, return and replacement policies, peaceful procedures for resolving disputes, and no risk of arrest. Surveys suggest that price is a key determinant of consumers' willingness to purchase stolen goods (Albers-Miller 1999). Rising demand for stolen goods, in turn, should strengthen incentives for those who supply underground markets with such merchandise acquired through robbery, burglary, and theft. Acquisitive crime rates should increase as a result.

If the economic logic linking the market for stolen goods to acquisitive crime is sound, the effect of inflation on crime trends should equal or exceed that of unemployment or economic growth. Compared with these indicators, the crime-relevant effects of inflation are widespread, instantaneous, and direct. The official unemployment rate, which excludes discouraged workers and others who have dropped out of the labor force, is a narrow and incomplete measure of joblessness. But even broader measures such as labor-force participation necessarily apply only to persons who are out of work (and their families). They do not capture the effects of changing economic conditions on those who remain employed, who—after all—constitute the large majority of the working-age population even under the worst economic circumstances. In addition, the full effects of job loss typically develop over a period of months, as savings are drawn down and unemployment insurance benefits are exhausted (Cantor and Land 1985). By contrast, although the effects of inflation are greatest for the poor (Easterly and Fischer 2001), it touches all consumers.

Unemployment influences consumer demand primarily to the extent that it reduces income. The effect of overall economic output and growth on demand is even less direct. Income obviously has a very close connection to demand, but only insofar as it keeps pace with prices. If price increases exceed income growth and real income declines, crime rates should rise along with demand for cheap stolen goods.

This proposition linking acquisitive crime increases to inflation is not meant to supplant earlier arguments regarding the effects of inflation on institutional legitimacy and socioeconomic stress, which may spur increases in violent as well as property crime. In addition, the same market dynamics that produce property crime may also, if less directly, lead to violence. Illegal commerce can be risky business. It is apt to occur after hours and in out-of-the-way places beyond the scrutiny of the police and other agents of formal social control (Venkatesh 2006). When disputes arise between buyers and sellers of stolen goods, they cannot be handled by store managers, customer service departments, credit agencies, consumer advocates, or the courts. In such "stateless" social contexts, violence is used to enforce agreements and punish wrongdoers. In addition, the legal vulnerability of the participants in illegal transactions makes them attractive targets of predatory crime (e.g., Jacobs 2000). These observations are now commonplace in the study of violence associated with illicit drug markets, but they apply in principle to any market arrangement in which participants have little access to formal social control and are vulnerable to predation.

In summary, there are ample reasons to bring inflation back into the suite of economic indicators included in research on crime trends. One reason inflation may have been overlooked in recent research is that it has been running at low ebb for over two decades. But that is precisely what makes it an attractive candidate for explaining the crime decline during the same period. The crime drop was not confined to the United States, nor was the taming of inflation after the tumultuous 1970s and 1980s. In the spirit of Fischer (1996), it is useful to consider recent crime trends in light of what may be a new period of price equilibrium in Europe and the United States.

IV. Data and Method

It is notoriously difficult to obtain reliable crime data for a large and diverse sample of nations over an appreciable period of time. Cross-national samples are typically small and assembled by convenience with available data. The analysis reported here is no different. It relies on data for three offenses—homicide, robbery, and burglary—spanning the period from 1981 (1980 for homicide) to 2010. The homicide and robbery data are for 13 European nations and the United States. The homicide data are from national public health sources for the European nations and the Uniform Crime Reports (UCR) for the United States. These data series cover the entire 30-year period.[3] The robbery and burglary data are from three sources: Interpol, for 1981–89; the European Sourcebook of Crime and Criminal Justice Statistics, for 1990–2007; and Eurostat, for 2008–10.[4]

---

[3] The European data were obtained from Marcelo Abei. The UCR data are from the US Bureau of Justice Statistics (http://www.bjs.gov/ucrdata/).

[4] See European Sourcebook of Crime and Criminal Justice Statistics, http://www3

Data comparability is always an issue with cross-national crime data, especially when multiple sources are used, which can lead to large "structural breaks" in time-series data where one source ends and another begins. That proved not to be a problem for merging the Eurostat and European Sourcebook robbery and burglary data in the latter part of the period. The Eurostat data were identical or very close to the European Sourcebook data for these offenses for several years prior to 2008, and no discontinuous break in series occurred between 2007 and 2008. The same was not true with respect to the transition from the Interpol to the European Sourcebook series. Implausibly large breaks, sometimes of an order of magnitude or more, occurred in the burglary series beginning in 1990 for six of the 13 European nations. These nations were dropped from the burglary series, leaving only eight nations in the sample.[5] Similar structural breaks were not evident in the robbery series.

Another consideration in sample selection was to minimize missing data. The main reason a nation was not included in the sample was extensive missing data on either the crime measures, explanatory variables, or both. For several nations included in the sample, data were missing for a single year and were imputed by linear interpolation or extrapolation. In a few instances, missing data over a few adjacent years were imputed by mean substitution. Robbery data were not available for Italy for the years 1983–89 and were left missing.

The resulting samples of 14 nations (for homicide and robbery) and eight nations (for burglary), listed in appendix A, are not strictly representative of Europe and North America, much less all "advanced" or "Western" nations. They do afford the opportunity, however, to examine the impact of inflation and other economic indicators on both violent and property crime rates across multiple nations during a period of pronounced swings in both crime and economic conditions. In a research area where comparative work remains quite limited, that is a good start.

.unil.ch/wpmu/europeansourcebook/date-bases/; Eurostat, http://appsso.eurostat.ec .europa.eu/nui/show.do?dataset = crim_gen&lang = en. The Interpol data were obtained from Marcelo Abei.

[5] The European sources exclude commercial burglaries from the category of "domestic" burglary. To make the US burglary series comparable, the burglary counts were adjusted by the proportion of total burglaries defined as "residential" in the annual UCR.

A. Explanatory Variables

The inflation measure used in the analysis is the year-over-year percentage change in consumer prices. Two additional economic indicators are included, the unemployment rate, defined as the percentage of the labor force "without work but available for and seeking employment," and real gross domestic product (GDP) per capita, in US dollars. The three measures are from the World Bank's cross-national data archive (http://data.worldbank.org). A measure of consumer sentiment has been used in prior cross-national research on crime trends (Rosenfeld and Messner 2009), but is not available for the full period under consideration here. Finally, it would have been desirable to include a measure of median income for individuals or households, but standardized income measures are not available from multination sources for cross-national comparison. Median income, however, should be highly correlated with GDP per capita.[6]

Three control variables commonly used in cross-national research on crime are incorporated in the analyses reported here: the percentage of the population residing in urban areas, the percentage between the ages of 15 and 24, and the infant mortality rate. Comparative researchers generally view the infant mortality rate as a valid measure of absolute poverty (Pridemore 2008). In addition to the substantive controls, year dummy variables are included in the panel regressions to capture unmeasured influences on homicide, robbery, and burglary rates that vary over time.

B. Measures and Models

Inflation, which represents the change in prices between one year and the next, is an inherently dynamic indicator. The crime outcomes and other explanatory variables, therefore, have been first differenced so that each yearly value reflects the change from the previous year ($X_{1\text{diff}} = X_t - X_{t-1}$). Prior to first differencing, all variables were transformed to natural logs to reduce extreme fluctuations and enhance interpretation of effects. When log transformed, a b percent change in the outcome is associated with a 1 percent change in the explanatory variable, where b is the coefficient on the explanatory variable.

The effects of inflation and other explanatory variables on the yearly

[6] For example, the correlation (r) between real GDP per capita and median household income between 1980 and 2010 in the United States is .941.

change in crime rates are estimated in random-effects panel models with robust standard errors to account for the clustering of observations within nations. A Hausman test disclosed no significant difference in the estimates from fixed- and random-effects models for any of the offense types. Under this condition, the random-effects estimator is more efficient (Wooldridge 2010, pp. 328–34). In addition, the random-effects estimates are based on differences between units (i.e., nations) as well as differences within units over time; both are of interest here.

Unless they are modified to detect nonlinearities, the panel regression models produce estimates of the linear relationship between changes in crime and the explanatory variables. Quadratic models are estimated to test for the possibility that the association between inflation and crime strengthens or even changes sign as inflation increases.

V. Results

Consumer prices surged in most Western nations during the 1970s, peaked in the early 1980s, fell over the next several years only to rise again for a year or so around 1990, and then fell throughout the remainder of the twentieth century. Inflation remained low and steady until the 2008–9 financial crash and recession, when consumer prices nose-dived in the United States and Europe. In the 14-nation sample I used in this analysis, inflation rates averaged over 10 percent in the early 1980s; they hovered around 2 percent between 2000 and 2010.

In fits and starts, crime rates followed suit. Figures 1–3 display the yearly percentage change in consumer prices and homicide, robbery, and burglary rates, respectively, in units of standard deviation from their respective means between 1982 and 2010. Despite the far greater volatility in crime than inflation, the two series exhibit a rough correspondence over the period, especially during the 1990s when both crime and inflation rates fell. But other economic conditions also improved, which makes it difficult to attribute the 1990s crime drop primarily to slowed inflation.

The case for connecting crime to inflation is strengthened, however, by the 2008–9 recession, when inflation and other economic conditions diverged sharply. Economic growth stagnated and unemployment rose steeply, but inflation fell. Crime rates behaved more like inflation. Homicide and robbery rates in the 14-nation sample barely budged. Av-

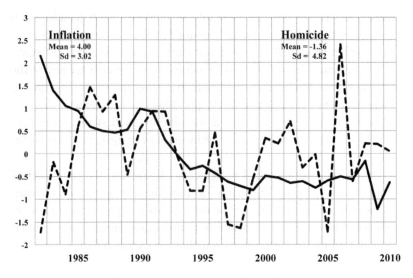

FIG. 1.—Percentage change in consumer prices and homicide rates in eight nations, 1982–2010 (z-scores).

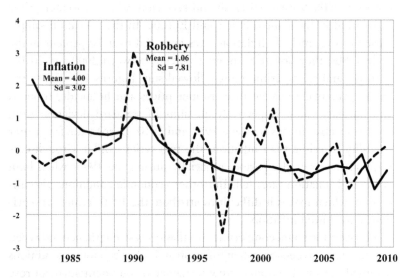

FIG. 2.—Percentage change in consumer prices and robbery rates in eight nations, 1982–2010 (z-scores).

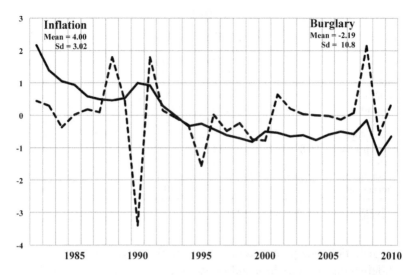

FIG. 3.—Percentage change in consumer prices and burglary rates in eight nations, 1982–2010 (z-scores).

erage burglary rates in the eight-nation sample did increase by 21 percent in 2008 over the previous year, but then fell by 9 percent the following year even as the recession deepened. Systematically disentangling the effects of inflation on crime from those of other economic conditions requires that we investigate a much longer time period in which each of the indicators undergoes appreciable change, but not at the same rate at the same time. The period from the early 1980s through the first decade of the twenty-first century—an era of enormous and variable shifts in prices, unemployment, economic growth, and crime rates—meets this criterion (see table 1).

A. Multivariate Models

Table 2 presents the panel regression results for the effects of inflation and yearly changes in unemployment and GDP per capita on yearly changes in homicide, robbery, and burglary rates between 1981 and 2010. The regression models include controls for urbanization, the infant mortality rate, and the percentage of the population between 15 and 24 years old. They also contain year dummy variables to absorb omitted time-varying influences on the outcomes (results not shown). Preliminary analysis revealed an outlier—a −4.5 percent price drop in Ireland in 2009—that remained an influential observation even when

TABLE 1

Descriptive Statistics

	Mean	SD	Min	Max	Observations
Homicide	1.68	1.72	.32	9.80	420
Robbery	78.3	57.9	1.00	273	413
Burglary	650	520	67	3,515	240
Inflation	3.96	3.98	−4.5	24.5	420
Unemployment	6.93	3.38	.185	18.1	420
GDP per capita (000)	26.7	14.7	4.59	95.2	420
Urban	73.6	8.40	56	87	420
Infant mortality	6.40	2.69	2.4	19.9	420
Percent ages 15–24	13.9	1.78	10	18.2	420

NOTE.—Variables in original metric.

logged. This data point was omitted from the regression analyses. First differencing the variables and omitting the influential case yields 419 observations for the homicide analysis. Missing data further reduces the number of observations for the robbery analysis to 397. The burglary analysis is based on 231 remaining observations after first differencing the variables and omitting the outlier in the eight-nation burglary sample.

Two panel regression models are presented for each offense type. Models 1, 3, and 5 specify a linear relationship between inflation and the yearly change in crime. Models 2, 4, and 6 include the square of the inflation measure in a quadratic specification to capture the possible curvilinear relationship between inflation and the change in crime. Beginning with the results for homicide, we observe a marginally significant linear effect of inflation ($b = .071, p < .10$) in model 1 and no evidence of a curvilinear relationship between inflation and the change in homicide in model 2. The linear effect is in the expected positive direction: increases (decreases) in crime are associated with increases (decreases) in prices. Changes in unemployment and GDP per capita are unrelated to homicide changes. The only other variable with a marginally significant effect on homicide is infant mortality. Given the direction of change in both homicide and infant mortality during the three decades under investigation, this result indicates that homicide decreased with decreases in absolute poverty, as indexed by infant mortality, both within and across nations.

Homicide rates are far higher in the United States than in the European nations in the sample, even after declining by more than 50

TABLE 2

Random-Effects Panel Regression Results for Homicide, Robbery, and Burglary Rates, 1981–2010

	Homicide		Robbery		Burglary	
	(1)	(2)	(3)	(4)	(5)	(6)
Inflation	.071[+]	.228	.069	−.574*	.112*	−.090
	(.040)	(.307)	(.052)	(.234)	(.056)	(.127)
Inflation^2	. . .	−.032	. . .	.137**	. . .	.041
	. . .	(.059)	. . .	(.044)	. . .	(.029)
Unemployment	.006	.005	.080	.088	.162	.164
	(.057)	(.056)	(.109)	(.109)	(.105)	(.105)
GDP per capita	.054	.051	−.170	−.149	−.245	−.241
	(.152)	(.152)	(.180)	(.171)	(.204)	(.210)
Urban	3.03	3.02	−.425	−.340	−1.25	−1.24
	(2.95)	(2.95)	(.933)	(.951)	(.796)	(.793)
Infant mortality	.800[+]	.766[+]	−.440	−.388	−.974*	−.953*
	(.439)	(.413)	(.488)	(.462)	(.384)	(.385)
Percent ages 15–24	−.653	−.574	.591	.205	.024	−.080
	(.577)	(.574)	(1.06)	(1.19)	(.484)	(.561)
R^2_{within}	.076	.076	.134	.140	.303	.304
$R^2_{between}$	.209	.168	.536	.602	.797	.802
Observations (n)	419	419	397	397	231	231

NOTE.—Robust standard errors are in parentheses. All variables transformed to natural logs and, except for inflation, first differences. Year effects not shown. Homicide series begins in 1981.

[+] $p < .10$ (two-tailed).

* $p < .05$.

** $p < .01$.

percent since the early 1990s. To determine whether this difference may have influenced the regression results, the homicide equations were reestimated with the United States omitted. The results of primary interest remain basically unchanged. The linear effect of inflation becomes significant at the 5 percent level ($b = .067$, $p = .017$), no significant curvilinear relationship emerges, and the change in homicide remains unrelated to changes in unemployment and GDP per capita. Infant mortality no longer has even a marginally significant effect on the change in homicide with the United States removed from the sample.

Moving to the results for robbery, inflation does not have a significant effect on the change in robbery, assuming a linear relationship between the two measures, as shown in model 3 of table 2. The inflation effects in model 4, by contrast, are statistically significant and in

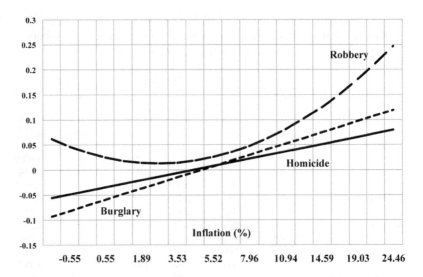

FIG. 4.—Predicted change in log crime rates by inflation rates

the expected direction, assuming that robbery rates begin to increase only after inflation reaches a minimum threshold ($b_{\text{infl}} = -.574$, $p < .05$; $b_{\text{infl}^2} = .137$, $p < .01$). The yearly change in robbery rates is not significantly associated with changes in unemployment, GDP per capita, or the three control variables.

The inflation results from model 4 imply that the relationship between inflation and the yearly change in robbery takes the form of a convex (U-shaped) curve. Robbery rates decrease as inflation increases to a threshold, after which robbery rates increase with further increases in inflation. Before the inflation threshold is reached, the slope of the relationship between robbery and inflation is negative; the slope turns positive as inflation increases beyond the threshold. This expectation is confirmed by the graph shown in figure 4 of predicted robbery rates by levels of inflation, with the other variables in the model set to their mean values.

It would be useful for theory and policy purposes to find the value of inflation at the minimum threshold of the relationship between inflation and robbery—the point at which the inflation slope equals zero. That point is given by the formula $-b_1/2 \times b_2$, where b_1 is the linear coefficient of inflation and b_2 is the quadratic coefficient of inflation. Applying the formula to the inflation and inflation^2 coefficients from model 4 of table 2, the minimum threshold value of inflation is 2.10. Exponentiating and subtracting the constant to return the logged inflation measure to original metric, the inflation rate at which robbery rates begin to increase is 2.67 percent. The average rate of inflation in the 14-nation sample dipped below this level for the first time in 1996 and did not exceed it through 2010.

The results shown in model 6 of table 2 do not offer evidence of a comparable curvilinear relationship between inflation and the yearly change in burglary rates in the eight-nation sample. Model 5 does reveal a significant linear effect, however ($b = .112, p < .05$). The only other variable with a significant effect on burglary is the change in the infant mortality rate: burglary rates rose with declines in absolute poverty within and across nations. The fit statistics indicate that the model fits the data reasonably well, especially the between-nation variation in the yearly change in burglary. The same pattern holds for the robbery models, whereas most of the variation in homicide, both between and within nations, is left unexplained by the models.

Model fit is typically reduced when the outcome and explanatory variables are first differenced. For the same reason, first differencing also tends to reduce correlations among explanatory variables when measured in levels and alleviate problems with multicollinearity. Variance inflation diagnostics reveal a mean variance inflation factor of 1.11 and a maximum of 1.18 for the explanatory variables in models 1, 3, and 5 of table 2, values far below levels indicating multicollinearity.

B. How Large Is the Impact of Inflation?

The results thus far indicate that, unlike unemployment and economic growth, inflation was statistically related to the yearly changes in homicide, robbery, and burglary rates across multiple nations during the past several decades. The remaining question concerns the magnitude of the relationship between crime and inflation. The inflation coefficients in table 2 can be used to estimate the change in the crime rates associated with changes in consumer prices. The estimates indicate that inflation had a nontrivial impact on crime rates over the period. Homicide and burglary rates declined by 1.19 percent and 3.03 percent per year on average, but would have been 24 percent and 15 percent higher, respectively, absent the effects of inflation. Robbery rates increased by 1.42 percent per year. As indicated above, the effect of inflation on the change in robbery becomes stronger at higher levels of inflation. At one standard deviation above its mean level, for example, inflation accounts for over three-quarters of the yearly change in robbery in the 14-nation sample (see app. B for computations).

VI. Discussion

The recession of 2008 and 2009 could conceivably reinstate the consensus of doubt that long characterized research on the effect of unemployment on crime rates. Unemployment soared during the recession, but crime rates dropped. It would be unwise, however, to abandon systematic investigation of the relationship between the economy and crime without fully exhausting the theoretical and empirical implications of multiple macroeconomic influences on crime rates. Recent studies have shown that alternative economic indicators, such as economic growth and consumer sentiment, are associated with change in acquisitive crime rates over time (Arvanites and Defina 2006; Rosenfeld and Fornango 2007). Yet these conditions also worsened during the recession, prompting the focus of the current analysis on the criminogenic effects of inflation. The results of this investigation suggest that continued attention to the influence of macroeconomic change on crime rates, including but not limited to inflation, is warranted.

In the analysis reported here, I found significant and appreciable effects of inflation on year-to-year changes in homicide, robbery, and burglary rates in multination samples between the early 1980s and 2010. A significant effect of inflation on income-producing crime has been documented in prior research, but in scattered studies limited to the United States and with little theoretical development. The current research situates the criminogenic effects of inflation in the demand features of underground markets, specifically markets for stolen goods. Consumer demand for cheap stolen goods increases, according to this argument, when prices rise or aggregate incomes fall. That, in turn, provides incentives for those who currently supply the markets with cheap stolen goods and perhaps entices others into robbery, burglary, theft, and the underground transactions that convert the goods to cash or other items of value. As the trade in stolen goods multiplies beyond the control of formal authorities, rates of violence also increase. The same mechanisms operate in reverse as inflation slows or turns negative.

Given the centrality of price changes in this scenario, inflation is a more direct and responsive indicator of the relevant market dynamics than other economic conditions. The current investigation finds, as expected, that the effects of inflation on crime are more robust than those of unemployment and GDP. It finds only partial support, however, for Fischer's (1996) hypothesis that inflation begins to influence crime rates only after reaching a minimum threshold.

My analysis here focuses on a single mechanism—illegal markets—to interpret the contribution of inflation to year-to-year changes in crime rates over a 30-year period. That is both a strength and limitation. The strength entails theoretical elaboration of how price changes influence crime by altering the dynamics of illegal markets. The limitation is the lack of direct empirical indicators of price changes in illegal markets. An ideal study design would contain measures of change over time in the price of stolen merchandise. Such data would have to be compiled by cross-national longitudinal surveys of the buyers (or sellers) of stolen goods, a daunting but not impossible research task. For example, items could be added to ongoing surveys that ask respondents whether they have been offered goods they thought were stolen, by type and price. Absent this information, the next-best option is to derive inferences regarding demand in illegal markets from consumer behavior at the lowest rungs of the formal retail market, as I have done here. Conclusions must remain provisional, however, until more direct evidence on the temporal dynamics of demand in illegal markets becomes available.

Several other limitations warrant caution in interpreting the results of this analysis. The most important are the small size and uncertain representativeness of the cross-national samples on which the results are based. The brevity of the time period under investigation is a related concern. The underlying theoretical argument assumes symmetry in the relationship between changes in prices and crime: crime rates should follow inflation, regardless of whether prices rise or fall. Yet the empirical base for the current findings is limited by and large to a period of falling inflation and crime rates. It would have been desirable to broaden temporal coverage to capture the equally precipitous rise in prices and crime that began in the 1960s. Evaluating the implied symmetry in most macrolevel theories of crime should become less difficult as the European Sourcebook of Crime and Criminal Justice Statistics and other sources continue to compile reliable cross-national crime data over extended time periods.

Future cross-national research should also incorporate, where possible, a measure of median income in order to evaluate the partial effect of price changes on crime, controlling for income, and to determine whether income conditions the effect of price changes. This will require searching national data sources for income data and converting the data to a common metric. Presumably, increasing incomes should weaken the contribution of inflation to crime increases, although some research suggests that consumers may respond adversely to price increases when an "inflation psychology" takes hold, even if their incomes are growing (Peretz 1983).

Just as income growth may weaken the effect of inflation on crime, so might lowering the punishment threshold for property crime. Evaluating the impact on crime rates of arrests and sentencing for property crime and receipt of stolen goods will require diligent data compilation from national sources. The expectation is that increasing risk of punishment for these offenses should dampen the impact of price increases on acquisitive crime. But harsh punishment could also have the perverse consequence of increasing violent crime. Policy makers should view the US war on drugs as an object lesson for how not to deal with the market for stolen goods. Substantially toughening criminal penalties for property crime and receipt of stolen goods may well drive the market for stolen goods even further underground and increase the utility of violence to resolve disputes among underground buyers and sellers (Rosenfeld 2009). A better way is to continue to expand target-hardening remedies, such as electronically "chipping" electronic and other consumer goods, which can reduce acquisitive crime by deterring theft and raising the price of stolen goods.

If the results reported here are replicated in future research, an additional policy implication would seem to follow. A chief policy objective of the US Federal Reserve and the central banks of other developed nations is to keep inflation rates low, between 2 and 3 percent per year. If effective, these monetary policies may have crime-control benefits, albeit unintentional. When inflation rises above the target threshold, corrective fiscal policies could be instituted to boost the incomes of the poor and make the purchase of stolen goods less attractive. Such policies may not be necessary for quite some time, however, at least in the world's developed nations, which appear to have entered a new era of price equilibrium and, if Fischer (1996) is correct, low and stable crime rates for the foreseeable future.

Meanwhile, it seems reasonable to conclude that restoring inflation to the repertoire of macroeconomic indicators used in the study of crime trends can yield new insights and help to resolve empirical anomalies, such as why crime rates drop when other indicators suggest they should increase. It is not yet time for theory and research on the economy and crime to succumb to a new consensus of doubt.

APPENDIX A

TABLE A1
Nations Included in the Analysis

Homicide and Robbery	Burglary
Austria	England and Wales
Denmark	France
England and Wales	Greece
Finland	Ireland
France	Norway
Greece	Scotland
Ireland	Switzerland
Italy	United States
Netherlands	
Norway	
Scotland	
Sweden	
Switzerland	
United States	

APPENDIX B

Estimating the Impact of Inflation on Crime Rates

Model 1 in table 2 indicates that a 1 percent change in consumer prices is associated with a .071 percent yearly change in homicide. Prices rose at an average rate of 3.96 percent per year between 1981 and 2010 in the 14-nation sample (see table 1). At the average annual rate of inflation, therefore, inflation is associated with an increase in homicide rates of .281 percent (3.96 × .071) per year. Homicide rates fell by −.020 incidents per 100,000 population per year on average, or by 1.19 percent of their mean value of 1.68 per 100,000 population (see table 1). The regression results imply that homicide rates would have fallen by an estimated 1.47 percent (1.19% + .281%) of their mean value absent the upward pressure of inflation. Put differently, homicide rates were 23.5 percent (1.47/1.19) higher on average than they would have been without the impact of inflation.

Applying the same logic to burglary, a 1 percent yearly change in prices is associated with a .112 percent change in burglary rates (see table 2). At an average annual rate of 3.96 percent, inflation is associated with a .444 percent (.112 × 3.96) change in burglary rates. Burglary rates fell by −3.03 percent of their annual average value over the period, and would have fallen by 3.47 percent (3.03% + .444%) absent the effect of inflation. Inflation boosted burglary rates, therefore, by 14.5 percent (3.47/3.03) in the eight-nation sample.

Given the curvilinear relationship between inflation and robbery, inflation has no single or fixed impact on the yearly change in robbery rates—its impact differs according to its level. The varying impact of inflation on robbery can be illustrated by comparing the inflation slopes at the mean value of inflation (3.96 percent), one standard deviation below the mean (3.96% − 3.98% = −.020%), and one standard deviation above the mean (3.96% + 3.98% = 7.94%) (see table 1). The corresponding inflation slopes from the curvilinear robbery equation in table 2, with the other variables set to their mean values, are $b_{-.020\%} = -.108$, $b_{3.96\%} = .042$, and $b_{7.94\%} = .138$. Only the latter coefficient is statistically significant ($p < .01$). A 1 percent change in inflation, therefore, is associated with a .138 percent change in robbery rates. At one standard deviation above the mean inflation rate, or 7.94 percent, inflation is associated with a 1.10 percent (7.94 × .138) yearly change in robbery rates. Robbery rates in the 14-nation sample rose at an average annual rate of 1.42 percent. Elevated rates of inflation, therefore, accounted for 77.5 percent (1.10/1.42) of the increase in robbery.

REFERENCES

Albers-Miller, Nancy D. 1999. "Consumer Misbehavior: Why People Buy Illicit Goods." *Journal of Consumer Marketing* 16:273–87.

Allen, Ralph C. 1996. "Socioeconomic Conditions and Property Crime." *American Journal of Economics and Sociology* 55:293–308.

Arvanites, Thomas M., and Robert H. Defina. 2006. "Business Cycles and Street Crime." *Criminology* 44:139–64.

Baumer, Eric P. 2008. "An Empirical Assessment of the Contemporary Crime Trends Puzzle: A Modest Step toward a More Comprehensive Research Agenda." In *Understanding Crime Trends*, edited by Arthur S. Goldberger and Richard Rosenfeld. Washington, DC: National Academies Press.

Becker, Gary. 1968. "Crime and Punishment: An Economic Approach." *Journal of Political Economy* 76:169–217.

Burke, Heather. 2008. "Discount Retailers See Sales Increase; Consumers Look for Bargain to Stretch Dollar." *USA Today*, May 9, p. 5A.

Bushway, Shawn D. 2011. "Labor Markets and Crime." In *Crime and Public Policy*, edited by James Q. Wilson and Joan Petersilia. New York: Oxford University Press.

Bushway, Shawn, Philip J. Cook, and Matthew Phillips. 2013. "The Net Effect of the Business Cycle on Crime and Violence." In *Economics and Youth Violence: Crime, Disadvantage, and Community*, edited by Richard Rosenfeld,

Mark Edberg, Xiangming Fang, and Curtis S. Florence. New York: New York University Press.

Cantor, David, and Kenneth C. Land. 1985. "Unemployment and Crime Rates in the Post–World War II United States: A Theoretical and Empirical Analysis." *American Sociological Review* 50:317–32.

Chiricos, Theodore G. 1987. "Rates of Crime and Unemployment: An Analysis of Aggregate Research Evidence." *Social Problems* 34:187–212.

Cohen, Lawrence E., and Marcus Felson. 1979. "Social Change and Crime Rate Trends: A Routine Activity Approach." *American Sociological Review* 44: 588–607.

Cook, Philip J., and Gary A. Zarkin. 1985. "Crime and the Business Cycle." *Journal of Legal Studies* 14:115–28.

Devine, Joel A., Joseph F. Sheley, and M. Dwayne Smith. 1988. "Macroeconomic and Social-Control Policy Influences on Crime Rate Changes, 1948–1985." *American Sociological Review* 53:407–20.

Easterly, William, and Stanley Fischer. 2001. "Inflation and the Poor." *Journal of Money, Credit, and Banking* 33:160–78.

Economist. 2010. "The Deflation Dilemma," June 3. http://www.economist .com/node/16274363.

Ehrlich, Isaac. 1973. "Participation in Illegitimate Activities: A Theoretical and Empirical Investigation." *Journal of Political Economy* 81:521–65.

Fischer, David Hackett. 1996. *The Great Wave: Price Revolutions and the Rhythm of History*. New York: Oxford University Press.

Gould, Eric D., Bruce A. Weinberg, and David B. Mustard. 2002. "Crime Rates and Local Labor Market Opportunities in the United States: 1979–1997." *Review of Economics and Statistics* 84:45–61.

Grogger, Jeffrey T. 1998. "Market Wages and Youth Crime." *Journal of Labor Economics* 16:756–91.

Jackson, Anna-Louise, and Anthony Feld. 2011. "Accelerating Inflation Spurs Consumer 'Trade Down' to McDonald's, Wal-Mart." *Bloomberg News*, June 16. http://www.bloomberg.com/news/2011-06-17/faster-inflation-causes-trade-down-to-mcdonald-s-wal-mart.html.

Jacobs, Bruce A. 2000. *Robbing Drug Dealers*. New Brunswick, NJ: Aldine.

Johnson, Ryan S., Shawn Kantor, and Price V. Fishback. 2007. "Striking at the Roots of Crime: The Impact of Social Welfare Spending on Crime during the Great Depression." NBER Working Paper no. 12825 (January). Cambridge, MA: National Bureau of Economic Research.

Krugman, Paul. 2010. "Why Is Deflation Bad?" *New York Times*, August 2. http://krugman.blogs.nytimes.com/2010/08/02/why-is-deflation-bad/.

LaFree, Gary. 1998. *Losing Legitimacy: Street Crime and the Decline of Social Institutions in America*. Boulder, CO: Westview.

LaFree, Gary, and Kriss A. Drass. 1996. "The Effect of Changes in Intraracial Income Inequality and Educational Attainment on Changes in Arrest Rates for African Americans and Whites, 1957–1990." *American Sociological Review* 61:614–34.

LaFree, Gary, Kriss A. Drass, and Patrick O'Day. 1992. "Race and Crime in

Postwar America: Determinants of African-American and White Rates." *Criminology* 30:157–88.

Lauritsen, Janet L., and Karen Heimer. 2010. "Violent Victimization among Males and Economic Conditions." *Criminology and Public Policy* 9:665–92.

Peretz, Paul. 1983. *The Political Economy of Inflation in the United States.* Chicago: University of Chicago Press.

Pridemore, William A. 2008. "A First Test of the Poverty-Homicide Hypothesis at the Cross-National Level." *Criminology* 46:133–54.

Ralston, Roy W. 1999. "Economy and Race: Interactive Determinants of Property Crime in the United States, 1958–1995." *American Journal of Economics and Sociology* 58:405–34.

Raphael, Steven, and Rudolf Winter-Ebmer. 2001. "Identifying the Effect of Unemployment on Crime." *Journal of Law and Economics* 44:259–83.

Rosenbloom, Stephanie. 2008. "Thrift Shops Thriving, but Running Low on Stock." *New York Times,* September 10, pp. C1, C8.

Rosenfeld, Richard. 2009. "Crime Is the Problem: Homicide, Acquisitive Crime, and Economic Conditions." *Journal of Quantitative Criminology* 25: 287–306.

———. 2011. "Changing Crime Rates." In *Crime and Public Policy,* edited by James Q. Wilson and Joan Petersilia. New York: Oxford University Press.

Rosenfeld, Richard, and Robert Fornango. 2007. "The Impact of Economic Conditions on Robbery and Property Crime: The Role of Consumer Sentiment." *Criminology* 45:735–69.

Rosenfeld, Richard, and Steven F. Messner. 2009. "The Crime Drop in Comparative Perspective: The Impact of the Economy and Imprisonment on American and European Burglary Rates." *British Journal of Sociology* 60:445–71.

———. 2013. *Crime and the Economy.* London: Sage.

Sutton, Mike, Sarah Hodgkinson, and Mike Levi. 2008. "Handling Stolen Goods: Findings from the 2003 Offending Crime and Justice Survey." *Internet Journal of Criminology.* http://www.internetjournalofcriminology.com/Sutton_Stolen_Goods.pdf.

Tang, Chor Foon, and Hooi Hooi Lean. 2007. "Will Inflation Increase Crime Rate? New Evidence from Bounds and Modified Wald Tests." *Global Crime* 8:311–23.

Venkatesh, Sudhir Alladi. 2006. *Off the Books: The Underground Economy of the Urban Poor.* Cambridge, MA: Harvard University Press.

Wilson, James Q. 1985. *Thinking about Crime.* Rev. ed. New York: Vintage.

Wooldridge, Jeffrey M. 2010. *Econometric Analysis of Cross-Section and Panel Data.* 2nd ed. Cambridge, MA: MIT Press.

Rossella Selmini and Suzy McElrath

Violent Female Victimization Trends across Europe, Canada, and the United States

ABSTRACT

Little work has sought to establish whether the homicide decline is affecting both male and female victims, and in the same or different ways, and whether patterns vary between countries. Little cross-national work has been done to establish whether rape rates are generally rising or falling and to explain similarities and differences between countries. The picture for homicide is straightforward. Rates are falling almost everywhere but usually more rapidly for men. The rape picture is complex, varies between countries, and often looks different depending on whether official or victimization data are consulted. In the United States, both show declines. Victimization data in Canada and Sweden show stable rates, though official data show declines in Canada and steep rises in Sweden. No generalizations can be offered about common, cross-national trends in rape. Much more can be learned. Focusing on gender differences in crime victimization demonstrates that they exist and need explanation. Both general and gender-specific theories must be considered if long-term trends are to be understood.

The early twenty-first century has been marked by strong interest in describing and explaining medium- and long-term crime trends, es-

Electronically published November 21, 2014

Rossella Selmini is associate professor of sociology, University of Minnesota, and formerly director of the Department of Police and Urban Security, Regione Emilia-Romagna, Italy. Suzy McElrath is a PhD student in the University of Minnesota's Department of Sociology. They are grateful to Eugenio Arcidiacono, Marcelo Aebi, and Tapio Lappi-Seppälä for facilitating access to data and to Eugenio for assistance with artwork.

pecially recent declines in crime rates in the United States and other Western countries. Most of that work has looked at overall patterns and trends. With only a few exceptions in the United States (e.g., Lauritsen and Heimer 2008) and Europe (e.g., Kangaspunta and Marshall 2012), studies of the "crime drop" have not explored whether violence experienced predominantly by women, such as sexual offenses, has fallen or whether trends in violent crime more generally differ for men and women.

Gender differences in offending and victimization have, however, always been a neglected topic, and the crime drop literature is not unusual in that respect (Kruttschnitt, McLaughlin, and Petrie 2004). Although males constitute the majority of crime victims, females account for significant shares of both offenders and victims. Studies of long-term trends in violent crime, however, often do not examine gender-specific trends. This has affected the range of explanations offered to make sense of rises and falls in crime rates. Most explanations of changes in violent crime have been gender-neutral and have focused on violence among males in public space. In this essay, we examine changes in rates of violence against females, namely, rape and homicide, in Canada, the United States, and Europe over the past two decades.[1]

The neglect of violence against women in cross-national analyses is an important gap. Violence, Mucchielli (2010) observes, encompasses a wide range of behaviors and is animated by diverse motivations. The trends in crimes against women may be different from those against men. Deeper knowledge of women's victimization and of gendered forms of violence is important in both scientific and policy terms (Heimer and Lauritsen 2008, p. 48). It will make clearer whether similar or different social forces affect men's and women's exposure to violence and whether with the same intensity and at the same time. Positioning violence against women within the context of broader trends can direct us toward explanations that incorporate general and crime-specific factors. Gender-specific analyses may also shed light on the validity of

---

[1] Violence against women includes a broad range of offenses, the forms and prevalence of which vary greatly around the globe (Alvazzi del Frate and Patrignani 1995; World Health Organization 2013). Intimate partner violence affects both men and women. However, we do not discuss intimate partner violence in general or forms of violent victimization of women (for instance, robberies) other than homicide and sexual offenses.

feminist perspectives in explaining gender violence and on the hypothesis that gender-related violence is different from other violent crime.

From a feminist perspective, gender-related crimes differ from other violent crimes, given that they have been argued to originate from and perpetuate gender inequities and male control over women (Dobash and Dobash 1979; Blau and Blau 1982). The relationship between gender and violence is heavily contested, however, and some have argued that "symmetry" in gender-specific trends in violence is suggestive of causes unrelated to gender (Jakobsen 2014). We believe, however, that similarities in gender-specific trends do not rule out the possibility of independent or "unique" causes of crime for men and women, nor negate the claim that violence perpetrated against both women and men may be gendered. Assessment of trends in crimes such as sexual violence, which has undergone extensive changes in cultural and legal definitions over the past half century, provides opportunities to test explanations that the crime drop is primarily a result of changes in criminal justice policy (Frank, Hardinge, and Wosick-Correa 2009). Emphasis on gender differences can also illuminate whether attempts to explain the rise and fall of crime through broader changes in sensitivity to violence (Eisner 2003), macro-level changes in self-control (Eisner 2008), or structural and economic developments in modern states (Austin and Young 2000; LaFree and Hunnicutt 2006) apply to violence against women. Examination of gender-specific trends can help direct scholarship toward more encompassing explanations of violence that incorporate both general and crime-specific factors. We examine rape and sexual assaults, crimes that predominantly affect women, and homicide, which predominantly affects men. We chose those offenses because the available data—though subject to important limitations—are more reliable than data on other forms of violence, especially intimate partner violence.[2] We assess the extent to which overall trends in crime and victimization, predominantly based on perpetration and victimization of men, also capture women's experience.

We consider these subjects in comparative perspective. Studies on the gender gap in violent female victimization mostly focus on the United States. A few cross-national analyses examine other countries

---

[2] Studies of physical and emotional abuse are much more limited than rape by cross-national differences in legal definition and cultural perceptions and by a paucity of statistical data in both official and victimization data (Hagemann-White 2001; Kangaspunta and Marshall 2012).

across the world. In this essay we compare the US and Canadian experiences with those of many European countries. We also compare the experiences of different European regions. These comparisons add complexity, owing to the variety of data sources for Europe and the differing kinds of data available in North America and Europe, but also add richness. We would have liked to extend our analyses to include other parts of the world, but reasonably reliable data are not available in many countries even for homicide (Alvazzi del Frate 2010; Harrendorf, Heiskanen, and Malby 2010; Lappi-Seppälä and Lehti 2014).

Our conclusions are necessarily tentative and exploratory. Cross-national study of trends in violence against women is at best an emerging field. We pose questions as to whether, or to what extent, women's victimization is affected by causal forces similar to those for victimization of men. Is women's victimization uniquely affected by changes in structural and cultural gender equality, or are there other general factors, common to both sexes and to different forms of violence, that affect changes in violence?

Our first interest is descriptive, albeit with important theoretical implications. We seek to understand whether violent victimization of women is following similar or different trends compared with victimization of men. If we were to adopt a narrow feminist perspective, we would assume that violence against women is the result of gendered asymmetry of power and of men's efforts to control women (Stanko 1985; Hanmer and Maynard 1987; Radford and Russell 1992) and thus that violence against women has motivations different from those of general violence. We assume that tolerance of violence against women has declined in most Western—and non-Western—countries in recent decades (Pierotti 2013), that women's conditions are generally, though slowly, improving, and that cultural understandings of gender relationships are changing. These assumptions imply that declines in violence against women are occurring for reasons that are at least partly different from those that explain violent victimization of men. If that is true, the timing of the declines in violence may also be different for men and women.

Analysis of gender-specific trends alone cannot make clear whether similar or different social forces are affecting men's and women's exposure to violence with the same intensity and at the same time. It is nonetheless a necessary first step in the examination of such questions.

Second, we examine whether there has been a general decline in rape and female homicide in Europe and North America or whether the declines have occurred only in some countries. Although there is general agreement that homicide and property crime rates (burglary, motor vehicle theft, personal theft) are declining in all wealthy Western countries (Eisner 2008; van Dijk, Tseloni, and Farrell 2012), there is no agreement about nonlethal violence. Both official and victimization data show that robbery and assault rates have been falling in recent decades in the English-speaking countries and in some continental European countries. In other continental countries, including all of Scandinavia, they have been rising. The disagreement is over how to interpret those apparently different trends. Some argue that they should be taken at face value: the incidence of nonlethal violence in some places is increasing (e.g., Aebi and Linde 2010, 2012). Others argue that real levels of nonlethal violence in those countries are almost certainly falling but that changes in victim reporting to the police, police recording of crimes, and changing cultural understandings of what counts as violence have generated artifactual and misleading increases in crime rates shown in official data (Tonry 2014).

Third, we explore similarities and differences in trends by analyzing data from different parts of Europe. Accordingly, we divided Europe into regions and used *European Sourcebook of Crime and Criminal Justice* (Aebi et al. 2010) and United Nations data to explore differences across regions for rape and female homicide. We speculate about possible reasons for differences we find.

Here are our main conclusions. First, there has been a decline in the United States in all forms of violence, including rape and female homicide, which are measured in official and victimization data. The declines are clear, are of several decades' duration, and are shown by different sources of information. Rape reported to the police and female homicide are declining as is self-reported rape victimization. Official data in Canada show similar declines, though victimization survey data show stable sexual assaults rates. We do not have Canadian victimization survey data for rape; however, victim-reported sexual attacks in that country are not declining. A variety of factors have probably been important.

Second, female homicide is declining almost everywhere in Europe. In most countries the trends closely resemble those for male victims, though in some, the declines in female homicide are less marked. Not all of this latter group of countries are characterized by unusual degrees of gender inequality or especially high prevalence of more traditional male and female roles (though this remains a relevant issue). Our broad findings for Europe show a fragmented picture that needs to be better understood.

Third, rape patterns in Europe only partly follow the American pattern. Rates in official data are increasing in many countries. The limited data available from victimization surveys show stability in rape victimization.

Explanations typically offered to explain the overall drop in violent crime do not take into account specific factors that may have influenced violence against women: improvements in gender equality, changes in masculine culture, long-lasting campaigns to change attitudes, and prevention programs aiming to reduce violence against women. In exploring explanations, we discuss the effects of statutory changes in rape law, changes in statistical routines, and—to a lesser extent—changes in police practices. We discuss developments in several countries that shed light on the effects these changes may or may not have had.

Here is how this essay is organized. In Section I, to provide context, we discuss research on gender violence in the United States, where the literature appears to be larger and more broadly focused than elsewhere. We also introduce themes from feminist and other theoretical writings that inform our discussions elsewhere. In Section II, we describe trends in female and male homicide in the United States, Canada, and Europe. We discuss our sources of information and their limits and consider whether female homicide is following similar or different patterns across countries. In Section III, we turn our attention to trends in rape. We discuss methodological issues that affect the reliability of available data on rape and explore the effects of legal changes and other developments on rape reporting (especially in Europe). Rape trends are compared—in some cases—with those for other violent crimes in order to explore hypotheses about changes in tendencies to report violent crime in general. In Section IV, we discuss our findings in relation to theoretical explanations that have been offered for crime trends in general and the drop in violence in particular. We explore how a gender-based perspective can interact usefully with other explanations for changes in general violence. Section V, the conclusion, briefly summarizes our main findings, discusses some of their limitations, and highlights open questions.

I. Theory and Context

Theorizing and research on gender differences in crime victimization remain rare. Even so, some important research and some theoretical works provide useful points of reference. For instance, for all national and cultural groups, males constitute the majority of crime victims and perpetrators. This is one of the most consistent findings in criminology. Gender gaps in female homicide victimization have been demonstrated over time and cross-nationally (Gartner, Baker, and Pampel 1990; LaFree and Hunnicutt 2006). Women, however, account for a significant share of both arrests and victimizations, and the size of the gender gap may change over time. Thus overall drops in levels of violence may be reflected in falling rates of violence against women or, alternatively, may be occurring despite rising or stable rates of female victimization.

To explain violence against women, feminist perspectives point to gender inequality. Several relationships between gender equality and women's violent victimization have been proposed. Below, we detail these approaches, as well as approaches incorporating routine activities theory, and hypotheses reflecting hybrid approaches.[3] The traditional feminist approach holds that gendered violence stems from gender inequalities. Thus, the corollary "ameliorative" hypothesis suggests that greater gender equality (on a variety of dimensions, including access to rights) would reduce the number of women victimized on a gendered basis (Brownmiller 1975). Women's victimization will persist when women are in disadvantaged positions relative to their male counterparts (Ellis and Beattie 1983). Additionally, absolute deprivations may leave poor women unprotected from frustrated and angry men they encounter in their daily lives (Bailey 1984). Studies of intimate partner homicide have emphasized exposure reduction that may have occurred through declining marriage rates, improvements in women's economic status, and the availability of domestic violence services (Rosenfeld 1997, 2000; Dugan, Nagin, and Rosenfeld 1999, 2003).

Feminist scholars have also hypothesized that gains in women's status relative to men may produce a "backlash": improved structural conditions may pose a threat to male dominance, which in turn may

---

[3] Feminist theories have been differentiated as traditional (ameliorative), radical (backlash), Marxist (absolute), and socialist (absolute and relative status; Vieraitis, Britto, and Kovandzic 2007).

provoke violence against women (Brownmiller 1975; Russell 1975). As Whaley (2001, p. 533) explains, an increase in women's status relative to men might be expected to increase the perceived threat to men's collective interests. In response to such threats, the importance of defining masculinity in contrast to femininity may increase. Rape—or other forms of violence—then becomes a medium by which men demonstrate their power over women.[4] Backlash effects may be time-graded, with gender parity having a positive relationship with female victimization in the short term but a negative one over longer periods as gender equality catalyzes broader cultural change (Russell 1975). Longitudinal analyses of rape in the United States have offered some support for this time-graded backlash thesis (Bailey 1999; Whaley 2001).

Gartner et al. (1990, p. 597) observe that "when women are free to move out of traditional roles their exposure to conflict with men increases both in and outside the home." Such exposure, in turn, increases women's risk for victimization.[5] Increased labor force participation has been associated with higher levels of homicide (Gartner et al. 1990; Bailey and Peterson 1995) and rape (Uggen and McElrath 2011).

Gartner et al. (1990) distinguish between improvement in women's lifestyles and roles and improvement in their status. Improvements in roles and lifestyles affect the general situational context and may increase female victimization in the short term, while changes in female status—a much slower process—in the long term can bring greater protection. When women achieve high status, they have more resources to protect themselves and are better positioned to influence changes in policy and culture. These ideas about differences in levels

---

[4] Gender equality, via threats to masculinity, may increase male propensities toward violence more generally, not simply violence targeted toward women (Whaley and Messner 2002). Recent downward trends in violence in homicide do not support this hypothesis.

[5] From a macro-level perspective, poor women in the United States face a greater risk of victimization. Yet, this American finding is not consistently replicated in victimization surveys in Europe. In Italy, for instance, female victims of both overall and gender violence typically have better educations and higher economic status (Istituto Nazionale di Statistica 2006). Violence against women in general is much higher in the more prosperous regions of countries characterized by higher levels of gender equality. In France, a one-time survey on violence against women in 2000 showed that—for victims older than 25—physical violence was more common among women with higher-level employment (Jaspard 2001). Findings from the British Crime Survey on the social status of victims, however, are similar to American findings (Finney 2006).

and characters of the broad category "gender equality" can usefully inform understanding of differences in the gender gap across space and time.

To date, evidence from the United States has proven largely inconclusive in testing the backlash hypothesis. The majority of findings, resulting from cross-sectional analyses, are consistent with it, but longitudinal studies have yielded support for an ameliorative hypothesis (Bailey 1999) or a short-term backlash followed by long-term amelioration (Whaley 2001). Longitudinal studies have also pointed to the importance of traditional gender norms (Pridemore and Freilich 2005) and absolute (Uggen and McElrath 2011) and relative (Xie, Lauritsen, and Heimer 2011) labor force participation as predictors of higher levels of homicide, rape, and nonviolent victimizations.

Results are even less clear in comparative studies. LaFree and Hunnicutt (2006), drawing on data from 35 countries in different areas of the world, found no clear evidence of a backlash effect as female homicide trends followed male trends in all but six of the countries they looked at. They did find a narrowing of the gender gap because the declines in men's victimization were greater than those for women.

Little research on the backlash hypothesis has been done in Europe. Though not directly addressing the backlash effect, a recent European study finds interesting variations between countries in rates of female homicide from 1985 to 2010 related to regional differences and to diverse economic and gender-related variables (Stamatel 2014).

At a national level, an exploratory attempt (Arcidiacono 2010), using data from a dedicated violence-against-women victimization survey in Italy, showed much higher levels of physical, sexual, and emotional violence against women in the north of the country. A multivariate analysis used indicators of women's greater emancipation in different areas of the country, especially in northern and southern regions historically characterized by great differences in gender equality. All three forms of gender violence were higher in areas in which gender equality (measured by educational attainment and women's presence in the labor force) is higher, in which women have more independent lifestyles, and in which rates of divorce are higher. The difference between changes in roles and status proposed by Gartner and her colleagues, and differences in timing, should be analyzed in depth and tested in case studies. In Italy, the much higher rates of female violent victimization in the north can be explained by greater adoption of nontraditional female roles and greater women's emancipation. Those characteristics, however, are not supported by a generalized increased presence of women in higher levels of society or by consistent changes in the masculine culture. A sort of "incomplete" level of gender equality seems to expose women to greater levels of violence in and outside intimate settings.

Studies on the gender gap and the backlash effect are strategically important if we want to improve our knowledge of violence against women and how it changes. Other interesting ideas elaborated by feminist scholars, however, suffer from their lack of engagement with empirical evidence. The case of "femicide," for instance, is illustrative. This is a promising theoretical initiative—conceptualization of a new category of homicide whose characteristics are defined by gender conflict (Radford and Russell 1992)—that has important implications for improvement in research on female homicide. It was primarily taken up by advocacy groups, international bodies, and nongovernmental organizations (and symbolically accepted in some Latin American countries as the basis for new legal definitions of homicide).[6]

Empirical investigations of femicide would require an improvement in the quality and quantity of data typically available on homicide, including characteristics of the event, relations between victims and perpetrators, and motives. In theory, femicide includes the killing of a woman for gender reasons (by a partner, ex-partner, acquaintance, or relative). It also includes killings for other reasons that are not gender-neutral, for example, killings of prostitutes by their clients, of women otherwise exploited in the sex market, and of trafficked or kidnapped women. It also includes suicides of violence survivors, killings of children and friends or relatives, and suicides of the perpetrator. Other categories include women killed for gender reasons because of patriarchal practices and cultures such as executions for adultery, widow burning, and female infanticide (ACUNS 2013). If statistics on causes of death included the data necessary to test femicide hypotheses, research on gender violence and therefore on violence generally would be much improved.

---

[6] Only in the United States and Canada have a few studies tried empirically to investigate female homicide using "femicide" as a starting point (e.g., Brawne and Williams 1993; Gartner, Dawson, and Crawford, n.d.). A more recent empirical examination of femicide in many countries appears in Alvazzi del Frate (2011).

II. Homicide

The gender gap in homicide is well known and long-standing. However, few crime trend studies take account of gender victimization differences across time and space, and macro-level studies of female victimization are rare, notwithstanding that the killing of women—and related global and national campaigns by feminist advocacy groups—has attracted the interest of international agencies, national governments, and public opinion.

In the United States, changes in the gender gap have varied over time, across types of crime, and across victim-offender relationships (Steffensmeier et al. 2005*a*, 2005*b*). For instance, Rosenfeld (2000) found that homicide rates during the 1990s for both males and females declined over the decade. Dugan et al. (1999, 2003) documented declines in intimate partner homicide but note that men's victimization rates have fallen more steeply than women's, reducing the gender gap in intimate partner homicide.

In Europe, macro-level studies are rare and mostly related to individual countries. Pioneering though controversial studies by Verkko (1951) introduced issues that are relevant to current debates.[7] He showed that it is important to distinguish female homicide trends from general trends because of the different social roles and conditions of women, because the proportion of female victims is higher when the overall homicide rate is low, and vice versa, and because rates of homicide committed by males are much more variable. Female homicide represented a more stable component of overall homicide (Verkko 1951; Kivivuori, Savolainen, and Danielsson 2012).

Work on crime trends stagnated for decades and has only recently resumed, though with little consideration of the gender gap. Two recent European studies offer insight into characteristics of gender-specific homicide victimization, but in only a few European countries and mostly cross-sectionally. A European Union–funded study is the first attempt to estimate mortality related to spousal violence at the European level (Psytel 2010). It gathered data for 27 European countries from Eurostat, the World Health Organization, the UN Office for Drug Control, Interpol, and national sources of information (in-

---

[7] Verkko's law of constancy in the rates of female victimization was characterized—consistently with the times in which he wrote—by "biological determinism" because the gender gap was seen as a consequence of biological differences between the sexes (Gartner et al. 1990, p. 594).

cluding the media). The largely cross-sectional study does not allow for an analysis of changes over time, though some longitudinal data were available for France, where overall homicide rates have been declining since the 1980s. The data show that the French decline was slower and weaker for female than for male homicide, as if the latter were "a more persistent and subterranean phenomenon" (Pystel 2010, p. 13).

On average, the study estimated that the killing of women by partners or ex-partners represented 33 percent of total homicides, with large variations ranging from 20 percent in Greece to 48.5 percent in Austria. "Gender-related homicide" was defined to include the killing of women by partners, ex-partners, or acquaintances; suicides of victims of intimate violence; suicides of perpetrators; collateral homicides; and homicides among people of the same sex in intimate relationships. There were 3,413 estimated deaths related to intimate relationships in 27 European countries in 2006: 1,409 killings of women by a partner or ex-partner, 1,010 suicides of women victims of violence, 272 killings of men by a partner, 186 collateral homicides, and 536 suicides of male perpetrators.

The second recent study compared female homicide victimization in Finland, Sweden, and the Netherlands (Ganpat et al. 2011).[8] The gender gaps were large. Women constituted 32 percent of all killings in the Netherlands, 38 percent in Sweden, and 28 percent in Finland. Women killed by strangers were 20 percent of all female killings in Finland and 24 percent in Sweden (data on the Netherlands were unavailable).

Trends in female and male homicide victimization were similar in the three countries through the 1960s, after which rates began to rise. They peaked, at slightly different times, in Finland and Sweden in 1980–90 and in the Netherlands in 1995. Declines occurred for both females and males; however, female homicide in the Netherlands was 70 percent higher in 2009 than at the end of the 1960s. In Sweden it was about the same, and in Finland it was 10 percent lower (Ganpat et al. 2011, p. 23).

---

[8] This is a pilot study in a 3-year project funded by the European Union that aims to build a database, the European Homicide Monitor, which will collect standardized data on homicide characteristics and trends in European countries. The information gathered includes types of homicide and victims' and perpetrators' characteristics and relationships. It has the potential to enable detailed and accurate comparative analyses of European homicide trends in general and female killings in particular.

Gender-related killing of women is mostly the subject in Europe of advocacy group reports, usually based on media sources. Scientifically speaking, these works are weak because of their sources of information, but they highlight a critical issue: to understand female homicide victimization, we need information on killers' motivations, something that to our knowledge is not available in any country. Only with this information can we single out gender-motivated killings. We can usually infer, however, that when perpetrators are intimate partners or ex-partners, the killing is based on gender reasons. This information about victim-perpetrator relationships, however, is often not available in official data sources and it is nowhere consistently available. Where data are available, they confirm that the vast majority of female homicide victims are murdered by males.

Homicide data on killings of women suffer from several limitations, even though they are more reliable than rape data because they do not depend largely on victim reports. However, even homicides are subject to underreporting, misreporting, and discrepancies in classification (Harrendorf et al. 2010; Lappi-Seppälä and Lehti 2014).

A. Sources and Data

We draw mostly on data from the Finnish National Research Institute on Legal Policy Comparative Homicide Time Series (NRILP-CHTS). Data are available from 1950 to 2012 and are mostly based on World Health Organization data on causes of death. For the United States and Canada we generally draw, respectively, on data from the Federal Bureau of Investigation's Uniform Crime Reports and Statistics Canada. The NRILP data set incorporates data on causes of death for 193 countries, 40 self-governing regions, and 15 historical administrative entities. Annual data by gender are available for 124 independent countries, 33 self-governing regions, and six historical administrative entities (Lehti 2013).[9] We use these data to present trends in male and female homicide victimization rates and to construct gender ratios. Even though these data are more reliable than police data because they are less influenced by statistical changes and police procedures, and above all by different counting rules in different countries,

[9] See Lehti (2013) and Lappi-Seppälä and Lehti (2014) for more detailed information, including citations to additional sources.

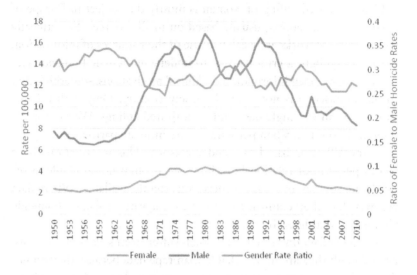

FIG. 1.—Male and female homicide rates per 100,000 same-sex population, United States, 1950–2010. Source: National Research Institute on Legal Policy Comparative Homicide Time Series (Lehti 2013). The 2001 spike reflects deaths from terrorist attacks on September 11, 2001.

we do not know how many women were victims of gender violence and lack information about victim-offender relationships.

B. United States and Canada

Male homicide rates in the United States have far outpaced female rates in the second half of the twentieth century, as figure 1 shows. There have been declines since the early 1990s for both men and women. Male victimization dropped most steeply in the 1990s and stalled in the 2000s, while female victimization rates fell more consistently. Between 1991 and 2000, rates for men fell by 45 percent and rates for women by 38 percent. Male rates fell an additional 15 percent between 2001 and 2010 when female rates fell 19 percent. The gender gap shrank. The ratio climbed between 1994 and 1999, as male homicide rates fell more steeply, only to reverse direction between 1999 and 2005.

Canadian police reported 543 homicides in 2012, for a rate of 1.56 victims per 100,000 population, the lowest since 1966 (Boyce and Cotter 2013). As figure 2 shows, this trend incorporated declines in both male and female rates, despite fluctuations in the 1970s and 1980s and

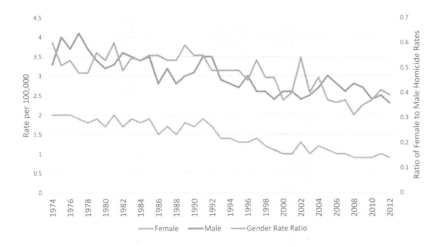

FIG. 2.—Canadian homicide rates per 100,000 population, male and female, 1974–2012. Source: Statistics Canada, Homicide Survey, Canadian Centre for Justice Statistics.

a rise in the early to mid-2000s, especially among males. Since 1991, the male rate has dropped by just over a third (35.3 percent), while the female rate has fallen by more than half (53.7 percent).

The gender gap has grown slightly. When men's rates continued to decline after 2005 while women's rates have held stable, the ratio increased to 0.4. A similar downward trend is evident in intimate partner homicides (Sinha 2013). By 2011, the rate of intimate partner homicides against women had fallen 51 percent since 1991 (and 15 percent since 2001). This resulted from a 46 percent drop in female homicides committed by spouses and a 65 percent drop in female homicides committed by nonmarried intimate partners.

Spousal homicides have also fallen for women. The intimate partner homicide rate in 2012 was 0.28 per 100,000 population, consistent with rates in the previous 5 years. Rates of intimate partner homicide continued to be higher for females than for males, regardless of the age group (Boyce and Cotter 2013). While there was no significant change in the proportion of women who experienced spousal violence between 2004 and 2009, there was a statistically significant decline between 1999 (8 percent) and 2009 (6 percent).

TABLE 1

Average Ratio Male to Female
Homicide Rates, 19 European
Countries, 1975–2011

Country	Average Ratio, 1975–2011
Italy	4.1
Bulgaria	3.1
Portugal	2.9
Spain	2.8
Greece	2.5
Finland	2.5
Romania	2.4
Poland	2.3
Netherlands	2.1
United Kingdom	2.0
Sweden	1.9
France	1.7
Norway	1.6
Czech Republic	1.6
Hungary	1.5
Denmark	1.3
Germany	1.2
Switzerland	1.1
Austria	1.0
European Union 19	2.1

SOURCE.—*European Sourcebook on Crime and Criminal Justice Statistics* (Aebi et al. 2010); UN Office on Drug Control.

C. Europe

The picture in Europe is more fragmented because of the existence of a diversity of countries and regions. We begin with ratios of male to female homicide victimization. Table 1 presents an average gender ratio in homicide victimization between 1975 and 2011 for 19 European countries. The ratio compares male and female homicide rates. In contrast to the preceding section, where we described the ratio as the female percentage of the male rate (e.g., 0.4), here we describe the ratio as the male multiple of the female rate (e.g., 2.5). The average ratio for the 19 countries was 2.1, ranging from near parity in Austria to 4.1 in Italy. Countries where gender inequality is greater, in southern and eastern Europe, have the highest ratios (as also Finland). Italy's ratio is highest because of the large number of men involved in organized crime, as is demonstrated by the ratio of the years 1989–91, when the male-to-female ratios were 8.1, 7.7, and 7.4 because of a peak in mafia killings that mostly involved men.

Figure 3 shows trends in homicide rates for men and women at the overall European level and for clusters of countries in four regions (eastern, northern, southern, and western Europe).[10] They take into account the "horizontal" boundaries between south and north instead of the traditional "vertical" division into three areas (western, central, and eastern Europe). The distinction between south and north is more relevant in understanding violence against women, in light of cultural differences in definitions of rape in these two areas and general differences in the conditions of women. Taking eastern Europe into account enriches comparative scope and healthily extends the conventional understanding of the "Western world."

Homicide rates for men began to fall in all European areas during the first half of the 1990s, after a peak that is most evident in eastern Europe and, at a lower level, in southern Europe. Female homicide follows a similar trend, but some differences are worth noting. Declines are clear for eastern and western Europe; less clear for northern Europe, where there are ups and downs; and not at all clear for southern Europe, where the homicide rates seem to be constant (and much lower than in other European areas). Female victimization has thus been stable in southern Europe, even though male victimization dropped steadily. Trends in male and female homicide are more similar in western, northern, and eastern Europe.

More detailed analyses for each country in the clusters, shown in figure 4, confirm that male homicide is declining everywhere but that there are no general patterns for women. Female homicide is clearly declining in some countries (all of eastern Europe, Germany, Austria, Finland, and the United Kingdom). In other countries there have been many ups and downs but no clear patterns (Norway, the Netherlands, Portugal, and Spain). In other countries, female victimization is decreasing slowly (Italy, France, and Sweden). In one case, it is clearly

[10] Northern Europe in the figures includes the United Kingdom, Finland, Denmark, Norway, and Sweden. Western Europe includes Austria, France, Germany, Netherlands, and Switzerland. Southern Europe includes Portugal, Italy, Spain, and Greece. Eastern Europe includes Hungary, Poland, Czech Republic, Romania, and Bulgaria. We include these countries but not others in the same areas because we believe that their official data are more reliable. However, we recognize that our categories do not reflect many other regional differences in Europe.

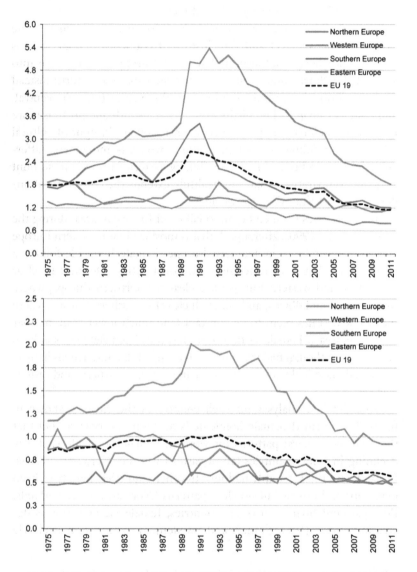

FIG. 3.—Male (*top*) and female (*bottom*) homicide rates per 100,000 population, by European regions and for 19 countries, 1975–2011. Source: National Research Institute on Legal Policy Comparative Homicide Time Series (Lehti 2013).

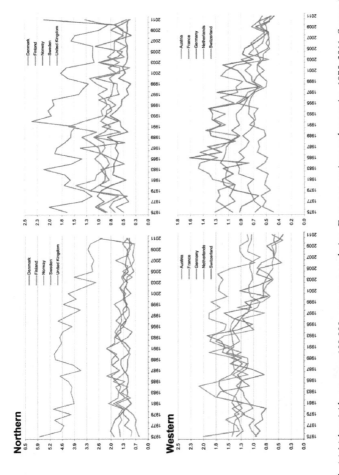

FIG. 4.—Male (*left*) and female (*right*) homicide rates per 100,000 same-sex population, European regions and countries, 1975–2011. Source: National Research Institute on Legal Policy Comparative Homicide Time Series (Lehti 2013).

385

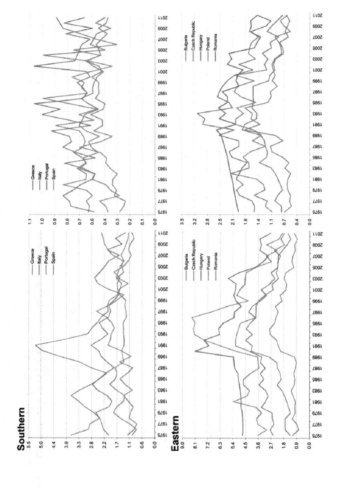

Fig. 4 (*continued*).—Male (*left*) and female (*right*) homicide rates per 100,000 same-sex population, European regions and countries, 1975–2011. Source: National Research Institute on Legal Policy Comparative Homicide Time Series (Lehti 2013).

increasing (Greece). The gender-specific trends are mostly convergent, however, including in Greece, where male homicide victimization also is increasing. Accordingly, we see a narrowing of the gender gap.

Female homicide victimization is thus declining in most European countries, but neither as sharply nor as clearly as male victimization. The timing of the onset of decline is also similar. The decreases start for both males and females in the first half of the 1990s, though for women the decline is more evident at the end of the decade. Despite these general trends, there are several outlying cases.

D. Discussion

In the United States and Canada, both male and female homicide rates have been falling since the early 1990s. In the United States, a narrowing of the gender gap is evident, but as a result of a steeper decline in men's victimization rather than an increase in women's victimization. During the 1990s, the decline in Canada was greater for women than for men. The gender gap in victimization thus grew slightly, as the ratio of women's to men's victimization fell from over 0.5 in the mid-1970s to a low of 0.3 in 2008. In recent years, the ratio has increased slightly as men's rates continued to decline while women's rates have held stable.

The European data, because they are disaggregated by region and country, permit more nuanced analyses. Where gender equality is higher, the relative number of women killed is much closer to the number of men, while in countries where gender equality is lower and traditional differentiations in male and female roles remain strong, there is a much higher homicide risk for men than for women.

Female homicide is thus declining in the United States, Canada, and a sizable majority of European countries, with the conspicuous exception of Greece. However, in a sizable number of European countries, the decline for females is much less pronounced than for males. In Spain and Greece, for instance, female homicide victimization in 2011 is at the same level as in 1975, and it declined only recently in Portugal and, slightly, in Italy. In the Netherlands, female homicide is still higher than in 1975, though lower than in 1990. Trends between men and women seem to be mostly convergent and suggest that similar forces are affecting both. The influence of these forces, however, seems to be weaker for women.

Unfortunately, we do not know whether declines in female homicide victimization result mostly from a decline in the percentage of women not killed other than in intimate relationships. Improved data on killers' motivations of crime and on victim-perpetrator relationships would further our understanding of these trends.

III. Rape and Sexual Assaults

For the analysis of rape, we need to use different kinds of sources in North America and Europe. For the United States and Canada, we examine trends in rape in police and victimization data. In Europe, we examine only police data, except for Sweden, for which we also examine victimization data.

Analysis of rape raises more methodological challenges than does homicide. This section therefore is primarily exploratory. We first briefly describe these challenges and the available sources of information and their characteristics and then describe trends and discuss our main, albeit tentative, findings.

A. Sources and Data

A threshold problem is that sexual offenses often are not reported to law enforcement authorities. Some proportion of all crimes goes underreported, of course, but among serious offenses, rape and sexual and other assaults by and against intimate partners are the least likely to be reported (Catalano 2006). In Italy, 90 percent of rapes are not reported to the police (Arcidiacono 2013, p. 175). In England and Wales, 87 percent go unreported (Ministry of Justice, Home Office, and Office for National Statistics 2013). The situation in other countries is not very different (Barbieri 2010).

In hopes of increasing victims' willingness to report to the police, many countries adopted legal reforms beginning in the 1970s (e.g., Kong et al. 2003). Recent research, however, suggests that many victims continue to perceive sexual victimization as a private matter and that most do not disclose their victimization to any official or agency (Felson and Paré 2005; Sable et al. 2006; Weiss 2010). Reasons why victims do not report sexual offenses to the police are well known. They include fear of reprisal, embarrassment, concern about maintaining a relationship with the perpetrator, and self-blaming (Baumer, Felson, and Messner 2003, p. 842).

Reporting to the police has increased in recent years in many of the countries we examine (e.g., Canada, the United States, and some European countries), but the gains have generally been modest. There are a few exceptions that we discuss below. Research from the United States shows that reporting of rape and other sexual offenses increased substantially between 1980 and 2005 and that the largest gains occurred in reporting victimizations by known assailants and by strangers (Baumer et al. 2003; Baumer and Lauritsen 2010).

Reporting of sexual victimizations varies by type of crime. Victims are more likely to report serious victimizations to the police. For instance, according to data from the 2009 Canadian General Social Survey (GSS), only 10 percent of offenses included in a broad category of "sexual assault" were reported to the police, but 37 percent of sexual assaults involving threats or use of physical violence were reported (Sinha 2013). A similar pattern is found in victimization data from the United States. According to National Crime Victimization Survey (NCVS) data, reporting rates are higher for rape and attempted rape than for the broader category of sexual assault (Baumer and Lauritsen 2010).

A second challenge, especially for cross-national analyses, is that legal definitions vary across time and space. The cultural meaning of rape and how women define it vary substantially in different times and different places. "Rape" is universally prohibited, but exactly how countries (and states, in the United States) define it in their criminal laws varies. Sexual assault, rape, violence against women, and gender-based violence are conceptualized in criminal codes in different ways. "Spousal rape," for example, has only recently been criminalized in most countries, and in some it has not been criminalized at all (Frank et al. 2009).

Despite these differences, a majority of countries have changed criminal laws on sexual offenses since 1950 following broadly common patterns. Most have broadened their laws' scope and liberalized provisions concerning sexual preferences (e.g., repealing "sodomy" laws). Major changes in Western countries have included criminalizing spousal rape, including men among possible victims, reclassifying rape as a crime against the person and not as an offense against public morality or honor, and broadening the range of acts that can constitute rape (Frank et al. 2009; Frank, Camp, and Boucher 2010).

Rape has broadened in two main ways. The first is to combine rape with penetration and other sexual assaults into a general category of "sexual violence" or "sexual offenses." The second is to define "consent" more narrowly: for example, that consent cannot be assumed if the victim was asleep or otherwise incapable of resisting. There is also a growing tendency to eliminate any requirement of proof of the victim's "resistance" (Eileraas 2012). Other recent statutory changes include rape shield laws, provision of legal and other resources to victims, and more severe punishments.

Finally, changes in statistical procedures and in police cultures affect the reliability of reported rape and sexual assault figures. Police conventions often limit recording to the most serious of several alleged offenses, thereby undercounting other crimes. It is unclear to what extent this affects police statistics on serious sexual victimizations, but inevitably it must affect them in different ways at different times and in different places. Only recently have police in many countries been encouraged or required to improve recording procedure and capacities to deal with rape victims and encourage them to report (e.g., Ministry of Justice, Home Office, and Office for National Statistics 2013, p. 8).

Because of these and other reasons to be skeptical about the reliability of official data, there is general agreement that victimization surveys provide better estimates of sexual offending, especially for violence against women (Kangaspunta and Marshall 2012, p. 105; National Research Council 2014). The best surveys for capturing the full complexity of gender violence are specialized efforts that target violence against women.[11] Very few countries, however, conduct targeted surveys. The first was Canada in 1993, followed by the United States in 1994, and later by a few European countries.[12] At the European level, the first dedicated survey on violence against women (42,000 women interviewed in 28 European countries) was carried out recently, with data released in 2014 (FRA 2014). These stand-alone surveys typically yield higher estimates of sexual assault incidence and prevalence

[11] See National Research Council (2014) for an overview of the limitations of victimization surveys as indicators of sexual offending.

[12] An intimate violence survey of men and women was conducted in the United States in 2010 (Black et al. 2011). Dedicated surveys in Europe are rare and are sometimes limited to regional areas (such as the Ile de France and Catalonia). The Italian survey "La sicurezza delle donne," conducted in 2006, was the largest dedicated survey in Europe, with a sample of 25,000 women. Estonia in 2008, Finland in 1997 and 2005, and France in 2000 have also conducted such surveys. Information about national and regional European surveys is not easy to find, partly because of some language barriers. For overviews, see Aromaa and Heiskanen (2008) and Kangaspunta and Marshall (2012).

than do ordinary victim surveys (Kangaspunta and Marshall 2012). In Italy, for example, only 0.6 percent of women interviewed in national victimization surveys in 1998 and 2002 reported being raped, compared with 2.2 of respondents in a dedicated survey in 2006 (Eugenio Arcidiacono, personal communication May 28, 2014).

Questions on sexual violence, rape, and domestic violence are often included in a specific module inside a general victimization survey. This is the case in the United States with the NCVS. NCVS estimates reflect a broader conception of sexual violence than do police data. The NCVS also provides additional information pertaining to the victims (e.g., age, sex, race, ethnicity, marital status, income, and educational level), offenders (e.g., sex, race, approximate age, and victim-offender relationship), and crimes (time and place, use of weapons, nature of injury, and economic consequences) and investigates whether victims reported to law enforcement or other third parties. As sexual violence has grown rarer, obtaining reliable estimates from victimization surveys has grown more difficult (National Research Council 2014).

In Europe, general victimization surveys are not easily available for each country.[13] Only England and Wales, for more than 30 years, has conducted victimization surveys that include a module on sexual violence on a regular basis. In Europe generally, the situation is fragmented and comparability is precluded because of many differences in national surveys concerning sample sizes, sampling procedures, timing and frequency, different questions, and other organizational details.

Some cross-national analyses rely on data from the International Crime Victimization Survey (e.g., van Dijk, van Kesteren, and Smit 2007). However, we do not analyze those data for a variety of reasons including small sample sizes, low participation rates, inconsistency from wave to wave in participating countries, and recurring changes in questions and statistical procedures. Nor do we use data from the International Violence Against Women Survey. It is a one-time survey in 11 countries around the world that provides no basis for examining trends (and that has major sampling and other methodological problems; Johnson, Ollus, and Nevala 2008).

In the following pages we present data from a number of national

---

[13] A European Crime Survey project started in 2007 (Aromaa and Heiskanen 2008). There has been discussion of a dedicated European survey on violence against women (Kervinen and Heiskanen 2013). A preliminary report has been published (FRA 2014).

and regional sources. For the United States and Canada, we rely mostly on the Federal Bureau of Investigation's Uniform Crime Reports and the Canadian Uniform Crime Reports compiled by Statistics Canada. The American UCR defines "forcible rape" as "carnal knowledge of a female forcibly and against her will" and includes attempts or assaults to commit rape (Truman, Langton, and Planty 2013).[14] The definition of "forcible rape" was unchanged between 1960 and 2011. Canada's official statistics have defined sexual offenses consistently since 1983, when Canada enacted legislation meant to increase victim reporting of sexual assaults to the police (Kong et al. 2003).

Despite limitations discussed above, national victimization surveys can be useful for looking at trends over time within a country. Below, we present survey data from the United States, Canada, and Sweden. In Canada, victimization data are obtained through the GSS, now in its fifth wave, which collects data from persons aged 15 years and older. Below, we present data from the most recent three waves, covering 1999–2009.

Sweden is the only European country from which we use victimization data.[15] The Swedish Crime Survey is a recurrent annual survey of the general population of Sweden aged 16–79 using telephone interviews supplemented by paper questionnaires from people who cannot be reached by phone or decline to participate by phone. The first survey was conducted in 2006 with 8,000 participants. Since then the survey has expanded to include 15,000 annual participants. Participation rates are high, typically more than 75 percent of those approached.

Because standardized European surveys do not exist and national surveys vary too widely in methods and measures to be used in comparative analyses, we rely on data from official statistics, mostly drawn from the *European Sourcebook of Crime and Criminal Justice* (ESCCJ). The ESCCJ has collected data on national criminal justice systems,

---

[14] In 2011, the FBI redefined forcible rape as "penetration, no matter how slight, of the vagina or anus with any body part or object, or oral penetration by a sex organ of another person, without the consent of the victim." Our analyses use earlier data and are not affected by the change.

[15] The Crime Survey for England and Wales (CSEW), formerly called the British Crime Survey, since 2004/5 has included a module on intimate violence. The CSEW is the longest-running representative national victimization survey using large samples in Europe. We do not discuss its findings because of the complexity of the raw data and problems in comparing data from different waves. We do provide information drawn from national reports on findings (Ministry of Justice, Home Office, and Office for National Statistics 2013).

including offenses recorded by the police, between 1990 and 2006/7 (Aebi et al. 2010). It was designed to facilitate cross-European comparisons by standardizing data into general definitions of offenses. It provides the best available longitudinal, comparative data on offenses reported to the police in Europe.[16] The ESCCJ defines rape as "sexual intercourse with a person against her/his will (per vaginam or other)." It includes penetration other than vaginal, violent intramarital sexual intercourse, sexual intercourse without force with a helpless person, sexual intercourse with force with a minor, and attempts. Other sexual assaults are not reported in the sourcebook. We also draw on data from the UN Crime Trend Survey data set for 2007–10. Data for these years are not yet available from the ESCCJ. The definition of rape used here is "sexual intercourse without valid consent" (Harrendorf et al. 2010). Comparisons of the data series from the two sources show perfect correspondence between 1990 and 2007.

For the period prior to 1990, we again use data from the UN Crime Trend Survey. Because data are not available for all countries for all years, we used estimates for the missing values.[17] For this reason, our discussion is largely limited to trends since 1990.

We first describe trends in reported rape in the United States, Canada, and Europe, divided into the four regions. We selected the 19 European countries because they provide the most reliable information on reported rape. We also analyze trends in the four regional clusters. For Sweden and Italy, we discuss trends on the basis of a variety of sources.

B. Broad Patterns

In the United States, the numbers and rates for reported rape grew steadily between 1960 and 1980, dipped in the early 1980s, and resumed a climb until the early 1990s. As figure 5 shows, rates dropped steeply in the 1990s and continued to fall to levels not known since the mid-1970s. Between 1992, the peak year, and 2012, the most recent year for which data are available, the rape rate fell by 37 percent from

---

[16] The ESCCJ is sponsored by the European Council and several European governments. It started in 1993. Four editions have been published, covering the period 1990–2007. The fifth edition will be available in 2014. The 2010 report discusses the project's methods and processes (Aebi et al. 2010). For detailed discussions of the challenges faced in compiling the ESCCJ, see Aebi (2008, 2010) and Harrendorf (2012).

[17] The system used to calculate the estimates is described in the methodological note (in the appendix).

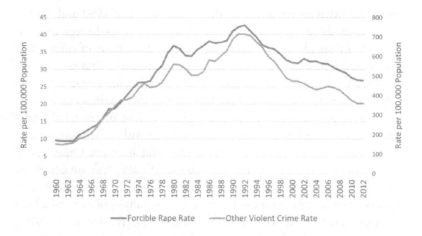

FIG. 5.—US rates of violent crimes except rape (aggravated assaults, robberies, and homicides; *right* axis) per 100,000 population and forcible rapes (*left* axis) per 100,000 female population, 1960–2012. Source: Federal Bureau of Investigation, Uniform Crime Reports, various years.

42.8 offenses to 26.9 per 100,000 female population. The pattern for rape closely paralleled that for other violent crimes (aggravated assault, robbery, and homicide).

Victim reporting of rape and other sexual offenses to the police has substantially increased since the mid-1970s. The declines in official data substantially understate the true declines (Baumer et al. 2003; Baumer and Lauritsen 2010).

The decline in rape shown in official data is supported by declines in reported rape victimization in the NCVS.[18] Victims' reports showed an even steeper drop. Between 1993 and 2010, rape victimizations fell by 75 percent, from 1.6 per 1,000 persons aged 12 and older in 1993 to 0.4 in 2010. Sexual assault victimization more broadly declined by 79 percent. Preliminary data for 2011 and 2012 suggest more stable rates of victimization and a smaller share of sexual victimizations reported to the police relative to the preceding decade (Truman, Langton, and Planty 2013).[19] Taken together, however, the UCR and NCVS

[18] Rape victimizations in the NCVS include completed and attempted rapes. In more recent years, data for rape separate from a more general category of sexual offenses are not available.

[19] These data should be interpreted with caution, as the NCVS implemented a change in counting procedures in 2011, affecting the victimization rate, and possibly police notification data (Lauritsen et al. 2012).

data show a substantial drop in sexual violence over the past 20 years in the United States.

Despite major differences in crime control policies and practices in the United States and Canada, violent crime patterns in Canada have largely mirrored those in the United States since the 1960s (Ouimet 2002; Tonry 2014). Since peaking in 1987, the police-reported violent crime rate in Canada has generally declined, in 2012 reaching its lowest level since 1972 (Perrault 2013).[20] Overall rates of police-reported violent victimization have been near parity for men and women in recent years, but the types of victimization differed. Women were more than 10 times more likely than men to be victims of a police-reported sexual assault. Men reported more physical assaults. The GSS showed similar patterns (Sinha 2013). Seventy percent of sexual assaults reported in 2009 involved a female victim. By contrast, 38 percent of victims of physical assaults were female.

As figure 6 shows, serious sexual offenses reported to the police have fallen steeply, declining annually between 1991 and 2000 and again from 2004 through 2012, except for an increase in 2010. Since peaking in 1992, the total violent crime rate (less serious sexual assaults) fell by 17 percent, while serious sexual assaults fell by 69 percent (Perrault 2013).

The GSS asks about a broader array of offenses (forced sexual activity, attempts at forced sexual activity, and unwanted sexual touching, grabbing, kissing, or fondling) than is included in the Canadian UCR classifications of sexual offenses. Nonetheless, we can still glean important information. Estimates of victimizations in 1999, 2004, and 2009, the most recent three survey waves, suggest that sexual assaults have remained at relatively stable levels over the past decade. There was no statistically significant change between 1999 and 2009. Sexual attacks, a narrower GSS category involving threats or physical violence, accounted for roughly one in five sexual assault incidents in 2009, 37 percent of which were reported to the police.[21] GSS estimates confirm that rates of sexual assault are higher among females than among males.

[20] Estimates are based on Canada's UCR1 reporting system, allowing for historical comparability. Exact numbers will differ from numbers recorded under the UCR2 reporting system, which employs a broader category of violent offenses (Perrault 2013).

[21] Estimated victimizations reported to the police in prior GSS waves are statistically unreliable, preventing analyses of changes in reporting over time (Perrault and Brennan 2010).

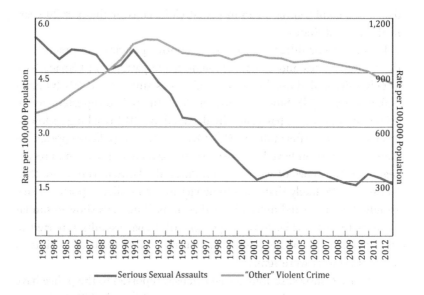

FIG. 6.—Violent crime (*right* axis) and serious sexual assault (*left* axis) rates per 100,000 total population, Canada, 1983–2012. Source: Statistics Canada, Uniform Crime Reports, various years.

On the basis of the 2009 survey, the self-reported sexual assault rate for females was twice that for males; 70 percent of all victims of sexual assaults were female (Sinha 2013).

We turn to Europe. The general European trend, represented by the dashed line in figure 7, shows a slow increase in reported rape that became more significant in the early 1990s and increased again after 2000. By 2011, rape rates in the 19 European countries were more than double those of the early 1990s. Rates in western Europe stabilized in the latter half of the 2000s after an earlier increase. They decreased in eastern Europe at the beginning of the decade. In all areas except eastern Europe, rates are higher than at the beginning of the 1990s. The rate of rape offenses reported to the police continued to grow in northern Europe, increasing a gap with the other regions that emerged in the early 1990s. Northern Europe, and to a much less extent southern and western Europe, contributed to the overall increase in reported offenses in Europe since the 1990s. Only eastern Europe shows a clear and longer decline.

This bird's-eye view obscures within-region variation. Figure 8 shows reported offenses for each region. Trends are much more ho-

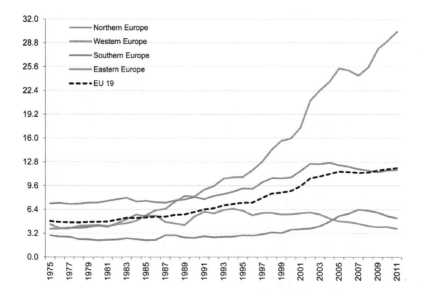

FIG. 7.—Rape rates per 100,000 population, European regions and countries, 1975–2011. Source: *European Sourcebook on Crime and Criminal Justice Statistics* (Aebi et al. 2010); UN Office on Drug Control.

mogeneous, and clearer patterns are evident in northern and western Europe. They are much more fragmented and characterized by ups and downs in southern and western Europe. This may be attributable to more systematic and organized recording procedures in the north and west. Several southern countries experienced political regime changes during the 1970s, as did all the eastern European countries in the 1990s. These changes affected crime reporting in addition to affecting broader social and cultural changes (e.g., Krajewski 2011; Gruszczynska and Heiskanen 2012).

Some of the eastern European countries experienced increases in reported crime immediately after the regime changes. That was particularly the case in Poland, where in 1989–90 the number of crimes reported to the police increased by 62 percent (Gruszczynska and Heiskanen 2012, p. 84). Krajewski (2011) attributes this to changes in patterns of reporting and recording offenses. Our rape data show clear increases in some countries, especially Romania, Bulgaria, and Hungary (with a time lapse compared with other eastern European countries). However, by the beginning of the 2000s, rape rates were falling in all four nations in the cluster. They still are.

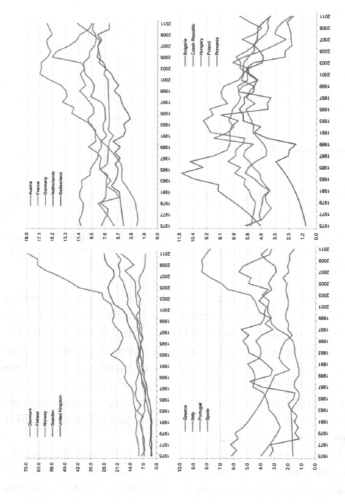

FIG. 8.—Rape rates per 100,000 population, European regions and countries, 1975–2011. Source: *European Sourcebook on Crime and Criminal Justice Statistics* (Aebi et al. 2010); UN Office on Drug Control.

Something different is happening in northern Europe. The high rates are driven largely by Sweden.[22] Yet, while omitting Sweden from the analysis would lower the average offense rates, there is a general upward trend. Only Denmark shows a decline in the last 5 years. The other countries have experienced major increases since the early 1990s. In the United Kingdom, reported rape was 14 times higher than in 1993. In Norway it was 10 times higher. In western Europe, France experienced an increase beginning in the mid-1980s that peaked in 2004. The increase stopped during the last decade, but in 2011, reported rape was more than five times higher than in 1975 and double the 1990 level. In the other countries in the cluster except Austria, rapes reported to the police decreased in recent years, though not sharply. In most cases rates remained higher in 2011 than in 1990.

In southern Europe, Italy shows the clearest increases in reported rape, starting in 1996 and peaking again in 2004. The countries that experienced transitions from dictatorship to democracy, Spain, Portugal, and Greece, had higher levels of reported rape at the beginning of the series, though we have to consider these data carefully since some of the years analyzed here are based on estimates (see the appendix). Compared with a starting point in 1990, the trends stabilized and became almost flat in Greece, with ups and downs in Portugal and Spain. The situation in these countries is fluctuating. There is not a clear decline.

C. Sweden

In this and the next section, we explore experiences in particular countries in greater depth. We start with Sweden, the country with the sharpest increase in reported rape and one for which additional sources are available.

Sweden has repeatedly changed its rape legislation since 1965, when intramarital rape was criminalized. In 1984, the offense became gender-neutral. In 1992, 1998, and above all in 2005, the behaviors that count as rapes were expanded. The law reforms and changes in statistical procedures are both important to understanding increases in rape in Scandinavian countries and above all in Sweden, where revisions of

---

[22] Yet we should not move too quickly past Sweden as the trend reveals an important cautionary note: despite the ESCCJ process to standardize statistics across various legal definitions, the outlying case of Sweden should give us pause. We return to Sweden below.

statistical routines occurred several times as well: in 1975, 1992, 1995, and 1999 (von Hofer 2000; von Hofer, Lappi-Seppälä, and Westfelt 2012). We need also to take into consideration other developments that precede or follow major changes in laws and may amplify their effects. These include advocacy campaigns meant to increase awareness and support among potential victims and extensive media coverage. These conditions, apparently, were present in Sweden, since the changes in rape law were part of a broader push of the Swedish government for enhancement of women's rights and protection from crime and other forms of exploitation.[23]

The soaring rates for rapes reported to the police in Sweden, shown in figure 8, attracted substantial media attention. Data on sexual offenses from the Swedish Crime Survey, however, paint a different or at least a more complicated picture. The survey asks about "sexual offenses" generally, not specifically about rape. Figure 9 shows trends in sexual offenses reported to the police from 2005 to 2012 and trends in sexual offense victimization reported by survey respondents for the same years. Sexual offenses reported to the police nearly doubled (Swedish National Council for Crime Prevention 2014a). However, the percentage of Swedish Crime Survey respondents who reported being a victim of a sexual offense has essentially been stable since 2005, varying between 0.7 and 0.9 percent (Färdeman, Hvitfeldt, and Irlander 2014). Extrapolating to the population aged 16–79 gives an estimated victimization rate of approximately 0.6 percent (Statistics Sweden 2014). The percentage of those who reported being a victim who also indicated that they reported the sexual offenses to the police fluctuated between 10 and 20 percent (Swedish National Council for Crime Prevention 2014b).

The Swedish data thus show an especially striking contrast between official data, which show a substantial increase in rape and in sexual offenses, and victimization data, which suggest that sexual offense victimization has been stable. This is different from what we found in the United States, where both data sources show a similar trend of sharply declining rates of rape. In short, assuming that rape patterns follow those for sexual offenses generally, official rates of rape in police data are increasing in Sweden for reasons that may not be explained by

[23] This broader context, which emphasizes feminist principles in a strict way, creating a widespread debate, has been analyzed for the change in prostitution law by Skilbrei and Holmström (2011) and generally by Tham, Rönneling, and Rytterbro (2011).

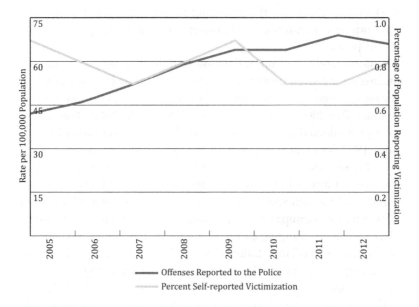

victimization by rape in real life. Reports by victimization survey respondents indicate that overall victimization by sexual offenses (and therefore, we assume, for rape as well) is stable. Differently from the United States, however, but similarly to Canada, there are no signs of a decline in the occurrence of sexual offense victimization in Sweden.

D. *Italy*

Italy is the only southern European country in which rape trends show clear increases. Rape rates in police data started to increase in Italy after 1996, when a new law changed the definition of the crime by broadening the behaviors that are included (sexual attacks without penetration are considered rape in Italian law) and by making the offense gender-neutral.[24] They increased again in 2004, in the wake of a

---

[24] The Italian Penal Code defines rape as any sexual intercourse committed with violence or the threat of violence, or abuse of authority, against any person. Aggravating circumstances are included for rape against minors and rape perpetrated by a group of persons. Punishments were increased.

fundamental change in the recording of crime that for the first time was entirely computerized and governed by standards applicable to all Italian police.[25]

Unfortunately, we cannot draw on victimization surveys to improve understanding, even though a well-designed targeted victimization survey on violence against women, with a large representative sample, was conducted in 2006 (Istituto Nazionale di Statistica 2006). The national surveys conducted every 5 years by the National Institute of Statistics since 1997–98 include a dedicated module on gender violence. However, because the questions have changed over the years, time-series data are not available to aid understanding of Italian trends in rape.

Italy and Sweden seem to be instances in which legal reforms—and related national campaigns to raise awareness and increase reporting—played a role in changing cultural understandings. The enormous Italian increase immediately followed the 1996 modernization of rape laws and a long period in which public debates on violence against women and the feminist movement gained momentum (Terragni 2002).

However, when trends in rape are compared with trends for assaults, in which most victims are male, we found only a partial confirmation of our hypothesis. Assault increased also, though not as sharply as rape did. The change in recording procedures by police, introduced in 2004 and fully implemented in the following 2 years, seems to have affected both offenses similarly. As figure 10 shows, trends for both crimes are very similar after 2004, thus demonstrating the importance of changes in statistical procedures for understanding trends in crime reported to the police.

E. Discussion

Our analysis provides evidence on which to base some strong conclusions but also leaves many open questions. The decline in the incidence of rape in the United States is clear and is supported by diverse sources of information. Drops were most steep in the 1990s, with slight declines in the 2000s. These trends map closely with those for other violent crimes. This raises the question whether the underlying causes of rape are different—as most feminist writers posit—from those of other violent crimes. Police data in Canada show a steep decline in

---

[25] There is clear evidence of the effects of the change in statistical routines in 2004 and that improving the recording system and related police training had a significant effect on crime trends (Selmini and Arcidiacono 2009).

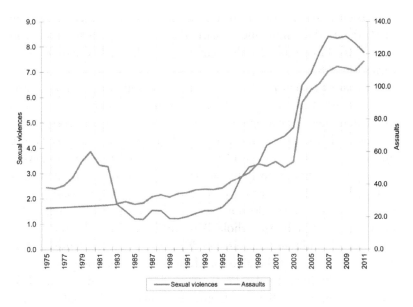

FIG. 10.—Sexual assaults and other serious assaults reported to the police per 100,000 population, Italy, 1975–2011. Source: Italian National Institute of Statistics.

serious sexual violence during the 1990s, followed by relative stability in the 2000s (Vaillancourt 2010). This is not significantly contradicted by the Canadian victimization data. At the very least, they do not show increases in sexual victimization. Between 1999 and 2009, Canadian victimization rates remained unchanged. In the United States, increased reporting to the police during a period when victimization was declining meant that the decline shown in police data was less than that in the victimization data. If victim reporting also increased in Canada, the police data should show increases. That they do not suggests that victimization in Canada was at worst flat but probably declining.

The European picture is somewhat different. Rape rates as shown in police data are increasing in most of Europe, including northern Europe (except Denmark), Italy, Austria, and France. In most European countries, rape rates remain several or many times higher than in 1990, including in the countries where there are indications of a decline. Yet, where victimization surveys have been conducted over time, in England and Wales and Sweden, rates of rape victimization appear to have held steady for at least the last decade.

Eastern Europe is the only European region where there appears to have been a general midterm decline. Declines also occurred in the Netherlands (but only since 2006), Portugal since 1998, and Spain since 2007. Greece is the only country where the decline started much earlier (in 1989).

The fairest conclusion to draw is that reported rape is rising in Europe, though there are signs of decreases in a few countries. Increases in Sweden, Italy, France, and the United Kingdom have been especially pronounced. To explain these patterns adequately, we would need more information than is now available. At this stage we offer somewhat informed speculation. In Italy, Sweden, and probably France, changes in rape laws and in statistical procedures may be a significant part of their explanations. We do not have other sources of information for the United Kingdom as a whole. A recent governmental report, however, shows continuing increases in 2012 for all sexual offenses in England and Wales, attributable mostly to changes in police recording procedures in 2008. England and Wales also broadened its legal definition of rape in the Sexual Offense Act 2003 and changed coverage of police-recorded sexual offenses (Ministry of Justice, Home Office, and Office for National Statistics 2013, pp. 8, 64). The British Crime Survey for 2004/5–2009/10 shows that victim reports of rape (including attempts) were stable (Smith 2011).

The comparison we offered on Italian trends in police data on assault and rape warrants further reflection. Assault is a complex category in Europe. Legal definitions vary widely between countries. According to the ESCCJ, assaults increased substantially between 1990 and 2007. Offenses known to police in sourcebook countries grew from a rate of 177.5 per 100,000 population in 1990 to 347.8 in 2011 (Aebi and Linde 2010, p. 12). That doubling needs explanation, and it might eventually prove to be the same explanation for all or part of the increases in rape rates.

Another recurring pattern warranting investigation is the differences in trend indications given by official and victimization data. In Sweden, as in Canada, there is a discrepancy between data from police statistics and victimization surveys. In both countries, general sexual offenses reported by victims are stable or slightly declining, but in Canada, reported rape has fallen and in Sweden it has increased dramatically. More research in these contexts is needed to prove that rape—among the sexual offenses included in the survey—actually decreased in its occurrence. Thus, while it is clear that the incidence of rape is falling in the United States and probably also in Canada and eastern Europe, the picture in other countries is mixed. In some, official data show marked increases. Although arguments can be made based on victimization data in some countries, and on possible shifts in formal policies and cultural attitudes in others, that the police data are misleading, our findings offer good grounds to be skeptical about the proposition that serious sexual violence is declining cross-nationally.

IV. Explaining Trends

By disaggregating homicide victimization by sex and analyzing rape and sexual offenses, which predominantly affect women, our findings show cross-national variation in long-term crime trends for men and women. These findings lay the groundwork for theoretical consideration. Explaining changes in crime rates is difficult because so many changing social, structural, and legal phenomena play roles. This is particularly true when female violent victimization is considered.

The explanatory literature on crime trends has improved remarkably in the attempt to find explanations for transnational crime trends (e.g., van Dijk and Tseloni 2012; Baumer and Wolff 2014; Eisner 2014). Many seek explanations that relate to broad structural, legal, and cultural changes. Distinctively female victimization has so far not received focused attention. It needs it, with particular attention to broader processes affecting male and female relationships and changes in female roles. Such explanations should also consider the massive structural, legal, and cultural changes that have occurred over the past half century with respect to women's status.

We have focused on homicide and rape. There are two different stories. When we comment on homicide, we contribute to the debate about changes in violence in the Western world. When we comment on changes in reported rape (as we do in general for Europe), we contribute to exploration of changes in general tolerance toward violent victimization of women (including as consequences of global and national campaigns to change attitudes and cultural norms and to criminalize this behavior). Both stories are important. They seem to confirm that violence in its most lethal forms is decreasing in most Western countries but that tendencies to criminalize and also probably to report "less" violent crimes to the police are increasing, at least in Europe.[26]

The likelihood that rapes are reported to authorities has increased in both North America and Europe. The timing has varied—later in Europe, earlier in North America and particularly the United States. Police data show clear and steady drops there in rape, but increases continue in many of the 19 European countries we looked at.

Only in the United States, however, is the rape decline in official data solidly supported by data from victimization surveys. In Canada and the few European countries for which we have data, rape victimization is stable. This means that we must be cautious in assuming or concluding that gender violence is declining cross-nationally. It suggests that changes in women's status and in cultural understandings about gender relationships may have been powerful enough only in the United States to affect the real occurrence of female sexual victimization. In Europe, even in Sweden, where gender equality is among the highest in the continent, we do not have clear signs of decline in data from victimization surveys, and rapes reported to the police are still mostly increasing. Thus, our findings support feminist theories that posit that violence against women is based on gendered asymmetry in power relationships and that real changes will occur only when these things change deeply and radically.

Most Western countries have fundamentally changed their laws and policies concerning rape since World War II. We briefly surveyed most of the major changes. Those efforts need to continue both for their narrow stated purposes of controlling, preventing, and appropriately responding to sexual offenses and also because of the complex interactions between law and culture. Important changes in laws in many countries followed major efforts by advocacy groups to identify victimization of women as a basic human rights problem and to change prevailing attitudes about it. Efforts by feminist law reformers in the United States in the 1970s and 1980s and in Sweden in the twenty-first century may be paradigm cases. One goal of the legal changes, however, is to confirm changing cultural norms about gendered vio-

---

[26] These processes go in parallel, according to Mucchielli (2010): while violence actually seems to be used less often to resolve conflicts, some forms of violence—and violence against women above all—are more and more stigmatized and "judicialized." Kangaspunta and Marshall (2012) and, for nonlethal violence in general, von Hofer et al. (2012) write of inflation in reporting behavior.

lence. Thus legal changes are often predicated on cultural shifts and aspire to cause more of them during the processes of implementation and enforcement of new laws.

The picture concerning trends in rape and other forms of violence against women is complicated. Concerning homicide, the story is different and vastly simpler. Female homicide victimization, like male victimization, is decreasing. However, there are differences. The female declines have not occurred in every country, and where they have, they are usually slower and smaller than male declines. In several European countries (from different areas of the continent) there has been no female decline. This sheds light on limitations of both conventional criminological theories (e.g., see Kivivuori et al. 2012) and conventional patriarchy explanations for violence against women. For instance, the feminist hypothesis of the "uniqueness" of gender violence cannot be rejected but needs to acknowledge other cultural and social changes.[27] These include recent attempts to understand changes in behavior through broader shifts "in culturally embedded images of conducting life" (Eisner 2008, p. 311). This approach tries to link changes in homicide rates "to change in norms and expectations about how young men interact in public space" (p. 312). Related questions arise. What about changes in norms and expectations about how men interact with women in private and public spaces? How much is behavior in intimate settings affected by general increases in self-control?

Female homicide victimization follows the same decreasing trend as male victimization. However, there are some differences. Female homicide follows a slower and weaker trend in decrease, and in several European countries (from different areas of the continent) it is still stable. We need more information about different components of female victimization: it could be, for example, that what is changing is the smallest part of overall female homicide, that of women killed outside intimate relationships. It seems therefore plausible to think that violence against women, though affected by broader cultural shifts that emphasize rejection of violence in general, is at the same time still characterized by the "uniqueness" that the feminist perspective has singled out and that the forces influencing crime trends for men and women are partly the same and partly different.

---

[27] Stamatel (2014) in her analysis of female homicide rates in Europe emphasizes the importance of bridging traditional criminological theories with "gender-sensitive explanations of female homicide" (p. 584) and consideration of regional differences.

Finally, we wonder whether and how Europe will follow the North American patterns of broadly declining rates for all traditional forms of property and violent crime. More narrowly, is it to be expected that in due course rape and female homicide victimization will fall steeply and be convincingly demonstrated by police and victimization data? Europe seems still to be engaged in a criminalization process of rape that expresses itself, among other ways, in increasing reporting in a remarkable number of countries. Homicide rates for both men and women are decreasing with slightly different timing and generally not so sharply as in North America. The crime drop is a phenomenon that, though having some similarities in all or nearly all wealthy developed countries, is still characterized by local peculiarities. We do not believe that Europe is following the North American pattern, at least not yet.

V. Learning More

The picture described in these pages indicates clearly the need for further research. First, we need to improve the quality of data for rape, above all in Europe, and for homicide everywhere. There is a need for a European victimization survey or at least for harmonization and standardization of national surveys in Europe as a first step to improve comparative studies on violence against women and rape in particular. Without improvements to the quality and richness of data in and outside Europe, cross-national comparisons will remain tentative.

Second, understanding of homicide could improve if more countries included in their statistical routines more information on the circumstances of the event, relationships between victims and perpetrators, and perpetrators' motives. In doing so, they should take account of the proposals for improved understanding of femicide (ACUNS 2013). Without better data, analyses such as ours can continue only at the level of speculation.

Third, another path to improving research in this field is to compare rape with other violent crimes, above all assault: a task that is still very difficult to do in Europe. More generally, future research must situate studies of violence against women within a broader context of national crime trends.

Fourth, future research in this area must engage in systematic analyses of legal changes and the broad contexts in which they occur. Understanding of the roles of law reforms and other initiatives aimed at raising public concern about rape and gender violence needs to be improved: trying to understand what kinds of law reforms can improve reporting; which other kinds of changes or arrangements must precede, accompany, or follow a law reform; and whether and how the reforms and these other factors are related and interdependent. Increases in women's self-awareness, changing sensibilities toward gender violence, law reforms, and national and international campaigns against gender violence may explain both increases in reporting by women and, in the long term, decreases in the occurrence of crime. Understanding social, political, and legal changes concerning rape will not explain changes in levels of violence directly but will help efforts to conceptualize broader explanations of the contexts in which crime trends unfold.

Fifth, we need to know much more about backlash effects. After pioneering work in North America, little additional work has been done. We need much more fully to understand what redefinitions of gender equality—and gender conflict—mean in different contexts, how cultural changes follow social and economic emancipation of women, and whether and how values of masculinity are changing. The process of improvement of gender equality in most countries is not always linear and progressive: there are steps and stops, backs and forths, that national case studies can shed light on.

Finally, it is clear that including gender violence in analysis of crime trends broadens understanding of overall crime trends and opens up new perspectives that can reinvigorate comparative work. General trends show local peculiarities that require different explanations. Violence against women forces us to overcome an "increase/decrease logic" (Mucchielli 2010) and to look for different explanations or at least for an integration of existing theories about changes in crime trends.

More generally, future research should be based on an integration of the gender perspective with more general explanations of crime trends. Traditional feminist perspectives should improve capacities to communicate with overall studies of violence. Conventional or less conventional theories of crime applied to crime trends should take into fuller consideration the importance of the different components, the heterogeneity of violent behaviors, and of explanations that include a gender perspective.

APPENDIX

Methodological Note

A. Estimation of Some Rape Data

Estimates for some years before 1990 were required because of incomplete data for some years for some countries in the historical UNODC data series. Estimates are based on the *tasso di incremento relativo* (rate of relative increase). The formula for the calculation is

$$^a r = tP - {_0}P/{_0}P \times t,$$

where $^a r$ is the rate of relevant increase, ${_0}P$ and tP are the statistical units (in this case, rape), respectively, at the beginning and the end of a predetermined lapse of time; t is the length of the lapse, defined by the number of years. As an example, for Austria, the historical series was interrupted in 1986 (547 rapes reported to the police) and resumed in 1993, with 533 rapes reported to the police. There was thus a slight decrease; intermediate numbers are assumed in table A1.

Applying the mathematical formula above, we have

$$^a r = tP - {_0}P/{_0}P \times t$$

$$= (533 - 547)/(547 \times 5)$$

$$= -0.0051.$$

On average, the annual decrease was less than 1 percent per year. Applying the coefficient found above (-0.0051) to the (real) number in 1986, we have the number of units we must deduct to obtain the estimated value for the year 1987. This formula in this case is

$$\text{estimate}^{1987} = {^a r} \times 1986.$$

Thus, $-0.0051 \times 547 = -3$. To calculate the value for 1987, we subtracted three cases from the 1986 total. Thus, $547 - 3 = 544$.

The estimated number of rapes for 1987 is 544. To estimate the number of rapes for 1988, we applied the same coefficient to the number for 1987 (which we just calculated) and so on for all the years. The base changes constantly while the coefficient remains constant. In this way we obtained the values of table A1.

This kind of estimation assumes that the phenomenon being estimated is following a linear and constant trend within the period of missing data (as is the case for linear interpolation). Like all estimation, this method can be

TABLE A1

Rapes Reported to the Police

Austria	1986	1987	1988	1989	1990
In UNODC	547				533
Estimate	547	544	541	538	533

TABLE A2
Countries and Years

Country	Years
1. Austria	1987–89; 1995–2000
2. Norway	2001–2
3. Greece	1981–89
4. France	1987–89
5. Norway	2001–2
6. Portugal	1991–92
7. Spain	1981–82; 1996

challenged. We used this method in order to connect the gaps in data to the two closest years for which we have data and inside which the lapses are included. This method ties the estimated data not to the whole historical series but to two reference times that are close to the missing data. The countries and years for which data are estimated in this way are shown in table A2.

For some countries, however, we did not have a starting data point for the historical series ($tP = 1975$) and could not use the method described. In these cases, we forced the application of the coefficient. If, for instance, in a country we lacked data from 1975 to 1980, we analyzed the trend in the years immediately following the gap, stopping when the trend changed direction. We calculated the rate of relative increase according to the formula previously explained. Once we obtained the coefficient, we applied it retrospectively starting from a base (e.g., 1981) in order to obtain values for the period 1975–80.

An example is Denmark. Data from 1975–78 were missing. From 1979 to 1981, the trend was increasing with a sudden interruption and a fall. We then calculated the rate of relative increase for the period 1979–81 and we applied it retrospectively using 1979, for which we had the data, as the base year.

TABLE A3
Countries and Years

Country	Years
2. Bulgaria	1975–79
3. Denmark	1975–78
4. Hungary	1975–79
5. Netherlands	1975–79
6. Portugal	1975–76
7. Romania	1975–85
8. Spain	1975–79
9. Switzerland	1975–80

We tied the estimate to a specific year in the historical series close to the available data. This reasoning assumes that social phenomena, including crime, follow a linear trend over time (decline or increase) that breaks at a certain point, with a peak or a drop. In the case of Denmark we hypothesized that the peak of 1981 was preceded by a constant increasing trend. The countries and years for which data are estimated in this way are shown in table A3.

B. Definitions of Rape in European Countries

The standard definition of rape used in the *European Sourcebook of Crime and Criminal Justice Statistics* (Aebi et al. 2010) is quoted in the text. Among the 19 countries considered, there are some differences in behaviors included or excluded. Penetration other than vaginal is excluded in police statistics in Switzerland. Violent intramarital sexual intercourse is excluded in Greece until 2005–6 (criminalized in 2006). Sexual intercourse with a helpless person in included in all countries considered except Austria, Greece, Netherlands, Switzerland, and the United Kingdom (England and Wales, Northern Ireland, and Scotland). Sexual intercourse with a minor with force is excluded in Greece and Switzerland. Sexual intercourse with a minor without force is included in Belgium, France, and Sweden. Attempts are excluded in Portugal. Other forms of sexual assault are included in Italy, Poland, and Switzerland.

REFERENCES

ACUNS (Academic Council on the United Nations System). 2013. *Femicide: A Global Issue That Demands Action.* Vienna: United Nations.

Aebi, Marcelo F. 2008. "Measuring the Influence of Statistical Counting Rules on Cross-National Differences in Recorded Crime." In *Crime and Criminal Justice Systems in Europe and North America, 1995–2004,* edited by Kauko Aromaa and Markku Heiskanen. Helsinki: European Institute for Crime Prevention and Control and United Nations.

———. 2010. "Methodological Issues in the Comparison of Police-Recorded Crime Rates." In *International Handbook of Criminology,* edited by Shlomo Giora Shoham, Paul Knepper, and Martin Kett. London: CRC Press.

Aebi, Marcelo F., and Antonia Linde. 2010. "Is There a Crime Drop in Western Europe?" *European Journal of Criminal Policy and Research* 16:251–77.

———. 2012. "Crime Trends in Western Europe According to Official Statistics from 1990 to 2007." In *Closing Doors: New Perspectives on the International Crime Fall,* edited by Jan van Dijk, Andromachi Tseloni, and Graham Farrell. New York: Palgrave Macmillan.

Aebi, Marcelo F., et al., eds. 2010. *European Sourcebook of Crime and Criminal Justice Statistics—2010.* 4th ed. The Hague: Boom Juridische uitgevers.

Alvazzi del Frate, Anna. 2010. "Crime and Criminal Justice Statistics Challenges." In *International Statistics on Crime and Criminal Justice*, edited by Stefan Harrendorf, Markku Heiskanen, and Steven Malby. Helsinki: European Institute for Crime Prevention and Control and UN Office on Drugs and Crime.

———. 2011. "When the Victim Is a Woman." In *Geneva Declaration Secretariat*, pp. 113–44. http://www.genevadeclaration.org/fileadmin/docs/GBAV2/GBAV2011_CH4.pdf

Alvazzi del Frate, Anna, and Angela Patrignani. 1995. *Women's Victimization in Developing Countries*. Issues and Reports, no. 5. Turin: UN Interregional Crime and Justice Research Institute.

Arcidiacono, Eugenio. 2010. "La violenza di genere in Emilia-Romagna." In *Violenza di genere e sicurezza delle donne in Emilia-Romagna*, edited by Rossella Selmini and Eugenio Arcidiacono. *Quaderni di Città Sicure* 35:33–75.

———. 2013. "La violenza contro le donne." In *Quaderni di statistica: Le donne in Emilia-Romagna*. Bologna: Servizio Statistica, Regione Emilia-Romagna.

Aromaa, Kauko, and Markku Heiskanen, eds. 2008. *Victimization Surveys in a Comparative Perspective*. Stockholm Criminological Symposium 2007. Helsinki: UN European Institute for Crime Prevention and Control.

Austin, Roy L., and Kim S. Young. 2000. "A Cross-National Examination of the Relationship between Gender Equality and Official Rape Rates." *International Journal of Offender Therapy and Comparative Criminology* 44:204–21.

Bailey, William C. 1984. "Poverty, Inequality, and City Homicide Rates." *Criminology* 22(4):531–50.

———. 1999. "The Socioeconomic Status of Women and Patterns of Forcible Rape for Major U.S. Cities." *Sociological Focus* 32(1):43–61.

Bailey, William C., and Rosemary Peterson. 1995. "Gender Inequality and Violence against Women: The Case of Murder." In *Crime and Inequality*, edited by John Hagan and Ruth Peterson. Stanford, CA: Stanford University Press.

Barbieri, Viola. 2010. "La violenza di genere nella ricerca internazionale." In *Violenza di genere e sicurezza delle donne in Emilia-Romagna*, edited by Rossella Selmini and Eugenio Arcidiacono. *Quaderni di Città Sicure* 35:21–30.

Baumer, Eric P., Richard B. Felson, and Steven F. Messner. 2003. "Changes in Police Notification for Rape, 1973–2000." *Criminology* 41(3):841–70.

Baumer, Eric P., and Janet L. Lauritsen. 2010. "Reporting Crime to the Police, 1973–2005: A Multivariate Analysis of Long-Term Trends in the National Crime Survey (NCS) and National Crime Victimization Survey (NCVS)." *Criminology* 48:131–85.

Baumer, Eric, and Kevin T. Wolff. 2014. "The Breadth and Causes of Contemporary Trends in Cross-National Homicide Rates." In *Why Crime Rates Fall and Why They Don't*, edited by Michael Tonry. Vol. 43 of *Crime and Justice: A Review of Research*, edited by Michael Tonry. Chicago: University of Chicago Press.

Black, Michele C., Kathleen C. Basile, Matthew J. Breiding, Sharon G. Smith, Mikel L. Walters, Melissa T. Merrick, Jiem Chen, and Mark R. Stevens. 2011. *The National Intimate Partner and Sexual Violence Survey (NISVS): 2010*

Summary Report. Atlanta: National Center for Injury Prevention and Control, Centers for Disease Control and Prevention.

Blau, Judith, and Peter Blau. 1982. "The Cost of Inequality: Metropolitan Structure and Violent Crime." *American Sociological Review* 47:114–29.

Boyce, Jillian, and Adam Cotter. 2013. "Homicide in Canada, 2012." 85-002-x. *Juristat* 2013. Ottawa: Statistics Canada.

Brawne, A., and K. Williams. 1993. "Gender Intimacy and Lethal Violence: Trends from 1967 through 1987." *Gender and Society* 7:78–98.

Brownmiller, Susan. 1975. *Against Our Will: Men, Women and Rape*. New York: Penguin.

Catalano, Shannan. 2006. *Criminal Victimization, 2005*. Washington, DC: US Department of Justice, Bureau of Justice Statistics.

Dobash, R. Emerson, and Russell P. Dobash. 1979. *Violence against Wives: A Case against the Patriarchy*. New York: Free Press.

Dugan, Laura, Daniel Nagin, and Richard Rosenfeld. 1999. "Explaining the Decline in Intimate Partner Homicide: The Effects of Changing Domesticity, Women's Status, and Domestic Violence Resources." *Homicide Studies* 3: 187–214.

———. 2003. "Exposure Reduction or Retaliation? Effects of Domestic Violence Resources on Intimate Partner Homicide." *Law and Society Review* 37: 169–98.

Eileraas, Karina. 2012. "Rape, Legal Definition of." In *Encyclopedia of Women in Today's World*, edited by Mary Zeiss Stange, Carol K. Oyster, and Jane E. Sloan. Thousand Oaks, CA: Sage.

Eisner, Manuel. 2003. "Long-Term Historical Trends in Violent Crime." In *Crime and Justice: A Review of Research*, vol. 30, edited by Michael Tonry. Chicago: University of Chicago Press.

———. 2008. "Modernity Strikes Back? A Historical Perspective on the Latest Increase of Interpersonal Violence (1960–1990)." *International Journal of Conflict and Violence* 2:288–316.

———. 2014. "From Swords to Words: Does Macro-Level Change in Self-Control Predict Long-Term Variation in Levels of Homicide?" In *Why Crime Rates Fall and Why They Don't*, edited by Michael Tonry. Vol. 43 of *Crime and Justice: A Review of Research*, edited by Michael Tonry. Chicago: University of Chicago Press.

Ellis, Lee, and Charles Beattie. 1983. "The Feminist Explanation for Rape: An Empirical Test." *Journal of Sex Research* 19:74–93.

Färdeman, Emelie, Thomas Hvitfeldt, and Åsa Irlander. 2014. *The Swedish Crime Survey, 2013: Concerning Exposure to Crime, Insecurity and Confidence*. English Summary of Bra Report 2014:1. Stockholm: Swedish National Institute on Crime Prevention.

Felson, Richard B., and Paul-Philippe Paré. 2005. "The Reporting of Domestic Violence and Sexual Assault by Non-strangers to the Police." *Journal of Marriage and Family* 67:597–610.

Finney Andrea. 2006. *Domestic Violence, Sexual Assaults, and Stalking: Findings from the 2004/05 British Crime Survey*. London: Home Office

FRA (European Union for Fundamental Rights). 2014. *Violence against Women: An EU-Wide Survey. Main Results.* Luxembourg: Publication Office of the European Union.

Frank, David John, Bayliss J. Camp, and Steven A. Boutcher. 2010. "Worldwide Trends in the Criminal Regulation of Sex, 1945 to 2005." *American Sociological Review* 75(6):867–93.

Frank, David John, Tara Hardinge, and Kassia Wosick-Correa. 2009. "The Global Dimensions of Rape-Law Reform: A Cross-National Study of Policy Outcomes." *American Sociological Review* 74(2):272–90.

Ganpat, Soenita, et al. 2011. *Homicide in Finland, the Netherlands, and Sweden: A First Study on the European Homicide Monitor Data.* Stockholm: Edita Norstedts Vasteras.

Gartner, Rosemary, Kathryn Baker, and Fred C. Pampel. 1990. "Gender Stratification and the Gender Gap in Homicide Victimization." *Social Problems* 37(4):593–612.

Gartner, Rosemary, Myrna Dawson, and Maria Crawford. n.d. "Women Killing: Intimate Femicide in Ontario, 1974–1994." Unpublished research report. Toronto: University of Toronto, Institute of Criminology.

Gruszczynska, Beata Z., and Markku Heiskanen. 2012. "Trends in Police-Recorded Offenses." *European Journal of Criminal Policy and Research* 18:83–102.

Hagemann-White, Carol. 2001. "European Research on the Prevalence of Violence against Women." *Violence against Women* 7(7):732–59.

Hanmer, Julia, and Mary Maynard. 1987. "Introduction: Violence and Gender Stratification." In *Women, Violence and Social Control*, edited by Julia Hanmer and Mary Maynard. London: Macmillan.

Harrendorf, Stefan. 2012. "Offence Definitions in the *European Sourcebook of Crime and Criminal Justice Statistics* and Their Influence on Data Quality and Comparability." *European Journal of Criminal Policy and Research* 18:23–53.

Harrendorf, Stefan, Markku Heiskanen, and Steven Malby, eds. 2010. *International Statistics on Crime and Criminal Justice.* Helsinki: European Institute for Crime Prevention and Control and UN Office on Drugs and Crime.

Heimer, Karen, and Janet L. Lauritsen. 2008. "Gender and Violence in the United States: Trends in Offending and Victimization." In *Understanding Crime Trends: Workshop Report.* Washington, DC: National Academies Press.

Istituto Nazionale di Statistica. 2006. *La violenza contro le donne.* Rome: Istituto Nazionale di Statistica.

Jakobsen, Hilde. 2014. "What's Gendered about Gender-Based Violence? An Empirically Grounded Theoretical Exploration from Tanzania." *Gender and Society* 28(4):537–56.

Jaspard, Maryse. 2001. "Violence against Women: The First French National Survey." *Population et Société* 364:1–5.

Johnson, Holly, Natalia Ollus, and Sami Nevala. 2008. *Violence against Women: An International Perspective.* New York: Springer.

Kangaspunta, K., and Ineke Haen Marshall. 2012. "Trends in Violence against Women: Some Good News and Some Bad News." In *The International Crime*

Drop: New Directions in Research, edited by Jan van Dijk, Andromachi Tseloni, and Graham Farrell. Basingstoke, UK: Palgrave Macmillan.

Kervinen, E., and Markku Heiskanen. 2013. *Study on International Activities in the Field of Data Collection on Gender-Based Violence across the UE*. Vilnius, Lith.: European Institute for Gender Equality.

Kivivuori, Janne, Jukka Savolainen, and Petri Danielsson. 2012. "Theory and Explanation in Contemporary European Homicide Research." In *Handbook of European Homicide Research: Patterns, Explanations and Country Studies*, edited by M. C. A. Liem and W. A. Pridemore. New York: Springer.

Kong, R., H. Johnson, S. Beattie, and A. Cardillo. 2003. "Sexual Offences in Canada." *Juristat* 23(6). Ottawa: Statistics Canada.

Krajewski, Krzysztof. 2011. "Crime and Punishment in Central and Eastern Europe during the Last 20 Years: Is the Region Different from the Rest of Europe?" Plenary lecture presented at the 11th annual conference of the European Society of Criminology, Vilnius, Lith., September 21–24.

Kruttschnitt, Candace, Brenda L. McLaughlin, and Carol Petrie, eds. 2004. *Advancing the Federal Research Agenda on Violence against Women*. Washington, DC: National Academies Press.

LaFree, Gary, and Gwen Hunnicutt. 2006. "Female and Male Homicide Victimization Trends: A Cross-National Context." In *Gender and Crime: Patterns in Victimization and Offending*, edited by Karen Heimer and Candace Kruttschnitt. New York: New York University Press.

Lappi-Seppälä, Tapio, and Martti Lehti. 2014. "Cross-Comparative Perspectives on Global Homicide Trends." In *Why Crime Rates Fall and Why They Don't*, edited by Michael Tonry. Vol. 43 of *Crime and Justice: A Review of Research*, edited by Michael Tonry. Chicago: University of Chicago Press.

Lauritsen, Janet L., and Karen Heimer. 2008. "The Gender Gap in Violent Victimization, 1973–2004." *Journal of Quantitative Criminology* 24:125–47.

Lauritsen, Janet L., Jennifer Gatewood Owens, Michael Planty, Michael R. Rand, and Jennifer L. Truman. 2012. "Methods for Counting High-Frequency Repeat Victimizations in the National Crime Victimization Survey." Washington, DC: US Department of Justice, Bureau of Justice Statistics.

Lehti, Martti. 2013. *NRILP Comparative Homicide Time Series (NRILP-CHTS)*. Research Brief 32:2013. Helsinki: National Research Institute for Legal Policy.

Ministry of Justice, Home Office, and Office for National Statistics. 2013. *An Overview of Sexual Offending in England and Wales*. Statistical Bulletin. London: Home Office.

Mucchielli, Laurent. 2010. "Are We Living in a More Violent Society? A Socio-historical Analysis of Interpersonal Violence in France, 1970–Present." *British Journal of Criminology* 50(5):808–29.

National Research Council. 2014. *Estimating the Incidence of Rape and Sexual Assault*. Washington, DC: National Academies Press.

Ouimet, Marc. 2002. "Explaining the American and Canadian Crime 'Drop' in the 1990's." *Canadian Journal of Criminology* 44:33–50.

Perrault, Samuel. 2013. *Police-Reported Crime Statistics in Canada, 2012*. Ottawa: Statistics Canada.

Perrault, Samuel, and Shannon Brennan. 2010. *Criminal Victimization in Canada, 2009*. Ottawa: Statistics Canada.

Pierotti, Rachael S. 2013. "Increasing Rejection of Intimate Partner Violence: Evidence of Global Cultural Diffusion." *American Sociological Review* 78:240–65.

Pridemore, William A., and Joshua D. Freilich. 2005. "Gender Equity, Traditional Masculine Culture, and Female Homicide Victimization." *Journal of Criminal Justice* 33:213–23.

Psytel. 2010. *Estimation de la mortalité liée aux violences conjugales en Europe*. IPV EU—Mortality. Rapport scientifique, Project no. JLS/2007/DAP-1/140. Paris: Psytel. http://www.psytel.eu/ehis/app/B.php.

Radford, Jill, and Diana E. H. Russell. 1992. *Femicide: The Politics of Woman Killing*. Boston: Twayne.

Rosenfeld, Richard. 1997. "Changing Relationships between Men and Women: A Note on the Decline in Intimate Partner Homicide." *Homicide Studies* 1: 72–83.

———. 2000. "Patterns in Adult Homicide: 1980–1995." In *The Crime Drop in America*, edited by Alfred Blumstein and Joel Wallman. New York: Cambridge University Press.

Russell, Diane E. 1975. *The Politics of Rape*. New York: Stein & Day.

Sable, Marjorie R., Fran Danis, Denise D. Mauzy, and Sarah K. Gallagher. 2006. "Barriers to Reporting Sexual Assault for Women and Men: Perspectives of College Students." *Journal of American College Health* 55(3):157–62.

Selmini, Rossella, and Eugenio Arcidiacono. 2009. "La criminalità in Emilia-Romagna." *Quaderni di Città Sicure* 34:17–108.

Sinha, Maire. 2013. *Family Violence in Canada: A Statistical Profile, 2011*. Ottawa: Statistics Canada.

Skilbrei, May-Len, and Charlotta Holmström. 2011. "Is There a Nordic Prostitution Regime?" In *Crime and Justice in Scandinavia*, edited by Michael Tonry and Tapio Lappi-Seppälä. Vol. 40 of *Crime and Justice: A Review of Research*, edited by Michael Tonry. Chicago: University of Chicago Press.

Smith, Kevin, ed. 2011. *Homicides, Firearms Offences and Intimate Violence, 2009/10*. Suppl. vol. to *Crime in England and Wales, 2009/2010*. London: Home Office.

Stamatel, Janet P. 2014. "Explaining Variations in Female Homicide Rates across Europe." *European Journal of Criminology* 11(5):578–600.

Stanko, Elizabeth A. 1985. *Intimate Intrusions: Women's Experience of Male Violence*. London: Routledge & Kegan Paul.

Statistics Sweden. 2014. "Swedish Population (in One-Year Groups) 1860–2013." http://www.scb.se/en_/Finding-statistics/Statistics-by-subject-area/Population/Population-composition/Population-statistics/Aktuell-Pong/25795/.

Steffensmeier, Darrell, Jennifer Schwartz, Hua Zhong, and Jeff Ackerman. 2005*a*. "An Assessment of Recent Trends in Girls' Violence Using Diverse

Longitudinal Sources: Is the Gender Gap Closing?" *Criminology* 43(2):355–405.

———. 2005*b*. "Gender Gap Trends for Violent Crimes, 1980–2003." *Feminist Criminology* 1:72–98.

Swedish National Council for Crime Prevention. 2014*a*. *Reported Offences, 1950–2013*. Stockholm: Swedish National Council for Crime Prevention.

———. 2014*b*. *The Swedish Crimes Survey, 2013*. English summary. Stockholm: Swedish National Council for Crime Prevention.

Terragni, Laura. 2002. "La violenza sessuale." In *La criminalità in Italia*, edited by Marzio Barbagli and Uberto Gatti. Bologna: Il Mulino.

Tham, Henrik, Anita Rönneling, and Lise-Lotte Rytterbro. 2011. "The Emergence of the Crime Victim: Sweden in a Scandinavian Context." In *Crime and Justice in Scandinavia*, edited by Michael Tonry and Tapio Lappi-Seppälä. Vol. 40 of *Crime and Justice: A Review of Research*, edited by Michael Tonry. Chicago: University of Chicago Press.

Tonry, Michael. 2014. "Why Crime Rates Are Falling throughout the Western World." In *Why Crime Rates Fall and Why They Don't*, edited by Michael Tonry. Vol. 43 of *Crime and Justice: A Review of Research*, edited by Michael Tonry. Chicago: University of Chicago Press.

Truman, Jennifer, Lynn Langton, and Michael Planty. 2013. *Criminal Victimization, 2012*. Washington, DC: US Department of Justice, Bureau of Justice Statistics.

Uggen, Christopher, and Suzy McElrath. 2011. "Gender Equality and the Great Rape Decline." Paper presented at the American Society of Criminology annual meeting, Washington, DC, November 16.

Vaillancourt, Roxan. 2010. *Gender Differences in Police-Reported Violent Crime in Canada, 2008*. Ottawa: Statistics Canada, Canadian Centre for Justice Statistics.

van Dijk, Jan, and Andromachi Tseloni. 2012. "Global Overview: International Trends in Victimization and Recorded Crime." In *The International Crime Drop: New Directions in Research*, edited by Jan van Dijk, Andromachi Tseloni, and Graham Farrell. London: Palgrave Macmillan.

van Dijk, Jan, Andromachi Tseloni, and Graham Farrell. 2012. "Conclusions—Understanding International Crime Trends: A Summing Up." In *The International Crime Drop: New Directions in Research*, edited by Jan van Dijk, Andromachi Tseloni, and Graham Farrell. London: Palgrave Macmillan.

van Dijk, Jan, John van Kesteren, and Paul Smit. 2007. *Criminal Victimisation in International Perspective: Key Findings from the 2004–2005 ICVS and EU ICS*. The Hague: Netherlands Ministry of Justice.

Verkko, Veli. 1951. *Homicides and Suicides in Finland and Their Dependence on National Character*. Copenhagen: G.E.C. Gads Forlag.

Vieraitis, Lynne M., Sarah Britto, and Tomislav V. Kovandzic. 2007. "The Impact of Women's Status and Gender Inequality on Female Homicide Victimization Rates: Evidence from U.S. Counties." *Feminist Criminology* 2:1–17.

von Hofer, Hanns. 2000. "Crime Statistics as Constructs: The Case of Swedish Rape Statistics." *European Journal on Criminal Policy and Research* 8:77–89.

von Hofer, Hanns, Tapio Lappi-Seppälä, and Lars Westfelt. 2012 *Nordic Criminal Statistics, 1950–2010: Summary of a Report.* 8th rev. ed. Stockholm: Stockholm University, Department of Criminology.

Weiss, Karen G. 2010. "'Too Ashamed to Report: Deconstructing the Shame of Sexual Victimization." *Feminist Criminology* 5(3):286–310.

Whaley, Rachel Bridges. 2001. "The Paradoxical Relationship between Gender Inequality and Rape: Toward a Refined Theory." *Gender and Society* 15:531–55.

Whaley, Rachel Bridges, and Steven F. Messner. 2002. "Gender Equality and Gendered Homicides." *Homicide Studies* 6:188–210.

World Health Organization. 2013. *Global and Regional Estimates of Violence against Women: Prevalence and Health Effects of Intimate Partner Violence and Non-partner Sexual Violence.* Geneva: World Health Organization.

Xie, Min, Karen Heimer, and Janet L. Lauritsen. 2011. "Violence against Women in U.S. Metropolitan Areas: Changes in Women's Status and Risk, 1980–2004." *Criminology* 50(1):104–43.

Graham Farrell, Nick Tilley, and Andromachi Tseloni

Why the Crime Drop?

ABSTRACT

The "crime drop" is the most important criminological phenomenon of modern times. In North America, Europe, and Australasia, many common crimes have fallen by half or more since the early 1990s, albeit with variation in the specifics. Seventeen explanations are examined here including demographics, policing, imprisonment, drug markets, and lead poisoning. Pioneering research relevant only to the United States now appears, with the benefit of hindsight, somewhat parochial. Sixteen of the 17 hypotheses fail one or more of four evidence-based standardized tests on which they are assessed. The one that passes is the security hypothesis, underpinned by crime opportunity theories. Here there is strong evidence that vehicle theft fell because of more and better security, and mounting evidence that improved security was critical in reducing burglary and other acquisitive crime. Many crime types are interrelated, while most criminal careers are dominated by property crime, so removing these volume crimes might be expected to reduce violence.

I. Introduction

Truth is stranger than fiction. Twenty-five years ago, had anyone the audacity to suggest that crime would soon embark on a steep and prolonged decline in most advanced countries, he or she would have been laughed out of the room. It was unthinkable! Hence while it is popular

Electronically published October 1, 2014

Graham Farrell is a professor at Simon Fraser University, Nick Tilley is a professor at University College London, and Andromachi Tseloni is a professor in the Department of Social Sciences at Loughborough University. They thank Gloria Layock, Louise Grove, Becky Thompson, Jen Mailley, and Laura Garius for collaboration; Michael Planty and Jennifer Truman for National Crime Victimization Survey data; Martin Andresen, Ron Clarke, Jan van Dijk, Chris Kershaw, and Martin Killias for sage advice; and the Economic and Social Research Council for grants RES-000-22-2386 and ES/K003771/1.

to start essays such as this by pillorying those criminologists who predicted crime's incessant rise, it is rarely acknowledged that such views were almost universally held. This essay will not make predictions. It will, however, provide theory and evidence to help explain why crime has declined and conclude with policy recommendations for sustaining the crime decline and extending it to crimes that are currently increasing, such as Internet-related crime, smartphone theft, and other iCrime.[1]

Has crime really declined? Where, by how much, and with what variation? This is the topic of Section II that follows. There is emerging scientific consensus regarding the existence of an international crime drop, with remaining debate focusing on the specifics. The most reliable sources of information are victim surveys, particularly the national surveys of England and Wales, France, the Netherlands, and the United States, all of which find many types of common or street crimes, such as assault, burglary, and car crimes, to have declined dramatically since the 1990s. National sources are buttressed by the International Crime Victims Survey, the only methodologically standardized general victim survey, and it indicates the international nature of crime's decline. While supplementary sources including police-recorded crime data, health data, and insurance data are each individually less reliable, the extent of supporting evidence they provide is rather overwhelming: the likelihood that so many different sources in different places point in the same direction by chance is infinitesimally small. There is variation in when, by how much, and which crime types have fallen, but such variation around the mean is to be expected in the real world and adds to overall credibility. An overview of this evidence is given in the first section of this essay, but there is no real diversion from the general theme: crime has declined in many advanced countries, though sometimes with considerable variation in the timing and trajectory.

Why has crime declined? This is the subject of Section III of this essay. Seventeen hypotheses are examined. Much of the pioneering research focused on declining violence in the United States, exemplified by the landmark collection of studies edited by Blumstein and Wallman (2000). This seems to form a natural "phase 1" of research

---

[1] Roman and Chalfin (2007) use the term "iCrime" to refer to theft of attractive electronic goods such as phones, computer laptops and tablets, GPS satellite navigation systems, and the like.

that was highly innovative and informative but that has been rather superseded by the emergence of what is here characterized as phase 2 crime drop research: growing recognition of the international nature of the crime drop and the importance of declining property crime. Explanations proposing that crime fell because of particular characteristics of the United States now appear somewhat parochial. The clearest evidence for this comes from Canada, which has similar crime trends and strong socioeconomic and cultural links but significantly different policies in many of the areas where explanation has been sought. The suggestions that crime fell because of legalized abortion or a decline in lead poisoning of children appear unable to account for the fact that offending rates fell among other age groups, not just those born in the 1970s who reached peak offending ages in the early 1990s. The demographics hypothesis suggests that crime rates fell because of an aging population. This and many other hypotheses suggest that crime fell because of a decline or relative decline in either the number or motivation of offenders, and such hypotheses seem unable to explain why some crime types, such as phone theft and e-crimes, have increased when others have fallen.

Some criticisms apply to more than one hypothesis, and these are identified and used as a series of "tests" to determine if any hypothesis passes each one. Of research to date it is concluded that only the security hypothesis passes each test. This hypothesis suggests that crime fell because of a reduction in crime opportunities caused by improved security, and this is the focus of Section IV of this essay. There is strong empirical support for the security hypothesis from independent research into the drop in car theft in four countries, which suggests that it was caused by improved vehicle security, particularly electronic immobilizers and central deadlocking systems. There is also mounting evidence that household burglary fell because of improved household security. It is suggested that while further research is needed, declines in several other crime types, including shoplifting and some types of robbery, may also have occurred because of improved security as business began to realize the cost of high crime rates. The link is made to criminal career research, which finds that most criminal careers are dominated by property crime and that property crimes are often the debut crimes that begin a criminal career. If security improvements have reduced the volume of property crimes, it is suggested that this may have caused the less prevalent violent crimes to decline also, because much violence would likely be linked with acquisitive crime in some way.

This essay concludes that the security hypothesis, nested in the theoretical framework of crime opportunity theory, rational choice, and routine activities, offers the most likely explanation for why crime has declined in many countries. On the basis of this conclusion, the main policy implication is that designing-out crime should be given far greater prominence: Government and police should seek to encourage both the public and private sectors to reduce the emission of crime opportunities. This is likely to require a mix of regulation and market-based incentives and policing to reemphasize crime prevention as its primary mission and to give a far greater emphasis to problem-solving approaches.

Here is a summary of the structure of this essay. Section II examines the extent and nature of the crime drop. Section III assesses 17 hypotheses that have been offered to explain the crime drop and finds 16 largely wanting. Section IV focuses on the the security hypothesis. It reviews strong evidence from independent research in multiple countries that greatly improved security-caused property crime and acquisitive crime to fall and that, since they are so prominent, it is possible that they triggered the fall in violence by various routes. Section V offers conclusions and recommendations.

The term "crime drop" is used in this essay in the same sense that it is used in much of the literature. It is a portmanteau term that identifies broad similarities in downward crime trends since the early 1990s while acknowledging significant variation in their timing, extent, and nature. Global or international crime trends remain rather elusive because of data limitations. Reasonable generalizations can nonetheless be made. Just as local crime patterns vary within countries' broad general national trends, so too can individual countries' patterns be expected to vary within broad international trends.

II. Extent and Nature of the Crime Drop

This section gives an overview of key trends and data sources. The importance of this section is that the evidence it provides underpins the assessment of the various explanations for the crime drop that have been offered that are the subject of Section III that follows.

This section shows that there is extensive evidence from multiple

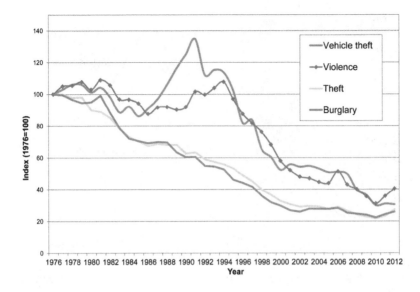

Fig. 1.—National Crime Victimization Survey crime rates 1976–2012 indexed to 100 in 1976. Source: Bureau of Justice Statistics.

independent sources and methodologies that indicates that crime has fallen substantially in many countries in recent years. It thereby demonstrates that the crime drop is not an artifact of statistics or method.

A. The United States

Figures 1 and 2 show trends based on the National Crime Victimization Survey (NCVS) and Uniform Crime Reports (UCR), respectively. Homicide, sexual violence, robberies, and assault rates declined rapidly from the early 1990s. While there has been some flattening of the trend from around the turn of the century, the crime drop has continued for two decades. By 2011, violence in the United States had fallen 70 percent since 1993 according to the NCVS (Truman and Planty 2012). Household burglary and larceny theft also fell over this period but had been in decline longer. Between 1973 and 1995, burglary fell by half and theft by 43 percent (Rand, Lynch, and Cantor 1997), trends that continued: burglary fell 56 percent between 1994 and 2011 (Hardison Walters et al. 2013). Figure 2 suggests a strong

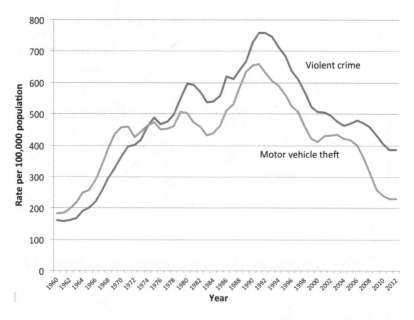

FIG. 2.—UCR violent crime (including homicide) and motor vehicle theft rates per 100,000 population, United States, 1960–2012. Source: Uniform Crime Reports.

relationship between car theft rates and rates of violence with a 2-year lag.[2]

B. Canada

There is a remarkable similarity between the UCR of Canada and those of the United States. These are held to be the best comparative source for present purposes. The reason is that while Canada conducts a national victimization survey every 5 years, its findings relating to crime trends have been significantly questioned and contradict the findings of all other sources that crime has been declining in a fashion similar to the United States. The Canadian national crime survey is conducted as part of a more general social survey by one part of Statistics Canada while its findings seem to have been openly contradicted by the Canadian Centre for Justice Statistics that is also part of Statistics Canada (see Farrell and Brantingham [2013] for further details;

---

[2] The Pearson correlation coefficient between auto theft and violent crime rates from 1960 to 2012 for the UCR is a remarkable .89 (and with a 2-year lag on auto theft it rises to .92) and .88 for the NCVS covering 1976–2005 as shown in fig. 2.

see also Greenspan and Doob 2011), and so Canada's UCR data are preferred here.

Figure 3 shows a panel of comparative crime trends for the United States and Canada for roughly similar crime types. Each chart is indexed to 100 in 1962 to facilitate comparison of the trends. This shows that trends in the homicide rates are very similar over time even though the per capita homicide rate in the United States is significantly higher.

A visual inspection of figure 3 suggests, and as others including Ouimet (2002), Zimring (2006), and Mishra and Lalumiere (2009) have concluded, that there is a strong relationship between crime trends in Canada and the United States. Burglary in the United States appears to fall earlier than in Canada. Car theft in Canada falls rather later than in the United States, and this seems likely to reflect differences in the timing of the introduction of improved vehicle security, an issue discussed at length later in this essay. Yet it is despite these differences that the strong similarities in crime trends in the two countries are apparent.[3]

C. England and Wales

The United Kingdom has data of good quality. The Crime Survey for England and Wales (CSEW; formerly the British Crime Survey) has been conducted since 1982. It identifies a crime drop with timing similar to that of the United States. Again following around three decades of increasing crime in the post–World War II period, the household crime rate peaked in 1993 and the personal crime rate in 1995 (fig. 4).[4] By 2012, relative to those peaks, all household crime had fallen 64 percent and all violent crime by 56 percent.[5] Figure 4, panel *B*, shows the rates indexed to 100 at the first survey sweep of 1981 to allow a clearer comparison of change. It demonstrates the similarity in

[3] Owing to a definitional difference, the comparison of rates of rape in the United States to sexual assault in Canada is not included here, but the chart was broadly similar in nature to the others with a correlation coefficient of .81.

[4] The CSEW category of "all household crime" covers vandalism, burglary, vehicle-related theft, and bicycle theft, and "all personal crime" covers theft from the person, other theft of personal property, assault (wounding, assaults with and without injury), and robbery. Unfortunately, the CSEW does not cover 1994, so the year in which crime peaked in England and Wales remains undetermined.

[5] From 2001 the CSEW coverage changes from a calendar year to be more akin to a financial year. For simplicity this essay refers to the main year, so that, e.g., when the CSEW refers to 2012/13, here we refer to 2012. This is less cumbersome for readers, and the same practice is used in chart labels.

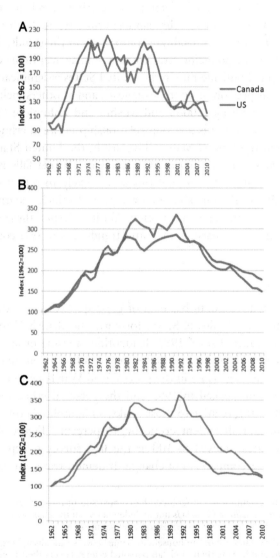

FIG. 3.—Uniform Crime Report data for Canada and the United States, 1962–2010, indexed to 100 in 1962. Source: Statistics Canada; Bureau of Justice Statistics. *A*, Homicide; *B*, theft; *C*, burglary.

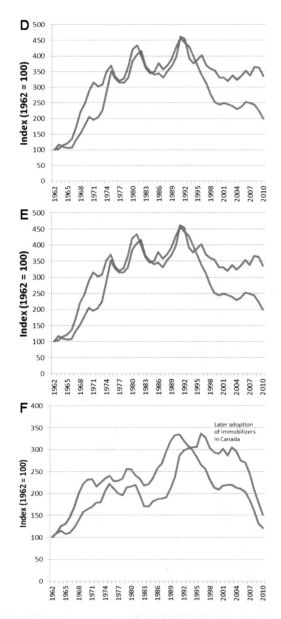

FIG. 3 (*continued*).—Uniform Crime Report data for Canada and the United States, 1962–2010, indexed to 100 in 1962. Source: Statistics Canada; Bureau of Justice Statistics. *D*, Robbery; *E*, assault; *F*, vehicle theft.

429

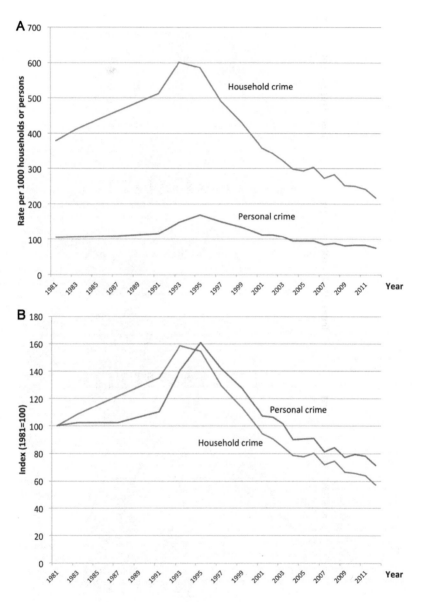

Fig. 4.—Household crime and personal crime, England and Wales, 1981–2012. *A*, Rates per 1,000 households or persons. *B*, Rates indexed to 100 in 1981. Source: Crime Survey for England and Wales.

the "crime drop" with the fall in household crimes including motor vehicle crime slightly preceding that of personal crime. The homicide rate is an anomaly in England and Wales. Unlike most other crime types, it continued to rise through the 1990s to a peak in 2002, after which it fell by half over the subsequent decade (Office of National Statistics 2014).

D. Australia and New Zealand

Australia and New Zealand have conducted national victimization surveys infrequently, so that information is supplemented from other sources, particularly police-recorded crime, to derive trends. Mayhew (2012) provides the authoritative review of the range of data sources and previous studies of crime trends in these countries. She concludes in relation to property crime that "the pattern of falling property crime in many industrialized countries in the last two decades or so is mirrored, then, in Australia and New Zealand. The timing of the 'turn' in property crime seemed to be around 2001 in Australia according to police figures. In New Zealand, it was about a decade before—more in line with other countries" (p. 98). In relation to violent crime, "in other countries, the picture for violent crime has been more mixed, although there is evidence of some stabilization in some countries. This seems to apply to Australia in the last decade and to New Zealand at least in the previous one" (p. 98).

Among prior studies, Morgan and Clare (2007) focused on household burglary in Western Australia while suggesting that trends were generally similar for other states. Following national burglary rate increases of 150 percent between 1973/74 and 1991/92, Western Australia experienced further increases of a quarter from 1993 to 1995 then fell by half between 1995 and 2005. This meant that the overall rate emerged a third lower in 2005, with Morgan and Clare suggesting that the decline was similar elsewhere in Australia.

From 2001, vehicle theft in Australia plummeted, falling around three-quarters over the next decade. Police-recorded crime data for car theft are generally held to be more reliable than most because incidents are reported for insurance purposes. Kriven and Ziersch's influential (2007) study examined the early years of this decline and links it strongly to improved vehicle security. In particular, and consistent with the work of Brown and Thomas (2003) and Brown (2004) in the United Kingdom, they find an aging of stolen vehicles, which would be expected when newer cars are more difficult to steal (see also Laycock [2004] and Webb [2005] in relation to the United Kingdom).

E. The International Crime Victimization Survey

The International Crime Victimization Survey (ICVS) is the only cross-national methodologically standardized general victim survey. It has smaller national sample sizes and hence larger standard errors than most national surveys. It has been conducted in 1988, 1992, 1996, 2000, 2004–5, and for six countries for 2010 (with the 2010 data supplemented by some complementary studies based on the ICVS method; see van Dijk 2013). This gives a spread covering more than two decades but for a maximum of six data points, making short-term variation less easy to specify. The ICVS reveals a crime drop that is broadly similar to what has been discussed so far but for a far wider set of countries. As an independent source, it further buttresses the evidence of widespread crime declines.

Aebi and Linde (2012) suggest that there is no "general" crime drop in Europe because of a variation between countries. Few would disagree that there is variation between countries or that there is variation within countries and across crime types. Whether or not that means it can be termed a general crime drop is a different issue. Their analysis uses police records of crime, police records of suspects, and court conviction statistics; while the multiple sources are useful, these data sources are not as appropriate for cross-national and over-time comparisons as the multiple survey sources examined by van Dijk and Tseloni (2012). Killias and Lanfranconi (2012) suggest, mainly with data from police and insurers, that Switzerland is the exception to the crime drop rule, though that conclusion is not borne out by the ICVS, which shows declines in most crime types in Switzerland (van Dijk et al. 2007). Overall, the preponderance of evidence seems to suggest that it is reasonable to refer to a general crime drop in Europe.

F. Evidence Relating to Violence against Women and Children

The nation-state has been the main unit of analysis so far, with particular crime types and groups discussed in that context. This subsection highlights key crime types or studies that tend to be excluded from such analysis or are often less comprehensively measured by some of the large-scale victim surveys.

With respect to violence against women, Kangaspunta and Haen

Marshall (2012) review data sources and measurement issues relating to trends in different countries. The methodological issues are myriad because of the hidden nature of violence against women. Despite those issues, they conclude that "[there are] some similarities in the violence against women trends: in all surveyed Western countries, partner violence is decreasing. Also, homicides against women are decreasing in nearly all countries, with the exception of Finland where the trend is stable" (p. 126). These positive findings were tempered by far more negative findings for violence against women in non-Western countries in particular. In a brief discussion of explanations, the authors suggest that declining violence against women in Western societies could be due to greater gender equality, improved resource availability, and changing relational lifestyles (p. 128). This hypothesis may warrant further close examination but is not discussed in detail elsewhere in this essay because there are not, to our knowledge, any existing attempts at empirical evaluation.

Finkelhor and Jones (2012) review evidence from different sources relating to trends in sexual abuse and physical abuse of children in the United States. The study was conducted because official sources, particularly the child protection system data, had been questioned, and so this review compared such sources to self-report surveys. Our summary of their findings, shown as table 1, gives very brief coverage of a lot of information and methodological issues that are covered in detail in the original studies and by Finkelhor and Jones (2004, 2006). The conclusion of Finkelhor and Jones is worth repeating at length:

> There is fairly consistent and convergent evidence from a variety of sources pointing to large declines in sexual abuse from 1992 to 2010. The idea that child protection system data is a misleading indicator on this trend is contradicted by the fact that the decline shows up in other sources that do not rely on CPS. The NIS [National Incident Study] study is particularly important because it uses consistent criteria across time, and confirms the child protection system trends. The self-report surveys are also very important because they represent victim testimony itself. It seems unlikely that, in the face of more public attention to sexual abuse and decreasing stigma, youth would be more reluctant to disclose in surveys. In fact one study shows greater reporting of sexual abuse to the authorities, but that the evidence relating to physical abuse is

TABLE 1
Abuse of Children, United States: Summary of Change in Crime Rates

Source	Definition	Period	Rate Change (%)
	A. Sexual Abuse		
National Child Abuse and Neglect Data System	Substantiated sexual abuse	1990–2010	−62
National Incident Study	Sexual abuse	1993–2005	−47
Federal Bureau of Investigation	Forcible rape	1990–2010	−35
National Crime Victimization Survey	Sexual assault against ages 12–17	1993–2008	−69
Minnesota School Survey	Sexual abuse	1992–2010	−29
National Survey of Family Growth	Statutory rape	1995–2008	−39
National Survey of Children Exposed to Violence	Sexual victimization	2003–8	−16
National Survey of Adolescents	Sexual assault—girls	1995–2005	−13 (NS)
	Sexual assault—boys	1995–2005	+9 (NS)
	B. Physical Abuse		
National Child Abuse and Neglect Data System	Substantiated physical abuse	1990–2009	−56
National Incidence Study	Physical abuse	1993–2005	−29

National Child Abuse and Neglect Data System	Child maltreatment fatalities ("majority are neglect and not physical abuse")	1993–2007	+46
Federal Bureau of Investigation	Homicide—children 0–17	1997–2007	−43
	Homicide—children 0–5	1997–2007	−26
Acute-care hospital admissions	Children < age 1	1997–2009	+10.9
	Children 1–18 admissions	1997–2009	−9.1
Admissions to 38-hospital sample	Children age < 6	2000–2009	+.79
	Children < age 1 (brain injury)	2000–2009	+3
National Survey of Children Exposed to Violence	Physical abuse by caregivers	2003–8	
National Survey of Adolescents	Physical abuse	1995–2005	−6 (NS)
Minnesota School Survey	Physical abuse	1992–2010	−20
National Crime Victimization Survey	Ages 12–17—simple assault	1992–2010	−59
	Ages 12–17—aggravated assault	1992–2010	−69

SOURCE.—Finklehor and Jones (2012).

NOTE.—NS indicates findings that were not statistically significant.

less clear and sometimes conflicting. (Finkelhor and Jones 2012, p. 3)

Finkelhor and Jones (2012, p. 3) conclude that the evidence of a decline in sexual abuse of children "is about as well established as crime trends can be in contemporary social science," which means that the evidence is compelling. Their review of trends in the physical abuse of children is slightly less conclusive, finding greater variation in the trends identified by different data sources (panel B of table 1). However, they conclude that the preponderance of evidence suggests that physical abuse of children has also declined, with the most methodologically rigorous evidence coming from the NIS: "The strongest evidence that overall physical abuse has declined is the evidence from the NIS. This study was specifically designed to monitor rates and it is unique in its use of exactly consistent criteria across time points" (p. 5).

G. Conclusion

This section painted a broad-brush picture of the nature of recent crime trends. It suggests that there is compelling evidence for the following conclusions:

- There has been a significant and prolonged "crime drop" in many industrialized nations.
- The extent and nature of the crime drop appear to be more similar between more similar countries (in Canada and the United States, e.g., there are marked similarities).
- The extent of the evidence means that the likelihood that crime drops in different countries are a coincidence is vanishingly small, which implies a causal link.
- These crime drops were generally preceded by several decades of rapidly rising crime.

While many common crimes have decreased, some, such as crimes facilitated by the Internet and theft of phones and similar electronic products, have increased. These conclusions are the basis for the assessment of explanations for the crime drop in Section III that follows.

III. Proposed Explanations

This section examines the competing explanations for the crime drop. The focus is those hypotheses that have been given some attention in the academic literature. The extent of supporting evidence varies by hypothesis, and some attempt is made to address this in what follows.

Each hypothesis is subjected to four evidence-based tests founded on the conclusions of the preceding section. It is proposed that each test must be passed for a hypothesis to be considered potentially viable. However, passing the four tests is considered a necessary but not a sufficient condition for a viable explanation of why crime has declined. The tests are straightforward, and variations on existing evaluation criteria. Part of their value lies in sidestepping many of the methodological dogfights in which some hypotheses appeared to be mired.

The assessment that follows finds that 16 of the 17 hypotheses fail one or more of the four tests. This is often in addition to other criticisms that have been leveled against them. The hypothesis that passes the tests is the security hypothesis. That hypothesis is covered only briefly in this section because it is the focus of Section IV of this essay. A summary of the results of applying the four tests to the hypotheses is given in table 3 below, but it is discussed at the end of this section.

A. The Identification of Crime Drop Hypotheses

The literature does not uniformly refer to a "crime drop" by that or a similar term and so, while it is hoped that the list of hypotheses in table 2 is comprehensive, others may exist. However, the four tests outlined here can be applied elsewhere.

Seventeen hypotheses are listed in table 2 with a brief description of each. Some potential hypotheses are not included here if they are largely speculative, that is, without supporting evidence, or if they lack a clear preventive mechanism or a reasonable chance of withstanding further scrutiny. For example, Farrell et al. (2010) speculated on what might be termed a "Jeffreys effect": the possibility that DNA fingerprinting, which began in the 1980s but spread most rapidly in advanced countries in the early 1990s and gained a lot of media attention, could have introduced a broad deterrent effect. Since there is not, to our knowledge, any further research on this issue, it is not included in table 2 even though, strictly speaking, it could still attract further research.

Some crime drop studies that provide useful insight are not included in table 2 if they do not offer a distinct causal hypothesis. This includes

TABLE 2

Crime Drop Hypotheses

Hypothesis	Summary
1. Strong economy	General economic improvement reduced crime
2. Concealed weapons laws	More concealed weapons increased deterrence
3. Capital punishment	Increased use of death penalty induced greater deterrence
4. Gun control laws	Gun control reduced crime due to gun control laws
5. Imprisonment	Increased imprisonment reduced crime via incapacitation and deterrence
6. Policing strategies	Better preventive policing reduced crime (i.e., Compstat and its progeny)
7. More police	Police staff increased, so crime fell
8. Legalization of abortion	Abortions in 1970s meant fewer at-risk adolescents in 1990s
9. Immigration	Immigrants commit less crime and promote social control in inner cities
10. Consumer confidence	Strong economy shifts consumers away from stolen secondhand goods
11. Declining hard-drug markets	Decline in hard-drug markets reduced related violence and property crime
12. Lead poisoning	Lead damaged children's brains in 1950s on, causing crime wave from 1960s when they reached adolescence; then cleaner air from 1970s caused crime drop of 1990s
13. Changing demographics	Aging population means proportionally fewer young offenders and victims, so crime rates fall
14. Civilizing process	Institutional control weakened in 1960s, causing crime increase, then strengthened in 1990s, causing crime drop
15. Improved security	Improved quality and quantity of security reduced crime opportunities
16. The Internet	Attractive displacement of offenders to e-crimes and changed lifestyles of victims
17. Phone guardianship	Portable phones spread rapidly in 1990s and provide guardianship

some empirical studies with important findings. Thus Mishra and Lalumiere's (2009) examination of how many types of declining risky behavior (such as accidents at work or in cars, sexual behavior including teen pregnancy and sexually transmitted diseases, and substance use including alcohol, tobacco, and marijuana) correlate with the decline in crime is insightful and informative but does not constitute a distinct

hypothesis. Similarly, studies showing that the crime decline is disproportionately concentrated in high-crime areas relative to others (Weisburd et al. 2004; Curman, Andresen, and Brantingham 2014; Ignatans
and Pease, forthcoming) and the fact that crime declines are disproportionately experienced for repeat victimization against the same targets (Thorpe 2007; Britton et al. 2012; Farrell and Pease 2014) are not
explanations per se. In each of these cases, however, it would be expected that a viable hypothesis should be consistent with these findings,
and while this is not included here as a separate requirement or "test,"
each warrants consideration in that respect. The ordering and termi-
nology of the table are based on that of Farrell (2013). For simplicity
in cross-referencing, the sections below use the numberings assigned
in table 2.

B. Four Tests for a Theory of the Crime Drop

The four tests are first outlined here. Clarification of the origins and
specifics of each test should emerge from what follows. The tests, with
brief justification for each that should become clearer as the tests are
applied to the hypotheses, are described briefly here.

1. *The Cross-National Test.*   Can the hypothesis be applied to different countries (e.g., to Canada for hypotheses developed for the United
States)?

The basis for this test is the earlier conclusions that a crime drop
has occurred in multiple countries and that this cannot be a coincidence. Marc Ouimet's comparative studies of crime in Canada and the
United States identified not only strong correlations between the crime
rates in these two counties but also key implications for crime drop
research. He observes that

> crime trends in Canada are very similar to those observed in the
> U.S. The quest for a general explanation should therefore focus on
> changes that have affected both countries. . . . If changes in the
> use of incarceration is to be invoked as an explanation, it would
> have to be shown why it worked in the U.S. but not in Canada. In
> terms of policing, contrary to the U.S., Canada has not increased
> the pro rata number of police officers . . . [and] there has been no
> move toward more aggressive policing as was observed in many
> U.S. cities. (Ouimet 2002, p. 46)

Zimring, shortly before publication of his book *The Great American Crime Decline*, declared his epiphany as follows:

> Closer inspection showed that the timing of the Canadian decline (1991–2000) fit perfectly with the timing of the declining in the United States. The extraordinary similarity of these trends in breadth, magnitude, and timing suggested that whatever was driving the decline in the United States was also operating in Canada. . . . But . . . Canada in the 1990s didn't increase its imprisonment, didn't hire more police per 100,000 population, and didn't have anything close to the economic boom we enjoyed south of the border. (2006, p. 619)

Others have made similar observations outside of North America. Van Dijk et al. (2007) and Rosenfeld and Messner (2009), for example, both observed that crime drops in Europe cannot be due to policy or legislation in the United States. Dills, Miron, and Summers (2008) similarly conclude that we "know little about the empirically relevant determinants of crime. This conclusion applies both to policy variables like arrest rates or capital punishment and to indirect factors such as abortion or gun laws. The reason is that even hypotheses that find some support in U.S. data for recent decades are inconsistent with data over longer horizons or across countries. Thus, these hypotheses are less persuasive than a focus on recent U.S. evidence might suggest" (p. 3).

Hindsight is 20/20, and the preference here is to celebrate the pioneering nature of crime drop research focused on the United States while noting the general dearth of research elsewhere until rather later (Ouimet being among the honorable exceptions). However, the key point is that the evidence suggests that a hypothesis should be applicable in different countries to warrant serious consideration, and any that does not, without appropriate justification, should be considered suspect. This is the basis for what is here termed the cross-national test.

2. *The Prior Crime Increase Test.* Is the hypothesis consistent, or at least not in contradiction, with the fact that crime was previously generally increasing for several decades?

The basis for this test is the earlier conclusion that, prior to the crime drop, crime in most advanced countries had been rising in previous decades: it is fair to say that there is scientific consensus on this issue. The extent and duration of crime increases varied, as with crime's more recent decline, and some evidence relating to some of the prior crime increase was touched on earlier in this essay. In short, any explanation for why crime has declined should not be in contradiction with the fact that crime was previously rapidly increasing. This may sound rather obvious and straightforward, but as the discussion of hypotheses below suggests, it is a test that is failed surprisingly often.

3. *The e-Crimes and Phone Theft Test.* Is the hypothesis consistent, or at least not in contradiction, with the fact that some crime types have been increasing while many have fallen?

The basis for this test is the fact that some types or subtypes of crime have increased during the "crime drop" when many crime types have decreased. The United Kingdom appears to have been ahead of the game in collating national crime survey data on phone theft since the 1990s and police data, at least for metropolitan London, since the early 2000s after the establishment of the National Mobile Phone Crime Unit. Mayhew and Harrington's (2001) landmark study shows how phone theft increased in the 1990s in Britain. Yet it is now increasingly recognized that phone theft and robbery, and theft of similar portable electronic products including laptops and tablet computers, have been increasing in many countries. It was observed that "in 2013, 3.1 million people [in the United States] reported their smartphones stolen, up from 1.6 in 2012. More people are misplacing their smartphones, too; last year, 1.4 million Americans lost their smartphones, up from 1.2 million in 2012" (Lowe 2014; reporting information from *Consumer Reports* [2014]) and "mobile device theft costs consumers $30,000,000,000 [$30 billion] each year according to the Federal Communications Commission" (Smartphone Theft Prevention Act of 2014 [HR 4065]). There is also strong evidence that e-crimes of various sorts relating to the Internet have increased in recent years. Clarke and Newman (2006), for example, examined e-commerce crime.

These increases in some crime subtypes run against the grain of the "crime drop." What is here termed the "e-crimes and phone theft test" is consequently straightforward. It proposes that any hypothesis should be consistent with this fact, or at least not contradict it. Again, this may sound obvious when viewed in isolation, but many of the crime drop hypotheses focus primarily on change in the number or motivation of potential offenders. If crime fell as a result of a change in demographics, abortion, or lead poisoning, which primarily reduced the number or motivation of offenders, then it might reasonably be expected that this would reduce all types of crime similarly. This is particularly true when it comes to phone thefts and robbery, which have increased. Theft and robbery have declined overall, but, because of phone thefts and robbery, perhaps less than other types of crime.

4. *The Variable Trajectories Test.* Is the hypothesis compatible, or at least not in contradiction, with variation in the timing, trajectory, and composition of crime falls both between countries and between crime types?

The basis for this test is the earlier evidence-based conclusion that there has been significant variation between and within countries in the nature of the crime drop. While the cross-national test implied an emphasis on the broad similarity in the fact that crime has declined significantly in different countries, the present test emphasizes differences within that picture. For instance, homicide in the United Kingdom did not begin its steep decline until considerably after the drop in most other crime types examined here. Likewise, in the United States, the NCVS identifies burglary and theft as having been in decline for around two decades before the major decline in auto theft and violence began. Similarly, there were significant differences in the timing of the crime drop in Australia and between the trends in property and violent crime in both Australia and New Zealand. Hence within the overall "crime drop," there are a range of significant differences. The variable trajectories test proposes that any explanation of the crime drop must be compatible with, or at least not in contradiction of, this evidence.

C. Review of Hypotheses

This subsection examines the 17 hypotheses in turn. Its sequence follows that of the listing of hypotheses in tables 2 and 3.

Hypotheses 1–4: Strong Economy, Concealed Weapons Laws, Capital Punishment, and Gun Control Laws. It has been suggested that crime fell because economies in the 1990s were growing rapidly, that laws allowing concealed weapons generated deterrence and guardianship, that the application of the death penalty deterred crime, and that stricter gun control laws meant that weapons were less freely available for use in crime.

Those four hypotheses are, on the basis of previous research, taken to be falsified. They were dismissed in two key reviews of crime drop research, being either formally discarded on the basis of the evidence offered in Levitt (2004) or implicitly dismissed by their absence from consideration in the review of Blumstein and Rosenfeld (2008).

For symmetry these hypotheses will be considered in relation to the other four tests, though it is not coincidental that they largely fail them. Many advanced countries had strong economies in the 1990s, and so that hypothesis is taken to pass the cross-national test. However, concealed weapons laws, increased use of the death penalty, and weak gun control laws are largely particular to the United States among advanced countries. They fail the cross-national test because legislation specific to that country is not responsible for reducing crime in the range of other countries experiencing the crime drop.

The basis for the original proposals that concealed weapons laws, capital punishment, and gun control laws may have caused the crime drop was that there appeared to be some fit in their timing. That is, although they may have subsequently been proved otherwise, they appeared to have some initial fit with the prior crime increase test. However, they do not appear consistent with the fact that some crime types have increased and fail the e-crime and phone theft test. Likewise, they all offer little by means of explaining differences in the timing of the crime drop between crime types or in the timing and trajectories between countries, and so they fail the variable trajectories test.

Hypothesis 5: Imprisonment. The possibility that increased imprisonment caused the crime drop is a hypothesis developed in relation to the United States. However, a recent National Research Council report notes that "over the four decades when incarceration rates steadily rose, U.S. crime rates showed no clear trend: the rate of violent crime rose, then fell, rose again, then declined sharply" (2014, p. 3). It concludes that "the increase in incarceration may have caused a decrease in crime, but the magnitude of the reduction is highly uncertain and the results of most studies suggest it was unlikely to have been large" (p. 4). This differs from some earlier findings, perhaps most notably the work of Spelman (2000), which suggested that a quarter of the crime drop in the United States was due to increased use of imprisonment.

Cross-national comparative analysis sheds useful light on the imprisonment hypothesis. Zimring's critique relating to neighboring Canada, where imprisonment policy is very different, cited earlier, was telling. According to van Dijk et al.,

Prison populations have since the early nineties gone up in many EU countries but not consistently so. Between 1995 and 2000 rates went down, for example, in Sweden, France, Poland and Finland (European Sourcebook, 2003). Sentencing policies in Europe as a whole are considerably less punitive than in the USA (Farrington, Langan, and Tonry, 2004) and yet crime is falling just as steeply in Europe as it is in the USA. No relationship between the severity of sentencing of countries and trends in national levels of crime is therefore in evidence. (Van Dijk et al. 2007, p. 23)

Rosenfeld and Messner (2009) add weight to this conclusion with their comparative analysis of European and American imprisonment rates, finding no significant relationship. Hence, it is fair to conclude that the imprisonment hypothesis fails the cross-national comparative test and thereby, via comparison with Canada in particular, also further impugns the hypothesis in relation to the United States. Further, the major increases in imprisonment that occurred in the United States before the crime drop occurred suggest that the imprisonment hypothesis fails what is here termed the prior crime increase test. Likewise, if imprisonment caused crime to drop, it is not apparent why phone theft or e-crimes would increase when other crimes fell, or how it might account for variation in the timing and trajectory of crime trends in different countries, and so it fails the third and fourth tests. Overall, there is little evidence that imprisonment played much, if any, role in the crime drop even in the United States, and no evidence that it played a role in most other countries experiencing a crime drop.

Hypotheses 6 and 7: Policing Strategies and More Police. Eck and Maguire's (2000) review of police numbers and policing strategy concludes that there is no real evidence supporting the notion that policing caused the crime drop. This is consistent with Bowling's (1999) study of New York City. However, a key role for policing in New York City has been claimed (Kelling and Sousa 2001), though while Zimring (2012) suggests that policing was a cause of the crime drop, he does not appear to identify the precise mechanism by which it is meant to have occurred. Ouimet (2002) summarizes the critical issues: "The main problem with the policing explanation is that innovative police practices such as gun patrols (stop and frisk) or Compstat type systems had been implemented after the crime rate had already begun declining. Moreover, the rate of crime dropped in cities that had not experienced major changes in policing" (p. 39). Note that this does not mean that policing strategies cannot affect crime. There is clear evidence that they can in some instances, particularly when resources are focused where crime is concentrated, and especially by use of problem-oriented policing focused on repeat victimization (Grove et al. 2012) or target crime hot spots (Braga, Papachristos, and Hureau 2012). Similarly, there is also evidence that increased police numbers may reduce the crime rate (Lin 2009). However, this is a different issue and does not overcome the timing problem noted above.

Both policing hypotheses also fail the cross-national test because other countries did not experience the increases in police numbers, or changes in strategies, that were proposed as causal for the United States. Similarly, if policing had induced the drop in many types of street crime, this could reasonably be expected to similarly have an impact on phone theft, and so it fails the fourth test. Neither policing hypothesis appears compatible with the variations in the timing and trajectory of declines in crime exhibited between countries and crime types, and so they fail the fourth test.

Hypothesis 8: Legalization of Abortion. Donohue and Levitt (2001) proposed that the legalization of abortion in the United States in 1973 was a cause of the crime drop. They argued that legalized abortion reduced the number of births of children who would otherwise be most at risk of becoming offenders in their teenage years. The evidence and methodology of this work have been revised and updated and remain significantly disputed, most notably by Joyce (2009, 2011). In particular, it is not clear that Cook and Laub's (2002, p. 23) criticism has been addressed. They concluded that "the timing of the downturn is simply wrong for legalized abortion to be the driving force" of the crime drop. They argue that the age cohorts that would experience reduced offending do not coincide with the timing of the crime drop. Thus Cook and Laub suggest that the crime drop must be due to period effects, that is, something changed at around the time that crime dropped rather than many years earlier. This is a significant criticism that also applies to the lead poisoning hypothesis addressed later in this essay. The point is reiterated by Blumstein and Rosenfeld (2008) in their review for the National Research Council. They conclude that "the important omitted variables in the initial analysis and the replications showing no significant effect suggest that any such effect [of this hypothesis] is likely to be quite small" (p. 27).

Once again, cross-national comparative analysis sheds significant further light on the validity of this hypothesis. An in-depth analysis of abortion rates and crime in the United Kingdom (Kahane, Paton, and Simmons 2008) could identify no evidence to support the hypothesis in that country, and Zimring (2007) suggests that this is true elsewhere. Dills, Miron, and Summers (2008) compare homicide rate trends from around 20 countries to the timing of abortion legalization laws. They conclude that "while the data from some countries are consistent with the [abortion legalization] hypothesis (e.g. Canada, France, Italy), several countries' data show the opposite correlation (e.g. Denmark, Finland, Hungary, Poland). In other cases crime was falling before legalization and does not decline any more quickly (20 years) after legalization (e.g. Japan, Norway)" (p. 17). Hence the hypothesis appears to fail the cross-national test. It can be taken to pass the prior crime increase test for present purposes since the purported fit with the timing of the crime drop is its key feature. However, it fails the phone theft and e-crimes test because, if abortion reduced crime across such a wide range of crime types, it is unclear why it would not also affect these crime types (phone theft in particular). Similarly, the timing of its effect would be expected to be somewhat uniform, and so it cannot account for the variations detailed in relation to the variable trajectories test even within the United States, where burglary and theft had been declining for significantly longer than violent crime. Overall, the preponderance of evidence suggests that the abortion hypothesis contributes little, if anything, to explanations of crime's decline.

Hypothesis 9: Immigration.   The notion that immigration might have induced the crime drop appears to have been floated in a news article by Sampson (2006) and furthered in Sampson (2008). In a more extensive empirical examination of the immigration hypothesis, Stowell et al. (2009) claim that it accounts for 6 percent of the crime drop.

For present purposes, and in the absence of evidence to the contrary, it is assumed that other countries have had immigration experiences with an effect similar to that of the United States, and so it is taken to pass the cross-national test. However, that assumption requires closer examination in further study because the nature of immigration in other countries is likely to be rather different in terms of both volume and the origins of immigrants. Unless the effect is the same for immigrants of all origins, which does not seem to be a proposition of studies focused on the United States, then it is quite possible that this hypothesis fails the cross-national test.

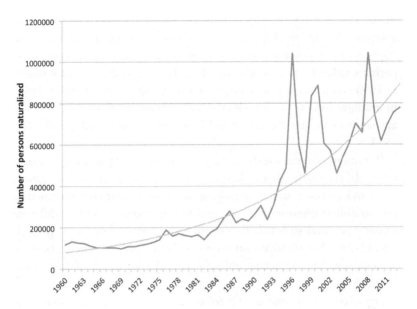

FIG. 5.—Number of persons naturalized annually in the United States (plus exponential trend line with R^2 = .88). Source: Department of Homeland Security, *Yearbook of Immigration Statistics 2013*, table 20.

Just as it was suggested that policing strategies can reduce crime but do not appear to have caused the crime drop, so it is possible that immigration may reduce crime in some instances but not account for the crime drop. There does seem to be evidence that immigration can reduce crime (see Martinez and Mehlman-Orozco 2013), but the evidence that immigration caused the crime drop appears less persuasive. In particular, while immigration in the United States may have increased in the 1990s, it was also increasing prior to the 1990s, when crime was increasing rapidly. This suggests that this hypothesis fails the prior crime increase test. Figure 5 shows the number of persons naturalized annually in the United States between 1960 and 2013. The significant increase in the 1990s is clear, though uneven, and it does not track (inversely) the decline in crime in any clear fashion. Perhaps more importantly, the trend in immigration prior to the 1990s, using naturalization as the proxy here, was also upward when crime was increasing. Why, if immigration reduces crime, was crime increasing so rapidly for several decades previously? It may suggest that while immigration may have increased more rapidly in the 1990s in the United

States, the relationship with rapidly decreasing crime may be somewhat spurious. At the very least this issue may warrant further examination. Aspects of two other key studies seem to lend weight to this suspicion: perhaps tellingly, Sampson's analysis (2008; see chart on p. 29) begins in 1990 and uses a 3-year average to iron out the large annual variation in immigration, while Stowell et al.'s (2009) pooled time-series analysis appears to consider the crime and immigration relationship only after 1994.

If immigration caused the crime drop, then it is unclear why it would affect differentially phone theft or e-crime, and so it fails the phone theft and e-crimes test. Similarly, it does not appear to accommodate the variable trajectories of crime in different countries and for different crime types, and so it fails the fourth test. Hence while we despise the xenophobia that immigration seems to bring out in some sections of society, immigration seems unlikely to underpin much, if any, of the crime drop.

Hypothesis 10: Consumer Confidence and Price Inflation. Rosenfeld (2009) and Rosenfeld and Messner (2009) proposed the consumer confidence hypothesis as the cause of the decline in violence in the United States. They suggested that consumer confidence increased when the economy was strong in the 1990s, causing consumers to move away from purchasing in secondhand markets that support the stolen goods trade, the converse being true when consumer confidence was less strong. They hypothesized that this reduction in property crimes moved offenders away from risky activity more generally such that it also caused the reduction in violence. However, the trend in violence is tracked rather better by auto theft than by an aggregate set of property crimes (as fig. 2 implies), and so the evidence underpinning the hypothesis is questionable. It also seems that since the global economic downturn in 2008–9 when consumer confidence has declined, the crime drop has continued, thereby appearing to falsify this hypothesis. Consumer confidence in many other countries may not have been as strong as that in the United States in the 1990s but can be taken to be moving in the same direction for present purposes, such that the hypothesis passes the cross-national test. However, while economies were particularly strong in the 1990s, they were also strong for significant periods prior to that when crime was increasing rapidly in the post–World War II period, and so the hypothesis does not pass the prior crime increase test. Similarly, the hypothesis does not appear to

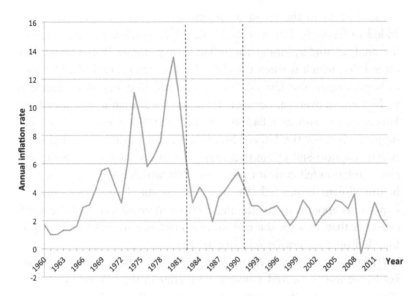

FIG. 6.—Annual inflation rate, United States, 1960–2013. Source: US inflation calculator, http://www.usinflationcalculator.com/inflation/historical-inflation-rates, accessed June 4, 2014.

offer an explanation for why some crimes increased when many decreased or for the variation in the crime drop between countries and crime types, and so it fails the third and fourth tests.

In a further iteration of the work, Rosenfeld (2013) proposed that crime is linked to inflation via a mechanism similar to the purchasing of stolen goods. Inflation rates are suggested to have declined across several countries studied, and they remained low when crime also remained low during the global economic downturn. The essence of the supporting evidence for hypothesis 10 is that "as inflation rates began to fall in the early 1990s, so did crime rates in both Europe and the United States" (p. 2). Data from 1982 onward are analyzed, and the annual change in consumer prices for eight nations is compared to that of homicide, robbery, and burglary, with some possible correlation evident. A limitation of the research is identified as follows: "the empirical base for the current findings is limited by and large to a period of falling inflation and crime rates. It would have been desirable to broaden temporal coverage to capture the equally precipitous rise in prices and crime that began in the 1960s" (p. 21). It is possible to overcome this limitation, at least for the United States. Figure 6 shows the annual inflation rate for the United States for 1960–2013.

In addition to the trend in inflation, two vertical lines have been added to figure 6. The first indicates 1982, which is the start date for the analysis underpinning the inflation hypothesis. The second indicates 1991, which is when the violent crime drop is typically identified as beginning in the United States. The inflation rate does appear to be higher, on average, between 1982 and 1990 than it was after 1990. However, the annual inflation rate before 1982 is telling. The chart suggests that, for the United States at least, a possible correlation between inflation and crime that may exist in recent years is likely spurious: inflation fell dramatically from 1980, which was a decade or more before violent crime fell. By this analysis the "crime and inflation" hypothesis appears to fail the prior crime increase test, and the implication is that, as with the consumer confidence hypothesis, it may be founded on a somewhat selective analysis.

Hypothesis 11: Waning Illicit Drug Markets. The waning crack market hypothesis appeared a strong contender in the United States (e.g., Blumstein and Wallman 2006; Blumstein and Rosenfeld 2008). A waning illicit heroin market has been suggested to account for a quarter or more of the crime drop in Europe (Morgan 2014). Use of these drugs increased in the 1980s, then declined in the 1990s, and so cannot account for the similar crime trends before and after. If improved security (discussed below) made acquisitive crimes harder to commit, this may have induced declines in the hard-drug markets. It is also unclear why phone theft and e-crimes would increase if most other types of crime fell as a result of the waning illicit drug market, and so it fails the third test. In addition, it is unclear how a declining crack market could explain variable trajectories in different countries and crime types, and so it fails the variable trajectories test.

Hypothesis 12: Lead Poisoning. Lead is a poison that can damage the brain of humans when ingested, with children particularly susceptible. From this foundation, Nevin's (2000) study in the United States posited that lead poisoning of children led to violent crime when they became adolescents. His work was extended by Stretesky and Lynch (2001, 2004) to include property crime (see also Reyes 2007, 2012). The evidence suggests that, with a 22-year delay, there is a strong aggregate correlation between lead exposure and the rates of some crime types. Following environmental laws requiring cleaner air and the removal of lead from petroleum gasoline in particular, this poisoning declined, and so, goes the theory, did crime 22 years or so later. A recent statement examining only lead compared to assault rates summarizes the lead hypothesis as holding "that present period rates of adult violence are associated with spatial and temporal variation in childhood [lead] exposure, linked together by the behavioral and cognitive mechanisms of impulsivity, aggressivity, and depressed IQ" (Mielke and Zahran 2012, p. 49). Nevin (2007) extended the analysis to a series of developed countries where lead appeared to correlate with crime many years later, such that the hypothesis can be said to pass the cross-national test.

As with abortion legalization, Cook and Laub (2002) define the lead poisoning hypothesis as a "cohort explanation" for the crime drop. Its effect should be produced primarily on the cohort that reaches adolescence at the time when crime begins to fall. They offer evidence showing that the crime drop was not experienced solely as the product of a single cohort, but that the range of age cohorts of offenders, including older offenders, experienced a reduction in offending rates at this time. Similarly, in their review for the National Research Council, Blumstein and Rosenfeld (2008) also seem to dismiss the lead poisoning hypothesis, suggesting that "there is a clear similarity between time trends in environmental lead levels and violent crime rates lagged by 23 years. But demographic trends—the arrival and waning of the baby boom generation from the high crime ages—coincided roughly with the arrival and departure of leaded gasoline, and so the apparent effect of exposure to lead on crime rates may be confounded with demographic change" (p. 27).

Dills, Miron, and Summers (2008) apply a longer-term version of what is here termed the prior crime increase test. They identify multiple measures of lead exposure for the United States dating from 1910 and conclude that "all proxies for lead increased dramatically from around 1910 through 1970. If the lead hypothesis is correct, then crime should have displayed a measurable increase between 1925 and 1985. The U.S. murder rate, however, decreased between the 1930s and 1950s. The murder rate does rise from the 1960s through the mid-1970s, but much unexplained variation remains between the mid-1970s and mid-1980s" (p. 16).

The prior crime increase test identifies a further issue, which is that lead poisoning is really a hypothesis of why crime increased before the fall. It is a theory of the crime drop only in its absence. Hence the hypothesis appears to claim to explain all major trends in crime over the last 50 years or so. In so doing it implies that routine activity theory does not offer the compelling explanation for the post–World War II crime increases, as most convincingly argued by Cohen and Felson (1979).

The lead poisoning hypothesis also appears incompatible with recent increases in phone thefts and robbery as well as Internet-related crime. Why would they experience such large increases at a time when the hypothesis suggests that the number of motivated offenders is sharply declining? Hence the hypothesis seems to fail the phone theft and e-crimes test. In addition, the lead poisoning hypothesis appears to fail the variable trajectories test. It is unclear how it would explain some within-country variations. Violent and property crimes fall simultaneously in some countries but at different times or at different rates in others. If the cause of both really is lead poisoning, then the patterns ought to be similar. Yet if the lead hypothesis applies only to violent crime, as implied by the omission of property crime by some studies, then how would it explain the drop in property crime? As a specific example, why would auto theft in the United States fall before violent crime? And why would homicide in England and Wales begin to plummet only several years after the decline in many other types of common crime including other types of violence? Hence while some of the correlations between levels of lead in the air and some crime rates a couple of decades later are quite compelling, the overall evidence implies that these may be spurious and that while lead is clearly a nasty poison, it does not seem to explain the crime drop.

Hypothesis 13: Changing Demographics. It is well known that most advanced countries are experiencing an aging population. Hence the fact that it is easily understood may be the basis for a popular belief that demographic change induced the crime drop. If the population is aging, then the proportion of younger people who constitute those most at risk as both victims and offenders will decline and so too will per capita crime rates.

In their review for the National Research Council, Blumstein and Rosenfeld (2008) give the demographics hypothesis short shrift, observing that "during the sharp crime drop of the 1990s, age composition changes were trending in the wrong direction: the number of 18-year-olds in the U.S. population was increasing while crime rates were declining for other reasons" (p. 20). This contradicts some earlier studies, perhaps most notably that by Fox (2000), which suggested that demographic change accounted for perhaps 10–15 percent of the crime drop. Hence the demographics hypothesis is included here but is likely to account for a small proportion of the crime drop at most. It passes the cross-national test since aging is occurring in many advanced countries and for present purposes is assumed to pass the prior crime increase test, though the turning point and rate of change in crime seem too sharp to be due to demographics.

If demographic change caused rates of crime to change, then it would not be expected that rates of some particular types of theft, notably phone theft, as well as fraud and other crime conducted via the Internet, would increase, and so it fails the phone theft and e-crimes test. In addition, since demographic change might be expected to affect crime types somewhat uniformly within a country, it does not appear to account for within-country variations across crime types and so fails the fourth test.

Hypothesis 14: The Civilizing Process. The "civilizing process hypothesis" is derived from the work of Norbert Elias ([1939] 2000). Elias's study is not about crime as we are discussing it here. The book's focus is largely feudalism and medievalism. Its 45 chapters cover, among other things, developments in each of going to the bathroom, blowing one's nose, spitting, and behavior in the bedroom. A nine-page chapter on "Changes in Aggressiveness" is mainly about the joys of battle and hunting and is closely followed by "The Life of a Knight." The index notes two references to violence: "The civilizing process does not follow a straight line. . . . But if we consider the movement over large time spans, we see clearly how the compulsions arising directly from the threat of weapons and physical force have gradually diminished, and how those forms of dependency which lead to the regulation of the affects in the form of self-control, gradually increased" (p. 157). The reference to "large time spans" is telling. It refers to a very gradual change over the centuries rather than to rapid change over the course of a few years, which is our focus here. More specifically, there is no identified mechanism in Elias's work that could explain the recent changes in crime.

Eisner (2008) gives Elias's work a criminological voice by linking it to evidence of declining violence over the centuries. Yet Eisner is skeptical about applying the civilizing process to the post-1990 crime drop, noting problems: "not the least of which is whether such a theoretical perspective could be moved beyond the level of speculation and be subjected to more rigorous empirical tests" (p. 312).

LaFree (1999), Rosenfeld (2000), and Ouimet (2002) have suggested that the civilizing process may have a role to play in explaining the current crime drop. More recently, and drawing on Eisner's studies of violence trends over the centuries, Pinker (2011) addresses the issue. Pinker's focus is on violence but also primarily the multiple-century time spans that concern Elias and Eisner. However, the book does discuss the recent crime drop, focusing on the United States, and proposes mechanisms of change similar to those suggested by LaFree: "It is possible that the recent declines in crime were related to the renewed legitimacy of three traditional, and the growing support for three newer, social institutions during the last decade of the twentieth century. Declining crime rates in the 1990s may have been produced by increasing trust in political institutions, increasing economic well-being, and growing institutionalization of alternatives to the traditional two parent American family. Increasing support for criminal justice, welfare, and educational institutions in the 1990s has also put downward pressure on crime rates" (1998, p. 1367).

Two issues are critical here. First, the mechanism by which the civilizing process occurs is extremely general—a notion that society improved by a wide variety of means—and so the way in which this is meant to have caused such a rapid and substantial decline in crime rates as detailed here is extremely unclear. Notions of "increasing trust" and "increasing support" in institutions are vague at best in terms of how they might reduce a range of types of crime ranging from property crimes to homicide, child sexual abuse, and intimate partner violence. For instance, one of Pinker's indicators of social improvement is the rate of increase in mentions of rights issues in literature in recent decades, despite the fact that these do not even really track changes in crime. Second, insofar as a mechanism can be identified, the brief section of the Pinker book on the recent crime drop provides no real evidence to support its assertion that institutional social control over the population declined in the 1960s (causing the crime rate to triple or more) and that it strengthened in such a way that caused the crime drop. On the other hand, if we interpret the civilizing hypothesis as so general that it means "something positive happened to society in the 1990s," then nobody could disagree, but it becomes sufficiently vague that it cannot be considered a scientific hypothesis. Hence, and in line with Eisner's suggestion as quoted above, the inclusion of this as a hypothesis here is generous.

The civilizing process could be assumed to have occurred cross-nationally, though the specifics of the human rights issues were likely different in the United States than in Europe and elsewhere. Similarly, in the absence of evidence to the contrary, the timing of improvements in institutional trust and support by offenders cannot be said not to coincide with prior increases in crime. However, this hypothesis fails both the e-crime and phone theft test and the variable trajectories test. If society has civilized so rapidly that homicide fell by half in a decade or so in some instances, then this is seriously contradicted by increased theft and robbery of mobile phones and the range of Internet-related crime. Similarly, if a civilizing process has occurred so rapidly and broadly, then why are there some quite significant anomalies both within countries and between countries? These are the primary reasons why this review concludes that the civilizing process offers little prospect of explaining the recent crime drops. In a 2000 study on US homicide rates, Rosenfeld is unable to identify an explanation and reverts to the civilizing process as a potential catchall hypothesis. Yet his skepticism is evident, and he brilliantly captures its vagueness: "If church is the last refuge of scoundrels, 'culture' is the final recourse of social scientists in search of explanations when existing economic, social and political theories have been exhausted" (2000, p. 157).

Hypothesis 15: Improved Security. Did improvements in the quality and quantity of security induce the crime drop? There is strong evaluation evidence from studies covering Australia, England and Wales, the Netherlands, and the United States finding that improved vehicle security (particularly electronic immobilizers and central deadlocks) caused dramatic declines in vehicle crime (Kriven and Ziersch 2007; Farrell et al. 2011; Farrell, Tseloni, and Tilley 2011; Fujita and Maxfield 2012; Brown 2013; van Ours and Vollaard 2013). There is also mounting evidence from the ICVS and from studies relating to England and Wales that improved household security caused the decline in household burglary (van Dijk et al. 2007; Tilley, Farrell, and Clarke 2014), which fits with a range of studies identifying household security as effective (see Tseloni et al. 2014). Hence this hypothesis passes the cross-national test. In each instance, the timing of the spread of security coincides with the start of the crime drop, and so it passes the prior crime increase test.

The security hypothesis is located within the crime opportunity theoretical framework, which suggests that the opportunities are crime specific. This framework means that it is theoretically compatible for some crime types to increase (as opportunities for those crimes increase) at the same time as other crimes decrease (as opportunities for those crimes decrease). Hence since valuable phones and the Internet offered new and enticing crime opportunities, those crimes increased, and this is compatible with the fact that security improvements induced declines in other types of crime. Hence, unlike most other hypotheses, this passes the phone theft and e-crimes test. In a similar vein, since opportunities and the spread of security occurred at different times in different places and in relation to different crime types, this hypothesis is compatible with the fact that there is variation in the timing and trajectory of the crime drop between countries and with the fact that there is variation between crime types within countries. Hence the hypothesis passes the variable trajectory test.

This hypothesis passes each of the four tests and is the only one that does so. It is examined in more detail in Section IV.

Hypothesis 16: The Internet-Induced Changes in Lifestyles. "The Internet" is included because although there have been few studies, there is some prima facie reason to suggest that its rapid increase coincides with the rapid decrease in crime, such that "the rise in the use of the internet has very roughly coincided with falls in crime (in 1995 use of the internet was not widespread). As it became more popular, it may have helped to occupy young people's time when they may otherwise have turned to crime. It also provides more opportunity for online crime which is not as easily quantifiable at present as traditional crime types" (Office of National Statistics 2013, p. 7). There is also the suggestion that "lifestyle and routine activity changes, plus perceptions, may have a larger explanatory role in relation to other crime types. The rise of the Internet has roughly coincided with the declines in crimes that get measured in traditional victimisation surveys, and took place sooner in the US. Coincidence? Perhaps the huge criminal opportunities presented by the Internet sucked some offenders away from traditional street crimes into online offending that is less routinely or easily recorded" (Farrell et al. 2008, p. 21).

For present purposes, the Internet began with its public release by America Online in 1994, but the crime drop began, at least in the United States, in 1991, with crime falling dramatically there in the first few years. This makes it implausible that the Internet caused the crime drop. Further, the spread of the Internet was most tardy in the least affluent areas and comprised dial-up connections (remember the screech?) and often pay-per-minute connections for many years. Any significant effect on the lifestyles of potential offenders and victims could have taken effect significantly only after the precipitous crime declines began. This review has not been able to identify a peer-reviewed study of the role of the Internet in the crime drop, but its importance is such that it receives attention in relation to most things and so is deemed worthy of brief discussion. At most, it is conceivable that the Internet has induced lifestyle changes for both potential of-fenders and potential victims (with consequent impacts on guardianship if everyone stayed home more) that have had a subsequent consolida-tion effect significantly after the crime drop began.

Hypothesis 17: Phone Guardianship. The final hypothesis included here is that the rapid spread of mobile cell phones occurred around the time that crime was falling, which may have a causal connection if phones enhanced personal guardianship (Farrell et al. 2010; Klick, MacDonald, and Stratmann 2012; Orrick and Piquero 2013). Orrick and Piquero examine the correlation between mobile cell phone own-ership and both property and violent crime in the United States. They conclude, "In sum, the relationship of cell phone ownership to the property crime rate between 1984 and 2009 indicates a negative, sig-nificant association . . . but virtually no relationship between cell phone ownership and violent crime" (p. 8). This seems counterintuitive in-sofar as, if mobile phones reduce crime via guardianship, we might expect any effect to be mainly on personal crime because phones are carried on the person. Hence while Orrick and Piquero acknowledge that an association does not identify causation, the nature and existence of that causation remains to be established. This suggests that the research to date does not really provide supporting evidence other than some correlation and some general argument, while it also reveals some inconsistencies. Overall this tends to suggest that phone guardianship is unlikely to prove to be a major contributor to the crime drop and that the supporting evidence to date is somewhat less than compelling.

D. Discussion and Conclusions

The tests utilized here are imperfect as formal evaluation criteria. They are better framed as broad guidelines that add some clarity with

TABLE 3

Findings from Four Tests

	Test			
Hypothesis	Cross-National	Prior Crime Increase	E-Crime and Phone Theft	Variable Trajectories
1. Strong economy	√	X	X	X
2. Concealed weapons law	X	√	X	X
3. Capital punishment	X	√	X	X
4. Gun control laws	X	√	X	X
5. Imprisonment	X	X	X	X
6. Policing strategies	X	√	X	X
7. More police	X	√	X	X
8. Legalization of abortion	X	√	X	X
9. Immigration	√	X	X	X
10. Consumer confidence	√	X	X	X
11. Waning hard-drugs market	X	√	X	X
12. Lead poisoning	√	√	X	X
13. Changing demographics	√	√	X	X
14. Civilizing process	√	√	X	X
15. Improved security	√	√	√	√
16. The Internet	√	√	X	X
17. Phone guardianship	√	√	√	X

NOTE.—√ = pass; X = fail.

respect to key issues. Each relates to evaluation issues more generally, and many published assessments include elements of some of the tests. Nevertheless, the tests add value through facilitating some standardization of assessment criteria and allowing the wood to be seen from the trees.

As summarized in table 3, one hypothesis fails all four tests, 10 hypotheses fail three, four fail two, and one fails only one but lacked basic evidence (phone guardianship). Most of the failures were accompanied by a range of other criticisms, some rather damaging. One hypothesis passes the four tests, and that is the security hypothesis. While the tests are proposed as necessary criteria for a valid theory of the crime drop, they are not deemed sufficient, and so the security hypothesis is examined in the next section.

IV. The Security Hypothesis

This section examines the security hypothesis. The most extensive supporting evidence to date relates to car theft, which is tackled first, followed by burglary of dwellings. The role that improved security may have played in reducing other crime types is then addressed. This is followed by an explanation and preliminary supporting evidence relating to how reductions in property crime, which accounts for most crime and the bulk of crime in criminal careers, may have also caused reductions in violent crimes of various types.

A. The Security Hypothesis

The security hypothesis proposes that change in the quantity and quality of security was a significant driver of declining crime:

- Security improvements, including specific security devices, vary for different crimes but have been widely implemented.
- Different security measures work in different ways to reduce the crimes to which they are applied: they increase actual or perceived risk to the offender, and/or they reduce actual or perceived reward for the offender, and/or they increase actual or perceived effort for the offender.
- The different ways in which security measures work produce variations in expected changes in crime patterns associated with crime drops. These include expected security device crime change "signatures."
- The specific falls in crime produced by improvements in security alongside their associated diffusions of benefit (preventive effects spilling out beyond the operational range of measures; see Guerette and Bowers 2009) to other targets and methods of committing crime are not matched by equivalent displacement.

A progenitor is identifiable in Clarke and Newman's (2006) book on terrorism. They list developments in security that they link to declining crime in many countries, concluding, "In fact, the one thing in common amongst all these countries, including the United States, is that they have all made a huge investment in security during the past 25 years, affecting almost every aspect of everyday life" (p. 220). A newsletter article by van Dijk (2006) made similar suggestions informed by ICVS data on the spread of security across Europe, later summarized as follows: "Perhaps a more significant factor inhibiting crime across the Western world is the universal growth in the possession and use of private security measures by households and companies over the past few decades. ICVS-based trend data on the use of precautionary measures confirm that in all Western countries, without exception, the use of measures to prevent property crimes such as car thefts and household burglaries has risen drastically over the past 15 years" (van Dijk

et al. 2007, p. 23). In the context of the existing criminological literature, the security hypothesis applied to the crime drop can be viewed
as simply a specific version of the more general notion that situational
crime prevention can be effective. In what follows, key empirical findings relating to the relationship between security and the crime drop
are examined.

B. Vehicle Theft

With crime close to its apex in many countries, Clarke and Harris
(1992) cited a study of 56 new cars that found that "the ease with which
locked cars can be broken into would be laughable if it weren't so
serious. Our security tester has got into nearly all cars he has checked
in a matter of seconds, using the unsophisticated tools of the car thief's
trade" (*Which?* 1988, p. 118; cited in Clarke and Harris 1992, p. 37).
Key studies of auto theft spanning Australia, England and Wales, the
Netherlands, and the United States lend support to the security hypothesis, suggesting that more and better vehicle security reduced vehicle crime and, thereby, may also have contributed to the collapse in
other crime types. The following subsections describe key data signatures that indicate both how and why improved vehicle security was a
determinant of declining vehicle theft. Eck and Madensen (2009) link
such data signatures to the broader evaluation literature.

1. *Turning Point and Trajectory.* Two data signatures are detailed
here. The first is the correlation between the growth of vehicle security
and the crime decline. Of course correlation does not establish cau-
sality, which is what the other signatures collectively indicate. The second signature is the assessment of the timing of the introduction of
improved security in different countries at different times and how in
each instance it occurs immediately prior to the downturn in car crime.

Fujita and Maxfield (2012) observe that the introduction and spread
of electronic immobilizers and central deadlocking systems in the
United States coincide with the start and trajectory of the crime drop.
They also show that, in contrast, the introduction of parts marking
does not. Brown (2013) notes that unlike in many other countries,
there was no national legislation to require electronic immobilizers in
the United States and suggests, rather, that it was indirectly promoted
by the Motor Vehicle Theft Law Enforcement Act of 1984 (HR 6257).
He notes that "the legislation, which came into force in 1987, required
manufacturers to mark the Vehicle Identification Number onto the

engine, transmission and 12 major body parts. The legislation also allowed for exemption from parts marking on some of the manufacturer's models if anti-theft devices were installed as standard equipment. It appears that these 'anti-theft' devices commonly consisted of electronic immobilisers" (Brown 2013, p. 12).

While the European Union formally mandated electronic immobilizers in new cars from 1998, the underpinning legislation had been passed in 1995, and the writing was on the wall for some time. In the United Kingdom, for instance, a car theft index had been published in 1992 (Houghton 1992), and government pressure brought to bear on vehicle manufacturers to tackle the car crime problem. Laycock (2004) identifies the car theft index and government leverage as instrumental in inducing the drop in UK car theft, and to the extent that both the introduction of immobilizers and the subsequent decline in car theft occurred in advance of other European countries, we might reasonably deduce that she is correct.

Figure 7 contains two panels. Panel A shows trends in vehicle insecurity (those without security) for immobilizers and central locking alongside the trend in theft of and from vehicles, for England and Wales 1991–2007. The CSEW did not distinguish between electronic and other vehicle immobilizers until the late 1990s, and so panel B extrapolates backward for the trend in electronic immobilizers prior to 1999. The exponential regression line fits the known data almost perfectly ($R^2 = .9988$), and assuming the extrapolation is correct, the timing of the introduction of electronic immobilizers since 1993 fits precisely with the initiation of the crime drop—just as Fujita and Maxfield (2012) found it did for the United States—and squares with Laycock's (2004) assessment. Van Ours and Vollard (2013) similarly link the introduction of immobilizers in the Netherlands directly to the timing of the major drop in car theft that occurred in that country and estimate the theft risks of cars with immobilizers at around half that of those without.

The emphasis here on the timing of electronic immobilizers partly reflects additional analysis that suggests they have been most effective in reducing vehicle thefts (Farrell, Tseloni, and Tilley 2011; Brown 2013). The evidence that the timing of electronic immobilizers in the United States, England and Wales, and the Netherlands coincides with crime's turning point is further supported by evidence from Australia. Australia also facilitates a natural experiment because high-quality

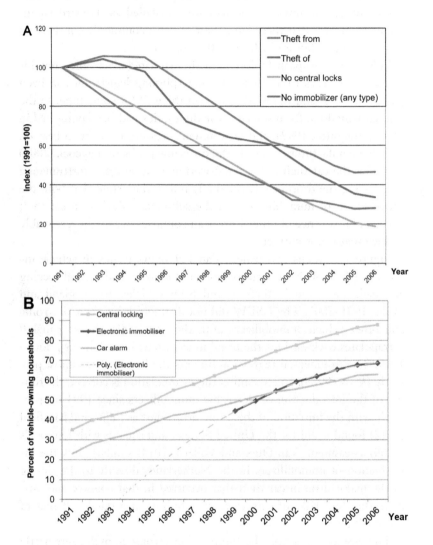

FIG. 7.—*A*, Theft of and from vehicles and percentage of vehicles without key security measures, 1991–2006, indexed to 100 in 1991. *B*, Percentage of vehicle-owning households with key security devices (with extrapolation for electronic immobilizers for years before 1999). Source: Crime Survey for England and Wales.

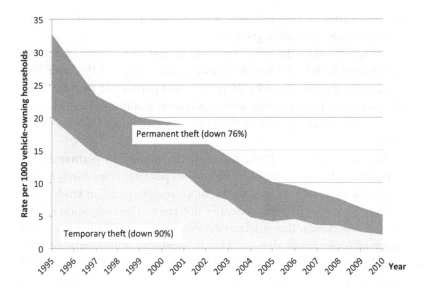

FIG. 8.—Temporary and permanent vehicle thefts per 1,000 vehicle-owning households, England and Wales, 1995–2010/11. Source: Office of National Statistics, Crime Survey for England and Wales.

immobilizers were introduced in the state of Western Australia ahead of elsewhere (Farrell et al. 2011). Consistent with electronic immobilizers being instrumental, the decline in vehicle theft in Western Australia began in 1998 (immobilizers had been subsidized from 1997 and were mandated in 1999), whereas immobilizers were mandated elsewhere for new cars in Australia in 2001, after which national car theft rates fell rapidly.

2. *Impact on Professional and Organized Crime.*   Figure 8 shows the decline in vehicle theft in England and Wales from 1995 to 2010, split into permanent and temporary thefts. In the 16 years from 1995 to 2010, the vehicle theft rate declined 84 percent, comprising a 90 percent fall in temporary thefts and a three-quarters (76 percent) fall in permanent thefts. Temporary theft, in which a vehicle is abandoned and recovered, is a reasonable proxy for thefts motivated by joyriding, theft for transportation, or theft for use of the vehicle in the commission of another crime (Clarke and Harris 1992). Permanent theft is a reasonable proxy for theft of vehicles to be sold for parts or "chopped" and vehicles to be resold. Hence temporary and permanent thefts are held to be good indicators of the relationship between more amateur

or early-career thieves and those who are more professional or working with an organized crime group.

Temporary theft declined more rapidly and to a greater extent than permanent theft in the first decade of decline. Between 1995 and 2001, temporary theft declined by 76 percent and permanent theft by "only" 44 percent. This conforms with expectation if improved vehicle security is more likely to disrupt thefts by less experienced adolescent car thieves.

Between 2005 and 2010, however, the decline in permanent and temporary thefts was similar (50 and 48 percent, respectively). This, we conjecture, may be due to the more recent spread in tracking devices, which prove a highly effective deterrent. The suggestion is based on the expectation that tracking devices are unusually disruptive of the work of professional thieves. This is consistent with results of Ayres and Levitt (1998) and with detailed analyses of CSEW data to 2007 by Farrell et al. (2011) and Farrell, Tseloni, and Tilley (2011), who concluded that tracking devices were highly effective but had not penetrated the vehicle fleet to a sufficient extent to have played a major role in prior crime drops. From the perspective of the security hypothesis, the fact that permanent theft also declined dramatically is notable because it suggests that security can be highly effective against professional and organized crime.

The findings reviewed here for England and Wales are largely replicated in Australia (Kriven and Ziersch 2007; Farrell et al. 2011). The decline in vehicle theft in Australia began around 2001, when electronic immobilizers were mandated, with overall vehicle theft declining by around half in the 6 years to 2007. Here, temporary theft declined 58 percent compared to a 13 percent reduction in permanent thefts, though the proportion of permanent thefts was always significantly lower than in England and Wales.

3. *Broken Windows and Forced Doors.*   Figure 9 shows trends in the means of entry for vehicle theft in England and Wales from 1995 to 2010. In 1995, the forcing of a door or lock was by far the most prevalent means of entry, accounting for almost two-thirds (65 percent). The decline in vehicle theft that ensued was experienced as primarily a decline in the forcing of doors and door locks. This pattern is consistent with improved central deadlocks on doors having induced the decline in crime. Over time, other means of entry also declined, but the way in which they did so is different. The second-most prevalent

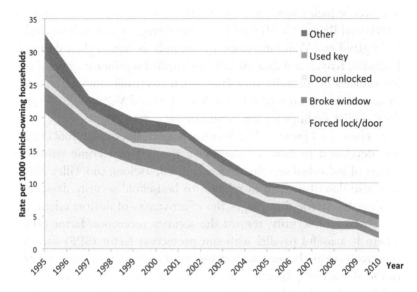

FIG. 9.—Means of entry for vehicle theft in England and Wales, 1995–2011. Source: Office of National Statistics, Crime Survey for England and Wales.

means of entry to vehicles in 1995 was window breaking. Yet there was no decline in the prevalence of window breaking as a means of entry between 1995 and 1997, and it subsequently declined less rapidly than door and lock forcing. Likewise, other means of entry also declined but can be interpreted as likely a diffusion of benefits: even if they could enter a vehicle, offenders had learned that they probably could not steal it because of the spread of immobilizers. Hence the general decline in most means of entry, driven by the decline in door and lock forcing, appears consistent with the expected impact of improved vehicle security.

The analysis of means of entry to vehicles was also conducted for Australian vehicle thefts for the period 2001–7 by Farrell, Tseloni, and Tilley (2011), extending the work of Kriven and Ziersch (2007), which covered 2001–4. The data cover a shorter period, but the findings are similar to those for England and Wales: lock forcing was the dominant means of entry prior to 2001 and accounted for the bulk of the decline in means of entry, falling disproportionately relative to other means of entry that fell later and less dramatically.

4. *Vehicular Demographics.* An increase in the average age of stolen vehicles is an important data signature. This is what would be expected

if newer vehicles were more difficult to steal. Brown and Thomas (2003) and Brown (2004) found that the average age of stolen vehicles in England and Wales increased significantly as vehicle theft declined. Likewise, Kriven and Ziersch (2007) identified significant aging of stolen vehicles in Australia after 2001 when electronic immobilizers became mandatory on new vehicles. Van Ours and Vollaard (2013) produce similar findings for the Netherlands.

5. *Horses for Courses.*   The Security Impact Assessment Tool (SIAT) was developed to assist in identifying the different crime reduction effects of individual security devices (Farrell, Tseloni, and Tilley 2011). It is also described later in relation to household security devices. It produced a metric that gauges the effectiveness of devices relative to the absence of security, termed the security protection factor (SPF). There is a useful parallel with sun protection factor (SPF) used for sunscreen cream, because each states the amount of time units, relative to the absence of protection, after which the owner is burned.

The analysis found considerable variation in the effectiveness of individual vehicle security devices. Tracking devices produced the largest effects, but mostly too recent to account for the drop in vehicle thefts of the early 1990s. Electronic immobilizers were found highly effective. Moreover, as might be expected, newer vehicles often included combinations of devices including built-in immobilizers, central locking, and alarms, and these produced positive interaction effects that improved overall security.

The best-ranked security combinations were found to reduce theft risk by a factor of 25 compared to a vehicle without security devices. The impact of devices and combinations worked better for some crime types than for others, and the patterns squared with theoretical expectation based on assessment of the preventive mechanism. For example, electronic immobilizers have an impact more on theft of vehicles than on theft from vehicles, while central locking systems affected both theft of and theft from vehicles. Alarms had a more modest effect generally, but this was greater against theft from vehicles than theft of vehicles. While the study acknowledges that the findings may conflate some effects of vehicle age and security quality, the strength of the findings is sufficient to conclude that, at minimum, security devices can have a considerable impact on crime and that the effect of individual devices and their combination varies by crime type.

6. *Implication for Other Hypotheses.*   While developed to examine the

role of security, the data signatures examined here can be assessed in terms of their implications for other crime drop hypotheses. None of the other hypotheses can explain these data signatures. Further, the data signatures would not be expected to demonstrate the detailed variation shown here if car theft trends were examined through the lenses of the alternative hypotheses. There would be no particular reason for any change in the proportions of different means of entry, for example, or for the aging of stolen vehicles, that were found in each of Australia, the Netherlands, and England and Wales and that we anticipate will be identified in North America and elsewhere should suitable data be analyzed. Hence while all of these data signatures are consistent with a security hypothesis, they also further refute rival hypotheses.

This does not mean that all data patterns relating to vehicle crime have been explained in terms of the security hypothesis, as much research remains to be undertaken. For instance, Fujita and Maxfield (2012) note that declines in car theft in the United States were geographically skewed, being higher in the Northeast, for example. A possible explanation is the differential rates of turnover of vehicles in different areas: areas where the car fleet is replaced more quickly, particularly affluent areas, would be expected to experience preventive gains more quickly.

C. Burglary

Comparative analysis of 18 EU countries using data from the 2005 ICVS concluded, "It is clear that levels of household security have increased in most European countries. Specifically the percentages of households with burglar alarms show upward trends in all countries for which trend data are available, with the possible exception of France. There have been particularly steep increases since 1992 in Sweden and Italy but also among the countries at the bottom of the scale (Poland, Estonia, Finland, Denmark and Spain)" (van Dijk et al. 2007, p. 84).

While the ICVS is the best source for extensive cross-national comparison, the in-depth analysis it facilitates is more limited in terms of both information and sample sizes. Tseloni et al. (2014) examine the effectiveness of household security devices and seek to identify the contributions to burglary reduction from each of individual devices and their combination. They use the SIAT approach mentioned previously in relation to vehicle security devices, with detailed data for England

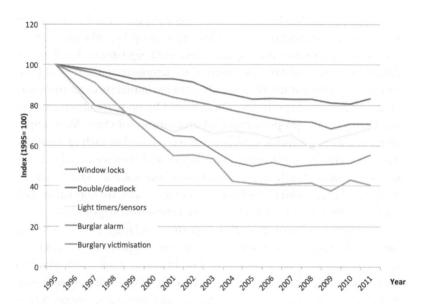

FIG. 10.—Household insecurity and burglary rate, 1995–2011. Source: Office of National Statistics, Crime Survey for England and Wales.

and Wales. Their findings are largely consistent with those of previous studies, concluding that combinations of devices, particularly dead bolt locks on doors, window locks, and internal and external lights, can dramatically reduce burglary risk. Figure 10 shows trends in the household burglary rate alongside trends in insecurity, measured as households without individual household security devices in England and Wales. Although household security was increasing while burglary was decreasing, the correspondence between the two is not as clear as it was for vehicle crime. That is, the increase in household security appears more modest and less rapid than was the increase in vehicle security. One possible explanation is the positive interaction effect of multiple security devices at the same property, which can sometimes be considerable (Tseloni et al. 2014). Another, offered by Tilley, Farrell, and Clarke (2014), is that there was an increase in the quality of security devices that is not apparent in the trend data of figure 10. In relation to auto theft, the timing and extent of the spread of electronic immobilizers and central locking coincided well, and this was most evident when legislation mandated immobilizers to meet particular standards (as in Australia and the European Union). In relation to households, however, security devices of various types were already quite prevalent by the early 1990s, and so not only is the increase in prevalence of devices per household more modest but any coincidence with the turning point in burglary rates is less obvious. Tilley et al. hypothesize that the spread of double-glazed windows for home insulation may have been particularly important in promoting the spread of better-quality security in new and replacement windows and doors. The data signature that they develop relates to a change over time in the means of entry to property. The rationale is that some burglaries do not require security to be overcome to gain entry whereas others do. Burglaries in which security had to be overcome were defined as those requiring

- the forcing of locks on doors, the forcing of locks on windows, the removal or breaking of a door panel, and the removal or breaking of a glass window.

Burglaries in which security was not overcome, that is, in which there was another entry method, were identified as those in which entry required

- a door (or window) was already unlocked or open, the burglar had a key, the burglar pushed past the occupant, or false pretenses (deception) were involved.

Trends in these two broad types of entry are shown for completed burglaries with entry in figure 11. In the early stages of the downturn in burglary, between 1996 and 1998, security-related burglaries decline 21 percent compared to 4 percent for burglaries with entry by other means. Over the longer term, between 1994 and 2003, burglaries that were security related declined 59 percent compared to 28 percent for burglaries by other means, consistent with security improvements having induced a diffusion of benefits that also reduced burglaries by other means of entry.

In addition, the decline in burglary via a window had a strong inverse correlation with the spread of double glazing where the whole household was double-glazed (fig. 12). Data were available for 1996–2008, during which time burglaries in which the window was the entry method fell by 70 percent compared to a 20 percent fall in burglaries by another entry method. The study concludes,

The importance of this analysis is, we think, as follows. Counts of

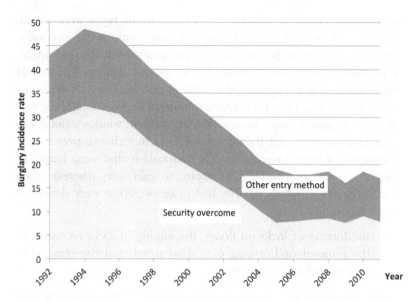

FIG. 11.—Means of entry as an indicator of the role of security: burglary with entry in England and Wales, 1992–2011. Source: Crime Survey for England and Wales.

numbers of security devices do not show changes in the quality of particular devices. Door and window locks in particular are much better than they once were, particularly when combined with double glazing and home insulation efforts. The result is that, in a survey's counts, a better device still just counts as one device. Further, when it is a new-for-old replacement, no change in the count of devices is registered. So, the finding that there is a greater decline in security-breaking burglaries relative to other means of entry is, we suggest, a signature of the improved quality of household security devices. (Tilley, Farrell, and Clarke 2014)

The amount of research linking security to falling burglary rates is less extensive than that for car crime. This likely reflects both the slow pace of research and the possibility that specific household security data may be less readily available as well as the fact that change in the quality of devices is less readily perceived. In addition, household burglary in the United States has been declining far longer than in many countries according to the NCVS. Examining double glazing and household insulation may not transfer to the United States because the housing stock is, on average, somewhat different. In particular,

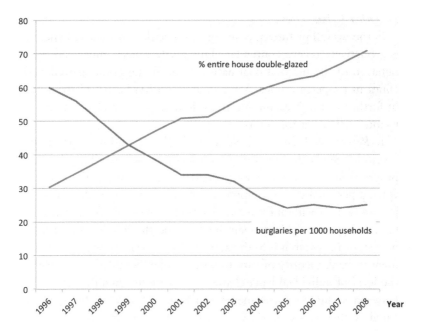

FIG. 12.—Change in levels of double glazing and burglary with entry, 1996–2008. Source: Crime Survey for England and Wales.

wooden-structure housing is far more common across much of North America than in England and Wales. Likewise, the need for insulation and the more extensive adoption of air conditioning offer somewhat different prospects for research. Central air conditioning is increasingly common and could promote the closing and locking of windows and doors. However, air conditioning units located in windows could conceivably afford an opportunity for illegal access, though, at the same time, perhaps less than that of an open window or door. Introduction of planning and building regulations to design out crime in the Netherlands in the late 1990s caused a 25 percent reduction in burglary in the areas with new housing. The benefits were spread across the entire country (diffusion): an estimated 5 percent of the national fall in burglary rates in the following 10 years is attributed to them (Vollaard and van Ours 2011). Hence there is an identifiable need for context-specific research in different countries.

D. Other Crime Types

In the overall picture of crime drop research, the security hypothesis is a relatively recent contender. This partly reflects more recent recognition of the international nature of declining crime as well as declines in property crimes. Yet a foundation has been laid for a range of further research examining the role of security, and situational and routine activity factors more generally.

1. *Robbery and Theft.* Tseloni et al. (2012) outline a preliminary research agenda that incorporates a learning process. They suggest a progression of research from property crime to acquisitive crime involving personal crime components (robbery and theft) that, they conjecture, will provide information to inform the study of violent crime. Certain types of robbery seem likely to be the low hanging fruit for next steps in research into the security hypothesis. If rates of improvement in bank security of various sorts can be identified, particularly at the level of individual bank chains and locations, then the relationship between security improvements and bank robbery might be investigated. Other types of risky facilities offer similar possibilities, and banks are just one for which good data may well be available. Were different types of bank security introduced at different branches at different times, for example, then this ought to facilitate the development of data signatures that parse out the security-robbery relationship. As with cars, if newer banks have better designs and security, then they ought to have lower crime rates. Security measures that are independent of capital infrastructure, such as exploding dye in money bags given to robbers, would be expected to produce particular data signatures, including perhaps an effect on the rate of repeat robberies at the same locations (Matthews, Pease, and Pease [2001] identify repeat bank robbery as extensive). Bank robbery is one obvious research possibility, but other types of risky facilities experiencing robbery or other crime types may offer other good prospects.

2. *Shoplifting.* Theft from stores, termed shoplifting, is a volume crime. It typically receives less attention than many crime types because it is not captured in victim surveys of the population (only in surveys of businesses) and because it is less serious, per average offense, than many crime types.

Prolific and violent offenders are also frequent thieves (and more evidence to that effect is offered in the next section of this essay). This means that shoplifting may, alongside car theft, be a keystone that,

once removed, leads to broader declines in other crime types. Purchasing of goods in stores used to take place primarily over the counter,
with store owners passing each item to the customer. This practice
changed largely in the post–World War II period, when it became
apparent that removing the counter and allowing customers to interact
with the products would increase sales. The opportunity, temptation,
and impulse purchases that access to goods on sale provided also provided major new crime opportunities for theft, and so shoplifting increased rapidly, likely promoted by larger stores and superstores with
reduced surveillance and increased anonymity as well as a proliferation
in consumer products that are suitable for theft (Tilley 2010). Consequent upon this wave of shoplifting, it has been suggested that

> bit by bit, countermeasures were introduced: staff were trained to
> be vigilant, cash tills were relocated to give better sight-lines down
> the aisles, window displays were changed to expose vulnerable cor-
> ners to glancing passers-by, mirrors and CCTV were introduced,
> store detectives and exit guards were recruited, high-value items
> were tethered or locked behind glass, dummy goods or packaging
> were put on display without the costly product inside, and a whole
> ingenious new industry was spawned to provide lockable cabinets,
> tell-tale markers, sensors, alarms, spider wraps, security gates,
> radio-frequency tags and extended families of visible deterrents.
> . . . Just as the removal of shop counters had led to a crime epi-
> demic, so restoring a semblance of security alleviated it. Shoplift-
> ing still accounts for almost half of all known commercial crime,
> but surveys suggest it fell 60 per cent in the decade up to 2012.
> (Ross 2013, chap. 2, section on "Shoplifting")

A report on victimization surveys of businesses in England and Wales
that compared crime rates in 2002 to those in 2012 found,

> In both 2002 and 2012, the crime type most frequently experi-
> enced by wholesale and retail premises was theft by customers,
> with 11.5 million of this type of incidents estimated in 2002 and
> 4.1 million in 2012. In both years, this was followed by theft by
> unknown persons, with 3.2 million incidents in 2002 and 1.8 mil-
> lion in 2012. . . . In addition, the proportion of wholesale and re-
> tail premises experiencing theft by customers (the crime most
> commonly experienced by wholesalers and retailers) fell from 43

per cent to 21 per cent between the 2002 and 2012 CVS [Commercial Victimisation Survey]. (Home Office 2013, p. 14)

Hence the incidence of shoplifting (theft by customers) fell 64 percent, the incidence of theft by unknown persons fell 44 percent, and the prevalence of shoplifting fell 51 percent across the decade. The time period covered here does not go back to the 1990s, when many other crimes were falling, but an earlier version of the survey had been conducted in 1994. The comparison of that survey with the 2002 survey identified a decline in crime, though not as steep as the decline that ensued, and concluded that "the findings are broadly consistent with trends in crime against individuals" (Taylor 2004, p. 2). Hence while only a small segment of the relevant research has been addressed here, it identifies a potentially fruitful line of inquiry for further research into the security hypothesis.

3. *Homicide.* Homicide appears to represent a challenge. While there is a body of research into homicide and the crime drop (e.g., Rosenfeld 2000), there is not, to our knowledge, a study of the widespread falls in homicide that focuses on its situational aspects. This, we suggest, may be a worthy avenue of inquiry.[6] From the perspective of crime opportunity theory, other changes in the opportunity structure in addition to security could influence homicide. Here there is a potential overlap with what are termed the debut crime hypothesis and the keystone hypothesis, described next.

E. The Keystone and Debut Crime Hypotheses

1. *Keystones and Criminal Careers.* Many types of crime are interrelated. Security improvements bringing dramatic reductions in volume crimes, including car crime and household property crimes, might reasonably be expected to have knock-on effects on other types of crime. There is an analogy with the removal of the keystone from an arch wherein the other stones tumble, such that this relationship has been termed the keystone hypothesis (Farrell et al. 2008, 2010). Reductions in car theft deny use of the road to offenders who steal vehicles for the commission of other types of crime. Stolen cars are instrumental in many burglaries, in which they are used for transportation. Cars stolen for transportation are relocating offenders who, cet-

---

[6] This suggestion owes a debt to discussions with Neil Boyd.

eris paribus, have a greater than average likelihood of being involved in further crimes, including violence, on arrival. Fencing of stolen goods is likely to decline when burglary is harder to commit and stolen transportation vehicles are less readily obtained. Shrunken stolen goods markets would likely incur lower rates of disputes, robberies, and assaults. Where stolen cars were used either to drive to drug markets or to provide a supply, this becomes increasingly difficult. Without a stolen vehicle, it may be more difficult to start and continue a gang feud. Retributive violence including drive-by shootings may be delayed and, where delayed, may be less likely overall, as is the case when suicide is delayed (Lester 2012). Inducing delay may be a technique of situational crime prevention that warrants further study.

Criminal career research provides a platform for investigating the keystone hypothesis. Offending careers are typically divided into the majority that are short and limited to adolescents and those that are long or life course persistent (Moffitt 1993). The "keystone" element of the hypothesis rests partly on the relationship between the commission of different types of crime for which career specialism and generalism might be used as a proxy. There is strong evidence that most offenders are versatile, or generalists, though there is some specialization. Most crime is property crime, not violence, and so the careers of most life course offenders tend to be dominated by property crime despite the fact that there can be some violence specialization. Farrington (1998) observed that "only a small proportion of offenses in criminal careers are violent: 15 percent up to age 40 in the Cambridge Study . . . 9 percent up to age thirty in the first Philadelphia age cohort study . . . and 5 percent up to age twenty-five in the Stockholm Project Metropolitan" (p. 435). While a more recent review indicates that "in a long-term analysis of specialization using conviction records from the South London male cohort through age 40, Piquero et al. (2007) found little evidence of specialization in violence and concluded that the strongest predictor of a violent conviction over the course of a criminal career was the number of convictions. More frequent offenders had a higher likelihood of conviction for a violent crime" (Piquero et al. 2014, p. 14). That review also suggests that serious theft offenders are more likely to be violent offenders, potentially linking reductions in acquisitive crimes to broader crime declines.

If property crime dominates the portfolio of most offenders, and it is property crime on which improved security has acted most dramat-

ically, then disrupting this primary component of the offending portfolio may have disrupted the less frequently committed, and probably
related, violent offenses. In particular, violence that is committed as an
instrumental or supporting part of property crime, as an inadvertent
consequence of involvement in property crime, or as the result of involvement with criminal peers (victimization rates among offenders being inordinately high; Lauritsen and Laub 2007) is likely to decrease
as natural wastage when the property crime keystone is removed. More
broadly, this suggests that preventing property crime may be the best
way to prevent violent crime. The review by Piquero et al. further
notes that "the analyses of specialization in criminal careers suggest
that there is little specific concentration within offense types among
most offenders. This overall conclusion holds with respect to different
samples, measures of offending (*including the incorrect presumption of
specialization among sex offenders*; Zimring et al., 2008, 2009), and time
periods" (Piquero et al. 2014, p. 15; emphasis added). The "incorrect
presumption of specialization among sex offenders" is particularly important in the present context. It potentially provides the missing link
that could explain why sexual victimization may have declined as a
result of security-induced reductions in property crime. From here it
is a small conceptual leap to suggest that child abuse and domestic
violence may also have declined as a beneficial knock-on effect of the
drop in property crime.

2. *Debuts and Legacies.* Among first-conviction offense types, "the
crime most readily identifiable as a strategic offence is vehicle theft,
but non-vehicle thefts and robberies (including mugging) are also predictive of a long and serious subsequent career in delinquency" (Svensson 2002, p. 395). More recently, Owen and Cooper (2013) found that
"offenders who committed robbery or vehicle theft as their debut offence were at the greatest risk of becoming chronic offenders" (p. 3).
Hence vehicle theft is a strategic debut crime offense, and preventing
vehicle theft may be a means of disrupting the onset of criminal careers, which in turn might be expected to reduce the frequency and
seriousness of offending. This is termed the debut crime hypothesis.
Cook and Laub (2002) observed that the prior crime peaks were an
"epidemic of youth violence," and Butts (2000) observed that the crime
drop in the United States has been experienced disproportionately as
a decline in adolescence-limited offending. This is shown in figures 13
and 14 as age-specific offense rates for aggregate groups of violent

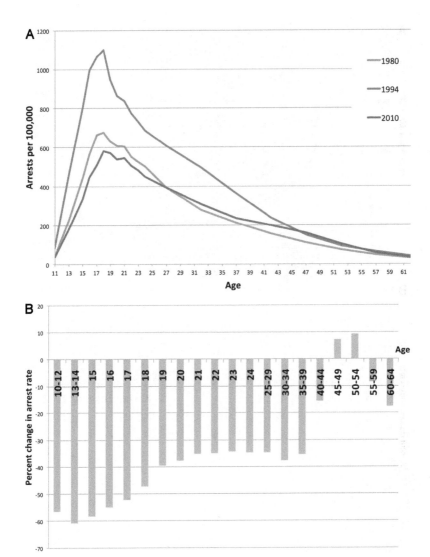

FIG. 13.—*A*, Violent crime age-specific arrest rates. *B*, Percentage change in violent crime arrest rates, 1994–2010. Source: Bureau of Justice Statisics.

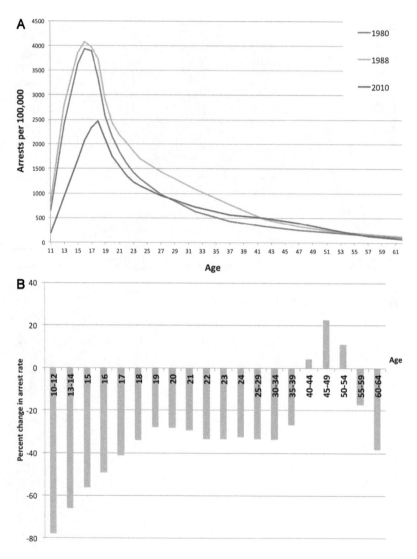

FIG. 14.—*A*, Property crime age-specific arrest rates. *B*, Percentage change in property crime arrest rates, 1988–2010. Source: Bureau of Justice Statisics.

crime and property crime in the United States, 1980–2010. Each of the figures contains two panels, of which the first shows a set of age-crime curves and the second the percentage change in arrest rates between the crime peak (measured by the UCR) and 2010. The change over time in the age-crime curves is consistent with the security hypothesis. That is, we suggest that the disproportionate drop in adolescence-limited offending is consistent with an interpretation that the number of crime opportunities declined, reducing offending among the less experienced and those less entrenched in a criminal career. This squares well with the fact that reductions in car theft occurred disproportionately as a reduction in temporary theft for joyriding and transportation.

The comparative age-crime curves demonstrate a decline in offending rates in most age groups by 2010, with the exception of those offenders aged in their 40s. This is shown in the second panel of each figure when the bars cross from negative to positive at the right-hand side or less obviously in each first panel when the age-crime curves cross to the right-hand side. That is, in 2010 the per capita rate of offending among those in their 40s is, in contrast to other age groups, higher than when crime was at its peak. Yet these offenders, close to age 40 by 2010, were at the peak offending ages when crime rates were highest 20 years previously. We interpret the higher offending rates among offenders in their 40s as a legacy of the plentiful crime opportunities of the late 1980s when these offenders learned their trade (Farrell, Laycock, and Tilley, n.d.). If plentiful crime opportunities of the 1980s increased the number of offenders who continued into lengthy criminal careers, this suggests that decisions to embark on criminal careers are significantly influenced by situational factors and that a substantial proportion of life course–persistent offenders could be swing voters who would be deterred were easy crime opportunities unavailable when they were adolescents.

3. *Discussion.* This section reviewed evidence that improvements in security reduced crime opportunities and caused the crime drop. The evidence that improved security caused some crimes to fall, particularly car theft, is strong, while evidence relating to other types of property crime is mounting.

Further research into the keystone and debut crime hypotheses that links the declines in violent crime to those of property crime might be pursued with cautious optimism. Most criminal careers are nonspecialist and dominated by property crime, while some violent crime is undertaken as an endeavor to support property crime, and the trends in age-specific arrest rates appear consistent with the security hypothesis. Together these facts suggest that some further exploration of this connection is warranted. However, this must be tempered by, and take account of, the empirical anomalies identified earlier including the later decline in car theft in Canada, the later decline in homicide in the United Kingdom, and the apparently significant variation in the decline across crime types in other countries.

V. Conclusions

There has been significant progress in crime drop research. The quest to identify the causes of the dramatic decline in crime has spurred a range of competing hypotheses, theory development and theory testing, innovative approaches, and methodologies. Hence it is proving an unusually productive research question. In that context it is surprising that there was perhaps never really the same drive among criminologists to explain the prior crime increases, where even the compelling routine activities approach seems to remain both underresearched and underappreciated. The routine activities approach is, we suggest, compatible with the security hypothesis, the main difference being that crime increases were argued to be due to inadvertent changes in the opportunity structure whereas security is deliberate.

Many influential criminological theories have not gotten out of the starting blocks when it comes to explaining the crime drop. This observation has become more apparent as the crime drop persisted through recession and the global economic downturn that began in 2008–9. Thus the long-term benefit to criminological theory of crime drop research should be extensive, requiring substantial revision to many theory texts.

Two key changes in the orientation of crime drop research emerged largely in its second decade that are characterized here as phase 2 research. The first was recognition that the crime drop has been international in nature, affecting many advanced countries in ways similar though far from identical to the United States. The second has been recognition of the importance of property crime. Within the United States, the drop in violence followed that in auto theft and seems to continue to track it remarkably closely. The available evidence suggests that the drop in auto theft in different countries coincided with the growth of vastly improved vehicle security, particularly high-quality electronic immobilizers and central deadlocking.

Blumstein and Wallman's *The Crime Drop in America* (2000) is rightly considered a landmark. It achieved sufficient recognition that a second edition appeared only 6 years later—somewhat unusual for an academic work that is not a textbook. Yet it has not dated well in the subsequent phase 2 decade of crime drop research, and much of its content seems now to be largely of historical value, with hindsight suggesting that its focus on violence and a single country was rather too narrow.

Seventeen explanations for the international crime drop from the academic literature were examined. In addition to an examination of the literature relating to each, some extra light was shed on them by subjecting them each to four evidence-based tests. While hindsight is 20/20, a surprising number of hypotheses now appear rather parochial and cannot explain the crime drop in more than one country, failing the cross-national test. Likewise, some hypotheses were inconsistent with what seems to be the basic fact that crime had previously been increasing for several decades. Most were irreconcilable with the fact that some crimes have increased at the time that many crimes have decreased, and few hypotheses could account for the variation between countries and crime types in the timing and trajectory of the crime drop. Sixteen of the 17 hypotheses failed at least one of the four tests, and most failed at least two.

The evidence examined here identifies the security hypothesis as the most promising explanation for crime drops. The framework of crime opportunity theory and routine activity theory in which it nestles provides flexibility in terms of addressing different types of crimes in different contexts. It is worth speculating on why security, and the theoretical areas of crime opportunity theory, principally rational choice and routine activities, seem to have featured little in earlier debates. Perhaps it was how the debate initially focused on violence, perhaps it was that rational choice and routine activities theories are not driven as much by an underlying ideology as many others, or perhaps it is the manner in which they tend to frame offenders as typically less able decision makers who are relatively easily influenced by their surrounding environment.

The main policy implications of the security hypothesis are straightforward. Architects, urban planners, product designers, and others should take account of crime in their blueprints. Governments should encourage this by all appropriate means, including regulation where necessary, but perhaps preferably through market-based incentives (Farrell and Roman 2006; Eck and Eck 2012; Tilley 2012). Problem solving and situational crime prevention would appear to offer the most viable approach to e-crime and to new crimes that emerge in the future. Policing might adapt to reemphasize crime prevention as its primary mission, using problem-solving approaches to modify the crime opportunity structure and playing a role in nudging business owners, place managers, and others into reducing their emissions of easy crime opportunities.

Further research into the security hypothesis is required, and several possible avenues have been suggested here. At worst it seems likely to prove a good explanation for the drop in car theft and other property crimes while providing insight for continued pursuit of explanations for violence. For the present authors it is a rather positive hypothesis insofar as it suggests that the solution to most crime lies in the hands of governments, and it provides a methodology—that of a problem-solving situational crime prevention—to achieve continued reductions in crime in the future. The best security is innocuous, liberating, and empowering—witness the electronic vehicle immobilizer—and offers no threat but many benefits to democratic society.

REFERENCES

Aebi, Marcelo F., and Antonia Linde. 2012. "Crime Trends in Western Europe According to Official Statistics from 1990 to 2007." In *The International Crime Drop: New Directions in Research*, edited by Jan van Dijk, Andromachi Tseloni, and Graham Farrell. Basingstoke, UK: Palgrave Macmillan.
Ayres, Ian, and Steven Levitt. 1998. "Measuring Positive Externalities from Unobservable Victim Precaution: An Empirical Analysis of Lojack." *Quarterly Journal of Economics* 113:43–77.
Blumstein, Alfred, and Richard Rosenfeld. 2008. "Factors Contributing to U.S. Crime Trends." In *Understanding Crime Trends: Workshop Report*. National Research Council Committee on Understanding Crime Trends, Committee on Law and Justice, Division of Behavioral and Social Sciences and Education. Washington, DC: National Academies Press.

Blumstein, Alfred, and Joel Wallman, eds. 2000. *The Crime Drop in America*. New York: Cambridge University Press.

Bowling, Ben. 1999. "The Rise and Fall of New York Murder: Zero Tolerance or Crack's Decline?" *British Journal of Criminology* 39(4):531–54.

Braga, Anthony A., Andrew V. Papachristos, and David M. Hureau. 2012. "The Effects of Hot Spot Policing on Crime: An Updated Systematic Review and Meta-Analysis." *Justice Quarterly* 31(4):633–63.

Britton, Andrew, Chris Kershaw, Sarah Osborne, and Kevin Smith. 2012. "Underlying Patterns within the England and Wales Crime Drop." In *The International Crime Drop: New Directions in Research*, edited by Jan van Dijk, Andromachi Tseloni, and Graham Farrell. Basingstoke, UK: Palgrave Macmillan.

Brown, Rick. 2004. "The Effectiveness of Electronic Immobilization: Changing Patterns of Temporary and Permanent Vehicle Theft." In *Understanding and Preventing Car Theft*, edited by Michael G. Maxfield and Ronald V. Clarke. Crime Prevention Studies, vol. 17. Monsey, NY: Criminal Justice Press.

———. 2013. "Reviewing the Effectiveness of Electronic Vehicle Immobilisation: Evidence from Four Countries." *Security Journal* 1–25. DOI:10.1057/sj.2012.55.

Brown, Rick, and Nerys Thomas. 2003. "Aging Vehicles: Evidence of the Effectiveness of New Car Security from the Home Office Car Theft Index." *Security Journal* 16:45–54.

Butts, Jeffrey A. 2000. *Youth Crime Drop*. Washington, DC: Urban Institute, Justice Policy Center.

Clarke, Ronald V., and Patricia M. Harris. 1992. "Auto Theft and Its Prevention." In *Crime and Justice: A Review of Research*, vol. 16, edited by Michael Tonry. Chicago: University of Chicago Press.

Clarke, Ronald V., and Graeme R. Newman. 2006. *Outsmarting the Terrorists*. Westport, CT: Praeger.

Cohen, Lawrence E., and Marcus Felson. 1979. "Social Change and Crime Rate Trends: A Routine Activity Approach." *American Sociological Review* 44:588–608.

Cook, Philip J., and John H. Laub. 2002. "After the Epidemic: Recent Trends in Youth Violence in the United States." In *Crime and Justice: A Review of Research*, vol. 29, edited by Michael Tonry. Chicago: University of Chicago Press.

Curman, Andrea S. N., Martin A. Andresen, and Paul J. Brantingham. 2014. "Crime and Place: A Longitudinal Examination of Street Segments in Vancouver, B.C." *Journal of Quantitative Criminology*, forthcoming. DOI 10.1007/s10940-014-9228-3.

Dills, Angela K., Jeffrey A. Miron, and Garrett Summers. 2008. "What Do Economists Know about Crime?" NBER Working Paper no. 13759. Cambridge, MA: National Bureau of Economic Research.

Donohue, John J., III, and Steven D. Levitt. 2001. "The Impact of Legalized Abortion on Crime." *Quarterly Journal of Economics* 116(2):379–420.

Eck, John E., and Emily B. Eck. 2012. "Crime Place and Pollution: Expanding Crime Reduction Options through a Regulatory Approach." *Criminology and Public Policy* 11(2):281–316.

Eck, John E., and Tamara Madensen. 2009. "Using Signatures of Opportunity Structures to Examine Mechanisms in Crime Prevention Evaluations." In *Evaluating Crime Prevention Initiatives*, edited by J. Knutsson and Nick Tilley. Monsey, NY: Criminal Justice Press.

Eck, John E., and E. Maguire. 2000. "Have Changes in Policing Reduced Violent Crime?" In *The Crime Drop in America*, edited by Alfred Blumstein and Joel Wallman. New York: Cambridge University Press.

Eisner, Manuel. 2008. "Modernity Strikes Back? A Historical Perspective on the Latest Increase in Interpersonal Violence (1960–1990)." *International Journal of Conflict and Violence* 2(2):289–316.

Elias, Norbert. 2000. *The Civilizing Process: Sociogenetic and Psychogenetic Investigations*. Oxford: Blackwell. (Originally published 1939.)

Farrell, Graham. 2013. "Five Tests for a Theory of the Crime Drop." *Crime Science* 2(5):1–8.

Farrell, Graham, and Paul J. Brantingham. 2013. "The Crime Drop and the General Social Survey." *Canadian Public Policy* 34(4):559–80.

Farrell, Graham, Gloria Laycock, and Nick Tilley. n.d. "Debuts and Legacies: The Crime Drop and the Role of Adolescence-Limited and Persistent Offending." Unpublished manuscript. School of Criminology, Simon Fraser University.

Farrell, Graham, and Ken Pease. 2014. "Repeat Victimization." In *Encyclopedia of Criminology and Criminal Justice*, edited by G. Bruinsma and D. Weisburd. New York: Springer-Verlag.

Farrell, Graham, and John Roman. 2006. "Crime as Pollution: Proposal for Market-Based Incentives to Reduce Crime Externalities." In *Crime Reduction and the Law*, edited by M. R. Stephens and K. Moss. London: Routledge.

Farrell, Graham, Nick Tilley, Andromachi Tseloni, and Jen Mailley. 2008. "The Crime Drop and the Security Hypothesis." *British Society of Criminology Newsletter* 62:17–21.

———. 2010. "Explaining and Sustaining the Crime Drop: Exploring the Role of Opportunity-Related Theories." *Crime Prevention and Community Safety: An International Journal* 12:24–41.

Farrell, Graham, Andromachi Tseloni, Jen Mailley, and Nick Tilley. 2011. "The Crime Drop and the Security Hypothesis." *Journal of Research in Crime and Delinquency* 48(2):147–75.

Farrell, Graham, Andromachi Tseloni, and Nick Tilley. 2011. "The Effectiveness of Car Security Devices and Their Role in the Crime Drop." *Criminology and Criminal Justice* 11(1):21–35.

Farrington, David P. 1998. "Predictors, Causes, and Correlates of Male Youth Violence." In *Youth Violence*, edited by Michael Tonry and Mark H. Moore. Vol. 24 of *Crime and Justice: A Review of Research*, edited by Michael Tonry. Chicago: University of Chicago Press.

Farrington, David P., Patrick A. Langan, and Michael Tonry, eds. 2004. *Cross-*

National Studies in Crime and Justice. Washington, DC: Bureau of Justice Statistics.

Finkelhor, David, and Lisa M. Jones. 2004. *Explanations for the Decline in Child Sexual Abuse Cases.* Washington, DC: Office of Juvenile Justice and Delinquency Prevention.

———. 2006. "Why Have Child Maltreatment and Child Victimization Declined?" *Journal of Social Issues* 62(4):685–716.

———. 2012. "Have Sexual and Physical Abuse Declined since the 1990s?" Durham: University of New Hampshire, Crimes against Children Research Center.

Fox, James A. 2000. "Demographics and U.S. Homicide." In *The Crime Drop in America,* edited by Alfred Blumstein and Joel Wallman. New York: Cambridge University Press.

Fujita, Shuryo, and Michael Maxfield. 2012. "Security and the Drop in Car Theft in the United States." In *The International Crime Drop: New Directions in Research,* edited by Jan van Dijk, Andromachi Tseloni, and Graham Farrell. Basingstoke, UK: Palgrave Macmillan.

Greenspan, E., and A. N. Doob. 2011. "Crunch the Numbers: Crime Rates Are Going Down." *Globe and Mail,* February 22.

Grove, Louise E., Graham Farrell, David P. Farrington, and Shane D. Johnson. 2012. *Preventing Repeat Victimization: A Systematic Review.* Stockholm: Swedish National Council for Crime Prevention.

Guerette, Rob T., and Kate J. Bowers. 2009. "Assessing the Extent of Crime Displacement and Diffusion of Benefits: A Review of Situational Crime Prevention Evaluations." *Criminology* 47(4):1331–68.

Hardison Walters, Jennifer, Andrew Moore, Marcus Berzofsky, and Lynn Langton. 2013. *Household Burglary, 1994–2011.* Report NCJ 241754. Washington, DC: Bureau of Justice Statistics.

Home Office. 2013. *Crime against Businesses: Headline Findings from the 2012 Commercial Victimisation Survey.* London: Home Office.

Houghton, George. 1992. *Car Theft in England and Wales: The Home Office Car Theft Index.* Crime Prevention Unit Paper 33. London: Home Office.

Ignatans, Dainis, and Ken Pease. Forthcoming. "Distributive Justice and the Crime Drop." In *Routine Activities and the Criminal Act,* edited by Martin A. Andresen and Graham Farrell. New York: Palgrave Macmillan.

Joyce, Theodore J. 2009. "Abortion and Crime: A Review." NBER Working paper no. 15098. Cambridge, MA: National Bureau of Economic Research.

———. 2011. "Abortion and Crime: A Review." In *Handbook on the Economics of Crime,* edited by B. L. Benson and P. R. Zimmerman. Cheltenham, UK: Elgar.

Kahane, L. H., D. Paton, and R. Simmons. 2008. "The Abortion-Crime Link: Evidence from England and Wales." *Economica* 75:1–21.

Kangaspunta, Kristiina, and Ineke Haen Marshall. 2012. "Trends in Violence against Women: Some Good News and Some Bad News." In *The International Crime Drop: New Directions in Research,* edited by Jan van Dijk, Andromachi Tseloni, and Graham Farrell. Basingstoke, UK: Palgrave Macmillan.

Kelling, George L., and William H. Sousa. 2001. *Do Police Matter? An Analysis of the Impact of New York City's Police Reforms*. New York: Manhattan Institute.

Killias, Martin, and Bruno Lanfranconi. 2012. "The Crime Drop Discourse— or the Illusion of Uniform Continental Trends: Switzerland as a Contrasting Case." In *The International Crime Drop: New Directions in Research*, edited by Jan van Dijk, Andromachi Tseloni, and Graham Farrell. Basingstoke, UK: Palgrave Macmillan.

Klick, J., J. MacDonald, and T. Stratmann. 2012. "Mobile Phones and Crime Deterrence: An Underappreciated Link." Research paper no. 12-33. Philadelphia: University of Pennsylvania Law School, Institute for Law and Economics.

Kriven, S., and E. Ziersch. 2007. "New Car Security and Shifting Vehicle Theft Patterns in Australia." *Security Journal* 20:111–22.

LaFree, Gary. 1998. "Social Institutions and the Crime 'Bust' of the 1990s." *Journal of Criminal Law and Criminology* 88(4):1325–68.

———. 1999. "Declining Violent Crime Rates in the 1990s: Predicting Crime Booms and Busts." *Annual Review of Sociology* 25:145–68.

Lauritsen, Janet L., and John H. Laub. 2007. "Understanding the Link between Victimization and Offending: New Reflections on an Old Idea." In *Surveying Crime in the 21st Century*, edited by M. Hough and Michael G. Maxfield. Monsey, NY: Criminal Justice Press.

Laycock, Gloria. 2004. "The U.K. Car Theft Index: An Example of Government Leverage." In *Understanding and Preventing Car Theft*, edited by Michael G. Maxfield and Ronald V. Clarke. Crime Prevention Studies, vol. 17. Monsey, NY: Criminal Justice Press.

Lester, David. 2012. "Suicide and Opportunity: Implications for the Rationality of Suicide." In *The Reasoning Criminologist*, edited by Nick Tilley and Graham Farrell. New York: Routledge.

Levitt, Steven D. 2004. "Understanding Why Crime Fell in the 1990s: Four Factors That Explain the Decline and Six That Do Not." *Journal of Economic Perspectives* 18(1):163–90.

Lin, Ming-Jen. 2009. "More Police, Less Crime: Evidence from U.S. State Data." *International Review of Law and Economics* 29:73–80.

Lowe, L. 2014. "U.S. Smartphone Thefts Doubled Last Year: How to Protect your Phone." *Parade*, April 18. http://parade.condenast.com/281418/linz lowe/u-s-smartphone-thefts-doubled-last-year-how-to-protect-your-phone/.

Martinez, Ramiro, and Kimberly B. Mehlman-Orozco. 2013. "Hispanic Immigration and Crime." In *Oxford Handbook of Ethnicity, Crime, and Immigration*, edited by Michael Tonry and Sandra Bucerius. Oxford: Oxford University Press.

Matthews, Roger, Catherine Pease, and Ken Pease. 2001. "Repeated Bank Robbery: Themes and Variation." In *Repeat Victimization*, edited by Graham Farrell and Ken Pease. Monsey, NY: Criminal Justice Press.

Mayhew, Pat. 2012. "The Case of Australia and New Zealand." In *The International Crime Drop: New Directions in Research*, edited by Jan van Dijk, Andromachi Tseloni, and Graham Farrell. Basingstoke, UK: Palgrave Macmillan.

Mayhew, Pat, and Victoria Harrington. 2001. *Mobile Phone Theft*. London: Home Office.

Mielke, Howard W., and Sammy Zahran. 2012. "The Urban Rise and Fall of Air Lead (Pb) and the Latent Surge and Retreat of Societal Violence." *Environment International* 43:48–55.

Mishra, Sandeep, and Martin Lalumiere. 2009. "Is the Crime Drop of the 1990s in Canada and the USA Associated with a General Decline in Risky and Health-Related Behavior?" *Social Science and Medicine* 68:39–48.

Moffitt, Terrie E. 1993. "Adolescence-Limited and Life-Course Persistent Anti-social Behavior: A Developmental Taxonomy." *Psychological Review* 100(4):674–701.

Morgan, Frank, and Joseph Clare. 2007. *Household Burglary Trends in Western Australia*. Perth: University of Western Australia, Crime Research Centre.

Morgan, Nick. 2014. *The Heroin Epidemic of the 1980s and 90s and Its Effect on Crime Trends—Then and Now*. Home Office Research Study 79. London: Home Office.

National Research Council. 2014. *The Growth of Incarceration in the United States: Exploring Causes and Consequences*. Washington, DC: National Academies Press.

Nevin, Rick. 2000. "How Lead Exposure Relates to Temporal Changes in IQ, Violent Crime, and Unwed Pregnancy." *Environmental Research Section* 83: 1–22. DOI:10.1006/enrs.1999.4045.

———. 2007. "Understanding International Crime Trends: The Legacy of Preschool Lead Exposure." *Environmental Research* 104:315–36.

Office of National Statistics. 2013. *Crime in England and Wales, Year Ending December 2012*. Newport, Wales: ONS.

———. 2014. *Crime in England and Wales, Year Ending September 2013*. Newport, Wales: ONS.

Orrick, Erin A., and Alex R. Piquero. 2013. "Were Cell Phones Associated with Lower Crime in the 1990s and 2000s?" *Journal of Crime and Justice*. DOI:10.1080/0735648X.2013.864570.

Ouimet, Marc. 2002. "Explaining the American and Canadian Crime 'Drop' in the 1990s." *Canadian Journal of Criminology and Criminal Justice* 44(1):33–50.

Owen, Natalie, and Christine Cooper. 2013. *The Start of a Criminal Career: Does the Type of Debut Offence Predict Future Offending?* London: Home Office.

Pinker, Steven. 2011. *The Better Angels of Our Nature: Why Violence Has Declined*. New York: Viking.

Piquero, Alex R., David Hawkins, Lila Kazemian, and David Petechuk. 2014. *Bulletin 2: Criminal Career Patterns*. Washington, DC: Office of Juvenile Justice and Delinquency Prevention.

Rand, Michael R., James P. Lynch, and David Cantor. 1997. *Criminal Victim-*

ization, 1973–93. Report NCJ-163069. Washington, DC: Bureau of Justice Statistics.

Reyes, Jessica W. 2007. "Environmental Policy as Social Policy? The Impact of Childhood Lead Exposure on Crime." NBER Working Paper no. 13097. Cambridge, MA: National Bureau of Economic Research.

———. 2012. "Lead Exposure and Behavior: Effects on Antisocial and Risky Behavior among Children and Adolescents." Working paper (February). Amherst, MA: Amherst College.

Roman, John, and Aaron Chalfin. 2007. *Is There an iCrime Wave?* Washington, DC: Urban Institute, Justice Policy Center.

Rosenfeld, Richard. 2000. "Patterns in Adult Homicide: 1980–1995." In *The Crime Drop in America*, edited by Alfred Blumstein and Joel Wallman. New York: Cambridge University Press.

———. 2009. "Crime Is the Problem: Homicide, Acquisitive Crime, and Economic Conditions." *Journal of Quantitative Criminology* 25:287–306.

———. 2013. "Crime and Inflation in Cross-National Perspective." Paper presented to the Modern Law Review seminar, University of Sheffield.

Rosenfeld, Richard, and Steven F. Messner. 2009. "The Crime Drop in Comparative Perspective: The Impact of the Economy and Imprisonment on American and European Burglary Rates." *British Journal of Sociology* 60:445–71.

Ross, Nick. 2013. *Crime: How to Solve It—and Why So Much of What We're Told Is Wrong*. London: Biteback. Kindle ed.

Sampson, Robert J. 2006. "Open Doors Don't Invite Criminals." *New York Times*, March 11.

———. 2008. "Rethinking Crime and Immigration." *Contexts* 7(1):28–33.

Spelman, William. 2000. "The Limited Importance of Prison Expansion." In *The Crime Drop in America*, edited by Alfred Blumstein and Joel Wallman. New York: Cambridge University Press.

Stowell, Jacob I., Steven F. Messner, Kelly F. McGeever, and Lawrence E. Raffalovich. 2009. "Immigration and the Recent Violent Crime Drop in the United States: A Pooled, Cross-Sectional Time-Series Analysis of Metropolitan Areas." *Criminology* 47(3):889–929.

Stretesky, Paul B., and Michael J. Lynch. 2001. "The Relationship between Lead Exposure and Homicide." *Archives of Pediatric Adolescent Medicine* 155:579–82.

———. 2004. "The Relationship between Lead and Crime." *Journal of Health and Social Behavior* 45(2):214–29.

Svensson, Robert. 2002. "Strategic Offences in the Criminal Career Context." *British Journal of Criminology* 42:395–411.

Taylor, Joanne. 2004. *Crime against Retail and Manufacturing Premises: Findings from the 2002 Commercial Victimisation Survey*. London: Home Office.

Thorpe, Katherine. 2007. "Multiple and Repeat Victimization." In *Crime in England and Wales, 2006/07*, supp. vol. 1, *Attitudes, Perceptions and Risks of Crime*, edited by K. Jansson, S. Budd, J. Lovbakke, S. Moley, and K. Thorpe. Home Office Statistical Bulletin 19/07. London: Home Office.

Tilley, Nick. 2010. "Shoplifting." In *Handbook on Crime*, edited by Fiona Brookman, Mike Maguire, Harriet Pierpoint, and Trevor Bennett. Cullompton, Devon, UK: Willan.

———. 2012. "Crime Reduction: Responsibility, Regulation, and Research." *Criminology and Public Policy* 11(2):361–78.

Tilley, Nick, Graham Farrell, and Ronald V. Clarke. 2014. "Target Suitability and the Crime Drop." In *The Criminal Act: The Role and Influence of Routine Activity Theory*, edited by Martin Andresen and Graham Farrell. London: Palgrave Macmillan.

Truman, J. L., and M. Planty. 2012. *Criminal Victimization, 2011*. Washington, DC: US Department of Justice, Office of Justice Programs, Bureau of Justice Statistics.

Tseloni, Andromachi, Graham Farrell, Nick Tilley, Louise Grove, Rebecca Thompson, and Laura Garius. 2012. "Towards a Comprehensive Research Plan on Opportunity Theory and the Crime Falls." In *The International Crime Drop: New Directions in Research*, edited by Jan van Dijk, Andromachi Tseloni, and Graham Farrell. Basingstoke, UK: Palgrave Macmillan.

Tseloni, Andromachi, Rebecca Thompson, Louise E. Grove, Nick Tilley, and Graham Farrell. 2014. "The Effectiveness of Burglary Security Devices." *Security Journal*. DOI:10.1057/sj.2014.30.

van Dijk, Jan J. M. 2006. "What Goes Up, Comes Down: Explaining the Falling Crime Rates." *Criminology in Europe—Newsletter of the European Society of Criminology* 5(3):3,17–18.

———. 2013. "The International Crime Victims Survey 1988–2010: Latest Results and Prospects." *Newsletter of the European Society of Criminology*, April 12. http://www3.unil.ch/wpmu/icvs/category/uncategorized/.

van Dijk, Jan J. M., R. Manchin, J. van Kesteren, S. Nevala, and G. Hideg. 2007. "The Burden of Crime in the EU." In *Research Report: A Comparative Analysis of the European Survey of Crime and Safety*. EU ICS, 2005. Brussels: Gallup Europe.

van Dijk, Jan, and Andromachi Tseloni. 2012. "Global Overview: International Trends in Victimization and Recorded Crime." In *The International Crime Drop: New Directions in Research*, edited by Jan van Dijk, Andromachi Tseloni, and Graham Farrell. Basingstoke, UK: Palgrave Macmillan.

van Ours, J. C., and B. Vollaard. 2013. "The Engine Immobilizer: A Nonstarter for Car Thieves." CESifo Working Paper: Public Choice no. 4092. Munich: University of Munich, Centre for Economic Studies and Ifo Institute.

Vollaard, B. A., and J. C. van Ours. 2011. "Does Regulation of Built-in Security Reduce Crime? Evidence from a Natural Experiment." *Economic Journal* 121: 485–504.

Webb, Barry. 2005. "Preventing Vehicle Crime." In *Handbook of Crime Prevention and Community Safety*, edited by Nick Tilley. Devon, UK: Willan.

Weisburd, D., S. Bushway, C. Lum, and S.-M. Yang. 2004. "Trajectories of Crime at Places: A Longitudinal Study of Street Segments in the City of Seattle." *Criminology* 42(2):283–321.

Zimring, Franklin E. 2006. "The Necessity and Value of Transnational Comparative Study: Some Preaching from a Recent Convert." *Criminology and Public Policy* 5(4):615–22.

———. 2007. *The Great American Crime Decline*. Cary, NC: Oxford University Press.

———. 2012. *The City That Became Safe: New York's Lessons for Urban Crime and Its Control*. London: Oxford University Press.

Index